Graham

This book fell apart the
minute I opened it.

EPIC AND EMPIRE

LITERATURE IN HISTORY

SERIES EDITORS

David Bromwich, James Chandler, and Lionel Gossman

The books in this series study literary works in the
context of the intellectual conditions, social
movements, and patterns of action
in which they took shape.

Other books in the series:

Lawrence Rothfield, *Vital Signs: Medical Realism
in Nineteenth-Century Fiction*

Alexander Welsh, *The Hero of the Waverly Novels*
(revised edition, forthcoming)

EPIC AND EMPIRE

POLITICS AND GENERIC FORM
FROM VIRGIL TO MILTON

David Quint

PRINCETON UNIVERSITY PRESS

PRINCETON, NEW JERSEY

LIBRARY OF CONGRESS CATALOGING-IN-PUBLICATION DATA

QUINT, DAVID, 1950–

EPIC AND EMPIRE:

POLITICS AND GENERIC FORM FROM VIRGIL TO MILTON / DAVID QUINT.

P. CM. — (LITERATURE IN HISTORY)

INCLUDES INDEX

ISBN 0-691-06942-5 (CL.)

ISBN 0-691-01520-1 (PA.)

1. EPIC POETRY—HISTORY AND CRITICISM.   2. LITERATURE AND HISTORY.

3. LITERARY FORM.   I. TITLE.   II. SERIES: LITERATURE IN HISTORY (PRINCETON, N.J.)

PN1303.Q56 1992

809.1′32—DC20   92-21709   CIP

THIS BOOK HAS BEEN COMPOSED IN BITSTREAM ELECTRA

PRINCETON UNIVERSITY PRESS BOOKS ARE PRINTED
ON ACID-FREE PAPER, AND MEET THE GUIDELINES FOR
PERMANENCE AND DURABILITY OF THE COMMITTEE ON
PRODUCTION GUIDELINES FOR BOOK LONGEVITY
OF THE COUNCIL ON LIBRARY RESOURCES

PRINTED IN THE UNITED STATES OF AMERICA

1 3 5 7 9 10 8 6 4 2

1 3 5 7 9 10 8 6 4 2

(PBK)

For Janet

CONTENTS

ACKNOWLEDGMENTS

THIS BOOK is the product of a happy period of teaching at Princeton University, and I am deeply grateful for the intellectual and human support of my Princeton colleagues and students. They remain close to my heart.

The writing of the book was generously supported by grants from the National Endowment for the Humanities and the John Simon Guggenheim Foundation. I worked on it during the academic year 1986–1987, when I was a fellow at the Villa I Tatti, the Harvard University Center for Renaissance Studies in Florence, and I want to thank Louise Clubb, the Director of the Villa, for her hospitality and scholarly counsel.

With a mixture of warm memories and sadness, I recall the beginnings of this project in conversations about Virgil with the late J. Arthur Hanson. I similarly mourn the loss of A. Bartlett Giamatti, a mentor and the "ideal reader" I kept in mind as I was writing.

Several friends read large chunks of the manuscript and offered me invaluable comments and advice. I owe much to Michael Murrin, who is preparing a parallel study of epic and modes of warfare. I have learned a great deal from his work, and he has furnished careful and constructive criticism of my chapters. Anthony Grafton has prodded me to sharpen my analytical arguments and given me the benefit of his encyclopedic erudition. Victoria Kahn has read sections of the book with keen intellectual scrutiny. In addition, she has let me read her own unpublished work on Milton, which has greatly shaped my thinking and approach to *Paradise Lost*. I am indebted to James Nohrnberg who, in the course of numerous conversations, has shared with me his incomparable understanding of epic mythopoesis. Ronald Levao has commented incisively on draft chapters and helped me to think about the wider implications of my study, and his friendship has sustained me during periods of self-doubt and flagging energy. My debts to all of these friends are more than intellectual in nature.

My chapters on classical epic have especially profited from the comments of Robert Fagles, Elaine Fantham, S. Georgia Nugent, Michael Putnam, and Froma Zeitlin. For readings of individual chapters I am also grateful to Rolena Adorno, John Archer, David Armitage, Albert Ascoli, Andrew Barnaby, Natalie Davis, Maria di Battista, Edwin Duval, Margaret Ferguson, Alban Forcione, Thomas M. Greene, Timothy Hampton, Richard Helgerson, Robert Hollander, Constance Jordan, John Logan, Eric MacPhail, Patricia Parker, Theodore K. Rabb, Lauren Scancarelli Seem, Michael Seidel, Walter Stephens, and Sergio Zatti. I want to acknowledge how much I learned from the participants of the 1990 Ariosto-Tasso Institute at Northwestern University.

I am grateful to David Bromwich, Lionel Gossman, and James Chandler, the editors of the Literature in History series, for their advice and criticism: particularly to David Bromwich, whose suggestions have greatly improved the later chapters of the book. I wish to thank the anonymous reader for Princeton University Press, as well as the literature editor, Robert Brown, and my copy-editor, Joan Hunter.

Earlier versions of parts of this book have appeared in articles: Chapter 1 in *Comparative Literature* 41 (1989): 1–32; Chapter 2 in *The Classical Journal* 78 (1982): 30–38, and in *Materiali e discussioni per l'analisi dei testi classici* 23 (1989): 9–54; Chapter 3 in *Representations* 26 (1989): 37–67; Chapter 5 in *Renaissance Quarterly* 43 (1990): 1–29, and in *Intersezioni* 10, 1990: 35–57; Chapter 6 in the collection, *Romance: Generic Transformation from Chrétien de Troye to Cervantes*, ed. Kevin and Marina Brownlee (Hanover and London: University Press of New England, by the Trustees of Dartmouth College, 1985), 178–202, and in *Intersezioni* 5, (1985): 467–98; Chapter 7 in the *Journal of the Warburg and Courtald Institutes* 54 (1991): 261–268; Chapter 8 in the collection, *Re-membering Milton*, ed. Margaret W. Ferguson and Mary Nyquist (London: Methuen, 1987), 128–147. I am grateful for permission to republish them here.

For the epic poems given principal attention in this study, I cite the following editions:

d'Aubigné, Agrippa. *Oeuvres*. Ed. Henri Weber. Paris, 1969.

Camões, Luis de. *Os Lusíadas*. Ed. Francisco da Silveira Bueno. São Paulo, 1960

———. *The Lusiad*. Trans. Richard Fanshawe, ed. Jeremiah D. M. Ford. Cambridge, Mass., 1940.

Ercilla y Zuniga, Alonso de. *La Araucana*. Ed. Ofelia Garza de del Castillo. Mexico City, 1972.

Homer. *The Iliad of Homer*. Trans. Richmond Lattimore. Chicago and London, 1951.

———. *The Odyssey of Homer*. Trans. Richmond Lattimore. New York, 1975.

Lucan. Trans. J. D. Duff. Loeb Classical Library. Cambridge, Mass. and London, 1962.

Milton, John. *The Poems of John Milton*. Ed. John Carey and Alistair Fowler. London and New York, 1968.

Tasso, Torquato. *Opere*. Ed. Bruno Maier. 5 vols. Milan, 1964.

Virgil. *P. Vergilii Maronis Opera*. Ed. R.A.B. Mynors. Oxford, 1969.

All verse passages in this book are cited in the original language with a following English translation. Prose citations from foreign languages are given only in translation. Except where noted, all translations are my own.

EPIC AND EMPIRE

INTRODUCTION

A S ACHILLES chases the panic-stricken Hector around the city of Troy in Book 22 of the *Iliad*,[1] the narrator draws out and heightens the suspense through comment and simile. One passage particularly reflects on the epic's aestheticization of warfare:

> It was a great man who fled, but far better he who pursued him
> rapidly, since here was no festal beast, no ox-hide
> they strove for, for these are the prizes that are given men for their running.
> No, they ran for the life of Hektor, breaker of horses.
> As when about the turnposts racing single-foot horses
> run at full speed, when a great prize is laid up for their winning,
> a tripod or a woman, in games for a man's funeral,
> so these two swept whirling about the city of Priam
> in the speed of their feet, while all the gods were looking upon them.

(158–67)

The lines are remarkable for the way in which the implied comparison of the footrace at the outset is followed by the full simile of the horserace, the two pivoting around Hector's customary epithet, "breaker of horses," which is now freighted with irony: the great horseman has been reduced to a horse (there is no mention of a rider); he is running for his own life. Hector's epithet may also bring to mind a corresponding epithet of his adversary, "swift-footed Achilles" (22.14, 229–30), an epithet that seems to have been lying in wait through the *Iliad* for this very moment: in this race, Achilles, the "far better" man, must be the prohibitive favorite. There is an ominous note in the amplification by which the simile turns the unspecified festal occasion of the footrace into funerary games. The wild chase around Troy is already a part of the games that will be celebrated in the following book in honor of the dead Patroclus, whose death, and the revenge it calls for, are the motives that bring Achilles into battle. Yet this is Hector's funeral as well, the last event celebrated in the *Iliad*. The comparison between the battlefield and the athletic arena is completed as the poet describes the gods looking down on the scene. What is life and death for the human warriors is a spectator sport for the gods.

The last thought is chilling, and would be more so did the reader not enjoy the gods' perspective on the poem's action. Like the gods the reader enjoys the sheer athleticism of warfare celebrated throughout the *Iliad*, now supremely embodied in the speed and strength of Achilles. The spectacle of concentrated power produces the heroic awe for which epic is noted, and it is matched by the power of the verse itself, producing the reader's awe before the great poem. For a moment, the poem contemplates both its action and itself as objects of aesthetic play. The Homeric poems themselves were recited on the same occasions as festal games. Yet the narrator insists upon the inadequacy of the games simile even before he employs it: the situation is, he says, "otherwise," the Greek "alla" at the beginning of verse 160 that Lattimore translates as "No." The stakes in the *Iliad* and in the epic genre it founds are higher than the aesthetic pleasure that the display of power affords. For the utmost expression of this power is to kill, and on the fate of the individual fighter Hector hangs the doom of a city and a people.

Achilles' power thus has political consequences, although in the *Iliad* it does not seem to be identified with a given regime, even if scholars have used the Homeric poems to try to reconstruct the prehistorical political arrangements of Greece from the twelfth to the seventh centuries B.C.[2] The hero acts for himself and for the demands of a private vengeance: notoriously at odds and barely reconciled with his commander Agamemnon, he makes a separate peace with the enemy king Priam in the epic's final book. But the individual heroism of Achilles could later be appropriated by and made to stand for the greatest concentration of power that Greece had seen. Plutarch reports in his *Life of Alexander* that the Macedonian conqueror carried on his campaigns a copy of the *Iliad*, which he kept under his pillow, together with a dagger; later he placed the poem in a precious casket that had been captured from the defeated Persian king Darius. Alexander claimed descent from Achilles, and just before setting forth on his conquest of Persia and Asia he visited Troy. According to Plutarch, he

> honored the memory of the heroes who were buried there, with solemn libations; especially Achilles, whose gravestone he anointed, and with his friends, as the ancient custom is, ran naked about his sepulchre, and crowned it with garlands, declaring how happy he esteemed him, in having while he lived so faithful a friend, and when he was dead so famous a poet to proclaim his actions.[3]

In this funerary tribute to the dead hero, Alexander reenacted both Achilles' race with Hector and the simile that described it. He self-consciously replicated Achilles' friendship with Patroclus in his own relationship with Hephaestion. Alexander thus made the exploits of Achilles at Troy a model for the conquests carried out by his own armies. As is attested by his well-known complaint that he lacked a Homer to celebrate his triumphs, Alexander pictured himself as an epic hero, competing for fame with the hero of an earlier poem.[4] Alexander was not, however, the first would-be conqueror to visit Troy. According to Herodotus, Xerxes had visited the city of Priam just before he crossed the Hellespont to invade Greece.[5] Perhaps Xerxes thought of himself as avenging the ghosts of Asian Troy, while Alexander, imitating *[handwritten marginalia]* Whether throughly / unflexable quites

both Achilles and Xerxes, may have seen himself, in turn, as the avenger of the Persian invasions, as he led a new and greater host to the Trojan shores.[6]

Alexander's taking on of the mantle of Achilles did not go uncontested within his own camp. Plutarch recounts a rival political application of the *Iliad* in his *Life*. Alexander famously murdered his lieutenant Cleitus, when the latter accused him of adapting the despotical mores of the Persian king he had conquered and then made the fatal mistake of citing verses from Euripides' *Andromache*, where Peleus, the father of Achilles, holds Menelaus and Agamemnon responsible for his son's death at Troy and complains,

> Do those who really sweated get the credit?
> Oh no! Some general wangles the prestige!—
> Who, brandishing his one spear among thousands,
> Did one man's work, but gets a world of praise.[7]

Alexander ran Cleitus through with his spear for suggesting that he, Alexander, was less like his heroic "ancestor" Achilles than the tyrannical Agamemnon, the king who basks in the collective achievement of his noble soldiers. The murder, however, seemed only to bear this suggestion out.

Plutarch recounts that Alexander himself became a model for Julius Caesar, and he parallels the lives of the two generals.

> It is said that another time, when free from business in Spain, after reading some part of the history of Alexander, he sat a great while very thoughtful, and at last burst out into tears. His friends were surprised, and asked him the reason of it. "Do you think," said he, "I have not just cause to weep, when I consider that Alexander at my age had conquered so many nations, and I have all this time done nothing that is memorable."[8]

The anecdote may recall one told of Alexander, who wept on learning of the Democritean doctrine of a multiplicity and infinity of worlds, because he had not yet conquered his own.[9] The chain of imitation that began with the epic hero Achilles, vanquishing Hector in single battle on the lonely fields of Troy, has transferred Achilles' individual power to the collective power of the great world empires of Macedon and Rome and to their imperial masters. The sixteenth-century humanist, Juan Luis Vives, could only look back with moral dismay at this particular continuum of the classical tradition.

> The name of Achilles enflamed Alexander, Alexander Caesar, Caesar many others: Caesar killed in various wars 192,000 men, not counting the civil wars.[10]

Plutarch puts at a million the number of the enemy killed during Caesar's ten-year conquest of Gaul, and modern historians have not hesitated to speak of a genocide. *[handwritten marginalia]* That is surprising, isn't it?

It is with a different, if related, critical spirit that Lucan surveys this chain of imitation when he restores Julius Caesar to epic poetry in the *Pharsalia*.

Caesar is the villain of Lucan's poem on the death throes of the Roman republic. At the opening of Book 10, Caesar disdains the other sights of Alexandria but eagerly pays homage to the tomb of Alexander (14f.). In fact, Caesar has just paid his own visit to Troy at the end of Book 9, and the two episodes of the poem together imitate the story of Alexander's pilgrimage to the city of Priam.[11] Caesar's tour of Troy is not mentioned in the historical chronicles and appears to be the invention of Lucan, who is returning here to a world of poetry. His treatment of the scene is frankly satirical:

> Circumit exustae nomen memorabile Troiae
> Magnaque Phoebei quaerit vestigia muri.
> Iam silvae steriles et putres robore trunci
> Assaraci pressere domos et templa deorum
> Iam lassa radice tenent, ac tota teguntur
> Pergama dumetis: etiam periere ruinae.
> Aspicit Hesiones scopulos silvaque latentes
> Anchisae thalamos; quo iudex sederit antro,
> Unde puer raptus caelo, quo vertice Nais
> Luxerit Oenone: nullum est sine nomine saxum.
> Inscius in sicco serpentem pulvere rivum
> Transierat, qui Xanthus erat. Securus in alto
> Gramine ponebat gressus: Phryx incola manes
> Hectoreos calcare vetat.[12]

> > (*Pharsalia* 9.964–77)

(Caesar walked about the famous name of burnt Troy, and sought the great remains of the walls of Phoebus Apollo. Now barren forests and rotten treetrunks cover the palace of Trojan Assaracus and their weak roots now grasp the temples of the gods, and all of Pergamum is covered with thickets; even the ruins perish. He sees the rock of Hesione and the hidden marriage-chamber of Anchises in the wood: the cave where the judge [Paris] sat, where the boy [Ganymede] was carried off into heaven, the peak where Oenone the Naiad mourned: no stone is without its story. Caesar crossed, without knowing it, a rivulet twisting through the dry dust which was the Xanthus. He stepped care-lessly on some high grass: his Phrygian native guide forebade him to walk over the remains of Hector.)

This rubble heap covered with rot is what is left of Troy. Its historical topography is irrecoverable, no matter what labels the local tourist industry may give to individual spots of the landscape in order to turn them into attractions. The buried Homeric city can hardly support vegetation that is not sterile, much less be the legitimating root and origin of the political dreams of Xerxes, Alexander, and Caesar in a line of murderous succession. (Lucan has already identified Caesar with Xerxes, when he compared in simile the causeway Caesar attempted to build across the port of Brindisi to Xerxes' bridge across the Hellespont [2.672–77]; this simile of imperial conquest would, in turn, be imitated by Milton to compare the causeway between Hell and Earth that Sin and Death build on the tracks of Satan in Book 10 of *Paradise Lost* [306–11], a "Hell's pont" indeed.) The episode is thus directly critical of the appropriation of Homeric epic, of its imaginative and aesthetic power that is inseparably bound up with its representation of the power of the hero, for the ends of empire: as a source of inspiration or authorizing model for political domination on a mass scale.

But Caesar's visit to Troy is not solely determined by his emulation of Alexander. He is seeking his family *roots*, however weak and rotten they may be. For, as Alexander had claimed Achilles as an ancestor, so Caesar claimed descent from the combatants at Troy, though on the Trojan side: it was from the refugee Aeneas and his followers that Rome and especially the Julian house—named after Iulus, Aeneas's son—supposedly derived their beginnings. Lucan's passage accordingly offers a particularly Trojan sightseeing tour, beginning at the palace of Assaracus, the ancestor of Aeneas (the putrid forest growing out of the palace's ruins offers a sardonic vision of the Julian family tree) and proceeding to the marriage cave of Anchises, the father of Aeneas, where the hero was presumably conceived, and to the tomb not of Achilles but of his Trojan victim, Hector. Caesar subsequently invokes the gods of "*my* Aeneas" (991; emphasis added).

It was, of course, Virgil who had made this political appropriation of Homeric epic into the stuff of epic itself: the *Aeneid* recounts the story of Aeneas's defeat in Troy and victory in Italy as the founding events of a Roman history that culminated in world empire and in the rise to power and the new principate of Julius Caesar's heir, Augustus. The delicious irony of Lucan's passage is that his Caesar seems to have read the *Aeneid*, composed twenty-five years *after* Caesar's death, some eighty years before Lucan wrote his anti-*Aeneid* in the *Pharsalia*. In the intervening years that had seen the reigns of such monstrous successors to Augustus as Tiberius, Caligula, Claudius, and Lucan's own contemporary, Nero, the *Aeneid* had become enshrined as Rome's national epic and as the ideological prop for the one-man rule of the emperor. Lucan's depiction of the ruined and barren foundations of Troy attacks the Roman foundation myth of the great predecessor epic, while in the *Pharsalia* he himself traces the foundation of the imperial ascendancy of Augustus and the Julio-Claudians back not to a hoary, Homeric past but merely to one generation earlier, to the civil strife between Julius Caesar and Pompey that had destroyed the republic.

With its dual focus, Lucan's episode suggests how the *Aeneid* had completed a politicization of epic that had already been under way when Alexander claimed Achilles and the *Iliad* as his own. Lucan implicitly equates the *Aeneid*'s poetic imitation of the *Iliad* and the *Odyssey*—Virgil's extraordinarily daring emulation of Homer, his continuing the story of the Trojans—with the chain of political imitation, drawing at its outset on the aesthetic power of the Homeric epics to fuel ambitions of imperial power, which had produced a Xerxes, an Alexander, a Caesar, and Caesarism. The *Aeneid* had, in fact, decisively transformed epic for posterity into both a genre that was committed to imitating and attempting to "overgo" its earlier versions and a genre that was overtly political: Virgil's epic is tied to a specific national history, to the idea of world domination, to a monarchical system, even to a particular dynasty.[13] From now on, future epic poets would emulate the *Aeneid* itself along with the Homeric epics; future imperial dynasts would turn for epic inspiration less to Achilles than to Aeneas, a hero deliberately created for political reflection. Epics of the Latin West subsequently took political issues as central subjects, whether they perpetuated the imperial politics of the *Aeneid* or, as in the case of the *Pharsalia*, sought to attack and resist empire.

Lucan mounts a twofold critique on the idea of "epic continuity." The term, which comes from Thomas M. Greene, describes the conservative tendency of the epic genre, which inclines to perpetuate—through imitation—its own formal structures of narrative and diction, its motifs and commonplaces of plot: the same story told over and over.[14] This is, it might be added, the particular consciousness of tradition that distinguishes a so-called "literary" epic from the orally inherited Homeric poems.[15] Lucan, as if prescient of a literary history that would last two millennia after him, correctly identifies and blames Virgil for this continuity—and for the continuity of an ideology of empire that a henceforth Virgilian epic tradition would encode and transmit. For Lucan recognized that even as his *Pharsalia* attacked both emperor and the *Aeneid*, it was nonetheless compelled to do so on Virgil's terms. His own allusions and imitations of the *Aeneid*, however much they may parody and send up the earlier poem, nonetheless participate in the very epic continuity they strive to break. Future, similarly antiimperial poets would imitate Lucan's model, forming an alternative tradition within epic poetry, but one that thus created its own continuity, a mirror of the Virgilian tradition it sought to displace.

The politicization of epic poetry is the subject of this book. In the course of telling this story, I have continually been impressed by the persistence of two rival traditions of epic, which are here associated with Virgil and Lucan. These define an opposition between epics of the imperial victors and epics of the defeated, a defeated whose resistance contains the germ of a broader republican or antimonarchical politics. The first, Virgilian tradition of imperial dominance is the stronger tradition, the defining tradition of Western epic; for, as I shall argue, it defines as well the norms of the second tradition of Lucan that arose to contest it.

One major unifying strand of the story I tell is how the *Aeneid* ascribes to political power the capacity to fashion human history into narrative; how, drawing on the two narrative models offered to it by the *Iliad* and the *Odyssey*, Virgil's poem attached political meaning to narrative form itself. To the victors belongs epic, with its linear teleology; to the losers belongs romance, with its random or circular wandering. Put another way, the victors experience history as a coherent, end-directed story told by their own power; the losers experience a contingency that they are powerless to shape to their own ends.

I am thus reexamining an old opposition between epic and romance, but romance in this case is peculiarly defined from the perspective of epic.[16] While the narrative romances that we are most familiar with, including the *Odyssey* itself, contain seemingly aimless episodes of wandering and digression—*adventures*—they also characteristically are organized by a quest that, however much it may be deferred by adventure, will finally achieve its goal.[17] But the romance that Virgilian epic sees as the "other" of its teleological plot is almost pure adventure—embodied in the wandering ship of Odysseus tossed by the winds of fortune, a literary figure that we shall see reappear in one epic after another. The Virgilian linking of this kind of romance narrative to the condition of defeat remains normative even for Lucan's rival tradition of the losers' epic, in which narrative structures approximate and may explicitly be identified with romance. Such epics valorize the very contingency and open-endedness that the victors' epic disparages: the defeated hope for a different future to the story that their victors may think they have ended once and for all. Nonetheless, this assimilation of Lucan's tradition to romance may already seem to be a capitulation to the terms dictated by the victors and their Virgilian epics.

The republican Rome idealized in the *Pharsalia* as an alternative to the imperial Rome of the *Aeneid* is an oligarchy. The resistance of Lucan's epic tradition to Virgil's contains an element of class conflict: a warrior nobility at odds with a central monarchy determined to limit their power. The conflict already exists in germ in the *Iliad*, where the supreme warrior Achilles has fallen out with his king and chieftain, Agamemnon, over the division of spoils. The historical king Alexander, nonetheless, chose to identify with the hero Achilles, and silenced Cleitus who reversed the analogy. Here, again, it was the *Aeneid* that "resolved" the conflict in favor of monarchy and the new Augustan principate by combining in its hero Aeneas the roles of both Agamemnon and Achilles at once: the king as both ruler-general *and* individual fighting man. Lucan and his successors spoke rather for the independent class identity of the martial aristocracy, an aristocracy whose members kings like Alexander cannot simply go around killing. Monarchs need the martial cooperation of their nobility—as Agamemnon's shaky reconciliation with Achilles bears out in the *Iliad*. It is the presence of a militarized class that Joseph Schumpeter, in his remarkable essay on imperialism, sees as the indispensable condition for a politics of expansion and conquest: the stuff of epic.[18]

A second story line that emerges from this study correlates the historical fortune and eventual demise of epic—after its revival along with other classical genres in the Renaissance—with the political position of the early modern European aristocracy. The nobility of the sixteenth and seventeenth centuries found their traditional role and their identity undermined both from below, in competition with a newly powerful mercantile bourgeoisie, and from above, as their role and identity were absorbed as instruments into the war machinery of modern absolute monarchy. This latter partnership, as Schumpeter and others have argued, may have ultimately suited the class interests of the nobility, but as it made politics, above all foreign policy, appear as the function of a "monarch's personal motives and interests," it gave the aristocrat little independent ideological stake in the wars of his sovereign.[19] This was a partnership fatal to epic. Paradoxically, at the moment of absolutist ascendancy in the seventeenth century, when European monarchies were acquiring power in unprecedented concentrations, the epic poems that should have celebrated that power failed artistically. These very poems, along with other, more successful contemporary efforts at heroic poetry, looked back nostalgically to a nobility and valor not yet subject to royal control. They looked as far back as Milton's Eden. Dying as a generic form, epic also looked back to its origins and to its preference for Achilles over Agamemnon: for the heroism of the individual distinct from the power of the corporate state. These nostalgic visions of aristocratic autonomy, moreover, characteristically employed the motifs and narrative structures of romance, by this time recognized as a separate genre by literary theorists. The stories that I want to tell about the epic of winners and the epic of losers, and about epic and romance, are intertwined.

·   ·   ·   ·   ·

The book is divided into two principal sections. Both go back and forth between the poems and perspectives of the winners and those of the losers. The first two chapters concern the Aeneid, in particular, and its legacy to the epic tradition. I begin in Chapter 1 with a case of epic continuity: the modeling of one epic battle after another—whether on land, on sea, or in Heaven—upon the battle of Actium depicted on the shield of Aeneas in Book 8 of the Aeneid. Virgil's description of Actium not only schematizes an imperialist ideology handed down to later epic fictions, but it also shows that the triumph of Augustus and the flight of the defeated Cleopatra are emblematic of the two narrative forms, epic and romance, that themselves become freighted with political meaning. The second chapter traces the opposition of romance and epic narrative through the Aeneid itself, with its division into Odyssean and Iliadic halves. This narrative opposition or progression that shows Aeneas and his Trojans transformed from losers at Troy to victors in Italy has a topical application to Virgil's Rome, a nation emerging from the trauma of civil war to a fresh start in the new Augustan state. But it also discloses an opposition, an unresolved contradiction in the official ideology of this new state, between Augustus's vaunted virtues of *clementia* and *pietas*, with their alternatives of forgetting or taking revenge on the past, alternatives that famously vie with one another at the end of the poem. If Virgil is a propagandist for emperor and empire—the position that he and his epic have occupied for the ensuing epic tradition—he is far from an uncritical one. A final section of the chapter also links the new ethos of the Augustan regime to the *Aeneid*'s substitution of a corporate heroism for the heroic individualism of Homeric epic. It proposes a new reading of the celebrated episode of the sacrificed helmsman Palinurus, and of its relationship to the leader-hero Aeneas, whose national, historical destiny will not allow him to be captain of his fate.

Chapters 3 and 4 concern the defeated. Chapter 3 observes how the vanquished enemy is depicted in the epics of the imperial victors. It also traces a continuous topos, repeated from poem to poem: the prophetic curse launched by the losers that constitutes a rival narrative of resistance coexisting alongside the triumphalist history that the epic proclaims for the winners. Yet, even as these poems acknowledge opposing voices, dissenting perspectives, other histories, they simultaneously depict the condition of defeat as one of self-defeat, the losers as born losers—monstrous, demonic, subhuman—condemned to a futile aimless repetition. As an extended reading of the figure of the cursing giant Adamastor in the *Lusíadas* of Camões suggests, the stories projected by and for the defeated have no place to go; they lack the teleology of the victors' epic narrative, and they fall into cyclical romance patterns that are finally *nonnarratable*. Chapter 4 discusses the losers' epic itself: the *Pharsalia* and two major poems of what I want to define as Lucan's tradition, Ercilla's *La Araucana* and d'Aubigné's *Les Tragiques*. It examines the ways in which these poems embrace the lack of narrative form already prescribed for the losers' stories by Virgilian epic—the episodic dismemberment of narrative in the *Pharsalia*, the inconclusive endings and romance digressions of the *Araucana*, and the spatially, rather than chronologically ordered tableaux of *Les Tragiques*—in the name of a still-contingent political history whose outcome has not been foreclosed and in which a defeat may be a temporary setback. But while the poems of Lucan's tradition criticize a Virgilian ideology that couples emperor-king and imperial conquest, and while their looser formal organization also argues for a *libertas* that connotes less centralized political arrangements, their own ideological contradictions nonetheless keep them from breaking free of Virgil's model. It is as if the very force of genre attaches them to an epic vision of concentrated power—the originally Homeric vision that now bears an indelibly Virgilian stamp.

The second section of the book repeats this alternation between the two traditions and between winners and losers by focusing on the two greatest modern epic poets: Tasso, the apologist, in Virgilian imperial terms, for a triumphalist Counter-Reformation papacy; and Milton, the Puritan poet of liberty and of a defeated republican Commonwealth. Chapter 5 examines the role of topical political allegory in the *Gerusalemme liberata*. The conflict of the Achillean warrior Rinaldo with his Agamemnon-like commander Goffredo (the latter is the ultimate hero of a poem that Tasso would title *Il Goffredo*) maps out the troubled relationship between Tasso's patrons, the Este dukes of Ferrara, and their feudal overlord, the pope. Likewise, the career of the Ethiopian heroine Clorinda, who fights on the side of the Muslim defenders of Jerusalem but eventually is granted a deathbed conversion to Christianity on the battlefield, alludes to recent efforts to bring the Ethiopian Coptic Church under obedience to Rome. In both cases, political resistance becomes interchangeable with heresy, and Tasso's epic upholds a Catholic unity and a papal one-man rule that constitute as much a temporal as a spiritual empire. Chapter 6 returns to the issue of epic and romance by tracing the figure of the errant ship, the boat of Fortune, both in the *Liberata* and, in the episode of Satan's space voyage to earth, in *Paradise Lost*. Tasso characteristically turns this traditionally romance figure into an instrument of providential epic destiny both in the action of his poem and by its role as a prophetic harbinger of Renaissance voyages of discovery; Milton reduces Satan's voyage—which, by a series of allusions to the *Lusíadas*, is similarly coupled with the voyages of discovery—to a familiar romance aimlessness. In this opposition of epic and romance, too, one can detect the beginnings of the romance of commerce and the emergence of a new moneyed class whose literary form—the novel—would displace the epic itself in the world of letters.

Chapters 7 and 8 assess the political content of Milton's epic poetry. Milton uses allusion, poetic and topical, to comment polemically on the Restoration of Charles II: it is (Satan's degraded epic plot in *Paradise Lost* suggests) a successful version of the Catholic gunpowder plot whose failure was celebrated in Phineas Fletcher's *Apollyonists* and in Milton's own youthful poem on the subject, *In Quintum Novembris*, and it is (the overdetermined reference to David's census in *Paradise Regained* implies) a continuation of the royal sins of Charles's father and a plague upon the English nation. I argue in Chapter 7 that in his depiction of the Fall of Adam and Eve, Milton, like other Puritan Arminians under attack in the Commonwealth, explored the psychology of his fellow Englishmen who were unable to live with the contingency of republican liberty and too eager to enslave their wills to a human power. For Milton as for Tasso, religious issues implicate political ones, but they point in different directions: to Tasso's epic subordination of all believers to a single authority, to Milton's contrary insistence on the autonomy of individual belief and will. The Miltonic emphasis on the contingency of free human choice generically assimilates the experience of Adam and Eve to romance, *both* before and after the Fall. In this respect, the central plot of *Paradise Lost* conforms to a general movement of the seventeenth-century epic in the direction of romance, an epic that appears increasingly unwilling or unable to celebrate the absolutist modern state and its centralizing institutions.

My final chapter looks for epic continuity in the revival of medieval heroic poetry through real and pseudo scholarship in the nineteenth century. The writing of epic declined after Milton, but Macpherson's Ossian poems provided a model for the recovery of "lost" national traditions of epic: poems that seemed to speak of loss and defeat and thus took the place of Lucan's tradition as an alternative to Virgil's imperial—universalist, multinational—epic. Even as bourgeois European nations created colonial empires on other continents, they celebrated their own origins in stories of doomed aristocratic heroism, often taking the form, or construed as taking the form, of resistance to foreign invasion. Sergei Eisenstein's communist film, *Alexander Nevsky*, may be seen as a last distinguished product of this revival of the heroic Middle Ages; a discussion of the film, with its conscious evocations of earlier epic, provides a retrospect on the entire tradition and concludes the book.

. . . . .

My analysis repeatedly shifts between the long-term continuity of epic—the political meanings that Virgil and Lucan attach to the genre and its narrative forms and which stick to it as later poems imitate their models—and the specific, topical political circumstances to which a single epic may address itself. These latter may take over the argument for long stretches, even chapters at a time. In emphasizing the *interplay* between tradition, with its long poetic memory, and the individual text, I am trying to establish a political genealogy of the tradition itself; that is, to show how the meanings of any one epic (the *Aeneid*, for a salient example) that originally were determined by a particular occasion (the ascendancy of Augustus) become "universalized" and codified as the epic becomes part of a larger literary history—and how that tradition, now *already* freighted with political ideas and expectations, becomes, in turn, an inseparable constituent of the political meaning of other epics that need themselves to be brought back to their own original occasions. I see this critical operation as skeptical and akin to Lucan's returning of Caesar to his supposed Trojan origins—and of the return of the *Aeneid* and Augustus to Caesarian origins, which, as we shall see, Virgil's poem is at pains to cover over—though the same operation is to be applied to the *Pharsalia* as well. It is also akin to that moment where, through its sporting analogies, the *Iliad* distances and distinguishes its own thrilling aesthetic play from the terrifying violence of the victorious Achilles, even as it acknowledges how these two may be bound up together.

My attempt to link the epic text with its historical occasion investigates *allusions*, both topical and poetic. These are the links by which the text already declares its connection to its political situation and to earlier epic tradition. I register here my methodological distance from, while acknowledging my indebtedness to, a poststructuralist critical practice that, in turning literary studies back toward history, has incorporated the models of structuralist anthropology. In this line of work, which is sometimes broadly called New Historicism, the literary text is one of an array of cultural products that share a single deep structure or mentality. The text, moreover, is conceived as an active shaper or mediator rather than the passive reflector of its surrounding culture, including the power arrangements that are enabling fictions of the culture and are thus themselves texts to be read and interpreted; in this sense, all cultural relationships are intertextual. In practice, the literary text is juxtaposed with some other manifestation—text, object, or event—of the culture, often from its popular or exotic margins, in order to disclose through their homology a common habit of mind. A relationship of metonymy—of historical contiguity—is thus turned into the cross-over pattern of metaphor. This method greatly expands the idea of historical context of the literary work; and its element of surprise—that what may at first seem an unconnected and arbitrary juxtaposition turns out to contain cultural analogies after all—is an essential part of its global explanatory claims.[20]

My reservations about this practice are partly conditioned by the more local explanations I have arrived at concerning epic and its relationship to the political order. In the widely conceived web of intertextual relationships that constitute the structuralist-historicist slice of history—in which all components of the culture are presupposed to develop at more or less the same rate at any historical moment—the literary text seems capable of being linked with almost any other text of the culture, and there appears to be no control to determine the juxtaposition. The text's own explicit allusive network becomes only one element of this intertextuality, and certainly not a privileged one. Politics, too, the social disposition of coercive power, becomes one more product of this patterned mentality or "poetics." That is, politics is *necessarily* aestheticized by the interpreter.[21] It is one thing to acknowledge that power to some degree depends on the manipulation of semiotic and symbolic order—I do, in fact, argue this—but quite another to conflate the two.

Furthermore, attention to synchronous historical relationships can cause the text's participation in a diachronic *literary* history to be overlooked. My preference for allusion over analogy aims to establish more precise and documentable links between the text and its historical situation—for more answerable criteria of evidence—and to link the text to its literary and cultural memory. Such memory seems to weigh particularly heavily on a genre as formally conservative and as dependent on imitation as is epic. I distinguish between where the text responds to historical occasion and where it repeats a generic convention or commonplace, although it may do both simultaneously. For I also want to argue that those conventions and commonplaces—indeed, generic form itself—carry their own history forward with them. The agency that current cultural theory grants to the text as shaper of its culture may be most fully released when the text draws on the force of an acknowledged tradition.

This last idea accounts for my double and elastic use of the term *ideology* in the book, as its focus moves between individual epic text and continuous epic tradition, between topical and literary allusion. In the first instance, when I am dealing with the single text, the term has a restricted sense and refers to an official party line that seeks to legitimate a specific historical regime, class identity, or political movement: an ideology that can be reconstructed from other texts and documents of the same historical moment and milieu. The epic text can both take this ideology as a given and subject it to an imaginative examination or critique. The latter process, Fredric Jameson argues, is itself ideological: an attempt "to invent imaginary or formal 'solutions' to unresolvable social contradictions" that the official ideology may itself disclose.[22] Ideology in this localized sense thus mediates between the individual reader and a topical political arrangement to which it seeks to command assent. This is the sense that I commonly use and intend, but it is not always easy to distinguish from a broader sense of the term. For official ideology often itself invokes what Jameson calls "master narratives" that subsume its own historically contingent situation. Such master narratives, I contend, are precisely what epic is in the business of producing: the equation of power and the very possibility of narrative is a defining feature of the genre. Although they can be returned to their original political occasion, these narratives also acquire a life of their own, especially as they draw on and, in turn, become part of a literary tradition whose very continuity seems to constitute another second-order master narrative, a kind of second nature. Here, I approach an analysis, again in Jameson's terms, of an "ideology of form"—above all of narrative or of an idea of narrative *itself*—carried through history by the epic genre.[23] This capacious sense of ideology attaches to epic's inherited formal and narrative structures a whole series of cultural and psychic associations (I shall try to outline some of these in my first chapter) that reach into other, less overtly political sectors of the reader's lived experience. These associations play at the edges of the ideology (in the narrower sense) of the historically situated poem. As they naturalize or universalize an official ideology, they also perform a legitimating function. In attempting to recover the literary tradition as well as the topical reference latent in a given epic passage, I want to account for the passage's imaginative power, which may be inseparable from its ideological force.

This is admittedly a partial view of epic, and in speaking of imaginative power I am aware that for many readers this power resides in epic's grandeur and energy of language, its descriptive scope, its dramas of human and divine heroism. These receive secondary emphasis here. I have given a privileged focus to the political or ideological dimension of the genre for the purpose of this study. I believe it to be an important dimension, among others, in the experience of reading epic poems. Topical political allusions and literary allusions that are themselves politically charged open up new perspectives on the poems' individual passages as well as on their larger structures and meanings. But I do not claim, as some present-day critics apparently do, that the political is the most important category, *tout court*, in the analysis of literary texts. Few of these critics, I imagine, were first drawn to imaginative literature because they wanted to find out how politics works. My interest in the politics of epic is to find out how the poems work.

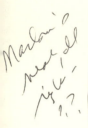

My book may be partial in another sense. In writing of winners and losers, my critical sympathies may lie on the side of the defeated; and, if so, my study continues the tradition of thought that I describe in my last chapter on the romantic reception of medieval epic in the nineteenth century. This book does make claims for the importance of Lucan's *Pharsalia* and its alternate tradition in the history of epic. To that extent it seeks to return attention to poems of the losers that have themselves lost out, poems that have been relegated to secondary, or *unread*, status in critical accounts of the genre, even though it is to this tradition that I would suggest Milton's epics are ultimately allied. But this does not mean that I think less of Virgil, Tasso, and Camões as poets, or am less moved by their fictions. I have tried to suggest the political and poetic complexity of both traditions: the winners' epic that projects the losers' resistant narratives, the losers' epic that is still deeply committed to the motives of the winners it opposes.

In this light I conclude with a passage from the *Araucana*, Ercilla's poem that is about the Spanish conquest of Chile in the sixteenth century, but even more about the resistance of the valiant native Indians. It thus belongs to Lucan's tradition. In canto 8, after the Araucanians have gained a victory over the Spaniards at Concepción, their chieftains gather at a council, where they wear the European clothing and armor of their victims (13–14). They are addressed by their captain, Caupolicán.

> según vuestros fuertes corazones,
> entrar la España pienso fácilmente
> y al gran Emperador, invicto Carlo,
> al dominio araucano sujetarlo.
>
> . . . .
>
> De vuestro intento asegurarme quiero,
> pues estoy del valor tan satisfecho,
> que gruesos muros de templado acero
> allanaréis, poniéndoles el pecho;
> con esta confianza, el delantero
> seguiré vuestro bando y el derecho
> que tenéis de ganar la fuerte España
> y conquistar del mundo la campaña.
> La deidad de esta gente entenderemos
> y si del alto cielo cristalino
> deciende, como dicen, abriremos
> a puro hierro anchísimo camino.[24]

$$(8.16.5-8; 18-19.1-4)$$

(Depending on your strong valor, I think it easy to invade Spain, and to subjugate the great Emperor, unvanquished Charles, beneath Araucanian rule.

. . . .

I want to assure myself of your desires, for I am satisfied as to your valor, for you will level stout walls of tempered steel with your opposing breasts; with this confidence I will stand, as your leader, behind your claims and your right to take possession of Spain and to conquer the world's battlefield.

We will determine the divinity of this people, and if they descend from the crystalline heaven, as they claim, we will cut open a wide highway up there with pure iron.)

The complex, shifting tone of this passage is remarkable. On the one hand, Ercilla is making fun of his Indian heroes, who in their boastfulness—they have been drinking around the campfire, too—threaten to invade Spain and engage in a campaign of world conquest. They have, in fact, no idea how minor are their guerrilla skirmishes on the frontier relative to the other concerns of Spain's vast international empire, how meager are their forces compared to the empire's true resources and power. There is a hint of the unevenness of the match in Caupolicán's own reference to their opposing their breasts against steel, which may remind the reader of the technological superiority that the conquistadors enjoyed fighting against peoples with stone weapons, though it is in their facing and sometimes overcoming these odds that the Araucanians demonstrate their true valor in the poem.

And yet, the imperial ambitions of the Indians, ludicrous though they may be, parody the actions of their would-be Spanish masters; dressed in the Spaniards' clothes, the Araucanians are playing at being Conquistadors. When Caupolicán speaks of the "right" ("derecho") that the Araucanians have to conquer Spain and take over the world, he raises some disturbing questions about the legitimacy of the Spaniards' own claims to possess the Americas and to impose dominion over the Indians' homeland. Might makes right, Caupolicán is saying, and he goes on to question the Spaniards' pretension that they are beings who have come from the sky.[25] Whatever the Indians may or not believe, Ercilla's Spanish readers know that this claim, frequently invoked by the Spaniards to awe the New World natives, is a lie.

The passage thus implicates both Araucanians and Spaniards in a critique of the imperial enterprise: the Indians present the conquistadors with a picture of themselves. Ercilla's poem belongs among the epics of the anti-imperial losers; but the passage also suggests with clear-sighted realism that the losers who attract our sympathies today would be—had they only the power—the victors of tomorrow. This realism is not cynical but hard-earned, and it plays against another idea, which we shall see explored with all of its tragic ambiguity in the *Aeneid*, that those who have been victimized losers in history somehow have the right to become victimizing winners, in turn. *but perhaps not in history.*

It is with such passages of moral as well as imaginative power that I hope my critical sympathies lie.

PART ONE

EPIC AND THE WINNERS

ONE

EPIC AND EMPIRE: VERSIONS OF ACTIUM

INSCRIBED on the center of the shield of Aeneas is an ideology of empire that informs the *Aeneid* and that Virgil bequeathed to subsequent literary epic. Virgil depicts the battle of Actium and its aftermath:

> in medio classis aeratas, Actia bella,
> cernere erat, totumque instructo Marte uideres
> feruere Leucaten auroque efffulgere fluctus.
> hinc Augustus agens Italos in proelia Caesar
> cum patribus populoque, penatibus et magnis dis,
> stans celsa in puppi, geminas cui tempora flammas
> laeta uomunt patriumque aperitur uertice sidus.
> parte alia uentis et dis Agrippa secundis
> arduus agmen agens, cui, belli insigne superbum,
> tempora nauali fulgent rostrata corona.
> hinc ope barbarica uariisque Antonius armis,
> uictor ab Aurorae populis et litore rubro,
> Aegyptum uirisque Orientis et ultima secum
> Bactra uehit, sequiturque (nefas) Aeygptia coniunx.
> una omnes ruere ac totum spumare reductis
> conuulsum remis rostrisque tridentibus aequor.
> alta petunt; pelago credas innare reuulsas
> Cycladas aut montis concurrere montibus altos,
> tanta mole uiri turritis puppibus instant.
> stupppea flamma manu telisque uolatile ferrum
> spargitur, arua noua Neptunia caede rubescunt.
> regina in mediis patrio uocat agmina sistro,
> necdum etiam geminos a tergo respicit anguis.
> omnigenumque deum monstra et latrator Anubis
> contra Neptunum et Venerem contraque Mineruam
> tela tenent. saeuit medio in certamine Mauors
> caelatus ferro, tristesque ex aethere Dirae,
> et scissa gaudens uadit Discordia palla,
> quam cum sanguineo sequitur Bellona flagello.
> Actius haec cernens arcum intendebat Apollo
> desuper; omnis eo terrore Aegyptus et Indi,
> omnis Arabs, omnes uertebant terga Sabaei.
> ipsa uidebatur uentis regina uocatis

uela dare et laxos iam iamque immittere funis.
illam inter caedes pallentem morte futura
fecerat ignipotens undis et Iapyge ferri,
contra autem magno maerentem corpore Nilum
pandentemque sinus et tota ueste uocantem
caeruleum in gremium latebrosaque flumina uictos.
at Caesar, triplici inuectus Romana triumpho
moenia, dis Italis uotum immortale sacrabat,
maxima ter centum totam delubra per urbem.
laetitia ludisque uiae plausuque fremebant;
omnibus in templis matrum chorus, omnibus arae;
ante aras terram caesi strauere iuuenci.
ipse sedens niueo candentis limine Phoebi
dona recognoscit populorum aptatque superbis
postibus; incedunt uictae longo ordine gentes,
quam uariae linguis, habitu tam uestis et armis.
hic Nomadum genus et discinctos Mulciber Afros.
hic Lelegas Carasque sagittiferosque Gelonos
finxerat; Euphrates ibat iam mollior undis,
extremique hominum Morini, Rhenusque bicornis,
indomitique Dahae, et pontem indignatus Araxes.

(8.675–728)

(In the center were to be seen brazen ships and the fighting at Actium; you would see all Leucate glowing with drawn-up forces of War and the waves glittering with gold. On this side Augustus Caesar is leading the Italians into battle with the fathers of the senate and the people, with the Penates and great gods; as he stands on the high stern, his happy brows pour out twin flames and his father's star appears by his head. In another sector is Agrippa, with the favoring winds and gods; lofty and proud, he leads on his formation; his brows gleam with the naval crown, decorated with ships' beaks, proud insignia of war.

On the other side, Antony, with barbaric wealth and varied arms, victor from the nations of the dawn and the ruddy Indian sea, draws with him Egypt, the powers of the East, and utmost Bactra; and (O shameful) his Egyptian wife follows him.

All rush together, and all the sea foams, uptorn by the drawn-back oars and the trident beaks. They seek the deep water; you would think that the uprooted Cyclades were floating on the sea or that high mountains were clashing with mountains: of such great bulk are the turreted ships in which the seamen attack. Their hands shower flaming tow and darts of flying steel, and Neptunes's fields grow red with new bloodshed. In the midst the queen summons her forces with her native sistrum, nor as yet does she look back at the twin serpents behind her. Monstrous gods of every kind together with barking Anubis wield weapons against Neptune and Venus and Minerva. In the midst of the conflict

Mars rages, engraved in steel, with the gloomy Furies from on high, and in her rent cloak Discord advances rejoicing, whom Bellona follows brandishing a bloody whip.

Beholding these sights, Actian Apollo was bending his bow from above: at that terror all Egypt and the Indians, all the Arabs and all the Sabaeans turned their backs in flight. The queen herself was seen to have invoked the winds and spread her sails, and now, even now, to let loose the slackened ropes. The God of Fire has fashioned her amid the slaughter, growing pale with approaching death, borne on by the waves and west wind, while opposite her he depicted the huge body of the mourning Nile, who was spreading open his folds and all his cloak and was inviting the vanquished to his azure lap and hidden depths.

But Caesar, brought into the walls of Rome with a threefold triumph, was dedicating an immortal votive gift to the Italian gods: three hundred great temples through the whole city; the streets resounded with joy and games, and applause; in all the temples there was a band of matrons; in all were altars and before the altars slain cattle strew the ground. He himself, seated on the snowy threshold of dazzling white Apollo, counts up the gifts of nations and places them on the proud doorposts of the temple: the conquered peoples file by in long formation, as varied in dress and arms as in languages. Here Vulcan portrayed the Nomad race and loosely robed Africans, here the Leleges and Carians and the arrow-bearing Gelonians; the Euphrates was flowing now with a more subdued current, and the Morini, the most distant of men, were there, and the double-horned Rhine, and the indomitable Dahae, and the Araxes, resentful of its bridge.)

The imperial ideology that is articulated in these verses is not identical to the "meaning" of the *Aeneid*, which devotes a considerable part of its energy to criticizing and complicating what it holds up as the official party line. The advantage of ideology, by contrast, is its capacity to simplify, to make hard and fast distinctions and draw up sides. At Virgil's Actium the sides are sharply drawn between the forces of Augustus and those of Antony, although the historical battle was, in fact, the climax of a civil war, Roman against Roman, where distinctions between the contending factions were liable to collapse. The construction of an apologetic propaganda for the winning side of Augustus brings into play a whole ideology that transforms the recent history of civil strife into a war of foreign conquest. There is a fine irony in the fact that epic's most influential statement of the imperialist project should disguise a reality of internecine conflict. But this irony points precisely to the function of the imperial ideology to which the *Aeneid* resorts: its capacity to project a foreign "otherness" upon the vanquished enemies of Augustus and of a Rome identified exclusively with her new master. The Actium passage defines this otherness through a series of binary oppositions that range from concrete details of the historical and political situation to abstractions of a mythic, psychosexual, and philosophical nature. These can be identified and listed in a kind of catalogue (see Figure 1 below). Through Virgil's artistry, each contiguous pair of opposed terms suggests their morphological similarity to the next as the description of the shield unfolds. Thus, even as these sets of oppositions are separated out to grasp their individual implications—both for the *Aeneid* and for the later epic tradition—they constitute a single ideological program, the sum of its parts.[1]

The struggle between Augustus and Antony pits the forces of the West against those of the East, continuing the pattern of epic confrontation that Virgil found in the *Iliad*. This pattern would subsequently be repeated in those Renaissance epics that portray an expansionist Europe conquering the peoples and territories of Asia, Africa, and the recently discovered New World: Ariosto's knights vanquish an Islamic army collected from Spain, North Africa, Samarkand, India, and Cathay; Tasso's paladins deliver Jerusalem from the Syrians, Egyptians, and Turks; Camões' Portuguese seamen lay the foundation for a commercial empire in Mozambique, India, and the Far East; Alonso de Ercilla's Spanish conquistadors attempt to wipe out the resistance of the Araucanian Indians of Chile, Indians who speak surprisingly in the Latinate accents of Virgil's Turnus and Mezentius. Milton may satirize this imperial pattern at one level of *Paradise Lost* when he depicts Satan intent on colonizing the eastern realm of Eden; yet, at another level, the same pattern occupies a central place in his poem. Milton's God wrests his "eternal empire" from the realm of Night, the darkest of dark continents, and Satan is described as a "sultan" whose palace in Pandemonium, built by diabolic art from the most precious materials in nature, far outdoes the wealth and splendor of an Oriental despot, "where the gorgeous East with richest hand / Showers on her kings barbaric pearl and gold" (2.3–4).[2]

Barbaric riches ("ope barbarica") from the East fill up Antony's war chest. The wealth at the basis of Eastern power—the gold upon which Dido's Carthage is founded (*Aeneid* 1.357–60) is another example—is proverbially fabulous to the European who covets it, and the Roman conquest of the East in the first century B.C. had, in fact, brought untold, unprecedented riches to the patriciate. But this wealth is also viewed with moral disapproval, for affluence produces indolence and luxury.[3] Virgil's Numanus in Book 9 is a spokesman for the Western work ethic. He praises the virility of the Latin youth whose time is consumed in tilling the fields and making war, "inured to work and accustomed to making do with little" (9.607). When, by contrast, the East's abundant wealth provides some respite from constant labor and opens up spaces of leisure time, a young man's fancy is free to wander, and the Oriental is inevitably addicted to womanizing (Antony in this respect has simply gone native) and hence becomes womanish, soft, and pleasure-loving. Numanus taunts the Trojan enemy for their idleness, fancy Asiatic clothes, and effeminacy (614–20). Numanus is himself a kind

FIGURE 1
Virgil's Actium

WEST	EAST
ONE	MANY
National unity (685)	variisque armis (685)
agens Italos (678)	Eastern overpopulation and *fertility*
patribus populoque (679)	
MALE	FEMALE
patriumque . . . sidus (681)	Aegyptia coniunx (688)
Agrippa (688)	
CONTROL	LOSS OF CONTROL
stans celsa in puppi (691)	ipsa uidebatur uentis regina uocatis /
parte alia uentis et dis Agrippa	uela dare (706–7)
secundis (682)	Cleopatra at the mercy of winds
Augustus at the rudder	
COSMIC ORDER	CHAOS
Apollo, the fastener of Delos	revulsas / Cycladas (691–92):
	Delos unfastened
	montis concurrere montibus (692):
	the *Giants*
OLYMPIAN GODS	MONSTER GODS
Neptune, Venus, Minerva (699)	omnigenumque deum monstra et
	latrator Anubis (698)
APOLLO	APOLLO
Apollo reacts to gods of war (704–5):	Egyptians, Indians, Arabs panic at the
Mars, Dirae, Discordia, Bellona	sight of Apollo (705–6)
(700–703)	
PERMANENCE, REASON	FLUX, NATURE, LOSS OF IDENTITY
uotam immortale (715)	Nile (711–13)
Augustus at the temple of Apollo (720)	Suicide, death wish
ORDER	
incedunt victae longo ordine gentes	
(722)	
ONE	MANY
Imperial unity out of many (728)	indignatus Araxes (728)
Conquered nations	Parthian hordes
Empire without end	End of empire?

of caricature of reactionary agrarian patriotism—to which Virgil may indicate his own antipathy by promptly having him dispatched by an arrow from the bow of Ascanius.[4] Yet the very manner of his death may confirm Numanus's insulting charges against his foes: the bow, which allows its user to strike from a distance and dispense with fighting man to man, is the Eastern weapon par excellence, as the "arrow-bearing Gelonians" on the shield of Aeneas attest (725); it is the weapon of the womanizer Paris, whom Diomedes taunts in the *Iliad* (11.385–95), and it is the weapon of Virgil's woman warrior Camilla as well. For all that he *is* a caricature, Numanus expresses well and clearly the censorious European attitude toward Eastern opulence and the corrupt pleasures it breeds.[5] The Easterners have more wealth than is entirely good for them, and the Westerner, with some minimal reservations that he might be corrupted in turn, may actually be doing them a favor by expropriating it.

Together with the gold of the East, Antony brings to Actium its human wealth of barbarian hordes, the "varied arms" (variisque . . . armis) drawn from its many teeming nationalities. This amalgam of foreign auxiliaries suggests what epic sees to be the dangerous excess of the East, whose populations multiply at an alarming rate and swell into armies that overflow toward the West. When their numbers reach the million mark, as they do in the pagan armies of Boiardo's *Orlando innamorato*, the poet may be suspected of tongue-in-cheek exaggeration, but epic combat typically finds the European troops outnumbered by their Oriental foes. Yet, like the wealth that softens up their fighting form, the immense size of the Eastern forces may be the ultimate cause of their defeat; the apparent assets that Antony draws from the East turn out to be liabilities instead. The huge numbers and varied composition of the Asiatic armies make them difficult to control and command; they make for "cumbersome / luggage," as Christ terms the Parthian host in *Paradise Regained* (3.400–401), a host that is compared to Boiardo's armies (336–43). The "myriad troops" (17.220) of allies who come to the defense of Troy in the *Iliad* appear to be confused by the diversity of the languges that they speak (4.437–38).[6] The great Saracen army in the *Gerusalemme liberata* is, according to the Crusader intelligence reports, for the most part useless, composed of men who do not listen to orders or bugle signals (19.122).[7] Such vast armies are apt to fragment in undisciplined routs, and Virgil suggests how Antony's composite forces fall apart when he describes the different peoples—Egyptians, Indians, Arabs, Sabaeans—in terror-stricken flight.

By contrast Augustus leads a unified patriotic army of Italians. It has been remarked that Virgil's appeal to a larger Italian rather than Roman nationalism reflects the new social basis of Augustus's power, and the poet was himself a provincial from Italian Gaul.[8] The depiction of a unified Italian front makes it seem as if the Social War had not taken place sixty years earlier.

Similarly the coupling "patribus populo," while it repeats the official formula, "senatus populusque," also suggests an end to the class warfare between *optimates* and *populares* by uniting them together on the same side. In fact, as the example of the *Iliad* first demonstrates, the European army must initially achieve unity in its own ranks before it can vanquish the foe. The dissension that it expels is often displaced into the enemy camp. In Ariosto's poem, a personified Discord descends upon the pagan host (27.35f.); Tasso's Armida herself embodies Discord, and she moves from the Crusader's tents early in the *Liberata* (5.60f.) to emerge later among the leaders of the Saracen army (17.41f.). Augustus's great achievement—depicted in his triumph that ends the description of the shield—is to impose order ("longo ordine") upon the defeated Eastern peoples. "Variisque . . . armis" is now amplified to "variae linguis, habitu tam vestis et armis" (723), indicating both the difficulty and the extent of this achievement. The Roman Empire creates a coherent political entity out of these disparate peoples, a unity of which they themselves were incapable.

This single entity implies a single master. The continuity between the unification of the Roman state and of the empire it builds turns into a brief for the one-man rule of Augustus. Augustus maintained the fiction that the senate still governed, and the "fathers" of that republican legislative body accompany him here, though distinctly as secondary players or even as the sign of his piety toward atavistic institutions—like the Penates, the ancestral household gods with which they are coupled in the verse. In fact, the shield scene suggests that only the autocratic *princeps* can hold together the Roman state and thus foster her empire. It was true that the greater part of Rome's imperial expansion had taken place during the years of her unruly republic. But the very vastness of Rome's conquered territories now demanded political consolidation both abroad and at home. Virgil's epic ideology is thus doubly "imperial," calling for both emperor and empire, as if neither could exist without the other.

The Western armies are portrayed as ethnically homogeneous, disciplined, and united; the forces of the East are a loose aggregate of nationalities prone to internal discord and fragmentation. The West, in fact, comes to embody the principle of coherence; the East, that of disorder. The struggle between the two acquires cosmic implications that appear to extend beyond alternative models of political and martial organization. The mythological analogies presented by verses 691–92, where the galleys of Augustus and Antony seem to be uprooted islands and onrushing mountains, suggest that the very coherence of natural creation may be at stake. The clashing mountains are reminiscent of the war of the giants on the gods, when the giants threw mountains at the Olympians and were, in turn, buried beneath mountainous masses. This gigantomachy is also recalled when the Roman gods oppose the monstrous gods of the East at verses 698–701. The image of the Cyclades swimming upon the sea may be more significant, for it alludes to the myth of Delos, the central isle of the Cyclades.[9] Virgil recounts (3.73–76) that Delos once wandered on the waves until it became the birthplace of Apollo. To express his gratitude to the island, the god chained it in place and made it his shrine. Propertius, in his poem on Actium (4.6), alludes directly to this story when he describes Apollo coming to the battle from Delos, which was once at the mercy of the winds but now stands anchored by the god's will. The image of Delos newly released from its mooring, like that of mountains torn away and wielded by giants, suggests a decreation of the cosmic order. The guarantor of this order is Apollo, the supposed divine father and patron of Augustus, who watches his triumph seated on the steps of the sun-god's temple. Apollo is the god of Western rationality, and his decisive intervention in the battle is apparently a reaction to the confusion and destruction bred by the Furies of War, Discord, and Strife. But, because it is the Eastern troops and Cleopatra who panic at Apollo's appearance, *they* become the embodiment of the disorder and violence that the god steps in to quell. Thus the sheer violence of warfare, in which both contending sides might seem to partake without differentiation—and all the more so in the case of a civil war—becomes an Eastern principle, and the Western soldier should be seen as the instrument not of war but of order and pacification.

The image of Delos wandering upon the seas is, in fact, repeated in Cleopatra's flight from Actium. The queen "gives" her sails to the winds she has summoned, and we next see her being passively carried away from the battle by wave and wind. With Cleopatra the opposition between East and West is explicitly characterized in terms of gender: the otherness of the Easterner becomes the otherness of the second sex.[10] If the Oriental is given to womanizing and effeminacy, here a woman has usurped the command of the Eastern forces. Much more than Antony, it is Cleopatra whose actions are followed on the shield. These actions mirror other episodes in the *Aeneid*. Cleopatra's pallor and future suicide verbally recall the suicide of Dido (4.644), and the resemblance between the two African queens is an important element in the poem's set of topical allusions. When, for example, at the end of Book 1, Dido embraces a Cupid who has been substituted for Ascanius, the scene suggests Cleopatra's love child Caesarion, whom she and Antony, at a ceremony in Alexandria in 34 B.C., attempted to pass off as Julius Caesar's heir.[11] In addition, Cleopatra's calling upon the winds—the formulaic "uentis . . . uocatis"—may return to the very beginning of the poem when Juno successfully entreats Aeolus to unleash his storm winds that scatter Aeneas's fleet in confusion (1.50f.). In the allegorical tradition, Juno-Hera is the goddess of air and thus particularly associated with the wind.[12] In Roman religion Juno also represents a universal feminine principle, and she, like Cleopatra, gives the name of woman to the anarchic forces inherent in the East, in the cosmos, and in the human psyche. Woman, like the boat of Cleopatra, is a passive, open vessel, unable to direct her destiny, subject to the everchanging winds of circumstance. As Mercury remarks of Dido in the accents of a man of the world, woman is an ever-fickle and ever-changing thing (4.569–70). By inference, the womanish Easterners cannot rule themselves and require the masculine government of their European masters.

In contrast to Cleopatra, who is carried away on what we might call her ship of state, Augustus stands firmly in control at the stern, beside the rudder, while his second-in-command Agrippa is posted at one side of the battle. With Agrippa are the favoring winds—"uentis secundis"—that ensure victory; the adjective "secundis" suggests that these winds, like Agrippa, are subordinates to Augustus, and that he, unlike the hapless Cleopatra, masters the shifting winds of chance. If Antony has Cleopatra for his consort, Augustus is accompanied by his *two* fathers: by Apollo and by the star of Caesar; *he* is the true Julian heir. The Western empire is an all-male business, a patriarchy that is marked by the use of "patribus" to describe the senators and thus by the repetition "patribus / patrium" in verses 679–81. Woman is subordinated or, as is generally the case in the *Aeneid*, excluded from power and the process of empire building. This exclusion is evident in the poem's fiction where Creusa disappears and Dido is abandoned, as well as in the historical circumstances that made Augustus the adopted son of Julius Caesar. Woman's place or displacement is therefore in the East, and epic features a series of Oriental heroines whose seductions are potentially more perilous than Eastern arms: Medea, Dido, Angelica, Armida, and Milton's Eve.

The danger for the West is to repeat the fate of Antony, to become Easternized and womanish. Such a fate implies castration and the loss of the sign of fatherhood that shines so brightly above Augustus's head. Woman cannot possess an independent identity, and there is more than a mere convention of Augustan political propaganda in the suppression of Cleopatra's name in this episode. This loss of identity is illustrated by Cleopatra's and Antony's absorption into the lap of the Nile, leaving no trace behind. As Odysseus remarks when he is adrift on Calypso's raft during a storm at sea (*Odyssey* 5.306–12), a watery death robs the epic hero of a funeral and of a grave, the commemorative monument—like the poem itself—to his existence. Aeneas in his opening speech, which imitates this Odyssean model, seems to desire just such an anonymous immersion into the waves of his native Simois (1.94–101), and the *Aeneid* must wage a campaign against this deathwish, drawing its hero away from the womblike waters of death.[13] This temptation is the greatest of Eastern temptations, and it accounts for the Oriental fatalism that, in such epic characters as Ariosto's Agramante, Tasso's Solimano, Ercilla's Caupolicán, and Milton's Satan, can rise to a tragic grandeur.[14]

In the last verses that describe the shield, the manifestation of the East becomes the river itself; to the Nile are added the Euphrates, the Rhine, and

the Araxes at the frontiers of the empire. The East is identified with its
fertility, with the cyclical fluid fertility of woman, and these both are identified, in turn, with the creative potential of nature. The river, the Heraclitean
emblem of flux, further redefines the imperial enterprise as the conquest
not merely of space but of time. Cleopatra's boat, swept about by the wind,
will become in the Renaissance the emblem of Fortune, representing time
as a purely random series of disparate events; and Fortune is also a capricious woman, a strumpet.[15] What may finally be at stake is how much can
be left to chance, or whether time can be marked off and enclosed like a
piece of foreign territory. Virgil's Jupiter promises Rome an empire without
end (1.279), and Augustus in return grants the gods an immortal pledge on
his triumphal march through the city depicted on the shield (715). Epic
takes particularly literally the axiom that history belongs to the winners.
Imperial conquest of geopolitical space—the imposition of a single, identical order upon different regions and peoples—becomes a process of history
making. The *Aeneid* appears to identify history itself with a new idea of
universal world history. Polybius, the Greek historian of the second century
B.C., argued that Rome's emerging empire had for the first time made such
a history possible, a history in which "the affairs of Italy and Africa have
been interlinked with those of Greece and Asia, all leading up to one end."[16]
Virgil's epic depicts imperial victory as the victory of the *principle of history*
—a principle lodged in the West, where identity and power are transmitted
across time in patrilineal succession—over the lack or negation of historical
identity that characterizes the everchanging, feminized nature of the East.
From such a perspective, the vanquished Easterner not only do not possess
a history, but also are virtually incapable of having one. Augustus's bridge
triumphs over the raging river Araxes, and an effigy of the river itself is
carried in his triumph; the image suggests that the victory at Actium, which
like all battles is in the last analysis a struggle for survival, is also a victory
over time.

But this final image of the shield, the Araxes indignant at the new bridge
built in place of the one put up by Alexander, the last Western conqueror
of the East, raises some questions about the permanence of Augustus's
achievement. The river had washed away Alexander's bridge and now chafes
at its subjection to Roman rule. The *Iliad* offered its own version of time and
nature destroying the works of human conquest: the great landward wall
that the Greeks have built to shelter their ships from the Trojans will eventually be overturned and swept away when Apollo and Poseidon turn loose
upon it the flooded rivers of Mount Ida (12.10–33). The Araxes, moreover,
by the convention of the Roman triumph, where depictions of river gods
were carried in the procession to symbolize the vanquished peoples residing
by their streams, here stands for the dreaded Parthians. The excessive natural energy and fertility of the East is once again associated with its great
hordes who stand poised to flood across the newly conquered territories. If

the glorious parade of Roman history in the underworld of Book 6 ended with the death of Marcellus, the male heir, and hence with the threat of new dissension and civil war destroying the empire from within, the shield's equally glorious triumph culminates with a nervous glance at the peril from without. The river's resentment echoes that of the pent-up winds of Aeolus (1.55), of the furious, dying soul of Camilla (11.831), and similarly of the soul of the wrathful Turnus in the final line of the *Aeneid*. How long can the forces of change and disorder be held in check? The rivers at the end of the description of the shield look back to the beginning of Book 8, where Father Tiber smoothes out his waters to give Aeneas's future Romans easy sailing up his stream (86–89). But Virgil's Rome was well acquainted with the periodic disasters of the Tiber's floods.[17]

Epic and Romance

The ideological dichotomies drawn between the winners and losers at Actium have formal implications for epic and its idea of narrative. This is best seen in the epic tradition that followed Virgil and that would repeatedly invoke, imitate, and rewrite the central scene on Aeneas's shield. Later epic poets found a normative narrative form embodied in the triumph of Augustus. In Cleopatra's flight, by contrast, they saw a rival generic model of narrative organization.

Epic loves a parade, perhaps because the procession that keeps its shape through both space and time resembles its own regular verse schemes— meter, rhyme, stanza—that similarly spatialize time and join the poem's beginning in interconnected sequence to its end.[18] Augustus's triumph can be assimilated with the military muster that instigates catalogues of ships or troops, or with the review of national heroes or dynastic descendants such as the procession of future Romans that Anchises displays to Aeneas in Virgil's underworld. This second category is a kind of historical pageant, and in fact the depiction of Actium culminates just such a review of Roman history (8.626–74) that now can be seen, even from its beginnings, to have been leading up to the victory of Augustus.

> illic res Italas Romanorumque triumphos
> haud uatum ignarus uenturique inscius aeui
> fecerat ignipotens, illic genus omne futurae
> stirpis ab Ascanio pugnataque in ordine bella.
>
> (8.626–29)

(There the Fire-god, not unacquainted with prophecy nor ignorant of the future, had sculpted the story of Italy and of the triumphs of Rome, every descendant to come from the race of Ascanius and the wars they fought depicted in order.)

The imperial triumph is one in a series of triumphs, itself a triumphal procession of Roman conquests that are presented in linear chronological order—"in ordine," like the "longo ordine" in which Augustus's defeated foreign subjects file by. The triumph thus gives its shape not only to the political unity of the empire but also to a unified narrative that imperial conquest has conferred upon Roman history. The shield depicts Augustus's victory at Actium as the triumph of history itself, of the very possibility of linking disparate events across time into a meaningful narrative; and that history turns out to link a sequence of victories, the constant growth and expansion of Roman arms.

The epic victors depict themselves as ever victorious and, by a kind of tautology, impose a unified meaning upon history. This same logic is at work when imperial themes reemerge in Renaissance epic, in another era of the expansion of empire. Camões recalls Virgil's Actium in *Os Lusíadas* (1572) to describe the recent imperial conquests of Portugal in the Indian Ocean.

> Nunca com Marte instructo e furioso
> Se viu ferver Leucate, quando Augusto
> Nas civis Áctias guerras, animoso,
> O Capitão venceu Romano injusto,
> Que dos povos da Aurora e do famoso
> Nilo e do Bactra Cítico e robusto
> A vitória trazia e presa rica,
> Preso da Egípcia linda e não pudica,
>
> Como vereis o mar fervendo aceso
> Co'os incêndios dos vossos, pelejando,
> Levando o Idololatra e o Mouro preso,
> De nações diferentes triunfando,
> E, sujeita a rica Áurea Quersoneso,
> Até o longínco China navegando
> E as ilhas mais remotas do Oriente,
> Ser-lhe-há todo o Oceano obediente.

(2.53–54)

(Leucate was never seen to burn with furious and drawn-up warfare, when, in the civil wars of Actium, the valorous Augustus defeated the unjust Roman captain who drew with him victory and rich captured booty from the peoples of the dawn, from the famous Nile, and from mighty Scythian Bactria—he himself captured by the fair and unchaste Egyptian woman—as you will see the sea burning, kindled with the fires of your warring Portuguese, taking captive the Hindu idolater and the Moor, triumphing over the various nations, and, once the rich Golden Chersonese is subjugated, sailing as far as distant China and the most remote islands of the East: the entire Ocean will obey them.)

These stanzas culminate the prophecy of Portugal's greatness (2.42–55) made by Camões' Jove to his daughter Venus in clear imitation of Jupiter's prophecy to Venus in Book 1 of the *Aeneid*. The father of the gods foretells a history that will be an unbroken string of Portuguese victories and conquests in East Africa (48), the Red Sea (49), and then, coasting down the western shores of India, at Diu (950), Goa (51), Cananor, Calicut, and Cochin (52). In fact, these last southernmost Indian cities were the first to fall to the Portuguese: the poet's strategy has been to present the course of empire in geographical sequence, as a single progression toward the East, which now, in stanza 54 cited above, continues past Malaya and China to Japan and the Moluccas. At the end the Portuguese rule the ocean itself; there is loosely present here the Virgilian analogy between the peoples of the East and the watery element, the latter a hardly less formidable obstacle to a maritime empire. Like the victory of Augustus, the Portuguese conquests assume the form of an orderly triumph—"De nações diferentes triunfando"—and their spatial mapping lends a linear shape to Portugal's imperial history. A reference to Magellan in the following stanza, which concludes Jupiter's prophecy (55.6), suggests that the final goal of the steady eastward expansion is world empire, an empire that circumnavigates the globe, one on which the sun never sets. The completion of this circle implies, in fact, a kind of timeless cessation of history itself, the ultimate dream of imperial power.[19] With this goal, epic linearity—the sequential linking of events—becomes a teleology: all events are led, or dictated, by an end that is their cause. The parade of history reaches a transhistorical or eschatological finish line, what in the *ethical* scheme of *Os Lusíadas* is the locus of eternal fame. Augustus's triumph similarly ended on the steps of the temple of Apollo.

The narrative shape of this history-as-triumph bears an affinity with the well-made literary plot—the plot that presents a whole with its linked beginning, middle, and end—defined by Aristotle in the *Poetics* (7c). In fact, it was apparently with the Aristotelian passage in mind that Polybius saw Rome's rise to empire forming a historical whole: "The subjection of the known parts of the world to the dominion of Rome should be viewed as a single whole, with a recognized beginning, a fixed duration, and an end which is not a matter of dispute."[20] If the plot of imperial history projected by Virgilian epic may already be modeled upon a classical idea of literary form, it, in turn, seems to lend its linearity and teleology to the epic narrative itself, which typically recounts a critical, founding chapter in that history. If epic usually begins *in medias res*, it moves toward a fixed end point, the accomplishment of a single goal or mission—the Trojans' settlement in Italy, Portugal's opening of the Indian trade route, the delivery of Jerusalem, the Fall of Adam and Eve. The formal completion of the epic plot speaks for the completeness of its vision of history: telling a full story, epic claims to possess *the* full story. Other accounts that might compete with the victors' version of history are dismissed as mere historical accidents, deviations from the straight line of imperial triumph; opposed to epic's end-directed narrative, these rival narratives appear directionless and beside the point.[21]

It is the possibility of just such a deviant and episodic narrative that Camões opposes to this triumphalist narrative of empire: the negative example of the captivated Antony, who at Actium leaves the scene of history making and follows after Cleopatra. Virgil's depiction of Cleopatra's fleeing, wind-tossed boat is related to the wandering ship of Odysseus and to an alternative, looser form of narrative organization that the *Odyssey* had introduced into epic; the first half of the *Aeneid* had explored the implications of this Odyssean model as it traced the Trojans' erratic voyage from Troy to Italy. For Borges and Northrop Frye, the wandering ship of Odysseus is the virtual emblem of *romance*: a narrative that moves through a succession of virtually discrete and unconnected episodes. The ship often finds these episodes on islands that reinforce their self-enclosed nature.[22] The romance episode thus resists being fitted into the teleological scheme of epic, and Virgilian epic consequently sees any deviance from the historical course of empire assuming the shape of romance narrative, whether this be the deviance of the Eastern conquered peoples whom we have seen to be without historical identity or that of the individual whose personal desire or very individuality is opposed to the collective goals of history and empire. The latter is the case of an Antony who thinks more of Cleopatra than of victory, and very nearly that of an Aeneas content to forget his Roman mission in Dido's Carthage. Epic views all such romance alternatives as dead ends (quite literally in the case of Antony and Cleopatra), stories that, unlike epic's own narratives of missions accomplished, have no place to go. For its part, the romance narrative bears a subversive relationship to the epic plot line from which it diverges, for it indicates the possibility of other perspectives, however incoherent they may ultimately be, upon the epic victors' single-minded story of history.

The affinity of Cleopatra's fleeing ship to the patterns of romance is documented by a literary history that would eventually transform the scene on Aeneas's shield into a central narrative complex in the great Italian romances of Boiardo and Ariosto, Renaissance poets who sought to invest their chivalric fictions with models from classical epic. The story of this transformation, as befits a romance plot, follows two interrelated paths. The *Aeneid* itself replicates the ship of Cleopatra in the boat that carries Turnus out of the battle in Book 10 (653–88), after he has pursued a phantom Aeneas set in his path by Juno. In both cases the epic protagonist briefly escapes an inevitable defeat and death, and Virgil underscores the analogy to Cleopatra by having the despondent Turnus briefly consider suicide (680–82). The Turnus episode is later imitated, in turn, by Boiardo in the fifth canto (46–55) of the *Orlando innamorato*. There the paladin Ranaldo, pursuing a similar phantom figure of his enemy Gradasso, is transported by an enchanted, pilotless boat to an island pleasure garden prepared for him by the beautiful and amorous Angelica. (Both the boat and the garden are familiar loci of chivalric romance;[23] I will take up the former again in Chapter 6.)

The same Angelica appears at the opening (1.10) of Ariosto's *Orlando furioso*, with her unbridled steed crashing headlong through the tangled woods of romance error.

> Il mover de le frondi e di verzure,
> che di cerri sentia, d'olmi e di faggi,
> fatto le avea con subite paure
> trovar di qua di là strani viaggi.
>
> (1.33)

(The sounds she heard from the movement of the branches and leaves of oaks, elms, and beeches gave her sudden starts and made her take odd paths now in this direction, now in another.)

Angelica is initially fleeing from the war between Charlemagne and the Islamic forces of King Agramante, and the scene recalls and verbally echoes the flight of the defeated Pompey at the opening of Book 8 of Lucan's *Pharsalia*; Pompey is escaping on horseback from the battlefield in Thessaly.

> Magnus agens incerta fugae vestigia turbat
> Implicitasque errore vias. Pavet ille fragorem
> Motorum ventis nemorum.
>
> (8.4–6)

(Spurring his horse, Pompey confused the indistinct tracks of his flight and tangled his path in his erratic course. He fears the noise of the woods moving in the wind.)

And behind Pompey's flight lies Cleopatra's. Lucan depicts Pharsalia as an earlier version of Virgil's Actium. Caesar's defeat of Pompey is presented as a victory of disciplined Western legions over a polyglot army collected from the East, numerically superior (7.360–68) but unreliable when the fighting starts (7.269–74, 7.525–44). Lucan, the enemy of the Caesars, draws the analogy between the two battles partly to explain why Pompey's republicans lost, but also to suggest that the victory at Actium was precisely what Virgil had said it was not: less a glorious triumph over foreign enemies than a continuation of Rome's civil wars and the final crushing of her liberty. In doing so he comes close to equating republican freedom with the cause of the conquered peoples of the East. The clearest evocation of Virgil's Actium comes in a description of Pompey and his army on the eve of battle.

Sic fatur et arma
Permittit populis frenosque furentibus ira
Laxat et ut victus violento navita Coro
Dat regimen ventis ignavumque arte relicta
Puppis onus trahitur. Trepido confusa tumultu
Castra fremunt, animique truces sua pectora pulsant
Ictibus incertis. Multorum pallor in ore
Mortis venturae faciesque simillima fato.

(7.123–30)

(So Pompey speaks and allows the nations to arm, and gives reins to their
frenzied wrath; so a sailor, vanquished by the violent northwest gale, forsakes
his skill and gives up his rudder to the winds, and is swept along, a listless
burden to the ship. The confused camp trembles with anxious hubbub, and
fierce spirits throb with irregular heartbeats in the soldiers' breasts. In the faces
of many there appeared the pallor of approaching death and their features were
the image of calamity.)

Pompey's Eastern troops share Cleopatra's and Dido's pallor, and the simile comparing their general to the sailor who gives up his vessel to the winds
is an evident recollection of Cleopatra's retreat from Actium ("uentis . . .
uela dare"). Pompey's loosing of the reins of war ("frenos . . . laxat") is a
conventional turn of speech that both may recall the ship ropes that Cleopatra lets fall slack ("laxat . . . funis") and suggest how his subsequent escape
from Pharsalia on horseback can be a rewriting of the Virgilian scene; the
confused pattern of his horse's tracks repeats her panicked flight. Ariosto's Angelica, in fact, gives up control of *her* reins and lets her horse carry
her wherever it will (1.13). Her flight is the opening image of the *Orlando
furioso*, and it announces a centrifugal trajectory that will eventually carry
Angelica out of the poem itself, still fleeing, as she seeks to return to her
home in Cathay (30.16).[24]

Both Boiardo and Ariosto thus present versions, mediated at second
hand, of the fleeing, errant Cleopatra and associate them with their central
female object of desire: Angelica's flight is the very emblem of the *Furioso*'s
wandering, entangled romance plots. Later in the *Furioso*, moreover, Ariosto includes a moral allegorization of the voyage of Boiardo's Ranaldo to
the island of pleasure. In canto 4, Ariosto's hero Ruggiero mounts on the
back of a winged hippogriff, which, like Ranaldo's boat, moves by enchant-
ment and which Ruggiero cannot rein in and control (4.49). Two cantos
later he is deposited on the East Indian island paradise of the fay Alcina, by
whom he is soon amorously enthralled. No less in love, Alcina regales him
with banquets that are compared to the Alexandrian feasts of Cleopatra
(7.20). When Ruggiero subsequently abandons Alcina, she follows him in

hot pursuit, and there ensues a sea battle between her armada and the forces of her sister fay Logistilla. Alcina's defeat and flight invoke the struggle at Actium.

> Fuggesi Alcina, e sua misera gente
> arsa e presa riman, rotta e sommersa.
> D'aver Ruggier perduto ella si sente
> via più doler che d'altra cosa aversa:
> notte e dì per lui geme amaramente,
> e lacrime per lui dagli occhi versa;
> e per dar fine a tanto aspro martìre,
> spesso si duol di non poter morire.
>
> Morir non puote alcuna fata mai,
> fin che 'l sol gira, o il ciel non muta stilo.
> Se ciò non fosse, era il dolore assai
> per muover Cloto ad inasparle il filo;
> o qual Didon finia col ferro i guai,
> o la regina splendida del Nilo
> avria imitata con mortifer sonno:
> me le fate morir sempre non ponno.
>
> (10.55–56)

(Alcina flees and her miserable troops remain behind, burned, captured, destroyed, and sunk. She feels much more sorrow at having lost Ruggiero than at any other of her calamities: she sobs bitterly for him night and day and her eyes pour out tears; and she often grieves that she cannot die to make an end of such cruel suffering.

No fay can ever die, while the sun turns or the heavens do not change their pattern. For if that were not the case, her grief was sufficient to move Cloto to wind out her fatal thread; or, like Dido, she would have finished her laments with the blade of a sword, or she would have imitated the splendid queen of the Nile with a deadly sleep: but fays may never die.)

Lest his reader miss the similarity between the fleeing Alcina and the fleeing Cleopatra on Aeneas's shield, Ariosto spells out the parallel.[25] In Virgil's scene, the historical combatants at Actium were transformed into personifications of reasoned order and directionless irrationality. Their struggle already suggested the kind of Prudentian psychomachia, an allegorical battle between warring principles in the human soul, that takes place in place in Ariosto's episode. Logistilla is the allegorical figure of reason, whose realm has been usurped by her illegitimate half sisters, Alcina and Morgana (6.43–45), the two lower forces, concupiscence and wrath, of the tripartite Platonic soul. Alcina makes war to recapture her erstwhile lover, and the battle is a fight both for and within Ruggiero's soul. The allegory comments on the wandering romance narratives of the *Furioso*: Ruggiero's journey on the hippogriff appears to be morally identical to the realm of the lower senses to which it leads, a realm that is revealed to be aimless and anarchic and, as the fate of its Eastern female ruler demonstrates, ultimately self-destructive. And yet Alcina cannot die. With his celebrated moral flexibility, Ariosto seems to suggest that appetites and desires are an ineradicable part of what constitutes the human. This is one of the truths that romance tells in opposition to a voice of reason, which would suppress or straighten out narratives of human experience that cannot be anything but wayward.[26]

Tasso's quarrel with Ariosto lies precisely over this question. It is with the conviction that reason can rule supreme and that the deviancy of romance can be contained and subordinated to epic form that he takes over Ariosto's moral, psychological allegory for his own imitation of the Alcina episode, the extended romance digression in cantos 14–16 of the *Gerusalemme liberata*. Tasso's hero Rinaldo, having rebelled against the jurisdiction of Goffredo, the commander in chief of the Crusader army, leaves the battlefront and wanders into a realm of romance. He captivates and is captivated in turn by Armida, the beautiful Syrian enchantress and enemy of the Crusade. Like Ariosto's Ruggiero and Alcina, the two lovers end up on a distant island paradise. The prose allegory that Tasso published along with his epic explains that the entire Crusader army stands corporately for the individual human soul. Goffredo, its head, is the figure for the rational faculty of the soul. Rinaldo embodies the second, irascible part of the soul, which, when it refuses the government of reason, becomes susceptible to Armida, who, Tasso's allegory hardly has to explain, represents the temptations of concupiscence.[27] This moral internalization of the *Liberata*'s action closely resembles Ariosto's personification allegory when it identifies the poem's central romance episode as a choice of appetite over reason, but Tasso goes quite beyond Ariosto by identifying reason with Goffredo's leadership and with the imperial enterprise of the Crusade itself. The power that speaks in the name of reason—a Machiavellian *ragione di stato* newly formulated in sixteenth-century political thought—becomes the guarantor of reason. This rationality, embodied by the teleological epic plot that aims at the conquest of Jerusalem, stands as a fixed pole in the *Liberata* against the sidetracking appetites. Rinaldo's choice receives a familiar imperial analogy in the scene of Actium that appears on the sculpted portals of Armida's palace (16.4–7).[28]

> Ecco (né punto ancor la pugna inchina)
> ecco fuggir la barbara reina.
>
> E fugge Antonio, e lasciar può la speme
> de l'imperio del mondo ov'egli aspira.

Non fugge no, non teme il fier, non teme,
ma segue lei che fugge e seco il tira.
Vedresti lui, simile ad uom che freme
d'amore a un tempo e di vergogna e d'ira,
mirar alternamente or la crudele
pugna ch'è in dubbio, or le fuggenti vele.

(16.5–6)

(And now behold—the outcome of the battle as yet inclines to neither side—
behold the barbarian queen in flight.

And Antony flees, and can leave behind the hope of world-empire to which
he aspires. He does not flee, no, that valiant man has no fear; he does not fear,
but follows her who flees and draws him with her. You would see him there, like
a man who at the same moment trembles with love and with shame and wrath,
gazing in turn now at the cruel fight which stands in doubt, now at her fleeing
sails.)

Cleopatra's flight becomes here again the archetype of the digressive romance narrative, a narrative that is explicitly posed as an alternative to the
martial epic and its pursuit of world empire. The hesitating Antony knows
better, as he chooses love over duty and a place in history. What is important here is the sense of choice itself, the availability of the epic arena as an
escape from the wanderings of romance desire. There is nothing inevitable
here about the option of romance, as there might be in the *Furioso*, the
poem of madness. Antony has simply made the wrong choice, and for the
moment Rinaldo, enthralled by Armida, has done the same.

The diversion of the Crusader soldiers from battle has been Armida's aim
from the beginning of the poem. Within the Virgilian dichotomies between
West and East that Tasso revives, romance becomes a deliberate stratagem
used by the female Easterner to impede the progress of the Crusade.
Armida plays the role of Cleopatra throughout the *Liberata*. Her first appearance in the Christian camp (4.28f.), where she turns the knights' sympathies toward her with her fetching feigned grief—"finto dolor" (77)—and
with an invented story that casts her as a princess whose realm has been
unjustly usurped, is modeled upon the other appearance of Cleopatra in
Roman epic, her audience in the *Pharsalia* (10.81f.) with Julius Caesar,
whom she persuades with her beauty and "simulatum . . . dolorem" (82) to
restore her to the throne of Egypt. The scene also recalls the opening of the
Orlando innamorato (1.1.20f.) where Boiardo's Angelica arrives at the court
of Charlemagne with her plot to capture and disperse all of his paladins.
Here again Cleopatra is assimilated with the leading heroine of Italian romance. Later, when Armida has joined up with the Saracen army, she participates in the final great battle for Jerusalem. She panics and flees from the

fighting, drawing several lovestruck pagan champions after her. She is explicitly compared to Cleopatra, turning this battle, too, into another version of Actium.

> Tal Cleopatra al secolo vetusto
> sola fuggia da la tenzon crudele,
> lasciando incontra al fortunato Augusto
> ne' maritimi rischi il suo fedele,
> che per amor fatto a se stesso ingiusto
> tosto seguì le solitarie vele.
>
> (20.118)

(So Cleopatra, in ancient time, fled alone from the cruel fighting, leaving her faithful lover to face the fortunate Augustus in the perils of the sea-battle; he, unjust to himself because of love, soon followed her solitary sails.)

Rinaldo, who has returned to the Crusader army and who has acquired a proper sense of the relationship of epic duty to love, now makes the correct choice. He first assures himself that the decisive battle has been won and only then turns his thoughts to following and regaining the fugitive Armida (121). He reaches her just in time to prevent her from killing herself, her face, too, colored with the Virgilian pallor of death: "già tinta in viso di pallor di morte" (127).[29] She is portrayed as a Cleopatra saved from suicide, he as an Antony/Augustus who resists Oriental temptations, notable among them the temptation to wander from epic to romance.

This subordination of romance to epic is the stated goal of Tasso's poetic theory, which attempts to accommodate the pleasing variety of Boiardo's and Ariosto's romances to a Virgilian epic teleology. But this subordination is also identical to the Western mastery—achieved by the Western male's self-mastery—of a feminized East whose disorder tends toward self-destruction. The Aristotelian "unity of the fable," which is Tasso's overriding theoretical concern, is the reflection of an imperial unity achieved both over the vanquished foreigners and within the victors' own ranks.[30] This unity depends on the logic of reducing the other to the same: to make different peoples and individuals march together in the triumphal procession, which is a model of political and narrative cohesion and singleness of purpose. Romance plots crop up in epic (and Tasso's treatment of his Italian romance predecessors repeats Virgil's similar gestures in the *Aeneid* toward the legacy of the *Odyssey* and *Argonautica*) to suggest alternatives to the imperial ideology of the unified and the same. These alternatives are multiple, precisely as epic accuses them of being, because difference from the same can take any number of shapes and meanings, and thus romance divergence can signify many different things within a single epic and differ in its significance from one epic to another. Formally, however, these paths of resistance to epic triumphalism assume a common shape: in opposition to a linear teleology that disguises power as reason and universalizes imperial conquest as the imposition of unity upon the flow of history, the dissenting narrative becomes deliberately disconnected and aimless. This is the case not only when a Virgilian poet like Tasso dramatizes what he sees as the perilous alternatives to the imperial order, which his epic upholds, but also when foes of empire like Lucan attempt to write a new kind of epic that would challenge Virgilian norms. There is something preemptive in the claim that the imperial epic makes to the high ground of classical form, of narrative unity and purpose: the critique of this epic and of the ideological agenda behind it appears to be condemned not so much to the construction of alternative literary forms as to the dismantling of form itself. Hence, it is liable to the charge of "bad form."

The War in Heaven

Elemental form is directly at stake in the War in Heaven in Book 6 of *Paradise Lost*, a conflict that closely imitates Virgil's Actium even as it verges on mock epic.[31] The battle between the rival angelic forces places in jeopardy, as does Actium, the very bonds of creation: "and now all heaven / Had gone to wrack with ruin overspread" (669–70). The angels have torn up the mountains of heaven and cast them at each other—"So hills amid the air encountered hills" (664)—a recollection of the classical battle between the giants and the gods that was also recalled by Virgil's description of the clashing ships of Augustus and Antony: "montis concurrere montibus altos" (692). It is at the point when the war threatens His creation that Milton's God intervenes and sends His Son, the Messiah, to decide the battle. The Son rides in "the chariot of paternal deity" (750). Like Virgil's Augustus, He fights in His Father's name, and the War in Heaven is a war of divine succession, fought over the Son's right to inherit His Father's rule. God shines His radiance upon the Son's face (719–21; Milton's scriptural source is Heb. 1:3), a sign of paternal legitimation that parallels the star of Julius Caesar shining upon Augustus's brow.

The Messiah's decisive appearance in the chariot of the Lord panics the rebel angels and sends them into a confused rout over the walls of Heaven, where they are swallowed up by Hell and "the wasteful deep" (862). The action typologically anticipates the absorption of Pharaoh's troops by the Red Sea; its epic model is Apollo's appearance at Actium that sends the Eastern forces into terror-stricken flight and Cleopatra and Antony into the embrace of the Egyptian Nile. Where Virgil's Apollo bends his bow at the Easterners, the Son is armed with a bow and a quiver of thunderbolts that, like Apollo's arrows, shoot "Plagues" (838) into the souls of His foes. Milton plays upon a pun that is commonplace in English sacred poetry. The Son is the true sun. It is Satan who earlier assumed the false pagan type.

> High in the midst, exalted as a god
> The apostate in his sun-bright chariot sat
> Idol of majesty divine.
>
> (100–102)

Satan presents himself in a kind of Apollonian solar chariot in emulation of the chariot of God. As an "Idol of majesty divine," he recalls the sun-kings of the seventeenth century—especially England's Charles I and Charles II—who equated their autocratic rule with the creative power of the sun. This equation goes back to the Roman emperors who identified themselves with the Mithraic cult of "Sol invictus," the invincible Sun.[32] Milton may create his own solar pun when the Son returns in triumph as "Sole victor" (880) from the expulsion of the bad angels.

There is a sense, then, in which the Son has conquered and cast out the very pagan imperial typology that Milton's version of Actium has imitated. Or rather, the typology can only belong to God, and Milton's account of the first events of history demonstrates that it originally *did* belong to God, before it was illegitimately imitated and taken over by demonic and human powers. Thus the triumph of the Son (880–93), which concludes Raphael's narration, is the sacred original of which the triumph of Virgil's Augustus is a profane copy.[33] The angels declare Him

> Son, heir, and lord, to him dominion given,
> Worthiest to reign: he celebrated rode
> Triumphant through mid-heaven, into the courts
> And temple of his mighty Father throned
> On high.
>
> (888–91)

So Virgil's Augustus will later ride through the general applause of Rome and seat himself in the temple of his divine father, Apollo, confirmed in an imperial power that, for the Puritan, staunchly republican Milton, is a blasphemous pagan attempt to play god.

The reversal by which Milton's classical models are discovered to be secondary imitations of his own fiction is a well-known strategy of *Paradise Lost* that needs no further comment here.[34] But Milton's attempt to divorce a divine, cosmogonic order from a human political order allows us to see just what is at stake in the Virgilian equation of the two. By holding the divine power of His Son in reserve until the third day of battle, Milton's God produces a temporary power vacuum and enables the poet to depict an alternative model of the universe, what it would look like without God: a state of perpetual civil warfare between the good and bad angels, in theological terms a Manichaean struggle in which neither side can gain ascendancy. This model is strongly reminiscent of, and in fact appears identical to, the state of Chaos described earlier by Milton in Book 2. The "intestine war in heaven" (6.259) threatens to return the heavenly landscape to the un-created, primordial condition of Chaos, and Chaos himself describes his realm as wracked by "intestine broils" (2.1001), a locus of "endless wars" (2.897) among elemental forces: without God's shaping hand, these "must ever fight" (2.914) and can never reach the stage of created form.[35] The Son's intervention, which ends the War in Heaven and puts the scenery back in place, is thus analogous to His act of creating the universe described immediately afterwards in Book 7, and indeed the Son is the creative Word of God by which all things first came into being (5.835–41; 7.216f.).

Both the as yet undecided angelic warfare and the neither/nor state of Chaos present images of formlessness, particularly of the absence of tempo-ral form. After the first day of battle, when Satan finds that, in spite of the pain they have suffered, his troops have survived to fight another day, he reasons in an aside, "And if one day, why not eternal days?" (424). Milton's God acknowledges that as long as He suspends the outcome of the war, "in perpetual fight they needs must last / Endless, and no solution will be found" (693–94). When the Son steps in to end the fighting, He thus em-bodies a *principle of ending*—"none but thou / Can end it" (702–3), His father tells Him. This is what we have already seen to be the teleology or eschatology with which epic shapes a master narrative of history. Otherwise the War in Heaven would always be plunged *in medias res*, without a before and after. It would revert to the condition of Chaos in whose continuous warfare "time and place are lost" (2.894), and where events come in such purely random succession, governed by "high arbiter / Chance" (2.909–10), that they cannot be sequentially narrated.

It is this loss of temporal coordinates that causes Milton to align Chaos, a "universal hubbub wild / Of stunning sounds and voices all confused" (2.951–52) with the "hubbub strange" of Babel, "the work Confusion named" (12.60, 62).[36] The War in Heaven joins this typology as well: "hor-rid confusion heaped / Upon confusion rose" like the Babelic tower itself. What is at issue in the war is the very possibility of narrative meaning. Like Chaos, the potentially endless war seems to be the final reduction of the cyclical view of time and creation advanced by Satan in Book 5 (859f.) whereby the universe is subjected to the arbitrary power of Fate and to the infinite creative and destructive cycles of nature, a nature devoid of narra-tive meaning. That meaning is ordered by language, whose syntax, in turn, depends upon temporal sequence—what is threatened by the apparent reversability or repeatability of cyclical time. Thus, at one level, the victory of the Son is the triumph of linguistic intelligibility—which the Son embodies as the creative Word of God—over an inarticulate nature, a nature of Babelic noise. At a higher, discursive level, this triumph is identical to the imposition of a finite narrative form upon time—the closed structure of Christian history—that transcends natural cycles. *Paradise Lost* thus aligns itself with other epic fictions that identify power with the capacity to create an order of historical meaning. It suggests, perhaps more clearly than any other epic, the dependence of its own capacity to signify upon the power whose victory it celebrates.

When Milton's version of Actium substitutes God for Caesar, it may appear to subsume the political altogether. But if the Son's power has no equivalent in human politics, the same is not true for the angelic civil war that the Son steps in to end. This conflict unmistakably evokes the recent English civil wars in which Milton had served as a propagandist. Satan's resemblance to Charles I has already been noted, and in the devil's mock-heroic exploits the War in Heaven satirizes an aristocratic martial heroism traditional to epic, the gallantry of the cavalier now outdated by gunpowder and artillery. While the war cannot be decided without the Son's intervention, the good angels nonetheless have their part; as they attempt to stand firm and maintain discipline, their very dependence upon God recalls the pious ranks of Cromwell's New Model Army.[37] And yet it was the same parliamentary forces who were famed for the cannonry that Milton ascribes to the devils' invention, and the good and bad angels become virtually interchangeable when they both resort to flinging the mountains of heaven at one another. This muddle of topical reference reflects the confusion of civil war that mixes friend and foe and seesaws back and forth in a seemingly endless chain of retaliation. For Milton, especially after the 1660 Restoration and the failure of his own republican hopes, this confusion has become the political condition of human history itself.

The Son's entrance into the heavenly war prefigures an apocalyptic end to history that is anticipated, in no small measure, as a solution to an unbearable political situation, a situation meaningless in itself. Milton's imitation thus finds common ideological ground with its Virgilian model in the two poets' shared experience of civil war, a state of political confusion that both equate with a threat to narratable historical meaning and, hence, to their own narrative projects, which are portrayed as depending upon that meaning. For Virgil, the way out of the impasse is achieved by the total victory of Augustus's faction, which allows the poet to rewrite the conflict with Antony *not* as civil strife at all, but rather as part, perhaps the culmination, of Rome's larger historical plot of empire: her conquest of foreign enemies who embody precisely the confusion that has been displaced from within the Roman state itself. Milton's Royalist contemporaries saw the returning

Charles II as a new Augustus similarly putting an end to the new threats of civil war, a horror they described with metaphors virtually identical to those that Milton would himself employ.

> What a strange Babell have we seen of late!
> Call it a larger Bedlam, not a State,
> Or second Chaos, greater than the first
> Where in a rude confused mass were nurst
> The seeds of all Antipathies.

So wrote William Uvedale in 1660 to welcome the king's return.[38] But Milton pointedly rejects the Augustan and cosmocratic analogies of Restoration propaganda. He reclaims the Virgilian typology for God alone, the only true bestower of an intelligible historical narrative, a narrative whose final shape is promised but not yet revealed.

The Narrative of Power

Narrative itself thus becomes ideologically charged, the formal cause or consequence of that Western male rationality and historical identity that epic ascribes to the imperial victors. Epic draws an equation between power and narrative. It tells of a power able to end the indeterminacy of war and to emerge victorious, showing that the struggle had all along been leading up to its victory and thus imposing upon it a narrative teleology—the teleology that epic identifies with the very idea of narrative. Power, moreover, is defined by its capacity to maintain itself across time, and it therefore requires narrative in order to represent itself. In this sense, narrative, like ideology, is itself empowering. The epic victors both project their present power prophetically into the future and trace its legitimating origins back into the past. The first of these narrative procedures in some sense depends on and is implied by the second: the victors can claim that they always will be protagonists in a continuing story of imperial and national destiny because they always have been. And it is this story that epic identifies with the possibility of narrative meaning itself. For, conversely, the ability to construct narratives that join beginnings purposefully to ends is already the sign and dispensation of power.

Epic's losers, the enemies of empire whom epic ideology assimilates with the East, woman, nature, irrationality, and chaos, consequently also embody a potential, indeed inevitable, collapse of narrative. This is what epic depicts in the undecided suspense and confusion of battle—the endless war that Milton's Satan would prolong into eternity—and in the circuitous wanderings of romance. Cleopatra's flight from Actium displaces the former confusion into the latter wandering and suggests how, from the perspective of epic, romance is a narrative representation of the nonnarratable. Also, Cleopatra's ship gives this epic version of romance a distinctly *political* genealogy: the condition of nonnarratability is the condition of the vanquished and powerless, those who drop out of the historical narrative written by the winners.

Epic indicates its allegiance to the winning side through the shape of its own narrative. The victors' achievement is restaged by a narrative that steadily advances to reach the ending toward which it has been directed from the beginning. Just as the victors' ideology ascribes principles of confusion and disorder to the enemy so that victory over them may be described as a triumph of reason and meaning, the epic narrative projects episodes of suspension and indirection in order that it may overcome them and demonstrate its ultimately teleological form. When these episodes expand or multiply to disrupt narrative unity and closure, epic may be suspected of going over to the side and perspective of the losers, as it does in the anti-Virgilian poems of Lucan and his successors. For if the teleological epic narrative is directed to answering the question "Who has won," the absence of an organizing teleology proposes the answer "Nobody wins," which might be seen as a deep truth (or cliché) about the absurdity of war and history. The losers console themselves that in the long run empire is a no-win affair and that its conquests are bound to perish, and even the staunchly imperialist epic may concede this possibility. But it is precisely empire's long run through history that informs epic's sense of narrative coherence and completion.

APPENDIX 1

MILTON AND HOMER

There is a second major epic model behind the war in Milton's heaven. When the Son intervenes on the third day and puts to rout the rebel angels, he recalls not only Virgil's Apollo at Actium but also the Achilles who returns to battle in the twentieth book of the *Iliad*, routing the Trojan forces, and who eventually wins the climactic duel with Hector in Book 22.[39] With this much delayed *aristeia*, Achilles confirms his central role as the hero of the *Iliad*; the epic is about *him* and his wrath, and the war for Troy can only be decided by his exploits. During his sulking absence, the fortunes of battle repeatedly change, particularly during the so-called Great Day of Battle that occupies Books 11–18. The advantage shifts at least seven times as the Trojans alternately flee for their city or drive the Greeks back to their ships.

The uncertainty of the battle's outcome during the Great Day is accompanied by the determining presence of projectile weapons in the warfare. In Book 11 Paris wounds Diomedes, Machon, and Eurypylus with his arrows, earning Diomedes' execration on an archery that equates the warrior with women and children (385f.). In Book 12, it is the Greek archer Teucer who wounds the Trojan ally Glaucus (389); and Locrian slingers similarly drive the Trojans back in Book 13 (711–22). In Book 15 Ajax appeals to Teucer to stop Hector and the Trojans with his arrows (437–70), then finds himself beaten back by the volleys of the Trojans. Finally, in Book 16, the overreaching Patroclos is struck down by the wrath of Apollo, "him who strikes from afar" (711).

These missile arms threaten to submerge beneath their often random and anonymous volleys the hand-to-hand exploits of individual warriors. Their prominence suggests that in the absence of the main hero, Achilles, heroism is itself in jeopardy. The Great Day of Battle thus bears a subversive relationship to the rest of the *Iliad*. Against the larger epic's ethos of individual martial glory, it presents an alternative picture of warfare: a confused melee of massed forces, a shower of flying weaponry that cannot be reduced—and thereby given meaning—to a narrative of the deeds of a single hero or small group of heroes. This is particularly true when one considers the nature of Achilles' own death that lies just beyond the events of the *Iliad* and that the epic does not recount. According to myth, he is killed by an *arrow*, shot either by Paris or by Apollo; but this myth may itself be based upon a reading of the *Iliad*.[40] Moreover, the indecisive stalemate of the Great Day of Battle suggests an unending warfare, similarly unnarratable, that would appear merely to prolong the fighting at Troy, which at the beginning of the *Iliad* has already dragged on for nine inconclusive years.

In Milton's imitation, this seemingly interminable war, with now one side, now the other, gaining the upper hand, becomes the dubious battle in heaven that Satan would endlessly perpetuate. The archery that puts the Homeric hero on a level with the common soldier becomes the devil's artillery and the flying mountains that overwhelm whole legions of celestial warriors. Milton openly mocks the individual martial heroics that the *Iliad* had at least seen threatened by mass warfare and projectile weapons. Beyond this undoing of the Homeric warrior code, the chaotic, potentially endless heavenly war endangers meaning itself. When Achilles returns to battle, he reinstates heroism; the intervention of Milton's Son brings into Christian history its principle of intelligibility. Both Achilles and the Son decide their respective wars, and both introduce closure into a narrative whose means or middle have threatened to expand indefinitely and to engulf its end.

The conflation by Milton's fiction of its Homeric and Virgilian epic models points up the difference between the two: the change that Virgil wrought upon the genre by appropriating Homeric epic for imperial politics. Milton follows Homer by portraying the undecidability of the heavenly war as the result of the hero's absence; and without the Son, the good and bad angels begin to look alike. But Milton also follows the pattern of Virgil's Actium and ascribes that undecidability—the possibility of endless strife and chaos—to the losers, the rebel angels who are not merely demonized but are literal demons. Epic reaches here its farthest extreme from the impartiality for which Homer is famous, an impartiality that is also a sympathy for Greeks and Trojans alike. Homer may achieve this evenhandedness because he celebrates the individual hero Achilles instead of one of the two rival sides—a hero who is, in fact, alienated from his own as well as the enemy camp. Virgil's politicized epic demands the conquest or sacrifice of this third, independent perspective of the hero as much as victory over the foes of Augustus and of Rome's imperial destiny.

APPENDIX 2

LEPANTO AND ACTIUM

In 1571 the battle of Lepanto was fought in waters not far from Actium. Here, West once again struggled against East, and the two naval battles were inevitably compared.[41] In the *Adone* (1623) of Giovanni Battista Marino, Venus passes by the site of the battles and invokes both the love story of Antony and Cleopatra and the defeat of the Turks, the latter being Heaven's punishment for the Ottoman capture and destruction of Venus's realm of Cyprus (17.168–75). The tradition of Spanish epic poems that celebrate Lepanto provides a further chapter in the imitation of Virgil's Actium. Juan Latino recalls Actium, in order to claim that Lepanto surpassed it in scale, in Book 2 of his brief epic, the *Austrias Carmen* (1573), and Cristobal de Virues couples ecphrastic descriptions of Actium and Lepanto in the fourth canto of his *Historia del Monserrate* (4.18–42).[42]

More extended Virgilian allusion and imitation can be found in the *Austriada* (1582) of Juan Rufo, which celebrates the career of Don Juan of Austria, the leader of the Christian Holy League, and in the Second Part of Ercilla's *Araucana* (1578), where Lepanto appears as a vision in the crystal ball of the Indian wizard Fiton. (The Ercilla passage will be discussed further in Chapter 4.) Both Rufo (22.93–95) and Ercilla (23.77) recall the ancient struggle between Augustus and Antony. Rufo describes Actium as an act of revenge for the murder of Julius Caesar, and he emphasizes the power of even the dead Caesar to sway the course of battle: "Que aun muerto César es fiero enemigo" (22.93). Three stanzas earlier the poet invoked the heavenly spirit of Charles V, and the analogy between the two battles suggests that at Lepanto, too, the son is fighting in the name of the father. In Ercilla's description of Lepanto, the Julian comet that shone above Augustus's head at Actium is replaced by an inscription written in gold upon Don Juan's helmet (and spelled out in capital letters in the text): DON JUAN HIJO DE CESAR CARLOS QUINTO" (24.8).[43] The Virgilian motif of paternal, Caesarian authorization is used by both poets to tie Lepanto back to Charles V and to his title of Holy Roman Emperor, and to make the battle indeed a second Actium, where Spain, allied to Papal Rome, renews and extends Roman imperial conquest. The emphasis is also dictated by a particular, awkward historical circumstance: Don Juan was, in fact, the illegitimate son of Charles.

TWO

REPETITION AND IDEOLOGY IN THE *AENEID*

THE POLITICALLY loaded narrative opposition that appears in emblematic form in Virgil's Actium—between the victors' epic teleology and the romance aimlessness and circularity of the vanquished—is repeated and written large in the *Aeneid*. The poem falls into two halves, and these correspond to two narrative forms. The first, modeled on the *Odyssey*, recounts the romance wanderings that detain Aeneas and his defeated Trojan compatriots on their way to Italy. The second, modeled on the *Iliad*, tells of the epic warfare from which they emerge victorious and gain the foothold in Latium that will eventually lead to the foundation and history of Rome. The process by which the Trojans go from being losers to winners thus matches the movement in the poem from one narrative form to another, from romance to epic.[1]

The Trojans' successive unsuccessful attempts to settle outside of Italy in the first six books of the epic constitute a pattern of repetition that threatens to keep them in continual wandering and blocks their progress to their destined future. These failed settlements all look back nostalgically to Troy and so conform to the model of the *Odyssey*, which stages a return to the homeland and to the father. But Troy has been destroyed for good, as Book 2 graphically demonstrates, and the *Aeneid* shows the repeated attempts of the survivors to found new versions and replicas of their city to be regressive—an obsessive circular return to a traumatic past that Book 3 will place under the rule of Aeneas's father, Anchises. The first half of the *Aeneid* describes the experience of the losers of the Trojan War who must rid themselves of their past, of their sense of loss and victimization—a process that involves as well the eventual removal of the father from the poem.

But in the second six books of the epic, Aeneas and the Trojans find themselves caught precisely in a repetition of the Trojan War—the war against the native Latins that seems uncannily to evoke and reproduce the events of the fighting before Troy. Here, Virgil's imitation of Homer becomes part of the thematic subject matter of the poem, for while Aeneas and the Trojans were not along on the voyage of Odysseus in the *Odyssey*, they were very much present in the action of the *Iliad*, fighting on the losing side. Thus the new *Iliad* of the second half of the *Aeneid* forces the Trojans to repeat their past struggle, but they will repeat it *with a difference*: this time they will be the winners.

The two ways of repeating the past in the two halves of the *Aeneid* and the alternative romance and epic narratives they respectively produce—the regressive repetition of the Odyssean wanderings, the successful repetition-as-reversal of the Iliadic war—conform to the two modes of psychic behavior that, for Freud in *Beyond the Pleasure Principle*, comprise the *repetition compulsion*. The victim of an earlier trauma may neurotically reenact his victimization over and over again. Alternatively, he may replay the original traumatic situation in order to create a new version of it, a situation of which he is now master, rather than victim, thereby "undoing" the past and gaining some control over his psychic history. The latter instance creates a teleologically structured narrative, a repetition that links the two events but demonstrates their difference and the overcoming of the first by the second. In a searching analysis of Freud's essay, Peter Brooks has argued that narrative itself is intimately linked to such plots of psychic mastery and empowerment. But Brooks points out an essential doubleness in repetition that potentially subverts mastery and unsettles any notion of narrative beginnings and ends.

> Narrative, we have seen, must ever present itself as a repetition of events that have already happened, and within this postulate of a generalized repetition it must make use of specific, perceptible repetition in order to create plot, that is, to show us a significant interconnection of events. An event gains meaning by its repetition, which is both the recall of an earlier moment and a variation of it: the concept of repetition hovers ambiguously between the idea of reproduction and that of change, forward and backward movement. . . . Repetition creates a *return* in the text, a doubling back. We cannot say whether this is a return *to* or a return *of*, for instance, a return to origins or a return of the repressed. Repetition through this ambiguity appears to suspend temporal process, or rather, to subject it to an indeterminable shuttling or oscillation that binds different moments together as a middle that might turn forward or back. This inescapable middle is suggestive of the demonic: repetition and return are perverse and difficult, interrupting simple movement forward.[2]

If narrative is built by repetition, Brooks notes, the risk is that its plotted events will become "merely"—regressively or endlessly—repetitious. Narrative emplotment requires a middle constituted by repetition that, because of the dual nature of repetition itself, may short-circuit and collapse upon itself rather than proceed to a desired ending from which, retrospectively, progress and mastery may be claimed: from which, we might say, the narrative may recognize itself *as* narrative.

The *Aeneid* plots out just such a struggle for empowerment and for a narrative that is both the result and the means of empowerment; but it is the struggle not of the individual psyche but of a collective political nation. The Trojans, obsessed with their fallen city in the first half of the poem, are condemned to a futile repetition and to a narrative of romance wandering that describes their experience of defeat as virtually nonnarratable. It is their victory in the epic contest of the last six books that produces a "positive" repetition of their tragic past and creates a narrative teleology. It is the first in the continuing series of victories that will constitute the narrative of Roman history. The two-part *Aeneid* thus identifies epic teleology with narrative itself—the winners' story made possible by conquest—and contrasts this story with the romance odyssey it supersedes: the losers' aimless course, their lack of story, their falling out of history. But this supersession of romance by epic represents the Trojans' victory not so much over defeated external foes as over themselves.

If Virgil casts the *Aeneid*'s narrative of political foundation—what is also the story of the political foundation of narrative—in terms of a repetition compulsion, he does so not only as a Freudian *avant la lettre*, but also in response to specific, opposing strains in the ideology of Augustus. In a kind of political allegory, the Trojans' story foreshadows the recent historical experience of the poet's Roman contemporaries. The negative and positive forms of repetition in the two halves of the epic correspond to the double message of Augustan propaganda: the injunction to forget a past of civil war (so as to stop repeating it), and the demand that this past be remembered and avenged (and so be repeated and mastered). These two ideological imperatives can be respectively assimilated to the personal virtues that Augustus claimed for himself—*clementia* and *pietas*—virtues that commentators on the *Aeneid* have long seen informing its fictions.[3] Virgil thus appears to dramatize the psychological implications, even the psychological basis of the workings of politics and of political ideology; at the same time we may begin to wonder whether Freud's model of the psyche empowered by narrative does not derive from influential political narratives like the *Aeneid* in the first place. These are not necessarily alternatives between which we must choose—the political or the psychic—for the displacement of repetition and narrative may oscillate between the two. But the political context of Virgil's poem should make us aware that its psychological depth may already be doing ideological work: it universalizes the historically particular, and, in what is one of ideology's central operations, it makes a given political and social arrangement appear to be *the* given, as if it were inevitable and somehow predetermined.[4]

Yet the *Aeneid* also uncovers the contradictions in the Augustan ideology that shapes it, the mutual incompatibility of *clementia* and *pietas*: precisely the contradiction between the admonition against history repeating itself and the call to repeat past history, if only to put that history finally in the past. This ambiguity haunts the repetition compulsion that the *Aeneid* locates at the heart of Roman experience—Brooks notes that regressive and progressive forms of repetition may not be easy to tell apart—and it accounts for the celebrated pessimism of the *Aeneid*. It is unfashionable at present, at least in this country, to read Virgil as the spokesman of the new imperial propaganda; it smacks of T. S. Eliot's blandly reactionary appropriation of the *Aeneid* for Church and Empire.[5] Yet Eliot is best countered by taking the poem's ideology seriously, by seeing the *Aeneid* questioning the Augustan regime and its party line *from the inside* and in its own terms. Playing these contradictory terms off against one another, the poem asks whether the new political foundation that the regime promises will be an escape from or merely a repetition of Rome's history of civil war. And in the process Virgil questions the therapeutic narrative of losers becoming winners—of "good" repetition replacing bad—that his epic presents as the founding model of Roman history.

The Return of the Past in *Aeneid* 3

The experience of Aeneas and his Trojan followers in Book 3 is reflected in the book's symbolic geography. On their wanderings from the fallen Troy, the Trojans stop to consult the oracle at Delos, the island that once floated and wandered upon the sea.

> sacra mari colitur medio gratissima tellus
> Nereidum matri et Neptuno Aegaeo,
> quam pius arquitenens oras et litora circum
> errantem Mycono e celsa Gyaroque reuinxit,
> immotamque coli dedit et contemnere uentos.
>
> (3.73–77)

(In the middle of the sea lies a holy island, most cherished by the mother of the Nereids and Aegean Neptune, which, as it wandered about the coasts and shores, was fastened by the grateful archer-god Apollo to lofty Myconos and Gyaros: he allowed it to lie immovable and to scorn the winds.)

Apollo repaid Delos, his birthplace, by fixing it in place and turning it into his shrine. Another story of a wandering island brought to rest is invoked when Aeneas subsequently makes a landfall in the Strophades, the islands of the Harpies.

> seruatum ex undis Strophadum me litora primum
> excipiunt. Strophades Graio stant nomine dictae
> insulae Ionio in magno.
>
> (209–11)

(The shores of the Strophades first take me and grant me safety from the sea. Strophades is the Greek name of islands in the great Ionian sea.)

Virgil calls attention to the name of the Strophades—"the islands of turning"—and asks that his reader remember how the islands first got this name, a story recounted in the *Argonautica* (2.296–97) of Apollonius Rhodius. Chasing the Harpies, the heroes Zetes and Calais reached these islands and then turned back to rejoin Jason and the Argo. The islands received their new name from this event, for before they had been called the Plotai (285, 297): the "floating islands." Like Delos, the Strophades were islands that once floated before they were fixed, and they seem to be related to the wandering Cyanean rocks that the Argonauts confront on the next leg of their journey (2.549f.); once the Argo successfully negotiates them, the rocks are rooted forever in place (2.604–6). Islands, like dangerous rocks and reefs, float and wander until sailors navigate, name, and chart them. They then become landmarks. For Aeneas and his men, the formerly wandering Delos and Strophades suggest the familiarity and stability of the eastern Greek Mediterranean. This had been their known world, the world of their past and, so they had thought, of their roots.

Italy, their eventual destination, is by contrast the world of the unknown. Its unfixed geography is described to Aeneas by the seer Helenus.

> haec loca ui quondam et uasta conuulsa ruina
> (tantum aeui longinqua ualet mutare uetustas)
> dissiluisse ferunt, cum protinus utraque tellus
> una foret: uenit medio ui pontus et undis
> Hesperium Siculo latus abscidit, aruaque et urbes
> litore diductas angusto interluit aestu.
>
> (414–19)

(These lands, they say, once burst asunder, rent by force and a great cataclysm [so great changes can be wrought by the hoary length of time] when the two were once one continuous stretch of land. The sea entered in by force between them and with its waves cut off the Italian from the Sicilian shore, and with its narrow tidal channel washes fields and cities severed by the shore.)

The tearing of Sicily away from the Italian mainland reverses the pattern of floating islands fastened in place. Sicily seems to have slipped its mooring and, as Etna shakes its foundation, to be on the move.

> fama est Enceladi semustum fulmine corpus
> urgeri mole hac, ingentemque insuper Aetnam
> impositam ruptis flammam exspirare caminis,
> et fessum quotiens mutet latus, intremere omnem
> murmure Trinacriam et caelum subtexere fumo.
>
> (578–582)

(It is storied that the body of Enceladus, half-scorched by Jove's thunderbolt, is weighed down underneath that mass, and huge Etna, placed above him breathes forth fire through its broken furnaces, and whenever he changes his weary side, all Sicily trembles with a groan and veils the sky with smoke.)

The island quakes beneath the Trojans' feet and suggests their own experience of uprootedness. They are themselves wandering, wrenched from their familiar past by the destruction of Troy and of the collective history it represented, a history now pervaded by defeat. Their future lies in the brave new world of Italy, which, precisely because it is new, initially appears unfixed and fluctuating.

The future is always uncertain, and it is little wonder that the Trojans prefer charted waters and recognizable landmarks. If the action of Book 3 describes their journey to Italy from their destroyed past of Troy, it also describes the pathos of their longing to find their past again in the course of their wanderings. Hence the paradox that the Trojans are most truly wandering when they feel they are on firm ground: when they think they have found the stability and security of a familiar past. And the Italy that seems to be breaking apart and wandering is their true destination and journey's end. It is because Italy is a terra incognita, lying outside their past experience, that it can be a virgin territory for the defeated Trojans, a site for a new and fresh beginning.

The emphasis which the whole first half of the *Aeneid* places upon the Trojans' need to break with their past, to stop looking backwards to Troy and to begin anew in Italy, is directly linked to the poem's political and ideological context. After the catastrophe of Rome's civil wars, the victorious Augustan party claimed to give the state a new foundation. Augustus was a second Romulus, and Virgil depicts a still earlier foundation of Rome before its foundation, with Aeneas as a shadowy antitype of Augustus.[6] The new regime dictated that Virgil's contemporary Romans were to put behind them the national trauma of civil strife in order to start over again, and the *Aeneid* is itself implicated in a program of Augustan propaganda that seeks to suppress and rewrite Rome's political memory. There is an evident analogy to be drawn between the defeated, war-weary Trojan remnant in search of a new beginning and Virgil's readers, the survivors of the recent civil wars, who are offered a fresh start in the new Augustan state; and we need to keep this analogy before us to construct a political reading of the *Aeneid*. The first six books of the poem describe the negative consequences of the Trojans' repeating or seeking to go back to their past—what for Rome would mean slipping back into its internecine conflicts. This is particularly the case in Book 3, which presents itself as a kind of condensed version of the first half of the poem, and whose dominant figure, Anchises, the hero's father and living reminder of the Trojan past, is also specifically tied to Julius Caesar, the adoptive father of Augustus and a major protagonist of the civil wars. But the same ideology is felt in the book's general depiction of the harmful effects of memory upon the Trojans' mission; and this has its counterpart at the end of the first half of the *Aeneid* in a depiction of the universal benefits of forgetting.

The Trojans' voyage in Book 3 is a miniature version of the wanderings of the *Odyssey* set within the Odyssean first half of the *Aeneid*; as such, the book performs in little and may be said to epitomize the action of Books 1–6.[7] In Book 3 the Trojans go from Troy to within a glimpse of the shores of Italy (519), the destination that they will finally reach at the beginning of Book 6. The *Odyssey* similarly delivers its hero from his wanderings, but while Odysseus *returns* to Ithaca, Aeneas and his followers have lost their homeland, and it is in pursuit of a new one that they are thrust out on an Odyssean voyage. It may be for this reason that the imitations of the Great Wanderings of the *Odyssey* in *Aeneid* 3 reverse Homer's narrative sequence, starting with the eating of the cattle on the Harpies' island that recalls the eating of the cattle of Helios in Book 12 of the *Odyssey* and ending with the visit to the coast of the Cyclopes that rewrites Book 9 of Homer's poem. Like its character Achaemenides (690–91), Virgil's book retraces backwards the wanderings of Odysseus.

Book 3 is also related to the larger first half of the *Aeneid* by the two storms that strike Aeneas's ships (192–208, 555–69) and drive them to the shores of the Harpies and the Cyclopes, respectively. These squalls, which are the plot device and emblem par excellence of the aimless and digressive wanderings of Odyssean romance, are smaller versions of the two great storms that send the Trojans into and away from Carthage at the beginnings of Books 1 and 5. For if, after a series of digressive episodes, Book 3 brings the Trojans within sight of Italy, the book is itself embedded within the narrative that Aeneas recounts to Dido at Carthage—in the most extended episode of his digressive wanderings. In the chronological sequence of the poem, the Trojans' arrival in Italian waters at the end of Book 3 is followed by their being blown off course to Africa in the very opening of the poem as Juno conspires with the wind-god Aeolus. The Homeric model lies in *Odyssey* 10 where, within sight of Ithaca, Odysseus's men release the winds of Aeolus from their bag (28f.) and the hero's ship is blown all the way back to the wind-god's realm from which it set out.

The *Aeneid* thus opens by evoking a pattern not only of narrative digression but also of narrative circularity: of romance wandering that brings the Trojans back to where they started, no closer to their destination. Their progress in Book 3 may only be apparent, and Book 3 also features a series of failed settlements that repeatedly force the Trojans to start all over again. They seem, in fact, to be caught in a vicious circle, and a regressive one at that, for in these settlements they build or find miragelike replicas of Troy. It is the Trojans' nostalgic attempts to repeat or relive their past that constitute their wanderings, steering them off course and away from the epic goal of Italy. The romance circularity that characterizes the narrative of the Odyssean first half of the *Aeneid* is thus assimilated thematically with an obsessive return to—and of—the past.

The problem of the past is directly raised in the third feature by which Book 3 stands as a smaller model of the first half of the poem. At the end of the book Anchises, the father of Aeneas, dies. But Anchises only disappears as a living character, and his influence upon the events of the poem is not over until the end of Book 6, where he leads his son through the underworld. The whole first half of the *Aeneid* may be read as an attempt to deal with the father and the past that he represents. Anchises plays a particularly prominent role in Book 3, a major surprise for the reader of the *Aeneid* who, at the end of Book 2, has seen Aeneas carry his apparently helpless father, a heavy and inert burden, out of the burning city of Troy, in probably the single most famous pictorial image of Virgil's poem. But in the ninth verse of Book 3 the suddenly recovered Anchises is found giving the Trojan fleet its orders to sail, and throughout the book he will share the leadership of the Trojan expedition with Aeneas. Aeneas defers to his father with the exemplary piety for which he is renowned, and it is difficult at times to determine just which of the two men is in charge.[8]

This collaboration begins to resemble a competition between father and son, between Trojan past and Trojan present, that lasts until Anchises' death at Drepanum (708–15) at the close of Book 3. Anchises' misreading of the oracle of Delos, which leads to the short-lived settlement on Crete, and the ways in which this episode is linked to others in the book, indicate how a fixation upon the former Troy threatens the Trojans' effort to make a new beginning. This thematic argument culminates in the book's central episode of Buthrotum. Through a series of Odyssean allusions and parallels, Virgil depicts the mimic Troy where Andromache and Helenus cling to their remembered past as a kind of underworld, inhabited by the living dead.

The oracle at Delos appears to be a dead giveaway. After having been addressed as "Dardanidae" (94), only a willful Trojan interpreter would not instruct his countrymen to head for the birthplace of Dardanus. Anchises' glaring mistake calls attention to itself. Perhaps swayed by the injunction to seek out his ancient motherland—"antiquam exquirite matrem" (96)—his thoughts about Crete turn to the cult of the mother goddess Cybele, imported from that island to Troy. His association of ideas thus parallels the first error that the Trojans commit in Book 3, the choice of Thrace for the site of their new city, a choice that seems to be influenced by the allied gods—"sociique Penates" (15)—of the Thracians. In both cases the Trojans are reassured by discovering that religious rites in the alien lands are identical to their own. In the episode of Thrace, Virgil reinforces this identity with a replication in the verse itself. The phrase "sociique Penates" echoes the one three lines earlier: "cum sociisque natoque, penatibus et magnis dis" (12; "with my companions and son, and the Penates and the great gods"). A similar repetition occurs in Anchises' interpretation of the words of the Delian oracle. His description of Mount Ida on Crete—"mons Idaeus ubi et gentis cunabula nostrae" (105; "where Mount Ida is, the cradle of our people")—is followed by a reference to the Phrygian Ida that overlooks Troy: "hinc Mater cultrix Cybeli Corybantiaque aera / Idaeumque nemus" (111–12; "hence came the Mother who inhabits Mount Cybelus, her Corybantian cymbals, her Idaean grove"). Anchises is, in fact, saying that the Trojan Ida received its name from the Cretan mountain. But here, too, the repetition "Idaeus/Idaeumque" reflects the Trojans' attempt to repeat their past by finding its likeness in alien lands, a likeness that now extends beyond commmon religious practices to a dim physical resemblance between Crete and Troy. Anchises' application of the oracle to Crete suggests a desire for what is familiar and recognizable—landmarks from the old Troy—rather than a willingness to confront a new and unknown future.

Aeneas is himself easily drawn to this frame of mind. He asks the gods to preserve another Trojan Pergamum—"altera Troiae / Pergama" (86–87)—and names his Cretan settlement "Pergamum" (133), suggesting that it is a kind of reconstruction of the old city. As late as Book 5 he creates an "Ilium" and Troy (756) for his weary countrymen who elect to stay behind in Sicily. Most notoriously, he infuriates the love-stricken Dido in Book 4 by telling her that, did his destiny not call him to Italy and were he free to choose, he would—and at this point Dido and the reader certainly expect him to say that he would remain beside her in Carthage—instead return to rebuild Troy and a restored—"recidiva"—Pergamum (4.344). The regressive implications can be heard in the adjective.

But to live in the past is to inhabit a state of death, and death haunts the Trojans' first attempted settlements. At Thrace they begin to build a city, but end up building the tomb of Polydorus; the verb "condimus" in the final verse of the episode (68) transforms the activity of city founding into one of burial. The fertile realm that Anchises expects to find in Crete turns out instead to be a wasteland in the grip of plague (137–42).

If Anchises directs the Trojans to Crete at least partly because he conceives of Idaean Crete as both an earlier model and a present replica of Idaean Troy, his reading of the oracle at Delos anticipates the focal episode of Book 3, the visit to Buthrotum and its miniature, mimic Troy. Here Aeneas finds a "simulataque ... Pergama" (349–50); this other Troy is a factitious copy, as false and empty as the tomb of Hector at which Andromache offers her sacrifice. This "tumulum" (303) also recalls the opening episode of Polydorus: here again, the nexus city/tomb describes a habitation of death. Moreover, a series of literary reminiscences links the episode at Epirus to Book 11 of the *Odyssey*, where Odysseus consults the shades of Hades. Reliving a dead past, Buthrotum's scale-model Troy is a kind of underworld.

At Buthrotum Helenus makes a prophecy to Aeneas of the white sow he will see in Italy, marking the site of the Trojans' first city, Alba Longa, and the end of their journey. The scene and his words verbally recall the moment in the *Odyssey* where the shade of the prophet Tiresias, summoned up from Hades, tells Odysseus that the wanderings of his second voyage will end when he finds a traveler who mistakes his oar for a winnowing fan (*Odyssey* 11.126–31). The man ignorant of ships is the sign that Tiresias promises for Odysseus, "σῆμα δέ τοι ἐρέω μαλ᾽ ᾽αριφραδές, οὐδέ σε λήσει" (126), a phrase that is repeated in Helenus's words, "signa tibi dicam" (388).[9] The Homeric model is appropriate enough; with the sign of the sow, Helenus similarly predicts a restful end to the Trojans' wanderings. David Bright has pointed out, moreover, the proximity of Buthrotum to the site of the Thesprotian Oracle of the Dead at Cichyrus, which Pausanias (1.17.5) had proposed as Homer's model for the landscape of the *Odyssey*'s underworld.[10] Thus, while Virgil's principal imitation of the Homeric episode of the dead is in Book 6, here, through allusion, he presents a second, ironic version. And if Book 6 occupies the same relative position—just short of the midway point—in the larger *Aeneid* that the underworld episode occupies in the twenty-four book *Odyssey*, the visit to Buthrotum is placed in the same position in the *Aeneid*'s Odyssean first half.

Beyond these verbal and structural parallels, the action of Virgil's episode contains further recollections of the underworld scene of the *Odyssey*. As he first arrives at Buthrotum, Aeneas encounters Andromache, who is performing a kind of necromancy, making sacrificial offerings and summoning the shade of Hector to his empty tomb (300–305). In her confusion at Aeneas's appearance, she seems to think that he may himself be a shade, coming in response to her invocation (310–12).[11] This initial meeting establishes the thematic argument of the Buthrotum episode: the dead Trojan past of Hector cannot be brought back to life; the Roman future of Aeneas has taken its place. The scene also evokes the situation of *Odyssey* 11, where Odysseus sacrifices and calls up the shades of the dead (23f.). But an ironic reversal of roles has taken place here. Andromache mistakes Aeneas for one of the shades she is trying to raise, but the Odyssean parallel suggests that it is she and Helenus who are, in fact, the dead shades with whom the living hero is to speak and consult.

Andromache begins to play the role of a shade in the *Odyssey* when she asks whether Ascanius is living and whether he is living up to the valorous examples of Aeneas and Hector (339–43). Her questions and her concern for the surviving child who carries on the family line recall the moments in *Odyssey* 11 when Agamemnon asks whether Orestes is still alive (458) and when Achilles inquires if Neoptolemus has grown up to be a warrior in the family mold (492–93). The pathetic situations are similar: the dead Homeric heroes and the past-obsessed Andromache inquire after offspring who embody their hopes in a future they cannot share. This similarity might appear to be merely coincidental had not Andromache only seven lines earlier described the fates of the same Orestes and Neoptolemus.

> ast illum ereptae magno flammatus amore
> coniugis et scelerum furiis agitatus Orestes
> excipit incautum patriasque obtruncat ad aras.

(330–32)

(But Orestes, inflamed by his great love for his stolen bride and stirred by the furies of his crime, catches him [Neoptolemus] unawares and cuts him down at his father's altars.)

Both of these sons have come to bad ends. Orestes, himself pursued by the Furies of matricide, has killed Neoptolemus. The death of Neoptolemus at his father's altar may thus be understood not only as a kind of poetic justice for having cut down Polites before Priam's eyes in Book 2 (525–32), but also, in this context, as a final answer to the questions of Agamemnon and Achilles about their sons in the *Odyssey*.

The *Aeneid* thus repeats the *Odyssey*'s own gesture toward the *Iliad*; by assigning the two heroes of the earlier poem to the underworld, the *Odyssey* clears the epic field for its own hero—while it improves on that gesture. Not only are Achilles and Agamemnon dead, but cut off, too, is the futurity of their heroic lineages for which the *Odyssey* had still allowed them to hope. Moreover, the visit to Buthrotum, haunted by the memory if not by the shade of Hector, reminds us of the end of another heroic line of the *Iliad*, this time on the Trojan side. It is Ascanius, not her own child, after whom Andromache asks, an Ascanius whom she sees as a kind of surrogate for Astyanax—"o mihi sola mei super Astyanactis imago" (489)—thereby evoking the fate of a third hero's son. The mantle that she bestows upon Ascanius (484) parallels the gift of Neoptolemus's armor that Helenus makes to Aeneas (467–69): the heroic line of the *Aeneid* receives a double legacy from Hector and Achilles, the adversaries of the *Iliad*, whose heroism and lineage are now part of an extinguished past. The episode is one in a series of Virgil's melancholy variations on the theme of the death of a son and the end of a genealogical line that stand for the end of a whole people and civilization.[12] The demise of Homeric Greece and Troy in the first half of the *Aeneid* will be matched in its last six books by the extinction or absorption of the native peoples of Italy and by the deaths of the Etruscan Lausus, the Arcadian Pallas, and the Latin Turnus. All of these sons die, of course, so that Rome may live and take over their inheritances, a Rome to which the future belongs and whose empire is a new amalgam built out of the past civilizations that the processes of history have brought to expiration and left behind. (The question of Rome's own future is addressed by the prophesied death of one more son, Marcellus, at the middle of the poem (6.860–86), a death that raises questions about the imperial succession and the stability of Augustus's political achievement.)

After the deaths of sons described at Buthrotum and in the opening episode of Polydorus, Book 3 closes with the loss of the father, Anchises, and his replacement by Aeneas, who is called by the title of "pater" as he ends his narration (716). However wrenching the death of Anchises may be for Aeneas, it provides in its context a reassuring image of generational continuity: the Roman stock will succeed to a future where other heroic lines have failed. And with its parade of replica Troys—each successively and more explicitly revealed to be a place of death—the fiction of Book 3 insists that this future can only be reached if the Trojans relinquish their past and its memories, if they can escape from a pattern of traumatic repetition. Anchises appears to embody that past, as the representative of an older generation too much part of a former Troy to begin anew. In Book 2, he stubbornly refuses to leave the fallen city (634f.), and, for all his surprising revitalization in Book 3, he still may be a deadweight for his son to shoulder: his misdirection of the Trojan expedition to Crete suggests the drag that the past can exert on Aeneas's historical mission. Anchises' death and the Trojans' first arrival in Italy complete the symbolic action of Book 3, which appears to accomplish both a physical and a psychological separation from the old Troy.

Once Anchises is dead, moreover, he increasingly becomes a source of aid and inspiration to Aeneas. He appears in dreams in Book 4 (351–53), urging his son to leave Dido's Carthage—still another, and the most insidious, version of a Troy doomed by history[13]—and again in Book 5 (722–40), when he directs the Trojans to set out from Sicily to Italy. The snake that emerges from Anchises' tomb in Book 5 (84–96) suggests his divinization, and in Book 6 he greets Aeneas as one of the elect of Elysium (744f.) and as the official spokesman for the glorious future of Rome.[14]

This transformation of Anchises from an emblem of the burden of the Trojan past to divine prophet and sponsor of the Roman future is hardly less surprising than his recovery between Books 2 and 3. This change might be explained in terms of the psychology of Aeneas: the dead father returns in idealized form to the hero as a kind of introjected superego. But, in fact, Anchises' transformation seems determined by the *Aeneid*'s loose-fitting historical allegory in which he plays the role of Julius Caesar, the adoptive father of Augustus.[15]

Julius Caesar was a problem for the Augustan propagandists. While Augustus claimed power as Caesar's heir, he also claimed to restore the senatorial authority and republican rule that had been destroyed by the same Caesar, the fomenter of civil war—and in this respect an embarrassment and political liability for his son. Ronald Syme has described this contradiction in the party line.

> Seeking to establish continuity with a legitimate government, Caesar's heir forswore the memory of Caesar: in the official conception, the Dictatorship and the Triumvirate were blotted from the record.[16]

As Syme points out, the *Aeneid* mentions the historical Caesar only once, without directly naming him, and then only in order to deplore his taking up the arms of civil war against the Pompeian defenders of the republic (6.834–35). But the deified Caesar whose temple was dedicated in 29 B.C., and from whom Octavian took his title as the "Divi filius"—or, in the words of the

Aeneid, "Augustus Caesar, Divi genus" (6.792)—appears at several moments in the poem (1.299; 6.790) as a kind of attribute of his adopted son, most notably, as we have seen, as the Julian comet shining above Augustus's head in the depiction of Actium (8.681) on Aeneas's shield.[17] The career of the living Caesar is a scandal for Augustus and his poets, but the dead and apotheosized Caesar is a source of divine authorization and guidance to his heir.

There is an apparent correspondence between this ambivalent Caesar and the *Aeneid*'s portrait of Anchises. Like that Caesar, Anchises is in life a burden and a liability. After his death and deification—one sign of which appears during the funeral games in his honor in Book 5, when the arrow of Acestes bursts into flames like a comet (522–28)—Anchises becomes in Book 6 part of the mythological apparatus that sanctions the wars that Aeneas will fight in Italy and that authorizes Rome's future mission in history. This identification of Anchises and Caesar, moreover, reinforces the topical analogy between the wandering Trojans and Virgil's Roman contemporaries and spells out the present-day political implications of the Trojans' adverse attempts to repeat their past in the first half of the *Aeneid*, and in Book 3 in particular. Following the lead of Anchises, their regressive return to versions of Troy indicate the dangers of Rome's falling back into its calamitous past of Caesarism and civil war.

This past must be both buried and forgotten, and then reinvented in the "memory" of the present, in the double process that characterizes Anchises' career in the *Aeneid*. Throughout its propaganda, the Augustan regime sought to rewrite the history of its own rise to power, passing over in silence its origins in triumviral strife and discovering instead its earlier republican roots. As part of this propaganda, the *Aeneid* rewrites Roman history even more radically, placing the origins that legitimate Augustan rule farther and farther back in time, beyond history to prehistory. According to the poem's fiction, the future advent of Augustus is built into Aeneas's original founding of the Roman people—a link that is confirmed by Augustus's descent, through the *elder* Julian line, from the Trojan hero.[18]

The action of Book 3 may comment upon and even allegorize the *Aeneid*'s larger strategy. The oracle at Delos directs the Trojans to make their new start at the place of their hoary ancestral origins in Italy, to return to a past that has been all but forgotten. The *Aeneid*'s readers are transported back to Rome's first beginnings, to a similarly mythical past that the poem offers as the propagandistic foundation for the Augustan national program. The Trojans sail by and must reject versions of their recent past. Virgil leaves out of his poem recent events that the present regime would prefer to suppress while he presents analogues to those events set in a distant, legendary past. The immemorial past, like the virgin territory of Italy, has the advantage of being a virtual blank where the poet, guided by the Muse of memory, can find whatever he wishes. Like the figure of Anchises that reveals the benefits that a mythological father can confer in place of a living one, the Trojans' journey back to their ancient homeland in Book 3 suggests the new sources of strength that the present can find in a past that it continually re-creates to serve its needs.

While the *Aeneid* offers its mythic fictions in place of historical memory, it also elevates the therapeutic effects of forgetting into one of its explicit themes. The Trojans' need to forget Troy and escape from a debilitating cycle of repetition in Book 3 is superseded at the end of the epic by the agreement reached by Jupiter and Juno (12.819–940), a passage to which we shall have occasion to return. By its terms, the Trojans and Latins will forget their differences and merge together until the very Trojan name will be no more.

> occidit, occideritque sinas cum nomine Troia.   (12.828)

> (Troy has fallen; let her perish along with her name.)

The divine decree that Rome's Trojan origins will be lost in the processes of history raises some interesting questions about the *Aeneid*'s own account of Rome's earliest past; here, too, the poem may comment self-consciously on its own procedures and acknowledge the purely fictional status of its founding narrative.[19] But the reconciliation of Latins and Trojans that the gods sanction also has unmistakable bearing upon the current political situation of Virgil's Rome. The old foes of the civil wars are similarly to be reconciled and to become one people again under Augustus; their former enmities and party allegiances are to be forgotten. Virgil's fiction may even represent a case of special pleading: the poet may have in mind an *amnesty*, a specific judicial act by which both the government and the former opponents and victims of the government agree to forget their mutual wrongs and grievances. Cicero had had such an amnesty enacted after the assassination of Julius Caesar, borrowing, as he was later to boast, a Greek word and the political wisdom of the Athenian democracy in order to restore the national peace (*Phil.* 1.1.1).

What is a political solution at the end of the *Aeneid* is revealed at the end of its first half to be a universal principle built into human existence itself. When, in the underworld of Book 6, Aeneas asks Anchises just why the souls of men would return to earth to live new lives after their experience of human suffering—Why, Aeneas asks, do they madly desire the light of day? (6.721)—his father responds with a famous disquisition on the transmigration of souls that draws attention away from his ultimate answer to the question: the returning souls have drunk from the river Lethe.

> has omnis, ubi mille rotam uoluere per annos,
> Lethaeum ad fluuium deus euocat agmine magno

scilicet immemores supera ut conuexa reuisant
rursus, et incipiant in corpora uelle reuerti.

(6.748–51)

(When these souls have rolled the wheel through a thousand years, the god
summons them all in a great troop to the Lethean river in order, you see, that
without any memory they may see again the vault of heaven and begin to desire
to return to their bodies.)

When the souls have forgotten the past, they will wish to live in bodies once
again. Forgetting is the prerequisite for the very continuity of the species,
and the juxtaposition of the two moments of forgetting, each at the climax
of its respective half of the *Aeneid*, suggests that the need for the survivors
of the Trojan war and later of the poem's Italian wars—and for the survivors
of Rome's own civil wars—to forget the tragic memories of their past is as
deep-seated as life itself, part of the basic processes of the psyche. Both a
fresh start in Italy under Aeneas and the national revival fostered by Augustus require the same collective act of oblivion that the souls undergo in
order to be reborn.

This analogy may be extended further. The souls in the underworld roll
on the wheel of time for a thousand years before they are led to the river
Lethe. This circular turning—by which they are slowly cleansed of their
former earthly existence—corresponds to, and may gloss, the circularity of
the Trojans' Odyssean wanderings and the romance narrative form that this
takes. The purgatorial process, which breaks the hold of the past upon the
soul, assumes the same cyclical pattern as the Trojans' repeated doubling
back to various versions of Troy that each time seems to return them to
where they started. At the same time, this psychic analogy leaves open the
question whether the succession of adventures the Trojans undergo in their
romance wanderings may not constitute a cumulative process of purgation
of their doomed past, rather than being merely the compulsive playing out
over and over again of that past. The Trojans do, after all, finally reach their
Italian destination in Book 6, where through the individual symbolic agency
of Aeneas they experience death and are reborn. This symbolism carries
over into the opening lines of Book 7 and the beginning of the second half
of the poem with the death of Caieta, the old nurse of Aeneas. Their revisit-
ing of their past in the first half of the poem may be read as a gradual
exorcism of that past—as well as a form of debilitating regression, a regression that has its narrative counterpart in episodic romance digression. The
Trojans may be thought of as taking two steps back for every three steps
forward; their narrative is a kind of spiral. In this sense the traumatic repetition that constitutes the Odyssean romance narrative of Books 1-6 may already contain within it a "working-through" that points the way out of this

narrative to the teleological epic narrative of the second half of the poem. The escape from this repetition still hinges on a repression or forgetting of the past (of the Trojans' forgetting their past as losers), and the narrative process, whether the Trojans' wanderings or the underworld souls' wheeling though purgatorial time, merely acts out at length what is symbolized in the single draught from the waters of Lethe. It is only when the past has been successfully repressed—when it ceases to repeat itself in its former version—that it can be repeated *with a difference* in order to be reversed and undone. The Trojans now become winners, and so Augustan Rome is restored to national health after the years of internal strife. At this point the *Aeneid* moves from romance to epic.

Undoing the Past in *Aeneid* 12

The first indication that the Trojans' fortunes are undergoing a process of reversal, the process that becomes the dominant pattern of the second half of the *Aeneid*, is already found earlier in the poem and concerns gift horses. The Trojans, who ignored Laocoön's warning against Greeks bearing gifts (48–49) and received the fatal wooden horse into their city, now become gift givers themselves as they journey into new lands. The presents they offer in friendship to their hosts are hardly less fatal than the Trojan horse itself. In parallel scenes, Dido in Book 1 receives the veil of Helen and the scepter of Ilione (647–55), Latinus in Book 7, a libation bowl of Anchises and the scepter and robes of Priam (244–48). These Trojan spoils carry with them a kind of curse, and their new possessors are condemned to play out the tragic roles for which the costumes fit them. Their cities now become new versions of the fallen Troy: Carthage's walls seem to be on fire with the flames of Dido's pyre (5.3–4); Laurentium's walls are literally burnt down (12.574f.). (Evander, we learn in Book 8, had already received Trojan gifts from Anchises on the latter's earlier visit to Arcadia: the pair of golden bridles that he has passed on to Pallas [166–68] similarly mark out the young hero for destruction.)

What do the Trojans receive in return, as Homeric *xenia*, guest-gifts? Horses. Dido gives Ascanius the horse (571) that he parades in the funeral games of Book 5; Helenus gives Anchises and the Trojan expedition horses (470) in Book 3; Latinus gives three hundred horses (274–85) to Aeneas in exchange for Priam's finery in Book 7; Evander gives horses to Aeneas and his companions (551–53) as they set out to join the Etruscans in Book 8. The Trojans, of course, need horses, since they can have taken few along with them on their storm-tossed voyages. But they need them for waging war, as Anchises indicates in his interpretation of the omen of the four horses sighted from off the coast of Italy (3.537–43), and the emphasis on cavalry fighting, particularly the light-horse combat involving Camilla in Book 11, is an intrusion of contemporary Roman battle tactics upon Homeric models of battle. There is an obvious irony when the Trojans are given horses—especially in the case of Latinus—that can be used in war against the giver. There is also an obvious reversal that the symbolic reciprocity in the gift exchange only underscores: the Trojans, victims of a gift horse, the most famous gift horse in history, now victimize others with their gifts while they become the beneficiaries of the gifts of horses.

The Trojans become winners by exchanging their past roles as losers with others. This is Virgil's poetic method in the second *Iliad*, the new Trojan war in Italy that takes up the last six books of the *Aeneid*. The scenario of the Italian war has already been prophesied by the Cumaean sibyl.

> non Simois tibi nec Xanthus nec Dorica castra
> defuerint; alius Latio iam partus Achilles,
> natus et ipse dea; nec Teucris addita Iuno
> usquam aberit, cum tu supplex in rebus egenis
> quas gentis Italum aut quas non oraueris urbes!
> causa mali tanti coniunx iterum hospita Teucris
> externique iterum thalami.
> tu ne cede malis, sed contra audentior ito,
> qua tua te Fortuna sinet.
>
> (6.88–96)

(You will find lacking neither a Simois, nor a Xanthus, nor a Greek camp: another Achilles has now been born in Latium, and he, too, the son of a goddess; nor will Juno anywhere be absent, pursuing the Trojans with hatred, while you, a suppliant in dire need, what peoples, what cities of Italy will you not beseech for aid! The cause of such great evil to the Trojans will again be a bride taken from foreign hosts, again an alien marriage. Do not give in to these hardships, but oppose them the more boldly, by means that your Fortune ordains you.)

"Iterum . . . iterum": the sibyl predicts that the Trojans will have to fight the Trojan War all over again. Thus, the second half of Virgil's epic, no less than the first, is shaped by repetition of the Trojans' tragic past. But the sibyl also predicts a change in their fortunes: it is a Trojan War that they will win. In a classic article on Virgil's second *Iliad*, W. S. Anderson demonstrated in detail how the Trojans thus play the parts of Homer's victorious Greeks while their own former roles are assumed by their defeated Italian foes.[20] If, in the first half of the poem, the Trojans actively sought to return to versions of Troy and consequently fell into a traumatic, obstructing repetition of their past history as losers, here, in the second half, the past seems to reappear unbidden—through Virgil's Homeric imitations—and the Iliadic war in Italy allows them to reexperience that past as winners and to move forward to found the future Rome, history's big winner. The Trojans now reach their new beginning not simply by forgetting and repressing, but by reversing and "undoing" the past as they repeat it. And this kind of repetition-as-mastery does not thwart narrative progress by circling back on itself in the pattern of Odyssean romance; it rather describes a teleological epic narrative that moves linearly to its final goal of victory. This narrative "sense of an ending," moreover, has its counterpart in an imperial ideology that wished to close off past conflict by finally settling old scores—at the very same time that it claimed to cast them into healing oblivion. Augustus's mastery of Roman history has a deadly finality about it.

At first, however, it is not quite clear that the Trojans have turned the tables on their past as they fight their new *Iliad* in Latium. The sibyl had predicted the appearance of another Achilles, and, as Anderson points out, the Italian Turnus will first attempt to appropriate this role for himself:[21] "hic etiam inuentum Priamo narrabis Achillem" (9.742; "you will bring word to Priam that here, too, an Achilles has been found"). So he taunts Pandarus in Book 9 before he kills him in his *aristeia* within the Trojan camp. Inside this camp, the Trojans once again play the roles of besieged defenders, and Turnus has earlier compared their earthworks to the walls of Troy (144–45); there, too, he compared himself to an Achilles who does not need the arms of Vulcan—"non armis mihi Volcani" (148)—to defeat the Trojans. Turnus is the victim of the irony of his own words, for in the preceding Book 8 the reader has just seen Aeneas receive his divine armor and shield from Vulcan and Venus and thus be confirmed in his identity as the new Achilles. Moreover, the Trojans' camp is just that, a camp, not a city, and it thus recalls not Troy but the Greek camp in the *Iliad*, the fortifications that protected the fleet of Agamemnon. Turnus has just unsuccessfully attempted to burn the Trojans' ships (69–122), and the action cast him in the role of Hector, who in *Iliad* 15–16 launched the counterattack that barely failed to destroy the Greek ships. And it is Hector whom Turnus will be doomed to play at the end of the *Aeneid*. Hector's exploits at Troy were only possible because of Achilles' withdrawal from battle, and it is similarly the absence of Aeneas—who is off seeking allies in Etruria—that permits Turnus and the Latins to hold the field in Book 9. When Aeneas reappears in Book 10, the tide of battle turns, and in Books 11 and 12 the site of the fighting shifts to before the walls of Laurentum. It is the Latins' own city that becomes the new Troy, besieged by Aeneas and his troops. Turnus now seems to concede that Aeneas is indeed the new and greater Achilles, Vulcanic armor and all.

> ibo animis contra, uel magnum praestet Achillem
> factaque Volcani manibus paria induat arma
> ille licet.

(11.438–40)

(I will boldly face him, even if he excels great Achilles, and wears similar arms made by the hands of Vulcan.)

The initial uncertainty about who is playing what role in the new *Iliad*—what corresponds to the uncertainty of battle—is gradually dispelled by the playing out of the Italian war and by the movement from the first three to the last three books of the second half of the poem, which thus hinges in its middle upon Aeneas's return to battle in Book 10. The confusion created by Turnus's rhetoric, in fact, emphasizes the reversal that has taken place: Aeneas and his Trojans go from being besieged to being besiegers, Trojans to "Greeks," losers to winners.

There is a second important, but little-noted pattern of Iliadic repetition and reversal enacted at the very end of the *Aeneid*, in the final events of the duel between Aeneas and Turnus.[22] It is a moment, however, that has been carefully prepared by the epic from its beginning in what is, I shall argue, the single, most extended network of Homeric allusion and perhaps the most significant symbolic nucleus in the poem. Anderson's study focused on the central characters of the *Iliad*, particularly Achilles and Hector, Menelaus and Paris, and the ways in which their roles are disputed between Aeneas and Turnus. But there was a minor player in Homer's epic, Aeneas himself, whose Iliadic career is remembered over and over again by the new poem that bears his name. And it is the way that this career is replayed in remarkably compressed form at the close of the *Aeneid* that measures the extent of the mastery that Aeneas—and the Trojans for whom this collective hero stands—have achieved over a past that they appear compulsively to repeat.

After the prolonged suspense of their combat—the loss and retrieval of Aeneas's spear and Turnus's sword, the flight of Turnus, the council of Jupiter and Juno, the apparition of the Dira, and Juturna's desertion of her brother—the two warriors face one another once again. Turnus makes the first move, his last offensive gesture in the poem.

> nec plura effatus saxum circumspicit ingens,
> saxum antiquum ingens, campo quod forte iacebat,
> limes agro positus litem ut discernet aruis.
> uix illum lecti bis sex ceruice subirent,
> qualia nunc hominum producit corpora tellus;
> ille manu raptum trepida torquebat in hostem
> altior insurgens et cursu concitus heros.

(12.896–902)

(Having said no more, he looked around and saw a huge stone, a huge ancient stone, which happened to be lying on the plain, placed as a marker in the countryside in order to settle disputes over the boundaries of fields; scarcely could twice six chosen men raise it on their shoulders, men with such bodies as

the earth now produces: the hero hurriedly seized it and was throwing it at his
foe, rising to his full height and running at full speed.)

The reader who comes to the *Aeneid* from the *Iliad* experiences a moment
of déjà vu, one that Aeneas himself presumably shares. The scene recalls and
echoes Aeneas's confrontation with the Greek hero Diomedes, the son of
Tydeus, in the fifth book of the *Iliad*.

> But Tydeus's son in his hand caught
> up a stone, a huge thing which no two men could carry
> such as men are now, but by himself he lightly hefted it.
> He threw, and caught Aineas in the hip, in the place where the hip bone
> turns inside the thigh, the place men call the cup socket.
> It smashed the cup socket and broke the tendons both sides of it,
> and the rugged stone tore the skin backward, so that the fighter
> dropping to one knee stayed leaning on the ground with his heavy
> hand, and a covering of black night came over both eyes.
>
> (*Iliad* 5.302–10)

Virgil's hyperbolic imitation of Homer—the stone that no two men could
carry in the *Iliad* is now too much for twelve—increases the heroic awe and
perhaps the desperation of Turnus's last martial act. But the scene is recognizably the same: once again Aeneas is faced by a stone-throwing enemy,
and both he and the reader hold their breath. Will history repeat itself? In
the *Iliad* Aeneas was saved from the hands of Diomedes only through the
intervention of Aphrodite and Apollo; the latter covered the wounded hero
with a dark mist (5.345). The scene was earlier recalled by Juno at the council of the gods in Book 10, when she angrily counters Venus's pleadings on
the Trojans' behalf.

> tu potes Aenean manibus subducere Graium
> proque uiro nebulam et uentos obtendere inanis.
>
> (10.81–82)

(You were able to remove Aeneas from the hands of the Greeks and to present
them with mist and empty air in place of the man.)

And Turnus himself alludes to this episode at the opening of Book 12, when
he boastingly seeks single combat with Aeneas to resolve the war.

> longe illi dea mater erit, quae nube fugacem
> feminea tegat et uanis sese occulat umbris.
>
> (12.52–53)

(Far away will be his goddess mother to cover the fugitive in womanish guise
with a cloud and to conceal herself in empty shadows.)

We should recall, too, that Diomedes is the hero who is conspicuous by his absence in the *Aeneid*. The envoy Venulus, sent out at the beginning of Book 8 (9–17) to summon Diomedes from his new city of Arpi in order to fight the Trojans a second time, returns empty-handed in Book 11 (225–95) with the discouraging news that the Greek hero has declined to come to the Italians' aid. Diomedes is himself haunted by the episode of *Iliad* 5, where he wounded Venus as she came to her son's aid—"et Veneris uiolaui uulnere dextram" (277). The boasting Turnus thus proposes to take Diomedes' place in Book 12, and in one incident in the battle appears to be doing just that: at verses 346–61 he kills Eumedes, the son of Dolon whom, we are reminded (351), Diomedes had slain in the *Iliad* (10.454–57). The poem has thus carefully set the stage for Turnus's casting of the stone, but at the moment when he appears about to duplicate Diomedes' feat and bring Aeneas down once again, Turnus falls short.

> sed neque currentem se nec cognoscit euntem
> tollentemue manu saxumue immane mouentem;
> genua labant, gelidus concreuit frigore sanguis.
> tum lapis ipse uiri uacuum per inane uolutus
> nec spatium euasit totum neque pertulit ictum.
> ac uelut in somnis, oculos ubi languida pressit
> nocte quies, nequiquam auidos extendere cursus
> uelle uidemur et in mediis conatibus aegri
> succidimus; non lingua ualet, non corpore notae
> sufficiunt uires nec uox aut uerba sequuntur:
> sic Turno, quacumque uiam uirtute petiuit,
> successum dea dira negat.
>
> (12.903–14)

(But he knows himself neither running, nor moving, nor as he raises his hands, nor when he is throwing the huge stone: his knees waver, and his blood congeals frozen with cold; his stone itself spins through the empty void, and it neither passed through all the intervening space nor brought the blow home. But as in dreams, when the languid repose of night weighs down upon the eyes, we seem to wish in vain to continue on eagerly running and, infirm, sink down in the midst of our efforts: our tongue is powerless, our usual strength does not imbue our body, neither voice nor words come out: so, to Turnus, by whatever powers he sought to win his way, the dire goddess denies success.)

Thwarted by the gods, Turnus cannot fill Diomedes' shoes, and the scene from *Iliad* 5 does not repeat itself. Aeneas instead enacts what seems to be a therapeutic reversal of his earlier victimization: this time he faces a stone-throwing Diomedes and defeats him. Moreover, when Aeneas subsequently wounds Turnus, the action and language recall his own wounding by Diomedes. Aeneas's flying spear is compared to stones—"saxa"—launched by a siege machine (921–22). The deliberately anachronistic simile balances the Homeric sense of modern distance from archaic heroism, expressed a few lines earlier; both the machine and the hero are able to do the stone throwing of many men, "such as men are now." The simile not only identifies Aeneas with future Roman power but suggests that it is *he* who will emerge as the new Diomedes when his weapon finds its mark.

> per medium stridens transit femur. incidit ictus
> ingens ad terram duplicato poplite Turnus.
>
> (12.926–27)

(Whistling, it passes through the middle of the thigh. Struck down, huge Turnus falls to earth on bended knee.)

In the *Iliad* Diomedes struck Aeneas in the thigh, and the Trojan hero fell to one knee; the scene is repeated and echoed here.[23] Aeneas appears to undo his past defeat at Troy, inflicting it upon another. But this is just what is disturbing in the reciprocity that transforms repetition into mastery: if Turnus fails to become a new Diomedes, he succeeds in becoming a second Aeneas.

And, in fact, the stone-throwing Turnus is *already* assimilated with the Aeneas of the *Iliad*: from the moment that he casts the stone in vain and fails to ward off the onrushing Trojan hero. He recalls the Aeneas who in *Iliad* 20 similarly picked up a stone to defend himself.

> Now Achilleus
> drew his tearing sword and swept in upon him
> crying a terrible cry, but Aineas now in his hand caught
> up a stone, a huge thing which no two men could carry
> such as men are now, but by himself he lightly hefted it.
> And there Aineas would have hit him with the stone as he swept in
> on helm or shield, which would have fended the bitter death from him,
> and Peleus' son would have closed with the sword and stripped the life from him
> had not the shaker of the earth Poseidon sharply perceived all.
>
> (*Iliad* 20.283–91)

The same Homeric formula used to describe Diomedes' combat with Aeneas recurs as Aeneas faces Achilles during the latter's great *aristeia*, the killing spree of *Iliad* 20–22 that climaxes with the death of Hector. Thus the Iliadic Aeneas could neither avoid the stone thrown by Diomedes nor bring down Achilles with a stone of his own. Once again, the gods intervene to save him; Poseidon puts a mist before Achilles' eyes and carries Aeneas off to the edge of the battlefield, safely out of range (318–39). The scene is a crucial one for the whole fiction of the *Aeneid*, for it is here that the god asserts that Aeneas is fated to survive the war and preserve the race of Dardanos (303–8), the Homeric basis for the Aeneas legend itself. Virgil's Neptune recalls the episode in his conversation with Venus at the end of Book 5.

> cum Troia Achilles
> exanimata sequens impingeret agmina muris,
> milia multa daret leto, gemerentque repleti
> amnes nec reperire uiam atque euoluere posset
> in mare se Xanthus, Pelidae tunc ego forti
> congressum Aenean nec dis nec uiribus aequis
> nube caua rapui.

(5.804–10)

(When at Troy Achilles drove the terrified Trojan troops to their walls and sent many thousands to death, and the rivers, choked with bodies, groaned, nor could Xanthus find a way to roll its waters to the sea, then I stole away Aeneas in a hollow cloud, as he, with neither equal strength nor equal favor of the gods, was contending with the powerful son of Peleus.)

The poem has thus foreshadowed its replaying of Aeneas's encounter with Achilles in the same way that its various allusions prepared the reader for a new version of his combat with Diomedes. With astonishing artistry, Virgil combines the two Iliadic episodes almost simultaneously in the final duel between Aeneas and the stone-throwing Turnus. He puts together the two most extended appearances of Aeneas in the *Iliad*, passages that the *Iliad* itself links by the motif of the stone. In both, Aeneas is shown about to be defeated by stronger Greek warriors, but rescued by favoring gods. At the end of the *Aeneid*, Aeneas is allowed to reverse both scenes and play the roles of Diomedes and Achilles, victorious over an Aeneas now played by Turnus.

As Aeneas's two most important and nearly fatal enemies, moreover, Diomedes and Achilles are linked together from the very beginning of the *Aeneid*, from Aeneas's first despairing words as the storm of Juno and Aeolus strikes his ships.

> o terque quaterque beati,
> quis ante ora patrum Troiae sub moenibus altis
> contigit oppetere! o Danaum fortissime gentis
> Tydide! mene Iliacis occumbere campis
> non potuisse tuaque animam hanc effundere dextra,
> saeuus ubi Aeacidae telo iacet Hector, ubi ingens
> Sarpedon, ubi tot Simois correpta sub undis
> scuta uirum galeasque et fortia corpora uoluit!

(Oh, three and four times blessed were those who were fated to fall beneath the high walls of Troy before the eyes of their fathers! Oh Diomedes, strongest of the Greeks, that I had poured out my soul by your right hand and fallen on the fields of Ilium, where fierce Hector and huge Sarpedon lie beneath the spear of Achilles, where the Simois seizes and rolls beneath its waves so many shields, helmets, and bodies of mighty men!)

This famous speech imitates the outcries of Achilles in the *Iliad* (21.273–83) and Odysseus in the *Odyssey* (5.299–312) when both heroes are faced with a watery death. Achilles exclaims:

> I wish now Hektor had killed me, the greatest man grown in this place
> A brave man would have been the slayer, as the slain was a brave man.

> (*Iliad* 21.279–80)

Achilles imagines a death by his nemesis Hector. Aeneas, in a similar situation, thinks of the Diomedes who almost did kill him at Troy, and his thoughts turn immediately to Achilles as well, the Achilles from whom he had a no less narrow escape. Both Greek warriors are clearly on Aeneas's mind; they are the emblems of his traumatic victimization and powerlessness at Troy. Aeneas begins the epic by wishing that they had finished the job, and the trajectory that the *Aeneid* charts from its opening scene to the duel with Turnus at its end is to overcome this regressive death wish by restaging Aeneas's experience in the *Iliad* so that he can exorcise the demons of his past.

But from the first book to the close of the poem Aeneas and Diomedes keep returning as a pair, in what becomes an obsessive motif. In Book 1 Diomedes appears in the bas-reliefs on the temple of Juno in Dido's Carthage (1.471), amid scenes otherwise devoted to Achilles and his victims. At the end of the book, Dido is asking Aeneas about the Trojan War, first about the nature of Diomedes' horses, then about the size of Achilles.

> nunc quales Diomedis equi, nunc quantus Achilles   (1.752)

In Book 2 the Trojans are taken in and destroyed by the wiles of Sinon, they whom neither Diomedes nor Achilles could overthrow.

> quos neque Tydides nec Larisaeus Achilles   (2.197)

In Book 10 the doomed Liger tauntingly declares that in Italy Aeneas will find neither the horses of Diomedes nor the chariot of Achilles.

> non Diomedis equos nec currum cernis Achilli   (10.581)

In Book 11 Turnus responds to Drances by reminding the Italians that the Trojans have twice been defeated; he sarcastically urges the Myrmidons to tremble now before the arms of Troy, and with them should tremble Diomedes and Achilles as well.

> nunc et Tydides et Larisaeus Achilles[24]   (11.404)

In Book 12, when the poem recalls the story of Dolon, the father of Eumedes, whom Diomedes killed as Turnus now kills the son, it also pointedly recalls that Dolon had dared to ask for the horses of Achilles as a reward for his spying upon the Greeks. Diomedes paid him in a different kind.

> ausus Pelidae pretium sibi poscere currus;
> illum Tydides alio pro talibus ausis
> adfecit pretio nec equis aspirat Achilli.
>
> (12.350–52)

Where the four preceding instances linked Diomedes and Achilles together in one line of verse, this last one sandwiches Diomedes between two verses in which the name of Achilles appears. This pairing of the two Greek heroes who were Aeneas's worst nightmares forms part of what now can be seen as a sustained verbal and symbolic chain running through the entire *Aeneid*. It gives the sensation of a textual tic, as if the poem experienced a repetition compulsion of its own.

The function of these insistent recollections of Aeneas's experience in the *Iliad* is to converge and focus attention upon the *Aeneid*'s final duel: upon the moment when Turnus casts the giant stone at the poem's hero. The double Homeric allusion creates a truly uncanny reading experience. In the one and the same motion of Turnus we see one episode of Aeneas's past history on the verge of repeating itself—only to turn into a reversal of another episode of that history. The moment of the overcoming of Aeneas's Trojan past comes at dizzying speed, and the reader cannot locate just when it takes place: just when his opponent Turnus exchanges Iliadic identities—from that of Diomedes, the successful wounder of Aeneas, to that of Aeneas, the failed assailant of Achilles. And Aeneas himself becomes both the new Achilles and—as he casts his own weapon—the new Diomedes as well. His assumption of the role of Achilles, claimed earlier in the poem by Turnus, is, of course, confirmed by the duel's primary Homeric model, Achilles' killing of Hector in *Iliad* 22. The simile of the dream that immediately follows the throwing of Turnus's stone (12.908–12) recalls *Iliad* 22.195–201, and assimilates Turnus once again with the victim Hector. But the *Aeneid* insists that Aeneas reenact and reverse not only Homer's central Trojan tragedy of Hector, but also his *own* failures at Troy before Diomedes and Achilles. His victory over Turnus is a vindication both for himself and for his defeated Trojan nation.

This vindication and the reciprocity of doing unto others what has been done to oneself amount to a taking of vengeance upon the past. Freud describes in *Beyond the Pleasure Principle* the child who masters his experience of powerlessness by repeating it in play.

> As the child passes over from the passivity of the experience to the activity of the game, he hands on the disagreeable experience to one of his playmates and in this way revenges himself on a substitute.[25]

The games of war and politics depicted by the *Aeneid* have more serious consequences. Revenge is, of course, a central Iliadic theme; Achilles' killing of Hector is a private act of vengeance for the death of Patroclus that also ensures the conquest of Troy: the city as well as the hero is mourned in the *Iliad*'s final lines. The *Aeneid* has its own version of this revenge plot in Aeneas's duty and desire to avenge Pallas: in the poem's final scene the sight of the baldric of Pallas on the fallen Turnus overcomes the inclination toward mercy that Aeneas momentarily shows for his enemy. But here, private vengeance seems secondary, almost tacked on to the historical plot of the poem, the conquest of Italy that leads to the foundation of Rome. Readers have often felt that Aeneas's feelings for Pallas cannot be compared to Achilles' grief for Patroclus.[26] But the conquest of Italy is itself presented, through the poem's pattern of Iliadic repetition, as the Trojan's reversal of, and (unconscious) vengeance for, the injuries of their past defeat. The theme of revenge is thus doubled in Virgil's second *Iliad*, and its imperative of revenge—to repeat the past in the name of retribution—speaks against the notion that the past can be forgotten so that the present can begin anew: the notion expressed in the Augustan ideology of a new national foundation that, we have seen, shapes the Odyssean first half of the *Aeneid*. That notion is enunciated again, only a few verses before Aeneas defeats and kills Turnus, in the settlement that Jupiter reaches with Juno.

The conference of Jupiter and Juno, in fact, represents an irruption into the Iliadic scenario of Book 12 of the sensibility and Odyssean models of the first half of the poem. Critics have noted Virgil's imitations of the dialogue of Zeus and Hera in Book 15.14–77 of the *Iliad*, where the king of the gods overcomes the obstructing designs of his wife, and of the exchange between Zeus and Athena that licenses her to seal the fate of Hector in *Iliad* 22.167–87.[27] One does expect Iliadic parallels in a book that so carefully plays itself off against *Iliad* 22. But the passage evokes another Homeric colloquy between Zeus and Athena, the one that ends the *Odyssey* (24.472–88).[28] Looking down at the civil strife that has arisen in Ithaca between Odysseus and the relatives of the slain suitors, Athena implores Zeus to intervene. Zeus sends her to earth to break up the fighting (529–32) and casts down his own thunderbolt to stop the raging Odysseus (539–40). But first he declares the terms of the future peace.

Now that noble Odysseus has punished the suitors, let them
make their oaths of faith and friendship, and let him be king
always; and let us make them forget the death of their brothers
and sons, and let them be friends with each other, as in the time past,
and let them have prosperity and peace in abundance.[29]

(24.482–86)

The *Odyssey* ends with the reconciliation between warring sides, and it is
such an act that Virgil's Jupiter ordains as a melding of Italian and Trojan
identities into the future Roman people (12.834–40). The Odyssean model
contains an act of forgetting—"ἔκλησιν" (24.485)—of burying the past. It
also reinforces the sense that the fighting in the *Aeneid* between two peoples
destined to live in eternal peace (12.504) is a form of civil war, and draws a
topical analogy to the civil wars of Rome's recent history. The Odyssean
Aeneid saw the Trojans escaping their past by a process of forgetting, and
here this new intrusion of Odyssean elements into Virgil's second *Iliad* also
indicates a policy of forget and forgive. The Augustan ideology that animated the first half of the poem—with its insistence on a new beginning
and a fresh slate—can now be seen as an extension of the vaunted *clementia*
of the new ruler. Augustus himself laconically claimed in his *Res Gestae*
(1.3): "I spared all citizens who sought pardon."

He was, of course, lying. Victims of the proscriptions knew better, including Cicero, the proposer of an amnesty that never went into effect. And
another cornerstone of Augustan propaganda as important as the promise of
clemency was the call to revenge, specifically the obligation of *pietas*: Augustus's obligation to avenge the assassinated Julius Caesar, the same Caesar
whose triumviral career his heir preferred to forget. Augustan poets celebrated the new *princeps* as the revenger—"ultor"—of his adoptive father,
and Augustus's filial piety became a screen behind which to eliminate his
enemies.[30]

At the end, and as the climax of, the *Metamorphoses*, Ovid retells the
story of Julius Caesar's death and apotheosis. Venus sees the assassination
coming and thinks back on the trials of her Trojans and of the precious
Julian line, beginning with her wounding by Diomedes at Troy (15.769). As
the swords are drawn, she tries to shield Caesar by concealing him in a
cloud, as Aeneas had once been rescued from Diomedes (803–5). But she is
consoled by Jupiter, who tells her of the future feats of Augustus

> qui nominis heres
> inpositum feret unus onus caesique parentis
> nos in bella suos fortissimus ultor habebit.
> illius auspiciis obsessae moenia pacem
> victa petent Mutinae, Pharsalia sentiet illum,
> Emathiique iterum madefient caede Philippi,

et magnum Siculis nomen superabitur undis,
Romanique ducis coniunx Aegyptia taedae
non bene fisa cadet, frustraque erit illa minata,
servitura suo Capitolia nostra Canopo.
quid tibi barbariem gentesque ab utroque iacentes
oceano numerem? quodcumque habitabile tellus
sustinet, huius erit: pontus quoque serviet illi![31]

(15.819-31)

(who, heir to the name of Caesar, will bear alone the burden imposed on him,
and as the most dauntless avenger of his father's murder will have us on his side
in his wars. Under his command the defeated walls of besieged Mutina will sue
for peace; Pharsalia will feel his presence, and Emathian Philippi will once again
be soaked with blood; the great name of Pompey will be defeated in Sicilian
waters, and the Egyptian consort of the Roman general, counting unwisely on
her "marriage," will fall and in vain will she have threatened that our Capitol
should serve her Canopus. Why should I enumerate to you barbarian lands and
peoples lying on either side of the ocean? Whatever habitable land the earth
supports will be his: even the sea will serve him.)

There is something peculiar about the way that this passage moves from the
avenging of Julius Caesar to the prospect of world conquest. The reason is
that while the wars against the assassins of Caesar and the surviving Pom-
peians may be justified by *pietas*, the struggle with Antony pitted two Caesarian factions against one another, each of whom could claim true heirship,
Antony through the child Caesarion that Cleopatra had born to Julius. And
so, following the same logic as the scene of Actium on the shield of Aeneas,
this Roman civil war is transformed into a foreign war, a war against Cleopatra rather than Antony—although it, too, is nominally sanctioned by the
duty of revenge.

Ovid is not above irony, and his narrator has earlier declared with a
straight face that Caesar had to be killed and made into a god in order that
his son would not be born of mortal seed (760–61). In addition to its flippancy, the passage forgets that Augustus was only the adopted son of the
slain dictator. It is small wonder that Augustus sent the poet packing into
exile.[32] Here Ovid is having fun, particularly with the *Aeneid* and the whole
apparatus of the Troy legend: the scene imitates the exchange between
Venus and Jupiter in *Aeneid* 1. We may even read it as a kind of political
gloss on the *Aeneid*'s reversal of the Trojans' fortunes at Troy, of which
Aeneas's personal reversal of his defeat by Diomedes is an emblem. Here
Diomedes is assimilated with the assassins of Caesar/political enemies of
Augustus whose past successes against Venus and her Julian line will be
reversed and revenged by the civil wars.

Even if Ovid's passage is sending up the party line, it demonstrates how central to that official line was the cry for vengeance. Augustus built the temple of Mars Ultor in his new forum, as well as the temple to the Deified Julius in the old one. The idea of vengeance was represented in a third propagandistic building project, the temple of Apollo on the Palatine, dedicated in 28 B.C.—the temple where the emperor is depicted sitting in triumph on Aeneas's shield (8.720–22). Its porticoes were decorated with the statues of the fifty Danaids killing their bridegrooms.[33] This is the scene portrayed on the baldric of Pallas (10.497–98), the sight of which produces Aeneas's final vindictive fury. The act of vengeance that concludes the poem thus seems to possess an imperial sanction.[34]

In fact we can now see how the final choice of Aeneas—whether to spare or kill the suppliant Turnus—corresponds in little to the larger division of the *Aeneid* into its Odyssean and Iliadic halves, each informed by the alternative ideological messages of *clementia* and *pietas* sent out by the new regime. Clemency and revenge are both strategies for overcoming the past, the first by forgetting, the second by undoing; the first sees repetition of the past as regressive, the second sees in such repetition the possibility of mastery, and these negative and positive types of repetition produce the opposing romance and epic narratives of the two halves of the poem. They are matched at the very end of the *Aeneid* in the moment of Aeneas's hesitation over the defeated Turnus, with the possibility of clemency and reconciliation it contains, and in the welling up of memory and vengeance at the sight of the fatal baldric. And the killing of Turnus is itself contrasted in Book 12 with the settlement reached shortly before by Juno and Jupiter to let bygones be bygones. The poem, like the regime, has it both ways, but in the process it discloses the contradictions in the regime's ideology: its promise to pardon and avenge at the same time.

And in the end, because it happens at the end of the poem, vengeance seems to win out. Yet Aeneas's revenge has been overdetermined from the beginning of the *Aeneid*, for he is the hero outstanding for his *pietas*—"insignem pietate" (1.10)—and it is in his final act that the full meaning is revealed of the virtue that links him with his descendant, Augustus. The entreating Turnus calls upon Aeneas to remember Anchises (933–34), and Alessandro Barchiesi has brilliantly studied how his words echo Priam's speech to Achilles in their sublime reconciliation scene in the last book of the *Iliad*.[35] We have seen how the first half of the *Aeneid* labored to get rid of the father, transforming Anchises as a figure of Julius Caesar from an emblem of the burden of the past into a divine source of strength, the blessed spirit of the underworld who famously instructs Aeneas to spare the defeated (6.853). But the evocation of filial piety in its second half may only bring the father back in the tragic role of a ghost crying for vengeance.[36]

The conquering of *clementia* by *pietas* at the end of the poem, moreover, follows the *narrative* sequence from its first to its second half. Within the poem's fiction and the psychological development it maps out for its hero and his people, this sequence may rationalize the contradiction in its double message. It describes a two-step process by which the Trojans may escape the hold of their past: they must first repress a compulsive repetition that returns them in the course of their wanderings to the scene and experience of their earlier loss; then, and only then, will they be able to repeat that experience therapeutically—if with no less compulsion—with a different outcome of victory. The Trojans' history, and the *Aeneid* itself, thus assume the shape of a teleological narrative in which the Trojans' past defeat can be treated as a closed chapter. But in the topical, ideological terms that inform the *Aeneid*, the same sequence suggests the supersession of a policy of clemency by one of revenge: the Augustan regime will put the past of civil war behind it not simply by (white)washing away its memory, but by settling accounts. The narrative logic of the epic thus seems to make inevitable its final moment: the killing of Turnus.

But will this revenge in fact be final, the last death demanded by a tragic past that Rome's history will now get over and go beyond? Augustus's pious revenge that claimed to put an end to the civil wars was itself a part and continuation of those wars. And in the killing of Turnus the *Aeneid* concludes with nothing less than *an image of civil war*, an ending that calls its own closure into question. For the repetition and reversal of Aeneas's Iliadic career in the final duel with Turnus not only constitutes the hero's personal revenge upon his own past, but it also makes the Turnus whom Aeneas defeats and kills a mirror image of Aeneas himself, the Aeneas who barely escaped Diomedes and Achilles at Troy.[37] This doubling effect is reinforced by Virgil's use of internal echoes. When Jupiter's fury assumes the shape of a bird of evil omen and beats its wings before Turnus's face, he is terrified.

> illi membra nouus soluit formidine torpor,
> arrectaeque horrore comae et uox faucibus haesit.
>
> (12.867–68)

(An unwonted numbness unknits his limbs with fear, his hair stood up on end with horror and his voice stuck in his throat.)

The bristling hair and voicelessness are traits that the reader has learned to associate with Aeneas in the early books of the poem (2.773; 3.48; 4.280). The numbness slackening Turnus's limbs prefigures the chill of death that fills his body in the penultimate verse—"ast illi soluuntur frigore membra" (12.951)—a phrase that, with stunning poetic virtuosity, recalls the very first appearance of Aeneas in the poem—"extemplo Aeneae soluuntur frigore membra" (1.92)—during the opening storm episode.[38] Turnus has completely assumed Aeneas's role as victim in the first half of the poem, and Aeneas thus kills his own double. A meliorative reading would see Aeneas overcoming a former self that he has now outgrown. But the scene is unmistakably one of civil war. No less than the fratricidal twins Romulus and Remus, this is a figure of Rome turning a sword upon herself in the act of foundation—"condit" (12.950). The burying of the hero's sword in Turnus's breast—"sub pectore" (950)—recalls Dido's self-inflicted wound (4.689), and this image may be equally suicidal.

In fact, the end of the *Aeneid* inverts the ideological project of the depiction of the battle of Actium on the shield of Aeneas—the project shared by Ovid in *Metamorphoses* 15—that transformed the civil war with Antony into a war of imperial, foreign conquest. Here the conquest of Italy by the Trojan foreign power contains a scenario of civil war. Like Cleopatra on the shield, the woman Dido represented the otherness of the foreigner in the first half of the poem, as it explored Rome's relationship with Carthage and the East. But Turnus, Aeneas's anatagonist in the second half, possesses the same gender as the hero, and the war in Latium is one of like against like; the Trojans, in fact, enter into a preexisting conflict of Italians against Italians. The sequence of the poem here follows the progress of Rome's history: first the Punic Wars and her rise to world domination, then her fall into internecine strife. What might have seemed a straightforward teleological plot of epic conquest, where a historically destined Rome creates narrative and history by defeating an external enemy who embodies a demonic, nonnarratable repetition—the never-say-die Turnus who is inspired by the infernal Fury Allecto—can now also be read as Rome wrestling with her own inner demons, the demons of a national repetition compulsion.

For the collapse of difference in civil war also introduces an ambiguity into the pattern of repetition-as-reversal that is the other teleological principle of Virgil's second *Iliad*. This is the ambiguity that Brooks sees already inhabiting the nature of repetition itself: "We cannot say whether this is a return *to* or a return *of*"—whether it is progress or regress. Once Turnus and Aeneas become interchangeable—both Romans—Aeneas seems to be victimizing himself even as he undoes his former victimization. What can be seen in one light as a therapeutic narrative mastering a traumatic past is in another only the perpetuation of that past, a mere repetition that cannot be narrated. Augustus repeats the violence of civil war that he seeks to end. His revenge may be part of a larger cycle of reciprocity rather than a final settlement. Or it may be both at once.

In a famous passage of the *Annals* (1.8–10), Tacitus describes the funeral of Augustus and the verdicts delivered upon the career of the first emperor. Intelligent persons—"prudentes"—differed, he says, in their praise and criticism.

One opinion was as follows. Filial duty and a national emergency, in which there was no place for law-abiding conduct, had driven him to civil war—and this can be neither initiated nor maintained by decent methods.[39] (1.9)

If Augustus had no choice in his methods, the results had been nonetheless impressive.

The empire's frontiers were on the ocean, or distant rivers. Armies, provinces, fleets, the whole system was interrelated. Roman citizens were protected by the law. Provincials were decently treated. Rome itself had been lavishly beautified. Force had been sparingly used—merely to preserve peace for the majority. (1.9)

But Tacitus reports a counter opinion as well.

The opposite view went like this. Filial duty and national crisis had been merely pretexts ("obtentui"). In actual fact, the motive of Octavian, the future Augustus, was lust for power. . . . His judicial murders and land distributions were distasteful even to those who carried them out. True, Cassius and Brutus died because he had inherited a feud against them; nevertheless, personal enmities ought to be sacrificed to the public interest. . . . After that there had certainly been peace, but it was a bloodstained peace. (1.10)

And the passage goes on to list Augustus's most notable victims.

It is apparent that Tacitus adheres to the second opinion, politically realistic, if not downright cynical.[40] But it is the first opinion that is more interesting here, for it seems very close to the perspective of the *Aeneid*. It was impossible for Augustus to refound Rome except through the base instrument of civil war. The violence of war makes the two contending sides look alike; it brutalizes even those whose cause is just. But the end of the *Aeneid* goes beyond the idea that warfare confuses its combatants. It does not let Augustus off so easily, for this is a special kind of war, a civil war in which the two sides were indistinguishable in the first place: where, Tacitus remarks, to take up arms at all is unjust. Virgil's hopes in the Augustan settlement may have been real enough, hopes that one-man rule might put an end to warring faction and institute good government, that the new regime might make good its general promise to provide clemency despite local exceptions, that it would thus offer a departure and escape from the calamities of recent history; but the end of the *Aeneid* does not disguise the part that the regime played in that history, nor the possible continuity with that history of its present policies.

It is impossible, however, to know where the poet's own convictions leave off and where the party line begins. The political contradictions of the *Aeneid* are those of an ideology that preached both forgiveness and revenge, that repetition of the past is disaster, that repetition is a way to overcome the past. The poem, in this sense, is never less than ideology. But this double ideology both plots out and unravels the narrative by which the *Aeneid*— and Augustus, too—would master and impose an ending on cyclical repetition. For the *princeps*, this is the cycle of retaliatory violence produced by civil war. The confusion of positive and negative repetition suggests that the poem's narrative of Roman foundation may collapse back upon itself as easily as it may achieve closure in a timeless imperial destiny, the empire without end. And thus the poem's progress from the Trojans' aimless, non-narratable wanderings of its little Odyssey to the teleological narrative of its second Iliad—its achievement of narrative itself—may be no progress at all. If we are to try to locate the poet behind the ideological terms that he negotiates into poetic form, we might say that to the extent that the *Aeneid* works toward and projects narrative completion, even as it calls the possibility of closure and narrative into question, Virgil seems to want to believe in the first opinion of Tacitus's *prudentes*; that questioning, however, contains a darker fear that their second opinion may be closer to the truth.

If that fear were to be confirmed, the *Aeneid* would look different; just how different may be seen in one of the first critical rewritings of the poem. Ovid's relationship to Virgil is rarely less than sardonic; his relationship to the Augustan regime earned him banishment. In Book 14 of the *Metamorphoses* he includes a version of the *Aeneid* itself in a miniaturized, literally belittling form. Here is his summary description of the war in Italy.

> perstat, habetque deos pars utraque, quodque deorum est
> instar, habent animos; nec iam dotalia regna,
> nec sceptrum soceri, nec te, Lavinia virgo,
> sed vicisse petunt deponendique pudore
> bella gerunt, tandemque Venus victricia nati
> arma videt, Turnusque cadit.
>
> (14.568–73)

(the war goes on, and each side has its gods, and what is equivalent to gods, they had spirits filled with animosity; and now neither the dowry of a kingdom, nor the sceptre of a father-in-law, nor you, Lavinian maiden, do they seek, but only to have conquered, and they wage war on account of the shame of yielding, until at length Venus sees her son's arms victorious and Turnus fell.)

This is a worst-case scenario of the *Aeneid* and of the Roman history that it seeks symbolically to represent. The later Augustan poet depicts the epic struggle as a contest of sheer power and will. The divinely sanctioned historical plan of the *Aeneid* is meaningless, not only because both Trojans and Latins have gods on their side, but also because the gods—through an ironic version of the proverbial "audentes deus ipse iuvat" (*Met.* 10.586)—are interchangeable with the animosity of the warriors. The ostensible causes, just or unjust, that might distinguish the belligerents are swept aside as the war progresses and is fought solely for the sake of domination. One cannot construct a narrative out of naked violence, and Ovid does not even try.

Palinurus and the Sacrifice of the Hero

When Aeneas appears to kill his alter ego in the duel with Turnus, the final scene of the epic also suggests the fate of heroic selfhood in the *Aeneid*. Virgil sings of arms and the man, but the man may not count for much: Aeneas himself may be reduced to one more piece of weaponry, the instrument of his historical destiny. What has been described as the hero's overcoming of his past identity—symbolized by the deaths of his wife and father at the endings of Books 2 and 3, respectively—is given an *ethical* construction by the poem as a process of self-sacrifice whose leading instance is the hero's renunciation of his love for Dido, the Dido who dies at the end of Book 4. The two forms of self-abnegation are as continuous as this formal pattern suggests them to be: the lost past persists into the present as memory, and present desire is an attempt to recover past losses; Dido and Carthage are another version of Troy. Aeneas is not allowed to transfer affective ties except to a collective Roman future; he is asked to give up the ties that constitute individual personality and will. The result is the lackluster, depersonalized hero for which readers have praised and (mostly) blamed Virgil, a hero stolid to the point of passivity—especially when Aeneas is compared to his Homeric prototypes, the passionate and willful characters of Odysseus and Achilles.[41] But individuality and selfhood may be beside the point so long as Aeneas has history on his side. The *Aeneid* thus redefines the epic hero, whose heroic virtue now consists in the sacrifice of his own independent will—a will independent from his national mission. It makes a virtue of historical necessity.

The *Aeneid* doubles its themes so that the imperative to escape the past is also the demand for the sacrifice of the individual. Here, too, it conforms closely to the prevailing ideological climate. The past that must be put behind in the poem refers topically to Rome's disastrous recent past of civil wars: and this had been an age of great individuals. After years of strife dominated by mighty warlords, Virgil's fellow Romans might have agreed with Brecht's dictum that a great man is a national calamity. The Augustan regime in any event declared an end to this personal style of politics. Syme describes its new moral program.

> It was not merely the vices of the *principes* that barred them from recognition. Their virtues had been pernicious. Pompeius's pursuit of *gloria*, Caesar's jealous cult of his *dignitas* and his *magnitudo animi*, the candour and chivalry of

Antonius—all these qualities had to be eradicated from the *principes* of the New State. If anything remained in the Commonwealth, it was to be monopolized by the Princeps, along with *clementia*. The governing class was left with the satisfaction of the less decorative virtues: if it lacked them, it must learn them.[42]

Where all power converged on the emperor, the supporting cast became faceless. Yet Augustus, too, projected a propagandistic image of selflessness. Not only did his clemency forbear personal enmities, but Augustus had publicly relinquished all power in 27 B.C. to the Roman Senate and People, and was ostensibly but the first among equals. The emperor set an example for others. Responsibility for the common good was to outweigh, though it could not dispense with, the cultivation of individual honor that was the traditional goal of Roman political life. There was to be little room, however, for great personalities and for the factions that might grow up around them. The suppression of a politically suspect individuality was thus fitted into an ethos of self-sacrifice. And in the *Aeneid* this ethos becomes heroic.

The *Aeneid* explicitly takes up the idea of sacrifice in the celebrated episode of the helmsman Palinurus, the single individual whom Neptune demands in sacrifice to ensure the arrival of Aeneas's fleet at its Italian destination. Placed at the end of Book 5, the death of Palinurus is thus the fourth in the series of deaths—following those of Creusa, Anchises, and Dido—that have stripped Aeneas of personal ties and identity, and it stands, I shall argue, for the sacrifice that Aeneas, in his role as leader of the Trojan mission, must make of his own individuality, even of his heroic agency in the poem. The self-sacrificing heroism of the *Aeneid* is defined in marked contrast to the model of the *Odyssey* and its individualistic hero, a model that Virgil's episode inverts and rejects. The random wanderings of Odyssean romance—which finally come to an end for Aeneas when he and his ships reach Italy at the beginning of Book 6—can thus characterize an errant individuality that the epic plot must overcome, just as it overcomes the Trojans' obsessive repetition of their past. Here, then, is another dimension of the *Aeneid*'s narrative opposition between epic and romance. As it distinguishes the experience of Iliadic victors and Odyssean losers, this opposition places the individual with the losers, for it is individuality—whether on the winning or losing side—that loses out in the larger epic scheme of Roman history. There is a further analogy to this opposition, in the Palinurus episode and elsewhere in the *Aeneid*, in the poem's use of the vocabulary of Fate and Fortune. The epic of the new imperial order places individuality in the domain of chance, at odds with the national plan that is preordained by destiny: as individual, even the poem's hero is expendable.

Just how little Aeneas may count in the historical scheme of things is revealed by Venus. The goddess is the hero's mother and special patron. Yet when the war in Italy seems to go against the Trojans in Book 9, she is ready with a fallback plan in which Aeneas will have no part. So she pleads at the divine council at the beginning of Book 10:

> liceat dimittere ab armis
> incolumem Ascanium, liceat superesse nepotem.
> Aeneas sane ignotis iactetur in undis
> et, quamcumque uiam dederit Fortuna, sequatur:
> hunc tegere et dirae ualeam subducere pugnae.
> est Amathus, est celsa mihi Paphus atque Cythera
> Idaliaeque domus: positis inglorius armis
> exigat hic aeuum. magna dicione iubeto
> Karthago premat Ausoniam: nihil urbibus inde
> obstabit Tyriis. quid pestem euadere belli
> iuuit et Argolicos medium fugisse per ignis,
> totque maris uastaeque exhausta pericula terrae,
> dum Latium Teucri recidiuaque Pergama quaerunt?
> non satius, cineres patriae insedisse supremos
> atque solum quo Troia fuit? Xanthum et Simoenta
> redde, oro, miseris iterumque reuoluere casus
> da, pater, Iliacos Teucris.

> (10.46–62)

(Let it be lawful for me to remove Ascanius safely from the clash of arms, let my grandson survive. Let Aeneas be tossed upon unknown seas, and let him follow whatever path Fortune will give him: let me avail to shield and withdraw Ascanius from the dire combat. I possess Amathus, lofty Paphus and Cythera, and the Idalian precinct: here, having put aside arms, let him live out his days inglorious. Bid Carthage in her great power to press down Ausonia: no opposition to the Punic cities will arise from Italy. What has it availed to have escaped the plague of war and to have fled through the midst of Greek fires, to have exhausted all the dangers of the sea and of desolate lands, while the Trojans seek Latium and a rebuilt Pergamum? Would it not have been more than enough to have settled on the last ashes of their country and on the soil where Troy once was? I beseech you, father, give back to the wretched Trojans the Xanthus and Simois and let them again repeat the lot of Troy.)

Venus's initial willingness to abandon Aeneas to Fortune and to the chance of the waves and winds is balanced by her final urging that the Trojans be brought back to Troy. In the poem's terms, these are identical fates: her speech spells out the equation that the first half of the *Aeneid* had made between the wanderings of the Trojans in the uncharted realm ("ignotis . . . undis") of Odyssean romance and a regressive ("recidiuaque Pergamaque"), circular ("reuoluere") repetition of their past. For Ascanius she requests a third alternative that, at first glance, is no less generically identified with romance. At the end of Book 1, Venus had substituted Cupid for Ascanius on the lap of Dido and carried away the sleeping boy for one night to her flowery Idalian grove (1.691–94). Now she is prepared to keep Ascanius permanently in her shrine, where he will lead an undoubtedly pleasant, but inglorious life. We are reminded of the choice that Achilles has in the *Iliad* to return to Phthia and live to a ripe old age in obscurity (9.414–16). We are also reminded of the pleasure gardens of Calypso and Circe that detain Odysseus and that are the models that lie behind Dido's Carthage. The temptation to forsake epic glory in order to dwell in a *locus amoenus*, a venereal garden of love, will become in the epic tradition that follows Virgil the romance alternative par excellence.[43]

But Venus's special pleading for Ascanius has its ulterior motive that belies her apparent attempt to isolate him from history. Ascanius-Iulus is the founder of the Julian line, the line of Augustus. Despite Venus's earlier disclaiming of empire (42), it is this Roman imperial future that the goddess is determined to safeguard. Venus knows that this future is destined by Fate—she has been told so by Jupiter back in Book 1—and her whole speech, with its specter of a historically victorious Carthage, is not to be taken altogether seriously; she is trying to sway opinion at the divine council. But Venus reveals her priorities nonetheless. The future Rome is to be founded with Aeneas or without him. As long as Ascanius survives unharmed, she is content to leave her son to the mercy of Fortune and the sea—"quamcumque uiam dederit Fortuna, sequatur."

Venus's words recall those of Palinurus when he and the Trojan fleet are caught in the storm that rises at the opening of Book 5:

> superat quoniam Fortuna, sequamur,
> quoque uocat, uertamus iter.
>
> (5.22–23)

(Since Fortune prevails, let us follow, and where she calls let us turn our course.)

The figure of Palinurus frames Book 5, and this turning before the storm of Fortune at its beginning will correspond at its end with his death, the random death of one for many arranged by Venus and Neptune (779–815). Palinurus confers during the storm with Aeneas, who agrees with the helmsman's decision to let the ships run off course before the winds toward Sicily (17–31); after Palinurus is swept overboard, Aeneas takes his place at the helm and laments the pilot's death (867–71).

Palinurus is, in fact, a surrogate for Aeneas in the hero's capacity as leader, as head of the ship of state. The episode of his death is the *Aeneid*'s symbolic substitution for that complete sacrifice of the hero that Venus will later offer to make for the sake of Ascanius and the Roman future. Palinurus is the logical—if apparently fortuitous—choice for sacrificial victim once Neptune agrees to guarantee the Trojan fleet's arrival in Italy. The helmsman becomes expendable. And, in fact, the opening storm has already shown his ineffectiveness. In contrast to the smooth sailing of divine purpose, the attempts of human beings to guide and control their destiny ultimately yield to Fortune and the wayward play of chance. And this may be Aeneas's situation as well as that of his pilot.

The episode of Palinurus has long posed an interpretive crux because of the discrepancies between the poem's third-person narration of his death at the end of Book 5 (835f.) and the first-person account that his shade itself gives to Aeneas in the underworld in Book 6 (337–83). Critics have viewed these discrepancies as evidence of the unfinished state of the *Aeneid* at Virgil's death.[44] In Book 5 Palinurus rejects the invitation of the god of sleep to rest from his vigilant labors; the god makes him drowsy by sprinkling the dew of Lethe upon his head, and casts him into the waters that Neptune has calmed. As he falls, Palinurus tears away the helm and stern with him. Aeneas takes over the drifting ship and, ironically, laments over what he takes to be an accident—"casu" (869). He complains that Palinurus had been too trusting in the sea and sky (870), whereas the pilot had resolutely refused to trust in the monstrous deep (849). But in Book 6 Aeneas asks Palinurus what god had been responsible for his death, and it is the helmsman who describes what happened to him as an accident: by chance— "forte" (349)—the helm was torn away by the rough seas, and the loyal helmsman was dragged along with it. After three nights clinging to the rudder on the stormy waters, Palinurus on the fourth dawn reached Italy, where the hostile inhabitants killed him. This story does not fit the time scheme of the poem, for only one day appears to go by between the death of Palinurus at the end of Book 5 and the visit to the underworld in Book 6.

Some of the discrepancies in the two versions of the episode—particularly those involving the perspectives of Aeneas and Palinurus—can be taken to be deliberate and not the product of changed plans that the poet did not live to revise and make consistent. Part of the pathos of the helmsman's story consists in the inability of mortals to perceive the workings of the gods upon them, in the story's own wavering between the sacrificial design of Neptune and the naturalistic explanation that Palinurus, for all his vigilance, fell asleep and was washed overboard: between divine plot and sheer accident. This uncertainty already suggests an opposition between Fate and Fortune: the course of destiny is experienced by human beings as chance contingency—the very randomness that casts on Palinurus the lot of sacrificial victim. Furthermore, many—though not all—of the discrepancies introduced in Book 6 can be explained as efforts to bring the episode closer to the Odyssean model that it both imitates and inverts.

The meeting with Palinurus in the underworld, where the helmsman complains that he has been left unburied and cannot enter the realm of the dead, has been rightly seen as an imitation of Odysseus's meeting with the unburied shade of Elpenor in the *Odyssey*'s underworld scene (11.51–63); Elpenor had fallen to his death from Circe's roof at the end of the preceding book (10.551–60) of Homer's epic. In each case the hero meets a companion who does not survive the trip and who is in need of burial. But the resemblance does not appear to go much farther: the slow-witted, drunken Elpenor—whose death really is an accident—is hardly at all like the responsible steersman of Aeneas's fleet. And exclusive attention to this Odyssean model has obscured a more significant pattern of imitation of the *Odyssey* that runs through and structures the entire story of Palinurus.

We should remember that Odysseus, too, loses his pilot.

> And at the stern of the ship the mast pole
> crashed down on the steersman's head and pounded to pieces
> all the bones of his head, so that he like a diver
> dropped from the high deck, and the proud life left his bones there.
> Zeus with thunder and lightning together crashed on our vessel,
> and struck by the thunderbolt of Zeus, she spun in a circle,
> and all was full of brimstone. My men were thrown in the water,
> and bobbing like sea crows they were washed away on the running
> waves all around the black ship, and the god took away their homecoming.
> But I went on my way through the vessel, to where the high seas
> had worked the keel free out of the hull, and the bare keel floated
> on the swell, which had broken the mast off at the keel; yet
> still there was a backstay made out of oxhide fastened
> to it. With this I lashed together both keel and mast, then
> rode the two of them, while the deadly stormwinds carried me.
>
> (12.411–25)

This is the storm of *Odyssey* 12 that not only kills the steersman of Odysseus's ship, but his entire crew as well, guilty as they are of eating the cattle of Helios. It is placed in the same position in the *Odyssey* that the episode of Palinurus occupies in the *Aeneid*: the last trial by sea that the poem narrates before the hero reaches his destination. For in the next book the Phaeacians bring Odysseus to Ithaca in their magic ship (*Od.* 13.70f.), while he falls asleep: "the sweetest kind of sleep with no wakening, most like / death" (13.80–81). This final Odyssean storm, moreover, has been recalled at the opening of Book 5 in the storm before which Palinurus turns his sails.

> ut pelagus tenuere rates nec iam amplius ulla
> occurrit tellus, maria undique et undique caelum,

olli caeruleus supra caput astitit imber,
noctem hiememque ferens, et inhorruit unda tenebris.
ipse gubernator puppi Palinurus ab alta:
"heu! quianam tanti cinxerunt aethera nimbi?
quidue, pater Neptune, paras?"

(5.8–14)

(As the ships reached the deep and no land at all is any longer in sight, but sea
and sky on all sides, then there loomed a blue raincloud overhead, bearing night
and storm, and the waves grew dark beneath its shadows. The helmsman Palinurus himself cries from the lofty stern: "Alas! Why have so many clouds encir-
cled the heavens? What are you preparing, Father Neptune?")

The passage is clearly modeled upon and virtually translates the rising of the
storm of *Odyssey* 12.

But after we had left the island and there was no more
land in sight, but only the sky and sea, then Kronian
Zeus drew on a blue-black cloud, and settled it over
the hollow ship, and the open sea was darkened beneath it.

(12.403–6)

Book 5 thus evokes twice—at its beginning and end, and around the figure
of Palinurus—the storm that wrecks the ship of Odysseus. The storm that
opens the book, moreover, looks back to the great storm that inaugurates
the action of the *Aeneid* in Book 1; the two tempests frame the Carthage
episode. Here, too, Aeneas lost a helmsman, Orontes, shaken headlong from
his ship (1.113–16), who, like Palinurus, seems to be the only casualty—
"unus abest" (584). To make the analogy clear, Virgil has the same Orontes
show up among the unburied shades in the underworld of Book 6 in the four
verses immmediately preceding the appearance of Palinurus (333–36).[45]
Aeneas and his companions are thus *twice* saved from storms that threaten
them with the fate of Odysseus's men, and in both cases a helmsman dies.
But although in Book 1 the pilot Orontes is a victim of the storm—like
Odysseus's own steersman in *Odyssey* 12—Book 5 emphasizes the sacrificial
substitution that is taking place by splitting off the death of Palinurus into
a separate episode at the book's end.

This substitution is also a carefully patterned inversion. For while his
helmsman and crew died, Odysseus survived by clinging to his ship's broken
mast: in the *Aeneid* Neptune demands one death for the larger collectivity—
"unum pro multis dabitur caput" (815)—and he calms the sea instead of
stirring it up. It is only in Palinurus's own account in Book 6 that the *Odyssey*'s storm scenario is reinvoked, although again with inversion. Pali-

nurus clings to the broken rudder and after three nights and four days at sea reaches Italy (6.355–57). It takes Odysseus longer to reach land after he escapes from Charybdis.

> From there I was carried along nine days, and on the tenth night
> the gods brought me to the island Ogygia, home of Kalypso.

> (12.447–48)

Virgil reverses night and day in the Homeric formula. Palinurus arrives at dawn in Italy, his destination, but there, ironically, he is killed; Odysseus arrives at night at the island of Calypso, as far from Ithaca as possible, but he survives. Nonetheless, by describing Palinurus's ordeal at sea holding on to a piece of the broken ship, Virgil, in the second, discrepant version of Palinurus's death in Book 6, brings his story into closer alignment with *Odyssey* 12. The contrast with the version told at the end of Book 5 further underscores the ways in which the episode turns its Odyssean model inside out.

The polemical relationship of the Palinurus episode to the *Odyssey* concerns the rugged individualism of the Homeric poem. Odysseus survives while his crewmen die. Just as in the episode of the sirens that opens *Odyssey* 12, where Odysseus alone may hear the sirens' song while his men stop up their ears—an episode fleetingly recalled by Virgil at the end of Book 5 (864–66)—the hero's companions are so many supernumerary, supporting players. And even when Odysseus returns to Ithaca to recover his kingship, he is pitted against the rest of the island—the suitors whom he kills and their relatives who seek revenge. As leader, Odysseus is fatal to his countrymen, but his antagonism with his community is just what defines the hero as individual. His individuality is not distinct from individualism: Odysseus is out for himself, and all others are expendable.

The reverse is true in the *Aeneid*. It is the collectivity of the Trojan remnant and the future Roman nation who count. They confer identity upon the hero as their leader and representative, and it is their survival for which he is responsible. The duties of leadership also preclude for Aeneas the other great model of Homeric individualism, that of Achilles, the chief warrior at odds with his commander and the rest of his army—although, interestingly enough, the Aeneas of the *Iliad* is on one occasion depicted as just such a sulking malingering hero,

> at the uttermost edge of battle
> standing, since he was forever angry with brilliant Priam
> because great as he was he did him no honour among his people.

> (*Il.* 13.459–61)

Homer suggests that Aeneas is a Trojan version of Achilles, angered by Priam as Achilles is angered by Agamemnon. But by the time of the *Aeneid* Priam and his ruling house are gone, and Aeneas has taken their place: he moves from periphery to controlling center of the action. His individualistic role of single combatant merges, to the point of being submerged, with the corporate role of king (1.544) and commander in chief. This emphasis on what Thomas M. Greene has called the "deliberative" as opposed to the "executive" function of epic heroism defines the communal, national ethos of the *Aeneid*.[46] It also has a basis in Roman warfare that—as distinct from archaic Homeric battle—brought into prominence the general, the leader and tactician, rather than the individual warrior. The model of Roman heroism described by the *Aeneid* is the *general*, in both senses of the word: leader and collectivity.

The sacrifice of Palinurus, of the individual for the community, defines this heroism in opposition to the Homeric ethos that individuates the hero at the expense of others. It is now clear why the surrogate figure of Palinurus is necessary. The logic of the *Aeneid*'s inversion of the model of the *Odyssey*, where the hero lives while the companions die, would require the death of its own hero. The "death" of Aeneas can instead be performed symbolically through that of his helmsman, and Palinurus's account of his fate in Book 6 indicates that this death is a figure of the self-sacrifice that the hero undergoes for his followers. Even as he was tossed upon the stormy waves, Palinurus declares, his thoughts turned not to himself but to his imperiled ship (351–54).

The Palinurus episode follows Aeneas's own major act of self-sacrifice, his parting from Dido in Book 4, and it precedes and overlaps with his visit to the underworld in Book 6, another symbolic death of the self where the hero is also incorporated with his Roman descendants. As a bridge between these two key moments in the hero's career, the sacrificial death of the loyal pilot suggests the peculiarly political and social dimension of Aeneas's heroic self-denial: his renunciation of his love for Dido is part of a larger surrender of personality and will demanded of the leader for the sake of community and nation. In fact, once he is identified with the community he leads—and with its future Roman destiny—the actions of Aeneas as individual may seem relatively unimportant. For if he was compelled to forsake his Carthaginian love affair because it went against the predetermined plan of Fate, neither is he permitted to do much to carry that plan forward. Neither he nor Palinurus were able to steer the Trojan fleet to Italy through the storm that opens Book 5, and when, at the book's close, Aeneas takes the place of the lost pilot and guides the ship—"rexit in undis" (868)—he is, as Michael Putnam has pointed out, steering a rudderless vessel.[47] It is Neptune who brings the fleet to Italy. The hero's individual agency is illusory, at best greatly diminished, even when he appears to promote his destiny. Thus the sacrifice of individuality that Aeneas makes as leader paradoxically includes his leadership initiative: he goes with the flow of a historical necessity that will not allow him independent action, either positive or negative. What is left is endurance, and the passivity that readers have found objectionable in Virgil's hero. He sits at a useless helm at the end of Book 5; in Book 10 (156–59) he is initially placed beside the *figurehead* of his ship.

The heroic individuality and agency that Aeneas gives up are associated with Fortune: the Fortune whose call Palinurus must finally allow the storm-tossed Trojan fleet to follow, the Fortune that Venus would permit to give a wandering course to Aeneas and his companions. The *Aeneid* doubles the motif of Fortune's guidance and, in both cases, links it to the epic loser. The ship at the mercy of the winds of chance—the virtual emblem of Odyssean romance—is the vessel of the defeated Cleopatra fleeing from Actium on the shield of Aeneas and of the defeated Trojans themselves as they wander through the Mediterranean in the first half of the poem. At the same time, the two great losers of the *Aeneid* will see their lives shaped by Fortune. Turnus echoes Palinurus's speech as he goes to his final showdown with Aeneas:

> iam iam fata, soror, superant, absiste morari;
> quo deus et quo dura uocat Fortuna sequamur.
>
> (12.676–77)

(Now, sister, now Fate conquers; cease to delay; where the god and where harsh Fortune call, let us follow.)

And Dido's last great pronouncement shares the same vocabulary, anticipating Venus's words:

> uixi, et quem dederat cursum Fortuna peregi.   (4.653)

(I have lived, and completed the course which Fortune gave.)

The enemies of Aeneas and Rome are condemned to a purely chance existence. By resisting the course of Roman destiny, they fall out of history itself, like the past-obsessed Helenus and Andromache to whom Aeneas bids farewell as he leaves them behind in their miniature Troy at Buthrotum.

> uiuite felices, quibus est fortuna peracta
> iam sua: nos alia ex aliis in fata uocamur.
>
> (3.493–94)

(Live happy, you whose fortune is now completed; we are called from one fate to another.)

Dido's subsequent echo of this passage—"Fortuna peregi"—suggests how she, too, as the representative of Carthage—the city that, even as it is being built, is doomed to fall—suffers the fate of historical supersession. Once the epic losers are denied a futurity in the history written by the victor, they have no coherent or meaningful story of their own, and their lives are prey to Fortune. The buried maritime figures in the words of Turnus and Dido make these lives into individual odysseys, the romance wanderings that epic assigns to the defeated as the deviant alternative to its plot of historical destiny. The *Aeneid* here already suggests the link between Fortune and romance that we shall see developed in later epic. But the Palinurus episode has also shown that the hero Aeneas *as individual* may be in the same figurative boat—a shipwrecked Odyssean boat, prey to Fortune—as the poem's losers, no less than they a victim of his epic destiny.

The imperative of that destiny is spelled out to Aeneas by the seer Nautes in Book 5, just before the episode of the sacrifice of Palinurus begins.

> nate dea, quo fata trahunt retrahuntque sequamur;
> quidquid erit, superanda omnis fortuna ferendo est.

> (5.709–10)

(Son of a goddess, where Fate drags us and drags us back, let us follow; whatever will be, all fortune is to be overcome by bearing its burden.)

This passage, too, echoes and is meant to be read in relation to the others I have cited. Aeneas, too, must follow the force that pulls him back and forth—but this force is not Fortune, but Fate; similarly, Aeneas tells Andromache and Helenus whose fortunes are played out that he is called from one fate to the next. While Turnus acknowledges that Fate has prevailed— "fata, soror, superant"—Nautes encourages Aeneas to prevail over Fortune by endurance. The language of this adage is, of course, Stoic; it is hard not to compare it with the celebrated dictum of the philosopher Cleanthes that Seneca (*Ep.* 107.11) translates: "ducunt volentem fata, nolentem trahunt" ("Fate leads the willing, drags the unwilling along"). But Stoic, too, is the language of Dido and Turnus; Seneca would cite with admiration her dying words about completing the course of Fortune.[48] In Stoic vocabulary, Fate and Fortune are notoriously hard to tell apart: Lucan will deliberately confuse the two, in no small part in reaction to Virgilian usage. For while we can see that Virgil himself plays with the tendency of the two terms to slide into one another, he nevertheless makes a distinction: Fortune denotes short-term contingency as opposed to the historical long run that is Fate.[49] History's losers only have the short term and must make the most of it. Their fortunes become personalized, allowing for the assertion of selfhood and the willfulness that make Dido and Turnus the most vivid characters in the poem.

The victors' lives can be seen in the larger teleological perspective of Fate, in which they individually count for much less. In this perspective, as Nautes' maxim suggests, Fortune takes the form of immediate vicissitudes—one damned thing after another, Aeneas may feel. The knowledge that he is fulfilling the plan of destiny thus may not bring much consolation to Aeneas, for he is still subject to outrageous Fortune—and to a Fate that, described in a plural form as dragging back and forth or going from one to another, seems to have lost any visible teleological drive. Again, Aeneas's experience as individual caught in history does not seem very different from that of the poem's losers who are driven by Fortune; and they, at least, indulge in personality and will. But, as Nautes tells Aeneas, it is precisely the hero's passivity, his simply bearing up, that allows him to withstand Fortune: the prospect of a fated future permits him to roll with present punches, to exercise a self-effacing *virtus* that may be the virtue of self-sacrifice itself.

This is the gist of Aeneas's famous words of farewell to Ascanius as he sets out for battle in Book 12:

> disce, puer, uirtutem ex me uerumque laborem,
> fortunam ex aliis.
>
> (12.435–36)

(Learn, my boy, virtue and true labor from me, fortune from others.)

"Some guys have all the luck," Aeneas seems to say bitterly, "I've only had hardship and hard work." Earlier in Book 10, when Jupiter leaves the battle between the Trojans and Italians open to Fate (113), "labor" had been directly opposed to "fortuna"—"sui cuique exorsa laborem / fortuna ferent" (111–12)—and given the sense of "misfortune": some will prosper and some will suffer in the fighting. It retains something of that former connotation in Aeneas's words, but it also indicates his heroic endurance. This, he tells Ascanius, is the true work of *virtus*. Hardship builds character—if not individual, literary character—and that, in turn, builds empire. The fortune, perhaps unearned, that others enjoy—with its alluring, but deadly individualism—is just what Aeneas and Rome must give up and resist in order to reach the national greatness promised by Fate.

This disavowal of fortune may contain a polemic against recent history: the warlords of the late Roman republic associated themselves with the goddess Fortuna. Both Sulla and Pompey styled themselves as "felix"—"lucky"—and Sulla rebuilt and refurbished the great temple of Fortuna at Praeneste. Caesar crossed the Rubicon declaring that the dice had been cast.[50] We are brought back to the ideological context discussed at the beginning of this section, to the Augustan state's distrust of great individuals and their propensity to faction and civil strife. Whether it is specifically topical or not, the politically repressive nature of the *Aeneid*'s either/or of Fate and Fortune is sufficiently clear. Allegiance to a destiny vested in nation and state requires an overcoming of fortune: of those chance human differences that constitute the individual. The hero of the *Aeneid* may not act by or for himself unless he also acts for the community.

The second half of the epic, through the subplot of Pallas that imitates Achilles and Patroclus, may try to give Aeneas a personal stake in the war against the Latins. But even as the hero's anger wells up and he plunges his sword into Turnus, his words curiously distance him from his deed.

> tune hinc spoliis indute meorum
> eripiare mihi? Pallas te hoc uulnere, Pallas
> immolat et poenam scelerato ex sanguine sumit.
>
> (12.947–49)

(Are you, clad in the spoils of my own, to be seized from me? Pallas, Pallas immolates you with this wound and exacts satisfaction from your guilty blood.)

The shifting of agency, not once but twice, to the dead Pallas and the language of religious sacrifice and legal punishment make the taking of private revenge ("meorum . . . mihi") indistinguishable from the impersonal, public act.[51] Once again, we cannot tell whether Aeneas has a will of his own.

The problem of the hero's volition, however, admits more than one construction. For if we are inclined to read this uncertainty about individual agency and will as a reflection of the *effects* of a repressive political order, we should remember that it was also an enabling fiction of that order: Augustus exercised personal rule by working through the senate and institutions of legitimate government to which he claimed to have given up all power. This suggests still another, quite different reading of the end of the *Aeneid*: private vengeance cloaking itself in legality, an act of judicial murder. Tasso, in the age of the Counter-reformation, may have committed no anachronism when he looked back and justified the killing of Turnus in terms of a Machiavellian "ragion di stato."[52]

For the subsequent literary tradition to which Tasso belonged, the *Aeneid* would decisively reshape the epic hero. Virgil's politicization of epic for the ends of empire demanded a curbing of the Homeric heroic will, and the flatness and passivity of Aeneas became the virtuous traits of other hero-leaders of the imperial epic: of Tasso's own Goffredo and Camões' Vasco da Gama. As opposed to the wandering Odysseus and the rebellious Achilles, the hero of empire became an executive type who places duty over individual desire, the goals of history over the present moment. The reaches of political power would thus extend not merely over space and time, but over the inner man. Heroic identity in this perspective seems a matter of chance, and in the epic struggle between imperial destiny and Fortune, even this residue of individuality becomes contested ground. For the poets of lost political causes, a Lucan or a Milton, this inner realm of identity is indeed the last line where a successful resistance can be waged. But even the heroes of their anti-Virgilian poems—the stoic Cato of the *Pharsalia* or the sacrificial Jesus of *Paradise Regained*—maintain their freedom from external power by practicing a repression that seems no less austere than the discipline that power seeks to exert upon them.

PART TWO

EPIC AND THE LOSERS

THREE

THE EPIC CURSE AND CAMOES' ADAMASTOR

W
HAT DO THE losers in epic have to say for themselves? What is their side of the story? The winners' epics, equating power with the power to narrate, suggest that they have no story or history at all. Yet these poems also project for the defeated ghostly narratives, as prophetic in their own way as the future vistas of imperial destiny that the epic offers to the victors. These rival narratives of the losers, we shall see, fail *as narratives*, and the characters who give utterance to them— the red man, the monster, the Eastern woman, the monster who is also a black man—provide a catalogue of types of the colonized "other" into which the imperial epic turns the vanquished. They and their stories can, as Chapter 1 argued, be finally assimilated with the forces of nature that the victorious builders of empire and history strive to overcome. Nonetheless, these voices of resistance receive a hearing, as the epic poem acknowledges, intermittently, alternative accounts vying with its own official version of history: they are the bad conscience of the poem that simultaneously writes them in and out of its fiction.

The Fall of Acoma

In 1610 Gaspar Perez de Villagrá published a minor epic poem in unrhymed heroic verse, the *Historia de la Nueva Mexico*. It chronicles the Spanish exploration and conquest of what is now the American Southwest. Villagrá was an eyewitness of and a participant in at the events he recounts, and while his poem is of small literary value, it is our chief, often exclusive historical source for the exploits of the New Mexican conquistadors. It is in the 1599 siege and destruction of the Acoma pueblo that Villagrá finds his true epic subject—events that inevitably evoke Troy, the model of all doomed epic cities.[1] The rebellious Acomans had ambushed and massacred eleven members of a Spanish patrol; the four-hundred-foot heights of their pueblo could not save them from a frightful retribution.

A punitive expeditionary force was sent out under the command of Vicente de Zaldívar, whose own brother lay among the Acomans' victims. It took only two days for the Spaniards to storm the seemingly impregnable pueblo, which they burnt to the ground. Hundreds of its Indian defenders died, many committing suicide by throwing themselves into the flames of their houses or over the pueblo's sheer cliffs. It was later alleged that Zaldívar butchered others who had surrendered, avenging his brother's death. The remaining inhabitants of the pueblo were subsequently put on trial and condemned for their revolt. All over the age of twelve were sentenced to twenty years of servitude; males over twenty-five were to have one foot cut off as well.

Villagrá's poem does not describe the trial or the fate of the survivors. It ends instead with a highly dramatic incident during the mopping-up campaign that followed Acoma's downfall. Two fugitives from Acoma, Tempal and Cotumbo, had been taken prisoner and held in a kiva in the pueblo of San Juan. The prisoners now barricaded themselves in the kiva and kept their captors at bay, hurling stones at anyone who approached them. After three days they asked the Spanish general, Don Juan de Oñate, for two daggers with which to kill themselves. After vain attempts to persuade them to surrender and convert to Christianity, de Oñate instead sent them two ropes. The captives made two nooses, placed them around their necks, came out into the open, and climbed into the branches of a nearby tree. Fastening the ropes to its boughs, they turned and spoke defiantly to their conquerors.

> Soldados advertid que aqui colgados,
> Destos rollizos troncos os dexamos,
> Los miserabiles cuerpos por despojos,
> De la victoria illustre que alcancastes,
> De aquellos desdichados que podridos,
> Estan sobre su sangre rebolcados,
> Sepulcros que tomaron, porque quiso
> Assi fortuna infame perseguirnos,
> Con mano poderosa y acabarnos.
> Gustosos quedareis, que ya cerramos
> Las puertas al vivir, y nos partimos,
> Y libres nuestras tierras os dexamos,
> Dormid á sueno suelto, pues ninguno,
> Bolvio jamas con nueva del cammino
> Incierto y trabajoso que llevamos,
> Mas de una cosa ciertos os hazemos,
> Que si bolver podemos a vengarnos,
> Que non parieron madres Castellanas,
> Ni barvaras tampoco en todo el mundo,
> Mas desdichados hijos que â vosostros.[2]

(Soldiers, take note that here we give you our miserable bodies, hanging from these sturdy boughs, as spoils of the famous victory which you have obtained, the reward for those wretched companions of yours we have killed who lie rotting drenched in their blood, the only burial which they found. Because infamous Fortune has thus wished to hound and destroy us with her powerful hand, you will remain here content, for now we close our gates on this life and take leave, and we freely give you our lands. Sleep with untroubled dreams, since no one ever returned with tidings from the uncertain and toilsome road upon which we set out; but we make you certain of one thing: that if we can return to avenge ourselves, no sons born to Castilian or Indian mothers in the whole wide world will be as wretched as you.)

With this ringing curse, the two Indians drop from the branches and hang themselves. Villagrá immediately brings his poem to an end with a brief address to his king.

This powerful closing scene transcends the doggerel verse in which it is told. The doomed but valiant Indians, cursing to the end, become their own executioners rather than surrender to the Spaniards. It makes a good story, and popular historians have included it in their narratives of Southwestern history.[3] But did the incident take place as Villagrá recounts it? One reason for doubt is that it repeats an episode in an earlier Spanish epic of New World conquest, the *Araucana* of Alonso de Ercilla, an account— here, too, by an eyewitness—of the wars in Chile against the Araucanian Indians.[4] Villagrá knew and modeled his own poem on Ercilla's epic, which was printed in three installments in 1569, 1578, and 1589 and remains a classic of Spanish literature. (The *Araucana* will be discussed at length in the next chapter.) He was a relation of Don Francisco de Villagrá, the conquistador of Chile who is one of the heros of Ercilla's poem. At the beginning of his twenty-seventh canto, Villagrá compares the punitive campaign against Acoma to the wars against "aquellos bravos barvaros de Arauco" (223r).

Ercilla's episode takes place in canto 26 of the *Araucana*. After the battle of Millarapue (1557), the Spaniards chose twelve chieftains from among the captured prisoners and sentenced them to be hanged. Ercilla writes that he himself was moved to pity and tried to save one of the condemned Indians from execution. But this prisoner turns out to be Galbarino, a major Indian character of the poem, whom the Spanish had captured once before; at that time they had cut off both of his hands as punishment for his rebellion (22.45–54). Galbarino then proceeded to the council of the Araucanian chiefs, where the testimony of his bloody stumps overcame the pleadings of the peace party and resolved the Indians to continue their struggle (23.6–17). Recaptured, he would prefer now to die, turning his sword upon himself, rather than grant to his conquerors the power to show him mercy (26.26).

> muertos podremos ser, mas no vencidos
> ni los ánimos libres oprimidos.
>
> (26.25)

(We can be killed, but not vanquished, nor can our free souls be enslaved.)

This defiance causes Galbarino to be condemned along with his counterparts. His death, however, is self-inflicted, just as he wanted it to be. For, Ercilla reports, there were no executioners available, and the sentence was carried out in an unheard-of way: each of the Indians took a rope, climbed into the trees, and hanged himself. One chieftain hesitated and begged the Spaniards for mercy, but, rebuked by the indomitable Galbarino, he, too, placed the noose around his neck and dropped from the treetop to his death. Last of all, Galbarino died in the same manner (26.31–37).

While Villagrá's poem is virtually the only firsthand report of what happened at Acoma, Ercilla's epic can be compared to other historical sources. The story of the Indians hanging themselves is confirmed in the 1558 chronicles of Gerónimo de Bibar,[5] but a somewhat different version of the aftermath of Millarapue is presented by Alonso de Góngora Marmolejo, another veteran and eyewitness of the wars, whose history of the Araucanian wars, composed in the 1570s, was first published in 1850.

> Ten caciques were taken prisoner, their chief lords who served the office of captain: Quepulican, the commander-in-chief, fled and escaped. Don Garcia ordered that all these chieftains be hanged. There was seen one cacique, a warlike man and a chief lord, who had served well in the time of Valdivia, an Indian of good understanding; he had endeavored that they grant him his life, but was unable to obtain it, although many tried to intercede for him because he was so well-known. Seeing that they had hanged the others, he greatly implored the constable that they hang him above the others on the highest branch of the tree, so that the Indians who passed by there should see that he died in the defense of his country.[6]

In Marmolejo's narrative, the central character is the Indian who first pleads for his life through Spanish intercessors and subsequently, when he realizes that he has no alternative, dies with patriotic dignity. Ercilla divides this character in two: the figure who implores mercy is relatively minor, the unnamed Araucanian whom Galbarino rebukes; Galbarino, probably a fictional composite of several historical figures, takes over center stage, rejecting efforts to intercede for him, choosing to die along with his like-minded companions. What Marmolejo recounts as a single noble gesture performed by an otherwise pathetic and even craven victim becomes for Ercilla a collective act of courage and firmness. Ercilla depicts the Indians' acting as their own hangmen—a feature that does not appear in Marmolejo's history—as an expression of their stoic valor. Their deaths become a mass suicide, like the one recounted in Lucan's *Pharsalia*, Ercilla's favorite epic model, where a surrounded band of Caesarian soldiers turn their swords upon each other (4.474–581). The Araucanians seem to have learned Lucan's stoic moral (576–77): "non ardua virtus / Servitium fugisse manu" ("It is no arduous feat of virtue to escape slavery by one's own hand").

When the two Indians hang themselves at the end of Villagrá's *Historia*, the scene is already an epic topos. The other component of the episode, the dying curse of the Acomans, can similarly be broken down into a series of traditional rhetorical attitudes assumed by the vanquished in epic poetry; but here, their literary provenance cannot be so clearly determined. It is Fortune who has led them to defeat, the Acomans say: so complains Turnus as he heads toward his fatal duel with Aeneas at the end of the *Aeneid* (12.676–77, 693–95); so the anti-imperial Lucan makes Fortune the god of the conquering Caesar in the *Pharsalia* (1.225; 5.570; 7.796); so Galbarino attributes the Araucanian downfall to "los fieros hados variables" (26.25)— to fates that are harsh, but also variable. The epic loser ascribes the victor's success to Fortune—to chance rather than to the victor's superiority or to some kind of historical necessity—thus leaving the possibility open that Fortune may change in the future. The Indians tell the Spaniards to sleep with untroubled dreams: after their great victory at Pharsalia, Lucan's poem recounts (7.764–68) that Caesar's troops were afflicted by nightmares as the ghosts of the dead rose to haunt their sleep. It is the possibility, however remote or unlikely, of such a return of the dead that the Acomans raise in their curse: similarly, the furious suicidal Dido threatens to become a Fury hounding Aeneas after her death in the *Aeneid* (4.384–86), and the defeated Solimano in Tasso's *Gerusalemme liberata* takes up her words:

> Risorgerò nemico ognor più crudo
> cenere anco sepolto e spirto ignudo.
>
> (9.99)

(I shall rise again, a still fiercer enemy, even as buried ashes and naked spirit.)

Solimano is modeled not only on Dido, who also prophesies the avenging Hannibal rising from her buried bones (4.625–29), but also on that Hannibal himself, as he is depicted in the *Punica* of Silius Italicus. Defeated at Zama at the end of the epic, Hannibal pledges to fight on so that Roman mothers will know no peace (17.614–15); at the poem's beginning, in a scene where Hannibal swears vengeance on Rome in the temple of Dido, it is said that his victories will cause the mothers of Latium to refuse to bear children (1.111–12). The Acomans suggest that Villagrá's Spaniards may come to regret the day their mothers gave them birth.

The historical factuality of Villagrá's final scene becomes more and more difficult to pin down. We can probably assume that the Spaniards hanged two rebellious Indians in the San Juan pueblo in 1599. The rest—their self-execution and curse—blends into an inherited poetic tradition. By isolating the traditional epic fictions and tropes that are interpolated into Villagrá's chronicle, we can observe their ideological function in a particular historical occasion. This function typically does not so much present a single official viewpoint; it rather seeks to contain, if not resolve, conflicting ideological messages. Moreover, it cannot be separated from the episode's *formal* function, its placement at the very end of the *Historia*: the form both determines and constitutes part of the ideological content itself.

The power of this epic ending is that it calls the idea of ending into question. Acoma has been destroyed, the war is over, the last rebels die at the hangman's tree—and yet the words of their curse echo on, a threat that all is not over. To be sure, the doomed Indians acknowledge their defeat and the loss of their lands; they admit that no one has ever returned from the realm of death. But they proceed to promise just such a ghostly revenge, an uncanny afterlife that reveals its affinity to other psychic forms by the Indians' reference to the dreams of their conquerors. Their curse raises the specter of a real future retribution, one that will take the shape of periodic insurrections, renegade raids, and acts of sabotage by a people who can never be reconciled to colonial rule. However gnomic its form, the curse amounts to an alternative history of resistance that competes with Villagrá's narrative of conquest, the narrative of the *Historia*, which presents itself as a complete and finished epic action, but which, at the very moment of formal closure, suggests a bloody and unending sequel.

The two Indians are thus lent a voice of their own—a momentary glimpse of what history looks like from the perspective of the losers, a voice that cannot simply be suppressed by Spanish force. They earn this voice by their invincible valor and self-execution. And even if this scene is lifted from the epic of Ercilla, who had himself embellished his historical narrative by portraying the Araucanians as stoic suicides, Villagrá's Indians are nonetheless linked to the other Acomans who jumped to their deaths from the heights of their citadel rather than surrender to their conquerors. There is a symbolic analogy between their mastery of their own deaths and their possession of an autonomous voice and history. Both the Acomans' self-execution and their curse are removed from the control of the victorious Spaniards, who can make complete and unconditional neither their conquest nor their version of the conquest: a stubborn core of native resistance remains and cannot be eradicated.

But this resistance can, perhaps, be contained within limits. The pose of stoic autonomy that the cornered Indians adapt as they hang themselves cannot disguise the fact that they are doing the Spaniards' work for them. The space in which they assert themselves as independent agents has been drastically reduced and circumscribed by their conquerors. The fate of Acoma recalls other cases of mass suicide by the defenders of besieged cities, Masada or Numantia; the latter, explicitly mentioned by Villagrá, held a special place in the sixteenth-century Spanish imagination.[7] These desperate measures are open to more than one interpretation. If the losers stake their claim to freedom and invincible heroism upon suicide, the victors can complacently view the same act as the inevitable outcome of their victory, an act of which they, the victors, are the true authors. Shakespeare's Octavius, soon to be Augustus, expresses this idea clearly when he appropriates the suicides of Antony and Cleopatra: "High events as these / Strike those that make them" (*Antony and Cleopatra*, 5.12.359–60). And Scipio Aemilianus, the conqueror of Numantia, adapted the title "Numantinus" as a trophy of its inhabitants' destruction.[8]

The Indians' curse may similarly be appropriated by their Spanish masters. This is obviously true in the sense that the curse is contained within Villagrá's poem, expressed in his language, and mediated, as we have seen, through the terms of his literary tradition. But it is true in a more sinister sense as well, for the curse can be used against the Indians. The undying hatred and resistance to which they give voice warrants the harshness of the Spaniards' countermeasures, such as the sentences meted out on the survivors of Acoma. De Oñate and Zaldívar were, in fact charged in 1609 and brought to trial in 1614 to answer for the brutal conduct of the Acoma campaign. Villagrá's *Historia* of 1610 is involved in a case of special pleading: the poet seeks to exonerate his commanders who, he suggests, had no other recourse against an enemy who admitted no quarter.[9] The Acomans' curse may thus be fitted into the conquistadors' own self-understanding. If it is a projection of their dread of future Indian revolts and retribution—and, hence, in some sense a veiled expression of their feelings of guilt—it also justifies, with the logic of a vicious circle, the severity of their present policy.

In this sense, too, the Indians' resistance is suicidal, for it only brings on further reprisals. And the same may be said for the future history that is projected by their curse, the narrative that would go beyond and compete with Villagrá's official history. The fact that this narrative is paired with and mirrored by the Indians' hanging themselves may suggest that it is, in fact, a narrative with no place to go, a chronicle merely of further, self-destructive defeats. If the curse challenges the formal closure of the *Historia*, it may not so much foretell an overthrow of Spanish rule, which has indeed been won once and for all in the completed action of the poem, as a series of abortive rebellions that can disturb, but not alter, the new political status quo. The Indians are condemned to a future of scattered suicidal gestures, ultimately without aim or direction. Thus if the Acomans' curse may represent the attempt of the victors' poet to identify imaginatively with the losers and to portray their fiercely independent version of history, it simultaneously suggests that they have no real history—their own story is rather a sequence of incomplete and unconnected events that cannot be linked together into a coherent narrative. They have a voice and role only within the history made by their Spanish masters. The ending of Villagrá's poem allows for diametrically opposed readings as it confronts the victims of the Spanish conquest, both endowing them with and denying them a separate identity and perspective. One cannot say whether this uncertainty and conflict of meaning is the effect or the cause of the epic tropes to which Villagrá has recourse in order to end his poem, but it is at such moments that these tropes seem most ideologically charged.

Because the epic forms at the end of the *Historia* are inserted into what presents itself as a factual history, they call attention to themselves and to their ideological function. By a reverse process, the particular historical occasion of the *Historia* may disclose ideological meanings in these forms that were latent or not fully articulated. A poem of small literary merit like the *Historia* can thus have something to say about the canonical epic tradition with which it claims affiliation. As a chronicle that reports, in however distorted a version, real historical events, it suggests that behind the fictions of epic poetry lie other similar events: episodes of political struggle and colonialist violence. Above all, it reminds us of the presence of real victims: the two Indians whom the Spaniards executed in the San Juan pueblo in 1599 and whom Villagrá's poem does not easily lay to rest.

The Indians' defiant curse invites us to reconsider other imprecations of epic losers against their conquerors, losers who appear initially to have mythical or fictional, rather than historical, identities. The epic curse, in fact, constitutes its own distinctive topos, whose morphology and history can be traced from the *Odyssey* and the *Aeneid* to a celebrated central episode in the *Lusíadas*. Camões' poem provides another, similar instance of a traditional epic-type scene imported into a historical narrative of Renaissance imperialism and native victims. But unlike Villagrá's *Historia*, it does so with the self-consciousness of "high" literature. Its representation of native resistance takes *both* historical and mythopoetic forms, and it plays these off against one another. It thus lays bare the process by which real events become transformed into epic fictions, fictions that depend—and Camões explicitly declares their dependence—upon earlier epic fictions. At the same time it interrogates the historical basis of those earlier epics. Yet even as Camões demonstrates how suppressed populations may find a voice—if only one that curses—in the epic fictions of their conquerors, his poem works to appropriate that voice, to contain and neutralize the unsettling implications that the inherited topos of the curse might have for its own triumphalist narrative of empire. The resources of the epic tradition are drawn upon here simultaneously to represent and disfigure the defeated and their version of history.

Polyphemus and Dido

The tradition of the epic curse properly begins when the blinded Cyclops Polyphemus cries out to his father Poseidon for vengeance upon Odysseus at the end of Book 9 of the *Odyssey*. His curse concludes an episode that has been recognized and well interpreted by modern critics, most notably

Horkheimer and Adorno, as a colonialist encounter between a "superior," civilized Greek and an underdeveloped barbarian.[10] Homeric scholars have associated aspects of Odysseus's wanderings with Greek colonizing ventures in the Mediterranean that began in the eighth century B.C., and Odysseus's glowing appraisal (9.131–41) of the island that lies off the Cyclopes' coast— fit for all crops, rich in meadows, a suitable site for vineyards, a good harbor, a freshwater spring—reveals a colonist's mentality.[11] The land is there for the taking, especially since the neighboring Cyclopes lack the ships to get there themselves; they also lack the agricultural skills to exploit it properly. But when Odysseus goes "to find out about these people, and learn what they are" (9.174), the Cyclopes turn out to be a pesky lot indeed. By means of verbal guile and technological improvisation, Odysseus is able to outwit and blind the backward cannibal Polyphemus, and he and the surviving remnant of his companions make good their escape. But they cannot escape the Cyclops's ensuing curse, which predicts and determines the subsequent plot of the *Odyssey*.

> Hear me, Poseidon who circle the earth, dark-haired. If truly
> I am your son, and you acknowledge yourself as my father,
> grant that Odysseus, sacker of cities, son of Laertes,
> who makes his home in Ithaka, may never reach that home;
> but if it is decided that he shall see his own people,
> and come home to his strong-founded house and to his country,
> let him come late, in bad case, with the loss of all his companions,
> in someone else's ship, and find troubles in his household.
>
> (9.528–35)

The curse shifts its focus midway through from ends to means. Polyphemus seems to concede Odysseus's homecoming, the narrative goal of the *Odyssey*, as predetermined and inevitable, and instead specifies the conditions that will defer the hero's return and make it a hollow achievement: the destruction of his ships and companions, the struggle with Penelope's suitors that awaits him before his homecoming can be complete. But the result of the curse will be to qualify the poem's completion as well: Teiresias later instructs Odysseus that to appease Poseidon for the blinding of his son he will have to depart from Ithaca again on a new voyage to the ends of the earth (11.10–138), instructions that Odysseus repeats to Penelope (23.264– 84) just before their much delayed sexual reunion in their marital bed.[12] Penelope takes heart in Teiresias's final words that promise Odysseus a prosperous old age after his sea of troubles, but the strength of the curse, greater than Polyphemus himself seems to imagine, is to prevent the *Odyssey* from ending happily ever after. Thus here, as in Villagrá's *Historia*, the victim's curse works against closure as the epic poem creates and defines it. The wrath of Poseidon affects the poem's ending both before and after: the god obstructs and delays Odysseus's homecoming through the storms that twice attack him at sea; the expiation required by the god demands that Odysseus leave home again.

The kinship of Polyphemus to Poseidon, the god of sea and storms, extends a process of dehumanization that has already begun by portraying the barbarian native as a Cyclopean giant, one-eyed and slow-witted because of his primitive culture, monstrously big because of his willingness to use force against the colonizing stranger.[13] Through his divine father, the native is further identified with the hostile elements that Odysseus must battle along his voyage. The conquest of native peoples becomes assimilated with efforts to dominate nature; but this familiar ideological equation merely suggests here how difficult and inconclusive such conquest may prove to be. The *Odyssey* presents a failed colonialist scenario in Book 9, even if it leaves a native victim behind. Odysseus loses six men, devoured by Polyphemus, in the course of the episode, and the curse of the Cyclops will eventually cost him the rest of his crew and literally untold hardships beyond the ending of the epic itself. The price of colonialist violence seems prohibitively high.

Virgil uses the curse of Polyphemus, cast at the fleeing ship of Odysseus, as a literary model for the great curse that the abandoned Dido utters as she sees the ships of Aeneas leaving Carthage and just before she mounts the funerary pyre she has constructed and commits suicide. This is well known, but critical commentary on the *Aeneid* has not discussed how the curse fits into larger patterns of Homeric allusion in the Dido episode; nor has it tended to recognize the full extent of Virgil's identification of Dido with the Homeric Cyclops. Dido does not at first look like such a monster. The Carthage episode in Books 1 and 4 of the *Aeneid* performs *through allusion* the same literary itinerary as Aeneas's narrative of his wanderings across the Mediterranean in Book 3: both retrace backwards the wanderings of Odysseus in Books 5–13 of the *Odyssey*, and both conclude with imitations of the Polyphemus episode, with Aeneas's own encounter with the Cyclops at the end of Book 3 and with Dido's curse at the end of Book 4.[14]

But before her curse and death, Dido and her Carthage suggest other Odyssean locales with their presiding female figures. When Aeneas shoots the deer in Book 1 to feed and comfort his companions, the African setting recalls the island of Circe (*Odys.* 10.156–84); when Mercury summons Aeneas to leave Dido (4.219–78), Carthage becomes a version of Calypso's isle (*Odys.* 5.43–147). Most obvious, Aeneas's enjoyment of Carthaginian hospitality and his inset narrative of his past wanderings at the banquet of Books 2 and 3 make the Punic city another Phaeacia (*Odys.* 6–13) in which Dido alternately plays the role of the wise woman ruler Arete and the enamored princess Nausicaa. But the first sighting of the Carthaginian coast in Book 1 casts Dido as still another Odyssean heroine, for the harbor into which the storm-tossed Trojan fleet sails (1.159–67) is a close imitation of Homer's description of the harbor of Ithaca with its Cave of the Nymphs

(*Odys.* 13.96–112). This momentary shadowy resemblance to Ithaca makes Carthage look like the longed-for homeland, and it casts Dido as the chaste and circumspect Penelope: she tells us in Book 4 that she has rejected the proposals of her local Numidian suitors (534–36).[15] This opening view of Carthage is particularly illusory and tragic, as if Aeneas and the Trojans could reach their destination in the first book of the *Aeneid* without the travails and sufferings of the rest of the poem, as if they could accept Dido's invitation to them to stay and settle in her newly founded city (1.572–74), as if she and Aeneas could be united in marriage. It is set in deliberate contrast to the final Odyssean characterization of Dido as Polyphemus in Book 4, and measures the extent of her erotic downfall. Once aroused through the combined agency of Venus and Juno, her passion for Aeneas will transform the Carthaginian queen from chaste consort and ruler into a monster.

But perhaps she has been a monster all along.[16] The encounter with the Cyclopes that Aeneas recounts retrospectively in Book 3 is the last extended episode of the Trojans' wanderings before they reach Carthage, hurled there by the storm of Book 1; this proximity in the chronological sequence of the wanderings is reinforced by the narrative sequence that reverts from Aeneas's story back to Dido's court in Book 4. This proximity has a Homeric basis, for we learn in the *Odyssey* (6.3–6) that the Cyclopes and the men of Phaeacia were once neighbors. Homer seems to suggest that the wealthy and hypercivilized Phaeacians are as alien to the Greek world as the primitive Polyphemus. Virgil takes this idea a step further, for opulent Carthage, closely modeled upon Phaeacia, is not only narratively adjacent to his Polyphemus episode, but it also offers a second version of that episode: in both Book 3 (666–67) and Book 4 (571–80), the Trojans cut the anchor cables of their ships in their haste to escape Cyclopean shores.[17] The two sides of the barbarian in the *Odyssey* have become one in a Carthage viewed in the anti-Eastern terms of Roman propaganda: the outward refinement of the city merely covers up a monstrous irrationality that, according to the same propaganda, associates the East with womankind and that here is embodied in Dido herself. Thus, alongside his dramatic version of Dido's progressive disintegration as she loves and is abandoned—a version that puts a share of the blame and guilt on Roman Aeneas—Virgil also presents a less sympathetic, ideologically colored view of Dido: her transformation into a raging Polyphemus merely allows her true nature to appear.

The *Aeneid* thus wavers between a human understanding and a demonization of Dido—and of the historical enemies of Rome whom she represents: the Carthage of the three Punic Wars and Cleopatra, the African queen of Virgil's own time. The history of this emnity is foretold in Dido's curse. The first part of her curse is much like the curse of Polyphemus: just as the Cyclops conceded that Odysseus might return home but called down the troubles in store for him there, Dido, acknowledging that Aeneas may be fated to reach Italy, invokes the hardships he will face in the second half of the *Aeneid*.

> si tangere portus
> infandum caput ac terris adnare necesse est,
> et sic fata Iouis poscunt, hic terminus haeret,
> at bello audacis populi uexatus et armis,
> finibus extorris, complexu auulsus Iuli,
> auxilium imploret uideatque indigna suorum
> funera; nec, cum se sub leges pacis iniquae
> tradiderit, regno aut optata luce fruatur,
> sed cadat ante diem mediaque inhumatus harena.
> haec precor, hanc uocem extremam cum sanguine fundo.

(4.612–21)

(If this detested creature must touch harbor and sail to the shore—if thus the fates of Jove demand, and if this end is fixed and determined: nonetheless harried by war and the swords of a daring people, exiled from his home and torn from the embrace of Iulus, let him beg for aid and watch the shameful deaths of his own people; nor, when he has yielded to the terms of an unjust peace, may he enjoy his kingdom or the light of day, but let him fall before his time unburied amid the sand. This is my prayer; I pour out these last words with my blood.)

The war with Turnus, Aeneas's alliance with Evander and the Etruscans, the death of Pallas: these are all contained in Dido's words. They are the immediate consequences of her curse for the rest of the poem. Moreover, whereas the effects of Polyphemus's curse was to send Odysseus off onto another protracted voyage and thus to unsettle the ending of the *Odyssey*, Dido predicts Aeneas's premature death after the Trojans' victory in Italy closes the *Aeneid*: here, too, the hero has little chance to live happily ever after. But Dido's curse does not stop here. She calls upon her compatriots to continue her hatred of the Trojans and her curse extends beyond the ending of the poem and enters into history.

> tum uos, o Tyrii, stirpem et genus omne futurum
> exercete odiis, cinerique haec mittite nostro
> munera. nullus amor populis nec foedera sunto.
> exoriare aliquis nostris ex ossibus ultor,
> qui face Dardanios ferroque sequare colonos,
> nunc, olim, quocumque dabunt se tempore uires.
> litora litoribus contraria, fluctibus undas
> imprecor, arma armis; pugnent ipsique nepotesque.

(4.622–29)

(Then you O Tyrians, practice your hatred against all his race and future stock, and send these offerings to my ashes. Let there be no love or treaty between our peoples. Rise up, you, unknown avenger, from my bones, to pursue the Dardan settlers with fire and sword, today, hereafter, whenever you have the power to do so. Let shore oppose shore in battle, I pray, sea against sea, sword against sword; let them and their children's children have war.)

It is now not simply the narrative ending of the *Aeneid* that is in question, but the closure that the *Aeneid* projects upon Roman history: the empire without end foretold by Jupiter. The curse operates as a rival prophecy, set alongside the prophecies in the *Aeneid* of future Roman greatness. Dido foretells the other side of the story, the saga of the conquered who refuse to stay conquered and of the repeated wars that the African foes of Rome will wage against her supremacy. Rome's unbroken rule will be periodically challenged, Dido predicts, every time that the defeated Africans regain sufficient strength. The defeated find consolation in the occasions that future history will offer them for retaliation and revenge.

Dido's call for an avenger rising from her bones, the avenger who will be Hannibal, is the most celebrated moment of her curse. It chilled Roman readers with historical memories and would continue to exert its fascination upon subsequent readers, including Freud, a Jew in a Catholic culture who identified with victimized Semites seeking revenge upon Rome.[18] Virgil's scene darkly evokes a mythic parallel: the Phoenix, the fabulous bird who, in one version of the myth, constructs the fragrant pyre upon which it will burn itself in order to be reborn from its ashes.[19] So Phoenician Dido—"Phoenissa," as Virgil repeatedly calls her (1.670, 714; 4.348, 531)—prepares the pyre for her own immolation. When Dido earlier unfastens her sandal and girdle (4.581), the ancient commentator Servius notes that she is summoning the presence of Juno in her aspect of Lucina, the patroness of childbirth.[20] Juno will send down Iris at the end of Book 4 to put an end to Dido's death agony and to release her struggling spirit from her confining, fastened limbs—"nexosque resolueret artus" (695); the action and language parody labor and delivery. Something terrible has been born, in place of the child that Dido longed to have had by Aeneas (327–30). It is Hannibal whom her curse raises up, Phoenix-like, from the remains of her pyre.

The Phoenix myth applies to Carthage itself, the city several times vanquished and destroyed that rises again and again from its defeat. Within Roman epic tradition, the cyclical repetition of Carthage's rise and fall is mirrored in a second myth, that of the Libyan giant Antaeus who falls to the earth, his mother, in order to rise even mightier from her sustenance. It is the myth of the autochthonous native par excellence, the native who must be literally uprooted from his elemental relationship to the land by his foreign conqueror. The story of Hercules' defeat of Antaeus is recounted in the *Pharsalia* (4.593–660), where Lucan treats it as a mythical analogue to

Scipio's victory at Zama over Hannibal, Dido's avenger himself.[21] Ariosto will later couple Antaeus and Hannibal when he cites them as native predecessors to his own African warrior, Rodomonte (*Orlando furioso* 18.24.4), and Tasso continues this epic typology, no longer African but more generally Eastern, with the figure of the sultan Solimano, the Turkish adversary of the first Crusaders in the *Gerusalemme liberata*. Tasso both models Solimano upon the Hannibal of the *Punica* of Silius Italicus and compares him to Antaeus when, after a career of defeats and comebacks, he is killed in the final decisive battle of the poem.[22]

> 'l Soldan, che spesso in lunga guerra,
> quasi novello Anteo, cadde e risorse
> più fero ognora, al fin calcò la terra
> per giacer sempre.
>
> (20.108.1–4)

(The Sultan, who often in long warfare, almost a new Antaeus, fell and rose again still fiercer, at last fell to earth to lie there forever.)

This is the same Solimano who promised, echoing Dido's words, to return from the grave as a naked, avenging spirit. Tasso depicts Solimano as an ancestor of the Saladin who would historically avenge the deaths of the defenders of Jerusalem. So, in some sense, the warrior sultan *does* return. And again and again: in Tasso's lifetime the invading army of a Turkish Sultan Suleiman had reached the gates of Vienna.

There is something demonic in this historical repetition—and Milton will compare his Satan to Antaeus at the end of *Paradise Regained* (4.563–68)— in a foe who refuses to die a natural death and whose hatred is transmitted to successive generations. Dido as Phoenix, Carthage as Antaeus, embody a life force that paradoxically both assimilates them to the regenerative cycles of nature and marks them as unnatural and monstrous. As her curse begets Hannibal, the otherwise barren, sexually frustrated Dido takes on the uncontrolled, diseased fertility of an Africa that is always producing monsters, a nature gone wild. This monstrosity reinforces Dido's similarity to Polyphemus, the controlling literary model behind her curse, and completes her dehumanization as a figure of Rome's foreign enemy, of a Carthage that must be destroyed. This figure should be read alongside the all-too-human Dido, wronged by the Roman she has loved and befriended, whose story has invited the Carthaginian Saint Augustine and other readers to weep for her and to identify with her loser's perspective, even with her curse and its projected history of resistance. Even if that history is not read—through the Roman victors' ideology—as a kind of demonic repetition, it is nonetheless marked by failure from the beginning, for, as was the case at the end of Villagrá's *Historia*, the loser's curse is accompanied by suicide; though, as opposed to the stoical autonomy and self-mastery displayed by Villagrá's

Indians, Dido's death marks an irrational loss of self-control.[23] It suggests that the harm her successors will inflict upon the Roman conquerors will always involve self-inflicted harm as well. The last of these, Cleopatra, took her own life, probably at the order, certainly with the connivance, of Augustus.[24] When Dido, *after* uttering her curse, declares that she will die unavenged—"moriemur inultae" (4.659)—this reversal may mean more than that she cannot have immediate revenge, that history must wait for the Punic Wars and Hannibal. In the long run, Rome's rule will be shaken but not overturned, and the continuing resistance of her subject peoples breaks down into a series of periodic, suicidal measures. Theirs is a repeated history of failures, a failed history.

Adamastor and the *Lusíadas*

In the fifth canto of the *Lusíadas*, Vasco da Gama is the guest of the African king of Melinde on the east coast of Africa. He narrates the story up to this point of his voyage from Portugal: Camões' obvious models are Odysseus telling his adventures to Alcinous in Phaeacia and Aeneas recounting his wanderings to Dido in Carthage. Da Gama describes the moment when his fleet is about to approach the Cape of Good Hope. Suddenly, there appears a black cloud out of which, in turn, an enormous giant emerges, looming over them in the air. This menacing figure announces to the Portuguese the punishments that await them for their daring and presumption—"atrevimento" (5.42.6)—in opening up the new maritime route to the Indian Ocean. He briefly mentions (5.42.7–8) the arduous wars they will have to fight to subjugate the seas and lands of their empire. Then he foretells at length (5.43–48) the storms and mishaps that the cape itself has in store for future Portuguese fleets, culminating in the terrible Sepulveda shipwreck of 1552. The monster would continue this dire prophecy, but da Gama interrupts him to ask his identity. He replies that he is Adamastor, one of the earthborn Titans who, during their rebellion against the gods, led an assault against Neptune to gain control of the sea. He was stirred by his love for the sea nymph Thetis, who lured him out of battle only to deceive and spurn him. In his shame and disdain he fled to the Southern Hemisphere, where the gods punished him for his presumption—"atrevimento" (5.58.8)—by turning him into the landmass of the cape itself. There he is still erotically tantalized and frustrated, for Thetis still swims around him in the encircling sea (50–59). Having told his story, the giant disappears as the black cloud dissolves, and the Portuguese sail by the cape (61) without further incident and continue their voyage.

It is a much admired scene: the giant rising up at the midpoint of Camões' ten-canto epic, at the geographical midpoint and boundary of da

Gama's journey. More than any other episode of the *Lusíadas*, it has given the poem its place in world literature, a place to which Camões and even his hero da Gama self-consciously lay claim. At the end of his narrative, da Gama favorably compares it to the maritime adventures recounted in the *Odyssey* and the *Aeneid*.

> Cantem, louvem e escrevam sempre extremos
> Dêsses seus semideuses e encareçam,
> Fingindo magas Circes, Polifemos,
> Sirenas que co'o canto os adormeçam;
> Dem-lhe mais navegar a vela e remos
> Os Cícones e a terra onde se esquecem
> Os companheiros, em gostando o loto;
> Dem-lhe perder nas águas o pilôto;
>
> Ventos soltos lhe finjam e imaginem
> Dos odres e Calipsos namoradas;
> Harpias que o manjar lhe contaminem;
> Descer às sombras nuas já passadas:
> Que, por muito e por muito que se afinem
> Nestas fábulas vãs, tão bem sonhadas,
> A verdade que eu conto, nua e pura,
> Vence tôda grandíloca escritura!
>
> (5.88–89)

(Let them sing, praise, and write, always in the highest terms, of those demigods of theirs and let them exaggerate, feigning sorceress Circes, Polyphemuses, Sirens that put men asleep with their song; let them still voyage with sails and oars among the Ciconians and to the land where their companions, having tasted the lotus, become forgetful, let them lose their helmsman in the sea;

Let them feign and imagine winds released from wineskins and enamored Calypsos, Harpies that foul their food; let them descend to the naked souls of the dead: for as much, as greatly as they refine these empty fables, so well dreamed-up, the truth that I tell, naked and pure, outdoes all their grandiloquent writings.)

The claim to historical truth certainly appears odd after da Gama has narrated the apparition of a prophesying cloud-born giant. The mention of Polyphemuses, moreover, is a tip-off that discloses the literary descent of Adamastor from the fantastic inventions of Homer and Virgil. But the burden of Camões' episode—and the basis of its alleged superiority to classical epic—is to show how such poetic inventions can be historical.

The commentators of the *Lusíadas* have noted that Adamastor is modeled upon Homer's and Virgil's depictions of the Cyclops Polyphemus.[25] His prophecy of future Portuguese hardships and disasters at the cape recalls the curse of the Cyclops in the *Odyssey*, while his monstrous body, "horrendo e grosso" (5.40.5), echoes Virgil's description of Polyphemus: "monstrum horrendum, informe, ingens" (3.658). Adamastor's name also seems to allude to Virgil's Cyclops episode, for Achaemenides, the companion of Odysseus whom Aeneas rescues from the Cyclopes' coast, tells us that he is the son of Adamastus (3.614).[26] But Adamastor's story of his passion for Thetis recalls still another Polyphemus, the one whose unrequited love for another sea nymph, Galatea, is recounted in *Idyls* 6 and 10 of Theocritus, in Virgil's *Eclogue* 9, and in the thirteenth book of Ovid's *Metamorphoses*. Following a typical Renaissance literary practice of imitative *contaminatio*, Camões has combined all the classical representations of Polyphemus into his mythical figure. In doing so he has also managed to capture something of Dido's spurned love and irrationality in Adamastor, for Virgil's queen is depicted as a kind of Cyclops in love. Ovid, in fact, remembering how the frenzied Dido became another Polyphemus, makes *his* enamored Polyphemus, as he turns upon Galatea's lover Acis (13.865–66), echo Dido's vindictive speech (4.600–601) seven lines before it turns into her great curse. Thus Dido and Polyphemus had achieved a kind of reciprocity—between monstrous passion and a passionate monster—in the classical literary tradition that informs Camões' fiction. Dido's presence can also be felt in the future orientation and historical concreteness of Adamastor's prophecy. Polyphemus cursed Odysseus alone, but, like Dido, Adamastor directs his words not so much against the epic hero as against his imperialist successors.

Da Gama's insistence upon the truth of his narrative is balanced by an earlier passage in canto 5, where he addresses those purely theoretical armchair scholars who deride the marvelous phenomena reported in sailors' tales, and insist that either the sailors have made them up or misunderstood what they have seen—"falsos ou mal entendidos" (17). Da Gama goes on to describe a waterspout, a prodigy of nature undreamt of by such scholars or by the ancient philosophers on whose works they rest their authority.[27] It is one of the many marvels he has himself encountered at sea: all can be narrated, without lying, as pure truth—"E tudo, sem mentir, puras verdades" (23). There is a polemic of moderns against ancients here, one that prefigures the experimental attitudes of the New Science. But the passage has a curious relationship to the later Adamastor episode, for if the landlubber scholars are wrong to doubt the factual existence of waterspouts, they may still be skeptical about a sailor's story of a giant hovering in the air above his ship—all the more since the waterspout itself offers a naturalistic explanation for the giant. Both are described as "a nuvem negra" (21.8; 60.3), and the poem suggests that the encounter with Adamastor is a second version of da Gama's sighting of the waterspout. The episode is true in the sense that he did really see a waterspout, and that waterspouts really do exist.

But the episode that immediately follows the description of the waterspout offers a second, historical explanation for Adamastor. The Portuguese make a landfall on the southern tip of Africa and, at stanza 27, they encounter a Hottentot who is gathering wild honey. He shows no interest in the gold and silver they show him, but he is delighted by their trade goods: beads, bells, and a red cap. The next day he returns with his fellow tribesmen who are eager to see the same trinkets. They appear so tame ("Domésticos":5.30.5) and friendly that one member of the crew, Fernão Veloso, dares ("atreva":30.7) to go off with them to see the manner of their land and customs. The next thing that da Gama sees is Veloso running at full speed down the hill toward the ships with the Africans in hot pursuit. Da Gama leads a rescue party to pick him up from the shore, where the natives have prepared a further ambush. The Portuguese drive them off, though da Gama receives a wound in the leg in the process. The tone of the episode is nonetheless lighthearted, for the narrator da Gama makes a joke about giving red caps indeed to the bloodied Hottentots, and it ends when all hands have safely returned on board ship with a humorous bantering between the crew and Veloso who is teased about his hasty retreat. But this mood quickly changes, for the apparition of Adamastor immediately follows.

The episode historically took place. It is recorded in the log of da Gama's ship and in Camões' sources, the histories of João de Barros and Damião de Góis.[28] It is an apparently trivial vignette of colonialist violence, but Camões evidently saw in it another version of the encounter between Odysseus and Polyphemus in the *Odyssey*. Veloso has an Odyssean curiosity to learn about the natives and their customs; as de Góis puts it, he wished "to go to see their dwellings, and the manner of life they kept in their homes."[29] But like Odysseus, the Portuguese explorer is forced to make a run for his ship. Camões invites us to note the analogy at the very beginning of the episode when he describes the honey-gathering Hottentot as "more savage than the brutish Polyphemus"—"Selvagem mais que o bruto Polifemo" (5.28.4)— and then directly follows the episode with the horrific spectral appearance of the Polyphemus-like Adamastor. The skirmish with the natives is paltry and one-sided enough; yet even so da Gama is wounded in the fray, and the giant Adamastor is a blown-up figure of the African natives and of the price that will be exacted by their resistance to Portuguese mastery and conquest. Adamastor's name means "the untamed one," and he suggests the nature of the Africans who turned out to be less domesticated than they first appeared. In this light it is significant that the first foreign lands that da Gama passes as he sets out on his voyage at the beginning of canto 5 are those of Muslim Mauretania, "the land over which Antaeus once reigned"—"Terra que Anteu num tempo possuiu"(5.4.6)—where the sixteenth-century Portuguese were involved in crusading and colonizing projects that would lead up to their disastrous defeat at Alcazar-kebir in 1578, six years after the

publication of Camões' poem. Like Antaeus, Adamastor is an autochthonous son of Earth (5.51) and a figure for an Africa that cannot be definitively subdued by European arms.[30]

Canto 5 thus moves in sequence from da Gama's description of the waterspout to Veloso's encounter with the Hottentots, then to the apparition
of Adamastor who is a demonic composite of the natural and human foes
faced by the Portuguese imperial enterprise. The canto self-consciously discloses the historical basis of its own act of mythmaking, both on the part of
the narrator da Gama and of the poet Camões. For the explorer, a native
chasing—and hitting—you with a spear can turn into a giant, a waterspout
can appear to be a supernatural power; for the poet an episode in the chronicles can suggest the story of Odysseus and Polyphemus and bring a whole
literary tradition—Homer, Virgil, Theocritus, Ovid—into play. This self-
consciousness allows the poet to assert a historicity and human truth for his
fabulous classicizing invention. At the same time it can restore the original
Polyphemus episode of the *Odyssey* to human dimensions: it suggests that
Homer's story is itself a mythic retelling of a similar encounter of colonialist
and native. The *Lusíadas* can indulge in a process of mythmaking by simultaneously exposing the mechanism of that process: the poem brings classical
myth forward into the modern world by simultaneously subjecting it to a
rationalizing, euhemerist critique. Camões' episode is thus able both to
enter into and to exploit the imaginative power of a classical epic tradition,
a power that in no small part accounts for the hold that the figure of
Adamastor has had upon readers: what has made the episode a part of
"world literature."[31]

If Camões can both demystify his mythic fiction and have it too, the same
may be said for its ideological content. The self-consciously constructed
nature of the Adamastor episode does not diminish its capacity for ideological manipulation; it may, on the contrary, augment it. The Africans' resistance to Portuguese rule, the retribution due for the violence done to
them—not only da Gama's skirmish with the Hottentots but the later destruction of Kilwa and Mombasa mentioned in the monster's prophecy
(45)—are summoned up in the apparition of Adamastor. But Adamastor
also embodies the raging elements that gave the cape its first name: the
Cape of Storms. If the kinship of Homer's Polyphemus to Poseidon suggested a relationship between the barbarian native and the natural elements, here the two become inextricably conflated in a third figure: the
cloud-born giant that is Camões' mythopoetic creation. This conflation is
already suggested when da Gama describes the black band of Hottentots
showering missiles at him as a thick cloud—"espessem nuvem" (33.1)—and
it is nicely maintained in the series of historical disasters that Adamastor
prophesies will befall the Portuguese: Dias, the discoverer of the cape, will

be lost in a hurricane at sea in 1500 (44); the first viceroy Almeida will land to provision there in 1509 and be massacred along with fifty of his men by Hottentots more successful than those who attacked da Gama (45); and the Sepulvedas will suffer both from the stormy elements and at the hands of the natives when they are shipwrecked in 1552 (46–48). In this curse the natives remain nameless, and the specificity of the events it foretells is determined by their notable Portuguese victims; there is no prediction here of any avenging Hannibal. The Africans fade into the workings of an anonymous nature. Such nature does not have a history, and if Adamastor might seem to project a loser's narrative that would rival the Portuguese victors' own version of history, the events he predicts are no more connected than recurrent storms.

Moreover, this assimilation of the native African resistance with the hostility of nature overlooks and suppresses the Portuguese aggression that kindled the resistance in the first place. Adamastor suggests that the storms of the cape rise out of some motive of retribution for the actions of the Portuguese, but, in fact, storms are impersonal and aimless; they are not even hostile, however much they may seem to be to those humans who happen to enter into their path. The natives' violence appears unmotivated. We do not know quite why the Hottentots should have turned on Veloso, whose sole crime is his explorer's curiosity and desire to penetrate into their territory, though their refusal to let him go any further (36) may be a miniature version of Adamastor's rage against the Portuguese for crossing the boundary of the cape and invading the seas that he has long guarded and controlled (41). Da Gama concludes that the Hottentots are simply bestial, brutal, and evil by nature—"gente bestial, bruta, e malvada" (34.4).[32] And according to his own mythic story, Adamastor was already an angry, literally tempestuous monster *before* the Portuguese ever arrived.

The resistance that the Portuguese face is thus reduced to a kind of blind fury of nature, a resistance that is not particularly directed at them or the result of their own acts of violence; they have simply wandered into a region of storms. And because such storms are not consciously out to harm the Portuguese, they may even help them. This is the case of the great storm that strikes da Gama's fleet in the following canto (6.70–91), and that actually drives his ships *toward* their Indian destination of Calicut. This tempest is carefully balanced against the apparition of Adamastor, and together the two episodes constitute the center of the ten-canto *Lusíadas*. Camões signals the relationship between the two episodes by having each follow a scene involving Fernão Veloso; in canto 6 Veloso has been telling the story of the Twelve of England when the storm suddenly strikes (70) with a telltale black cloud—"nuvem negra" (70.8)—that recalls Adamastor himself. The poem's mythological machinery at first makes the storm seem to be an enactment of the monster's curse, for it has been sent by Neptune (35), and thus is a reminder of the storms that Poseidon unleashes in the *Odyssey* to avenge Polyphemus. But the storm is subsequently ended by Venus, who sends a band of sea nymphs to woo and calm the winds. The episode pointedly inverts the opening scene of the *Aeneid*, where it is Neptune (1.124f.) who must calm the storm that has risen from the sexual bribe, in the form of the nymph Deiopea (72) that Juno offered to Aeolus, god of the winds. In Camões' fiction, moreover, the nymph sent to tame the south wind, Notus, is none other than Galatea (90), the Galatea loved unsuccessfully by Polyphemus and the model for Adamastor's stormy romance with Thetis. As opposed to Adamastor's failure and continuing frustration, his desire for the tantalizingly close but unattainable Thetis, canto 6 features a second mythic story of storm demon and nymph that concludes with a promise of sexual consummation. As the storm at sea subsides, da Gama's lookouts catch sight of the coast of Calicut, the desired end and consummation of his voyage. The storm which has seemed to reverse the beginning sequence of *Aeneid* 1 thus also reverses the digressive movement of the Virgilian model: whereas Aeneas was blown away from the Italy he sought into the potential dead end of Carthage, da Gama is driven across the Indian Ocean from the hospitable, Carthage-like Melinde to his goal in southern India. In fact, the storm probably represents the violent monsoons of the Indian Ocean region. The historical da Gama took advantage of these winds, and their seasonal repetition was a vital part of the Portuguese trade route.

Furthermore, the marriage of winds and sea nymphs looks forward to the final two cantos of the *Lusíadas* where da Gama's crew are sexually rewarded for their successful labors. Venus sends an enchanted island floating into their path and populates it with enamored Nereids—willing native girls in a thin mythological disguise (9.18). Da Gama himself receives Tethys (85) as his consort. Her name ("Tétis") closely resembles that of Thetis ("Tetis"), so much so that Renaissance mythographers were at pains to keep them apart.[33] So, in the symbolic economy of the poem, Adamastor's loss looks very much like da Gama's gain. This final consummation, a reward to the Portuguese for their mission accomplished, becomes in the last canto of the epic an eschatological allegory of the pleasures of immortal fame and a prophecy of Portuguese empire without end.

It is this sense of ending—both of the completed narrative action of the poem and of the finality of an imperial conquest that claims to remain permanent throughout history—that we have seen unsettled by the topos of the epic curse, by the promise of the defeated to return, in some form, to disturb the victor's achievement and rule. Adamastor and his dire prophecy are indeed symbolically connected to the ending of the *Lusíadas* and the celebration on Venus's island of love. But the relationship between these two most famous episodes of the epic is one of inversion: the Portuguese get the girls, and consummate fame and power, while the enemy monster is consumed with frustration. The diametrical contrast suggests how completely the epic, by its end, has overcome the resistance, including the resistance to its own closure, that Adamastor represents. But, in fact, this resistance has already been overcome and left behind well before the celebratory ending of the poem. The first of the two middle cantos of the *Lusíadas* raises the specter of storms and disasters that might stop or sidetrack the Portuguese progress to India—that might halt Portuguese history as it is in the making. But the second immediately dispels this specter: one such storm rises, merely to turn to the advantage of the Portuguese, propelling them toward their destination and imperial destiny. The prophecy of Camões' Jupiter in Book 2 (44–55) describes Portuguese history as an undeviating line of conquest across world geography: the center of Camões' epic narrative turns potential deviation into linearity. By confining Adamastor to its narrative center, the poem turns the prophecy into a question of means—the costs that empire will incur along its way—rather than final ends. And because those imperial ends are assured and untouched by the prophecy, the costs, while they may be more considerable than a mere scar on da Gama's leg, are no less incidental.

What is particularly remarkable is the way in which the monsoon of Book 6—a seasonally recurring storm that crosses the Indian Ocean from west to east—manages to combine the aimless repetition of Adamastor's squalls with the narrative direction and teleology of da Gama's voyage, and how it manages to transform the former into the latter. In terms of literary structure, the middle of Camões' poem enacts the twofold dynamics of what we saw in the last chapter to be the typical *narrative middle*, that indeterminate space described by Brooks where the repetition that constitutes narrative either may become purely, compulsively repetitive, and hence collapse back upon itself, or may move forward, repeating with difference, toward a predetermined goal. In epic this moment of narrative suspension is characteristically dramatized in the suspense of battle, where the power of the emergent victor ensures the possibility of narrative, what epic identifies with its own teleological plot; the losers come to embody a principle of nonnarratable repetition.

And epic, we have also seen, identifies this latter principle generically with romance: that random and finally endless wandering that finds its prototype in the storm-tossed vessel of Odysseus. The losers threaten to reduce their conquerors to their own condition, and we might say that the curse of Polyphemus condemns Odysseus to an all but perpetual romance, requiring the hero, according to Tieresias, to set out again from Ithaca on his voyage to the ends of the earth: a kind of Flying Dutchman.

Camões self-consciously aligns the storm of Book 6 with the literary genre of romance by causing it to strike during Fernão Veloso's narration of the legend of the Twelve of England, a dozen late-fourteenth-century Portuguese knights who, led by the paladin Magriço, performed feats of chivalry and derring-do at the English court. Veloso, like da Gama, proclaims the historical truth of his story and pointedly opposes it to the dreamed-up fables—"fábulas sonhadas" (6.66.4)—of romancers who waste the reader's time with their tedious decriptions of tournaments and duels. He has Ariosto in mind, the modern poet whom he seeks to overgo in this episode just as da Gama claimed superiority to the classical fictions of Homer and Virgil at the end of the preceding canto. At the opening of the *Lusíadas*, Camões had referred to the fabled dreams—"as sonhadas, fabulosas" (1.11.6)—of the *Orlando furioso* and its heroes, Rodamonte, Ruggiero, and Orlando; and in this same passage he had explicitly promised to present the story of Magriço and the Twelve of England as a rival and better version of Ariosto's twelve peers of France (1.12). Veloso's tale is thus self-consciously labeled as romance, and as a digression from the epic narrative, recounted as a means to keep his fellow sailors awake: this is literature as pastime. His story itself seems to digress. His listeners protest as he is about to drop the exploits of Magriço in order to tell about another of the Twelve whose knight-errantry took him to Germany. Their complaints about this deviation—"tal desvio" (6.69.6)—is a sly reference on the part of Camões to the sixteenth-century critical debates over the multiple, digressive, and deliberately confusing plot threads of Ariosto's poem: these were the debates that first identified the *Furioso* as a separate genre called "romance."[34] It is at this precise moment of romance deviation within an episode that is itself a romance deviation from the epic plot of the *Lusíadas* that the storm of Book 6 strikes, the storm that we might now expect to set the whole epic enterprise of da Gama's voyage adrift and wandering into an aimless romance. But this monsoon, instead, puts an end to romance digression and hastens the Portuguese on their way to India.

In the uncertainty whether the storm of Book 6 will carry out Adamastor's curse and drive da Gama off course to destruction or will blow his ships to their epic goal, alternative forms of narrative repetition—and the alternate genres of romance and epic—are as clearly politicized as they are in the undecided epic battle. And here, in addition, they are sexualized. The monsoon winds move in a fixed direction and therefore arrive at a destination that Camões' poem characterizes as a union with the nymphs of the sea: similarly, the Portuguese conquest of the waves and lands of the East will turn into a sexual conquest. By contrast, the aimless storms of Adamastor, rising only to subside just as the risen giant himself dissolves along with his cloud, mirror his unconsummated passion for Thetis, and his sexual frustration itself perpetuates the original failure of his rebellion against the gods. The storms and disasters that Adamastor foretells are the product of an impotent fury, the rage of those powerless to stop, hardly able even to slow, an inevitable Portuguese triumph.

In Adamastor the human identity of the Africans has begun to disappear as they are merged with the storms of the cape. We have already seen how epic can dehumanize foreign and subject peoples in order to characterize imperial conquest as the triumph of culture over nature. The continuing resistance of these peoples turns into a cyclical repetition that seems to be a version of nature's repeated regenerative cycles, but one that has been unnaturally thwarted and has become demonic: like Dido's barrenness, Adamastor's frustration begets a monstrous future. But quite beyond this familiar ideological trick, the *Lusíadas* makes available a further reading of the figure of Adamastor that would displace the natives altogether. Or perhaps, it suggests, they were never quite present in the figure in the first place.

The readings of Adamastor advanced so far have depended on an implicit relationship between the apparition of the giant and the two episodes that precede it—the description of the waterspout and the encounter with the Hottentots. The poem offers clues to this relationship and invites the reader to draw it out of its text, especially by its self-conscious assertion of its historical truth. But in a literal reading of the poem that simply follows its narrative sequence, Adamastor's apparition and prophecy constitute a discrete episode, unconnected to what has gone before. Adamastor makes no mention of Veloso and the natives. Rather, he tells the Portuguese that they will be punished for their daring, their "atrevimento"—the word suggests pride and presumption—in going into seas where no (European) men have gone before. In fact, this also glosses the curiosity of Veloso, who dares—"atreva"—to go off to visit the Hottentots, as a kind of overweening pride.

But it so happens that it was for Adamastor's own "atrevimento," the proverbial pride of the rebellious giants, that the gods transformed him into the cape. In this context, Adamastor's love for Thetis is another version of his presumptuous rebellion, for according to myth, the nymph was prophesied to give birth to a son destined to be greater than his father, one who might therefore pose a threat to the rule of Zeus. Thus Adamastor becomes an image of the transgressive pride and daring of the Portuguese themselves.[35] By venturing into uncharted seas, the Portuguese had been earlier compared to the proud, aspiring giants (2.112), and the monsoon that assails da Gama's ships in Book 6 is likened to the destruction wrought by heaven upon the warring giants (78) and upon their biblical counterparts, the builders of the Tower of Babel (74).[36] The Portuguese transgress not only geographical limits but a whole vision of the world that had endured since antiquity and that the voyages of discovery were to change forever. Adamastor's presumption mirrors the pride of the modern, no longer content to be a dwarf standing on the shoulders of giants, but claiming to be a giant himself—the modern who claims to be mightier than the classical fathers he dislodges. We are brought back to da Gama's reference to the "antigos filósofos" (5.23), who had no knowledge of the lands and marvels he has seen at first hand, and to the end of his narrative and his assertion that his story surpasses the poems of Homer and Virgil: Camões' own presumptuous claim to overgo his ancient models.

The Portuguese and their poet may see themselves in the hubris of Adamastor and stand back in awe of their own achievements. This specular gaze seems to involve as much self-satisfaction as dread at having gone too far. For when the gigantomachy is read as an allegory of the moderns' attempt to outdo the ancients and overthrow their authority, the Portuguese may claim victory where the mythical giants met defeat. The continuing contrast in the poem between Adamastor's failure and da Gama's success can be reinterpreted to suggest just how successful the revolutionary accomplishments of the Portuguese have been.

But what is most striking in this potential moment of self-knowledge—as the Portuguese find their daring mirrored in Adamastor—is that the African natives have vanished from sight. The "other" in which the Portuguese are reflected is the monstrous mythopoetic figure, not the natives whose historical encounter with da Gama's fleet might seem to have generated the black giant in the first place. Indeed, if that historical episode still stands behind Adamastor's apparition, the giant now seems to have grown out of Veloso's overconfident daring rather than from the wrath of the natives. The poem avoids a mutual recognition between colonialist and native, and in this reading of Adamastor as the projection of a (justifiable) Portuguese pride, the Africans are virtually canceled out. The production of self-knowledge that might be held to be laudable in itself is here involved with a twofold suppression of the other, one by which the figure of Adamastor is both substituted for the Africans and simultaneously emptied of their presence and made to point instead to their Portuguese masters. This suppression repeats the original act of violence against the Hottentots, a violence that was doubled in Camões' text by da Gama's joke about the wounded natives and the comic dismissal of the whole episode.

This self-reflection that takes place at the expense of the natives can be linked to the remarkable self-consciousness of the Adamastor episode as a whole: the way in which the epic announces and points to its own act of creating a new myth out of the stuff of history. We are accustomed, I think, to see such self-consciousness as an undoing of ideology. Insofar as it insists upon the historicity of Adamastor, Camões' poem may indeed allow us to glimpse the violence and victims that lie behind its own and other epic fictions. But its calling attention to the constructed nature of the giant figure does not necessarily question the ideological operation that the figure effects: an assimilation of the African natives with the storms of nature that

deprives them once again of an historical identity and of an identity as victims. Moreover, in his very self-consciousness, the poet seems to become
complicit with a reading that still further erases the historical natives by
turning Adamastor into an image of Portuguese pride and achievement. For
Camões stakes his own claim to excel Homer and Virgil upon the figure of
the giant who not only lends a proper heroic awe and epic magnitude to da
Gama's relatively uneventful journey but also presents the poet with an
occasion to demonstrate his powers in a kind of epideictic display. The figure of Adamastor can be read to be what it literally declares itself to be: the
poet's daring and aggrandizing figure of his own daring and greatness and
that of his Portuguese heroes. When the figures of poetic language are read
as self-reflexive figures, history and human beings begin to disappear.

The African natives have indeed disappeared for readers of the poem, in
which the textual strategies may work only too well: the relationship between Adamastor and da Gama's encounter with the Hottentots has virtually escaped previous commentary on the episode. And equally submerged
in the implicit symbolic relations of the text and its web of poetic and historical sources is the topos of the epic curse, the classical model that informs
the fiction of the giant, but which the ideology of the *Lusíadas* deforms in
turn. We have seen that the curse typically lends the epic loser something
of an autonomous voice and identity. But here it issues from a giant cloud
rather than a human agent. Its characteristic prophecy of a future history of
resistance that may unsettle the political dominance and closed histories of
the victors turns into a weather forecast. And even the storms it predicts as
obstacles to the Portuguese have the capacity to turn into their opposites
and facilitate the building of a Lusitanian empire without end. This deformation of the topos suggests even more forcefully than our earlier examples
that epic's representation of its losers—its attempt to adopt their perspective—may not be able to escape appropriation by the victors' ideology. And
such appropriation would become complete when the representation, the
giant Adamastor, is read no longer as a figure of the native loser but as a
mirror image of the Portuguese victor himself.

And yet the episode of Adamastor has not failed to produce an uncanny
frisson in subsequent readers. This may be due precisely to the way in which
the not-so-hidden presence of the natives—and with it the topos of the
curse and the earlier literary voices of Polyphemus and Dido—are displaced
and swallowed up in Camões' giant, the way they are covered over, as it
were, by alternative readings: a textual suppression that creates the effect of
a return of the repressed. In *Billy Budd*, Melville writes of the "wars which
like a flight of harpies rose shrieking from the din and dust of the fallen
Bastille," and then shifts epic figures to remark of the Napoleonic period:
"the genius of it presented an aspect like that of Camoens' 'Spirit of the
Cape,' an eclipsing menace mysterious and prodigious."[37] Melville suggests

a genealogical posterity for Adamastor and his curse, of oppressed voices and insurgent ghosts heard at last, that is no less distinguished than their Homeric and Virgilian ancestry. Camões' monster, born of the initial encounter of Portuguese imperialism and its native subjects, is the first in a line of specters haunting Europe.

APPENDIX

FRACASTORO'S *SYPHILIS* AND BARLOW'S *COLUMBIAD*

In *Syphilis* (1530), his celebrated Neo-latin poem that gave the new epidemic its name, Girolamo Fracastoro provides a further example of the topos of the epic curse functioning in the context of Renaissance exploration: in this case in an account of the very first contact between Europeans and the New World. Book 3 of the poem narrates a highly fictionalized version of the first landing of Columbus and his men on Hispaniola. They have hardly come ashore when they see and begin to hunt with their guns the myriad bird life of the island (3.151ff.). This episode recalls the violence that Aeneas and his men commit against the Harpies in *Aeneid* 3 (234ff.), and it ends with one of the birds, like Virgil's Harpy Celaeno, launching a prophetic curse against the attackers.[38]

> Qui Solis violatis aves, sacrasque volantes,
> Hesperii, nunc vos, quae magnus cantat Apollo,
> Accipite, et nostro vobis quae nunciat ore.
> Vos quanquam ignari, longum quaesita, secundis
> Tandem parta Ophyrae tetigistis littora ventis.
> Sed non ante novas dabitur summittere terras,
> Et longa populos in libertate quietos,
> Molirique urbes, ritusque ac sacra novare,
> Quam vos infandos pelagi terraeque labores
> Perpessi, diversa hominum post praelia, multi
> Mortua in externa tumuletis corpora terra.
> Navibus amissis pauci patria arva petetis,
> Frustra alii socios quaeretis magna remensi
> Aequora: nec nostro deerunt Cyclopes in orbe.
> Ipsa inter sese vestras discordia puppes
> In rabiem ferrumque trahet: nec sera manet vos
> Illa dies, foedi ignoto quum corpora morbo
> Auxilium sylva miseri poscetis ab ista,
> Donec poeniteat scelerum.

(3.174–92)

(You who have done violence to the birds of the Sun, his sacred flying creatures, you men of Hesperia hear now what almighty Apollo prophesies, what he declares to you by our mouth. Although you do not know it, you have with favouring winds at last touched and gained the shores of the Ophyre you sought so long. But it will not be granted you to place in subjection new lands and a people which has enjoyed long liberty and peace, to construct cities and change rites and customs, until, having suffered to the bitter end unspeakable trials by land and sea, and after battling against men on all sides, many of you bury dead bodies in a foreign land. Ships will be lost so that few of you will make for your home lands; others retraversing the mighty seas will search for comrades in vain. Nor will Cyclopes be wanting in this hemisphere. Discord herself will drag your crews into mad and murderous disputes; and a day lies in wait for you, close at hand, when, your bodies filthy with an unknown disease, you will in your wretchedness demand help of this forest until you repent of your crimes.)[39]

This curse, apparently uttered on behalf of the soon-to-be-subjected natives of the New World but not by them, may well have been a model for Camões, and it enacts a series of displacements that are similar to those performed by the curse of Adamastor. Unlike Adamastor's curse that followed, this curse immediately precedes an encounter with the human natives, which here is entirely amiable: the people of Hispaniola feast and trade with Columbus, and there are no unfriendly incidents. The shooting of the birds and the ensuing curse thus acknowledges, if only symbolically, the historical violence inflicted by the gun-toting Spaniards upon the natives of America. The mention of Cyclopes joins the curse of Fracastoro's Hispaniola bird (probably a parrot) back to Homer's Polyphemus and the origin of the topos. At the same time it refers to the cannibalism that was the most notorious trait of the Amerindian peoples. It reduces the Americans, on the one hand, to a part of the wildlife and, on the other, hints at a monstrous savagery that equally dehumanizes them. The Spanish violence, for its part, while it has something of the mythical resonance of Odysseus's men eating the cattle of the Sun—a violation of nature—is comparatively innocent and trivial: a hunting scene.

Yet the impression of dread remains, not least because of the association that the curse makes in this poem about syphilis—between the threat of the disease and the retribution that awaited the Europeans for their treatment of the American natives. For syphilis was widely, probably correctly, thought to have been brought back to Europe by Columbus's crew, the true curse and revenge of the New World upon the Old. But here, too, the power of the curse is displaced and contained. At the opening of his poem (1.33ff.) Fracastoro explicitly rejects the idea of an American origin for syphilis. If we can see the curse bringing this idea back once again, we should also note that it ends *not* simply with the disease—which the poem will shortly depict the Spaniards bringing with them to the New World *from* Europe (3.381ff.)—but rather with the prospect of its *cure*: by means of the guaiacum tree growing in the American forests. In this instance, the curse—and the discovery and conquest of America—turn into a blessing.

If this episode in the *Syphilis* anticipates and may have provided a model for Camões' Adamastor, the episode of the *Lusíadas*, in turn, was the inspiration for the high point, poetic and moral, of Joel Barlow's *Columbiad*, first published in 1807. In this epic poem celebrating the American Revolution, Christopher Columbus, imprisoned in Spain, receives a series of prophetic historical visions from the spirit Hesper, the spirit of the new Western world he has discovered. These culminate in the war that the American colonists fight to achieve their independence from Great Britain, accomplished by the end of Book 7; the last three books describe the triumphant extension of American commerce and America's federal system of democracy to the rest of the world. But the transitional Book 8 contains an unsettling moment. As Barlow's prose summary puts it, the spirit Atlas, the "guardian Genius of Africa, denounces to Hesper the crimes of his people in the slavery of the Africans."[40] This Atlas is clearly inspired by his brother African Titan, Adamastor, whom Barlow encountered in the celebrated English translation of the *Lusíadas* by William Mickle, first published in 1776.[41] As Adamastor is the personification of the Cape of Good Hope and the guardian of the southern gateway of Africa, so Atlas is the spirit of the Moroccan mountain that bears his name and the guardian of the continent's northern shores. He inveighs against the moral hypocrisy of the fledgling American nation.

> Enslave my tribes! what, half mankind imban,
> Then read, expound, enforce the rights of man! (8.223–24)
>
> . . . .
>
> Enslave my tribes! and think, with dumb disdain
> To scape this arm and prove my vengeance vain! (8.245–46)

Republican freedom and slavery cannot coexist, Atlas sarcastically declares, and he goes on, like Adamastor, to foretell the consequences, the revenge of history, upon the oppressors of Africa. Africa itself will take reciprocal vengeance, he suggests, when Americans will find themselves the prisoners and slaves of the Barbary pirates (239–60). Still more cataclysmic punishment awaits the new American nation, however, if it does not renounce slaveholding.

> Nature, long outraged, delves the crusted sphere
> And molds the mining mischief dark and drear;
> Europa too the penal shock shall find,
> The rude soul-selling monsters of mankind.
> Where Alps and Andes at their bases meet,
> In earth's mid caves to lock their granite feet,
> Heave their broad spines, expand each breathing lobe
> And with their massy members rib the globe,
> Her cauldron'd flood of ire their blast prepare;
> Her wallowing womb of subterranean war
> Waits but the fissure my wave shall find,
> To force the foldings of the rocky rind,
> Crash your curst continent, and whirl on high
> The vast avulsion vaulting through the sky,
> Fling far the bursting fragments, scattering wide
> Rocks, mountains, nations o'er the swallowing tide.
> Plunging and surging with alternate sweep,
> They storm the day-vault and lay bare the deep,
> Toss, tumble, plow their place, then slow subside,
> And swell each ocean as their bulk they hide;
> Two oceans dasht in one! that climbs and roars,
> And seeks in vain the exterminated shores,
> The deep drencht hemisphere. Far sunk from day,
> It crumbles, rolls, it churns the settling sea,
> Turns up each prominence, heaves every side,
> To pierce once more the landless length of tide;

Till some poised Pambamarca looms at last
A dim lone island in the watery waste,
Mourns all his minor mountains wreckt and hurl'd,
Stands the sad relic of a ruin'd world,
Attests the wrath our mother kept in store
And rues her judgments on the race she bore.
No saving Ark, around him rides the main,
Nor Dove weak-wing'd her footing finds again;
His own bald eagle skims alone the sky,
Darts from all points of heaven her searching eye,
Kens thro the gloom her ancient rock of rest
And finds her cavern'd crag, her solitary nest.

(8.277–304)

Atlas's prophecy of an earthquake that will destroy and submerge the Americas beneath the now joined Atlantic and Pacific oceans evokes the story of Atlantis, the island kingdom that vanished beneath the sea, a realm of which, according to Plato (*Critias* 114), Atlas—or his twin brother— was the mythological founder. From the moment of its earliest discovery America was frequently linked with this lost continent—the natives of Hispaniola in Fracastoro's *Syphilis* (3.265f.) in fact claim to be descendants of the inhabitants of Atlantis—and here Barlow's fiction predicts another disaster that will befall this new Atlantis, as Nature itself rises up in repugnance against the American institution of slavery. Like the storms summoned up by the curse of Adamastor, the earthquake and tidal wave prophesied by Atlas suggest a primal link between the peoples of Africa and elemental creation.

Barlow is even more self-conscious than Camões about his cursing Titan. He immediately distances himself and his reader from his impressive mythopoetic episode.

Fathers and friends, I know the boding fears
Of angry genii and of rending spheres
Assail not souls like yours; whom science bright
Thro shadowy nature leads with surer light;

. . . .

You scorn the Titan's threat; nor shall I strain
The powers of pathos in a task so vain
As Afric's wrongs to sing;

. . . .

The tale might startle still the accustom'd ear
Still shake the nerve that pumps the pearly tear,
Melt every heart and thro the nation gain
Full many a voice to break the barbarous chain.

(8.309–12, 319–21, 327–30)

In an age of reason and science, Barlow is unsure whether the mythical creations of poetry retain any persuasive power—no one believes in giants any more—and he goes on (331–94) to make the case against slavery on the grounds of rational self-interest. Yet, he holds out the hope that the epic figure of Atlas and his chilling prophecy may still rouse his countrymen to emotional sympathy. Both Barlow and Camões, anxious about the continuity of a kind of classical epic awe in a modern era increasingly skeptical toward poetic fictions, vest that awe in personifications of the victimized: the African human casualties of this new era of exploration and of the creation of America. Such poetic awe may now be identical to the guilt feelings of an enlightened culture, whose central enterprise of dominating nature has its corollary in the domination of other human beings: for which nature may take an awesome revenge. But the moral and political sensibilities of the sixteenth-century imperialist and of the nineteenth-century republican abolitionist are nonetheless greatly different. As a successor to Adamastor, Barlow's Atlas launches another epic curse on the part of the victims of history, promising retribution on their oppressors. But whereas the disasters that Adamastor's prophetic curse seems to call into being do little to impede or call into question Portugal's progress toward world empire, Atlas predicts nothing short of national cataclysm, and by the time of Shiloh and Gettysburg half a century later this prophecy had come true.

FOUR

EPICS OF THE DEFEATED: THE OTHER TRADITION OF LUCAN, ERCILLA, AND D'AUBIGNE

The *Pharsalia*

THERE ARE FEW poems as moving in Roman literature as the ode that Statius dedicated to Polla, the widow of Lucan, on the occasion of the dead poet's birthday (*Silvae* 2.7). The tribute to the genius of Lucan, author of the unfinished epic, the *De Bello Civili*, or, as it is commonly known, the *Pharsalia*, is tinged with the pathos of his untimely death. Involved in a botched conspiracy against Nero, Lucan was forced to commit suicide in A.D. 65 at the age of twenty-six. Statius must demonstrate that in so brief a life Lucan had achieved a full poetic career, that however premature his death he had reached maturity as a poet and adulthood as a man. The latter is attested to by Lucan's marriage to Polla, whose devotion to his memory is invoked in the final section (120f.) of the ode.

The issue of Lucan's poetic adulthood is addressed through a series of agonistic comparisons with Virgil. The ode first forbids Mantua, Virgil's native city, to challenge the preeminence of the Spanish river Baetis near Córdoba, the birthplace of Lucan: "Baetim, Mantua, provocare noli" (35). It then recounts the prophetic speech that Calliope made over the newborn Lucan, admonishing her darling to forswear the example of the *Aeneid*.

> nocturnas alii Phrygum ruinas
> et tardi reducis vias Ulixis
> et puppem temerariam Minervae,
> trita vatibus orbita, sequantur:
> tu carus Latio memorque gentis
> carmen fortior exseris togatum.[1]

(48–53)

(Let others follow the tracks worn by the wheels of other poets: the nocturnal destruction of Troy, and the paths of the slowly returning Ulysses, and the bold ship of Minerva: you dear to Latium and mindful of your own people, more strongly unveil an epic of the Romans, those who wear the toga.)

Lucan receives praise for having written the *true* national epic, the *Pharsalia*, the historical poem on the Roman civil wars. The Virgil of the *Aeneid* is here reduced to an imitator of Greek models—the *Iliad*, the *Odyssey*, and the *Argonautica*—and Lucan is lauded for his originality: precisely the originality of not having, in turn, imitated Virgil's poem. In fact, in the verses immediately following, Calliope foretells that Lucan in his early precocious years—"primum teneris adhuc in annis" (54)—will write on the subject of Troy, before advancing in young manhood—"coepta generosior iuventa" (64)—to the *Pharsalia*. His Virgilian stage thus represents the juvenilia of Lucan's very young career, and the implication is that he has brought Roman poetry to a new maturity. And yet he will still produce the *Pharsalia* at an earlier age than that at which Virgil had written his own juvenilia, the *Culex*.

> haec primo iuvenis canes sub aevo,
> ante annos Culicis Maroniani.
>
> (73–74)

> (You will sing these things as a youth in your early prime before the years of the Virgilian gnat.)

Thus Virgil is doubly juvenilized by the comparison: the *Aeneid* is a kind of imitative school exercise or preparation for the *Pharsalia*; the *Pharsalia* was itself but a token of what might have been had Lucan lived. And thus the *Aeneid* will join the other great Roman epics, the *Annales* of Ennius, the *De Rerum Natura*, Varro's *Argonautica*, and the *Metamorphoses* (75–78)—and bow before Lucan's poem.

> ipsa te Latinis
> Aeneis venerabitur canentem.
>
> (79–80)

> (The *Aeneid* itself will do homage to you as you sing among the Latins.)

These lines are followed by Calliope's prophecy of Lucan's wedding day (81–88): his coming to full manhood just before he is cut off by the Fates (89).

The question of Lucan's poetic maturity thus becomes a case of the anxiety of influence: of anxiety toward the poetic father Virgil, whom the ode belittles and to whom it denies the status of adulthood, hence of paternity itself.[2] Statius's strategy is the more striking given the reverence for Virgil expressed at the end of Statius's own epic poem, the *Thebaid*. Statius addresses the finished poem and enjoins it to keep a respectful distance behind the unrivaled *Aeneid*.

> nec tu divinam Aeneida tempta,
> sed longe sequere et vestigia semper adora.
>
> (*Thebaid* 12.816–17)

> (Do not compete with the divine *Aeneid*, but follow after and always venerate its footsteps.)

Statius may willingly accept for himself the role of epigone and imitator, following in the footsteps of Virgil. But his ode recognizes that Lucan's *Pharsalia* stakes all upon its emulation and overgoing of the *Aeneid*.

These stakes are not merely poetic but political. For Lucan, Virgil was the apologetic spokesman for the institution of the emperor, of the tyrannical one-man rule of the Caesars. The *Pharsalia* is the epic of the lost Roman republic; it takes the side of the senatorial forces of Pompey and Cato, defeated by Julius Caesar in the civil war. The anxiety that the ode suggests about a literary father so powerful as to inhibit his successor's own poetic voice is thus bound up with Lucan's opposition to the imperial establishment that made the *Aeneid* its official poem and that might silence other, dissenting versions of Roman history. The Nero—"nefas rabidi tyranni" (100)—whose command cut short Lucan's life and epic is thus a sinister double in Statius's poem of the Virgil who is felt as a threat to the poet's growing up to maturity. The *Pharsalia* gives back to the vanquished republicans their story of resistance and keeps that story alive in historical memory. It allegorizes its own activity in the episode where Pompey's body is rescued from the waves off the Egyptian coast and given a burial and marked grave (8.712–872), while the soul of the leader of the fight against Caesarism soars laughing to the empyrean and then returns to earth to enter into the tyrannicide Brutus (9.1–17). This is the episode that Statius recalls as he describes Lucan, immortalized by the fame of the *Pharsalia* itself, looking down at the earth and laughing at his grave—"terras despicis et sepulchra rides" (110)—while the ode as a whole celebrates the annual rite of the poet's commemoration. Neither Lucan, nor his poem, nor its political message and cause can die.

This is an assertion of faith. Statius's ode is the more affecting because it affirms what its author probably knows is not the case: Lucan would not supplant Virgil as the great Roman epic poet (as the end of the *Thebaid* attests); nor would the republic return. Lucan did, however, initiate a rival, anti-Virgilian tradition of epic whose major poems—the *Pharsalia* itself, *La Araucana* of Alonso de Ercilla, and *Les Tragiques* of Agrippa d'Aubigné— embrace the cause of the politically defeated. These works have been consigned, or perhaps consigned themselves, to a secondary canonical status in the history of the genre, never quite achieving the same rank as the *Aeneid*, the *Lusíadas*, or the *Gerusalemme liberata*, the poems of the dominant tradition—the tradition on the side of the victors. Statius's ode shrewdly exposes the double anxiety that runs through the project of the *Pharsalia*. Lucan's desire to break free from the prestigious model of Virgil is already based as much upon opposition to what Virgil stands for politically as upon a dread of the great poetic father. At the same time, Lucan's capacity to overgo the *Aeneid* is impaired because he speaks from the side of the losers, contesting a vision of history upheld not only by Virgil's epic but by the reality of imperial power. Lucan and his subsequent imitators sing of the failure of history to turn out as it ought to have done, and they thus deny to themselves the closed classical form of Virgilian epic, the form which that epic assimilates with a *closure upon history* achieved by political conquest.

The resulting lack of form, or bad form—always measured against Virgilian standards—has dismayed even Lucan's admirers sympathetic to his anti-imperial politics. Thus Joel Barlow, the American Revolutionary War poet, could write in the preface to his own epic, *The Columbiad* (1825):

> Lucan is the only republican among the ancient epic poets. But the action of his rambling tho majestic poem is so badly arranged as to destroy, in a poetical sense, the life and interest of the great national subject on which it is founded.[3]

Barlow, who might have looked to Lucan as a model, finds in the *Pharsalia* an episodicity and sprawling misshapenness that runs counter to the "poetical sense" he has learned to appreciate from the linear, teleological narratives of the *Iliad* and the *Aeneid*. Of the latter he writes: "Its poetical or fictitious design, the settlement of his hero in Italy, is well delineated and steadily pursued."[4] Similar charges of narrative disorder and excess have been leveled against *La Araucana* and *Les Tragiques*, and they account in large part for the failure of Lucan's tradition to obtain pride of place in the epic canon. But Barlow is mistaken in trying to separate the political ideas of the *Pharsalia* from what he sees as the epic's formal shortcomings. Lucan's deliberate deformation of Virgilian narrative structure is part, perhaps the largest part, of the political message of his poem—and of the poems of his followers.

The unshapeliness of the *Pharsalia* appears to stem from its adherence to historical annals. The poem presents itself as a chronicle of the relatively recent civil war. This subject matter allows Statius to make the surprising claim that Lucan, not Virgil, is the author of a truly Roman epic; to oppose, that is, the historical events of the *Pharsalia* to the *Aeneid* with its story of mythical national origins and its dependence on Homeric models. But it also causes Tasso, epic's greatest theorist, to argue that Lucan is not a poet at all.

> The order observed by Lucan is not the order proper to poets, but the exact, natural order in which past events are narrated: and this is the usage of the historian.[5]

Tasso's judgment follows a long tradition that goes back to Lucan's Roman critics.[6] It would later be echoed by Voltaire, who labels the *Pharsalia* a "declamatory gazetteer" in his influential *Essay on Epic Poetry* (1727), and complains that Lucan has recounted the historical events of his epic in their chronological sequence without forming them poetically into a coherent narrative.[7] In fact, as more recent critical studies have shown, Lucan carefully juxtaposes episodes of the *Pharsalia* to create patterns of meaning; his numerous digressions have little to do with the historical record, from which, in fact, he omits important events.[8] Nor was he the first Roman poet to narrate events of national history. He was preceded by Ennius and Naevius, the founders of Latin epic, and would be followed by Silius Italicus; all of them gave accounts of the Punic Wars against Hannibal's Carthage.[9] The special impression of the historical factuality of the *Pharsalia* nonetheless remains, and it is tied to Lucan's authentic generic innovation, one that Silius significantly did not follow: his dispensing with a Homeric divine machinery.

The removal of the Olympian gods to the periphery of the *Pharsalia* secularizes its historical narrative, and makes it seem more immediate to the raw events themselves.[10] It also precludes the gods from sanctioning or predetermining the outcome of those events—from imposing a closed narrative form on Roman history. Their place is taken by the forces of Fortune and Fate, which Lucan's epic notoriously confuses together.[11] If the vanquished in the *Aeneid* saw their lives governed by a capricious Fortune while the victors were consoled by the long-term perspective of Fate, the *Pharsalia* identifies the conquering Caesar with Fortune—she virtually becomes his patron goddess—and denies any meaningful historical teleology to either winners or losers. Lucan portrays a world ruled by chance, whose radically contingent events form self-contained episodes and can only be organized into narrative according to the chronicler's criterion of temporal succession. This desacralization of history—at least of history as it has been written by the victors—is an enduring feature of Lucan's tradition.

The point of banishing the gods and placing Roman history under the domain of Fortune is to deny the necessity—and the permanence—of the imperial establishment. Rome's destiny is thus not closed and irreversible as the *Aeneid* had claimed, both through its own narrative teleology and through its several passages of prophecy foretelling the ascendancy of Augustus. In one of his favorite figures, the rhetorical question, Lucan's narrator asks why the Delphic oracle of Book 5—during an episode that wickedly parodies Aeneas's visit to the sibyl of Cumae in *Aeneid* 6—has refused to prophesy the future: a question that could be addressed to the *Pharsalia* as a whole.[12]

> Vindicis an gladii facinus poenasque furorum
> Regnaque ad ultores iterum redeuntia Brutos
> Ut peragat fortuna taces?
>
> (5.206–8)

(Are you silent so that fortune may carry out the deed of the vindictive sword, exact punishment for the fury of civil war, and bring tyranny around once again to meet its avenging Brutuses?)

The immediate idea here is that the gods do not wish to foretell the assassination of Julius Caesar lest it be thwarted. But there is also a more complex, secondary meaning, contained in the cyclical connotations of "redeuntia," in the repetition suggested by "iterum," and in the use of the plural "Brutos," that tyrannicide may continually reappear in Roman history to remove imperial pretenders, including the present ruler Nero. The problem, however, with imagining history as open-ended and given over to chance, free to produce avenging Brutuses and eventual political restitution, is that no historical or prophesied future settlement—whether of tyranny or of the desired freedom—can be definitive.[13] As the very form of the narrator's question suggests, as well as the fact that it consigns retribution to the agency of fortune, the avenger may come or he may not; should he come, the republican order he restores may or may not last. Against the victors' Virgilian narrative of imperial destiny, the losers' epic does not oppose an equally closed and end-directed narrative of the losers' own eventual political restoration, but rather a narrative of historical contingency that has no end in sight.

To reverse the terms of the Virgilian model of epic narrative may not constitute a break with the model itself. The *Pharsalia* takes up a vision of history-as-chance and a corollary sense of narrative aimlessness that the *Aeneid* had *already* assigned to the epic loser. The looser, episodic structure of Lucan's poem draws close to the open-endedness and cyclicality of *romance*, a conjunction that will be consciously articulated by Ercilla and d'Aubigné, writing in an age that had begun to recognize romance as a distinct generic form. But Virgilian epic projects romance narrative as the rival to its own plot of empire and uses it to represent the condition of nonnarratability with which it characterizes the experience of the defeated. Similarly, Virgilian epic gives voice to the losers' alternative vision of history in the great curses they launch against their conquerors; but, as the last chapter argues, these curses foretell not the definitive overthrow of the victors' rule but a story of continued resistance against it, a narrative of repeated, endless struggle that—compared to the victors' teleological plot of conquest—also represents the nonnarratable. The epics of Lucan's tradition can be seen as extended versions of these losers' curses—particularly *Les Tragiques*, which seems to be a long string of wrathful imprecations against the persecutors of the Huguenot saints; and their misshapen narratives can appear to signal a failure of narrative itself. This alternative, anti-Virgilian epic tradition thus conforms to what the *Aeneid* had all along suggested would be the alternative to its own models of narrative and imperial history: it is just the way Virgil supposes that the defeated and powerless would tell and shape their side of the story. The anxiety of poetic secondariness that Statius brilliantly intuits in Lucan's career may stem from this inability to escape from the norms and expectations of the epic genre as Virgil had already decisively defined them.[14]

One such generic expectation is that epic will contain the glorification of a national destiny of power and conquest, that it will conform to an aristocratic martial ethos, and here Lucan and his Renaissance followers are more Virgilian than they might perhaps wish to think themselves. This is obviously the case of Ercilla, whose poem celebrates Spanish victories at the same time that it recounts the Araucanians' stubborn resistance. But it is also true of the Huguenot d'Aubigné, who hymns the predestined triumphs of an international Protestantism, and of Lucan himself, who, at those points of the *Pharsalia* where Rome's *imperium* is at stake—her foreign conquests and world domination as opposed to the imperial principate—reveals the contradictions of his anti-Virgilianism. There are accordingly ideological stakes that militate against a total break with the model of the *Aeneid*, however much it may relegate Lucan's tradition to a secondary position. Even as they contest Virgilian norms by telling the losers' other side of the story, the poems of Lucan and his imitators remain epics of empire.

Caesar's Boat Ride

The deformation of narrative in the *Pharsalia* is epitomized in one emblematic episode of Book 5: the nocturnal sea voyage that Julius Caesar takes into a threatening storm (476–677). Impatient with and distrustful of his lieutenant Antony, who has failed to follow orders and transport his army from Italy to Epirus, Caesar decides to voyage to Italy himself. The historically based episode allows Lucan to put Caesar in the same position as the Aeneas of the first half of the *Aeneid* who wanders at sea in search of receding Italian shores: Caesar even repeats Aeneas's route from Epirus (Buthrotum). Critics have noted that when the storm subsequently rises and strikes the little boat of Caesar and Amyclas, the poor mariner who accompanies him as helmsman, the scene imitates the storms of the *Aeneid* that cause Aeneas to deviate off course away from his Italian destination. Principally, it imitates the great opening storm of Virgil's poem with its recollection of the storm of *Odyssey* 5, but it also brings to mind the squall that strikes the Trojan fleet as it leaves Carthage at the beginning of Book 5.[15]

Amyclas's exchange with Caesar at verses 567–93 rewrites the speeches of Palinurus and Aeneas in the later Virgilian passage.[16] Aeneas acceded to Palinurus when the helmsman despaired of reaching Italy and turned his ship over to Fortune.

> magnanime Aenea, non si mihi Iuppiter auctor
> spondeat, hoc sperem Italiam contingere caelo.
>
> . . . .
>
> superat quoniam Fortuna, sequamur,
> quoque uocat, uertamus iter.
>
> (Aeneid 5.17–19, 22–23)

(Greathearted Aeneas, not even if Jupiter should authorize it do I hope to reach
Italy with this threatening sky.

. . . .

since Fortune prevails, let us follow and where she calls, there let us turn our
course.)

By contrast, Lucan's Caesar tells the apprehensive Amyclas, who has correctly read the signs of the oncoming storm, to sail on nonetheless, for Fortune is on his side.

> Italiam si caelo auctore recusas,
> Me pete. Sola tibi causa est haec iusta timoris,
> Vectorem non nosse tuum, quem numina numquam
> Destituunt, de quo male tunc fortuna meretur,
> Cum post vota venit.
>
> . . . .
>
> Quid tanta strage paretur,
> Ignoras: quaerit pelagi caelique tumultu,
> Quod praestet Fortuna mihi.
>
> (*Phars.* 5.579–83, 591–93)

(If you refuse to seek out Italy by the authority of the sky, seek it by mine. The
only just cause of your fear is that you do not know your passenger—he whom
the gods never abandon, whom Fortune treats badly when she only responds to
and fails to anticipate his prayers . . . do you not know what this storm portends:
by this tumult of sea and sky Fortune seeks to benefit me.)

Lucan recasts the scene where the Virgilian helmsman relinquishes control
and gives his ship up to the winds of chance: a scene, I have argued in
Chapter 2, that demonstrates the inability of the human individual to guide
or determine historical destiny. It anticipates the ending of *Aeneid* 5, where
the superfluous Palinurus—a surrogate for the hero Aeneas himself—is
swept overboard and Neptune directs the Trojan ships to their Italian destination. Lucan makes a similar point about the agency of Caesar, who abandons himself to Fortune, although Caesar, with supreme self-delusion,
claims at the same time to have a special relationship with Fortune and
represents his voyage as a proud act of heroic will. Whereas Palinurus, in the
face of the storm, would not acknowledge the authority of Jupiter himself,
Caesar tells Amyclas that he, Caesar, is authority enough for their venturing
out into the gale. When, directly following these words, the storm hits and
tears away the sails of the little boat, Caesar's confidence seems comically
misplaced. His proud claims are subjected to a literal cold bath, and for the
rest of the episode, throughout Lucan's gorgeous, hyperbolic description of
the storm, we are in suspense over whether or not the would-be conqueror
of the world will be lost at sea.

But in another sense, Caesar is perfectly correct. His salvation in this episode, and his success in the larger poem, are due to Fortune, whom he chooses as his lone companion at the beginning of the boat trip—"Sola placet Fortuna comes" (510)—and who greets him on shore at its end.

> Pariter tot regna, tot urbes
> Fortunamque suam tacta tellure recepit.
>
> (676–77)

(He touched land, and in the same moment regained so many realms, so many cities, and his own Fortune.)

No Neptune appears, as in both the first and fifth books of the *Aeneid*, to smooth the waters and steer the hero to port. Caesar's success is not of his own making—in this sense he is much like Palinurus and Aeneas—but neither is it directed by a divinely sanctioned destiny of the kind that directs the action of Virgil's poem. Caesar speaks of the gods ("numina") who take his part, but these, in a way that is typical of the *Pharsalia*, are quickly conflated with Fortune: goddess and abstraction. Caesar is brought to shore not as part of an intelligible, predetermined narrative of history distinct from the chance confusion of the storm—a traditional emblem of Fortune—but by the storm itself, which only blows him back to Epirus where he started.[17] Caesar is simply very, very lucky. He plunges recklessly ahead in a series of happy blunders, and survives. Lucan may have to cóncede that Caesar's delusions of grandeur give him an energy and willfulness that partly account for his success—Fortune aids the daring—but the success does not go by plan, and it is not to be confused with necessity.[18] The *Pharsalia* thus denies history to its winner for, as the episode suggests, history is a matter of chance: it is virtually unnarratable.

This nonnarratable condition was associated by the *Aeneid* with the epic loser and was represented in the narrative form of Odyssean romance, whose emblem is precisely the wandering, unguided ship, tossed by the winds and storms of Fortune: Cleopatra fleeing Actium, Turnus carried away from the battle of Book 10, the defeated Trojans themselves buffeted by the storms of the first half of Virgil's poem. We have seen that Lucan, too, uses the figure of the pilotless ship in a simile that portrays Pompey on the eve of his defeat at Pharsalia (7.125–27), in a passage that directly recalls the flight of Virgil's Cleopatra. The motif describes the vanquished who lose control over history itself and fall out of an ordered epic narrative into the aimlessness of romance. Caesar's boat ride thus has further generic implications: Lucan appears aware of the political distinction that Virgil draws between epic and romance, but only to break that distinction down. His episode shows the victorious Caesar, as well as the defeated Pompey, cast in the role of a helpless romance wanderer. The losers' epic insists that the victors enjoy no greater mastery over history than the vanquished, and it thus dispenses with epic—a Virgilian teleological—narrative altogether.[19] Guided by the random whim of Fortune, the narrative of the *Pharsalia* collapses into episodic fragmentation, which in this Odyssean episode reveals its generic affinity to romance.

The episode emphasizes not only its digressive but also its self-contained nature; it is in this sense sheerly episodic. Caesar gets nowhere, returning in a circle to where he embarked, and there is clearly no need for the inclusion of his boat ride at all. The description of the storm occasions one of Lucan's greatest poetic displays, a rhetorical *amplificatio* of the storms of the *Odyssey* and the *Aeneid* that reaches its hyperbolic climax when it appears that Chaos and Night are about to return (634–37). This tour de force would in fact become *the* great epic storm scene, imitated in turn by subsequent poets, but its very nature as an epideictic set piece, like Lucan's famous passage on the Libyan snakes in Book 9, marks it off as a separate episode.[20] The frequent tendency of Lucan's poetry to turn into rhetorical showpieces called forth Quintilian's judgment that the *Pharsalia* was more fitting to be imitated by orators than by poets (10.1.90). But these purple passages that are to be admired for their own sake, rather than for their connection to a continuous narrative, may have a rationale and function that rescue them from the charge of empty display. As a series of sublime—and, to be truthful, often sublimely ridiculous—highlights, they participate in the poem's larger strategy of narrative disjunction, its preference for the part over the whole.

Broken Bodies

Modern criticism has argued that Lucan's fragmentary narrative is a deliberate choice. Gordon Williams comments on the disunity of the *Pharsalia*:

> . . . the major part of the epic is constructed from digressions. . . . Connectedness of plot—such that it formed a story with a linear progression from beginning, through middle, to end—must have been something to avoid rather than to seek; and as a corollary there must have been a premium on episodic construction.[21]

Williams finds a precedent for this episodicity in Ovid's *Metamorphoses*. Ovid's poem had already established a contestatory relationship with the linear narrative of the *Aeneid*, and it provided in the very subject matter announced in its opening line—bodies changed into new forms ("In nova . . . mutatas . . . formas corpora")—a figure of its own narrative processes. For the model of the narrative unity of which Williams speaks had been the body: in Chapter 7 of the *Poetics*, where Aristotle elaborates the doctrine of beginning, middle, and end, he compares the well-made plot to a living animal, whose body parts are harmoniously ordered together.

> To be beautiful, a living creature and, every whole made up of parts, must not only present a certain order in its arrangement of parts, but also be of a certain definite magnitude. Beauty is a matter of size and order. (1450b)[22]

The comparison of narrative unity to the unified body is probably indebted to rhetorical theory, where a similar analogy describes the ordering of the sections of a speech.[23] In the *Phaedrus*, Socrates contends that

> any discourse ought to be constructed like a living creature, with its own body, as it were: it must not lack head or feet; it must have a middle and extremities so composed as to suit each other and the whole work. (264c)[24]

And, a little further on (265e), Socrates warns against asymmetrical logical divisions in the rhetor's argument: "We are not to hack off parts like a clumsy butcher." Cicero takes up the metaphor; the opening of a speech, he declares in *De Oratore*, should fit the rest, appearing to be a limb cohering to the other parts of the body: "cohaerens cum omni corpore membrum esse videatur" (2.325).[25] It is against this theoretical background, with its advocacy of poetic and rhetorical unity, that Ovid's treatment of the body in the *Metamorphoses* is to be read, both of the bodies that change and lose their shape in the fables of the poem and of the narrative body of the poem itself, deformed by constant digressions and interwoven episodes. Ovidian metamorphosis seems to realize and revel in precisely that bad poetic form that Horace admonished against at the opening of the *Ars Poetica*, the human head on the horse's neck, the beautiful woman with the tale of a fish. Lucan indeed learned from Ovid, and the episodicity by which the *Pharsalia* departs from and resists classical form also finds a corollary thematic reflection in its depiction of the body. But this is not so much the Ovidian body changing and exchanging shapes as a body subjected to a more direct violence: the violence of Plato's butcher image, and its breaking apart of discursive logic. The narrative disunity of the *Pharsalia* corresponds to a body in pieces, mutilated until it is beyond recognition.

The master image of the *Pharsalia* is the divided body politic itself— Rome plunged into civil war. Here, as in the *Metamorphoses*, the poem's opening lines announce its subject matter in terms of the body:

> populumque potentem
> In sua victrici conversum viscera dextra.
>
> (1.2–3)

> ([I sing] of how a powerful nation turned its victorious right hand upon its own viscera.)

And later in Book 10, Lucan epigrammatically notes:

> Latium sic scindere corpus
> Dis placitum;
>
> (10.416–17)

(It pleased the gods thus to sever the body of Rome.)

We may note that these two metaphors will be actualized in the deaths of the poem's two heroes: Pompey, betrayed and beheaded by the minions of Ptolemy—"trunco cervix abscissa" (8.674)—and Cato, who, in the celebrated episode that Lucan did not live to recount, committed suicide in hara-kiri fashion, driving his sword into his entrails. (Caesar, the third major protagonist of the poem, will also be sliced up at his assassination on the Ides of March.)

The slippage from metaphor to individual acts of violence also characterizes the memories of the earlier period of civil war retold by an anonymous Roman in Book 2: after a roll call of the patrician victims of Marius, including the dismembered Baebius (119–21), the speaker recalls the vengeance taken by Sulla, who, with his proscriptions, operated as a surgeon on the sick commonwealth.

> dumque nimis iam putria membra recidit,
> Excessit medicina modum,
>
> (2.141–42)

(While he excessively cut off the putrid limbs, his medicine went beyond the proper bounds.)

Sulla's civic amputation turns into indiscriminate mutilation, and the effects of the larger policy are written out upon Marius Gratidianus, a minor adopted relation of the enemy. The verse lovingly details how the Sullan mob tore him to pieces.

> Cum laceros artus aequataque volnera membris
> Vidimus, et toto quamvis in corpore caeso
> Nil animae letale datum moremque nefandae
> Dirum saevitiae, pereuntis parcere morti.
> Avolsae cecidere manus, exsectaque lingua
> Palpitat et muto vacuum ferit aera motu.
> Hic aures, alius spiramina naris aduncae
> Amputat; ille cavis evolvit sedibus orbes,
> Ultimaque effodit spectatis lumina membris.
> Vix erit ulla fides tam saevi criminis, unum
> Tot poenas cepisse caput. Sic mole ruinae
> Fracta sub ingenti miscentur pondere membra,

Nec magis informes veniunt ad litora trunci,
Qui medio periere freto. Quid perdere fructum
Iuvit et, ut vilem, Marii confundere voltum?
Ut scelus hoc Sullae caedesque ostensa placeret,
Agnoscendus erat.

(2.177–93)

(We saw the lacerated limbs and the wounds distributed evenly on all his limbs, and although the whole body was mutilated, no death-stroke given to its life; we saw the terrible form of unspeakable cruelty: to spare death to the dying. The hands and arms wrenched from their joints, fell down, the cut-out tongue quivered and beat the empty air with silent motion. One man cuts off the ears, another the nostrils of the hooked nose; that one there rolled out the eyes from their hollow sockets and dug the eyes out last, after they had seen the other limbs scattered. There will be scarcely any belief in so savage a crime or that one body could encompass so much punishment. So limbs are mangled and broken beneath the huge weight of a fallen building, nor do the bodies of those who perish in the middle of watery straits come to shore more mangled and misshapen. What made them lose their reward and destroy the features of Marius, as if he were a common nobody? His face ought to have been recognizable, the murder to be proven, if this crime were to please Sulla.)

Although the passage is spoken by one of his characters, it is pure Lucan.[26] Its horror is real: the poet wants to rub the noses of his readers in the gory facts of civil war, to violate a Virgilian decorum that, for all the bloody descriptions of battle in the *Aeneid*, now seems, in contrast, to have aestheticized war and politics. Yet Lucan's horror has its own ghastly aesthetic. The eyes of the unfortunate Marius that are torn out last of all, after they have witnessed the rest of the body's dismemberment, are carefully balanced against the speaker's own vision—"vidimus"—that governs the first four lines, and suggests the fascination of the spectacle alike for onlooker, victim, and reader who now beholds it again. Because it is unspeakable, the scene of horror elicits hyperbole and exaggeration, but these often slip over into poetic playfulness and virtuosity, into a kind of perverse wit.[27] Lucan cannot resist the detail of the still-flapping tongue, the fractured epigram about sparing death, the double simile, or the sarcastic rhetorical question at the end. Here, too, the poem's brilliant rhetorical surface calls attention to itself, and thus creates distance from the very horrors it seeks to bring home. The passage is marked off as a separate set piece, and the description of dismemberment is itself further fragmented into a group of vivid, individual tropes.

The fate of Marius Gratidianus announces and anticipates a whole series of bodily mutilations in the *Pharsalia*: the gory carnage at the sea battle before Marseilles, where one soldier is torn in two (3.635f.) and another crushed between the beaks of onrushing ships (3.652f.); the feat of Caesar's centurion Scaeva, who holds off Pompey's army while he is struck by countless spears and arrows (6.138f.); the various atrocities performed on the corpses of the dead by the witch Erictho (6.538f.); the mutilations of the bodies of their kinsmen by the combatants at Pharsalia (7.626–30) and the feeding on the corpses after the battle by beasts and birds (7.825f.), the latter raining down gobbets of flesh upon the conquering army (838–40); and the grotesque distortions of the bodies of Cato's soldiers bitten by the poisonous snakes of Libya (9.762f.). Most important, perhaps, is the death of Pompey, who, after suffering the swords of his treacherous enemies, is still alive when they behead him.

> spirantiaque occupat ora
> Collaque in obliquo ponit languentia transtro.
> Tunc nervos venasque secat nodosaque frangit
> Ossa diu; nondum artis erat caput ense rotare.
>
> (8.671–73)

(He seizes the breathing head and laid the languishing neck upon a crossbeam. Then he saws through the sinews and veins and hacks away for a long time at the knotty bones: it was not yet an art to send a head spinning with a single blow of the sword.)

It is not a clean death. Lucan wants the reader and the still-sentient Pompey to feel the prolonged effort to sever the head. But amid the horror, the narrator's aside about spinning heads and the artistry of the modern executioner has the macabre flippancy of the *Mikado* ("Now though you'd have said that head was dead . . ."). Even at this solemn moment when the Roman body politic has itself become headless, the poet's wit turns bitterly upon itself to emphasize its own gory artistry.

It is the apotheosized Pompey himself who laughs from heaven (9.14) at the mockery ("ludibria") done to his headless trunk at the opening of Book 9, perhaps the most famous moment of the epic.[28] The distance that wit creates upon Lucan's horrific scenes of bloodshed has here become literalized. Pompey becomes a stoic sage in death—already when his murderers strike, he is granted a moment of detached composure as if he were standing outside of himself (8.613–37). The mutilations that the poem inflicts upon its protagonists may be viewed as an acting out, carried to a sensational extreme, of the Stoic's contempt of the body. Seneca advises Lucilius in epistle 66 to regard the body as one of Fortune's capricious gifts, one that has no effect upon the virtue of the good man.

You will not praise your virtue more if fortune has favored it with a whole ("integrum") body than with one maimed ("mutilatum") in some member. (23)[29]

In one piece or mutilated: it is all the same to the sage, as are the various modes of death that Seneca holds up for contemplation.

> Now compare . . . those who have been transfixed by the sword, or killed by the bite of serpents, or crushed beneath ruins, or tortured bit by bit by slow crippling of nerves and sinews. Some of these departures may be said to be better, some worse: but death is equal to all. The ways of ending are different, but the end is one. (43)

If the body is held indifferent, then what happens to it ultimately does not matter. This is Seneca in a particularly severe mood; he can be more indulgent toward the body and its infirmities. But it is a mood that seems virtually to prescribe the terrible images of his nephew Lucan's poem. The bizarre, spectacular deaths inflicted by the Libyan snakes on the bodies of Cato's men seem to have an inverse relationship to the ascetic composure of their Stoic leader.

The Stoic sense of death as the great equalizer merges in the *Pharsalia* with the lack of differentiation produced by the civil conflict itself: in the war of like against like, all bodies are indeed the same. Thus the dead Pompeian soldier whom the necromantic art of Erichtho restores to brief life on the eve of Pharsalia prophesies nothing more than death for both Pompey and Caesar.

> Quem tumulum Nili, quem Thybridis adluat unda,
> Quaeritur, et ducibus tantum de funere pugna est.
>
> (6.810–11)

(The question is whose tomb the waters of the Nile will wash, whose the Tiber's; and the battle is merely over what burial awaits the leaders.)

The death of Pompey encompasses Caesar's as well. At the moment of his murder, Pompey draws his cloak up over his head to hide his face (8.613–15), an act that looks forward proleptically to Caesar's similar famous gesture at his own assassination;[30] after flying through the empyrean, Pompey's liberated soul will settle down as an avenging spirit in the breast of Brutus (9.17). History will thus accomplish what had been the witch Erichtho's great desire: to mutilate the two rival Roman generals.

> Hic ardor solusque labor, quid corpore Magni
> Proiecto rapiat, quos Caesaris involet artus.
>
> (6.586–87)

(This is her sole desire and scheme: what she may seize from the exposed body of Pompey, what limbs of Caesar she may steal away.)

Whether determined by the reciprocity of civil war or the leveling process of death, the body in Lucan's poem suffers a common fate. And if bodies become interchangeable, they are also further lopped apart and reduced to mere chunks of flesh.

The *Pharsalia*, in fact, insists upon the unrecognizability of the bodies of the victims. The rhetorical question addressed to the killers of Marius, asking what good it did them to mutilate his corpse to the point where Sulla could not identify it and reward the murderers, looks forward to the episode in Book 9 where Caesar carefully scrutinizes the head of Pompey—death has changed the once-familiar features—to make sure it really is that of his onetime son-in-law, and then feigns anger and tears (1033f.). Pompey's body, meanwhile, had been tossed by the waves until it lost all shape, identifiable only by the absence of the severed head: "nullaque manente figura /Una nota est Magno capitis iactura revolsi" (8.710–11). The passage recalls both the simile of the formless sea-washed corpse used to describe the body of Marius (2.189–90) and the extraordinary final verses of Book 3 that describe the funeral in Marseilles after the sea battle.

> Coniunx saepe sui confusis voltibus unda
> Credidit ora viri Romanum amplexa cadaver,
> Accensisque rogis miseri de corpore trunco
> Certavere patres.
>
> (3.758–61)

(Wives often embraced an enemy Roman corpse, believing the face, its features disfigured by the waves, to be that of their husbands: having lighted the pyres, wretched fathers strove against each other for the possession of a headless body.)

Here bodies, robbed of their identifying features, have really become interchangeable.[31] There is a contrasting impiety among the soldiers at Pharsalia, one who deliberately beheads his brother, another who mutilates the face of his father, in order to hide the horror of their deeds (7.626–730). But this loss of identity is the final effect of almost all of Lucan's scenes of violence. Of the snakes of Libya, the seps destroys the body altogether (9.788), the prester causes it to swell until its features are lost, an "informis globus" (801), the haemorrhis reduces the whole body to a single wound (814). And finally there is Scaeva, who survives, but only after he pulls an arrow out of his eye, taking the eyeball with it.

> Perdiderat voltum rabies, stetit imbre cruento
> Informis facies.
>
> (6.224–25)

(Rage had destroyed his facial features; his countenance was formless with streams of blood.)

This is the face of war: a bloody, unrecognizable pulp.

I dwell on these passages because Lucan himself dwells on them: on epic violence as a drive to dismemberment and formlessness. And this drive characterizes aspects of the larger poem, which resists what it sees as the illegitimate unity that imperial one-man rule has claimed to confer upon the Roman body politic. The imperial regime, moreover, claims to have unified into a closed form the history of which the human body is the instrument: the vicissitudes of the body in the *Pharsalia*, to the contrary, reflect the shapelessness of recent Roman history as the poem conceives it, and as it imagines and portrays that history through a narrative of episodic disunity. The epic narrative, which classical literary theory describes with the metaphor of the whole, well-knit body, is deliberately fragmented by Lucan to depict a world out of joint, a history that cannot be organized by imperial apologists into the plot of destiny. This is a history whose very features have become effaced in the confusion of civic strife: history as Humpty-Dumpty, for all of Caesar's horses and men—and for all of his poets, most especially Virgil. To portray history from the perspective of the lost republican cause and to counter the unifying historical fictions and narratives of imperial ideology, both bodies and poems must fall into pieces.

The Never-Ending Story

The formlessness of narrative and history in the *Pharsalia*, which might otherwise appear merely horrific and nihilistic, thus affords some consolation when it is construed as a resistance to form: to the political unity and uniformity that the imperial regime sought to impose upon its subjects, to the formal closure it placed upon its version of history. The poem speaks against the desire for endings that would freeze history into any final shape and unalterable political configuration. At the end of Book 1, the astrologer Nigidius Figulus attempts to prophesy. He first enunciates the poem's typical either/or between chance and necessity (641–45), and then reads the ominous signs in heaven that indicate the impending disaster of civil conflict. He concludes by hyperbolically wishing that the war might go on forever.

> Et superos quid prodest poscere finem?
> Cum domino pax ista venit. Duc, Roma, malorum
> Continuam seriem clademque in tempora multa
> Extrahe, civili tantum iam libera bello.

(1.669–72)

(And what is the use of praying the gods for an end? With peace will come a master. Prolong, Rome, a continuing series of sufferings and draw out the destruction for many ages: you will be free only as long as the civil war lasts.)

As bad as the civil war is, it is preferable to the outcome of imperial rule. The idea is repeated with variation early in the following book when a Roman matron urges others to weep while they can, while the fortunes of war are still suspended—"Dum pendet fortuna ducum" (2.41)—for they will be forced to rejoice by the victor.[32] This is not merely a paradoxical nostalgia for the civil war as the last period of republican freedom, however great the sufferings it contained. Lucan's objective is to persuade the reader that all is, in fact, not over, that the struggle against Caesarism persists, that the civil war events he recounts are continuous with the present of Nero—which is not the end. The words of Figulus plead: Don't give up the fight.

The depiction of the battle of Pharsalia in Book 7 is shaped around the issue of a premature desire for closure, for a decisive, final battle, and—once the battle is lost to the republicans—the question of whether the results are indeed decisive and definitive. Pompey holds an advantageous strategic position in Thessaly and has separated Caesar from supplies from the sea; he can wait and starve his enemy into submission. But Pompey's followers have become impatient and clamor for battle. His Eastern allies, who will prove unreliable when the fighting begins, want to return home, and the war-hating Cicero, who himself wants to return to the Forum from which his voice has been long absent, urges Pompey on, allowing Lucan to indulge in a wicked parody of the orator's style (7.67–85). The entire camp is overtaken by a desire to get on with the fighting.

> Dira subit rabies; sua quisque ac publica fata
> Praecipitare cupit
>
> (51–52)

(A dreadful rage for battle comes over them; each is eager to precipitate his own and the collective, public fate.)

This precipitate haste is echoed and repeated at the very onset of the battle; when Crastinus strikes the first blow, the "dira . . . rabies" becomes "O praeceps rabies!" (474). The rush to battle not only plays into Caesar's hands but also, as the narrator remarks of Crastinus who had the audacity to strike before Caesar (475–76), takes over Caesar's own characteristic trait. For it is Caesar who is precipitate in all things:

> Caesar in omnia praeceps   (2.656)
>
> Neque enim iam sufficit ulla
> Praecipiti fortuna viro   (3.50–51)
>
> praeceps facit omne timendum
> Victor   (9.47–48)
>
> Caesar semper feliciter usus
> Praecipiti cursu bellorum   (10.507–8)

"Praeceps" is virtually the epithet of Caesar, who rushes headlong into action, who in Book 7 has been praying for the occasion to stake all on a final gamble—"in extremos quo mitteret omnia casus" (239). The desire for imminent decision is also a desire to get things over and done with; it is a Caesarian temptation against which Pompey admonishes his followers in vain.

> Multos in summa pericula misit
> Venturi timor ipse mali. Fortissimus ille est,
> Qui promptus metuenda pati, si comminus instent,
> Et differre potest.
>
> (104–6)

(The very fear of future evil has driven many into the greatest dangers. The bravest man is he who is prompt to face fearful things if they are close upon him, and, when they are not, is also able to wait and defer action.)

Those who cannot stand the suspense, Pompey asserts, seek after premature endings. True courage entails living with uncertainty, waiting it out. The urge to precipitate events is a measure of despair—so Caesar's own soldiers tell him after his boat ride in Book 5 (692–94)—and those most eager for the trial of battle are also disposed to regard its verdict as final: they have placed all their hopes on the result. To lose is thus to lose forever, to accept an ending, any ending, so long as it relieves the individual of the fears (and the risks and responsibilities) of the future.

The narrator can adapt this despondent mood: Pharsalia, he declares, when the battle has been decided in Caesar's favor, settled the shape of Rome's history once and for all.

> in totum mundi prosternimur aevum.
> Vincitur his gladiis omnis quae serviet aetas.
> Proxima quid suboles aut quid meruere nepotes
> In regnum nasci? pavide num gessimus arma
> Teximus aut iugulos? alieni poena timoris
> In nostra cervice sedet. Post proelia natis
> Si dominum, Fortuna, dabas, et bella dedisses.
>
> (7.640–47)

(We are conquered for all the ages of the world. By these swords are conquered all the ages that will be enslaved. What did the sons and grandsons of the fighters do to deserve to be born beneath a monarchy? Were we cowards in battle or did we shield our throats from the sword? We bear on our necks the penalty for the fear of others. If you gave a master, O Fortune, to those born after the battle, you should also have given the chance to fight further wars.)

As a member of the future generations condemned by the republican defeat, the narrator complains that nothing further can be done. The shift to the present tense emphasizes the continuing effect of Caesar's victory in the past. Though even here he hints at a new round of armed resistance: *we* are ready to take up the struggle, he seems to say. But this is perhaps the starkest moment of a dark poem: a recognition that all may well be over, and that imperial tyranny has come to stay.

This despairing passage is, however, sandwiched between two other narratorial interventions in Book 7 that belie its sense of finality. Earlier, just before he begins to recount the battle itself, the poet steps forward in his narrator persona to comment on the intended effect of his poem on its future readers.

> Haec et apud seras gentes populosque nepotum,
> Sive sua tantum venient in saecula fama,
> Sive aliquid magnis nostri quoque cura laboris
> Nominibus prodesse potest, cum bella legentur,
> Spesque metusque simul perituraque vota movebunt,
> Attonitique omnes veluti venientia fata,
> Non transmissa, legent et adhuc tibi, Magne, favebunt.
>
> (207–13)

(These events among later peoples and their descendants—whether their fame by itself will come down to future ages, or whether my work and study can do some service to the famous participants—when the story of battle is read, will elicit hope and fear together with unanswered prayers; and all, amazed, will read of them as if they were still to come and not past, and will side with you, Pompey.)

The experience of retelling the battle plays it out once again: for the moment the poem keeps the war against Caesar imaginatively alive; and by repeatedly returning readers to Pharsalia, it fulfills Figulus's prayers—that the war may never come to an end.[33] Moreover, the reading of the events of the battle becomes prophetic: it is not merely the vivid you-are-there quality, the rhetorical *enargeia*, of Lucan's narration that makes the reader seem to witness events that are yet to come rather than those that have transpired in the past. The passage also implies that the *Pharsalia*, as it wins adherents to Pompey's cause, may pave the way to future action, new Pharsalias. And this sense of futurity and transhistorical continuity becomes explicit in the narrator's famous declaration at the end of the battle, when Pompey has fled the scene. The absence of the warlord leader allows the true political significance of the conflict to become clear:

> sed par quod semper habemus,
> Libertas et Caesar erit.
>
> (695–96)

(but the struggle which we always have with us will be between Freedom and Caesarism.)

The confusion of tenses—present and future describing a past event—again spells out the message. Precisely at the moment of crushing republican defeat, the poem announces a sequel of ongoing resistance: this is the war we are still fighting, despite setbacks.[34] Such assertions at the beginning and ending of the narration of Pharsalia counterbalance the despairing declaration of finality that lies between them. The narrator's differing reactions—of jumping to pessimistic conclusions about history or holding out hope in the openness of the future—mirror the alternatives that faced Pompey of rushing to a single decisive battle or staying the course of a larger drawn-out strategy. Where Pompey, who knew better, chose badly and failed, the narrator stakes the project of his poem upon bravely keeping faith and waiting upon history.

The political hope-against-hope of the *Pharsalia* lies in this insistence upon historical open-endedness at a time when the hated imperial regime had long been confirmed in power. The very fact that the poem continues rambling along after the battle of Pharsalia denies a sense of an ending to Caesar's victory. The struggle between Liberty and Caesar goes on and on, and the epic projects no goal or teleology for its narrative: moreover, it warns against the very desire for such endings, which imperial narratives of history are only too willing to provide. To the epic loser endings always seem premature; and so, in retrospect, do the actions that lead to them. The poem thus seems to adapt for its own narrative what it saw as Pompey's better strategy of deferral ("differre"): its episodic digressions put off and defeat any linear movement toward closure.[35] This is not to say that Lucan did not intend to end his poem, but critics can only guess where. With Cato's suicide, with the battle of Munda, with Caesar's assassination, with the battle of Philippi?[36] The poet's tragic suicide left the poem unfinished, but there is something appropriate about the absence of its conclusion.[37] And the point where the poem does break off as we have it is also appropriate: with Caesar at Alexandria, hemmed in by the troops of Ptolemy and the crush of his own forces, reduced almost to despair. It is one of many moments depicted in the *Pharsalia* where history might have turned out differently. And, perhaps, since history, too, is unfinished, it still may.

Freedom for Whom?

When Lucan's narrator asserts that at Pharsalia "we are conquered ("prosternimur") for all the ages of the world" (640), it is not clear just who is included in the "we." For the preceding verses have emphasized the international cast of the participants at the battle, a reference to the foreign auxiliaries in Pompey's army.

> quod militis illic,
> Mors hic gentis erat; sanguis ibi fluxit Achaeus,

Ponticus, Assyrius; cunctos haerere cruores
Romanus campisque vetat consistere torrens.
Maius ab hac acte quam quod sua saecula ferrent
Volnus habent populi; plus est quam vita salusque
Quod perit: in totum mundi prosternimur aevum.

(7.634–40)

(For every soldier who died there, a nation died; there the blood of Achaea,
Pontus, and Assyria flowed, and all the blood which the torrent of Roman gore
forbids to stick and linger on the fields. Peoples received a wound at this battle
greater than their own times could bear; more than life and survival perished:
we were conquered for all the ages of the world.)

The Eastern allies, peoples subject to Roman dominion, seem to be grouped
with the republicans as victims of the battle that will deprive them and their
future descendants of liberty. But what kind of liberty is it? The poem may
come close here to a recognition that the freedom that the republicans seek
from Caesarian tyranny is to be equated with the freedom the conquered
peoples can obtain only by throwing off Roman rule. The imperial ideology
of the *Aeneid* had indeed wished to demonstrate the continuity between
Roman world-conquest and the one-man rule of Augustus—the geographical unification achieved by empire seemed to have its corollary in the concentration of power upon a single leader.

The reversal of this equation would identify resistance to the emperor
with resistance to empire: the cause of freedom would comprise the dismantling of the imperial system. This is a position that Lucan entertains but
does not embrace, for it would mean his rejection not only of the recent
history of the principate, but of the history as well of his beloved republic,
during whose time Rome had achieved the bulk of her foreign conquests.
W. R. Johnson observes: "Lucan cannot bring himself to think that freedom
is incompatible with empire, but this underground thought . . . haunts the
poem."[38] The *Pharsalia* thus produces a dissonance of meaning when it contemplates the freedom of non-Romans. The contradiction is fully evident in
the passage that evokes Johnson's comments, an earlier intervention by the
narrator in Book 7.

Hac luce cruenta
Effectum, ut Latios non horreat India fasces,
Nec vetitos errare Dahas in moenia ducat
Sarmaticumque premat succinctus consul aratrum,
Quod semper saevas debet tibi Parthia poenas,
Quod fugiens civile nefas redituraque numquam
Libertas ultra Tigrim Rhenumque recessit
Ac, totiens nobis iugulo quaesita, vagatur,

Germanum Scythicumque bonum, nec respicit ultra
Ausoniam . . .

(427–36)

(As a result of that day of bloody battle, India does not fear Latin standards, no consul forbids the Dahae to roam where they will and leads them into city walls, nor leans upon a plough in Sarmatia [drawing up the boundaries of a Roman colony] with his toga girded up; because of Pharsalia Parthia still awaits from you, Rome, her dire punishment; and Freedom, fleeing from the civil war, has withdrawn beyond the Tigris and Rhine, never to return, and many times sought by us with our throats exposed to the sword, she wanders away, a good enjoyed by the Germans and Scythians, nor does she look back on Italy . . .)

The narrator initially complains that the decimation of Roman ranks at Pharsalia has placed a halt upon imperial expansion. The energy and manpower expended in achieving rule over Rome has prevented the extension of her foreign dominion: the emperor, it seems, is bad for empire. When, however, he contemplates the receding figure of Liberty, he acknowledges that it is only outside the empire's boundaries that she may be found. But are the Scythians and Germans the beneficiaries of freedom because of (a) the liberty of their institutions celebrated by Herodotus and later by Tacitus? (b) the fact that they are beyond Roman rule and therefore exempt from Caesarian tyranny? (c) their being outside the empire, altogether—not among the subject peoples of Rome? This last idea—that Rome's world-conquest, effected during the "freedom" of the republic and now jeopardized under the emperor, is the enemy of the freedom of others—is both glimpsed at and subsumed in the ambiguity of the passage.

This idea, and the ideological fissure that might potentially be produced by a sympathetic identification with the enslaved subjects of the empire, surface again in Book 10. In Alexandria, Caesar visits the tomb of Alexander the Great, the prototype both of the world conqueror and of the tyrant.[39] The scene occasions another long tirade by the narrator.

sacratis totum spargenda per orbem
Membra viri posuere adytis; fortuna pepercit
Manibus, et regni duravit ad ultima fatum.
Nam sibi libertas umquam si redderet orbem,
Ludibrio servatus erat, non utile mundo
Editus exemplum, terras tot posse sub uno
Esse viro. Macetum fines latebrasque suorum
Deseruit victasque patri despexit Athenas,
Perque Asiae populos fatis urguentibus actus
Humana cum strage ruit gladiumque per omnes

Exegit gentes; ignotos miscuit amnes
Persarum Euphraten, Indorum sanguine Gangen:
Terrarum fatale malum fulmenque, quod omnes
Percuteret pariter populos, et sidus iniquum
Gentibus. Oceano classes inferre parabat
Exteriore mari. Non illi flamma nec undae
Nec sterilis Libye nec Syrticus obstitit Hammon.
Isset in occasus mundi devexa secutus
Ambissetque polos Nilumque a fonte bibisset:
Occurrit suprema dies, naturaque solum
Hunc potuit finem vaesano ponere regi;
Qui secum invidia, quo totum ceperat orbem,
Abstulit imperium, nulloque herede relicto
Totius fati lacerandas praebuit urbes.
Sed cecidit Babylone sua Parthoque verendus.
Pro pudor! Eoi proprius timuere sarisas
Quam nunc pila timent populi. Licet usque sub Arcton
Regnemus Zephyrique domos terrasque premamus
Flagrantis post terga Noti, cedemus in ortus
Arsacidum domino. Non felix Parthia Crassis
Exiguae secura fuit provincia Pellae.

(10.22–52)

(They placed the limbs that should be scattered across the entire earth in a sacred tomb chamber; fortune spared his remains, and the destiny of his reign endured to the last. For if Liberty should ever return to the earth, his body would have been preserved for mockery, he who was born as a bad example to the world: that so many nations should be in the power of one man. He left his own obscure realm of Macedon, disdained Athens conquered by his father, and, driven by the urging of destiny, he rushed through the peoples of Asia with human slaughter and drove his sword through all the nations; he mixed hitherto unknown rivers, the Euphrates and the Ganges, with Persian and Indian blood: he was a fatal pestilence to the nations, and a thunderbolt that struck all peoples alike, a malign comet to mankind. He was preparing to launch his fleet on the Ocean by way of the outer sea. He was deterred neither by heat, nor sea, nor barren Libya, nor the Syrtes, nor the desert of Hammon. Following the curve of the earth, he would have gone towards the west, around the two Poles, and drunk from the Nile at its source. Death opposed him, and Nature alone could put an end to his mad reign; he jealously took with him the power with which he had seized the whole earth, and, leaving no heir to his greatness, he offered the nations up to be torn apart. But he died in Babylon and was feared by the Parthians. For shame! The eastern peoples feared the Macedonian pikes more than they now fear the Roman spear! Although we are permitted to reign to the North and the dwellings of the West Wind, and to rule the lands that lie beyond the burning South Wind, we will yield in the regions of the dawn to the Parthian lord. Parthia, unlucky to the Crassi, was a secure province of paltry Macedonian Pella!)

Alexander's body awaits the fate of dismemberment shared by so many characters of the poem—like Pompey's corpse (9.14), his body should be subject to mockery ("ludibrio") and defilement—a fate that overtook his empire, lacerated and broken to pieces after his death. Alexander's conquests fell apart because they belonged to him alone, the jealous tyrant— rather than, for example, to the collective senate and people of the self-perpetuating Roman republic. The passage powerfully condemns imperial violence as a crime against humanity, but it simultaneously backs away from a blanket condemnation by casting this violence as an extension of tyrannical (Caesarian) monarchy. It further suggests the boundless nature of imperial ambition in Alexander's quest for the source of the Nile, a quest that, as the later digression of Acoreus makes clear (10.256–85), has foiled other great conquerors as well. (In Lucan's time, Nero would, in turn, send out an unsuccessful expedition.)[40] Natural limits, both geographical expanses that are too vast and the temporal space of Alexander's own life which was too short, demonstrate the ultimate futility of empire. And yet, by the end of the passage, the narrator envies the success of Alexander against the Parthians, the formidable present-day Eastern enemy still unsubdued by Roman arms. The Macedonian and Roman empires have become comparable, and the reader must decide to what extent the criticism of the former applies to the latter. Does it make a difference to the conquered foreign peoples whether they are ravaged and spoiled by a monarchical army or a republican one? Should Rome, in fact, be *more* like Alexander and vanquish the Parthians?

It is to Parthia, the victor over Crassus at Carrhae in 53 B.C., that Pompey sues for aid after Pharsalia (8.211–37). (We will see Milton later imitate the episode in *Paradise Regained*, when Satan tempts Jesus to use the arms of Parthia against the Roman oppressors of Judaea.) But when Pompey proposes a Parthian alliance to his followers, he is sternly opposed by Lentulus, whose long speech of over a hundred verses (8.331–453) contains the most extended and virulent attack on the Easterner in Roman poetry.[41] As Frederick Ahl has pointed out, Pompey's willingness to ask for the help of enemy Parthian arms shows him to be out for himself just as much as Caesar—so Cato had foreseen back in Book 2 (319–23)—and completes the separation of Pompey from the republican cause that had begun with his flight from Pharsalia.[42] But the sheer vehemence of Lentulus's speech is hard to account for, even given Lucan's fondness for overblown rhetoric and *amplificatio*. The East, Lentulus asserts is the place of effeminacy.

Quidquid ad Eoos tractus mundique teporem
Ibitur, emollit gentes clementia caeli.
Illic et laxas vestes et fluxa virorum
Velamenta vides.

(8.365–68)

(With every step taken towards the East and the warmer regions of the earth
the peoples become softer with kindness of the climate. There you see loose
garments and flowing robes worn by men.)

The Parthians fight with arrows rather than man to man with swords (382–
90): thus they are of questionable military value to Pompey. And they are
given to insatiable womanizing and outlandish sexual practices, including
mother-son incest (397–410) in the royal family. Parthia is to be conquered,
as is demanded by the ghost of Crassus, imaginatively evoked by Lentulus
(431–35), not brought into an alliance against Caesar. There is considerable
irony, however, in the advice that Lentulus gives instead and that Pompey
reluctantly follows: he seeks refuge and aid in Egypt, another effeminate
Eastern kingdom (543) where royal incest takes the brother-sister form
(693), and the home of the greatest sexual threat to Rome of all, Cleopatra
(10.59–67). Not only does Egypt claim the life of Pompey, but even Caesar,
shamefully allied with Cleopatra, barely escapes the treachery of Ptolemy.

Outside of the world of *romanitas*, there are no real alternatives between
which to choose. The womanish, barbarian nature of the Easterners justifies
their subordination to Roman rule, and in this racist perspective the question of the freedom of the subject peoples of the empire finally becomes a
moot point. Lucan can acknowledge, intermittently, the sufferings that imperial conquest brings upon its foreign victims, but he cannot go so far as to
identify the cause of their liberty with the lost *libertas* of the republic. For
the poet and the nostalgic aristocratic class for which the *Pharsalia* particularly speaks, the empire is the very manifestation of the virtue of free republican Rome. And in the Neronian age, the senate still administered the more
established and pacified provinces through its governors; the empire might
still appear and function as a largely republican institution.[43] For Lucan,
imperial conquest need not in itself have produced the Alexander-like Caesar; this is a logic of Roman history that he will not bring himself to recognize or accept.

When it comes, then, to Rome's foreign empire rather than to the rule of
the emperor, the *Pharsalia* reverts to generic type: it refuses to give up the
Virgilian dream of empire without end. And thus, for all its antagonism to
the *Aeneid*, the *Pharsalia* reveals a Virgilian strain that inflects both its
ideology and its sense of epic identity. For Virgil, following earlier Roman
poets, had decisively transformed Homeric epic into the celebration of a
history of national greatness. The *Aeneid* had depicted Rome's history as

shaped into a linear and teleological narrative by two interrelated and finally identical principles: the expansion of her empire to world dominion and the establishment of the Augustan monarchy. Lucan's quarrel is with this second historical principle, not the first; he is as much of an imperialist as Virgil. And thus Lucan claims allegiance to the tradition of patriotic epic. He takes as a given the history of Rome's unswerving rise to imperial greatness even as the *Pharsalia* portrays the Caesarian emperor *not* as the culmination but rather as the fall or disruption of that history. The celebrated opening simile of the epic (1.72–80) compares the city's descent into civil war and tyranny to the destruction of the universe itself, a dark variation on the *Aeneid*'s analogy between cosmos and imperium.[44] But the universe had not, in fact, come to an end; the outer frame of the empire had remained standing while the Republic crumbled from within. (And though Lucan implies otherwise, the Julio-Claudians added to and consolidated the imperial system.) Lucan's own imagination balks at the prospect of the conquered peoples of the empire regaining their liberty, of a dissolution of the political achievement that had invested Virgilian epic with its sense of narrative organization and unified form. Thus the anti-Virgilian rhetoric with which Lucan describes the perspective of the lost republican cause—the rule of Fortune, the imagery of formlessness and fragmentation, a historical narrative indefinitely suspended and left open—*has* to be measured against a Virgilian plot of imperial destiny, unity, and historical continuity, which, when applied to Rome's foreign rule, the *Pharsalia* scarcely questions and whose factuality the poet could not deny if he wanted to. And he does not want to. This is not, then, simply the dilemma of the latecomer poet who can only react against the great predecessor in the predecessor's own terms. Lucan's ideological position as both republican *and* imperialist—a position whose potential contradictions his poem both hints at and backs away from—places him both outside and inside Virgil's camp. So, too, does the sheer weight of epic tradition, whose formal conventions, themselves by now heavily freighted with nationalist and imperialist ideas, Lucan satirically bends out of shape, even to the breaking point, but never abandons. Just as Lucan will not entertain for long the thought of freedom for the subject peoples of Rome and, hence, the dismantling of her empire, so he cannot fully free the *Pharsalia* from its secondary dependence on the model of Virgil's imperialist epic.

The Araucana

If the *Pharsalia* both rejects and still cannot help but follow the example of the *Aeneid*, Ercilla's *Araucana* imitates *both* Roman poems, the epic of the victors and the epic of the defeated. The combination of models is evident in cantos 23–24, roughly in the middle of the second of the poem's three installments and thus near its center. Here is Ercilla's most extended imitation of Lucan, the narrator's descent into the cave of the Araucanian sorcerer Fitón, which is based on the episode of Erictho in *Pharsalia* 6. Fitón shows him a crystal ball in which he can view the Spanish victory over the Ottoman Turks at Lepanto on the other side of the world, a sea battle that specifically recalls Virgil's description of the battle of Actium and that is another imperial triumph of the West over the "barbarian" (24.80, 82, 91) East.[45] The great victory in the European theater seems to provide an analogue for the main action of the *Araucana*, the deeds of the conquistadors who attempt to make the "barbarian" (1.13) Indians of Chile subject to a worldwide Spanish empire.

Yet this Virgilian insertion into an episode chiefly modeled on the *Pharsalia* contains within it a further imitation of Lucan. The speeches to their troops by the rival commanders at Lepanto, the bastard Spanish prince Don Juan of Austria and the Ottoman renegade Ochali, are respectively based on the speeches of Lucan's Pompey and Julius Caesar before the conflict at Pharsalia. The effect of this second model is paradoxically to turn the triumph at Lepanto, led by Don Juan, the son of the "César" Charles V (24.8), into a defense against the Caesarism of the Ottomans: Ochali disparages the multinational forces of the Holy League as a rabble of barbarians—"bárbara canalla" (34)—whom the Turks will incorporate into their own empire stretching from the Ganges to Chile (36). By casting the Ottomans as the true "evil empire," Ercilla depicts Lepanto not only as another Actium but as a second Pharsalia as well, this time a Pharsalia won by the "Pompeian" side, whose Christian cause is just (18). Yet, in so doing, he breaks down the symmetry that appears to link the Spanish victory at Lepanto with the Spanish conquest of the Chilean Indians. Instead, the Spanish combatants against the Turks are placed in a position similar to that of the Indian "barbarians" themselves, Indians whose valor the *Araucana* has earlier compared to the virtue of the great Roman republicans (3.43–44), and who are fighting for their freedom against what *they* see as Spanish tyranny (2.24).

The superimposed models of Virgil and Lucan thus provide alternative interpretations of Lepanto and, more importantly, of Ercilla's larger poem.

(VIRGIL)

Lepanto (Actium): Imperial Spain (Augustus Caesar) conquers Turkish barbarians.

  Araucana: Imperial Spain conquers Araucanian barbarians.

(LUCAN)

Lepanto (Pharsalia): Spain (Pompey) resists Turkish imperialism (Julius Caesar).

  Araucana: Araucanians resist Spanish imperialism.

The choice between the two models determines whether the subject matter of the *Araucana* is imperial conquest or freedom fighting, whether its heroes are the Spanish conquistadors or the leaders of the Araucanian resistance, whether it takes the side of the winners or the losers. The inclusion of both models allows Ercilla to avoid this choice, to celebrate both Spanish imperialism and the Indians' defense of their liberty. Yet the models are not held in equilibrium, and the predominance of the poem's imitations of Lucan over its Virgilian elements corresponds to what has made the *Araucana* perennially surprising to its readers: the tilting of its sympathies to the Araucanian chiefs and their desperate struggle.[46]

Nonending Endings

Ercilla both acknowledges and defends his inclination toward the Indian enemy in the 1569 prologue to his epic.

> And if it seems to some that I show myself somewhat inclined ["inclinado"] to the side of the Araucanians, treating their matters and deeds of valor more extensively than is required for barbarians, should we wish to consider their education, customs, modes and exercise of warfare, we will see that many have not surpassed them, and that there are few who have with such constancy and firmness defended their lands against such fierce enemies as are the Spaniards. And certainly, it is a cause for wonder that, though they do not possess more than twenty leagues of frontier and do not have within them a town, wall, or fortress built for their defense, nor arms, not even defensive ones, for the drawn-out war and the Spaniards have wasted and consumed them, and that on level ground, encircled by three Spanish towns and two fortresses in the center, with pure valor and stubborn determination they have redeemed and sustained their liberty, shedding in sacrifice so much blood, both their own and that of the Spaniards, that in truth one can say that there are few places that are not stained with it and peopled with bones, and that few of the dead lack those who succeed them to carry their cause forward, for sons, desirous of vengeance for their dead fathers, with the natural rage that moves them and the valor that they have inherited, hastening the course of the years, take up arms before their time and offer themselves to the rigors of war, and so great is the lack of people because of the multitudes who have perished in this struggle that, to give strength and to fill out their squadrons, women as well go out to the great war, and sometimes fighting like men, they submit with great courage to death. All of these things I have wished to cite in proof and token of the great valor of these people, worthy of greater praise than I can give them with my verses. (Prologue, 11–12)

And in the address to the reader that prefaces the second part of the *Araucana* (1578), Ercilla notes that the Indians are still fighting, long after the wars of 1553–1559 recounted by the poem: "for the Araucanians deserve everything ["pero todo lo merecen los araucanos"] because it has been more than thirty years now that they have been upholding their cause, without ever having let their weapons fall from their hands" (227). Their valor made these Indians—they called and still call themselves the Mapuche—a special case, different from most other adversaries of the Spaniards in the New World, and their resistance continued unflaggingly from one generation to the next. Pedro de Oña, a Chilean-born successor to Ercilla, who published a second, rival epic account of the events of the *Araucana* in his *Arauco Domado* of 1596, had to acknowledge ruefully that, despite his poem's title, the Araucanian territory was still to be subdued and tamed.[47] In fact, the Mapuche kept fighting for three centuries, until 1882.

This unending conflict already belied sixteenth-century attempts to give it the closed narrative shape of a Virgilian epic of achieved and enduring conquest. De Oña's triumphalist poem remained unfinished. On the other hand, the ongoing war lent itself quite well to Lucan's digressive, open-ended narrative form, particularly if it were read as the Araucanians' story as much as the Spaniards'. The *Pharsalia*'s resistance to narrative teleology and closure had contained a message of political resistance: an injunction to the defeated republican cause to keep up the fight even after an apparently decisive victory of imperial tyranny. This may have been largely wishful thinking on Lucan's part, but the Araucanian wars provided a living example of a people who, no matter how many times they might be vanquished, refused to give up their struggle for their liberty. It was not, then, merely because Ercilla wrote an epic about real historical events, some of which he had witnessed himself, that he was drawn to imitate the *Pharsalia*, the epic traditionally viewed and criticized as a historian's chronicle: it was the nature of those events themselves, the story of a losing side's unending resistance.

Because he wrote and published the *Araucana* in three parts, Ercilla was able repeatedly, at the end of each installment, to contest the idea of narrative closure: he specifically opposes the model of the *Aeneid* to insist upon his poem's open-endedness. The action of the First Part reaches, in cantos 14–15, the death of the Araucanian leader, Lautaro, and the terrible defeat of the Indians at the battle of Mataquito by Francisco de Villagrán. But canto 15 does not end with this military solution, and instead turns to the voyage that the new Spanish commander, Don García Hurtado de Mendoza, is making from Peru toward the shores of Chile. Don García takes with him the poet himself, who now becomes an eyewitness to and character in the events of his own poem. The fleet reaches Chilean waters near a region of winds and storms that Aeolus himself cannot keep imprisoned, and it is soon overtaken by a tempest sent by Fortune (15.67) that threatens to sink it then and there.

> Allí con libertad soplan los vientos,
> de sus cavernas cóncavas saliendo
> y furiosos, indómitos, violentos
> todo aquel ancho mar van discurriendo,
> rompiendo la prisión y mandamientos
> de Eolo, su rey, el cual temiendo
> que el mundo no arrüinen, los encierra
> echándoles encima una gran sierra.
>   No con esto su furia corregida
> viéndose en sus cavernas apremiados
> buscan con gran estruendo la salida
> por los huecos y cóncavos cerrados.

(15.58–59)

(There the winds blow in freedom, rising from their hollow caverns, and, furious, indomitable, violent, they course all across that broad sea, breaking the bonds and commandments of Aeolus, their king: he, fearing lest they bring the world to ruin, confines them, hurling a great mountain range on top of them.

Their fury is not tamed by their seeing themselves oppressed in their caverns, and with great clamor they seek an outlet through the empty and hollow enclosures.)

These freedom-loving, indomitable winds are obviously analogous to the Araucanian inhabitants of the region, who from the first canto of the poem we learn have never submitted to any king (1.2, 47). Here, as we have seen in the Adamastor episode in the roughly contemporary *Lusíadas*, the native resistance is refigured in the natural forces of the storm. But, unlike Camões, Ercilla is less interested in dehumanizing the natives than in suggesting the difficulty of the Spanish project of domination. The winds are incorrigible: Aeolus intervenes to stop the storm threatening Mendoza's ships, but matters only get worse.

> Eolo, o ya fue acaso, o se doliendo
> del afligido pueblo castellano,
> iba al valiente Bóreas recogiendo,
> queriendo él encerrarle por su mano;
> y abriendo la caverna, no advirtiendo
> al Céfiro que estaba más cercano,
> rotas ya las cadenas a la puerta,
> salió bramando al mar, viéndola abierta.

(15.76)

(Aeolus, either by chance or because he felt sorry for the afflicted Castilian folk, went to lock up the valiant Boreas, seeking with his own hand to imprison him, and opening the cavern, did not take notice of Zephyr who was standing nearby and, now that he saw the chain of the door broken and the exit open, went out in search of the sea.)

The North Wind is no sooner imprisoned by Aeolus than the West Wind escapes, and stirs up the squall to even greater heights and fury. The episode thus allegorizes the preceding action of the canto: what appeared to be a decisive victory over the Indian enemy at Mataquito leads simply to further and greater resistance. The military solution has not worked.

The canto and the whole First Part of the *Araucana* end with the ships still caught in the middle of the storm and with little hope in sight: an image of suspense and narrative suspension that stands in place of closure. This ending is pointedly anti-Virgilian, for the presence of Aeolus alludes to the *opening* of the *Aeneid* and to the storm unleashed by the winds of the god upon the Trojan fleet—a storm that Virgil had explicitly compared in the famous first simile of his epic (1.148f.) to the violence of political discord. The nonnarratable confusion from which the *Aeneid* had started is thus where the first installment of the *Araucana* arrives; no narrative progress seems to have been made. When, moreover, the poem takes up the storm again at the beginning of the Second Part in canto 16, it proffers a second epic model.

> No la barca de Amiclas asaltada
> fue del viento y del mar con tal porfía
> que aunque de leños frágiles armada,
> el peso y el ser del mundo sostenía.
>
> (16.10)

(The boat of Amyclas was not assaulted by the wind and sea with such insistence, which, even though it was armed only with fragile wood, bore the weight and being of the world.)

Ercilla appears to be aware of how Lucan's own storm scene in *Pharsalia* 5, which his description of the storm off Chile now imitates, was itself a revision of *Aeneid* 1 (and, as we have seen, of *Aeneid* 5 as well). The boat of Amyclas was subjected to a storm that showed its passenger, the world-conqueror Caesar, to be the plaything of Fortune: Lucan's episode made a mockery of any attempt by the victorious Caesarian party to impart a narrative teleology to its account of Roman history, including and especially the account presented by the *Aeneid*. The episode, moreover, became emblematic of the deliberate narrative aimlessness of the *Pharsalia* itself. Ercilla similarly draws a connection between the storm scene and his larger epic by invoking at the beginning of canto 16 the traditional figure of the poem as a ship he hopes to bring to port: "Espero que la rota nave mía / ha de arribar al puerto deseado" (16.4).[48] But the *Araucana* appears here precisely to deny itself the comfort of a final, fixed goal and safe haven.

If the close of the First Part of the *Araucana* invokes the beginning of the
Aeneid, the close of the Second Part in canto 29 recalls the ending of Virgil's
epic—but only to suspend ending once again. Two Indian heroes, Rengo
and Tucapel, fight a duel before the convoked chieftains. After long battle,
Tucapel, possessed with infernal furor (52), raises his sword to rain a fatal
blow down upon his rival. But the narrator intervenes.

> ¡Guarte, Rengo, que baja, guarda, guarda
> con gran rigor y furia acelerada
> el golpe de la mano mas gallarda
> que jamás gobernó bárbara espada!
> Mas quien el fin deste combate aguarda
> me perdone si dejo destroncada
> la historia en este punto, porque creo
> que así me esperará con más deseo.

(29.53)

(Take heed, Rengo, for now falls, look out, look out, with great strength and
hastening fury, a blow from the most valorous hand that ever governed a barbarian sword! But let whoever awaits the end of this combat forgive me if I leave
the story truncated at this point, since I believe that thus he will wait for me
with greater desire.)

The final octave of the canto masterfully switches perspectives, as the narrator first addresses the beleaguered Rengo, warning him of a blow that is
felt in all of its impending imminence, and then turns to the reader who is
to be left in prolonged suspense: for eleven years as it turned out, until the
final installment of the poem appeared in 1589. Once again, as in the storm
that menaces the Spaniards and their poet at the end of the First Part, the
poem presents a case of life or death, and then breaks off, seemingly in mid-
sentence.

The scene is recognizably Virgilian, a duel at the end of a poetic narrative
that recalls the combat of Aeneas and Turnus at the end of the *Aeneid*
and, perhaps equally, Ariosto's imitation of Virgil's fiction in the fight between Ruggiero and Rodomonte at the end of the *Orlando furioso*. But
where the duels in these literary models climax with the deaths of Turnus
and Rodomonte and thus signal the removal of the last resistence to the
victors, Ercilla's duel is anticlimactic in more than one sense. We have to
wait to find out whether Tucapel's sword stroke will prove mortal and
final—and it will turn out that it does *not* when the action resumes in canto
30 at the beginning of the Third Part: Rengo survives the blow, he and
Tucapel fight on until they reach mutual exhaustion, and they are eventually reconciled by Caupolicán, the Araucanian commander in chief. This
duel is, in any case, a personal affair between two Indians who are on the

same side against the Spaniards, and it has no bearing on the larger war. It recalls the various private duels fought by Ariosto's paladins, and the technique of narrative suspension, both here, and in the interrupted account of the storm, is also clearly indebted to the romance narrative form of the *Furioso*, which frequently cuts short its narrative threads at points of greatest suspense.[49] The relationship of Ercilla's narrative to romance forms will be taken up again below. Here we may briefly note that Ercilla's metaphor of narrative interruption as amputation—"destroncada"—recalls the mutilated bodies and fragmented textual body of Lucan's epic. The *Araucana*, as critics have commented, is similarly full of broken bodies—the "miembros sin cuerpos, cuerpos desmembrados" of the Indians riddled by Spanish artillery at Penco (32.8)—that draw inspiration from the horrors recounted in the *Pharsalia*.[50] This, too, is an epic that deliberately falls apart in order to defeat narrative incorporation of a violence that exceeds explanatory or ideological structure.

Rengo's deliverance at the opening of Part Three, moreover, continues a consistent pattern that the *Araucana* ascribes to his heroic career, a pattern that, we shall see, also has implications for its narrative structure.[51] After the death of Lautaro in the climactic battle of Part One at Mataquito, a death that echoes the death of Turnus in the last verses of the *Aeneid*—

> la alma, del mortal cuerpo desatada,
> bajó furiosa a la infernal morada.

(14.18)

(the soul, loosened from its mortal body, went down furiously to its infernal dwelling-place.)

—and thus conveys a momentary sense of finality to the war and poetic narrative, the attention shifts to the single combat between Rengo and the Genoese soldier Andrea. Here, too, at the end of canto 14, the poet interrupts the conflict as both warriors are poised to strike, and then resumes their duel at the beginning of the following canto. Despite the fact that the conquistador is covered with armor and the Araucanian warrior's body is unprotected (15.6), they fight on and on and eventually wrestle hand to hand. Andrea recalls the mythical Hercules raising up Antaeus from the earth: "Lo que el valiente Alcides hizo a Anteo, / quiso el nuestro hacer del araucano" (15.14). The comparison of Rengo to Antaeus, the autochthonous child of the earth, who keeps coming back with greater strength each time that he is thrown down, was already made by the poem in a still earlier episode, a wrestling match with the warrior Leucotón, this time in sport rather than in earnest battle, in the Indians' heroic games in canto 10. Rengo falls by accident, only to spring up like Antaeus (10.56) and go after his opponent with furious rage and shame. Here, once again, the end of a canto interrupts the struggle, which continues in canto 11 until Caupolicán breaks in to reconcile the two warriors—just as he does later in canto 30 to end the duel between Rengo and Tucapel. In canto 15, however, the combat between Rengo and Andrea ends when the Genoese strikes the Indian across the head with the flat of his sword and leaves him for dead (29) in a field covered with the corpses of the Araucanians who preferred to die rather than surrender: the last survivor, Mallen, commits suicide to join his comrades, and the Spanish victory appears to be complete (49–55). Complete, however, except for Rengo himself, who, it later develops, was only stunned and who reappears at the beginning of the Second Part in canto 16 (40). His salvation from a seemingly certain death between the second and third parts of the poem thus merely repeats a more spectacular return from the dead between the first and second.

Rengo has no sooner come back from Mataquito in canto 16 than he enters into contention with Tucapel; the two demand the duel, which is deferred until canto 29 and the end of the whole installment, which their rivalry thus comes to frame. Midway through, Tucapel saves Rengo's life when the latter, after he and his old foe Andrea have vainly sought each other on the battlefield (25.46), finds himself winded and imperiled. The rescue of a rival whom Tucapel wishes to preserve for his own private quarrel is an example of Araucanian magnanimity and gallantry (25.65–72); it is also one in a series of related episodes in which Rengo is momentarily down and nearly counted out only to revive and fight another day. We are told that both he and Tucapel were exempted from the massive slaughter of the Indians at Cañete (32.21–22), the last battle recounted by the poem: their sense of honor—"una arrogancia generosa" (32.23)—would not allow them to participate in an ambush prepared by fraud, an ambush that backfires when the less scrupulous Spaniards counter with fraud of their own.[52] The two allusions to Antaeus link Rengo to what we have seen in the preceding chapter to be a stock epic figure—deriving ultimately from the *Pharsalia*—for a native resistance that refuses to accept defeat and rises up again and again to oppose its would-be conquerors. Rengo is thus the poem's emblematic survivor and continuator of the Araucanian struggle: unlike the Turnus-like Lautaro who goes down to the infernal shades, he has the properties of a ghostly revenant, a Turnus who refuses to be killed off at the various end points of the poem. He is accordingly associated with the larger narrative of the *Araucana* that refuses to end where it is supposed to: he is repeatedly involved in single combats—his wrestling match with Leucotón, his fight with Andrea, his duel with Tucapel—that are interrupted and left suspended at the end of one canto and spill over into the next. The last of these suspends the action at the end not only of a canto but also of the larger narrative unit that is the poem's Second Part. The poem's resistance to formal closure is thus thematically linked and built around the undying resistance of the Indian defenders.

This resistance continues to the very end of the *Araucana*. The crushing defeat and massacre of the Indians at Cañete is followed by the capture and execution of Caupolicán, whose election to commander by the Araucanian senate began the action of the poem in canto 2. The poem compares him to the defeated Pompey after Pharsalia (34.2), and its action appears to have run its full course. But the defiant Caupolicán asserts that a thousand other Caupolicáns are out there to take his place: "que luego habrá otros mil Caupolicanos" (34.10).[53] His words are soon confirmed when the Araucanians assemble to choose a new general (34.38–43). At this point, however, the narrator breaks off his account of the Araucanian wars and never returns to them, although later, in the penultimate canto of the poem, he describes what he *could* narrate if he so chose.

> Volveré a la consulta comenzada
> de aquellos capitanes señalados,
> que en la parte que dije disputada
> estaban diferentes y encontrados,
> contaré la elección tan porfiada,
> y cómo al fin quedaron conformados;
> los asaltos, encuentros y batallas,
> que es menester lugar para contallas.[54]

(36.43)

(I will turn to the council that had begun among those famous captains who in the part I was last speaking about were debating factiously and contentiously; I will tell of the election of a captain after so much rivalry, and how in the end they remained in agreement; of the attacks, fights, and battles which need leisure to be fully recounted.)

The poem has simply begun anew: the Araucanians choose a new leader, another Caupolicán, and embark on a new series of wars. The narrator, that is, would have *to tell the poem all over again*, and it is no wonder that he abandons the project. The epic action that seems to have been completed by Spanish victory turns out to be part of an ever-repeating cycle of Araucanian insurgency.

The narrator meanwhile turns in the last cantos to other subjects. In cantos 34–36, a passage added to the posthumous 1597 edition of the poem, he recounts the long journey of exploration that Don García leads into southern Chile. In the final canto 37, he seems to attempt to bring the epic to a triumphalist conclusion by returning to Europe to describe the Spanish invasion and annexation of Portugal in 1580: like the vision of Lepanto and the still earlier description of the victory of Philip II over the French at Saint-Quentin (cantos 17–18), the conquest of Portugal would depict an ideologically justified victory of Spanish arms and imperial expansion in the Old World—canto 37 begins with a discussion of the nature of the just war—that has not been available in the inconclusive Araucanian war in the New.[55] But both of these new narrative subjects are themselves notably inconclusive. The Spaniards are warned by the crafty Araucanian exile Tunconabala that in place of enemy warriors they will encounter formidable natural obstacles on their march south (35.17). They, in fact, suffer terrible hardships on their way to Ancud, where their course is finally stopped by an unfordable, raging torrent: only the poet himself manages to cross with a small party to "see the end of this journey" (36.26). The expedition is reminiscent of Lucan's description of the failed attempts by various conquerors to reach the source of the Nile, and the endless Indian resistance that thwarts the conquistadors finds its spatial analogue in the endless tracts of the South American continent that defeat and swallow up Spanish attempts to chart it.[56] The end of this frustrated voyage, moreover, was the cutting short of the poet's own career in Chile, an incident that very nearly cost him his life. On his return (36.33), Ercilla was accused of starting a duel with a fellow Spaniard. He was condemned to be beheaded by Don García and was reprieved only at the last minute—rather like his character Rengo—after which he was imprisoned and then sent to Lima never to return to Chile: an ending/nonending of sorts, and certainly an ignominious one.

The invasion of Portugal, on the other hand, never gets started in the poem: Ercilla describes the Spanish preparations and the efforts of the Portuguese regent, the Archbishop Henry, to draw out and suspend negotiations—"con larga dilación impertinente / el negocio suspenso entretenía" (37.60)—but leaves the actual campaign for other poets to celebrate (65). The *Araucana* consistently falls short of the narrative goals it projects, and in its final octaves the poet returns to the figure of the poem as ship, a ship still caught in stormy weather.

> y al cabo de tan larga y gran jornada
> hallo que mi cansado barco arriba
> de la fortuna adversa contrastado
> lejos del fin y puerto deseado.
>
> (37.71)

(And at the end of such a wide and extensive journey, I find that my weary ship draws towards the lee shore in distress, opposed by fortune's adverse tempest, far from its desired goal and haven.)

Ercilla surely has the end of the *Orlando furioso* in mind, but this is not Ariosto's poem-as-ship coming into port in its final canto, but a vessel still sailing *in medias res* at the mercy of Fortune and charting an errant course; three stanzas later this ship becomes as well a figure for the poet's soul anxious for salvation (74). Having failed to find a narrative ending and coherence in his historical poem, the narrator seeks one in his life history, and, in the final two stanzas, he turns toward God.

Ercilla finishes his poem three times, at the ends of each of its installments, but in each case he provides images of aimless confusion, interruption and suspension, cyclical repetition. He does so knowingly imitating and overturning epic models of closure, particularly Virgilian models that equate narrative completion with definitive military victory and political settlement. The *Araucana* rather follows the example of the *Pharsalia*, which dismantles teleological narrative structures in the name of a losing political opposition for whom nothing is settled and history remains an open book. With its nonendings and the concomitant sense that the Spaniards are fighting an unwinnable war, the poem and poet incline toward the side of the repeatedly defeated, but unconquerable Araucanians.

Ideological Divisions

It may appear possible for Ercilla to acknowledge that the Indians are still fighting—and that his poem cannot end until they are beaten once and for all—without his taking their side and approving what it is they are fighting for. The celebration of their heroism might merely build them up into worthy opponents for the Spaniards, as the narrator seems to suggest in the second stanza of the poem.

> que más los españoles engrandecen:
> pues no es el vencedor más estimado
> de aquello en que el vencido es reputado.
>
> (1.2)

(For they aggrandize the Spaniards all the more: since the victor is never more highly esteemed than by the reputation of the vanquished.)

And Ercilla the epic poet may need to build up the Araucanians into classical heroes—their feats and language imitating those in the poems of Homer, Virgil, Lucan, and Ariosto—in order to give the *Araucana* an epic dignity that will place it within a canonical literary tradition. The fact that the Indians fight man to man and without guns helps to keep that anachronistic tradition alive in an age of rapidly changing military tactics: their individual heroism is easier to turn into the stuff of epic than the Spaniards' grouped and, as the poem describes it, relatively anonymous fighting.[57] Some such possibility lies behind all epic representations of the defeated: the greater their valor, the greater the achievement of their conquerors.

But, in fact, the depiction by the *Araucana* of the Indians' valor and of their stubborn, ongoing resistance does more than merely enhance the prestige of the conquistadors and of the epic itself. As we shall see, to depict them resisting *at all* already takes a position in support of the Indians in the ideological debates that surrounded the Spanish conquest.

Unlike the other European nations engaged in imperial and colonial expansion in the New World, the Spaniards seriously worried about the legality and morality of their project. By midcentury, when Ercilla came to Chile, the lines of ideological support and opposition to the conquest of America had become clear.[58] The central issue was the institution of the *encomienda*. This was a district or group of villages whose Indian inhabitants were placed under the "protection" of a Spanish colonist; he was obligated to defend and govern them, to oversee their religious instruction, and to maintain the local clergy. In return, this *encomendero* was entitled to a number of days of forced labor from the Indians, either free or at a fixed wage. In practice, especially for the exploitation of gold and silver mines that were initially the Spaniards' primary concern, this system could amount to little more than slavery. It was immediately criticized by reforming friends of the Indians like Bartolomé de Las Casas, an ex-encomendero himself, who described how on Hispaniola, the first Spanish colony, not only were the Indians' wages insufficient to feed themselves and their families, but, because they were kept away at the mines for eight months of the year, they were unable to keep their fields in cultivation. In eight years, Las Casas maintained, ninety percent of the population had died of starvation and maltreatment, and his figures are probably not exaggerated, although European diseases also played a large part in this genocide.[59]

Such reports did not fall on deaf ears in Spain, and in 1542 laws were promulgated that abolished the encomienda: the crown had an interest as well in promoting the authority of its viceroys and administrative bureaucracy over that of the local encomenderos, who had divided the spoils of conquest among themselves without royal sanction. The new edicts caused open rebellion and civil war among the colonists in Peru, and they were suspended in Mexico; in 1545 they were revoked and the encomienda restored, although the encomenderos were now subjected, on paper at least, to strict legal regulation; and tribute was supposed to be substituted for forced labor.

The colonists meanwhile found their spokesman in Juan Ginés de Sepúlveda and his *Democrates secundus*, written in 1544 and widely circulated in manuscript but, significantly enough, suppressed by royal and ecclesiastical authority and only published in 1892. Sepúlveda drew on the already current Aristotelian doctrine of natural slavery to justify legally the subjection of the barbarian Indians to the control of the Spaniards, who were to educate them not only in religion but also in the arts of civilization. But Sepúlveda did not concede that the Indians would *ever* be capable of governing themselves, although they might with time be granted greater freedom. Inferior beings by nature, they were at worst, his language suggested, sub-human brutes. The proof of this racist doctrine was the very ease with which the Indians had been conquered by the Spaniards. Sepúlveda cites the example of Moctezuma and the Mexica, "considered the most prudent and valorous" of the Indians, who were terrified by the paltry force of three hundred Spaniards led by Cortés and let them into their city.

> Cortés, for his part, having thus taken possession of the city, held in such contempt the cowardice, passivity, and primitiveness of those people that he not only, using terror, obligated the king and his chief subjects to receive the yoke and rule of the King of Spain, but went so far as to put the King Moctezuma in chains, on account of suspicions he held that the king was plotting the death of some Spaniards in a certain province: and this before the stupor and abjectness of the king's fellow citizens who stood quietly by and by no means plotted to take up arms and free their sovereign. And thus Cortés at the beginning and for many days, and with the the the assistance of such a reduced number of Spaniards and a few natives, held oppressed and in fear such a great multitude that gave the impression of lacking not only activity and intelligence, but even common sense. Can there be a greater, clearer example that declares that some men have the advantage over others in intellect, industry, strength of mind, and valor? And that demonstrates that those Indians are slaves by nature?[60]

The initial success of Cortés—Sepúlveda simply omits the Mexicans' uprising that drove the Spaniards out of Tenochtitlán on the *Noche Triste* and their subsequent fight to the bitter end during the siege of the city—demonstrates the cowardly servility and lack of rational intelligence of the Indians.[61] And since, Sepúlveda goes on to maintain, the Mexica were the most civilized people of the New World and boasted the most advanced public institutions—institutions that failed them—they prove the general barbarity of all Indians, incapable of self-government and rightfully subjugated by the conquistadors.

The stage was set for the great public debate between Sepúlveda and Las Casas at Valladolid in 1550. The arguments of Las Casas are preserved in his unpublished *Apologia* and in the published treatise *Aqui se contiene una disputa* (1552). He asserts that the Indians could not be considered to be "barbarians," if that term were taken to describe men without reason and social organization, wild men living a quasi-bestial existence: they were thus not Aristotle's natural slaves.[62] Las Casas insists, to the contrary, on the sophistication of the great Amerindian civilizations. Perhaps they were not as advanced as the Europeans, but could one people justify aggression against and conquest of another simply by claiming to possess a higher culture? This was the logic, Las Casas asserts, of Sepúlveda's argument, which he refutes by a clever apppeal to patriotic history: he asks whether the ancient Romans were justified in conquering the natives of Spain, whom they called wild and barbaric.[63] And the logic had a modern-day application.

> Now if on the basis of this utterly absurd argument, war against the Indians were lawful, one nation might rise up against another and one man against another man, and on the pretext of superior wisdom, might strive to bring the other into subjection. On this basis the Turks, and the Moors—the truly barbaric scum of the nations—with complete right and in accord with the law of nature could carry on war, which, as it seems to some, is permitted us by a lawful decree of the state. . . . I am of the opinion that Sepúlveda, in his modesty, thinks Spain regards other nations as wiser than herself. Therefore she must be forced to submit to them according to the eternal law![64]

Any nation can pretend and even believe itself to be culturally superior: even the Ottoman Turks, Spain's Islamic archenemies. Las Casas ridicules the Spanish claim to be civilizing an already civilized New World, and he further argues that the goal of conversion to Christianity does not justify political subjugation; here, too, he uses Islam as a counterexample: "Leading to faith by massacre and terror is Mohammedan, since Mohammed said that he was sent in the terror of the sword and the violence of weapons."[65] While Las Casas defends the public institutions that Sepúlveda had denigrated, he does not contest the latter's version of the ease of Spanish conquest. He emphasizes the gentleness and tractability of the Indians that make the use of force unnecessary: the peaceful persuasion of missionaries could do the work of conversion without depriving the Indians of their liberty.[66]

The *Araucana* does, however, refute Sepúlveda's picture of craven Indians submitting without much struggle to Spanish arms. Ercilla does not idealize the Indians as meek lambs readily disposed to enter the universal sheepfold of the Church, but his depiction, perhaps equally idealized, of fierce, undying Araucanian valor dispels the notion of a naturally servile people who deserved to be conquered.[67] If raising the Indians into worthy epic opponents makes the Spanish military victory more impressive, it simultaneously removes one of the contemporary ideological justifications for that victory: this, too, is a defense of the Indians, but on different grounds from those of Las Casas. Elsewhere, Ercilla follows Lascasista lines of thought: we have seen that he also uses the example of the Turks (who in the poem's version of Lepanto seek to conquer Spaniards and other European Christians, whom they regard as "barbarians") as a foil that calls into question the imperial project of the conquistadors in Chile.[68]

Ercilla's pro-Indian position, which both determines and is determined by his adaptation of the model of the *Pharsalia* and of Lucan's rhetoric of freedom, can partly be understood as a contribution to this ongoing debate in Spain over the legitimacy of her New World empire. The debate tended to divide between the hard-line colonists on the spot in America, who wished to preserve the encomienda system that they regarded as their right by conquest, and the servants of the Spanish crown, who came later and sought to place the Indians under royal protection, in part to break down the local privileges and power of the settlers. Ercilla belonged very much to the latter royalist camp: he had been a page to Philip II, and on his return to Spain was a figure of some importance at court. He spent a total of seven years, from 1556 to 1563, in the New World, only two of them, 1557 to 1559, in Chile, and he never lost the outsider's critical perspective upon the colonial situation.[69] This was all the more the case because of his run-in with his commander, Don García Hurtado de Mendoza, who ordered and then rescinded the poet's execution. In return, Ercilla largely leaves Don García—the son of the Peruvian viceroy, the Marquis de Cañete, and thus himself a crown representative—out of the action of the Araucana. It was partly to rectify this omission that de Oña declares that he wrote his Arauco Domado, in which the Chilean wars are treated as a celebration of Mendoza's exploits and which is dedicated to his son.[70]

Ercilla identifies with the power and interests of the king over those of the colonists, and he applauds the terror tactics with which de Cañete put down the rebellion of the encomenderos in Peru (12.76–13.5). Don García's Spaniards issue proclamations at the beginning of the Second Part of the Araucana asserting that the Indians have similarly rebelled against the feudal loyalty they had pledged to Charles V and the Spanish monarchy (16.29–30) and thus justified the measures taken against them;[71] Ercilla's narrator earlier speaks of the Araucanians as "gente / a la Real Corona inobediente" (13.29). But this legal formula insufficiently describes the poem's view of the political status of the Indians and of the justness of the war waged by and against them. Ercilla presumably could not stomach the idea of presenting his personal enemy, Mendoza, as a triumphant figure of royal authority and justice. Moreover, the identification with the crown against the local colonists often carried with it a more sympathetic, protective attitude toward the Indians whom the colonists were charged with mistreating. The Indians, Las Casas and others maintained, were justified in resisting their oppression by the encomenderos, and this is what the Araucanians had been doing throughout the First Part of the epic, prior to Ercilla's arrival in Chile with Mendoza. But now that Don García was on the scene, the Indians appeared to have extended their rebellion from the Chilean colonists to their royal master as well, if such a distinction could, in fact, be maintained. Ercilla and his poem can be seen once again as divided among several ideological options, depending on how they construe the position of the Spanish king as liege lord of colonist and Indian alike.

Spaniards (the king) subdue Spaniards (colonists, rebel vassals).

Spaniards (colonists) oppress Indians (freedom fighters).

Spaniards (the king) subdue Indians (rebel vassals).

The comparison with the *Arauco Domado* is instructive here. In the third canto of de Oña's poem, Don García arrives in Chile, and, in the words of the poet's own prose summary, "seeing the excess with which the peaceful Indians are treated by their encomenderos and the great disorder that there is in employing them, driving them beyond measure to exhaustion, makes some brief ordinances, by which he relieves them of their heavy load."[72] De Oña's narrator excoriates the encomenderos' thirst for riches (21) and tells how Mendoza (27–31) stopped the abusive labor practices in the mines, exempting women and old men from the work force and stipulating fair wages; he did not, however, do away with the encomienda system. The canto begins with a praise of moderation (1–5), and Mendoza's viceregal intervention has found a middle way that is supposed to have satisfied everyone, as the poet's epigrammatic couplet suggests.

> El indio con su carga moderada,
> Y el amo su conciencia descargada.[73]

(The Indian with his burden lightened, the Spanish master with his conscience unburdened.)

This is the encomienda as it should work. De Oña, a native-born colonist, concedes that there were past problems and excesses, but says they have been corrected. His poem, moreover, can now proceeed with its own clear conscience, for once Mendoza's reforms are in place, the rebellious Araucanians no longer have a cause for complaint, and they can be depicted as justly subjugated by the heroism of Spanish arms.

Ercilla makes a passing reference in one stanza to Don García's reforms (30.31) that have removed excesses and disorders introduced by the "new greed" ("nueva codicia").[74] But this is too little and comes too late in his poem, at least for the Araucanians, who are not fighting for better working conditions but for their liberty and homeland. The Indian spokesman, Galbarino, who has had both of his hands cut off as an exemplary punishment ("ejemplar castigo") by the Spaniards (22.45), urges his fellow soldiers on by reminding them that the alternative is slavery.

> Que si en esta batallaa sois vencidos
> la ley perece y libertad se atierra,
> quedando al duro yugo sometidos,
> inhábiles del uso de la guerra;
> pues con las brutas bestias siempre uncidos,

habéis de arar y cultivar la tierra,
haciendo los oficios más serviles
y bajos ejercios mujeriles.

   Tened, varones, siempre en la memoria
que la deshonra eternalmente dura,
y que perpetuamente esta vitoria
todas vuestras hazañas asegura:
considerad, soldados, pues, la gloria
que os tiene aparejada la ventura,
y el gran premio y honor que, como digo,
un tan breve trabajo trae consigo.

(25.38–39)

(For if you are vanquished in this battle, the law perishes and liberty is overthrown; you will remain subjected to the hard yoke, deprived of and unfit for the
exercise of war; then, forever yoked with the brute beats, you will have to plough
and cultivate the fields, doing the most servile tasks, base and womanly work.

   Keep always in mind, gentlemen, that dishonor endures forever, and that this
victory will perpetually insure the memory of all your exploits: think further,
soldiers, on the glory that fortune keeps readied for you, and the great reward
and honor that such a brief effort brings with it.)

The Araucanians were nomadic herdsmen who practiced occasional and ru-
dimentary agriculture. Reform or no reform, the imposition of the encomienda would turn them into peasant serfs and end their independent way of
life. Ercilla portrays the Indians, in terms contemporary Europeans could
understand, as warrior aristocrats, men of honor, who would rather die than
fall under a foreign domination that would also occasion their fall in social
caste. The issue is again whether the Indians are naturally servile and fitted
for plantation labor, as Sepúlveda had maintained and as de Oña implicitly
appears to believe; the *Araucana* depicts them rather as nature's noblemen,
as soldiers who fight above all for the prize of glory;[75] or, to put it another
way, they fight for the very possibility of their going on *as fighters*, to perpetuate their aristocratic, martial identity.

   The epic thus assimilates the Araucanians with a feudal nobility already
becoming outmoded in Europe. This was the age of the "crisis of the aristocracy," occasioned by the emergence of strong and centralized national
monarchies that sought to break the power and autonomy of local magnates, to demilitarize the nobleman or to channel his martial training and
disposition in service to the crown.[76] From the very second stanza of the
poem we learn that the Araucanians' most distinguishing feature is that they
obey no king—"gente que a ningun rey obedecen" (1.2). And there is a kind
of nostalgia in Ercilla's attribution to the fiercely independent and unyield-

ing Chilean Indians of the values and attitudes that were being relinquished—not without struggle and various atavistic revivals—by *his own*
aristocratic class. For if the poet was the king's servant, his decision to serve
his monarch with his sword (13.29) in Chile, rather than at the court where
he had grown up, proclaimed his adherence to an older code of martial
nobiliary identity; and the crime for which he was nearly executed and for
which he was banished from Chile—his reaching for his sword to fight a
duel—was that code's emblematic exercise of a personal honor that the
nobleman placed outside the jurisdiction of the king or, in Ercilla's case, of
the king's viceregal representative.[77] The poem's depiction of the duel between Rengo and Tucapel thus shows the Indians to be more "honorable"
than the Spaniards, for whom, the narrator notes, such combats were legally
prohibited, even if still sanctioned by custom (30.6). The Indians' fight for
independence acquires a peculiarly conservative cast: it becomes a displaced
version of the struggle between crown and nobility in Spain and the reflection of the divided class allegiances of the poet, who is at once the prototypical new royal servant and the nostalgic aristocrat yearning for an earlier class
identity. If the Indians are indeed rebels against the Spanish king, the poet
allows himself an imaginative identification with them that he does not, for
example, permit with the mutinous Peruvian encomenderos who were, in
their own way, trying to perpetuate in the New World a feudal society that
was being dismantled in the Old. No small part of Ercilla's sympathy for the
defeated, but obstinate, Araucanians stems from his projection upon them
of the ideology clung to by a European aristocracy itself in the process of
historical defeat.

The ideological divisions and contradictions of the *Araucana* are mani-
fold: the poem treats the Indians alternately as natural noblemen or barbarians, as fighters against enslavement by the local encomenderos or subjugation to legitimate crown authority, and, if the latter, as seditious rebels
against the king or defenders of aristocratic independence and honor. A
similar division marks the poet's discussion of the conduct of the war. In his
chief and perhaps only important appearance in the poem, Don García is
made a spokesman for moderation and restraint in battle; he urges his
troops to spare the defeated.

> pues cuando la razón no frena y tira
> el ímpetu y furor demasïado,
> el rigor excesivo en el castigo
> justificar la causa al enemigo.

(21.56)

(For when reason does not bridle and restrain an unmeasured force and fury,
excessive rigor in punishment justifies the cause of the enemy.)

The poem repeatedly tries to find a balance between "rigor" and "clemency," such as de Cañete displayed in Peru (13.5). The poet recognizes the need for the political use of force and approves the "exemplary punishment" (13.6) meted out on the Peruvian rebels: it was, in fact, the lack of just such an exemplary punishment that occasioned the rebellion of the Araucanians in the first place (1.72). Yet the poem's main instance of such punishment, the amputation of Galbarino's hands, backfires on the Spaniards and only strengthens the resolve of the Araucanians who had been considering coming to terms (23.5f.). And in the final canto of the poem, the narrator concedes that there are occasions when clemency may be the only workable policy (37.18–24); at the end of the same passage he also concedes that here and there he can be accused of contradicting himself: "algún curioso / dirá que aquí y allí me contradigo." Earlier, when describing the great massacre at Cañete, the narrator is "suspended" between "just pity and just hatred" (31.49) for the enemy. But this balance tilts once again as he recognizes that the balanced restraint urged by Don García has not been observed and maintained.

> La mucha sangre derramada ha sido
> (si mi jüicio y parecer no yerra)
> la que de todo en todo ha destruido
> el esperado fruto desta tierra;
> pues con modo inhumano han excedido
> de las leyes y términos de guerra,
> haciendo en las entradas y conquistas
> crüeldades inormes nunca vistas.
>
> Y aunque ésta en mi opinión dellas es una
> la voz commún en contra me convence
> que al fin en ley de mundo y de fortuna
> todo le es justo y lícito al que vence.

(32.4–5)

(The great spilling of blood has been [if my judgment and opinion do not err] that which all in all has destroyed the fruit that was hoped for from this land; for they have exceeded the laws and limits of war, in their invasions and conquests committing enormities and cruelties such as were never seen before.

And although this occasion is one of those excesses in my opinion, the common voice persuades me to the contrary that ultimately in the law of the world and of fortune everything is just and licit for the victor.)

This passage has been rightly identified as a high moral moment in the epic.[78] Questions about ideological justification and about the status of the Indians are superseded by the poet's revulsion at the killing, which he goes on to describe in horrific detail. Like Las Casas, Ercilla, as eyewitness to the events of the conquest, is sickened by what he has seen. As Don García had said, such cruelty justifies the cause of the Araucanian enemy.

The narrator takes his position against the *voz commun* that tells him that all is fair in war provided one wins, a doctrine that is reasserted in the final canto: in a *just* war "all is permitted to the victor" (37.7). But Galbarino, at the end of his exhortation to the troops in canto 25, had suggested that the justice of war was itself determined by the victor,

> que no hay vencido justo y sin castigo
> quedando por jüez el enemigo.
>
> (25.40)

(for among the vanquished there is none who is just and left unpunished when his judge is his enemy.)

Vae victis! This is what the *voz commun* asserts and what a triumphalist epic, cheering the winners on, would finally be reduced to. Ercilla maintains his distance from this attitude by parodying it in a remarkable passage where he "goes over" to the Araucanian side at the end of canto 9, after the Indians have won an early victory at Concepción.

> Con la gente araucana quiero andarme,
> dichosa a la sazón y afortunada;
> y, como se acostumbra, desvïarme
> de la parte vencida y desdichada;
> por donde tantos van quiero guiarme,
> siguiendo la carrera tan usada,
> pues la costumbre y tiempo me convence
> y todo el mundo es ya ¡viva quien vence!
>   ¡Cuán usado es huir los abatidos
> y seguir los soberbios levantados,
> de la instable Fortuna favoridos,
> para sólo después ser, derribados!
> Al cabo estos favores, reducidos
> a su valor, son bienes emprestados
> que habemos de pagar con siete tanto,
> como claro nos muestra el nuevo canto.
>
> (9.112–13)

(I want to go with the the Araucanian people, happy on this occasion and blessed by Fortune, and, as the custom is, to turn away from the vanquished and unlucky side: for where so many go I too wish to guide my steps, following the common path so frequently taken; for custom and time persuade me and all the world says: Long live the victor!

How customary it is to flee those who are down and defeated and to follow the proud raised on high, favored by unstable Fortune only later to be felled. At the end her favors, reduced to their true value, are borrowed goods that we have to pay back with high interest, as the next canto clearly shows.)

The ironies of this passage work in several directions. Epic, like everyone, loves a winner, and the poet's rapid switches in allegiance depend on fortunes of war that can turn from one canto to the next. The language of chance and luck—another legacy from the *Pharsalia* that runs through the *Araucana*—denies any ideological explanation for political and military success.[79] Rather, the passage teaches distrust of such explanations by suggesting that they are constructed by writers who, as Ercilla's narrator claims he does, will follow and uphold the victorious side, whichever it may be. Here, for the moment, the narrator becomes an Indian lover. But the incongruity of this picture of the poet as a flag-waving Araucanian hints that it needs to be read with irony, an irony, however, that extends to the larger epic where the Spaniards are more generally victorious: the poem should not be read as an opportunistic endorsement of their conquest or as a taking of sides with might regardless of right. The narrator and the *Araucana*, that is, do *not* simply follow the way of the world—the way, it may be implied here, of a more traditional Virgilian epic—and celebrate the winners, deserting the losers in their adversity. This refusal of triumphalism not only allows for the poem's genuinely divided, inconsistent sympathies, for the poet really does go from one side to the other. It permits those sympathies to be based on other criteria than power, and it thus permits a critique of ideology.

The Turn to Romance

Ercilla's narrator goes his own way, in spite of his ironic profession to follow the path taken by so many, while the poet himself becomes an increasingly important protagonist in his poem, the one fully individualized character on the Spanish side. The *Araucana* gives the Indians more than their due, with various individual figures—Lautaro, Caupolicán, Colocolo, Rengo, Tucapel, Galbarino—giving voice to the aspirations of liberty and the determined resistance of the losing side. But it is through the actions and perceptions of Ercilla, the character, as well as through the comments of the narrator—and these two may finally be impossible to tell apart—that a *Spanish* subjectivity is introduced into the epic that registers horror at the war, and sympathy and pity for the Indians.[80] Thus *all* human individuality in the poem distances itself from the victors. In the poet's case, this distance is spatialized in the Second Part of the epic where he quite literally goes off on his own in a series of episodes in which, alternately, marvelous agents (the goddess Bellona, the Indian sorcerer Fitón) will show him visions of a larger world history and geography—the siege of Saint-Quentin (17–18), the battle of Lepanto (23–24), the view of the globe and of the Spanish New World empire (26–27); or he will listen to novelistic stories told to him by Araucanian women who have been separated from their true loves by the war—Tegualda who causes the poet to mourn with her over the body of her slain husband Crepino (20), Glaura whom the poet himself reunites with her beloved Cariolano (28).

These episodes are self-consciously digressive. At the beginning of the poet's visit to Fitón, the sorcerer asks him what fate or chance has drawn him so far from his path: "tan fuera de camino" (23.34); and at its end the poet apologizes for the digression that has diverted him from his narrative: "en larga digressión me he divertido" (24.98). In the opening of canto 20, the narrator complains that his dry subject matter of war and battle keeps him from going among gardens and forests where he might collect varied flowers and mix into his account of martial exploits "tales, fictions, fables, and love stories"—"cuentos, ficciones, fábulas y amores" (20.4)—and then introduces Tegualda and her tragic history of love some twenty stanzas later. The *Araucana* contains several such pleas for variety and for the inclusion of love interests. In his address to the reader at the beginning of the Second Part, Ercilla justifies the insertion of the Saint-Quentin and Lepanto episodes to complement the "poca variedad" of his Chilean war story. The opening of canto 15 asks rhetorically, "What good thing can there be without love?" (1), and here, too, the narrator uses the figure of a field of diverse flowers to describe the variety he would like to employ in his poem (5). This is also an instance where the narrator's complaint points self-reflexively at what the poem is already doing, for the previous two cantos have seen the introduction of the first erotic scene into the epic, the conversation between the Indian hero Lautaro and his beloved Guacolda on the eve of the battle that will claim his life (13.44–14.18).

Ercilla's appeal to a criterion of narrative variety seeks consciously to justify his epic's turn to romance—to both the narrative form and the erotic content of the great Italian chivalric romances of Boiardo and Ariosto. These *romanzi* had been recognized as a modern genre, distinct from classical epic, by Italian literary theorists who noted the romancers' fondness for digressions and for loosely connected episodes, their use of multiple plots and heroes in preference to Aristotle's prescriptive model of a single, completed epic action centered around one hero.[81] Boiardo had himself described the variety of his poem, alternating between stories of love and of battle, as a mixed bouquet of flowers with something for everyone (*Orlando innamorato* 3.5.1–2), and the theorists validated this variety and multiplicity—the basis of the generic difference of romance—by the pleasure that they produced in the reader. So wrote Giovambattista Giraldi Cinzio in his *Discorso intorno al comporre dei romanzi*, published in 1554.

I say this because the diversity of actions carries with it the variety that is the spice of delight and so allows the writer a large field to use episodes, that is, pleasing digressions, and to bring in events that can never, without risk of censure, be brought into poems of a single action.[82]

As examples of such digressions, Giraldi lists "jousts, tourneys, love affairs, beauties, passions of the mind, fields of battle, buildings."[83] The *Araucana* has versions of them all: the jousts that are replaced by the Indian wrestling match through which Crepino won Tegualda's hand and by the duel of Tucapel and Rengo; the various love stories of the Indian maidens; the praise of famous Spanish beauties, including the poet's future wife, Maria de Bazán, during his dream vision in canto 18 (64–73); the battles in Europe; the descriptions of Fitón's marvelous palace and gardens.

The *Araucana* thus incorporates the variety and episodic structure of romance into its narrative—that romance that the recent enormous success of the *Orlando furioso* had caused to be identified and categorized as a new and independent genre. The *Furioso* joins the *Pharsalia* and the *Aeneid* as a major model for Ercilla's poem. Critics have noted how all of the Indian love episodes—Lautaro and Guacolda, Tegualda and Crepino, Glaura and Cariolano—contain imitations of Ariosto, who is mentioned by name in the exordium to canto 15 (2); and the *Furioso* provides elements for the other digressive episodes of the poem as well.[84] This is an evident switch from the opening lines of the *Araucana*, which banish romance love-plots from its epic subject matter,

> No las damas, amor, no gentilezas
> de caballeros canto enamorados . . .

(I sing not of ladies, love, nor the gentle feats of enamored knights . . .)

lines that pointedly reject the opening line of the *Furioso*,

> Le donne, i cavallier, l'arme, gli amori . . .

and, perhaps, behind it, the opening of the *Orlando innamorato* as well:

> Non vi par già, signor, meraviglioso
> Odir cantar de Orlando innamorato.
>
> (1.1.2)

As the poem progresses, however, the poet has a change of heart, and he turns increasingly to romance models. At the opening of canto 22, his enamored narrator complains once again that the epic subject he undertakes precludes the treatment of love, and that he will accordingly take the most direct path without twisting deviations—"la más corta senda, sin rodeo" (22.5). But the figure of the narrator tormented by love is itself an invention of the *Orlando furioso*, and while this canto devotes itself dutifully to a narration of battle, the ensuing narrative of Part Two follows a course that is anything but straight.

Ramona Lagos, in an important critical discussion of the *Araucana*, argues that by the end of the poem its deviations and digressions have become the norm;[85] toward the end of canto 36, the narrator asks how it is that he has left behind the subject matter with which he started.

> ¿Cómo me he divertido y voy apriesa
> del camino primero desvïado?
> ¿Por qué así me olvidé de la promesa
> y discurso de Arauco comenzado?

(36.42)

(How is it that I have been diverted and hasten in deviation from my first path? Why have I thus forgotten my promise and the subject of Araucania which I began?)

Lagos interprets the poet's repeated flights into diversionary episodes— which we have seen that he himself more or less explicitly identifies with the narrative forms of the Italian *romanzi*—as a deliberate turning away from his story of Spanish conquest and from his initial promise to celebrate the deeds and prowess of his victorious countrymen. Revulsion at Spanish cruelty and treachery, and sympathy for the suffering and heroism of the Indians, lead Ercilla in search of alternative episodes. He cheers on Spanish victories in the Old World (Saint-Quentin, Lepanto, the annexation of Portugal) about which he feels no similar moral ambivalence; he expresses his individual solidarity with the lamenting Araucanian women. In both cases he distances and detaches himself from the killing fields in Chile.

The digressions of the *Araucana* thus bear a critical relationship to its epic plot with which they compete and which they begin to displace. These digressions, in fact, constitute a rival genre, the newly defined romance; and to take Lagos's arguments a step further, this generic conflict within the *Araucana* embodies an ideological conflict as well. As the romance episode contests the formal linearity and teleology of the poem's narrative of epic conquest, it contains a message of resistance to the conquistadors' enterprise; at the very least, it voices the poet's individual disaffection with the brutality of the war. At the level of narrative structure and strategy, there is thus an overlap in the *Araucana* between its digressive episodes, delaying and sidetracking its movement "forward" to an ending, and the inconclusiveness that we have seen to typify its various formal end points. The cliffhanging narrative suspension at the ends of Parts One and Two imitates not only Ariosto but also Lucan, whose influence is ever present in the poem, and we can further redescribe this overlap as a conscious superimposition of the model of Ariostesque romance and the model of the *Pharsalia*: Lucan's poem works equally to subvert a Virgilian epic teleology and to dismember its textual body into separate, often digressive episodes; and it does so similarly to counter an ideology of political domination. The conflation of models recognizes their generic affinity: the anti-Virgilian *Pharsalia* becomes a form of romance.

The *Araucana* thus reads the relationship of the *Aeneid* to the *Pharsalia* as an opposition of epic to romance: it provides a case *within the epic tradition* of the same "anachronistic" reading of Latin epic that I have pursued in this study, a reading that recognizes in the poems of Virgil and Lucan the narrative structures of a romance genre that was only identified as such in the sixteenth century. This reading further acknowledges the potentially political nature of this generic opposition, that *within epic* the digressive "formlessness" of romance can embody the oppositional itself, either projected by the victors' poem in order to be overcome by its own epic form (*Aeneid*) or as the dominant narrative principle of the losers' poem that swallows up the victors' epic story inside it (*Pharsalia*). Epic form and romance formlessness can alternately be seen to win out in Ercilla's poem, whose representation of the Araucanian war, by turns pro-Spanish and pro-Indian, may once again be construed as a war of poetic and generic models, but now as a three-way, if still two-sided, battle: Lucan meets and overlaps with Ariosto in the *Araucana*, and together they put up a fight against Virgil.

The anti-Virgilian nature of the poem's turn toward romance becomes explicit in the principal narrative digression of Part Three, the poet's retelling of the story of Dido in cantos 32–33. The episode, which is placed between the defeat and massacre of the Araucanians at Cañete and the capture and execution of Caupolicán, is in fact a double one. It begins with the third of Ercilla's encounters with Indian women: this time it is Lauca, whose husband of one month was mown down by the Spanish artillery at Cañete and who was herself wounded in the battle (32.35–37). She begs to die along with her beloved, but the poet sees to it that her wound is cured and that she is sent back with safe-conduct to her people. Her steadfast loyalty to her husband's memory puts the poet in mind of Dido, whose *true* story he now tells to counter Virgil's slander of the Carthaginian queen in the *Aeneid*.

Lauca thus both inspires the long story of Dido that follows and links that story to the earlier episodes of Indian heroines—Tegualda, Glaura—whose models lie in Ariosto's romance. Dido's history is, then, another similar attempt to lend romance variety to the epic narrative by interweaving episodes of love, and Ercilla explicitly introduces the passage as an escape and

deviation from his harsh subject and narrow path into an open field—
"anchura y campo descubierto" (32.50)—where his poetic imagination can
roam at liberty. He speaks both as a character within the poem to his fellow
soldiers and as narrator to his readers:

> Viendo que os tiene sordo y atronado
> el rumor de las armas inquïeto
> siempre en un mismo ser continüado
> sin mudar són ni varïar sujeto,
> por espaciar el ánimo cansado,
> y ser el tiempo cómodo y quïeto,
> hago esta digresión, que a caso vino
> cortada a la medida del camino.

(32.51)

(Seeing that the unquiet sound of war keeps you deafened by its thunder,
always continuing the same without changing vein or varying subject matter—
in order to give space and recreation to the tired mind, and since the time is
undisturbed and gives the opportunity, I make this digression, which perhaps
was fitted to the length of our journey.)

This is to be another self-conscious departure from the one-track martial
subject of epic into the multiple paths of romance, which here are characterized by stories of romantic love and, hence, by the presence of female
protagonists. These women belong to the side of the defeated enemy—their
husbands slain or captured—and they will now be linked in the narrator's
digressive tale to a prototypical epic figure of the enemy woman-in-love:
Dido. But this is not Virgil's Dido, who, for all the sympathy the poet ac-
cords her, nonetheless in her uncontrolled female passion embodies a monstrosity that characterized Carthage itself, the great barbarian foe of Rome.
The Araucanians are assimilated instead with a "barbarian" queen who is
the model of true love and patriotic self-sacrifice.

That Virgil had slandered Dido was well known.[86] The "real" Dido, as the
Aeneid recounted, had fled Tyre after her greedy brother had murdered her
wealthy husband. She had founded the city of Carthage. But here her history diverged from Virgil's fiction. A local African king, Iarbas, had demanded her hand in marriage and threatened to go to war against the new
city if he were refused. Assembling her fellow citizens, the queen had committed suicide before them, thus at once preserving her country and her
faith to her dead husband. Virgil's departure from the historically accepted
legend of Dido was noted by Servius, the ancient commentator on the
Aeneid. The "true" story of the Carthaginian queen's suicide had been preserved by Justin and widely transmitted by Boccaccio in his De Claris Muli-

eribus, in which Dido became an exemplary figure of chaste widowhood. Significantly, Ariosto had cited Virgil's calumny of Dido in a passage of the *Orlando furioso* (35.28) that depicted poets as self-interested prince pleasers, and asserted that Augustus had not been as pious and benign as his greatest poet made him out to be: the *Aeneid*, in other words, had an ideological *parti pris*.

When Ercilla retells the story of Dido, in which Aeneas plays no part and Dido's suicide is a patriotic act that establishes the greatness of Carthage— not, as in Virgil's version, a prophetic anticipation of the city's fall—he reminds us that the defeated have their own stories that rival and may be more reliable than the history told about them by the winners and their poets. At the same time, he contests the ideological nexus of woman-barbarian-romance that Virgilian epic projects as the alternative to its narrative of imperial (Western, male) conquest, an alternative that must be overcome and/or excluded. Rather, Ercilla contests the negative valorization of this nexus: the barbarian foes of empire, Araucanian and Carthaginian, may be represented in his poem's romance episodes by women—and to this extent the *Araucana* repeats Virgil's terms—but Dido's example shows the woman and the Eastern barbarian to be the equal of the Western man in fortitude and as state builder, the founder of that Carthage which rose, Ercilla notes at the end of his story, to challenge Rome at the peak of the latter's power (33.53). Her chastity shows her to be not the victim of a self-destructive appetite—the romance femme fatale whose temptations must be resisted by the state-building Aeneas—but a being who is fully as capable as Virgil's hero of the rationality and erotic sublimation required for civilization and political rule. Ercilla's correction and repudiation of Virgil's slander of Dido is thus a repudiation of a larger Virgilian ideology of empire—and of the redeployment of that epic ideology to describe the present-day Spanish conquest of Araucania. The episode collapses dichotomies between male and female, West and East, civilization and barbarism, and, not least, epic and romance. It announces itself as romance digression and thus apparently as an entertaining diversion from the world of epic history into a realm of literary fiction: but, instead, it recounts the true facts of history against the very authority of Virgil's epic, which turns out to be the maker of fictions. The romance episodes of the *Araucana* that seem ready to crowd out and take over from its central narrative of war and conquest are no less true, no less part of the historical record than that narrative; but they tell the other— the losers'—side of the story.

The alternative story of Dido, moreover, presents a different model of how to colonize a foreign land.[87] Dido and her band of refugees from Tyre are themselves colonists in North Africa. She can stand in Ercilla's fiction both as a figure of Araucanian virtue and resistance and as a foil to the colonizing Spaniards. Dido founds her city by purchasing from the natives, "los moradores" (33.7), enough land to be covered by the hide of a bull. Her famous subterfuge of cutting the hide into narrow strips and thus enclosing an area large enough for settlement is a piece of sharp dealing, and the natives cry foul (33.8). But Dido pays as she goes.

> Pero recompensó la demasía
> dejándolos contentos y pagados.
>
> (33.9)

(But she paid them what remained owing, leaving them contented and satisfied.)

Rather than cheat the native inhabitants, the queen uses the treasure she has stolen away from her avaricious—"codicioso" (32.72)—brother Pygmalion to satisfy them for taking their land. Dido's story pointedly opposes her both to the greed—"codicia" (32.55, 56, 64; 33.2)—of her brother *and* to the hungry and wretched greed—"la hambrienta y mísera codicia" (1.68; 2.87–88; 3.1–3)—of the Spanish conquistadors for which the poem from its very beginning has blamed the war in Chile.[88] She brings her own wealth to the new colony, founding it on a mutual agreement and exchange with the natives, while the Spaniards have sought to expropriate the Indians' wealth and lands by force. In this description of a peaceful colonization to the advantage of both colonist and native—and Ercilla knew of the rival Portuguese empire in the East and its trading-post colonies purchased, though often not without force, from local rulers—the romance episode of Dido once again suggests an alternative to the larger epic plot of historical destiny: how the very plot of Spain's history in America could have, perhaps should have, taken a different turn.[89]

Les Tragiques

The turn within the losers' epic to romance, as an alternative narrative to an apparent history of defeat, is spelled out in a simile in Agrippa d'Aubigné's poem of Huguenot resistance. In *Vengeances*, the sixth and penultimate book of *Les Tragiques*, the poet addresses the victims of the massacre of Saint Bartholomew's Day and all others who have died for the Protestant cause.

> O martyres aimez! ô douce affliction!
> Perpetuelle marque à la saincte Sion,
> Tesmoignage secret que l'Eglise en enfance
> Eut au front e au sein, à sa pauvre naissance,
> Pour choisir du troupeau de ses bastardes soeurs
> L'heritiere du ciel au milieu des mal'heurs!

Qui a leu aux romans les fatales miseres
Des enfans exposés de peur des belles meres,
Nourris par les forests, gardez par les mastins,
A qui la louve ou l'ourse ont portés leur tetins,
Et les pasteurs aprés du laict de leurs oüailles
Nourissent, sans sçavoir, un prince et des merveilles?
Au milieu des troupeaux on en va faire choix,
Le valet des berger va commander aux Rois:
Une marque en la peau, out l'oracle descouvre
Dan le parc des brebis l'heritier du grand Louvre.
  Ainsi l'Eglise, ainsi accouche de son fruit,
En fuyant aux deserts le dragon la poursuit,
L'enfant chassé des Rois est nourri par les bestes:
Cet enfant brisera de ces grands Rois les testes
Qui l'ont proscript, banni, outragé, dejetté,
Blessé, chassé, battu de faim, de pauvreté.
Or ne t'advienne point, espouse et chere Eglise,
De penser contre Christ ce que dit sur Moyse
La simple Sephora qui, voyant circoncir
Ses enfans, estima qu'on les vouloit occir:
"Tu m'es mari de sang", ce dit la mere fole
Temeraire et par trop blasphemante parole!
Car cette effusion, qui lui desplaist si fort,
Est arre de la vie, et non pas de la mort.
  Venez donc pauvreté, faim, fuittes, et blessures,
Banissemens, prison, proscriptions, injures;
Vienne l'heureuse mort, gage pour tout jamais
De la fin de la guerre et de la douce paix!
Fuyez, triomphes vains, la richesse et la gloire,
Plaisirs, prosperité, insolente victoire,
O pieges dangereux et signes evidens
Des tenebres, du ver, et grincement de dents![90]

(*Vengeances* 703–40)

(O beloved martyrs! O sweet affliction! Perpetual mark for Holy Zion, a secret witness that the infant Church possessed from her humble birth on her forehead and breast: to choose and distinguish her from her bastard sisters as the heir of heaven, in the midst of her adversities!

Who has read in romances of the destined misfortunes of infants exposed because of the fear of their stepmothers, nourished in the forests, guarded by wild dogs, to whom the she-wolf or the mother bear have offered their teats? and of shepherds who afterwards have unknowingly raised with the milk of their sheep a prince and marvels? Election is to be made in the midst of flocks, and the servant of shepherds will command kings: a birthmark on the skin, whence the oracle discovers the heir of the mighty Louvre in the sheepfold.

Just so the Church, just so, having delivered her newborn, fleeing into the wildernesss is chased by the dragon. The infant pursued by Kings is nourished by beasts: this infant will break the heads of those mighty Kings who have proscribed him, banished, outraged, thrown him down, wounded, hunted after, afflicted him with hunger and poverty. Now do not ever let it come about, dear, espoused Church, that you should think against Christ, what the simple Zippo-rah said of Moses, on seeing him circumcise their children, and thinking that he wanted to kill them: "You are my husband of blood." Thus spoke the foolish mother, overly rash and much blaspheming words! For this spilling of blood, which displeased her so, is the token of life, and not of death.

Come then poverty, hunger, flights and wounds, banishments, prison, pro-scriptions, injuries; let happy death come, the promise for all time of an end to war and of sweet peace! Away with you, vain triumphs, riches and glory, plea-sures, prosperity, insolent victory: o dangerous traps and evident signs of dark-ness, of the worm, of the gnashing of teeth!)

The passage gives a good idea of the vehement energy and rhetorical com-plexity of d'Aubigné's verse, a brilliance that can be found almost wherever one chooses to sample *Les Tragiques*.[91] Here the simile of the literary ro-mances is enriched by associations with the pastoral imagery of Jewish (David, the shepherd who becomes king) and Christian (Jesus, the good shepherd and King of Kings) Scriptures. The conceit that the blood of Prot-estant martyrs is a sign on their foreheads, similar to the birthmarks by which the hero of romance foundling stories is discovered to be heir to a kingdom, depends, as does so much of d'Aubigné's imagery, on the Book of Revelation, in this case on 7:3–4, where the angels of God place their seal upon the foreheads of the elect before the Last Judgment.[92] D'Aubigné's Calvinist twist on the image describes this seal precisely as a birthmark, as the *invisible* or *unreadable* sign of predestination, of God's secret choice ("on en va faire choix") of the saints from the birth of the Church, itself; that is, from the beginning of history. It is a mark whose significance only becomes apparent at the end of time—or in the life history of the individ-ual, only after the moment of death—when God will recognize His own and offer them a place in His Kingdom.

From the same Book of Revelation (12:1–6, 13–17), the poet draws the figure of the true Church as the woman driven into exile in the Wilderness, the place of wandering, and thus again assimilates the history of the Church with a romance plot.[93] But when his narrator admonishes the Church—his Huguenot coreligionists—not to complain against God for the blood-shed they have suffered for His sake, the ensuing comparison to Zipporah's complaint against Moses appears subtly to shift the terms of his conceit. Circumcision, which Paul asserts in Rom. 4:11 was a sign and seal of Abraham's righteousness—like the eschatological seal of Revelation 7—is granted to the male child at birth, but it is not a birthmark. It is rather inscribed on the infant from the outside, and it is a *visible* and *readable* sign. The logic of the whole passage is thus circular, and something of a tautology. The wounds of martyrdom, the violence that history visibly inflicts upon the defeated Huguenots, are taken to be signs of a divine election that, according to strict doctrine, is in fact invisible and inscrutable. Yet this election has, by the divine commandment of circumcision given to Abraham and repeated to Moses, been ratified by a visible sign, an act of ritual violence upon the infant body, that is, in turn, assimilated with the literal violence of martyrdom that initiated the string of conceits. History marks those whom God chooses; or, conversely, to be of the elect is to be a marked man.

The poem wavers, if only momentarily, over the legibility of a recent history of persecution and defeat. This history, which otherwise seems to be a senseless series of horrors—and this is how it is depicted for much of *Les Tragiques*—nonetheless contains a secret romance narrative within it: not so secret, however, that the eye of faith cannot detect it in the signs of the times. These signs can be misread, however. Zipporah thinks that by circumcision Moses is killing her sons. A despairing Huguenot Church may think that the very real killings and other tribulations of its faithful have no significance beyond death. The narrator believes differently and embraces affliction and death as the tokens of a final triumph and victory in the afterlife: while earthly victory is itself a manifest sign of eternal damnation.[94] His conviction is borne out rhetorically in the two second-person addresses, first to the Church and then to the list of adversities he welcomes upon himself (these are linked by the semantic relationship between the verbs, "ne t'advienne point" and "venez"): these vocatives, repeated throughout the poem, recall the style of the biblical prophets and confer a similar prophetic status on the poem's narrating voice.

The assertion that apparent defeat in this world is the sign of victory in the next indicates what happens when the losers' epic in the tradition of the *Pharsalia* is adapted to Christian and sectarian use; a similar pattern is found in *Paradise Lost*. For the faithful Christian is in a no-lose situation. According to the Beatitudes that Jesus delivers in the Sermon on the Mount, it is the meek (Matt. 5:5) and those persecuted for His sake (5:10–12) who will respectively inherit the earth and the Kingdom of Heaven. Christianity itself provides an alternative narrative of hope—which, in this slide between earthly and eschatological inheritance, does not exclude political hope—that counters a reality of persecution and oppression. Thus, *Les Tragiques*, like the *Pharsalia* and the *Araucana*, seeks to undo the triumphalist historical narrative of the victors, in this case of the majority Catholic party in France, to deny a meaningful epic teleology to that history and to break it down into nonnarratable violence, while ascribing to the losers' experience of tribulation the pattern of romance, still open-ended in history and therefore alive to hope. And d'Aubigné's epic indeed goes further than those poems by offering, particularly in its last two books, *Vengeances* and *Jugement*, a triumphalist narrative of its own, in which God punishes the Catholic persecutors and, in the ultimate teleology, executes His Last Judgment on humanity, separating the saved from the damned. Where the opening simile of the *Pharsalia* (1.72–80) hyperbolically and despairingly described the fall of the Roman republic as the end of the world, the Stoic *ekpryrosis*, d'Aubigné's poem views the sufferings of the Huguenot Church as events that will usher in a real apocalyptic destruction of the earth (*Jugement* 923–31). The passage may be modeled on Lucan's simile, but this apocalypse promises a divine restoration of the Church and the heavenly reward of the Protestant elect. And where the *Pharsalia* attributes the victory of the Caesarian party to Fortune and therefore places it within a history that is forever open-ended, *Les Tragiques* sees the providential hand of God operating even in the defeat of the Huguenot cause, a testing of His saints that will lead to their ultimate victory. The story of the Church exiled to the wilderness is not, then, one of indefinitely prolonged romance wandering; in the end, as the happy endings of the *romans* themselves suggest, it will turn into a plot of epic destiny.

What I have referred to as a potential slide in Christian thought between worldly, political hopes and eschatological hope is apparent in the relationship between d'Aubigné's simile of the shepherd become king and heir to the "grand Louvre"—a Davidic example of the meek inheriting the earth—and the figure to which the simile refers: the messianic Christ born to the Church at the end of time who will break the heads of earthly kings. Indeed, the political Israel of the Hebrew Scriptures functions as the typological figure for the purely spiritual or apocalyptic Kingdom of God of the New Testament, but the distinction normally became confused for Calvinists, who thought of their Church and their own political entities (and the two were often inseparable), as versions of the New Israel, whether Geneva, the Low Countries, or the English Commonwealth under Cromwell.[95] There is a particular historical poignancy, however, in d'Aubigné's simile, for in Henry of Navarre the Huguenot party had produced its own David, a prince, as the verse Préface to *Les Tragiques* puts it, chosen from the tents of Judah (281–82): a prince, who had, in fact, become heir to the Louvre. D'Aubigné had fought beside and once even saved the life of the future Henry IV; he had been a member of the inner circle of the Huguenot war leader. But in 1593 Henry had abjured his Protestant faith in order to become king of a predominantly Catholic France, dashing the political hopes of many of his Huguenot supporters, the poet among them.[96]

D'Aubigné began *Les Tragiques* in the late 1570s, but only published the poem in 1616, six years after Henry's assassination and during the regency of Marie de' Medici, when it seemed to many French Protestants that they would have to begin their armed struggle all over again. The appearance of the epic seemed to be a call for further resistance, and four years later d'Aubigné, after participating in a failed revolt against Charles de Luynes, the favorite of Louis XIII, was forced to flee into exile in Geneva; his own life had come to conform to the typological exile of his Church.[97] Because of the long period of composition and revision of Les Tragiques, it is often difficult to date passages or to determine where its historical ironies are part of the poet's original design.[98] This is the case here, where the shift from the simile, in which the Louvre may seem within the reach of God's elect, to an eschatological kingdom that is not of this world may suggest a move to a fallback position once the earlier political aspirations of the Huguenot cause have been disappointed: cheated of earthly victory, the poet welcomes the defeat that assures him of a celestial reward. However, this is anything but an attitude of resigned quietism, and the very presence of the simile suggests that d'Aubigné would like to have it both ways, that his hopes for a successful outcome to the Protestant political struggle now within history are not canceled out, even if they are superseded by his confidence in a final vindication at history's end. And the awaited kingdom of heaven may be a displaced version of the hoped-for Huguenot kingship that history has failed to provide.

The Model of Lucan

The combination of a commitment to ongoing political resistance together with a strong sense that defeat has caused the world of human history and politics to lose almost all meaning links Les Tragiques closely to the spirit of the Pharsalia, and it is Lucan's epic that is invoked from the opening lines of the first book of the poem, where d'Aubigné's narrator contemplates an assault upon the legions of Rome,

> Puisqu'il faut s'attaquer aux legions de Rome . . .

the Rome of Catholic tyranny and error.

> Je brise les rochers et le respect d'erreur
> Qui fit douter Cesar d'une vaine terreur.
> Il vid Rome tremblante, affreuze, eschevelee
> Qui en pleurs, en sanglots, mi-morte, desolee,
> Tordant ses doigts, fermoit, defendoit de ses mains
> A Cezar le chemin au sang de ses germains.
>   Mais dessous les autels des idoles j'advise
> Le visage meurtri de la captive Eglise,
> Qui a sa delivrance (aux despens des hazards)
> M'appelle, m'animant de ses trenchans regards.

Mes desirs sont des-ja volez outre la rive
Du Rubicon troublé: que mon reste les suive
Par un chemin tout neuf, car je ne trouve pas
Qu'autre homme l'ait jamais escorché de ses pas.

(Misères 7–20)

(I break through the alpine rocks and the mistaken reverence that made Julius Caesar hesitate with vain terror. He saw Rome, trembling, ghastly, dishevelled, who, in tears, with sobs, half-dead, desolate, wringing her fingers, stopped, forbade Caesar with her hands from taking the path towards bloody, fratricidal war.

But beneath the altars of the idols, I see the murdered face of the captive Church, who calls me, whatever the dangers, to her rescue, emboldening me with her penetrating glance. My desires have already flown to the other bank of the troubled Rubicon: let the rest of me follow them along a brand new path, for I find no other man who has marked it with his feet.)

At the beginning of the action of the *Pharsalia* (1.186–205), Caesar is momentarily deterred from crossing the Rubicon and inaugurating civil war by a vision of a personified Roma. The narrator of *Les Tragiques* has no inhibitions about singing of civil strife or about attacking his native country when it wears the mask of Rome; the recollection of Lucan is immediately superseded by an allusion to Rev. 6:9–10, where the souls of martyrs buried beneath the altar of sacrifice call upon God and ask how much longer they must wait for His vengeance and judgment. The poet writes in response to their call, and when, a little later in *Misères* (97–130), he presents his own version of a personified France, inspired by Lucan's Roma, it is of a mother holding twins.[99] The Catholic majority, identified typologically with Esau, fights to keep the Huguenot minority, the chosen Jacob, from receiving the nurture of their mother's milk: the just struggle (109, 122) of the younger child for survival has created a war that has torn apart the body of the motherland. The horrors of fratricidal strife give d'Aubigné and Lucan a common subject matter, and both are partisans of the losing side. In these early passages of his epic the French poet is claiming affiliation with his Roman predecessor, but with a difference: for d'Aubigné, as a partisan convinced of the sanctity of his cause, embraces civil war itself, and places his narrator in the position of Lucan's villainous Caesar, the instigator of the Roman conflict. Whatever sense the poem might offer that the reciprocity of civil warfare makes guilty parties of both sides—Mother France curses *both* of the sons (127–30) who are destroying her—disappears at the end of *Misères*, where the poet calls upon God to distinguish between the elect and their foes.

Tes ennemis et nous sommes esgaux en vice
Si, juge, tu te sieds en ton lict de justice;
Tu fais pourtant un choix d'enfans ou d'ennemis,

Et ce choix est celui que ta grace y a mis.

. . . .

Distingue pour les deux, comme tu l'as promis,
La verge à tes enfans, la barre aux ennemis.

(1277–80, 1291–92)

(Your enemies and we ourselves are equal in vice, if, as a judge, you sit on your throne of justice; you make a choice, however of children or enemies, and this choice is one that your grace has made. . . . Differentiate for the two, as you have promised, the rod of parental chastisement for your children, the iron rod of doom for your enemies.)

The potential equivalence between French Catholic and Protestant fighters, equal according to Calvinist doctrine in their lack of human merit, is overcome by the election of divine grace. They may share an identity as twin children of a war-torn France, but only the Huguenots are God's children. Patriotic sentiments here give way to the poet's sectarian allegiance: the fate of France takes second place to the destiny of a transnational Protestantism.

D'Aubigné described his feeling of kinship with Lucan in a Latin poem that served as a postscript to a longer poem on the French civil wars composed as a cento of verses from Book 1 of the *Pharsalia*; Lucan's epic, this poetic exercise suggested, could easily be made applicable to current political history.

Haec lego Lucani concepta vocabula nobis,
   Mens eadem studio scripsit uterque pari.
Lucano stilus est durus: mihi durior, utque
   Non tractim serpit, sic mihi comma placet.
Libertatis amans, vixitque tyrannidis osor.
   Illa fuit portus; haec mihi naufragium.
Principibus placuit, placui sic Regibus: illi
   Carmina noxia, me talia fata manent.
Non leve discrimen; moritur Lucanus inermis,
   Non imbellis ego victima sponte cadam.
Tum fama insonti dono servata Neronis;
   In me vera mei fama Neronis erit.[100]

(I have collected these words of Lucan arranged by me; each of us wrote with the same mind and equal zeal. Lucan's style is harsh: mine is harsher, and that verse period pleases me that does not crawl slowly along. Loving Liberty, he lived as the hater of Tyranny; Liberty was his haven in death; Tyranny is the cause of my shipwreck. He pleased Princes, so I pleased Kings: his poetry was harmful to him; a similar fate awaits me. There is a not insignificant difference between us: Lucan died unarmed; I will not die as a willing victim without a fight. Back then the fame of Nero was preserved by his inadvertent gift; the true fame of my Nero will be preserved in me.)

Here again, d'Aubigné distinguishes himself from his poetic father by his bellicosity, his willingness to attack Rome and her legions: the poem seems to be written for the sake of the magnificently defiant line, "Non imbellis ego victima sponte cadam." He shares with Lucan a style that can be epigrammatic and violently abrupt; d'Aubigné's verse repeatedly bursts out of the symmetrical structures of its alexandrine couplets, with startling enjambments and caesuras.[101] And he will depict the Huguenot struggle as a fight against tyranny: Catherine de' Medici (*Misères* 815–34), Henry III (*Princes* 819–28), and Charles IX (*Fers* 963–1018) are by turns compared to Nero by *Les Tragiques*, a Nero who is both tyrannical emperor and persecutor of the early Church. The comparison reveals what the poet claims are their true natures. Catherine is further defamed by being described as a conjurer of infernal demons in a lengthy passage (*Misères* 885–949) that is closely modeled on Lucan's grotesque depiction of the witch Erictho.

There are numerous other imitations and echoes of the *Pharsalia* in *Les Tragiques*. One of these is the central passage of the fifth book, *Fers*, the description of the Saint Bartholomew's Day Massacre in Paris, "the tragedy that effaces all others" (703–4). In the book's fiction, the blessed souls in heaven, led by Admiral Coligny, one of the chief victims of the massacre, are visiting a celestial gallery in which they see pictures portraying scenes from the history of the French wars of religion.[102]

> D'un visage riant nostre Caton tendoit
> Nos yeux avec les siens, et le bout de son doight,
> A se voir transpercé; puis il nous monstra comme
> On le coupe à morceaux: sa teste court à Rome,
> Son corps sert de jouët aux badauds ameutés,
> Donnant le bransle au cours des autres nouveautés.
> La cloche qui marquoit les heures de justice,
> Trompette des voleurs, ouvre aux forfaicts la lice;
> Ce grand palais du droict fut contre droict choisi
> Pour arborer au vent l'estendart cramoisi.
> Guerre sans ennemi, où l'on ne trouve à fendre
> Cuirasse que la peau ou la chemise tendre.
> L'un se defend de voix, l'autre assaut de la main,
> L'un y porte le fer, l'autre y preste le sein:
> Difficile à juger qui est le plus astorge,
> L'un à bien esgorger, l'autre à tendre la gorge.

(*Fers* 831–47)

(With a laughing face, our Cato directed our eyes with his own and with his pointing fingertip to where he was depicted being run through; then he showed us how they cut him to pieces: his head travels to Rome: his body served as a plaything for the stirred-up mob, setting in motion a series of other enormities. The clock which marked the hours of the lawcourt, was a trumpet signal to the thieves, opening the lists to the murderous crimes; this great Palace of Justice was unjustly chosen to unfurl a blood-red banner to the breeze. A war without an enemy, where one found no armor to cut through except skin and a thin shirt. One side defends itself with its voice, the other attacks with its hand. One bears a sword, the other puts forth its breast. It is difficult to judge who acts more dispassionately: he who readily cuts throats, he who offers his throat to the sword.)

The poem has earlier described Coligny in a similar attitude, glancing down from heaven:

> Coligni se rioit de la foulle
> Qui de son tronc roullé se joüoit à la boulle.

> (*Princes* 1430–31)

(Coligny laughed at the mob that played ball with the rolling trunk of his body.)

Both passages depend on the laughter of the spirit of Lucan's Pompey as it watches the mutilation of its former body. D'Aubigné has significantly identified Coligny with a different hero of the *Pharsalia*, preferring Cato, Lucan's martyr of republican liberty as well as the ideal figure of stoicism: the *constance* and *fermeté* in the face of death that characterized the Protestant martyrs of *Feux*, the fourth book of the poem, are viewed as superior forms of the stoic virtue by which "Caton d'Utique et tant d'autres Romains" (803) died for their country.[103]

A similar firmness is demonstrated by the victims of Saint Bartholomew who proffer their bodies to the sword. The one-sidedness of the massacre contains a second recollection of the *Pharsalia*, the onset of the battle of Pharsalia itself.

> Civilia bella
> Una acies patitur, gerit altera; frigidus inde
> Stat gladius, calet omne nocens a Caesare ferrum.

> (*Pharsalia* 7.501–3)

(One side suffers civil war, the other wages it; on Pompey's side, the sword is cold: all harmful blades heat up on the side of Caesar.)

> . . . .
> Perdidit inde modum caedes, ac nulla secuta est
> Pugna, sed hinc iugulis, hinc ferro bella geruntur.

> (7.532–33)

(Then the slaughter lost measure, though what ensued was no battle; instead war was waged on this side with the throat, on that with the sword.)

These passages also attracted Ercilla, who adapted them vividly to describe the technological inequality of the warfare between the Spaniards and the Araucanians.

> todos al descargar los brazos gimen
> mas salen los efetos desiguales:
> que los unos topaban duro acero,
> los otros al desnudo y blando cuero.
>
> Como parten la carne en los tajones
> con lo corvos cuchillos carniceros,
> y cual de fuerte hierro los planchones
> baten en dura yunque los herreros,
> así es la diferencia de los sones
> que forman con sus golpes los guerreros:
> quién la carne y los huesos quebrantando,
> quién templados arneses abollando.
>
> (*Araucana* 14.34–35)

(All groaned to swing their arms, but with unequal results: for one side struck against hard steel, the other against bare and soft skin.

As butchers cleave meat on the block with their curved knives and as blacksmiths beat plate out of strong iron on a heavy anvil, so is the difference of the sounds that the warriors make with their blows; one side breaking flesh and bones, the other denting suits of tempered armor.)

Lucan's strategy, well understood by his imitators, makes a virtue out of losing: the defeated republicans seem unwilling to engage in civil war and to make their swords guilty ("nocens") of fratricidal killing. Similarly, Ercilla shows the odds unfairly stacked in the Spaniards' favor and turns the battle into a massacre, or, as his simile suggests, sheer butchery: for all their valor, virtually no Indians survive the fighting at Mataquito. D'Aubigné reverses the equation: the echo of the *Pharsalia* momentarily elevates the massacre of Saint Bartholomew's Day into an epic battle, even if it is a war without an enemy. But in doing so, it criticizes epic warfare itself, and in all three instances this warfare is reduced to murder. In such a war, it is better to be defeated, an innocent or helpless victim, and, in the case of *Les Tragiques*, a willing martyr to the faith.

The tableaux of the massacres of Saint Bartholomew, first in Paris and then in the various cities of France, culminate the pictures in the heavenly gallery, a poetic invention that d'Aubigné feels the need to defend in his prefatory address to the readers of *Les Tragiques*. In the poem (*Fers* 1195f.), he claims to have viewed these celestial paintings himself when, as he lay unconscious while recovering from an attack on his life in the months following the massacres, his soul was detached from his body and enjoyed a series of divinely inspired visions. Critics have pointed out that the paintings in heaven continue and typify the larger poem, which presents a whole series of mostly static tableaux and portraits, whether the figure of Mother France in *Misères*, whom the poet wishes to paint—"Je veux peindre la France une mère affligée (97)—the debate between the allegorical personifications of Fortune and Virtue in the poet's dream vision in *Princes* (1175–1487), or the whole rogues' gallery of caricatured vices in *La chambre dorée*.[104] There is, in fact, little narrative action in *Les Tragiques*: God, Himself, visits the earth and sees the persecution of his Protestant faithful in *La chambre dorée* and *Feux*; in *Fers* He allows Satan to test the French Huguenots in particular;[105] the last two books contemplate the retribution and rewards of His judgment. This is the overarching narrative, the secret and not-so-secret romance of the Church, that *Les Tragiques* opposes to other possible profane narratives of history. But as the poem insists that God is watching and weighing earthly events, it adapts His atemporal point of view and describes those events as so many pictures frozen in time. Such narrative stasis informs even the middle books, *Feux* and *Fers*, that come closest to chronicle histories and describe events from the contemporary or near-contemporary Catholic-Protestant conflict.

This is, in fact, the principal difference that separates *Les Tragiques* from both the *Pharsalia* and the *Araucana*, poems that, for all their episodic deviations, present themselves as historical annals and narrate events in a chronological sequence. While the books *Feux* and *Fers* are carefully structured, the latter centered around the death of Coligny, the former around the profession of faith of the Italian martyr Montalchine—which thus becomes the center of the larger poem as well—their series of discrete vignettes or tableaux are not organized chronologically; nor are they linked by cause and effect. In *Fers*, the account of the battles and massacres of the Wars of Religion shifts back and forth across both time and the geography of France, described by her rivers: the Loire (466, 650, 665, 1065), the Rhone (517, 669, 1071, 1086,), the Seine (585, 665, 869, 886, 1093), and the Garonne (665).[106] In an extended elaboration of a passage in the *Pharsalia* (2.214–20) that describes the Tiber choked with the corpses and blood of the victims of the Roman civil wars, d'Aubigné depicts the French rivers both as the instruments of death by which the Huguenots are drowned and as the receptacles of their murdered bodies (585–91, 611–18, 867–75, 901–20, 1066–72, 1083–92). Their bloody waters are the Red Sea (524) through which God's elect must pass, and the martyrs repeat the experience of the crucified Christ from whose pierced side flowed "living waters" (John 7:38, 19:34) as well as blood.

> Là mesme on void flotter un fleuve dont le flanc
> Du chrestien est la source et le flot est le sang.
>
> (559–60)

(There, too, one sees flowing a river whose source is the side of a Christian and whose stream is blood.)

The conceit that organizes the book culminates in its final vision (1446–1532) of a personified Ocean who first refuses, then piously receives into his breast, the blood-stained waters of the Seine, Gironde, Charente, Loire, and Vilaine.

But the watery conceit of *Fers* itself is part of a larger baroque conceit begun in *Feux*, in which martyrology is given variety as much by the different, horrifying modes of the martyrs' deaths as by the individuality of the Protestant victims. Most of them, as the title of the book suggests, die at the stake. But an Avignonese maker of tennis balls (391–426) is suspended in an iron cage at the mercy of the elements so that the injuries "de l'air" (417) might serve as his executioners. And in Flanders, Protestant women, including "la constante Marie," are buried alive beneath the earth (515–42).

> Le feu avoit servi tant de fois à brusler,
> Ils avoyent fait mourir par la perte de l'air,
> Il avoyent changé l'eau à donner mort par elle;
> Il faloit que la terre aussi fust leur bourrelle.
>
> (523–26)

(Fire had served to burn so many times; they had killed by causing a loss of air; they had transformed water in order that it might deal death: it was necessary that the earth too should be their executioner.)

The four elements—fire, air, and earth in *Feux*, water in *Fers*—provide the ways to kill a Protestant in *Les Tragiques*; later in *Vengeances* (315–26), they will become willing instruments of divine vengeance upon the Catholic persecutors by whom they have been defiled; and in *Jugement* (770–94), they will protest before the throne of God against their desecration.[107] The pollution of elemental nature by religious strife anticipates—and may already be part of—a final apocalyptic dissolution.

> Tout se cache de peur: le feu s'enfuit dans l'air,
> L'air en l'eau, l'eau en terre; au funebre mesler
> Tout beau perd sa couleur.
>
> (*Jugement* 929–31)

(Everything hides in fear; fire flees into the air, the air into the water, the water into the earth; at this somber confusion, beauty loses her features.)

As it links the historical books of the poem to its eschatology, the grisly baroque conceit of the elements provides those books with an ordering frame. It holds together, if only barely, what seem to be the almost randomly arranged tableaux of war and persecution against the saints.

It is a history that cannot be narrated. Just as the heavenly pictures give atemporal, spatial representation to events of the Huguenot struggle, so the device of the four elements transfers the poem's organization of those events from historical time to space—and at that to a space broken down into its component parts. Both the times and the physical universe are out of joint in *Les Tragiques*, and the poem carries to an extreme the narrative disjunction that characterizes the anti-Virgilian losers' epics of Lucan and Ercilla. And here, too, an emblem of this disjunction, matching the breaking apart both of the elemental body of nature and of the political body of France, is the dismembered human body: the tortured bodies of the Huguenot victims and preeminently Coligny's body torn to pieces by the mob of Saint Bartholomew's Day.

There was, of course, an alternate Catholic interpretation of Coligny's murder. The pictures in the heavenly gallery are pointedly opposed to the frescoes of the Saint Bartholomew's Day Massacre in the Sala Regia, the papal throne room in the Vatican, painted by Vasari but attributed by d'Aubigné to demonic artists (*Fers* 256–60); Coligny's death is there the central scene in what is celebrated as a glorious victory of the Roman Church. And there were poetic renditions, too. Jean Dorat, the beloved teacher of the poets of the Pléiade, had gloatingly detailed the dismemberment of the Huguenot leader's corpse both in Latin epigrams and in French verse.

> Cil qui estoit iadis chef des voleurs d'Eglises
> Gaspar, a mis sans chef, fin à ses entreprises.
> Cil qui profane & sainct de ses mains ravissoit,
> En luy manchot de mains figure on n'appercoit.
> Cil qui la part honteuse ostoit à la gent sacre,
> Est sans partie honteuse un hontuese simulachre.[108]

(This Gaspar who was once head of the thieves of the Church ended his deeds without his own head. He who used to steal prophane and sacred goods with his hands, one sees as a figure lacking hands. He who used to show off his shameful member to holy people is a shameful image without a shameful member.)

From a Catholic perspective, the mutilated bodies of Coligny and his coreligionists are full of meaning and perfectly narratable: they are the visible signs of the punishment of heresy and of the triumph of the true faith. Vasari's frescoes juxtapose the death of Coligny with the victory at Lepanto one year earlier that is depicted on another wall in the same room, thereby raising Saint Bartholomew to the same epic dignity as the great Actium-like victory over the Turkish infidel.

It is with such possible triumphalist narratives in mind that we should view the refusal of d'Aubigné's anti-epic to narrate or to make sense out of a senseless horror. His disembodied Coligny can only laugh down at the mutilation of his corpse, the figure of a violent human history that has no meaning on its own visible and sheerly physical terms. But the nonnarratibility of this history is inversely correlated to the poet's faith in an invisible/barely visible plot of redemption and eventual apocalyptic judgment. What is at one level a desacralization of history, and a reduction of the victors' narrative from claims to epic formal coherence to the disjunction and randomness that epic contrasts to itself in *romance*, corresponds at another to the sanctification and elevation of the losers' own historical romance of earthly wandering and tribulation into a heavenly epic.

A King and No King

In *Princes*, the second book of the poem, d'Aubigné ascribes the dismemberment of the body politic of France to its head, that is, to the monarchy.

> Le peuple estant le corps et les membres du Roy,
> Le Roy est chef du peuple, et c'est aussi pourquoy
> La teste est frenetique et pleine de manie
> Qui ne garde son sang pour conserver sa vie,
> Et le chef n'est plus chef quand il prend ses esbats
> A coupper de son corps les jambes et les bras.
> Mais ne vaut-il pas mieux, comme les traistres disent,
> Lors que les accidens les remedes maitrisent,
> Quand la playe noircit et sans mesure croist,
> Quand premier à nos yeux la gangrene paroist,
> Ne vaut-il pas bien mieux d'un membre se deffaire
> Qu'envoyer laschement tout le corps au suaire?
> Tel aphorisme est bons alors qu'il faut curer
> Le membre qui se peut sans la mort separer,
> Mais non lors que l'amas de tant de maladies
> Tient la masse du sang ou les nobles parties:
> Que le cerveau se purge, et sente que de soy
> Coule du mal au corps duqel il est le roy.
>
> (*Princes* 467–84)

(The people are the body and the members of the king, the king is the head of the people, and this is why the head is thus insane and full of madness that does not protect its blood in order to preserve its life, and the head is no longer the head when it takes pleasure in cutting the legs and arms away from its body. But would it not be better, as traitors say, when afflictions prevail over remedies, when the wound blackens and grows without measure, when gangrene first appears to our eyes, would it not be better to do without one limb than faintheartedly to send the whole body to the shroud? That aphorism is good when one must cure a member that one can sever without causing death, but

not when the sum of so many maladies has taken hold of the whole blood or of
the noble parts: Let the brain purge itself and realize that it is from itself that
the disease flows to the body of which it is king.)

Catherine de' Medici and her sons had thought to amputate the Huguenot
members of the state—we are reminded of Lucan's Sulla—but this spilling
of France's lifeblood had only demonstrated that these rulers themselves
were the cause of the contagion of civil war they sought to heal. *Princes* is an
extended satirical invective against the French monarchy, particularly
Charles IX and Henri III; as it attacks monarchical institutions themselves,
it includes Henri IV as well.

In his address to his readers, d'Aubigné felt the need to defend himself
from the charge of being a "republican" and of preferring an "aristocratic"
form of government, alleging that Henri IV, then only king of Navarre, had
read the poem himself several times and found nothing politically objectionable in it. The king had personally asked the poet his views on the best
form of government and was answered

> that it was monarchy according to its founding (*institution*) among the French,
> and that after that of the French he thought that the best was that of the Poles.
> Pressed further on that of the French, he replied "I hold with everything that du
> Haillan says about it and hold as unjust all that has been changed about it, even
> when it were only the submission to the Popes. Philip the Fair was a brave ruler,
> but it is difficult to believe that he who submits to another's yoke can give a
> bearable yoke to his own subjects." (8)

D'Aubigné's profession of political belief is both disingenuously evasive for
the censor and forthright for those who can read between the lines. The idea
that submission to papal authority would be the least exceptionable of the
changes undergone by the French monarchy since its beginnings is, of
course, ironic in the mouth of the Huguenot writer; and it is laced with
historical irony in the context of this interview with the then still-Protestant
Henry IV. Moreover, it places d'Aubigné within a tradition defending Galli-
can independence in ecclesiastical matters, a respectable enough position
for Catholics themselves to hold. But it is, above all, a red herring that
distracts attention from the more radical assertion that it is the *original*
French monarchy that the poet prefers before all others. For as the historian
du Haillan had observed, the first kings of France were *elected* by their aristocracy, and this was also the practice of the Polish monarchy, d'Aubigné's
runner-up for the best form of government: Henry III had been elected king
of Poland before the early death of Charles IX brought him to the throne of
France.[109] Thus the poet's politics are in sixteenth-century terms aristocratic
and republican after all: his ideal king, like the doge of Venice, possesses an
executive power that is carefully held in check by the great nobility.[110] With-

out such a control, the absolutist king becomes a "tyrant"; and in his preface (3), it is tyranny, not royalty, that d'Aubigné claims to attack in his poem.

In the somewhat later, unpublished treatise, *Du Debvoir mutuel des Roys et des subjects*, d'Aubigné—with what kind of sincerity it is difficult to determine—distances himself from those who "affect" du Haillan's portrait of an original, elective kingship.[111] The opening of this work, nonetheless, names and joins a tradition of Huguenot resistance literature that included Hotman's *Francogallia*—which specifically bases its political thought on the elective basis of the first French monarchy—and the *Vindiciae contra tyrannos*, attributed to de Mornay.[112] Like those works, d'Aubigné's own tract insists on the contractual nature of royal government, which subjects the king to the laws of the country that he is pledged to uphold, and on the right of his people to take measures, including the resort to arms, in order to ensure that the king keeps faith with them. The people's resistance has constitutionally authorized channels in the assemblies of nobles and the Estates-General, and d'Aubigné calls for a greater role for the aristocracy in the government of the country.

This attack on royal prerogative is of course in large part the product of the wars of religion and of the actions that Charles IX and Henri III had taken against their Huguenot subjects; in his treatise (483), d'Aubigné says that the Huguenots had insisted on the integrity of the king's faith in order that they themselves would not "be cut to pieces" ("mis en morceaux"). But in his poem these monarchomach sentiments, that after the accession and conversion of Henry IV ran counter to a prevailing absolutism and the emerging doctrine of the divine right of kings, are conflated with a more general tension between the nobility and the centralizing power of the crown. As Ercilla had depicted the Araucanian chiefs as warrior noblemen who obeyed no king, d'Aubigné places the Huguenots among a larger trans-European aristocracy in crisis, resisting monarchies that would deprive them of their customary martial identity and turn them into servile courtiers. The final long section of *Princes* features a debate between Fortune and Virtue that d'Aubigné had beheld in a dream vision when as a young man he had come to court (1099ff.) but had proved to be a "mauvais courtisan" (1175), unable to adapt to its corruption and dissimulations.[113]

Fortune upbraids the poet for his naive humanist study of classical authors who taught the paths of her rival, Virtue.

> Je t'espiois ces jours lisant, si curieux,
> La mort du grand Senecque et celle de Thrasee,
> Je lisois par tes yeux en ton ame embrasee
> Que tu envios plus Senecque que Neron,
> Plus mourir en Caton que vivre en Ciceron;
> Tu estimois la mort en liberté plus chere

Que tirer, en servant, une haleine precaire:
Ces termes specieux sont tels que tu conclus
Au plaisir de bien estre, ou bien de n'estre plus.

(1214–22)

(I observed you these days reading, so curiously, the death of the great Seneca
and that of Thraseas; I read from your eyes that in your kindled soul you envied
Seneca more than Nero, preferred to die as Cato than live as Cicero; you esteemed a death in freedom more dear than to draw a precarious breath as a
servant: these specious terms are those that you decided in favor of living, or
else of living no longer.)

Fortune reads the young d'Aubigné reading the ancient exemplars: he has
become one of his heroes, a Stoic foe of Nero who chose suicide rather than
a life as a servile courtier of the emperor, or one of those Stoics' heroes,
Cato, the enemy of Caesar. Fortune mocks this sequence of imitation by
citing the deplorable fates of the modern-day Huguenot exemplars of virtue, the Prince of Condé and Coligny, later to be identified as "our" modern
Cato: "Murdered, thrown down, dragged, mutilated, stripped naked"—
"Meurtri, précipité, traisné, mutilé, nu" (1230). This is where virtue gets
you, Fortune says. She notes parenthetically that her argument about the
great Huguenot nobles and war leaders depends on the poet's reading their
histories according to his own human judgment without giving heed to the
judgment of God (1237–38): here we are on the by now familiar ground of
the poem where the Stoic doctrine that virtue is its own reward is replaced,
though not invalidated, by the promise of Protestant election and of a divine reward. But Fortune continues with her secular reasoning and groups
the Huguenot magnates with other European high noblemen and military
heroes, both Catholic and Protestant, whose virtue went unrewarded or
even caused their disgrace and death at the hands of their ungrateful monarchs: the Duke of Parma, Gonsalvo de Cordoba, Don Juan of Austria, the
Duke of Alba, the Earl of Essex (1246–50). These men of arms have been
displaced by sycophantic and effeminate courtiers, and Fortune now advises
the poet how to succeed at court—her proper domain where favor is bestowed at the random caprice of the king. Her speech is a satirical attack on
the putatively homosexual court of Henri III and his *mignons*: the poet is
first counseled to prostitute himself, and then, as his own youthful charms
fade, to pimp for others.

Je reviens à ce siecle où nos mignons viellis,
A leur dernier mestier vouëz et accueillis,
Pipent les jenes gens, les gagnent, les courtisent;
Eux, autresfois produicts, à la fin les produisent,

Faisans, plus advisez, moins glorieux que toy,
Par le cul d'un coquin chemin au coeur d'un Roy.

(1313–18)

(I return to this century where our aging mignons, welcoming and devoted to their last project, entrap, win over and court young men; they, having formerly been produced, at the end produce them in turn: wiser, less proud than you, by the backside of a knave they make a path to the heart of a King.)

This perpetuation of a series of royal favorites in the school of vice that is the court is a kind of counterpart to the transmission of virtue through humanist reading and imitation.

The brilliantly nasty final verse, with its alliteration and internal rhyme, "coquin/chemin," is too much for Virtue who has been standing by and listening at the door. With the young poet's manhood at stake, she intervenes, driving Fortune away before her, and directs the poet on the path of honor, not the false *honneur* (1338, 1373, 1398, 1464) of titles and office given out by the monarch to his soft-living courtiers, but the honor of the battlefield.[114]

Cerche l'honneur, mais non celuy de ces mignons
Qui ne mordent au loup, bien sur leur compagnons;
Qu'ils prennent le duvet, toy la dure et la peine,
Eux le nom de mignons, et toy de capitaine;
Eux le musc, tu auras de la meche le feu;
Eux les jeux, tu auras la guerre pour ton jeu.

. . . .

Puis que ton coeur royal veust s'asservir aux Rois,
Va suivre les labeurs du Prince Navarrois,
Et là tu trouveras mon logis chez Anange,
Anange que je suis et (qui est chose estrange)
Là ou elle n'est plus, aussi tost je ne suis;
Je l'aime en la chassant, la tuant je la suis;
Là où elle prend pied, la pauvrette m'appelle;
Je ne puis m'arrester ni sans ni avec elle;
Je crain bien que, l'ayant bannie de ce Roy,
Tu n'y pourras plus voir bien tost elle ni moy.
Va t'en donc imiter ces eslevez courages
Qui cherchent les combats au travers des naufrages;
Là est le choix des coeurs et celui des esprits;
Là moi-mesme je suis de moi-mesme le prix.

(1449–54, 1470–82)

(Seek honor, but not that of the mignons who do not bite at the wolf, but readily at their companions; let them take the soft downy mattresses, you the hard earth and its pain; them the name of mignons, you that of captain; them musk, you the perfume of gunpowder; them courtly games, you will have war as your game.

. . . .

Since your royal heart wishes to place itself in the service of kings, go follow the labors of the Prince of Navarre, and there you will find my dwelling place by the side of Necessity, Necessity who I myself am and—a strange thing—where she no longer is, I am immediately absent: I love her while I pursue her, and in killing her, I become her instead; wherever she goes, the poor thing calls me, and I cannot rest either with or without her; I very much fear that when she has been banished from this King, you will no longer be able to find either her or me beside him. Go then and imitate those exalted courageous spirits who seek for combat in the midst of shipwreck; there is the chosen place of great hearts and souls; there I am myself the reward of myself.)

D'Aubigné literally makes a virtue out of Necessity ("Anange"): his younger self is instructed to seek out the hardships of the battlefield, to take over the traditional martial role of the aristocrat rather than the new courtly identity offered to him by the centralizing monarchy. The strategy of the passage is to exhort noblemen—not only Huguenots but also members of the Catholic majority—to take sides with Henry of Navarre against a corrupt king and a royal power encroaching on their independence, and it announces the destabilizing pattern of allegiances that would afflict French politics until the defeat of the Fronde. The failed revolt against de Luynes in 1620, which d'Aubigné joined with a group of intransigent Protestants, was one chapter in a continuing struggle between the nobility and the crown, colored by issues of religion. At the time of the young poet's vision, the Prince of Navarre is still on the outs with the Valois kings and can thus be a rallying point for aristocratic virtue and honor. But, as Virtue herself predicts, in a passage that was probably added in retrospect at a later date, once Navarre reaches the throne as Henri IV, the situation will change, both because of his conversion to Catholicism and because he will form a court of his own.[115] Virtue can only flourish in adversity and in an adversarial relationship to the king.

Lucan's epic had depicted the struggle of an aristocratic patriciate to preserve its control over the Roman republic against the threat of imperial monarchy. The epics in his tradition continue this pattern: in the *Araucana*, the freedom-loving Indians are seen as nature's noblemen resisting the imposition of a king over them; in *Les Tragiques*, the Huguenots, seeking to preserve an aristocratic life of honor apart from the corruption of the court, rebel against royal authority. And Richard McCoy has shown that Samuel Daniel's unfinished poem, *The Civil Wars*, the main English epic on the model of the *Pharsalia*, similarly explores, in its treatment of the War of the Roses, the conflict between the crown and the factious nobility, between "order or honor."[116] In epic, this political struggle goes back to the genre's very beginning, to the quarrel between King Agamemnon and his greatest fighting man, Achilles; the *Iliad* clearly takes the side of Achilles against his selfish and even ignoble ruler. We have already seen how Virgil "resolves" this struggle for an Augustan ideology of one-man rule by making Aeneas both commander in chief and chief warrior at the same time. And sixteenth-century Virgilian epics that uphold central political authorities over their feudatory subordinates will present Agamemnon figures as their central heroes: Tasso's popelike Goffredo, to whom the Achillean Rinaldo must submit; Spenser's Arthur, the monarchical figurehead who is, Spenser notes in his Letter to Raleigh, modeled on Agamemnon in whom Homer "ensampled a good governour." The choice between the epic traditions of Lucan and Virgil is thus at one level a choice between aristocracy and king. D'Aubigné's choice seemed clear enough, especially to his enemies, according to whom "il affectoit plus le gouvernement aristocratique que monarchique."

And yet, d'Aubigné's personified Virtue presupposes that the young nobleman with a "royal heart" needs a king to serve. For, however much he may chafe at the prospect of being transformed from warrior into courtier, of losing traditional privileges and local autonomy, the aristocrat needs the monarchy at the top of the social hierarchy precisely in order to preserve his own rank and identity within it. How can the nobleman have a king's heart—with all the assertion of aristocratic autonomy and honor that it implies—without the very king he seeks to emulate? This is the paradox noted by Norbert Elias in his analysis of the court society that came definitively into being under Louis XIV, and it helps to explain the failure of the Fronde and of other revolts against the name of the king.[117]

Not least of these was the resistance from 1590 to 1594 of the Catholic League inside Paris against Henri IV. The shoe was now on the other foot: a Catholic rebellion against a Huguenot king. One of the celebrated documents to emerge from this event was a League propaganda pamphlet, the *Dialogue d'entre le maheustre et le manant* of François Cromé, published in December of 1593 after Henri's abjuration of Protestantism in July of that year. Both speakers of the dialogue are Catholics: the *maheustre* is a nobleman who had gone over to his king; the *manant* is a Parisian bourgeois and *ligueur*, who refuses to credit the sincerity of Henri's conversion. And the *manant* extends his attack on the king to include the nobility itself.

Manant: The general species of nobility is founded only on the basis of the virtue that one acquires, and not on that acquired from others; and the title of nobility must be personal, and not hereditary, so much so that he who is not virtuous cannot be noble. And I beg you to believe this solely by the experience that we have seen and heard for the last thirty or forty years: that the nobility at present is nothing but an imaginary species, without any effective deeds, and the fault is due to nothing but the fact that your children are contented with their high birth and do not seek out the path of virtue; and there have been, as there still are, more monsters of tyranny than of a virtuous and valorous nobility.

Maheustre: We'll show you just how much force and valor we retain: your League and rebellion won't succeed at all. You will see how you will be more harshly punished, and you'll recognize how much the nobility of nowadays is worth, and that you should not disdain it, but, on the contrary, seek it out and honor it, and the people must believe in and obey the nobility.

Manant: It would be better if they believed in and obeyed their God and His Church than in a heretical king and a false nobility. The belief of a people and their obedience to their King is founded on that to their God, and if the Prince forgets God and goes against His Church, the people no longer have an oath of obligation or obedience to him. Furthermore, it is better to disobey and flee from a nobility that is ambitious and upholds the party of the heretic, than to favor them and lose both Religion and State; and as long as the nobility follows the party of the heretic or wishes to tyrannize, the people cannot favor and obey them; but if, on the other hand, the nobility wishes to band against the heretic, to exterminate him and throw him out of the kingdom, and elect a Catholic king, full of piety and justice, and wishes no longer to make war against the people, but rather to maintain and favor them, than you will see all the people in return honor and gratify them, and submit themselves in devotion to them, and no sooner.

Maheustre: If you don't do so, all your arguments won't save you; you will see that the sword of the nobility is stronger than that of the people, and what you won't do out of love, force will make you do to your great distress.[118]

While the idea that nobility is based on virtuous deeds rather than on birth is a commonplace, here it contributes to the stirring of class conflict: the *ligueurs'* opposition to the king constitutes an attack on the aristocracy as well. The *maheustre* earlier declares that one of his reasons for joining the royalist forces of Henri IV against the League is that "we are French Catholics who are resisting a popular violence that wishes to emerge to the prejudice of the privileges of the nobility, to extinguish it and to form a democracy" (51). The threat of popular unrest from the bottom drives the nobility toward their king, however doubtful his religious convictions. The *maheustre's* position, in fact, so conformed to Henri's own appeal to the French aristocracy, Catholic and Protestant, to rally behind him against the Parisian *ligueurs* that he had the *Dialogue* reprinted in a revised version as part of his own propaganda.[119]

The extremists of both sides of the French religious conflict sought to justify resistance to monarchical authority—and both Henri III and Henri IV would die at the hands of assassins. But for the aristocracy the prospect of no king could be as daunting as that of royal tyranny. D'Aubigné's portrait of the sick French body politic infected from the head downwards by its corrupt kings is balanced by an earlier passage in *Misères*, where France appears as a diseased giant.

> Son corps est combatu, à soi-mesme contraire:
> Le sang pur ha le moins, le flegme et la colere
> Rend le sang non sang; le peuple abat ses loix,
> Tous nobles et tous Rois, sans nobles et sans Rois;
> La masse degenere en la melancholie;

(Misères 141–45)

(His body is fought over, enemy to itself: it has the least part of pure blood, phlegm and choler make the blood no longer blood; the people destroy their laws, all nobles and kings, without nobles and kings; the mass degenerates into melancholy.)

Here the contagion rises from below: the people disregard the law and aspire to be nobles and kings, destroying degreees of rank and the entire social order. The clinical conceit of blood and "humours" also contains the mystifying notion of an aristocratic purity of blood, of a nobility conferred by birth, as opposed to the meritocratic basis of nobility argued by the *manant*. As this pure blood is displaced by baser strains, the body politic *degenerates*. The destinies of the nobility and the king are linked together, as they face a common popular enemy. D'Aubigné may be a republican, but he is no democrat. (The Calvinist poet who would defend regicide and a kingless republic would be instead the middle-class, if hardly more democratic Milton.) D'Aubigné's social conservatism tempers his monarchomach radicalism, leaving him in the dilemma that would be shared by more than one European aristocrat in the following century: he can live neither with nor without a king.

Poetry and Power

D'Aubigné's ambivalence toward the necessary evil that is kingship, his resistance both to a concentration of power in the monarch and to a leveling of power in popular rule, characterizes the aristocratic republicanism of all three epics of Lucan's tradition. It is also a corollary of the ambivalence of these poems toward the genre of epic itself, particularly toward the rival Virgilian epic of empire to which they set themselves in opposition, but to which they nonetheless share a class allegiance, both ideological and aesthetic. This underlying allegiance suggests why these anti-epics of the losing side cannot escape the terms of the Virgilian model they contest, and why they have been relegated to a secondary place in literary history.

In a famous discussion of Shakespeare's *Coriolanus*, William Hazlitt describes the nature of the poetic imagination that is by turns aristocratic, royal, and tyrannical.

> The language of poetry naturally falls in with the language of power. The imagination is an exaggerating and exclusive faculty: it takes from one thing to add to another: it accumulates circumstances together to give the greatest possible effect to a favourite object. The understanding is a dividing and measuring faculty: it judges of things not according to their immediate impressions on the mind, but according to their relations to one another. The one is a monopolising faculty, which seeks the greatest quantity of present excitement by inequality and disproportion; the other is a distributive faculty, which seeks the greatest quantity of good, by justice and proportion. The one is aristocratical, the other a republican faculty. The principle of poetry is a very anti-levelling principle. It aims at effect, it exists by contrast. It admits of no medium. It is everything by excess. It rises above the ordinary standard of sufferings and crimes. It presents a dazzling appearance. It shows its head, turetted, crowned, and crested. Its front is gilt and blood-stained. Before it, "it carries noise and behind it leaves tears." It has its altars and its victims, sacrifices and human sacrifices. Kings, priests, nobles, are its train-bearers, tyrants and slaves its executioners.—"Carnage is its daughter." Poetry is right-royal. It puts the individual before the species, the one above the infinite, might before right.[120]

This brilliant passage outlines the psychology of the epic sublime, as well as the egotistical sublime,[121] and it may offer the terms to explain the *poetic* disadvantage at which the losers' epic finds itself next to the Virgilian victors' epic where poetry and power mutually support one another to impose themselves on the human mind: an epic that "accumulates circumstances together" into a master narrative in order to promote the idea of a single, centralizing power ultimately vouched in an individual ruler. It is against this kind of "monopolizing" teleological narrative that the epics of Lucan's tradition practice their narrative disjunction and episodic digression. When Hazlitt talks of a prosaic, republican understanding that divides and distributes power itself, we may see an analogy to their deliberate rejection of formal unity.

Yet these poems of lost republican causes are still products of an aristocratic imagination, giving voice to the ambitions of an oligarchy that may as much seek a partnership with the monarch in the monopoly of power as it resists monarchical domination. They cannot give up the idea of power that for Hazlitt, as later for William Empson, inheres in that habit of poetic thought or metaphor that makes the one stand in place of the many.[122] Thus

Lucan can at once lament the loss of the free Roman republic and hope for the perpetuation of Rome's imperial domination of her subject peoples; Ercilla at once celebrates the Araucanian resistance to the Spanish conquistadors and extols Spain's world empire; d'Aubigné at once portrays the Huguenots as helpless victims of persecution and as victorious saints accompanying an all-powerful King of Kings at the end of time. As Hazlitt suggests, the aristocratic and monarchical imaginations, whatever differences they may have between them, are of one piece: a patrician imagination, dreaming epic visions of martial power and princely splendor, opposed to an unpoetic plebeian common sense.

A simpler, more obvious way of putting this is that the losers' epics would all—not so secretly—like to be epics of history's winners. Not only do their poets long for a reversal of history that would put their side on top, but they also long to write with the same concentration of poetic energy that the imagination of power grants to the victors' epic: the poetic power that attracts them to the epic genre itself. But these writers cannot have it both ways. In order to contest the claims that their victorious enemies make to have the last word on history, they have to open up and break apart their own poems, to focus on a series of parts rather than the whole—though d'Aubigné's poem also counters such a final verdict by invoking an alternative Last Judgment that is outside of history itself. The losers' epic risks above all a loss of form, and the history it recounts begins to resemble the indefinite wandering plots of romance: as d'Aubigné writes, he and his Church are still exiled in the wilderness. These poems knowingly condemn themselves to formal shortcomings relative to the closed classical structures of Virgilian epic and, hence, to an indefinite generic status: critics have debated whether they are epics at all, and the secondary canonical place that they have historically enjoyed among the "classics" only seems to bear out Hazlitt's uneasy view that power makes the best poetry. Only by bravely embracing a position of poetic, as well as political, weakness can Lucan and his successors make epic speak on behalf of the defeated.

PART THREE

TASSO AND MILTON

FIVE

POLITICAL ALLEGORY IN THE

GERUSALEMME LIBERATA

SINCE the post-Risorgimento criticism of Francesco De Sanctis, literary historians and critics have generally deplored the political ideology of Tasso's *Gerusalemme liberata* without, however, inquiring too closely or curiously into its details. The poem was written in the world after the Council of Trent, when Italy had surrendered its political and intellectual liberty to Spanish and papal domination. Seeking the cultural origins of the new unified Italy of his own day, De Sanctis found them in a tradition of resistance to the ideological closure effected by the Counter-Reformation Church.

> The virility of intellect in Italy was not with Rome but with the opposition. And if we want to trace the beginnings of the new Italy, we must seek them in the opposition that it raised to Spain and the pope, for the history of this opposition is the history of the new life.[1]

Incipit vita nuova. But on the face of it, the religious and political themes of the *Liberata* do not belong to this new life, this history of opposition, but to Rome itself. To save Tasso's epic for the national tradition, De Sanctis declared that its poetic value lay elsewhere: in its idyllic and elegiac episodes.[2] The gesture by which the great critic deflects attention away from the poem's objectionable ideology and toward its purple passages was repeated by subsequent criticism that was influenced as well by the Crocean rejection of ideology, itself, as "non-poesia." In place of idyll and elegy, Eugenio Donadoni finds the true poetry of the *Liberata* to lie in a closely related "passionalità" that transcends the poet's historical moment; Giovanni Getto locates this poetry instead in Tasso's melancholy lyricism, tinged by intimations of death.[3]

Thus if Tasso's politics were a scandal, they were best declared unpoetic and dismissed from closer scrutiny; only recently has such scrutiny begun to enter critical discussions of the *Liberata*.[4] The two parts of this chapter examine episodes in the epic that suggest the extent to which topical allusion and contemporary ideological writing are inscribed in Tasso's language and fictions. They examine, respectively, the careers in the poem of two rebels: the hero Rinaldo whose insubordination toward the Crusader captain Goffredo is mirrored in the open mutiny of Argillano; and the Ethiopian heroine Clorinda, who is a "rebel"—"rubella" (12.65;87)—to the

Christian God. Here, indeed, are representations of that resistance to the papacy that De Sanctis longed to find in the Italian literary tradition. But the ways in which their rebellions are put down reveal a Tasso who not only is an apologist for papal supremacy, but who also upholds this supremacy at the expense of Italian political aspirations, and who repeatedly conceives of political struggle in terms of a conflict between orthodoxy and heresy. The poet's politics may be more scandalous than De Sanctis even suspected.

Argillano's Revolt

In 1553, six years before Tasso first began to sketch out the poem on the First Crusade that was to become the *Gerusalemme liberata*, the Catholic monarchs Philip II and Mary Tudor acceded to the throne of England, after the Protestant reigns of Henry VIII and Edward VI. The event was celebrated in an encomiastic oration, *De restituta in Anglia religione* ("On the restoration of religion in England"), by the minor Modenese humanist, Antonio Fiordibello. In one passage Fiordibello searches for a precedent to the achievement of the new English rulers.

> The deeds of what kings or emperors were ever so great, magnificent and glorious that they can be compared, for piety, greatness, and glory to this act of yours? Most frequently and especially admired are the exploits of Godfrey, Bohemund, and Baldwin, those most famous of commanders, who once marched out of these western regions into Asia, and having defeated and overcome enemy armies in the name of Christianity, recovered the city of Jerusalem and the holiest sepulchre of our saviour Christ. And truly they were the most deserving of merit from the republic of Christendom, nor were any more glorious or outstanding deeds of prowess ever performed against enemy forces by our ancestors. Even so, in my judgment, this action of yours is the most glorious and outstanding. For they opened the way to Christ's sepulchre for those Christians who wished to make a pilgrimage for the sake of religion: you have opened the entrance to the celestial homeland and to Christ Himself for this great nation. They restored to the Church those places that were, so to speak, the cradle of our Religion. You restored to the Church her own great and especially noble part, which had been lost to her. Finally, they performed their exploits with a great slaughter of those peoples who were indeed barbarian pagans, but nonetheless men: you have recalled to life this English people, who, because of their separation from the Church, were perishing. Moreover, you have accomplished so great a deed without an army, without force, without weapons, but with such great piety, wisdom, and authority.[5]

For Fiordibello the heroism of the First Crusade finds its modern equivalent in Philip and Mary's reclamation of England for Catholicism, in the efforts of the Counter-Reformation to recover the territories of the Church lost to heresy. The armed struggle against the Muslim infidel is superseded by the reconversion of Protestants. Fiordibello describes this reconversion as a purely spiritual process of persuasion, and praises it for its lack of violence or coercion—thus glossing over its political character and failing to anticipate the events that gave Bloody Mary Tudor her sobriquet.

This linking of the Crusades with the reunification of the Church, suggesting that the reunification is indeed a new crusade, is shared by the ideology and fiction of the *Liberata*. Tasso's epic portrays the taking of Jerusalem by the knights of the First Crusade under the leadership of Goffredo (Godefroi) of Boulogne. But Goffredo finds himself fighting on two fronts. Before he can conquer the Muslim defenders of Jerusalem, he must restore unity in his own ranks, particularly with regard to the hero Rinaldo, whose defection and eventual return to the Christian army imitates the model of Achilles and gives the poem its generally Iliadic shape. Goffredo's task is spelled out from the first octave of the epic.

> Il Ciel gli diè favore, e sotto a i santi
> segni ridusse i suoi compagni erranti.
>
> (1.1.7–8)

(Heaven favored him and he brought back his errant comrades beneath his holy banners.)

The "santi / segni" refer both to the army banners that indicate allegiance to Goffredo's command and to the cross that is displayed upon the banners: the political errancy of Goffredo's recalcitrant knights is equated with a spiritual, religious error. The equation becomes explicit in one episode of the *Liberata*, Argillano's revolt against the authority of Goffredo's captainship in canto 8, where a series of topical and literary allusions draw an analogy to the Protestant schism of Tasso's own day. The epic thus depicts a double crusade: against the infidel outside the Church, against disunity and potential heresy within. Moreover, the link that the poem makes between Argillano's rebellion and the disobedience of Rinaldo draws us to a further level of topical allusion involving Tasso's patron, the Este duke of Ferrara, and his relationship with the papacy, the Church in its guise as a temporal, political power.

The seeds of Argillano's revolt in canto 8 are planted when a party of scouts returns to the Crusader camp with the report (8.47–56) that a corpse missing both its head and right hand has been found and is believed to be that of Rinaldo, whom Goffredo banished three cantos earlier for his unruly violence and insubordination. The belief is false and is the result of a deception engineered by the young pagan sorceress Armida (10.53–56): the corpse is one of Rinaldo's own victims that Armida has clothed in the hero's discarded armor. She has, moreover, planted one of her servants disguised as a shepherd near the body; he hints (8.55) that Rinaldo was killed by soldiers from his own Christian army. That evening the diabolic Fury Aletto (Allecto), following plans made at the opening of the canto with her fellow devil Astragorre (1–4), appears in a dream to Argillano, an Italian soldier and compatriot of Rinaldo. In the dream Argillano sees (59–62) the trunk of Rinaldo's body, which bears the hero's head in its left hand: the head speaks and tells Argillano that he was murdered by Goffredo, who plans to kill Argillano and his companions as well. Argillano addresses the Italian troops and, after voicing indignation at their common subordination to the foreign Frankish captain, discloses the contents of his dream, accusing Goffredo of having envied the "valor latino" (67) of Rinaldo. The ensuing rebellion spreads (72) to include the Swiss and English soldiers as well. Informed of the uprising, Goffredo prays to God, protesting his abhorrence of civil strife (76), and then goes to meet the mutineers unarmed. Divinely inspired, his face resplendent with celestial majesty, Goffredo is able to restore order to the army simply by his speech and presence. He pardons all except Argillano, who is turned over to him for execution.

There is an epic model for Tasso's episode in the mutiny of Julius Caesar's army in the fifth book of the *Pharsalia* (237–374). There are no direct echoes, but the scenario is much the same: the general faces down the rage of the mob, puts an end to the rebellion merely by his undaunted words and countenance, and demands the execution of the ringleaders. We might be initially surprised that Tasso should model the pious Goffredo on Lucan's Caesar, the clear villain of the *Pharsalia*. Yet Goffredo plays this same Caesar elsewhere in the *Liberata*. His interview with Armida in canto 4, I have noted in Chapter 1, recalls the meeting of Caesar and Cleopatra in Book 10 of the *Pharsalia* (80f.)—though Goffredo, unlike Caesar, proves impervious to feminine wiles and charms. His speech to the Crusader army before the climactic battle in canto 20 (14–19) is closely modeled on Caesar's speech to his troops in Book 7 of the *Pharsalia* before the battle of Pharsalia, while the Egyptian Emireno's speech (25–27) imitates the corresponding speech of Lucan's loser, Pompey (369–73). We have seen how Ercilla uses the same speeches from the *Pharsalia* as models for the harangues to the fleets of the Ottoman and the Spanish sides in his depiction of Lepanto, but the Spanish poet is careful to cast the Turkish commander, Ochali, as the unjust Caesar. Tasso's adherence to the Virgilian, imperial model of epic causes him to rewrite the alternative model of Lucan and make Caesar into the hero of the *Pharsalia*. The identification of Goffredo with Caesar, Lucan's enemy of republican liberty, suggests just how authoritarian is the political thought of Tasso's poem. And if these politics determine his reading of the *Pharsalia* against the grain, they also inform Tasso's revision of the *Iliad*: for Goffredo is also modeled on Agamemnon, an Agamemnon who is in the right while Rinaldo's Achilles is in the wrong.

A further series of literary models and topical allusions give the episode a layer of contemporary political meaning. The dream vision of Aletto in the guise of the mutilated Rinaldo is drawn from Dante's headless figure of Bertran de Born, who appears among the sowers of discord and schism in *Inferno* 28.112–42. The Dantesque emblem of the lacerated body politic is appropriate to the dramatic situation of Argillano's revolt against the head of the Crusader forces. Bertran's placement, moreover, in a canto whose central character is Mohammed (28–63) and which alludes to Fra Dolcino (55–60) suggests that, already for Dante, the crucial body politic in question is the body of the Church, threatened by heretical schism. This idea is confirmed in Tasso's episode when, according to the plan announced by Astragorre at the beginning of canto 8 (3), Argillano's rebellion spreads first to the Swiss, then to the English troops: to the sixteenth-century Protestant enemies of Rome.

An anti-Protestant polemic may underlie the Virgilian imitation in the episode as well. Conflated with the mutilated ghost of Hector, who appears to the dreaming Aeneas in Book 2 (268–97) of the *Aeneid*, the apparition of Aletto to Argillano more clearly recalls the passage of Book 7 (415f.), where the same Fury assumes a disguise to visit the sleeping Turnus and to instill in him the furor of battle, leading to the war in Italy that takes up the second half of Virgil's epic. Tasso's choice of this model for his episode of rebellion is logical enough: it is Virgil's great depiction of how the irrational violence of war is instigated, and the Virgilian fury is easily assimilated with Christian devils. But I would suggest that this choice was mediated by a recent anti-Lutheran tract by Girolamo Muzio, *L'Heretico infuriato*, published in 1562. Muzio was a humanist at the court of Urbino, where between 1557 and 1558 he had been a teacher of the young Tasso, at that time the thirteen-year-old school companion of the ducal heir, Francesco Maria della Rovere.[6] Muzio wrote the *Heretico infuriato* as a polemic against a certain Matthew of Jena, the Protestant Matthaeus Iudex, who in 1561 had published a pamphlet urging the emperor Ferdinand I to march on Rome and overthrow the pope.[7] At the beginning of his tract, Muzio explains its title.

Someone may perhaps wonder on seeing the title of this little pamphlet that, inasmuch as all heretics are not only furious, but diabolically possessed, that I should have given the name of furious to one in particular. Wherefore I think it fitting that I should give the reason for this before turning to other matters. I say, therefore, that in reading his writings, which have moved me to write a response, there was represented to my mind that infernal fury described by Virgil, which with her deadly trumpet blast kindled the peasants of Latium to take arms against the nobility of Troy. For not otherwise does a certain Matthew the judge and professor (as he titles himself) of the Academy of Jena, a city in Saxony, and author of the writing of which I speak, as if prompted by the burning torches of one of the infernal furies, go ranting, raving, and raging to arm against us men of all conditions.[8]

Muzio associates Virgil's Allecto with the diabolic inspiration of Protestantism, and views the Italian war of the *Aeneid* as a Lutheran Peasants' Revolt; he expresses a typical Counter-Reformation horror at the prospect of Protestantism setting the lower orders against their aristocratic social betters. Tasso similarly depicts Argillano's rebellion as a mutiny of the "vulgo folle" (74; 82). And he portrays Argillano as the recipient of a new spiritual inspiration—"gli spira / spirto novo di furor pieno" (62)—that equates the individual inspiration by which the Protestant claims authority outside the community and consensus of the Church with the suggestion of the devil: it is contrasted with a genuine working of the Spirit, the new and unwonted warmth—"un novo inusitato caldo" (77)—that Goffredo feels in response to his prayer.[9] Moreover, Argillano proposes a deviation from the Crusaders' goal that spells out the nature of his schism in typological terms.

> o pur vorrem lontano
> girne da lei, dove l'Eufrate inonda,
> dove a popolo imbelle in fertil piano
> tante ville e città nutre e feconda,
> anzi a noi pur? Nostre saranno, io spero,
> ne co' Franchi commune avrem l'impero.
>
> (8.69)

(Or shall we rather wish to travel far from Goffredo's power, where the Euphrates washes the land, where it nourishes and makes fruitful so many towns and cities on the fertile plain for a people unused to war—let it be for us instead? They will be ours, I hope, nor will we share our dominion with the Franks.)

Urging the Italians to leave Jerusalem to the Franks and to carve out a kingdom of their own, Argillano would lead them into the plain watered by the Euphrates—what appears to be the plain of Shinar (Sennaar) of the Bible (Gen. 10:10)—the site first of Babel and its tower, later of Babylon. It was common for sixteenth-century Catholics and Protestants to accuse each other of building Babylon, the earthly city of confusion, in opposition to Jerusalem, the true Church; both exploited the biblical analogy that had been decisively reshaped by Augustine in his discussion of the two cities in Book 14 of *The City of God*. Tasso may here again follow Muzio, who in Chapter 20 of his treatise, identifies Babylon with Saxony, the home of his Lutheran adversary.

And this Protestant doctrine was born and nourished in Germany; and principally in Saxony, whence as I have said issued the book of this furious spirit, and thence, catching like a plague, goes travelling through the world. This is therefore that proud and bold woman, this that whore, that goes fornicating with the Princes of the Earth, removing them from the true worship of God; this is she who is stained with the blood of the saints and prophets, who have been oppressed by the Princes and by the people who have endeavored to destroy the Catholic Faith. She has made herself the habitation of devils and the haven of all unclean spirits; and this is the great Babylon that is fallen; Babylon signifies confusion: and where was there ever greater confusion and where are Catholics more travailed and persecuted than in those regions? where did so many heresies ever exist at one time? . . . Fallen is the great Babylon, fallen from religion, fallen from devotion, and from the true faith. . . . Great Babylon, the largest among Christian nations, and which used to be unified like one city, now is divided against itself between Catholics and heretics, and the heretics among themselves.[10]

Argillano's exhortation to seek out a Babylonian realm by the Euphrates is thus inscribed by the language of Renaissance religious controversy. The secessionist alternative he offers reinforces the analogy between his revolt and Protestant schism.

As a fomenter of rebellion, Argillano has a prior history of participation in civil strife.

> nacque in riva del Tronto e fu nutrito
> ne le risse civil d'odio e di sdegno;
> poscia in essiglio spinto, i colli e'l lito
> empié di sangue e depredò quel regno,
> sin che ne l'Asia a guerreggiar se 'n venne
> e per fama miglior chiaro divenne.
>
> (8.58)

(He was born on the banks of the Tronto and raised amid civil quarrels of hatred and wrath; then, cast into exile, he filled the hills and shore with blood, and plundered that realm, until he came to do combat in Asia and became renowned with a better fame.)

Argillano's experience is one too often repeated in Renaissance Italy: an exile from his faction-torn city who becomes a bandit and scours the surrounding countryside. The city here is Ascoli Piceno. Located on the banks of the Tronto, it was subject to frequent civil violence and outbreaks of banditry in the sixteenth-century. Tasso may have modeled Argillano upon a particular historical bandit, Mariano Parisani, who was active around Ascoli in the 1560s. In 1561 Parisani went into exile from Ascoli after having killed three fellow citizens: a woman cousin, her husband, and her eighty-year-old father-in-law. For the next five years Parisani preyed upon the territory of Ascoli as the leader of a formidable troop of bandits. After defeating several papal forces sent against him, he finally left the region altogether and served as an honored mercenary in the employ of the dukes of Savoy and Tuscany.[11] Parisani's career is strikingly parallel to that of Tasso's Argillano, the bandit who turns his prowess to a better military cause. But Argillano has not, in fact, put his strife-ridden past behind him.

The real significance, however, of Tasso's topical allusion lies in the fact that Ascoli belonged to the States of the Church and that its bandits fought against papal troops: it casts Argillano's rebellion as another similar revolt against papal authority. This reading overlaps with the anti-Protestant overtones of the episode: when the revolt spreads to the Swiss and the English, the idea seems to be that opposition to the temporal power of the Church is the first dangerous step toward heresy and schism. Conversely, Protestantism is reduced to a purely political problem, a defiance of Rome that is equivalent to the acts of seditious bandits in the Papal States. Yet here, as was the case in Fiordibello's oration, the political problem is given what appears to be a spiritual solution: the sole presence and persuasion of Goffredo are enough to quell Argillano's mutiny. Tasso adds, however, a marvelous supplement at the very end of the episode: legend has it that a winged warrior was seen shielding Goffredo and brandishing a sword still dripping with blood:

> sangue era forse di città, di regni,
> che provocar del Cielo i tardi sdegni.
>
> (8.84)

(It was perhaps the blood of cities and kingdoms that provoked the delayed anger of Heaven.)

Goffredo's spiritual defense may possibly contain force after all, though it is a force transferred to God and his angel of wrath.

Implicit in this reading of Argillano's rebellion as political allegory is the identification, at some level, of Goffredo with the authority of the papacy; the unity that he seeks to maintain in the Crusader forces is the unity of the Church. Peter the Hermit has described what will be the nature of Goffredo's office at the beginning of the *Liberata*.

> Ove un sol non impera, onde i giudìci
> pendano poi de' premi e de le pene,
> onde sian compartite opre ed uffici,
> ivi errante il governo esser conviene.
> Deh! fate un corpo sol de' membri amici,
> fate un capo che gli altri indrizzi e frene,
> date ad un sol lo scettro e la possanza,
> e sostenga di re vece e sembianza.
>
> (1.31)

(Where there is not one ruler, on whom depends the determination of rewards and punishments, by whom are allotted tasks and duties, there government must be unstable. Ah, make one single body of loving members, make a head that directs and checks the others, give to one alone the sceptre and power, and let him undertake the role and guise of king.)

Here, too, Tasso's language derives from the polemics of the Counter-Reformation; as head of the Crusader body politic, Goffredo resembles not only king, but pope, the Vicar of Christ who on earth assumes the headship of the Church, which is the body of Christ.[12] Writing a confutation of Luther's arguments, Gaspare Contarini asserts:

> Therefore just as there is one body of Christians of which we are the members, so is there also one Pontiff in the Church, by whom this unity may be kept together on earth. For a multiple sovereignty is evil and is greatly detrimental to unity. . . . Of one Church, therefore, there should be one head, one ruler.[13]

The idea was a commonplace, but a Calvin would challenge it, arguing that the pope was "neither appointed leader of the Church by the Word of God, nor ordained by a legitimate act of the Church, but of his own accord, self-elected."[14] Tasso begins his poem with God Himself choosing Goffredo as captain of the army; He sends down Gabriel, the bearer of His Word, in a scene that recalls the Annunciation (1.13–17). When Goffredo is subsequently elected by a council of his peers under the inspiration of the Holy Spirit (32), we are meant to think of a papal election in the College of Cardinals.

Argillano's rebellion against Goffredo's duly constituted authority is not an isolated episode in the *Liberata*. Argillano is a mirror figure of the poem's central hero, Rinaldo, in whose name he leads his revolt.[15] He repeats Rinaldo's own earlier act of insubordination against Goffredo: Rinaldo's refusal to submit to Goffredo's judgment in canto 5 (42–44) after he has killed the insulting Norwegian prince, Gernando. On that occasion Tancredi persuaded Rinaldo not to fight Goffredo—"con le piaghe indegne de' cristiani / trafigger Cristo, ond'ei son membra e parte" (5.46; "and with unworthy wounds upon Christians to wound Christ, of whom they are members and limbs"). Argillano's rebellion thus inflicts the civil strife and wounds on the Christian body politic that Rinaldo had been on the point of inflicting himself. Conversely, Rinaldo's eventual decision to leave the Crusader camp in exile is much like the schismatic departure from Jerusalem that Argillano will later urge upon his followers.[16] The two characters are further linked by the issue of Italian political subjugation. Possessed by the devil, the proud Gernando scorns Rinaldo who was born "ne la serva Italia" (5.19), and Gernando's death at Rinaldo's hands is a kind of vindication of Italian honor against the northern "barbaro signor." (This idea was more forcefully articulated in an earlier version of the poem that survives in manuscript. The character Gernando was formerly named Ernando and was the prince of Castile: the episode was explicitly directed against Spanish hegemony over Italy before Tasso prudently revised it.)[17] But when Argillano makes a similar patriotic gesture, it is *he* who is depicted as diabolically possessed, inciting the Italian troops to rebel against their Frankish captains and a "popolo barbaro e tiranno" (8.63), to avenge affronts that would make Italy and Rome burn with scorn and anger for a thousand years—"tal ch'arder di scorno, arder di sdegno / potrà da qui a mill'anni Italia e Roma" (64).

Argillano is thus a stand-in for Rinaldo, one who discloses the more serious dangers and consequences of the hero's actions, of Rinaldo's assertions of (Italian) independence from Goffredo's rule. And Argillano is also a fall guy, punished by the poem so that Rinaldo can be forgiven and rehabilitated. In fact, Goffredo demands that Argillano be handed over for justice in the same breath with which he pardons the absent Rinaldo (8.80–81): the hero is welcomed back to do submission to Goffredo (18.1–2), while the revolt of the minor character is sternly put down. The repentant Argillano will later escape from prison to be killed in battle by the pagan warrior Solimano (9.87); it is probably significant that Solimano *beheads* him.[18] Rinaldo escapes this fate by killing the same Solimano (20.107) in the poem's final battle.

Argillano and Rinaldo are further, and perhaps most significantly, linked by topical allusion. Rinaldo is the fictional ancestor of the Este dukes of Ferrara, the last of whom, Alfonso II, was Tasso's patron. Ferrara was a papal fief, and the Este ruled the city as knights of Saint Peter and vassals of the Apostolic See. Thus Rinaldo's relationship to Goffredo, no less than that of Argillano, the rebellious bandit from Ascoli Piceno, can point to a contemporary conflict between a refractory dependent subject and the Church as a temporal, territorial power. Read as topical allegory, Rinaldo's differences and eventual reconciliation with Goffredo map out a sufficiently ambivalent relationship between the Este and the papacy. In fact, this relationship had been far from easy. Julius II and Leo X had schemed militarily unsuccessfully to drive the Este dukes out of Ferrara early in the century; their successors sought the same objective by diplomatic means, and recent history had produced new sources of antagonism.

The Este grievances with Rome are neatly listed in a document drawn up for Alfonso II in 1578, entitled "Document in which appear the reasonable suspicions that His Highness could continually have had that the Popes of his time were about to move against him."[19] This memorandum notes the various disputes, conflicts, slights, and accusations that Alfonso had endured from the papacy, listing them year by year and month by month from 1562 up to the present of 1578, and labeling them in the margin under various reappearing categories, such as "saltworks," "precedence," "reprisals," "borders" (with the neighboring papal territory of Bologna), "war," "imputations," and "complaints." The first two of these were the major causes of irritation and discord between the two powers. The saltworks of Comacchio were a major sector of Ferrara's economy, but they constituted competition for the papal saltworks at Cervia. Pius IV and Pius V forbade the production and transport of salt through the duchy to Lombard markets, prohibitions that Alfonso defied, continuing the salt trade unabated while sending ambassadors to negotiate endlessly before ecclesiastical courts in Rome. The other major issue dividing the Este from the papacy was their precedence controversy with the Medici; it became their overriding diplomatic concern during the decades of the 1560s and 1570s, and it had international repercussions.[20]

The controversy dated back to 1541 when Duke Ercole II claimed for his ambassador a place of greater honor at the papal court than that accorded to the Florentine ambassador of Cosimo I de' Medici. For while the Este could trace their lordship back to the feudal twelfth century, the Medici banker-princes had only recently been ennobled. A diplomatic battle ensued, waged by both ducal houses with elaborate negotiations and hefty bribes. In the 1560s, jurisdiction to determine the question was claimed both by the Emperor Ferdinand, who favored the Este, and by the pope, Pius IV, who was pro-Medici. It was the latter's successor, Pius V, who in 1569 named Cosimo Grand Duke of Tuscany, raising him to a higher rank and to the titles of "Serenissimo" and "Altezza," and thus guaranteeing him precedence over Alfonso II. The pope was partly moved to his action by his irritation over the issue of the saltworks. Alfonso reacted by refusing to join the Holy League created by Pius in 1570 to fight the Turks—the "Scrittura" makes the unlikely charge that, instead, the pope "excluded the person of the Lord Duke of Ferrara who had been proposed to be the General of the League against the infidels"[21]—and the bad blood created by the affair contributed to the emperor's absence from the League as well. Thus Tasso, the poet of the First Crusade, wrote under the patronage of one of the few major Italian courts that did *not* participate at Lepanto.

There was a third question, not mentioned in the "Scrittura," that lay ominously in the background of Este relations with the papacy. The same Pius V had on May 23, 1567, issued a bull that forbade illegitimate family lines from inheriting feudal titles in papal domains. The bull seems to have been aimed particularly at Alfonso, who was widely (and, as it turned out, correctly) believed to be sterile—so the Medici ambassador to Ferrara, Bernardo Canigiani, reported in December of the same year[22]—and who had no legitimate collateral heirs. The very future of the Este in Ferrara was menaced, and, in fact, after Alfonso's death in 1597 the duchy would finally be swallowed up into the States of the Church. The threat was real, but, as the omission from the "Scrittura" suggests, it does not seem, as some modern scholars have maintained, to have been a central objective of Este diplomacy in the decade following 1567, the period when Tasso was composing his poem. Only in the second half of the 1580s did Alfonso begin to make vain attempts to obtain legitimacy for first one, then another bastard cousin.[23]

Relations between Ferrara and Rome were thus strained, and Alfonso sought alliances with other powers to play off against his papal overlords. The Este were also dukes of Modena and Reggio, which they held as imperial fiefs, and Alfonso's marriage in 1565 to Barbara of Austria, the daughter of Ferdinand I, brought him closer into the sphere and protection of the Hapsburg empire. But the duke sought other alliances in the north as well. In 1575 the Venetian ambassador, Emilio Maria Manolesso, reported, mildly scandalized, that Alfonso had gone to the great trouble of learning German, "a language which isn't learned for pleasure, because it is most barbarous," and that he maintained close relations with the Lutheran duke of Saxony.[24] But those in the know, Manolesso continued, thought that the duke had no other goal in his friendship with the German Protestants than to use the fearful prospect of their descending upon Italy as a weapon against the pope and Florence. The Florentine ambassador, Canigiani, recounts actual threats against the pope voiced by Ferrarese courtiers. On July 12, 1568, he wrote back to Cosimo I:

> One hears that the cause of the saltworks in Rome is not going according to the Duke's wishes, with all the good offices done for him by the Emperor, by the Catholic King of Spain, by many cardinals, and in the person of Signor Don Francesco d'Este: and I begin to think, that as much as they may boast that their cause is so just, they're telling lies as usual and believing them: But the beauty of it is that these intriguers and their servants are secretly letting out that this pope, irritating so great a prince, and a relation of the Emperor and of so many great kings and princes is looking to have him summon down here a swarm of Huguenots: now let Your Most Illustrious Excellency see with what weapons we here want to defend the wrong, and make His Holiness behave, which to my way of thinking is a way to lose the benevolence of all Christian princes: however I don't know whether this or similar things come from the mouth of His Excellency the Duke and I also don't know how much I believe it.[25]

And Canigiani writes again to Cosimo on January 16, 1570, when the Este were seeking allies in other Italian princely courts to oppose the new title of Grand Duke granted the Medici ruler.

> Sunday morning I saw at court the Ambassador Guerrino [Guarini] returned from Savoy and one can't find out anything about his answer, from which I conjecture that it isn't according to their intention, for they would make a song

out of it to send me into a stupor if it were, especially Bentivoglio, who would like to be able to light a fire between the pope and the emperor; it seems to him that in all Europe there is no soldier his equal to serve his imperial Majesty, and he lets out that he would bring down a swarm of Lutherans if this pope keeps causing irritation and similar poisonous vanities, which at a moment will make me burst with laughter.[26]

A swarm of Huguenots, a swarm of Lutherans. These anticipations of another sack of Rome, the first carried out in 1527 by the Lutheran mercenaries of the emperor Charles V, suggests how the resistance of the Este to papal power could seem to ally itself with Protestant heresy. And the Este, in fact, had played a role in 1527, allowing the imperial army to cross through their territory on its way down the peninsula, for which they were still being blamed by the papacy forty years later.[27] There was, moreover, real discussion at the imperial court in 1568 of a new military campaign against Rome: of the kind promoted by Matthaeus Iudex seven years before.[28] Entering into the causes of friction between emperor and pope was their backing of Ferrara and Tuscany, respectively, in the precedence controversy. Canigiani is dismissive, but his friend Tasso may have taken the loose talk in Ferrara seriously, and with some reason. Tasso's epic doubles the insubordination of the Este avatar Rinaldo with the crypto-Protestant revolt of Argillano.

If at home in Ferrara the Este could assume an aggressive posture toward Rome, they publicly sought reconciliation and a return to the favor of the pope. On July 22, 1569, their ambassador at Rome, Francesco Martello, received a long letter of instructions, outlining the arguments he was to use to ingratiate the Este to Pius V.[29] The burning issue was the precedence controversy, and Martello was ordered to read or present to the pope a "succinct abstract" of nineteen pages, entitled "Services rendered the Holy Apostolic See by the most serene house of Este beginning in the year 773 through the year 1474."[30] By heeding this document, Pius was to see "the many and signal services that these Princes have done the Church, exposing their own persons, and how they have continued to aid and serve Her always with every readiness, and often to their notable detriment: and with the loss of their own lives and also of many of their dominions."[31] In return, the document proclaimed, earlier popes had given the Este "privileges with widest concession of every tax and every sort of jurisdiction so that they could repair to them according to their needs, and also created them Grand Dukes ["Duchi Magni"], equal to any other Grand Duke, as grand as he might be."[32] It continues with a list of sixty-nine episodes from the dynastic history of the Este, all attesting to their services, primarily military, to the Church. The list is drawn from and offers a kind of prepublication preview of Giovan Battista Pigna's *Historia dei Principi d'Este*, the major work of literary propaganda produced for the Este during the precedence controversy: a book that, Pigna himself wrote to a Ferrarese ambassador in Rome, was similarly to be presented to the pope as witness to how greatly "the predecessors of His Excellency have been devoted to the Apostolic See and perpetual defenders of the Church."[33] But between the letter to Martello and the first printing of Pigna's *Historia* in November, the perfidious Pius had declared in favor of Cosimo on August 24, 1569, and given him the title of Grand Duke that Alfonso claimed for himself.

Defeated, the Este waited until Pius's death in 1572 to renew their suit with his successor Gregory XIII. Alfonso now hoped to have Cosimo's title revoked or at least to be awarded the same rank himself. A delegation was sent to Rome on December 18 that included Tasso and Battista Guarini, later the author of the *Pastor fido*. On December 31, Guarini presented before Gregory and the papal court an accomplished Latin oration that was subsequently published.[34] This was a typical *obedientia* oration in which a new pope was to receive congratulations on his accession and a pledge of obedience from the foreign prince.[35] Guarini used the occasion to take up again the theme of previous Este service and military assistance to the Apostolic See, this time with the elegant variation of recalling the occasions when such aid had been rendered to popes with the name of Gregory.

> If anyone should diligently contemplate the annals of past times, in no other series, however numerous or often repeated, as in this most noble one of Gregorys will he ever find so many pontiffs, who with a greater consensus of minds, or on more frequent occasions, have embraced the faith and observance of this family, or received from them more numerous or more outstanding services worthy of their own dignity as much as of the dignity of the Church.[36]

Guarini invokes the cases of Gregory V, Gregory VII, Gregory IX, and Gregory XI, all paired with their respective Este lords and auxiliaries. The series of odd-numbered Gregorys irresistibly leads to the present Gregory XIII, whom Guarini assures of Alfonso's devotion.

> Therefore this constant and most famous series of Roman pontiffs and Este Princes, conserved together through so many centuries to our present times by a binding chain of beneficial services seems—if traces of divinity in human affairs can do anything to excite the minds of men—clearly indeed to admonish our Prince Alfonso II that, beyond that which he owes you, supreme Pontiff, because of your immortal merits, that he should venerate you with the greatest and most outstanding honor and reverence: you, indeed, excellent Father, as you carry on the title and name of those popes, will also imitate their benevolence towards this family so worthy of merit from the republic of Christendom.[37]

The quid pro quo is clearly spelled out. Este devotion and service in return for papal favor in the disputed areas of the saltworks and precedence, particularly in the latter: what most struck Guarini's audience was his audacious reference to Alfonso by the Grand Ducal title of "Serenissimo."[38]

Just what service Alfonso really had to offer Gregory became clearer when the duke himself came to Rome to see the pope in January 1573. The Florentine ambassador in Rome, Alessandro de' Medici, wrote to Cosimo that the Duke of Ferrara had come

> beyond all other reasons with the design of procuring entrance in the [Holy] League, where once it is conceded him to enter, he offers to the Pope to draw in the Emperor, too, hoping with his presence, and with such an offer not only to make good his present intent, but also to gain the mind of His Blessedness in order to effect all his other desires.[39]

Alfonso was now willing to enter the Holy League he had earlier spurned and promised to guarantee imperial participation as well. The Medici ambassador thought this offer to be a weak bargaining chip, and, in fact, nothing came of it.[40] Alfonso and his delegation returned empty-handed from Rome, and the differences between Ferrara and the Church remained unresolved.

The Este did not obtain a reconciliation with the papacy, but their poet appears to offer an idealized version of such a reconciliation in the submission that Rinaldo shows to Goffredo. Goffredo has been instructed by a divinely inspired dream (14.13–14) that he needs the Este knight as much as the latter needs him, and when the repentant Rinaldo comes to renew obedience to him, Goffredo rises from his throne to meet him halfway (17.97.7–8). He urges that bygones be bygones.

> Ogni triste memoria omai si taccia
> e pongansi in oblio l'andate cose.
> E per emenda io vorrò sol che faccia,
> quai per uso faresti, opre famose.
>
> (18.2.3–6)

> (Henceforth let every unhappy memory be left unspoken, and let past events be placed in oblivion. And to make amends I shall only wish that you do those famous deeds which you would be wont to do.)

The scene is a much revised version of Achilles' reconciliation with Agamemnon and return to battle in Book 19 of the *Iliad*. There, it is Achilles who relinquishes his anger and Agamemnon who acknowledges his fault and makes amends. But inscribed in this traditional epic plot of commander and chief warrior is the identification of Rinaldo with the Este and Goffredo with papal power and authority: it suggests here a vision of the dukes of Ferrara settling their quarrel with the papacy and resuming their vaunted role as defenders of the Church. This identification is made quite explicitly in the earlier prophecy of Peter the Hermit, who urges the recall of Rinaldo to the army in canto 10 and predicts, in Virgilian accents, the future part that both Rinaldo and his Este descendants will play as champions and upholders of Papal might.

> Ecco chiaro vegg'io, correndo gli anni,
> ch'egli s'oppone a l'empio Augusto e 'l doma;
> e sotto l'ombra de gli argentei vanni
> l'aquila sua copre la Chiesa e Roma,
> che de la fera avrà tolte a gli artigli;
> e ben di lui nasceran degni i figli.
>
> De' figli i figli, e chi verrà da quelli,
> quinci avran chiari e memorandi essempi;
> e da' Cesari ingiusti e da' rubelli
> difenderan le mitre e i sacri tempi.
> Premer gli alteri e sollevar gli imbelli,
> difender gli innocenti e punir gli empi
> fian l'arti lor: così verrà che vole
> l'aquila estense oltra le vie del sole.
>
> E dritto è ben che, se 'l ver mira e 'l lume,
> ministri a Pietro i folgori mortali.
> U' per Cristo si pugni, ivi le piume
> spiegar dee sempre invitte e trionfali,
> ché ciò per suo nativo alto costume
> dielle il Cielo e per leggi a lei fatali.
> Onde piace là su che in questa degna
> impresa, onde partì, chiamato vegna.

(10.75–77)

(Lo, I see him clearly, as the years course by, oppose and conquer the impious emperor, and I see his Este eagle shelter beneath the shade of its silvery wings the Church and Rome which he has wrested from the claws of that beast, and his sons and descendants will be born worthy of him. Hence the children of his children and those born from them will follow his famous and memorable examples, and they will defend papal mitres and the holy temples of God from unjust and rebellious Caesars. To subject the proud and aid the unwarlike, defend the innocent and punish the wicked, these will be their arts: and thus it will come about that the Este eagle will fly higher than the course of the sun. And it is just, if it sees the truth and the light, that it should put its deadly thunderbolts in the service of Peter. Where there is combat for the sake of Christ, there it must ever spread its wings unconquerable and triumphant, for this is the inborn custom that the fatal laws of Heaven have assigned it. Wherefore it is the pleasure of Heaven that Rinaldo be recalled to this worthy enterprise from which he departed.)

Rinaldo, who will defeat Frederick Barbarossa, the oppressor of the Church, will be followed by other Este rulers who will sustain the papacy against the emperor during the Investiture Controversy and otherwise lend their support to Rome. The logic of the last octave conflates the present Crusade with the future defense of the Church: it is because the Este are divinely destined to be the protectors of the papacy that Rinaldo should be brought back now into Goffredo's service. Tasso's fiction, which draws here upon the same sources as Pigna's *Historia*, repeats the Este diplomatic line that ascribed to the family a special relationship to the Church, a relationship that Alfonso would offer to renew in 1573, pledging military service that he had earlier withheld from the Holy League.[41] For Tasso, the Este become the chosen ministers of papal power, just as, in the fiction of the poem, Rinaldo has been elected by Providence to be the "essecutor soprano" (14.13.4) of Goffredo's orders. This exaltation of the Este as champions of the Church is given prominence by the position of Peter's prophecy at the end of canto 10, at the very midpoint and center of the *Liberata*. The plot and structure of the poem hinge upon the divinely sanctioned return of the errant Rinaldo under Goffredo's command, and in the same way Heaven seems to have decreed the continuation of the historical partnership between the pope and his Este vassals.

If the *Liberata* thus gives voice to an offical line of Este propaganda, Tasso's attitude toward his patrons remains sufficiently ambivalent. Alfonso must presumably have been gratified to see reflected in the story of Rinaldo his family's claims to be the special military servants of the papacy—and thus entitled to special papal consideration. But he would have found less to his liking—had he been able to decipher them—the poem's encoded linkings of Rinaldo to Argillano and of Argillano to heretical schism: i.e, the suggestion that the Este quarrels with Rome might ally them with the Protestant enemy.[42] Moreover, for all the benevolence that Goffredo shows to the penitent Rinaldo, he remains in charge of the situation, and it is Rinaldo who must declare submission to him. Tasso may plead for the return of the Este into the good graces of the pope, but his reconciliation is based on their acknowledging and bowing to the Church's higher authority. The depiction of this submission may have given some satisfaction to the poet, whose resentment at his own subordination and powerlessness vis-à-vis his Este patrons should not be excluded from the political equations of his epic. Tasso may have chosen to identify with his patrons' "patron"—the feudal overlord of the dukes of Ferrara.[43] There is no necessary contradiction here: Tasso may enjoy portraying the Este's humiliation and still advocate their cause. Within this sadomasochistic dialectic, moreover, it is possible to identify with the rebellious son as well as with the punishing paternal authority, and Tasso can sympathize with his Este hero and with the local Italian political interests he represents when he shows Rinaldo upholding Italian independence and nationalistic honor against the arrogant foreigner

Gernando. But by suggesting that behind Rinaldo lurks Argillano, the specter of lawlessness and Protestant heresy, Tasso argues for the subordination of those local interests to papal rule. By the same token, the identification of Goffredo's supreme power with the Church allows for an Italian nationalism of another kind. A sixteenth-century Italian poet aiming to revive the imperialist formula of Virgilian epic could find in the papacy the only peninsular power with genuinely international claims. In the last chapter of the *Prince*, Machiavelli had himself looked, perhaps with mere utopian wishful thinking, to a ruler who could use the power of the Church to unite Italy and drive out her foreign conquerors.

The *Liberata* thus celebrates the triumph of the imperial, Counter-Reformation papacy: this is the significance for the larger poem of the specific topical allusions that gather around Rinaldo and Argillano. The peculiar trick of these allusions is to portray the two rebels against Goffredo's authority literally as *political subjects* of the Church, inhabitants of papal domains. This does not necessarily reduce the universal political concerns of the epic to provincial squabbles in central Italy; rather, it transforms all members of the ideal Church imagined by the epic into similar subjects: this Church is conceived as much as a temporal political power as a spiritual institution, and indeed these two identities become as confused and inseparable in the poem as they do in the Papal States. The resulting political picture turns Tasso's First Crusade into an emblem of the Church Militant, whose quest for souls is finally indistinguishable from the imperialist conquest of new territories and dependent subjects.

Alfonso II died in 1597, two years after the death of Tasso, sixteen years after the first edition of the *Gerusalemme liberata*. By December of that year a papal army of thirty thousand men stood poised on the borders of Ferrara, and on December 23, Pope Clement VIII excommunicated Cesare d'Este, Alfonso's cousin and chosen heir, and placed Ferrara under an interdict. After some hasty negotiations, Cesare fled the city for Modena, where the Este continued to reign until 1859. On January 29, 1598, papal troops headed by Cardinal Pietro Aldobrandini, the nephew of Clement, marched into and occupied Ferrara.

The event was celebrated in a Latin hexameter poem of 166 verses, the *Ferraria recepta*—"Ferrara Regained"—of one Giuseppe Castiglione, Roman jurisconsult, who published it in Rome in 1598 and dedicated it to Cardinal Aldobrandini.[44] The poem, which is a kind of miniature epic, rehearses a number of familiar motifs and topoi of the genre. It begins with the death of Duke Alfonso without legal heir. The devil now sees a chance to stir up trouble and to check the power of the Roman Church. He summons a council of his fellow demons.

> Ergo Tartareus qui dudum haec ipsa satelles
> Tempora captabit; qui socios immania monstra

Cogit, et hos inter sic orsus, Quae tenet, inquit
Nos mora? cur rapidum tandem non subdimus ignem
Italiae, exsultat longum quae pace per aevum.
Ite citi mecum, populos impellite ad arma,
Et serite ingentis passim nova crimina belli
Ne quisquam ferat augeri maioribus Urbem
Romam opibus, sed sit suspecta potentia cunctis.

(33–41)

(Therefore the Tartarean servant, who was watching for this very occasion, assembled his associates, frightful monsters all, and thus began to speak to them: What delay, he asks, holds us back? Why do we not set a fast-spreading fire under Italy which presently rejoices in a longstanding peace? Go quickly with me and urge the peoples to arms, and everywhere sow new crimes of tremendous war. Let no one allow the city of Rome to grow greater with further power, but let her might be feared by all.)

The passage echoes Juno's words to Allecto in Book 7 of the *Aeneid*—"sere crimina belli" (7.339). It also may be compared to the words of Tasso's devil at the diabolic council in canto 4.

Ma perché più v'indugio? Itene, o miei
fidi consorti, o mia potenza e forze:
ite veloci, ed opprimete i rei
prima che 'l lor poter più si rinforze.

(4.16.1–4)

(But why do I further delay you? Go, my faithful companions, my power and my might: go quickly and put down these guilty ones before their power grow yet stronger.)

As the infernal denizens scatter to carry out their mission, their leader makes a nocturnal visit to Cesare d'Este, assuming the disguise of an aged friend: the model is the visit of Virgil's Allecto to the sleeping Turnus, the same model imitated by Tasso in Argillano's dream. The devil speaks:

Quid cessas? populi iussu quin sceptra capessis?
Praesidiisque urbem firmas, agrumque tueris?
Finitimas tibi iunge manus, atque extera regna
Concilia, bellum prior infer. ius sit in armis.
Quos veterum ingentes auri congessit acervos
Dextera, in hos usus ne parce insumere, multo
Conductus pretio tibi confluet undique miles.
Talibus incendit Iuvenem, qui luce sub ipsa
Corripit e stratis artus, atque ordine narrat
Visa suis, actus stimulis, & consulit unum

Quemque, quid in tanto moliri cardine rerum
Debeat. Insedit stolidi sententia coetus
Deterior, furiisque quos inflammaverat Orcus.

(46–58)

(Why are you idle? Why not seize your sceptre by the command of the people?
Why not fortify the city with troops and defend your territory? Join your neighbors' hands to yours, and gain the favor of foreign powers; be the first to attack.
Let justice reside in arms. Do not forbear to use in these urgent times those
great heaps of gold which the prosperity of your ancestors amassed. Attracted
by large payment, soldiers will flock to you from all directions. With these
words he set the youth on fire, who, at the verge of day, tears himself out of bed,
and tells in order to his men the things he has seen, driven by the diabolic spurs
and goads, and he consults each one about what course he should take at such
a critical state of affairs. The worse opinion fixed itself in the stupid crowd,
those whom Hell inflamed with its furies.)

With this sound practical advice, the devil takes possession of Cesare and
persuades him to hold on to Ferrara. Much as Argillano's narration of his
dream, together with Aletto's fire, incites his followers from the "vulgo
folle" to rebel against Goffredo, Cesare gathers behind him the Ferrarese
mob to confront Clement. The pope, meanwhile, has received news of Ferrara's revolt and of the conflict that is brewing. Like Goffredo, he first turns
to heaven and prays that war may be averted.

Hic vero intrepidus versat dum pectore CLEMENS
Omnia, suppliciterque Deum veneratur, & orat,
Ne detrimenti capiat quid Romula tellus,
Neve suo e populo rapiat quem funere Mavors.

(72–75)

(While here the truly intrepid Clement considers all these things in his breast,
and, supplicating, worships and prays to God lest any harm befall the land of
Romulus and lest Mars carry off any of his people by death in war.)

In answer to the prayer, Peter and Paul descend from heaven and pledge
their support to Clement's cause, urging him to keep to his resolve. With
this divine sanction, the peace-loving pope raises an army of epic pro-
portions.

Non tot & ad Iliacos misisse examina fines
Graecia narratur, nec Tarchon duxit ab oris
Tyrrhenis acies, quot millia vidit in arma
Ire virum Oenotriae tellus ripisque minari
Eridani, tanta subigi virtute Propontis
Posset, & ab Solymis expelli finibus hostes.

(98–103)

(Not so many were the multitudes they tell were sent from Greece to the confines of Troy, nor did Tarchon lead from the Tyrrhenian shores so many troops, as the thousands of men the land of Italy saw go in arms and threaten the banks of the Po, enough might to subjugate the Propontis and expel the enemy from the territory of Jerusalem.)

Not only does the enterprise against Ferrara outdo the *Iliad* and the *Aeneid* in grandeur, but the papal army could reconquer Constantinople from the Turks and deliver Jerusalem as well. The war has assumed the shape of a crusade against the infidel. And on the other hand, Cesare's army, correspondingly numerous, is tinged with a suggestion of heresy.

> Interea stimulos populis sub pectore diros
> Versat avernali pestis progressa barathro.
> Quotquot ad Hercynios nutrit Germania saltus,
> Infestasve Urbi gentes Helvetia tellus,
> Sollicitat flammis Caesar furialibus actus
> Infandumque parat summo conamine bellum.
>
> (108–13)

(Meanwhile the pest advancing from the depths of Hell pours dreadful incitements into the breasts of the people. Cesare, himself driven by the flames of the furies, stirs up as many troublesome folk as Germany nourishes in the Hercynian woods or the soil of Switzerland in the region of Orbe, and he prepares unholy war with an all-out effort.)

The Ferrarese troops are compared to the warlike northern hordes who fought the ancient Romans. But Germany and Switzerland are also the homes of the contemporary Protestant enemies of Rome. As was the case with the reference to the Swiss and English partisans of Argillano's rebellion, resistance to the temporal power of the Church here begins to look like heretical schism, inspired by infernal demons. And there is the same accompanying confusion between temporal and spiritual force. While the Roman matrons are frightened by the rumors and prospect of war, Clement stands firm, and pledges to shed his own blood and life for the "maiestate Latini /Imperii" (122–23). But this sacrifice proves unnecessary when he launches his interdict against Ferrara. The result is immediate.

> Ille ubi se addictum tristi cognovit Averno,
> Dilabi & comites videt, O qui me abstulit, inquit,
> Ater, & a summo desciscere compulit error
> Principe. iam sceleris tanti me poenitet, & quae
> Inconcessa tuli, depono insignia regni,
> Moenibus, atque agris abeo, sanctoque resigno
> Cuncta Patri, flammas satis, evassisse barathri.
> Quis te sic meritum non tollat ad aethera Caesar

Laudibus, ad studium pacis quem nuper ab armis
Traduxit pietas, & summi reverentia Patris?

(141–50)

(Cesare, when he sees himself destined for the miserable underworld, and that his associates have slipped away from him, says, "O what black error has carried me away and compelled me to revolt from the supreme Monarch! Now I repent my great crime, and I lay down the insignia of lordship that I took up unlawfully; and I will leave the city walls and its territory, and resign all to the Holy Father: it is enough for me to have escaped from the flames of Hell." Who does not raise you, thus worthy Cesare, to the skies with praise, whom piety and reverence for the supreme father led from recent arms to the study of peace?)

The revolt fizzles out with the display of papal authority and the unleashing of Clement's spiritual weaponry. The excommunicated Cesare's change of heart is attributed more to his fear of damnation than to the defection of his followers or to the huge army at his border. His penitent recognition of the supreme power of the pope turns him from demonic agent into the subject of the poet's reconciliatory praise, praise that covers over Cesare's ignominious flight from Ferrara. The poem ends with more fulsome praise of Clement and Cardinal Aldobrandini, the city's new masters.

This piece of papal propaganda uncannily repeats the motifs of Argillano's rebellion and offers a peculiar confirmation of the political reading that I have proposed for the episode, a reading that sees it as a shadowy double of the larger quarrel and reconciliation of Rinaldo and Goffredo, itself a reflection of the relationship between the Este and the Church. It does not matter whether, in invoking a series of epic models, Castiglione was consciously imitating the *Liberata* or not, though by 1598 he must have been aware of Tasso's vastly popular epic and the very title of his little poem suggests its influence. It is further unclear to what extent he was aware of the irony that his work casts in retrospect upon the *Liberata*. For, by equating the Crusade with the political triumph of the Church, Tasso turned out to be celebrating not only the delivery of Jerusalem, but of Este Ferrara as well.

Why Is Clorinda an Ethiopian?

The *obedientia* oration, such as the one Battista Guarini delivered on behalf of the Este before Gregory XIII, was a common-enough papal ceremony to constitute a distinct literary subgenre in the sixteenth century. But few such speeches declaring the submission of earthly monarchs to the authority of the pope could have been as curious as one printed in Giovanni Battista Ramusio's *Navigazioni e viaggi* of 1550. Addressed to Pope Clement VII, it had been translated by Ramusio into the Tuscan tongue from the Latin, into Latin from the Portuguese, and into the Portuguese from the Abyssinian. Here is one more translation of its opening section.

> In the name of the omnipotent God the Father, creator of heaven and earth, of visible and invisible things. In the name of God the Son, of Jesus Christ, who is the identical essence with Him from the beginning of the world, and is light from light, true God from true God. In the name of the Holy Spirit, the living God, who proceeds from God the Father. These letters I send to you, I the king whose name is revered by lions, and who by the grace of God am called Atani Tingil, that is Incense of the Virgin, Son of King David, Son of Solomon, Son of the King by the hand of Mary, Son of Nau by carnal succession, Son of the saints Peter and Paul by grace. Peace be with you, O Great Lord, Holy Father, powerful, pure, consecrated, who is head of all pontiffs and fears no one, there being no one who can cause you, who are most watchful governor over souls and friend of pilgrims, consecrated master and preacher of the faith, and capital enemy of those things that offend the conscience, lover of good customs, holy man, praised and blessed by all.
>
> O happy Holy Father, with great reverence I obey you, since you are the father of all and merit all goods: and thus it is the duty of all to render obedience, after God, to you, as the holy apostles command. This is truly said of you, and they also command, that we reverence bishops, archbishops, and prelates; similarly that we should love you in place of a father and reverence you in place of a king, and have faith in you as we do in God. Wherefore I, humbly with bended knee on earth, say to you, Holy Father, with a heart entirely sincere and pure, that you are my father and I am your son. O most powerful holy father, why have you never sent someone here to us, so that you could learn more certainly about our life and wellbeing, since you are shepherd and I am your lamb?[45]

Ramusio tells us that this letter from King David of Ethiopia—the European name of Atani Tingil—was presented to Clement VII in a ceremony at Bologna on January 29, 1533. Francisco Alvarez, a Portuguese priest who had accompanied the Portuguese expedition that had reached the Ethiopian court over a decade earlier in 1520–1521, acted as the king's ambassador. He kissed the foot, hand, and mouth of the pope and offered him a gold cross as a small gift from the African monarch, who had sent him, he said, to offer as well "true obedience and subjection in the name of his majesty and of all his realms."[46] The same Alvarez wrote an account of the voyage into Ethiopia to the kingdom of "Prester John" ("Prete Ianni") that was published first in Portuguese in 1540, then translated and printed in an Italian version in Ramusio's 1550 *Viaggi*.[47]

Here was indeed sensational news. The Portuguese had finally made contact with—and returned to tell of—the great Christian kingdom in Africa, long separated from Europe by the iron curtain of Islam and shrouded in legend. Europeans had long fabled of the great and powerful kingdom of Prester John, whose forces might be joined with theirs in a crusade against the infidel. This appeared to be a hope shared by Atani Tingil, who, in a second letter to Clement, writes that he hopes, once his armies and forces are linked up with those of Portugal, that "we will open a way both by land and sea through the provinces of the evil Moors, and we will attack them with such fury that we will drive them from their thrones and kingdoms, and so Christians will be able easily to go back and forth to the temple of Jerusalem at their own good pleasure."[48] Reunited with her fellow European Christians, Ethiopia could throw her forces against the rear flanks of their common enemy, the advancing Turkish empire. Moreover, the acquisition for the Roman Church of this great African dominion might make up for the recent defections of Protestant sectarians. This was hardly less encouraging news for the cause of the Counter-Reformation imperial papacy than the subsequent repossessing of England by Mary and Philip: but it turned out to be equally short-lived.

For something had been added, rather than lost, in the translations that separated the Christian king of Ethiopia and the pope. The Ethiopian Church followed its own version of Coptic theology and ritual, and Atani Tingil had no intention of submitting his religion to Roman jurisdiction. Alvarez recorded a conversation that he and the king had held over matters of ecclesiastical obedience.

> Then came another question, if we did everything that the pope commanded us to do; I said yes, that thus we were obliged by the article of our holy faith, which confessed one holy and catholic church. On this I was answered that, if the pope commanded them something that the apostles had not written, they would not do it, and the same was true if their own patriarch (*abuna*) were to command it: they would burn such a commandment.[49]

Arguing from apostolic precedent, these Ethiopians were just as bad as Protestants when it came to Church authority. And their alien Judaizing religious practices, such as circumcision and observance of the Saturday Sabbath, were unmistakably heretical. When the Erasmian Damião de Góis published a treatise in 1540 that described, nonjudgmentally, the theology and very ancient customs of the Ethiopian Church, the Portuguese Inquisition stepped in to suppress the book.[50] In 1554, the members of a Jesuit mission, personally chosen and instructed by Ignatius Loyola, set out to convert their schismatic Christian brethren in Ethiopia.

Nor did the Ethiopians prove to be the hoped-for allies who would help to deliver a beleaguered Europe from the Turkish peril. Quite the opposite: Muslim tribesmen from Somalia, backed by Turkish mercenaries and artillery, invaded and overran Ethiopia itself in 1527, and Atani Tingil was involved in constant warfare, defending his remaining mountain strongholds, until his death in 1540. It was an expeditionary force of 400 Portuguese soldiers, led by Cristóvão da Gama, the son of the great explorer, that in 1541 heroically came to the rescue of Galâwdêwos, Atani Tingil's son and successor. Two thirds of the Portuguese army perished, and Don Cristóvão was captured and horribly tortured to death; but the European intervention turned the tide of battle, and by 1543 the resurgent Ethiopian kingdom had reestablished itself and recovered its dominions.[51] When the Jesuit missionaries reached Ethiopia in the next decade, the Portuguese sacrifice was still fresh in memory. They were welcomed, but Galâwdêwos, who died in 1559, defended the evangelical purity of Ethiopian Christianity and denied that his father had ever pledged the obedience of his throne and church to the dictates of Rome.[52] The Jesuit missionary efforts persisted nonetheless and seemed finally to have come to fruition in 1626 when King Suseynos pronounced his adherence to Catholic dogma and performed a genuine public act of submission to the pope. But the result was an armed rebellion by Ethiopians faithful to their own church and an ensuing religious war parallel to the conflicts between Catholics and Protestants in Europe. Suseynos was forced to give up his project of imposing Catholic uniformity upon his subjects, and two years after his death, his son and successor expelled the Jesuits from Ethiopia in 1634: again European parallels come to mind.[53]

The re-establishment in the sixteenth century of contact between Ethiopia and Catholic Europe and, in particular, the letters and historical narrative of Father Alvarez translated and collected in Ramusio's *Viaggi* form the context of topical reference for the career of the Amazon-like Clorinda, the famous Ethiopian heroine of the *Gerusalemme liberata*. Tasso explicitly cites Alvarez in a short unpublished work, *Dubbi e risposte intorno ad alcune cose e parole concernenti alla Gerusalemme liberata*, which survives in an autograph manuscript and was finally published in 1892. He replies to an imaginary interlocutor, who asks why Clorinda had not received baptism at her birth.

> According to the custom of the Ethiopian Church, which had to be observed by her [Clorinda's mother], it was not lawful in any way, for the Ethiopians do not baptize their female children until forty days after their birth, and if they die first, they let them die without baptism: furthermore the act of baptism brings with it greater difficulty among them than one might suppose. One can read on this point Francesco Alvarez in his *Voyage in Ethiopia*, chapter 22.[54]

This issue of baptism will turn out to be central to Clorinda's story.

Clorinda is Ethiopian and of Christian parentage without knowing it, for she was born with white skin afer her pregnant mother, the black queen of Ethiopia, had prayed before a picture in her bedchamber of Saint George saving a white virgin from the dragon. Afraid lest the white baby lay her open to the charge of adultery, the queen entrusted her newborn daughter to her eunuch servant Arsete, meanwhile invoking the protection of the

saint over her child. Arsete had taken the infant Clorinda with him back
to his native Egypt. On the way, Saint George intervened twice to save the
baby girl from harm and, in a dream, revealed himself to Arsete and commanded him to baptize Clorinda. But the eunuch chose instead to raise
her in his own religion of Islam. Over the years Clorinda has grown up into
a great warrior like her tutelary saint; but, rather than fight, as he did, for
the true faith, she uses her prowess against Tasso's Crusaders, aiding her
besieged Muslim coreligionists in Jerusalem. All of Clorinda's life story is
finally revealed to her by Arsete, as Clorinda prepares to leave on a nocturnal
raid to burn the Crusaders' siege machines, in canto 12: the eunuch has
been troubled by a new dream vision of an angry Saint George, who threatens to make Clorinda his at last. Undeterred by Arsete's pleas that she
remain inside the city, Clorinda goes out and completes her mission, but
on the way back she is spotted by the Christian champion Tancredi, who
engages her in a prolonged duel and fatally wounds her. In the last minutes
of her life Clorinda asks for and receives baptism from the hands of
Tancredi. He is himself in love with Clorinda, but he recognizes her only
as he loosens her helmet to baptize her—the most famous moment of
Tasso's story.

As this complicated plot of recognition and mistaken identity suggests,
Tasso's Ethiopian fiction depends upon literary sources as well as upon Alvarez's contemporary traveler's report. The episode, in fact, is a remarkable
contamination of a fanciful, literary view of Ethiopia with up-to-date details
and commentary on a historical Ethiopia. In placing a character who is both
an Ethiopian and an Amazon fighting on the side of a beleaguered city,
Tasso was following a long epic tradition. If we ask why Clorinda should be
an Ethiopian in the first place, we may trace her *literary* genealogy back to
the verses in *Aeneid* 1 that describe the temple reliefs in Carthage depicting
the Trojan war. There Aeneas sees himself portrayed as well as the foreign
auxiliaries of his defeated city.

> se quoque principibus permixtum agnouit Achivis,
> Eoasque acies et nigri Memnonis arma.
> ducit Amazonidum lunatis agmina peltis
> Penthesilea furens mediisque in milibus ardet.

> (1.488–91)

(He recognizes himself fighting among the Achaean chieftains, and the troops
of the Dawn and the arms of black Memnon. Furious Penthesilea leads the
squadron of Amazons with their halfmoon shields and burns in the midst of the
warriors.)

After the death of Hector, the Trojans fought on, their cause sustained by
the Ethiopian Memnon, the son of the goddess Dawn, and Penthesilea,

queen of the Amazons, until each of these allies, in turn, was killed by Achilles. Tasso's Clorinda is clearly a composite of these two figures coupled together in Virgil's verses—a black Ethiopian in the guise of a white Amazon. Virgil recounts no more, but Tasso read of the further fighting at Troy in the fourth-century Byzantine epic of Quintus of Smyrna, the *Posthomerica* or *Fall of Troy*: Penthesilea's death occupies the first book of the poem, Memnon's the second. (It is Achilles' turn to die in the third.) The celebrated moment when Tancredi loosens Clorinda's helmet and recognizes his beloved, whom he himself has slain (12.66), is modeled on the description by Quintus of Achilles smitten by love for Penthesilea after he has killed her and beheld her features, still beautiful in death (1.656–74).[55]

The same pairing of Amazon and Ethiopian determines the more complex contamination of imitated models in the account of Clorinda's marvelous infancy: her trip with Arsete into Egypt and subsequent nurture recall at several points the story of Virgil's Amazonian Camilla (*Aeneid* 11.535–84), whom the Roman poet compares in a simile to Penthesilea (11.661–63); her birth as a white child is imitated from the *Ethiopian Romance* of Heliodorus, in which Persinna, the black queen of Ethiopia, gives birth to the white heroine Chariclea, after she, when conceiving the child, had gazed at a painting in her chamber of the fair-skinned Andromeda rescued by Perseus: alarmed, Persinna exposes her daughter, placing with her the necessary birth tokens to generate the foundling romance of Heliodorus's novel. In this same passage, Heliodorus describes Chariclea's descent from the hero Memnon.[56]

There was also a precedent for an Ethiopian episode in the *Orlando furioso*, the most important predecessor poem within Tasso's own Italian tradition. In canto 33, the paladin Astolfo, carried by the winged hippogriff, reaches Ethiopia, the realm of the Senapo, the king whom Europeans call Prester John (106). Like Phineus in the *Argonautica*, the Senapo has been blinded and plagued by Harpies: this was a divine punishment for his sacrilegious attempt to scale the local mountain at the top of which stands the original Garden of Eden. Astolfo chases away the Harpies, and, with an herb from the same Eden bestowed to him by Saint John the Evangelist, he restores the monarch's eyesight (38.24): in the same general episode, Astolfo famously ascends to the moon and recovers the lost wits of Orlando, whose madness is revealed to be a similar divine chastisement. The providential resolution of the war between Christian and Saracen in the *Furioso* requires, in fact, both the return of Orlando to fighting form and, simultaneously, the intervention by the grateful Senapo with a hundred thousand African troops to fight as allies of Charlemagne against the infidel. The parallel may suggest either a "realistic" military scenario that gives the credit for defeating the Muslim troops less to the individual prowess of Orlando than to the huge reinforcements from Ethiopia, or a fabulous one that attributes to

Orlando the strength of a hundred thousand fighting men. And there may be a more distanced ironic sense that Orlando's exploits are as make-believe as the fabled kingdom of Prester John.

But a decade after the first publication of the *Furioso* in 1516, Ethiopia had become less fabulous as accounts of the Portuguese embassy began to circulate in Europe. Tasso also gives his Ethiopian king the name or title of "Senapo" (12.22), and his Heliodorean fiction of a white African princess seems hardly less marvelous than the Harpies in Ariosto's tale. Yet his story's transformation of the painting of Perseus's rescue of Andromeda in the *Ethiopian Romance* into a votive picture of Saint George rescuing the maiden from the dragon contains an element from Ramusio's translation of Alvarez. Other writers were struck by the parallel between the Perseus and Saint George stories—Mantuan, in his *Georgius*, compares the maiden that the saint rescues to Andromeda (v. 268)[57]—and Tasso's Christianizing of Heliodorus may in itself be unremarkable. But Alvarez describes pictures of Saint George as being ubiquitous in Ethiopia.

> On all the walls of the churches are pictures of our Lord and of our Lady and of the apostles, prophets and angels, and in every one there is Saint George.[58]

Here was the kind of "historical" element that Tasso liked to claim for his marvelous fictions, a basis for the presence of a painting of the saint in the chamber of an Ethiopian queen and for the Christian updating of an ancient novel already set in Ethiopia.

The Ethiopian fictions of Ariosto and Tasso are thus separated within the sixteenth century by the European encounter with a real Ethiopia that henceforth began to displace a legendary one. Next to legend, reality was bound to be disappointing, even alarming. The massive troop support that the Senapo brings to the aid of Charlemagne in the *Furioso* reflects both an epic tradition in which Ethiopians are cast in the role of allies and the long-cherished hope that the Ethiopian realm of Prester John, once found, would come to the aid of Christendom and crush her Islamic enemies. By midcentury that hope had faded considerably as Ethiopia was discovered to be itself in need of military aid and—perhaps much worse—to have fallen prey to heresy. In the *Liberata* Clorinda plays the part of epic ally, but she is fighting on the wrong side.

It is the eunuch Arsete who appears to be most responsible for Clorinda's religious confusion; he had failed to heed the words of Saint George and had carried the infant princess off into the Egyptian captivity of Islam. In doing so, Arsete had reversed and undone the work of another Ethiopian royal eunuch. In the Acts of the Apostles (8:27–39), Philip explains a passage of Isaiah to the eunuch servant of Queen Candace of Ethiopia and then baptizes him in the new religion of Christ. As Alvarez reports, the Ethiopian Church regarded this scripturally attested conversion as the founding event in its history and as the witness to the preeminent antiquity of its faith and traditions.

> And they say that there was fulfilled the prophecy, in which it is said that Ethiopia will rise and stretch out her hands to the Lord God [Psalms 68:31]; and thus they say that they were the first to convert to the faith of Christ, and that the Eunuch returned at once very joyously towards Ethiopia, where lay the house of his sovereign, and that he converted and baptized her together with all her family and household, because he told her all that had happened to him, and thus the queen had baptized all her realm and domains.[59]

Tasso's fiction thus pointedly substitutes for a eunuch who was responsible for the original baptism of the Ethiopian queen and her subjects a royal eunuch, Arsete, who denies baptism to the queen's daughter. Where the eunuch of Queen Candace had brought the faith to Ethiopia, Arsete takes Clorinda away from the land of religion and into the realm of the infidel. The very history of Ethiopian Christianity seems to have been turned around and canceled out, and Clorinda is thus an Ethiopian who must be converted all over again to Christianity.

But Clorinda's dilemma, however she may have been kidnapped into an alien Muslim faith, also has its root in the Ethiopian form of Christianity itself. Arsete tells Clorinda that her mother gave her to him unbaptized and remarks that this was the religious custom in Ethiopia.

> a me che le fui servo e con sincera
> mente l'amai, ti diè non battezzata;
> né già poteva allor battesmo darti,
> ché l'uso no 'l sostien di quelle parti.
>
> (12.25)

(She gave you unbaptized to me, who was her servant and loved her with a pure mind; nor could she have given you baptism anyway, for the usage in those regions did not allow it.)

The eunuch puts his finger on the feature of Ethiopian ritual that above all scandalized Catholic Europeans. In the passage that Tasso cites in his *Dubbi e risposte*, Alvarez reports on the local practice:

> They confer baptism in this way: they baptize male infants after 40 days, females after 60, and if they die before this they go without baptism. And I many times and in many places have said that they do a great error in this, and that they were practicing against the Gospel of our Lord, that said: "Quod natum est ex carne, caro est, et quod natum est ex spiritu, spiritus est," that is: what is born of the flesh is fleshly, and what is born from the spirit is spiritual. To this they answered me many times that the faith of the mother was sufficient, and the communion that she took while she was pregnant.[60]

And later, Alvarez, records having been asked to baptize the son that had been given to one Pietro Cordiero of Genoa by his Ethiopian wife, "and he asked me to baptize the child after eight days, because they did not baptize male children there except after forty days."[61] Clorinda, who was smuggled out of the country before the sixty-day waiting period for girl infants, was deprived of the baptism that the Catholic Church bestowed on all newborn souls to ensure their salvation.

Nor was this the only peculiarity of Ethiopian baptismal custom. Alvarez reports that yearly on the feast of Epiphany the entire population, beginning with the emperor himself, underwent a mass baptism, marching naked, both men and women, into a large tank built into the ground for the occasion and fed with mountain streams.

> All that night a great number of priests ceaselessly sung until morning, saying that they were blessing the water; and almost at midnight, a little after or before, they began the baptism, and they say (and I believe it was the truth) that the first to be baptized was the Prester, and after him the patriarch Marco and the queen, the wife of the Prester: and these three persons had clothing around their shameful parts, and the others completely naked as they came into the world. . . . [The officiating priest] was naked as he had issued from the body of his mother and was almost dead with cold, because that night there had been a great frost, and he stood in the water up to his shoulders, for that was the depth of the pool, where those who were to be baptized descended by stairs, all naked, with their backs turned to the onlooking Prester, and when they departed they exposed their frontal parts, the women as well as the men.[62]

Repeatedly asked if he and his fellow Portuguese would like to participate in the ritual, Alvarez responded that it was their custom to be baptized only once, and that when they were little. This was not merely a reluctance to be plunged into the freezing waters flowing in January through the high Ethiopian plateau, or a European prudery about nakedness. The Epiphany baptism smacked of the heresy that neither European Catholics nor their Lutheran and Calvinist opponents could tolerate: anabaptism, with its practice of adult baptism. When Prester John (Atani Tingil) himself explained that the Ethiopian practice could be directed to Christians who had lapsed into Islam and then repented or to those whose faith in their first baptism was not firm, Alvarez replied that

> as for those who did not believe firmly, it was enough to instruct them and to pray to God for them, and if this did not bear fruit, to burn them as heretics, because thus Christ had said "Qui crediderit et baptizatus fuerit salvus erit, qui vero non crediderit condemnabitur." And as for those, who had been renegades and, recognizing their error, had demanded mercy, that the Patriarch should absolve them, giving them penitence for the salvation of their souls, since he

had power in this; if not he should send them to Rome where all powers lay. And for those who did not repent, if they could be caught, they should be burnt, according to the custom of the Franks and the church of Rome.[63]

Burning is better than adult baptism, Alvarez seems to say, and this was, in fact, the shortest way of dealing with Anabaptists in Europe. The Council of Trent explicitly condemned rebaptism "in one converted to repentance after having denied the faith of Christ among the Infidels," as well as the Anabaptists' insistence that baptism could only be valid when conferred upon adults who willingly chose faith in undergoing the rite.[64] The practice of adult baptism may be the "greater difficulty" in the Ethiopian version of the sacrament to which Tasso referred in the *Dubbi e risposte*. It was a practice troubling enough to Catholic sensibilities to be mentioned twice in Loyola's letter of instruction to the first Jesuit missionaries sent into the African kingdom. He suggests the institution of ecclesiastical ceremonies such as processions bearing the Host "in place of their baptisms, etc.,"[65] and also notes:

> It would be well that it be taught to them the administering of the sacrament of Baptism and its ceremonies, and that baptism should be one and not many, as they do, customarily baptizing themselves every year.[66]

But Pêro Paez, the Portuguese Jesuit historian, reported in the early seventeenth century that the Ethiopians had not heeded the missionaries' teachings and persisted both in allowing infants to die unbaptized and in rebaptizing themselves—and not only on Epiphany, but also at other feasts: the transit of the Virgin, Pentecost, and Holy Week.[67] By then Paez had declared his African brethren to be openly schismatic.[68]

Tasso's Clorinda is a soul in search of baptism. Born Christian, turned Muslim, inspired at death to return to the faith of her parents, she would not need to be baptized as an adult had the error of her native church not prevented her from receiving the sacrament at birth in the first place. And so she has to die in order to be baptized. Her battlefield conversion is a literary topos of the chivalric romances: Pulci's Orlando baptizes the giant Marcovaldo after felling him in combat (*Morgante* 12.63–71); Boiardo's Orlando does the same for the Tartar king Agricane (*Orlando innamorato* 2.19.12–16). Tasso incorporates this conventional scene into the scheme of his epic where the pagan male warriors, notably Argante and Solimano, die in combat while the pagan heroines Armida and Erminia fall in love with Christian knights and become their obedient "handmaidens"—"ancella" (6.71; 16.48; 19.101)—and, presumably, convert handmaidens to Christ (20.136) as well.[69] This is war, where men are killed and women enslaved, but the gender distinction also suggests the two modes in which the crusading ideology of the poem can conceive of the pagan enemy: either as demonized, irreconcilable foes who can only be fought and destroyed or as kindred souls who may be loved as neighbors and guided to salvation.[70] Clorinda, because of her double identity as warrior *and* woman, is both slain and converted. As she falls to Tancredi's sword, Clorinda is suddenly filled with faith, hope, and charity,

> virtù ch'or Dio le infonde, e se rubella
> in vita fu, la vuole in morte ancella.

(12.65)

(virtues that God now infuses in her, and if she was a rebel against Him in life, He wants her as His handmaiden in death.)

So, too, Clorinda's mother had prayed to Saint George that Clorinda should be his faithful "ancella" (28), and the saint (39), as well as a higher God, now claims her as his own. But the nature of Clorinda's conversion is also punitive: up until now she has been warring against Christianity as a rebel and the penalty for such rebellion is death.

But just who and what are being punished—and saved—in Tasso's fiction? Clorinda is a mass of overlapping and contradictory identities: a woman warrior, a white Ethiopian, a person of Christian birth and Muslim nurture. In terms of the painting on the wall of her mother's bedchamber, it is unclear from moment to moment in the poem whether Clorinda emulates the knight, Saint George, the white virgin whom he saves from the dragon and converts to Christianity, or the monster-dragon—"mostro" (12.23)—of religious error itself.

That beneath Clorinda's armed Islamic exterior—hidden beneath her armor—lies a Christian woman ready to become the bride of Christ may be meant to remind us that *historically* the Holy Land was itself once Christian and that the present Muslim domination is merely a recent overlay and usurpation: Tasso calls the Saracens "gli usurpatori di Siòn" (1.81), and begins his narrative by describing the persecutions against the Christian population of Jerusalem enacted by the "new king" Aladino (1.83f.). In this sense, Clorinda's story is a legitimating emblem of the Crusade itself, which restores to Palestine its "proper" Christian identity that was there all along, although politically supplanted and covered over by a false religion.

But when Clorinda's real Christian origins are revealed in Arsete's narrative, it turns out that she belongs to the wrong kind of Christianity: she has been born into a heretical Ethiopian Church that denied her the needed baptism she will only receive from a Latin Crusader. Tasso has conflated the errors of Ethiopian Christianity concerning baptism with the error of the Muslim Arsete who refused to confer baptism on Clorinda, as commanded by Saint George, and raised her in his faith. Clorinda is thus a rebel against God on two scores, as a heretic and as an infidel, and these seem to be much the same thing. Her long-deferred baptism represents, that is, the conversion not simply of a Muslim to the Christian faith, but of a schismatic Ethiopian to the Church of Rome. As royal Clorinda finally becomes the handmaiden of Christ, she fulfills the same act of obedience that King Atani Tingil had, it was once thought, pledged to the pope in Bologna, placing his national church under the authority of the Apostolic See. Tasso thus depicts an ideal return of Ethiopia into the Roman fold that was being disappointed by historical events, and this gap between Catholic European expectations and the frustrating reality of Ethiopian religious politics may partly account for the violence of his fiction. Clorinda does not heed the warning of Arsete—or of her own prophetic dreams (12.40)—and is only converted when overcome in battle; similarly, the conversion of Ethiopia to Catholicism may be obtainable not by missionary persuasion but by the use of force.

The pagan foe Clorinda turns out to be a Christian heretic: the enemy without is in reality the enemy within. Clorinda is thus a counterpart of the rebellious Rinaldo and of Rinaldo's surrogate, Argillano, whose mutiny inside the Crusader camp also carries overtones of heresy, this time Protestant, within the Catholic body politic. And the two topical political issues to which the stories of Rinaldo and Clorinda refer—the problems of Tasso's Este patrons at home in Ferrara and the question of orthodoxy in exotic Ethiopia—boil down to the same issue: submission to the power, temporal and spiritual, of the Church of Rome.

Clorinda is, in fact, linked to Rinaldo in the poem's symbolic economy. Her errancy into paganism confuses gender identities as she takes on male armor; Rinaldo's errancy on Armida's island of love makes him, conversely, act and dress effeminately (16.30): he is implicitly compared by the sculpted reliefs on Armida's palace to Hercules wearing women's garments in erotic servitude to Iole (16.3).[71] Whereas Rinaldo is dissuaded from fighting a duel with Goffredo (5.43.5–8), and Argillano's revolt against his commander comes to nothing, it is Clorinda who wounds Goffredo with her arrow in the battle before Jerusalem in canto 11 (54), one canto before her death.[72] And Clorinda's last-minute baptism reintegrates her into the Christian body politic in a way that parallels the errant Rinaldo's own reconversion to the Crusade and to the authority of Goffredo. As the penitent Rinaldo prays on the Mount of Olives in canto 18 (15), the morning dew physically washes over his head as he sacramentally washes away his sins. The similarity to the baptism of Clorinda reflects the doctrine of the Council of Trent that penance "has rightly been called by the holy Fathers a laborious kind of baptism."[73] (But the council strenuously warned against the confusion of the two sacraments, and it was penance that Alvarez and later Jesuit missionaries attempted to substitute for the Ethiopian practice of rebaptizing lapsed believers.) The resplendent whiteness that transforms Rinaldo's ash-colored armor in this episode (18.16) has its opposing counterpart in the black armor that Clorinda dons for her night exploit (12.18), a blackness that is a funereal harbinger of her impending death, but also the mark of her true, Ethiopian identity.

Clorinda is punished—as she is converted—for her violence against Goffredo and her rebellion against the true faith, just as the rebellious Rinaldo is humbled before both Goffredo and God. And, as is the case with Rinaldo, Tasso's sympathies appear to be divided between the authorities and the chastened rebel—registered here in the reaction of Clorinda's baptizer Tancredi, who has killed the thing he loved and considers himself a monster—"mostro" (12.76)—pointedly recalling the dragon and not the savior knight of the Saint George story. He is sobered by the fire-and-brimstone preaching of Peter the Hermit admonishing him that Heaven is punishing him for his sinful infatuation with "a girl in rebellion against God"— "una fanciulla a Dio rubella" (12.87). But the normally authoritative hermit is ironically unaware of Clorinda's miraculous conversion in death.[74] Tancredi receives a dream vision of Clorinda seated in glory among the blessed, thanking him for her salvation, and proclaiming her eternal love for him (12.91–94). The dream comforts Tancredi, but in the celebrated episode of the enchanted forest that follows in the next canto, he is once again overcome by his guilt before the demonic simulacrum of Clorinda trapped in the bark of one of the forest's trees.[75]

As these double ghostly reappearances suggest, Clorinda is not so easily laid to rest. Tancredi's reaction suggests the bad conscience of Tasso's epic, a chink in its ideological armor. For how can one both love and kill one's neighbor, especially when it transpires, in Clorinda's case, that the neighbor is a fellow, albeit a schismatic, Christian? The *Liberata* exalts a militant papacy whose universalism is an alibi for empire and whose spiritual power is a disguise for temporal political violence. In contrast to Clorinda, the penitent Rinaldo gets off lightly, and the element of coercion in his submission to Goffredo is covered over by their mutual, face-saving reconciliation; even in the case of Argillano's rebellion, the force that backed up Goffredo's authority was displaced by God's avenging angel. But there is no hiding the punitive violence of Clorinda's death—all the more naked and sadistically charged because of Tancredi's love for the woman he unwittingly kills.[76] Tancredi is the author of this violence, which seems to exceed containment by the poem's politico-religious ideology; as a stand-in for the author Tasso, he at least casts a measure of doubt on the capacity of that ideology to resolve its own inner contradictions.

Tasso's discomfort with the killing of his Ethiopian heroine is suggested by his rewriting of the episode—Clorinda's final reappearance—in a minor vignette during the great battle before Jerusalem that concludes the poem in canto 20, a passage that also brings in Rinaldo. At stanza 54, Rinaldo kills as the first victim of his *aristeia* another Ethiopian warrior, Assimiro of Meroe, first introduced in the catalogue of the army of the caliph of Egypt in canto 17 (24) and brought briefly back to prominence. On the one side, Rinaldo has now gotten over the errors of his rebellion and of his romance sojourn with Armida, done submission to Goffredo, and been rehabilitated as the chief warrior and executor of Goffredo's orders in the Crusader army.[77] On the other, Assimiro has been purged of all the confusing ambiguities of Clorinda's identity: her whiteness, her womanhood, her Christianity; he is black, male, and comes from the part of Ethiopia that is Muslim. Tasso's poem has, in fact, reverted to normative epic type—its Achillean hero fights and kills a straightforward Memnon figure, an Ethiopian ally— and this rewriting of Clorinda's story appears to be ideologically normative as well.[78] That grey area of identity and ideology constituted by the figures of both Rinaldo and Clorinda—that area of internal division, rebellion, and potential heresy—has been replaced at the end of the epic by a politics that spells out its terms literally in black and white.

SIX

TASSO, MILTON, AND THE BOAT OF ROMANCE

THE TWO foremost modern epics are directly opposed in their politics, as the inversion of the title of the *Gerusalemme liberata* into *Paradise Lost* might suggest. Tasso's epic celebrates the absolute power of a triumphant, imperial papacy; Milton's is the poem of defeated Puritan republicanism and liberty. This opposition is also felt at the level of generic form. Tasso eliminates romance, with its potential aimlessness and dependence on random chance, or rather incorporates such romance into his poem's epic plot of conquest and manifest political destiny. Milton, as this and the next chapter will argue, satirically collapses such epic plots into the bad romance of Satan, while his larger poem, the story of Adam and Eve, reclaims and revalorizes the open-endedness and contingency of romance. Reserving the imperial typology of Virgilian epic for its God alone—as we observed in Chapter 1—*Paradise Lost* effectively moves away from epic altogether.

The opposition of epic and romance finds an instance in the present chapter in the two poems' respective treatments of the Renaissance voyage of exploration; and these depend on intertextual allusion. Tasso's allusions to Boiardo's *Orlando innamorato* involve the integration of the romance adventure into a "higher" epic context, while Milton demotes from the rank of epic the exploits of discovery celebrated in the *Lusíadas* and recasts them into the pattern of adventure. Renaissance interpretations of the discoveries saw them alternately as heroic acts of military conquest or as commercial trading ventures. Epic traditionally aligns itself with aristocratic, martial values; when, in the context of the voyages of discovery, it casts romance as its alternative "other," it lends a mercantile, bourgeoise cast to the romance adventure. The generic split between epic and romance thus yields here an ideology of class distinction that begins to suggest the historical demise of epic itself.

The Fortunate Isles

In cantos 7 and 8 of the *Rinaldo*,[1] the chivalric romance that Tasso composed at the age of eighteen, Rinaldo of Montalbano and his faithful companion Florindo take a trip in an enchanted boat that is called the "barca aventurosa" (7.73). Its purpose is to carry knights-errant to whatever adventure may be currently available to give them an opportunity to demonstrate their prowess. The enchanted boat, which travels without human guidance carrying the hero from episode to episode, is a common topos of chivalric romance. It is a close relative of the wandering ship of Odysseus, whose storm-tossed course maps out the apparently random, deviating structure of the romance plot. We have seen versions of this ship before: in the fleet of the wandering Trojans of the first Odyssean half of the *Aeneid*, in the little boat on which Julius Caesar sails into the teeth of the tempest and the mercy of Fortune in Book 5 of the *Pharsalia*, in Vasco da Gama's ship beset by the storms promised by Adamastor in Book 6 of the *Lusíadas*; that is, at points in those poems where epic teleology comes into question and threatens to fall into what the epic perceives as romance aimlessness. But in romance narratives such as the *Rinaldo* (or the *Odyssey*) the ship embodies an adventure principle that counterbalances an equally constitutive quest principle: while digressive adventures and subplots delay the quest's conclusion, they also come to acquire an attraction and validity of their own. Georg Simmel describes the adventure as an "island of life which determines its beginning and end according to its own formative power,"[2] and the romance boat often travels to a series of islands and discrete episodes. This series may be random. In epic narrative, which moves toward a predetermined end—where the quest is all—the magic ship would signal a dangerous digression from a central plot line, but the boat of romance, in its purest form, has no other destination than the adventure at hand. It cannot be said to be off course. New adventures crop up all the time, and the boat's travels describe a romance narrative that is open-ended and potentially endless.[3]

When the boat is encountered again in Tasso's writings, at the opening of canto 15 of the *Gerusalemme liberata*, it has become the boat of Fortune. Its pilot is an allegorical figure, whose description (15.4–5) recalls the character of the Fata Morgana in Boiardo's *Orlando innamorato* (2.8.43). Boiardo's version of Morgan le Fay personifies Fortuna (2.9.25) or Ventura (2.9.19). The etymological link suggests why the "barca aventurosa" should now belong to the province of Ventura-Fortuna; the chance of the moment bestows adventures, and the adventurer takes chancy risks. The iconography of Fortune and her boat is a Renaissance commonplace, part of a humanist conflation of the concepts of Fortune and Occasion ("kairos") that redefines the experience of time; it transforms the contingent moment into an opportunity for human action and exploitation.[4] For Boiardo, the seizure of occasion—the forelock of Fortune that dangles before Morgana's brow—is the ideological emblem of romance adventure itself. In Orlando's successful pursuit and mastery of Morgana in the second book of the *Innamorato* (2.8–9, 13) he allegorizes the triumph of heroic virtue over whatever adventures Fortune or the romance narrative may present, adventures that are Ventura's infinitely variable forms.[5] Similarly, the iconography of Fortune's boat assimilates her with the ever-changing winds and tides—contingent forces that man cannot control but which, through foresight and exertion—the twin Renaissance virtues of prudence and fortitude—he can learn to time properly and turn to his advantage.

But if Tasso assimilates the boat of romance adventure with Boiardo's figure of Fortune, the animating principle of such adventure, he simultaneously transforms both Fortune and her boat into epic, rather than romance, entities. Like Dante (*Inferno* 7.61–96), Tasso represents Fortune as the minister of Providence (*Liberata* 9.57); her apparently random actions in fact carry out a larger divine plan for human history. Here she tames the seas in order to convey the knights Carlo and Ubaldo on their divinely sanctioned mission to rescue Rinaldo (who is no relation to the Rinaldo of the *Rinaldo*) from the island of Armida, to bring him back beneath the command of Goffredo at Jerusalem, where he is destined to lead the victorious final assault on the city. Fortune's boat no longer sails into digressive romance adventures but has become an essential part of the epic machinery that drives forward to the providential goal and narrative end point of Tasso's poem.

Moreover, as her craft passes through the Gates of Hercules, Fortune prophesies the voyage of a future Atlantic sailor:

> Tu spiegherai, Colombo, a un novo polo
> lontane sì le fortunate antenne,
> ch'a pena seguirà con gli occhi il volo
> la fama c'ha mille occhi e mille penne.
> Canti ella Alcide e Bacco, e di te solo
> basti a i posteri tuoi ch'alquanto accenne:
> ché quel poco darà lunga memoria
> di poema dignissima e d'istoria.

> (15.32)

(You, Columbus, will extend your fortunate sails so far in the direction of a new world that Fame will scarcely be able to follow you and keep you in sight, Fame with her thousand eyes and thousand wings. Let her sing of Hercules and Bacchus, and let it suffice that she give only a little mention of you to your posterity: that little will afford a long record of events worthy of poetry and history.)

The final epic transformation of Fortune's boat is into the ship of Columbus with its "fortunate antenne." The journey of Carlo and Ubaldo outside the Mediterranean world becomes the prototype for the Renaissance voyages of exploration and colonial expansion, voyages that could similarly transvalue romance adventure into the stuff of epic. The Age of Discovery provided real-life adventures that not only were the equal of fabled ones—Portuguese soldiers in India compared their own exploits favorably with those of Amadís[6]—but also were seen to be chapters in historical plans that would bring Christianity to the newly discovered world and fulfill the destinies of various European nation-states. The enterprise of discovery and conquest provided sixteenth-century epic poetry with one of its two great contemporary subjects, the other being the struggle between Christian Europe and the Ottoman Empire, the subject reflected in Tasso's fiction of the First Crusade. By Tasso's own literary theory, the subject that merits both poetic and historical treatments is by nature an epic one, and in the *Liberata* he elevates Columbus into an epic hero of undying fame. Columbus's voyage is placed within a providential scheme, the first step in evangelizing the peoples of the Americas; Fortune tells her passengers:

> la fé di Piero
> fiavi introdotta ed ogni civil arte.

> (15.29)

(The faith of Peter and every civil art will be introduced there.)

In keeping with the politics of the *Liberata* discussed in the last chapter, Tasso's passage describes the triumph in the New World of the Roman Church and its faith; the passage is pointedly opposed to an analogous episode in the *Orlando furioso* (15.19–35) where Ariosto celebrated the voyages of discovery as extensions of the power of the Hapsburg emperor Charles V.[7] Tasso thus transforms the boat of Fortune twice over into an epic ship: just as it receives a fixed course and destination in Tasso's plot, the boat prefigures future voyages of discovery that carry out God's plot for history. No longer the emblem of the fortuitous at all, the boat escapes the aimless pattern of romance wandering, of adventure for its own sake.

Such wandering into romance adventure is also depicted by the *Liberata*. While Carlo and Ubaldo travel to Armida's island on Fortune's boat, Rinaldo falls into Armida's clutches one canto earlier by entering a little skiff that he finds moored by the bank of the Orontes (14.57f.). This boat, which promises to take him to the greatest "meraviglie" the world has to offer— the marvels that sixteenth-century theorists and readers alike considered to be the chief pleasure of romances[8]—is a second version of the "barca aventurosa" of the *Rinaldo*. The Rinaldo of the *Liberata* has left the Crusader army after his quarrel with Goffredo and intends to take up knight-errantry. He proposes a voyage of discovery of his own, a journey to the source of the Nile (5.52), and he enters the world of romance by sailing to the little enchanted island in the Orontes, an island of adventure. Presiding over this romance world is Armida, who takes the place of Boiardo's Fortuna; indeed, we are to see her as a version of that Fortune figure. The Orontes island where Armida first captures Rinaldo foreshadows her garden paradise in the Fortunate Islands (14.70; 15.37) or, as the Canaries are also known, the Happy Islands (15.35). The labyrinthine structure of Armida's palace

(16.1.8) and the bas-reliefs on its doors (16.2–7) recall the reliefs of the labyrinth of Crete on the gates of the Fata Morgana's realm in the *Orlando innamorato* (2.8.15–17), and the celebrated tableau of Armida gazing at her mirror (16.20) similarly echoes Boiardo's description of Morgana embracing her captive favorite Ziliante in the same episode: "Mirando come un specchio nel bel viso" (2.13.22). These allusions cast the rescue of Rinaldo from Armida's palace as a rewriting of Orlando's rescue of Ziliante from an overly favorable Fortune.

Tasso's fiction thus contains and juxtaposes two versions of the boat of adventure, two versions of Boiardo's figure of Fortune—both the allegorical Fortune who pilots their ship and the fallacious maidens on Armida's island address Carlo and Ubaldo as "fortunati" (15.6.62)—to distinguish the epic enterprise from its romance double. The romance adventure on which Rinaldo embarks is the hero's individualistic alternative to the collective epic mission of the Crusade. It quickly emerges as a mistaken choice of Achilles, an opting for hedonistic ease outside of the heroic arena of history, by an Achilles figure who was also mistaken to have rebelled against the higher political authority of his commander in chief, Goffredo, who plays in the authoritarian *Liberata* the role of a just Agamemnon. Rinaldo's romance wandering is thus the figure as well as the consequence of his political errancy. His insubordination removes him from the scene of history at Jerusalem into a realm of Fortune, where time is broken down into a series of contingent, unrelated moments, isolated from one another and from any larger historical or narrative plan, where Boiardo's humanist imperative to exploit occasion shades into the *carpe diem* theme contained in the song of the rose recited by Armida's parrot (16.14–15), and where the adventure becomes an end in itself. It is a dead end, however. Tasso insists that to live in a world of Fortune is to become her prisoner, and he portrays Rinaldo not as Boiardo's Orlando, the master of Morgana, but rather as Ziliante, her beloved captive. Much as Virgil suggested about Aeneas (*Aeneid* 10:48–49), Tasso ascribes his hero's individual personality and career—once he is removed from a corporate political destiny—to the accidents of chance; but this chance, Rinaldo's good fortune that Armida has fallen in love with him and taken him, chained with flowers (14.68), along with her to her island paradise, is all-determining and nullifies any autonomous agency on the hero's part. By refusing to subject himself to Goffredo's authority—and from the beginning of the poem Rinaldo has belonged to the band of "avventurieri" (1.52) in the Crusader army, adventuring soldiers of fortune or knights-errant whose allegiance to the central command is already suspect—Rinaldo merely turns into Armida's thrall.

Escape from the romance prison, from an existence that is merely episodic, is offered by epic and its politico-historical mission which posits a goal that transcends the adventure of the moment and organizes what may otherwise seem random events into a coherent narrative. The goal of Tasso's epic, the liberation of Jerusalem, is, as we have seen, inseparable from the political unification of the Crusader army, Goffredo's reimposition of his authority over his "compagni erranti" (1.1.8); and Goffredo's achievement, in turn is closely analogous to the poet's uniting of his poem's episodes into a single end-directed plot, his incorporation of the romance models of Boiards and Ariosto into the epic framework of the *Liberata*. This epic teleology characteristically invokes a "higher" vertical dimension of synchronic meaning to explain the horizontal world of diachronic action in which the romance adventurer is normally confined. Tasso's boat of Fortune, ferrying Rinaldo back to fulfill his divinely appointed destiny, back to do submission to Goffredo, is an emblem of the assimilation of romance into such epic structures of meaning. The boat and the actions to which it carries its passengers are no longer subject to Fortune the personification of chance and contingency but rather to Fortune the servant of Providence. In the epic world, nothing is left to chance.

Satan in Chaos

The voyage to the Canaries in the *Gerusalemme liberata* is one of the many epic models to which Milton alludes in Satan's journey to earth through Chaos in Book 2 of *Paradise Lost*, a journey that is cast as a sea voyage. Beelzebub describes earth as "the happy isle" (2.410), and later Satan passes through stars that seem to be "happy isles, / Like those Hesperian gardens famed of old, / Fortunate fields, and groves and flowery vales, / Thrice happy isles" (3.567–71). But while Milton's fiction recalls Tasso's and other earlier epic voyages—those of Odysseus, Jason, Aeneas, and Spenser's Guyon—his principal subtext is the journey of Vasco da Gama around the Cape of Good Hope to India in the *Os Lusíadas*. Scholars have noted how the initial comparison of the flying Satan to a fleet returning from "Bengala, or the isles / of Ternate and Tidore" (2.638–39) and heading for the cape is balanced in Book 4 (4.159–65) by the simile that likens the archfiend outside Eden to "them who sail / Beyond the Cape of Hope, and now are past / Mozambic." These similes at either end of Satan's trip invoke the Indian Ocean world of Camões' epic.[9] I should like to point out a further series of recollections and direct echoes of the *Lusíadas*—more specifically of Sir Richard Fanshawe's English translation of the poem published in 1655—which constitute a whole pattern of Miltonic allusion. Camões describes the palace of Neptune on the ocean floor; on its doors are sculpted bas-reliefs (6.10–12) that depict first Chaos and subsequently the four elements, evoking a traditional identification between the ocean and the sources of material creation. Milton's Chaos is described as a "dark / Illimitable ocean" (2.890–91), where prime matter has not yet disposed itself into elemental form, "neither sea, nor shore, nor air, nor fire" (2.912).[10] On its way to India, da Gama's fleet is caught in the terrible monsoonlike storm of Book 6:

> The *thund'ring's* such, that there are now no hopes
> But that HEAV'N'S *Axles* will be streight unbuilt:
> The ELEMENTS at one another tilt.
>
> (6.84)

Milton's Chaos, a realm of incessant storms, is described in strikingly similar terms. Its noise peals no less in Satan's ear

> than if this frame
> Of heaven were falling, and these elements
> In mutiny had from her axle torn
> The steadfast earth.
>
> (2.924–27)

Later compared to a "weather-beaten vessel" (2.1043), Satan makes his way through the gusts of Chaos to the court of Chaos himself. When he asks this anarch for directions to get to earth, the action parodies da Gama's visit to the king of Melinde from whom he seeks a pilot to guide him to India. His address to Chaos—

> I come no spy,
> With purpose to explore or to disturb
> The secrets of your realm
>
> (2.970–72)

—has precedents in the *Odyssey* (2.71–74) and the *Aeneid* (1.527–29), but these were in turn imitated by Camões in da Gama's speech to the Muslim king. Milton's choice of the word "spy," which has no counterpart in the classical epics, indicates that his model was indeed Fanshawe's translation:

> We are not Men, who spying a weak *Town*
> Or careless, as we pass along the shore,
> Murther the *Folks*, and burn the *Houses* down.
>
> (2.80)

Finally, the alliance that Satan forges with Chaos and Night, offering to turn over all the profits of his mission to earth to his partners—"Yours be the advantage all, mine the revenge" (987)—recalls and echoes another moment in Camões' poem, the similar proposition that da Gama offers the Zamorin of Calicut on behalf of his Portuguese king: "*His* shall be the *glory*, *thine* the *Gain* be found" (7.62).[11]

Like the voyage of Columbus, da Gama's expedition inaugurated the Age of Discovery. Tasso's encomium to Columbus celebrated the voyages of discovery as providential events; Milton's fiction, by recasting the events of the *Lusíadas* into Satan's journey, suggests that the voyages are the work of the devil. As da Gama opened up a route to the Indies for the trade and imperialism of Europe—particularly Catholic Europe—so Satan blazes a trail for Sin and Death to build their bridge by "art / Pontifical" from Hell to earth (10.312–13). Adam and Eve, who after their fall don fig leaves, which liken them both to the Indians of Malabar and to the Native Americans whom "of late / Columbus found" (9.1099–1118), assume the roles of innocent natives victimized by their European conquerors.

It is not surprising that the Puritan poet Milton should reject the providential interpretations of the exploits of Renaissance discovery advanced by Catholic epic poets such as Camões and Tasso. His criticism is in keeping with a general rejection in *Paradise Lost* both of imperialism and of the Virgilian epic of empire. This criticism, moreover, runs along generic lines. For whereas Tasso had seen the voyages of discovery as events that raised the adventures of romance to the level of epic, Milton's fiction suggests a reverse process. When Satan enters Chaos where "high arbiter / Chance governs all" (2.909–10), he finds himself at the mercy of the warring elements.

> At last his sail-broad vans
> He spreads for flight, and in the surging smoke
> Uplifted spurns the ground, thence many a league
> As in a cloudy chair ascending rides
> Audacious, but that seat soon failing, meets
> A vast vacuity: all unawares
> Fluttering his pennons vain plumb down he drops
> Ten thousand fathom deep, and to this hour
> Down had been falling, had not by ill chance
> The strong rebuff of some tumultuous cloud
> Instinct with fire and nitre hurried him
> As many miles aloft.
>
> (2.927–38)

In addition to the larger model of the *Lusíadas*, this scene recalls Caesar's boat ride in *Pharsalia* 5. Commentators have suggested how Satan buffeted by the winds of Chaos is modeled on Caesar caught in the stormy Adriatic, an episode that I have already analyzed as Lucan's farcical deflation of the epic conqueror into romance wanderer under the aegis of Caesar's patroness Fortuna, a particularly dark version of romance fortune.[12] Milton's passage turns all its models into a tour de force both of science fiction space fantasy and of slapstick comedy. Satan's wings are like a ship's sails waiting to be filled by favoring winds. The phrase "Uplifted spurns the ground" wittily indicates that while Satan's trip may seem to be a haughty act of individual will, he is not in fact traveling under his own power but is rather swept off the ground by an updraft from Chaos. When these winds fail, moreover, the becalmed Satan plummets, flapping his useless wings, and still would be falling through the infinite reaches of space to this day if a chance explosion had not sent him hurtling back up into the air again. This cartoonlike reduction of the archfiend to a plaything of Chaos is highly comic, but it also presents a startling idea: that Satan would never have accomplished his journey to earth in order to seduce Adam and Eve but for a piece of very bad luck. Milton demonstrates that the evil will gives itself up to the play of chance, that its activities are ultimately random and fortuitous: there is only one coherent plan of action in the universe, and it belongs to God.[13]

Chaos is a realm of Fortune, hence a world of adventure, and Satan is transformed from epic voyager to a romance adventurer who takes advantage of, but is also, like Lucan's Caesar, dependent on, the occasions that chance brings his way; it is not surprising to hear the same Satan in *Paradise Regained* tempting Christ to seize "occasion's forelock" (3.173). It is as an "adventurer" that Satan returns from earth to Hell in Book 10 (10.440, 468), and the devils who remained behind in Book 2 on their own mission of reconnaissance through Hell, a "bold adventure to discover wide / That dismal world" (2.571–72), are similarly "adventurous" (2.615) explorers whose endeavors find "no rest" or final destination. The deflation of the epic deed into an adventure that has no more than a momentary significance not only undercuts the heroic posturings of Milton's devils but also represents Milton's judgment on the enterprise of discovery as a literary subject matter. Other Renaissance poets may assert that the voyages of discovery serve higher ends and merit inclusion among the transcendent fictions of epic. For Milton those voyages accomplish merely temporal (hence Satanic) ends and accordingly belong exclusively to the world of time and chance. The flying Satan is figuratively a ship sailing through the seas of Fortune, a boat of romance.

Heroes and Traders

There is a further argument latent in this same opposition between the epic voyage and the romance adventure within the context of the Age of Discovery, an argument that depends on the allegiance of epic fictions to the class ideology of a martial aristocracy. The terms of this ideology are vividly spelled out in a passage of the *Lusíadas* that Milton chose to parody—the trading agreement that da Gama offers to the Zamorin of Calicut. India will receive the profits of their transaction; the king of Portugal will reap the glory: "De ti proveito, e dele glória ingente" (7.62; "*His* shall be the *glory*, *thine* the *Gain* be found"). Camões' hero claims that Portugal's aim in opening up new trade routes, the general goal of all the voyages of discovery, is the acquisition not of the wealth that traders normally seek but of fame. The claim is on the face of it implausible. Yet it is central to the ethos of the *Lusíadas* and reflects a larger split in sixteenth- and seventeenth-century attitudes toward the enterprise of discovery.

Propaganda for the discoveries ran up against a time-honored aristocratic disdain for mercantile activities. This prejudice was institutionalized by six-teenth-century statutes in Spain and France that forbade noblemen from practicing trade.[14] The situation was somewhat different in Portugal. Con-servative noblemen might complain that expansion in the Indies was caus-ing their fellows to neglect their landed estates and turn merchant.[15] But the Portuguese nobility generally followed the lead of their king, investing and taking an active part in the lucrative Eastern ventures. The royal monopoly on the Indian trade, in fact, made commerce appear to be a patriotic duty. The Portuguese empire, moreover, was based on the tribute of conquest as well as on trade; it was gained and maintained through a series of wars with Muslim trading rivals.[16] If profit was a matter in which a gentleman was not supposed to take any interest, the Portuguese aristocracy could view its par-ticipation in the imperial enterprise primarily in terms of its traditional role as a military caste, in terms of personal honor, patriotism, and religious zeal.

These are the terms of the *Lusíadas*, and indeed they are the traditional terms of epic, a genre historically linked to aristocratic values. The overrid-ing ethical imperative of Camões' poem is the acquisition of martial fame, both for oneself and for one's country. Missionary and crusading motives are also ascribed to da Gama's expedition; though important, they are decidedly secondary to the pursuit of fame. Camões' Portuguese hero disdains money and the gifts of Fortune (6.98). Greed and desire for wealth are attributed instead to the Indian natives—the Zamorin's chief official is eventually won over by a bribe, occasioning the narrator's execration upon gold (8.96–99) at the very moment when da Gama's men gain access to the Indian markets—and to Portugal's European neighbors (7.11). Exchanging gain for glory, Camões provides a version of the Portuguese ventures in the East that plays down their commercial character, a version that was both consonant with epic norms of behavior and congenial to the self-image of a noble reader.

In England the gentry similarly persuaded themselves to invest in New World ventures by appealing to the idea of a glorious national destiny. They contrasted their nobler motives with those of their merchant partners, con-cerned primarily with the return on their investments.[17] Here, too, epic themes could come into play. Writing in 1577, Abraham Fleming laments the lack of a Homer to celebrate the return of Martin Frobisher, "our Ulys-ses," whose fame deserves to live forever:

> A right Heroicall heart of Britanne blood,
> Ulysses match in skill and Martiall might:
> For Princes fame, and countries speciall good,
> Through brackish seas (where Neptune reignes by right)
> Hath safely saild, in perils great despight:
> The Golden fleece (like Iason) hath he got,
> And rich returned, saunce losse or lucklesse lot.[18]

As a propagandist for empire, Fleming does not wish to dispense with the incentive of riches altogether, but they are an added incentive, mentioned after the primary motives of personal glory and patriotism. The English adventurer could think of himself less as a businessman, more as a soldier and epic hero. The notorious early experience of the Jamestown settlement, where idle gentlemen were found bowling in the streets while the colony faced starvation, is an example of how counterproductive such aristocratic attitudes could be when the adventurer arrived in the New World.[19]

The Renaissance voyage of discovery could be described as an epic voyage to distinguish it as an aristocratic rather than a mercantile pursuit. But voyages of seafaring epics might themselves need to be differentiated from commercial doubles or false twins. In the *Odyssey* the travels of Odysseus are carefully distinguished from less-heroic maritime activities. The prominence of Phoenician traders—"gnawers of other men's goods"—in the lying stories that Odysseus recounts about himself to Athena (13.255–87) and Eumaios (14.192–359), as well as in Eumaios's narration of his own life story (15.390–483), suggests a parallel between these masters of the sea and the poem's wandering hero. To prevent the reader from drawing such a parallel, Homer inserts a scene in Book 8 where Odysseus declines to compete in the Phaeacians' athletic games and is consequently insulted by a young nobleman, Euryalos:

> No stranger, for I do not see that you are like one versed
> in contests, such as now are practiced much among people,
> but rather to one who plies his ways in his many-locked vessel,
> master over mariners who also are men of business,
> a man who, careful of his cargo and grasping for profits,
> goes carefully on his way. You do not resemble an athlete.

> (8.159–64)

Odysseus promptly repudiates this slur by picking up the heaviest discus and throwing it farther than any of the Phaeacians' casts.[20] The episode is strategically placed, however, for it precedes Alcinous's decision to ask all the men of Phaeacia to assemble gifts for Odysseus; in fact, the same Euryalos presents the hero with a special gift to make amends for his ill-measured words (8.396–411). This is the wealth with which Odysseus returns to Ithaca, more wealth, Poseidon will complain (13.134–38), than Odysseus could have attained had he brought back his share of the plunder of Troy—the normal means for an epic hero to acquire portable property. Homer takes pains to demonstrate that the Phaeacians' gifts are a tribute to Odysseus's heroism—to the fact that he is not a base merchant as Euryalos had charged—in order to distinguish his wealth from the profits of a trading expedition. Nonetheless, ancient critics noted the pecuniary motives of the heroes of the *Odyssey*. The second-century author Aelian wrote that Odysseus and Menelaus "traveiled from region to region, after the custome of the Marchantes of Phenicia, for they did hourde and heape up money lyke mountaines, the desire whereof spurred them forward, and imboldened them to attempt dangerous journeys by lande, and perilous voyages by sea."[21]

Similarly, Jason's quest for the Golden Fleece, the subject of the *Argonautica* of Apollonius Rhodius, was regarded in antiquity as a commercial venture; Juvenal (6.53) refers to this second voyager of classical epic as "mercator Iason." In Fleming's verses, the Golden Fleece is equated with the riches brought back by Frobisher's expedition, and Spenser's *Faerie Queene* would later allegorize the Libyan Syrtes upon which the Argo is caught in the fourth book of the *Argonautica* (1228f.) as the "quicksand of Unthriftyhed," upon which merchants' ships are seen to founder (2.12.18–19).

When the actions of the *Odyssey* and the *Argonautica* are transferred to the sea, the domain of traders and sailors, epic fiction collides with social reality, and uncertainties arise about their heroes' motives and behavior. These uncertainties correspond to generic uncertainties about the poems themselves. If they claim relationship to the martial world of epic—Odysseus returns from the world of the *Iliad* and greets the hero of that poem in the underworld, Jason is the shipmate of the greatest of heroes, Hercules— the episodic wanderings of their heroes into a world of the marvelous indicates a turn toward romance. The *Odyssey* was regarded by Renaissance critics as the first *romanzo*—as it still seems to be regarded by Frye.[22] There is, I wish to argue, a link between the disposition to view the voyages of Odysseus and Jason as trading ventures and the resemblance of these voyages to romance adventures. This link is clearly visible in the most extended Renaissance rewriting of the Jason story in economic terms. We are brought back to the fiction of the *Orlando innamorato*.

In the first book of Boiardo's poem, Orlando accepts and overcomes the trials proposed to him by the Fata dell'Isola del Lago. They are the same obstacles that Jason faced at Colchis: the enchanted bulls, the dragon, and the armed men springing up from the dragon's teeth.[23] In canto 25, Orlando is rewarded with what he is told is the greatest "ventura" (4) for which a knight can hope: a little dog with which he can hunt down a marvelous stag with golden horns. The stag is Boiardo's version of the Golden Fleece, for it molts its horns six times a day and is guaranteed to make its capturer infinitely rich. Orlando, however, flatly refuses to have anything to do with this adventure. He does not regret having undergone the trials, for danger and toil are the source of chivalric honor (13). But the search for wealth, he declares, is an unending one, because the searcher is never satisfied.

> Che qualunque n'ha più, più ne desia:
> Adunque senza capo è questa via.
>
> Senza capo è la strata ed infinita
> De onore e di diletto al tutto priva.

(1.25.14–15)

(For he who has more, desires more: therefore this road is without end. It is an endless and infinite road, totally lacking in honor and pleasure.)

Because, Orlando maintains, one can never have enough money, its pursuit will be as endless as it is inglorious. Without a final goal, such activity will bear a disturbing likeness to the open-ended structure of Boiardo's own romance narrative, to the apparently endless, loosely connected string of adventures upon which Orlando will himself embark. The likeness is reinforced by the episode's play on the word "ventura." Orlando voices his desire, "Dio me doni alta ventura" (1.25.2; "God grant me a high adventure"), the characteristic desire of the knight-errant for some marvelous adventure. The phrase is very similar to formulas that recur, often as salutations, in the letters of a sixteenth-century Venetian merchant: "che'l Signor Dio li doni venttura . . . lo eterno Dio ve dono quelo dexideratte e a noi tan bien venttura . . . si che staremo alla vedetta et aspettar venttura che Idio la mandi . . . che'l nostro Signor Dio ne manda venttura"[24] ("The Lord God should grant him luck . . . the eternal God grant you what you desire and such good luck to us . . . so we are on the lookout and await opportunity, which God send us . . . our Lord God send us good luck"). The merchant prays for good fortune and the specific chance to make a fortune: such an opportunity is offered to Orlando in place of the adventure that he craves. But the knight rejects the offer of fabulous wealth. Like Homer, Boiardo finds it necessary to dissociate his hero from the economic activity that so closely resembles the hero's adventures in the realm of romance.

The enchanted stag, moreover, returns us to Boiardo's figure of Fortune, for the stag, first described at 1.17.57–58, is the property of the Fata Morgana, none other than Ventura herself. Like her stag, Morgana is also a kind of Golden Fleece, for her forelock, the forelock of occasion, is golden (2.8.58). The seizure of Fortune by her forelock, representing the humanist idea of man exploiting time to his advantage, can easily bear an economic interpretation: for the merchant, time is money. In one sense, the *Innamorato* may be said to disclose the social origins of its romance ideology, for the idea that fortune can be mastered through fortitude and prudence was developed by Florentine humanists who were either merchants themselves or closely associated with mercantile society, and their terms were drawn from a traditional mercantile vocabulary.[25] But the hero of the aristocratic poet Boiardo wants nothing to do with this aspect of Fortune, and Orlando's further encounters with Morgana contain two further rejections of wealth: first when he rebukes his cousin Rinaldo for trying to carry off some of the golden furnishings of Morgana's subterranean realm (2.9.33), later when he refuses Morgana's offer of riches and treasure, a bribe to prevent him from rescuing Ziliante from her clutches (2.13.23–24). Ziliante is the son of King Manodante, who has amassed more than half the wealth of the world (1.21.49; 2.11.46), and Boiardo's fiction allegorizes the dangers of being Fortune's favorite, of being the prisoner of one's own wealth and good fortune.[26] The tenor of all these episodes in the *Innamorato* is the same: the knight should grasp all opportunities to make a trial of his strength and virtue in the adventures that Fortune sends his way without turning into a grasping Fortune hunter. He should be a Jason who turns down the Golden Fleece.

Boiardo's romance conceded, if only to forswear, a resemblance between its adventures and moneymaking ventures. This resemblance can enter into the generic distinction that epic draws between its closed form and the open-ended romance narrative. The higher, transcendent goals toward which epic narrative is directed correspond to the ethical goals by which a martial aristocracy claims to distinguish itself from social inferiors who—in the eyes of the aristocrat—care only for their day-to-day temporal needs and the accumulation of wealth. To the extent that the romance adventure remains autonomous from these goals—that it remains merely the adventure presently at hand, dealt out by an everchanging Fortune—it remains, from the perspective of epic, immersed in contingent time and inevitably directed toward temporal goods. The hierarchy of genres may thus reflect an ideology of social hierarchy.[27] When, moreover, Renaissance epic describes the recent voyages of discovery, this dichotomy between epic and romance finds a specific ideological application. It reflects the divergent interpretations of the voyages that ran along class lines. The enterprise of discovery could alternately be understood as a heroic endeavor in the epic, aristocratic mold or as a business expedition undertaken by adventurous merchants in search of their fortunes. It is in this light that we may return to the fictions of Tasso and Milton.

Tasso's encomium of Columbus, whose ship of discovery is a future epic extension of the providential boat of Fortune of canto 15, is juxtaposed with a repudiation of the romance Fortune figure Armida, who replays the role of Boiardo's Morgana, the "Fata del Tesoro" (2.12.24) and dispenser of all worldly wealth. Her captive Rinaldo takes the place of the rich heir Ziliante in the *Innamorato*. In the immediate fiction of the *Liberata*, Armida tempts Rinaldo with concupiscence, but in the play of allusion to Boiardo's poem that produces two opposing figures and concepts of Fortune, the temptations of her realm are all of Fortune's temporal gifts. The celebration of Columbus juxtaposed with the rejection of this worldly Fortune—which is also a generic rejection of the romance adventure—and the implication that Columbus's voyage represents an alternative to that Fortune fit into an ideological scheme that elevates the voyages of discovery into epic events by dissociating them from economic pursuits. The symbolic geography that places Armida's garden in the Canaries, where Columbus provisioned before sailing west in 1492, makes of Rinaldo a kind of Columbus *manqué*, one who got sidetracked along the way. The Canaries were a flourishing trading center by the sixteenth century, and the historical Columbus had modeled his title and prerogatives as the Admiral of the Ocean Sea on those of the Admiral of Castile, who controlled shipping to the Canaries and was entitled to a one-third rake-off on the profits.[28] There were indeed fortunes to be made on the Fortunate Isles.

In the figure of Ubaldo, the knight who journeys on the boat of Fortune to rescue Rinaldo, there is a further hint that Tasso's rejection of romance is also a rejection of a mercantile interpretation of the voyages of discovery. For Ubaldo is a former romance adventurer—and he, too, belonged to the crusading "avventurieri" (1.55)—chosen for this epic mission because of his wide travel experience in his youth, when he wandered through various countries and regions of the earth. He is like a man "che virtute e senno *merchi*" (14.28), one who trades in virtue and wisdom. His journeying makes him an Odyssean figure,[29] particularly reminiscent of Dante's Ulysses, who told his men to follow "virtute e canoscenza" (*Inferno* 26.120); it is Ubaldo's curiosity about Atlantic navigation (15.24) that prompts Fortune to discuss the earlier Dantesque Ulysses (25), whose aimless wandering ended in shipwreck, before she goes on to prophesy the future, providential voyage of Columbus. There is a sense, then, in which Ubaldo, no less than the boat of Fortune itself, is a piece of romance machinery that Tasso transforms and rehabilitates by placing it in an epic context and to which, in the figure of Ulysses, he opposes a demonic romance double.

Like Homer's Odysseus, moreover, Ubaldo in his earlier wanderings already possessed a commercial double, for trading in wisdom can resemble trade itself. Conversely, the Renaissance merchant could be praised for the wide experience of the world he acquired through his business ventures. In his *Suma de Tratos* of 1569, the Spaniard Tomás de Mercado asserts of merchants that

> conversing with many peoples, dwelling in different realms, trading with various nations, experiencing different customs, considering the differing governments and political institutions of peoples, they make themselves universal men, practiced and apt for whatever business ventures may offer themselves to them. They acquire and build up a great store of prudence and experience by which to guide and govern themselves, in particular circumstances as well as general ones. They are useful to the state because of their knowledge of the various things which they have seen and heard in their travels.[30]

The ideal merchant has become a universal Renaissance man and also an Odyssean man of many turns, and he is described here in terms remarkably similar to those with which Tasso describes Ubaldo. Ubaldo's wealth of experience is the kind sought by romance heroes such as Boiardo's Orlando, but, as was the case in the *Innamorato*, such wealth may be difficult to separate from the material, monetary wealth with which it seems to come hand in hand. Ubaldo's voyage to Armida's island is shown, however, to be a rejection of his former adventuring: romance adventure as an end in itself is figured in the fate of the drowned Ulysses, while the formerly wandering Ubaldo is placed on the formerly wandering boat of Fortune, and both are set upon a straight epic course—what will be the future course of Renaissance exploration. Tasso's depiction of the discoveries as epic events seems to require first the exorcism of a romance spirit of adventure, which, it is intimated, may be identical to the spirit of trade.

The effort to distinguish heroic from moneymaking pursuits may find a specific context in the ideology of Renaissance discovery, but it also conforms, as we have seen in the *Odyssey*, to a normative epic ethos. The verb "mercare," which describes Ubaldo's former activities, appears one more time in the *Liberata*. It is, in fact, the very last word spoken by a character in the poem. Just before Goffredo reaches the Holy Sepulcher he turns down the offer of a large ransom from the captured Altamoro, king of Samarkand. He spares Altamoro's life, but declares:

> de la vita altrui prezzo non cerco:
> guerreggio in Asia, e non vi cambio o merco.
>
> (20.142)

(I do not seek a price for another's life: I wage war in Asia, and do not change money or trade there.)

The passage contains a rich overlay of allusion. It directly echoes the speech in *Paradiso* 16 of Dante's ancestor Cacciaguida, who decries the degeneration of Florence and her noble families; because of the city's political sins:

> tal fatto è fiorentino e cambia e merca,
> che si sarebbe vòlto a Simifonti,
> là dove andava l'avolo a la cerca.

$$(61-63)$$

(Such a man has become a Florentine and changes money and trades, who would have continued to live in Semifonte, there where his grandfather went peddling.)[31]

The canto has begun with the apostrophe of Dante the narrator to nobility of blood—"O poca nostra nobiltà di sangue!"—and with the slightly sheepish admission that he had gloried in heaven in his own noble family as Cacciaguida had revealed it to him (6). Dante now dissociates that family and an older virtuous Florence from the new outsiders, merchants whose ancestors were even lesser entrepreneurs before them. This Dantesque moment of aristocratic hauteur is woven into Tasso's other imitative gesture in Goffredo's response to Altamoro: his revision of episodes in the *Iliad* (21.34–113) and the *Aeneid* (10.521–34) where Achilles and Aeneas refuse to spare suppliants who beg to ransom their lives. Part of the purpose of the scene is to end the *Liberata* with an act of clemency amid the general massacre (143) of the Saracen army. But it also closes Tasso's epic with an assertion of a heroism untainted by baser desires for gain, with Goffredo's refusal to turn merchant.[32] The taking of ransoms and selling of prisoners were common enough features of sixteenth-century warfare, both between different European nations and between Europeans and the Ottoman Turks. The privateering Knights of Malta and the knights of Saint Stephen, the modern-day crusaders of Tasso's own time, combined warfare with business and were not likely to pass up offers of ransom from their Muslim captives in the manner of Goffredo.[33] Tasso may thus find both heroic arenas of his century—the exploits of discovery *and* the crusade against Islam—threatened by mercenary behavior inadmissible within the ethical code of epic. He closes his poem by reasserting epic's traditional class prejudice, its exclusion of money and trade from the heroic world.

Milton, in keeping with his general criticism of the earlier epic tradition, exposes as false the distinction which that tradition draws between martial heroism and mercantile activity. He accompanies his reduction of Satan from epic voyager to chance adventurer by depicting Satan as a commercial traveler:

> As when far off at sea, a fleet descried
> Hangs in the clouds, by equinoctial winds
> Close sailing from Bengala, or the isles
> Of Ternate and Tidore, whence merchants bring

Their spicy drugs: they on the trading flood
Through the wide Ethiopian to the Cape
Ply stemming nightly toward the pole. So seemed
Far off the flying fiend.

(2.636–43)

This simile is the first to develop the comparison between Satan's journey and a sea voyage. The voyage in question is a trading venture, engaged in bringing back the Eastern spices that were the initial goal of Renaissance discovery. The passage retrospectively lends a mercantile note to Beelzebub's earlier talk of "enterprise" (345) and "some advantageous act" (363), and it colors the exchange between Satan and Chaos about "recompense" (981), "advantage" (987), and "gain" (1009). If Satan and the devils are "adventurers," they are also Merchant Adventurers.[34] The conversation between Satan and Chaos, I have already noted, is an ironic rewriting of the moment in the *Lusíadas* where da Gama claims to seek a trading agreement with Calicut for the sake of Portugal's glory rather than her profit. Milton's fiction not only casts doubt upon da Gama's protestations of heroic disinterestedness, but in the character of Satan the trader it also reflects upon other heroes of maritime epic like Odysseus and Jason, long suspected of being merchants in disguise.

By the middle of the seventeenth century, the Portuguese monopoly on the Indian Ocean trade had long been broken by the Dutch and British. These new commercial rivals had waged two wars by the time *Paradise Lost* was first published in 1667, and a third was fought before the second edition of the poem appeared in 1674.[35] The focus of Milton's criticism constantly shifts between a revision of the earlier epic tradition and an indictment of European expansion and colonialism that includes his own countrymen and contemporaries. Moreover, Milton may be aware of the implications for epic poetry of the emergence of a merchant class whose interests had begun to shape the imperial destinies of the nation. The merchant not only contested with the nobleman for power but also laid claim to the nobleman's very nobility. In 1641, Lewis Roberts, merchant and Captain of the City of London, argued in *The Treasure of Traffike* that trade ennobled its practitioners:

And if true Nobilitie should have taken its foundation, (as the Iudicious and Learned have observed heretofore) from the courage of men, and from their Valour, there is no vocation wherein there is so many usefull and principall parts of man required, as in these two, for they are not only to adventure and hazard theire owne persons, but also their estates, goods, and what ever they have, amongst men of all nations, Customes, Lawes, and Religions, wheresoever they are inhabited.[36]

Roberts comments further in another passage:

> It is not our conquests, but our Commerce; it is not our swords, but our sayls, that first spred the English name in *Barbary*, and thence came into *Turkey*, *Armenia*, *Moscovia*, *Arabia*, *Persia*, *India*, *China*, and indeed over and about the world; it is the traffike of their Merchants, and the boundless desires of that nation to eternize the English honour and name, that hath enduced them to saile, and seeke into all the corners of the earth. What part is there unsearched, what place undiscovered, or what place lyes unattempted by their endeavors, and couragious undertakings?[37]

Roberts speaks proudly for a merchant class that asserts self-worth by claiming the heroic virtues that had been heretofore the exclusive property of the aristocracy. The merchant shows as much if not more valor, courage, and patriotism in his ventures as the nobleman does in his soldierly profession. Moreover, trading exploits, rather than martial ones, are the source of England's national glory and her achievements in the enterprise of discovery. Insisting that the true heroes of exploration are merchants, Roberts provides an alternative to an aristocratic ideology that interprets the discoveries in terms of imperial conquest. While such a mercantile version of the voyages of discovery may preserve their heroic nature—at least in the merchant's eyes—it cannot be accommodated to epic terms, for epic does not celebrate bourgeois heroes, however heroic they may be. Milton's deflation of the epic voyager Satan into a representative of the East India Company suggests that the aristocratic ideology that animated earlier epic has by now become obsolete. Just as the leveling artillery in the War in Heaven reveals the uselessness of a warrior class—a lesson that was learned, as always imperfectly, by the Royalists during the civil wars—so the presence of traders on the oceans of the East suggests that a new social group has taken over the heroic arena that formerly belonged to the gentleman soldier.

Epic and Novel

Renaissance epic insists on the mercantile cast of the romance adventure in order, in Tasso's case, to distinguish the voyage of discovery from its false commercial twin; or, in Milton's, to disclose the true economic nature of that voyage. This epic characterization of the adventure was in some ways prophetic of the future of romance. It points up the relative flexibility of romance's open forms vis-à-vis epic's more rigid classical structures and greater commitment to social hierarchy. This flexibility, which led Renaissance critics to consider romance the genre of innovation, allowed it to change to meet the demands of a new audience in ways that epic could not. The example of the voyages of discovery itself suggests the failure of aristocratic ideology and literary forms to describe a reality that was increasingly pervaded by early capitalism. As a bourgeois reading public began to command the literary marketplace, epic was doomed and romance had to adapt quickly to survive. A late flowering of courtly and pastoral prose romances—these will be touched upon in the following chapter—proved to be a dead end. The future for romance, as epic had already intimated, lay with the new world of money and materiality[38]—and with the novel.

In Chapter 29 of the second part of *Don Quixote*, Don Quixote and Sancho come across an oarless little boat on the river Ebro. The ingenious hidalgo concludes that some enchanter has placed the craft in his path to carry him to the aid of some other knight or important person in distress. Cervantes' probable source is an episode in *Palmerín de Inglaterra*, but it might just as well have been Tasso's "barca aventurosa." The knight and squire settle in this boat of romance and set it adrift. In spite of Sancho's protests that they have not traveled five yards from the river bank, Don Quixote believes that they have already been transported seven or eight hundred leagues, and he speculates whether they have crossed the equator: "according to those Spaniards and others who embark in Cádiz in order to go to the East Indies, one of the signs by which they know that they have passed the equinoctial line that I have spoken of is that the lice die on board the ship." Ordered to search his body, Sancho confirms that they have not yet reached the equator.[39]

Here again the romance boat of adventure has turned into the Renaissance ship of discovery, and we may speculate whether that ship is on a heroic epic voyage or just on a mercantile adventure.[40] But to do so is to remain inside Quixote's mad imagination, where literary genres and other things are impossibly confused. The novel does not allow us to remain there long. A few moments later, the knight and squire collide with a water mill, their vessel is smashed to pieces, and its enraged former owner demands to be paid for its loss. The boat of romance turns out to be nothing more than a boat.

SEVEN

PARADISE LOST AND THE FALL OF THE

ENGLISH COMMONWEALTH

ADAM'S SPEECH toward the end of Book 12 of *Paradise Lost*, when he and Eve are to be expelled from Eden, appears, if translated into Milton's biographical context, to affirm a withdrawal from collective political action to individual acts of piety and peaceful resistance, whose master model will be the passion of Christ. Adam's attitude, readers have presumed, corresponds to that of John Milton himself: politically disappointed by the failure of the republican Commonwealth he had served, forced to lie low during the first decade of the Restoration, and condemned to the internal exile of his blindness.[1]

> Henceforth I learn, that to obey is best,
> And love with fear the only God, to walk
> As in his presence, ever to observe
> His providence, and on him sole depend,
> Merciful over all his works, with good
> Still overcoming evil, and by small
> Accomplishing great things, by things deemed weak
> Subverting worldly strong, and worldly wise
> By simply meek; that suffering for truth's sake
> Is fortitude to highest victory,
> And to the faithful death the gate of life;
> Taught this by his example whom I now
> Acknowledge my redeemer ever blest.

(12.561–73)

Critics as different as Northrop Frye and Christopher Hill warn us not to confuse this attitude with a mere quietism.[2] As the delayed object of "obey" in the first two lines suggests, Adam has learned the good of obedience, but only to God, not to the worldly powers he still may subvert; and in *Samson Agonistes* the not so peaceful resistance of the blind, defeated hero brings down ruin upon his enemies. Moreover, critics tend to overlook the angel Michael's response: "only add / Deeds, to thy knowledge answerable" (581–82); this Miltonic version of works and faith is no formula for passivity. Nonetheless, this inward turn to individual spirituality, even as it claims to subsume politics, appears to represent a turning away from the public spirit of Milton's controversialist prose: there is an especially pointed moment of pathos in *Paradise Regained* when, during the temptation of Athens, Milton's Jesus rejects Satan's suggestion that he master the techniques of republican oratory and follow the example of Demosthenes and Pericles "whose resistless eloquence / Wielded at will that fierce democraty" (*PR*4.268–69)—those classical models whom Milton boasted he had equalled in his *Defenses* of the English people.[3]

We might, then, be tempted to equate Milton's inward turn with his turning to poetry itself after the Restoration. And yet the great poems of Milton's captivity continue to echo many of the politico-religious polemics of his earlier prose. After a period when critics rather unpersuasively tried to demonstrate that Milton had turned against the Commonwealth in *Paradise Lost* and that his Satan was a kind of caricature Cromwell, more recent studies from a different ideological bias have shown the persistence of anti-Royalist sentiments in the poem, voiced by topical allusions and citations that connect Satan instead with Charles I and that echo Milton's pamphlets of the 1650s.[4] The use of allusion and indirection to criticize the old Stuart king—and by implication the regime of his restored son as well—was no doubt conditioned by the problem of censorship, especially when the criticism came from an already marked man like Milton. The notorious ambiguity of its language makes poetry an appropriate medium for veiled political utterances.[5] In this respect, Milton's turn to poetry from his controversialist prose may not have been such a drastic departure after all: it kept alive, if in disguised form, a dissenting partisan voice.

The three sections of this chapter offer separate, if interrelated approaches to the politics of *Paradise Lost*. The first two treat, respectively, the plot of the poem's divine machinery—Satan's conquest of the earth and his defeat by the Son—and its human plot, the Fall of Adam and Eve. By examining the heavy dependence of the early books of the epic on *The Apollyonists* of Phineas Fletcher, a poem on the Gunpowder Plot that appears to have haunted Milton's career, the first section detects a pattern of political reference in *Paradise Lost* that topically links Satan's possession of the earth to the Stuart restoration. The Fall and loss of Eden of the epic's title thus suggest analogies to the failure of the Commonwealth, and the second section looks at how the poem's depiction of the psychology of Adam and Eve attempts to understand the reasons not only for their sin but for this political failure as well; the characters' psychological motives are linked, we shall see, to a contemporary theological dispute over the doctrine of assured predestination and its significance for religious politics. Instead of such assurance with its built-in teleology, Milton emphasizes the contingency of both Christian and republican liberty. Hence, this section also suggests how, in the terms of our larger study, the losers' story of Adam and Eve belongs to Lucan's rather than to Virgil's epic tradition, how Milton's Eden belongs to the romance side of an epic versus romance opposition. The chapter's third section carries this last argument further by placing *Paradise Lost* within a broad movement of seventeenth-century epic in the direction of romance, and by suggesting some of the political and historical implications of this generic trend.

Plots and Counterplots: Milton and Fletcher's *Apollyonists*

Let us return to Satan's journey to earth in *Paradise Lost*. In the preceding chapter, we saw how a series of epic allusions, notably to Vasco da Gama's travels in the *Lusíadas*, turned the devil's space trip into a seventeenth-century voyage of exploration and mercantile colonialism along the new trade routes to the East and West Indies. But there is a second pattern of allusion and symbolism contained in this journey that brings it much closer to home for Milton. Satan reaches the earth, "the happy isle" (1.410) described by Beelzebub, by passing through stars that seemed other

> happy isles,
> Like those Hesperian gardens famed of old,
> Fortunate fields, and groves and flowery vales,
> Thrice happy isles.
>
> (3.567–70)

Raphael later spots the earth on his own trip from heaven as a

> pilot from amidst the Cyclades
> Delos or Samos first appearing kens
> A cloudy spot.
>
> (5.264–66)

Both the Fortunate Isles and Delos were conventional figures for England. As a westerly island, it had long been identified with the Fortunate Isles of classical poetry, and the identification survived the discovery and conquest of the Canaries.[6] Drayton's reference to England as "this Island Fortunate" occasions the first annotation of *Poly-olbion*; Jonson's masque, *The Fortunate Isles*, depends on the same commonplace.[7] In Jonson's preceding masque, *Neptune's Triumph for the Return of Albion*, the floating island that conveys Albion, who is both Prince Charles and England itself, is compared to "a Delos" (131). The comparison became frequent in the political poetry of the civil war period: England's travails likened her to an island drifting without mooring until a strong leader, a Cromwell or Charles II, fixed her, as Apollo chained Delos, to a firm foundation.[8]

The stabilizing of Delos was a favorite Restoration trope, taken up by the Oxford poets who celebrated the Stuart king's return in the 1660 collection, *Britannia Rediviva*.[9]

Resembling Great Apollo, where you please
To plant your station, headlesse Tumults cease;
And we not owe to you a mercy less,
Than to bring *Delos* to our *Cyclades*.

(Ja. Vaughan)

England was then, what *Delos* was before,
The floating Island; stood, like that, all'ore
Surrounded with a sea of Blood, more red
Than that which all the Egyptians buried
. . . You first set on this happy shore
Did fix it so (by a Magnetick Power
Much stronger than its own) that now we stand
Firm as the Rocks i' th'midst of waves and sand.

(William Uvedale)

Milton provides a dark parodic version of this Restoration when he depicts Sin and Death building the bridge across Chaos that will fasten the Delos-like Earth to Hell "with pins of adamant / And chains" (318–19).[10] The myth is directly invoked in the solidifying of Chaos by the "Gorgonian rigor" (279) of Death.

The aggregated soil
Death with his mace petrific, cold and dry
As with a trident smote, and fixed as firm
As Delos floating once.

(10.293–95)

This Restoration indeed puts chains upon Earth-Delos-England. The causeway of Sin and Death is also compared to the pontoon bridge by which the Persian king Xerxes sought to yoke the liberty of Greece (306–11), and it is easy to see here a similar enslavement of England's free Commonwealth to the royal tyranny of Charles II—though with the suggestion that Charles will ultimately be no more successful than Xerxes.[11] Once we read the causeway as a route leading to England as well as to the New World and the Far East, the "art / Pontifical" (312–13) of its builders suggests that the Stuart monarch whom Milton suspects of being a secret Catholic will tie the island to Rome.

This second, topical reading of Satan's journey turns the story of Adam and Eve's Fall into the Fall of the English Commonwealth to the Restoration, itself a Catholic plot. And indeed, Milton's imagination was obsessed from the beginning to the end of his poetic career by another Catholic plot, the Gunpowder Plot of 1605, when Guy Fawkes and his confederates sought to blow up the Houses of Parliament, and by the literature that described that event, most importantly *The Apollyonists* of the Spenserian poet, Phineas Fletcher. Milton never outgrew his own juvenile poem on the subject, *In Quintum Novembris*, and critics have argued for the continuing presence of that earlier work in *Paradise Lost*.[12] But Milton's return to the conspiracy of Guy Fawkes was also filtered through Fletcher's work, which appeared almost simultaneously with *In Quintum Novembris* and made an enduring impression upon the teenage apprentice poet.[13]

In the *Poems* of 1645, Milton states that he had written *In Quintum Novembris* in his seventeenth year; the miniature Latin epic of 226 lines, as well as his four Latin epigrams on the Gunpowder Plot, have consequently been dated to 1626. In 1627 Fletcher published his own Latin poem on the Gunpowder Plot, *Locustae*, together with its English version, *The Locusts or Apollyonists*. Was Milton's dating in error or did he have access to manuscripts of Fletcher's much longer and more ambitious works?[14] The textual evidence is inconclusive. The young Milton's emulation of Fletcher may indeed have come after the fact. He would have completed his short poem on the Gunpowder Plot only to find rival versions, both in Latin and English, appearing in print from the older and at that time more established poet, Fletcher, and experienced the uncanny sensation of having called a poetic father into being. However it came about, the relationship of emulation between *In Quintum Novembris* and *Locustae* would reemerge in Milton's career, but it would be transferred to his English poetry, with its imitations, echoes, and rewritings of *The Apollyonists*.

The Apollyonists is not a very good poem, and it is not surprising that few Miltonists have cared to read it.[15] Milton's dependence on Fletcher's crude anti-Catholic work may even seem an embarrassment, a lapse by a youthful poet that tact enjoins us to pass over in silence. Nevertheless, this five-canto poem in Spenserian stanzas is one of the chief models for *Paradise Lost*, particularly for its first two books, with their description of Hell and the council of the fallen angels.

At several points, Milton directly imitates and verbally recalls Fletcher's poem. His description of Sin and Death in Book 2 draws upon Fletcher's figure of Sin, who, like her Miltonic counterpart, is the gatekeeper of Hell.[16]

> The Porter to th'infernall gate is Sin,
> A shapelesse shape, a foul deformed thing,
> Nor nothing, nor a substance:
>
> . . . .
>
> Of that first woman, and th'old serpent bred,
> By lust and custome nurst; whom when her mother
> Saw so deform'd, how faine would she have fled
> Her birth, and selfe?
>
> . . . .
>
> Her former parts her mother seemes resemble,
> Yet only seemes to flesh and weaker sight;

> For she with art and pain could fine dissemble
> Her loathsome face: her back parts (black as night)
> Like to her horride Sire would force to tremble
> The boldest heart.[17]
>
> (*Apollyonists* 1.10.1–3; 11.1–4; 12.1–6)

Milton divides Fletcher's description of Sin between his two infernal guardians, Sin and Death, standing like Scylla and Charybdis on either side "before the gates" (649) of Hell. It is Death who is a "shapelesse shape":

> The other shape,
> If shape it might be called that shape had none
> Distinguishable in member, joint, or limb,
> Or substance might be called that shadow seemed,
> For each seemed either;
>
> (*PL* 2.666–70)

while Sin takes on the more specific description of Fletcher's Sin, the dissembled woman's face and horrid serpentine back parts:

> The one seemed woman to the waist, and fair,
> But ended foul in many a scaly fold
> Voluminous and vast, a serpent armed
> With mortal sting.
>
> (650–53)

The figure also resembles Spenser's Errour (*Faerie Queene* 1.1.4) and the personification of Hamartia (Sinne) in another Fletcher poem, *The Purple Island* (12.27–29): there, too, Fletcher ascribes her genealogy to Satan and Eve.[18] Milton transfers the horror that causes Fletcher's Eve to flee after giving birth to sin, to the flight—"I fled ... I fled" (787–90)—of Sin from her offspring Death.

The episode of Sin and Death further echoes *The Apollyonists* at the moment when Death learns that Satan intends to lead him to a new feeding ground on earth: he

> Grinned horrible a ghastly smile, to hear
> His famine should be filled, and blessed his maw
> Destined to that good hour.
>
> (*PL* 2.846–48)

Death recalls none other than Fletcher's Guy Fawkes himself, contemplating the ruin of the Houses of Parliament.

> Thus nurst, bred, growne a Canniball, now prest
> To be the leader of this troup, he blest
> His bloody maw with thought of such a royall feast.
>
> (*Apollyonists* 5.10)

As they bless their unholy appetites, both Death and Fawkes slaver in anticipation of impending havoc and carnage. But Satan's plot to take over Eden
and the earth succeeds—and Sin and Death build their pontifical, chain-
link bridge to annex Hell's new possession—where the plot of the Catholic,
cannibal (i.e., Eucharist-worshipping) Fawkes fails.

Fletcher describes the deliverance of England and of her Protestant religion from the conspiracy of Fawkes as a providential act that is an extension
of the care with which God oversees His creation and keeps in harmony its
potentially warring elemental forces. In a passage that looks back to Spenser's praise of the works of constancy-in-change in the *Mutabilitie Cantos*
(7.25), *The Apollyonists* concludes with a hymn to God the Creator.

> For Earth's cold arme cold Winter friendly holds;
> But with his dry the others wet defies:
> The Ayer's warmth detests the Water's colds;
> But both a common moisture joyntly ties:
> Warm Ayre with mutuall love hot Fire infolds;
> As moist, his drythe abhorres: drythe Earth allies
>   To Fire, but heats with cold new warres addresse:
>   Thus by their peacefull fight, and fighting peace
> All creatures grow, and dye, and dying still increase.
>
> Above them all thou sit'st, who gav'st all being,
> All every where, in all, and over all:
> Thou their great Umpire, all their strife agreeing,
> Bend'st their stiffe natures to thy soveraigne call:
> Thine eye their law: their steppes by overseeing
> Thou overrul'st and keep'st from slipp'ry fall.
>   Oh if thy steady hand should not maintaine
>   What first it made, all straight would fall againe
> And nothing of this All, save nothing would remaine.
>
> (*Apollyonists* 5.25–26)

The prospect of cosmic decreation that arises in the last tercet—and which
Fletcher's poem implicitly equates with the destruction of the English
Church, narrowly averted by the last-minute exposure of the Gunpowder
Plot—is just what greets Milton's Satan on the other side of the gates of
Hell in the realm of Chaos.

> For Hot, Cold, Moist, and Dry four champions fierce
> Strive here for mastery, and to battle bring
> Their embryon atoms; they around the flag
> Of each his faction, in their several clans,
> Light-armed or heavy, sharp, smooth, swift or slow,
> Swarm populous, unnumbered as the sands

Of Barca or Cyrene's torrid soil,
Levied to side with warring winds, and poise
Their lighter wings. To whom these most adheres
He rules a moment; Chaos umpire sits,
And by decision more embroils the fray
By which he reigns; next him high arbiter
Chance governs all.

(*PL* 2.898–910)

The passage both echoes and inverts Fletcher's account of the "peacefull fight and fighting peace" by which God keeps the physical universe in working order. Chaos is a site of "endless wars" (897) that prevent even the four Aristotelian elements individuated by Fletcher's text from assuming distinct shape: "neither sea, nor shore, nor air nor fire" (912). Chaos himself has replaced Fletcher's God as "umpire" sitting over his domain.

We saw in our last chapter how Satan promises Chaos to return the newly created earth back beneath the sway of that "anarch old," just as earlier in the War in Heaven he would have reduced Heaven itself to "wrack, with ruin overspread" (6.670–71). Satan's weapon on that occasion was the gunpowder that he found when he turned up

Wide the celestial soil, and saw beneath
The originals of nature in their crude
Conception; sulphurous and nitrous foam
They found . . .

(*PL* 6.510–13)

Heaven itself appears to be built out of the primordial matter of Chaos— "the originals of nature"—and this matter has the explosive properties of gunpowder.[19] So Satan discovers again when he is comically buffeted amid the elemental forces of Chaos.

The strong rebuff of some tumultuous cloud
Instinct with fire and nitre hurried him
As many miles aloft.

(*PL* 2.935–37)

The depiction of Chaos as a kind of natural minefield ready to go off at any random moment reinforces the analogy that the poem draws between its endless "intestine broils" (2.1001) and the civil "Intestine war in heaven" (6.259), which the rebellious angels wage with their newly invented guns. Satan's decreative impulse, the impulse of evil to bring about a reversion of God's works back to the volatile state of Chaos, is thus a kind of Gunpowder Plot:[20] the same type of plot against which Fletcher's God intervenes in *The Apollyonists*, employing the power with which He preserves the order and harmony of His creation.

But the parallel between the two plots and the full extent of Milton's debt to Fletcher emerges when one moves beyond these textual echoes of *The Apollyonists* in *Paradise Lost* and compares the respective infernal council scenes of the two poems. Milton drew from a tradition of demonic underworld assemblies—from Vida's *Christiad*, from the *Gerusalemme liberata*, and from their many imitators. But the assembly of the angels in Pandemonium in Book 1 and the council debates in Book 2 find their closest model in Fletcher's poem, which itself draws on the same tradition.

The Apollyonists, in fact, presents two council scenes, one in Hell and one in the Papal Curia in Rome, and these are, in Fletcher's heavy-handed treatment, mirror images of one another. In canto 1, Fletcher's Satan calls the council and considers what action to take now that the Reformation, particularly in England, has broken his forces of Catholic superstition and error; in canto 2, the demon Equivocus pledges to continue the infernal struggle against God's rule and providential plans by employing the Jesuit Order. In canto 4, Equivocus throws one of his serpents into the breast of Pope Paul V, who calls "a Senate" (5) of his cardinals; after the pope, like Satan, complains of recent setbacks—he cites the defeat of the Spanish Armada—the Jesuit cardinal Robert Bellarmine rises, like Equivocus, and discloses a plan to blow up the Houses of Parliament. Thus three of the five cantos of Fletcher's poem on the Gunpowder Plot are taken up by plotting itself, with Rome's plots as diabolical as the devil's own.

Milton borrows from both of these council scenes in *The Apollyonists*, and he redistributes their narrative elements through Books 1 and 2 of his epic. When joined to the direct echoes of Fletcher's text, these reminiscences, perhaps less persuasive as evidence of influence when taken individually, add up cumulatively to a case of systematic imitation. Fletcher's Satan counts up his assembled followers—"his fiery eye / Much swol'ne with pride, but more with rage and hate, / As Censour, muster'd all his company" (1.18)—much as Milton's Satan: "Their number last he sums. And now his heart / Distends with pride, and hardening in his strength / Glories" (1.571–73). Fletcher's description of Satan, "To be in heaven the second he disdaines: / So now the first in hell, the flames he raignes" (1.20), rings changes on the proverbial Caesarian sentiment that Milton's Satan will echo: "To reign is worth ambition, though in hell: / Better to reign in Hell, than serve in heaven" (1.262–63).[21] Fletcher's Book 1 ends with a simile that belittles his devils by comparing them to a swarm of gnats (1.40); Milton's Book 1 similarly ends with the devils shrinking themselves to fit into Pandemonium and being compared in simile to bees (768f.). In his long address to his fellow devils, in which he considers their various choices of revenge and resistance, Fletcher's Satan takes up or considers options that Milton will divide up among Moloch, Belial, Mammon, Beelzebub, and his own Satan.[22] The murmuring of the devils that follows Mammon's speech is compared to "when hollow rocks retain / The sound of blustering winds, which all night long / Had roused the Sea, now with hoarse cadence lull / Seafaring men . . . After the tempest" (*PL* 2.285–88); the outcries of the devils following the speech of Fletcher's Satan are also compared to "angry winds" that subside following a storm at sea (2.4).

Beelzebub, whose speech follows Mammon's and whose proposal sways Milton's demonic assembly—a proposal we subsequently learn to have been conceived by Satan himself (379–80)—corresponds to Fletcher's Equivocus and Bellarmine in their respective councils. He proposes, of course, the se-duction of mankind and the possession of the "happy isle" (410) of an Edenic Earth. Equivocus plots against "that little Isle (our envy, spight / His Paradise)" (2.34), Bellarmine against "That blessed Isle" (4.30), that is, against Protestant England. Fletcher's Satan has already singled out England, "That little swimming Isle above the rest" (1.26):

> There God hath fram'd another Paradise
> Fat Olives dropping peace, victorious palmes,
> Nor in the midst, but every where doth rise
> The hated tree of life, whose precious balmes
> Cure every sinfull wound: give light to th'eyes,
> Unlock the eare, recover fainting qualmes.
>   There richly growes what makes a people blest;
>   A garden planted by himself and drest:
> Where he himselfe doth walke, where he himselfe doth rest.
>
>   (1.27)

The English island and its Protestant Church is a second Eden—or, as the most famous version of the idea puts it, an "other Eden, demi-paradise." *The Apollyonists* thus already provides the typology that both makes Guy Fawkes's conspiracy into an attempt to bring about a second Fall and, con-versely, gives to Milton's story of the original Fall the dimensions of another Gunpowder Plot. To complete the series of parallels, the pope embraces his "sonne" Bellarmine (4.37) and promises him that for his plot against En-gland he will be worshiped as a saint with his gold statue set "next highest Jove: / To thee wee'l humbly kneele, and vowe and pray" (4.39); the fallen angels similarly adore Milton's Satan for his venturing to the island Earth on their behalf:

> Towards him they bend
> With awful reverence prone; and as a god
> Extol him equal to the highest in heaven.
>
>   (2.477–79)

These scenes, which go back to Ascanius embracing Euryalus before the latter and Nisus set out on their unsuccessful nightraid in *Aeneid* 9, are shown by Milton in Book 3 of *Paradise Lost* to be unholy parodies of the true self-sacrifical mission of the Son: at His volunteering himself on behalf of fallen humanity, His almighty Father commands the angels of heaven to "Adore the Son and honor him as me" (343).[23]

This close borrowing from *The Apollyonists* reinforces the political topicality of *Paradise Lost*. Fletcher's poem describes the failed attempt of the devil and his Roman Catholic agents to subdue a British isle that is likened to Eden. Milton's epic depicts the Fall to Satanic forces of a paradisal Earth that is compared to islands—the Fortunate Isles, Delos—that, in turn, stand for England, an England that has, with the poet, "fallen on evil days" (7.25) of monarchy and popery. His imitation of Fletcher's work is thus one more way in which Milton portrays the Fall as the Stuart Restoration, and the Restoration itself as a kind of successful Catholic conspiracy or Gunpowder Plot.

That this Restoration government might be laid low in turn is the dream of Milton's *Samson Agonistes*. At the play's end, the blind hero brings down the temple upon the assembled Philistines, a transparent-enough figure for the blind poet's final blow against his political enemies.[24] What is less immediately apparent is that Samson's destruction of the temple is another reenactment of the Gunpowder Plot, carried out this time *upon* rather than by the Catholic or crypto-Catholic foes of the true English Protestantism. But an earlier event, when a Catholic temple had fallen in London, had already provided the typology that made Samson, in his last heroic feat, into an antithetical or "good" version of Guy Fawkes.

On October 26, 1623, a Catholic chapel attached to the French ambassador's house in the Blackfriars district of London collapsed during a celebration of the Mass led by the Jesuit Robert Drury. Drury and ninety-five worshipers died in what came to be referred to as the "Fatal Vespers."[25] The date of the disaster corresponded, according to the Catholics' own new Gregorian calendar, to November 5, Guy Fawkes Day. The hand of providence did not fail to be detected: God had brought down their own house upon those who had tried to bring down the Houses of Parliament. Fletcher describes the event in canto 4 of *The Apollyonists*:

> So when of late that boasted Jesuite Priest
> Gath'red his flocke, and now the house 'gan swell,
> And every eare drew in the sugred spell,
> Their house, and rising hopes, swole, burst, and head-long fell.
>
> (4.2)

This passage is then echoed later in the canto in Bellarmine's description of his plot against James and Parliament:

> And when with numbers just the house gins swell,
> And every state hath fill'd his station,

When now the King mounted on lofty sell,
With honeyed speech and comb'd oration
Charm's every eare, midst of that sugred spell
I'le teare the walls, blow up the nation.

(4.35)

The internal textual echo suggests that the Fatal Vespers were the true enactment of, and retribution for, the failed Gunpowder Plot.

This idea is explicitly formulated by Samuel Clarke in *England's Remembrancer*, published in 1657 and reprinted again in 1671, the same year as *Samson Agonistes*. It is the scriptural figure of Samson that Clarke invokes when he includes the Fatal Vespers in his narrative of the realm's two great deliverances from the Catholic peril: the Armada and the Gunpowder Plot.

> Shall *Herod*, whilest he is priding himself in the flattering applause of the people, be eaten of worms? Shall *Haman*, whilest he is practicing to destroy all the people of God, be hanged on a gallows fifty foot high which he had prepared for *Mordecai*? Shall the house where the *Philistines* met together to sport with *Sampson* fall upon their heads? Shall these and such like judgments overtake men in the very act of their sin, and yet be accounted no judgments, no evidences of Gods revenging justice, or signes of his indignation? Truly then we may deny all providence, and attribute all to chance: But add hereto, that this fel upon their fifth of *November*, and it will be as clear as if written with a Sun-beam, that the pit which they digged for others, they themselves fell into it.[26]

If Haman is the figure of the perfect reciprocity of God's judgment upon those who sympathized and may even have conspired with Fawkes and his confederates, Samson fits the event itself: the fall of the Catholic chapel is a new version of the Philistines' temple of Dagon. The figure of Samson had already been invoked immediately after the Fatal Vespers by Alexander Gil in his short Latin poem on the event, *In ruinam Camerae Papisticae*.

> Sic, cum *Israeli* populus infestus sacro
> Illuderet *Samsonis* invicti malis,
> *Dagonis* aedes corruit, & altissimi
> Inopina clades stravit inimicos Dei.[27]

(43–46)

(Just so, when that people who were the foes of holy Israel, made sport of the misfortunes of the unbowed Samson, the house of Dagon tumbled down and unexpected slaughter prostrated the enemies of the highest God.)

Gil was the friend, poetic critic, and correspondent of the young Milton. He was the son of Alexander Gil, Sr., Milton's teacher at St. Paul's School. It is very likely that Milton read *In ruinam Camerae Papisticae* soon after its composition in 1623, and that the younger Gil's anti-Catholic Latin poem on the sequel to the Gunpowder Plot was an inspiration for his own *In Quintum Novembris* three years later.[28]

When Milton took up the Samson story at the end of his career, he had available to him a tradition that read the destruction of the Philistine's temple as a figure of the divine retribution for the Gunpowder Plot, a punishment in kind that returned the evil that God's enemies sought to perform back upon themselves. This tradition motivates his recourse once again to the literary version of the Gunpowder Plot in *The Apollyonists*. The "theatre" in the temple of Dagon described by *Samson Agonistes*, "With seats where all the lords and each degree / Of sort, might sit" (1607–8), resembles a hierarchically arranged parliamentary chamber like the one described by Fletcher's Bellarmine in canto 4, where "all the States in full assembly meet, / and every order rank't in fit array." Bellarmine's plot is to destroy all of England's rulers while they are gathered together in one place.

> Kings, Nobles Clergy, Commons high and low,
> The Flowre of England in one houre I'le mow,
> And head all th'Isle with one unseen, unfenced blow.
>
> (4.30)

The cadence and wording of this passage are recalled by the Messenger of *Samson Agonistes* as he recounts Samson's final act of heroism.

> He tugged, he shook, till down they came and drew
> The whole roof after them, with burst of thunder
> Upon the heads of all who sat beneath,
> *Lords, ladies, captains, counsellors, or priests,*
> *Their choice nobility and flower,* not only
> Of this but each Philistian city round
> Met from all parts to solemnize this feast.
>
> (SA 1650–56; my emphasis)

Where Guy Fawkes aimed to assassinate the English government en masse, so Milton's Samson kills the ruling elite of all of Philistia. "The vulgar only scaped," notes the Messenger (1659).

But the slaughtered Philistines are themselves figures of the present English government in 1671, the government of the restored Charles II. "Where is Guy Fawkes, now that we need him?" seems to be the idea that is contained in Milton's echo of Fletcher. This imagined overthrow of the Stuart monarchy is conceived precisely as a reversal or undoing of a Restoration that *Paradise Lost* already depicted as a reenactment of the Gunpowder Plot. And if the Fatal Vespers had wrought a Samson-like divine vengeance for Fawkes's failed conspiracy, *Samson Agonistes* expresses the hope that a similar disaster and countercoup will overtake the new, successful Fawkeses of its own day. The play is thus an answer to the earlier epic and its portrait of the Fall not only of mankind but of a potentially godly Commonwealth as well; it is not for nothing that the play was coupled and printed with *Paradise Regained*.

The inverse political relationship between *Paradise Lost* and *Samson Agonistes* may be clear enough without the third term of Guy Fawkes, but his spectral presence in both works—via *The Apollyonists*—provides a specific link of reciprocity between them. A similar reciprocity, moreover, gives a shape to Milton's larger career, and locates in his poetry a continuous political strain derived from a tradition of militant Protestantism. He began and ended that career with the Gunpowder Plot, and by the end, he had envisioned a heroic response that would, as the Fatal Vespers had done, turn the tables on his and England's enemy. *In Quintum Novembris*, written forty-five years earlier, turned out to have been prophetic, for in the Gunpowder Plot Milton had found the recurring plot of history itself.

Adam, Eve, and Assurance

The Satanic plot of *Paradise Lost*—the devil's conquest of the earth for Sin and Death—of course functions in the poem only secondarily as an allusion to the Stuart Restoration: even at the level of such topical reference it points equally, as the last chapter just argued, to the building of European colonial empires in the "new world" of America and along the trade routes to the Far East. By the same token, the Fall of Adam and Eve and their loss of Eden is not primarily a figure for the failure of the Commonwealth and of England as a godly nation. Nonetheless, by its topical allusion, Milton's epic aims to disclose the true, diabolical nature of the restored monarchy. Moreover, as its attention shifts from Satan and the divine machinery in its first half to the human psychological dynamics that lead Adam and Eve to fall into the servitude of sin, it seeks by analogy, if not by one-to-one allegory, to understand what would cause a free people to embrace the political sin of servitude. The two slaveries are explicitly linked in Book 12 (82f.), where kingly tyranny over the "outward freedom" (95) of men and women is viewed as a divine punishment for the inner "servitude" (89) of reason to the passions that is the result of original sin. For in Milton's Eden the devil proposes, but man disposes: Adam and Eve choose to fall by their own free will. Similarly in his England the English people invited Charles II back to rule and subjugate them.

The shift in the poem's focus from the divine superplot that pits Satan against the Son down to the level of its human protagonists seems a virtual shift in literary genre.[29] For it is in the actions of the devil and the deity that

Paradise Lost includes, often in parodic form, the conventional plots of epic—the Iliadic war, the Odyssean voyage, and the combination of these two Homeric plots in a third, Aeneas's founding of empire. In the Son's defeat of the rebel angels in the War in Heaven, an anticipation of his eschatological victory that will send Satan back to the burning lake of Hell forever (Revelation 20:7–10), the poem provides the teleology that supports its overarching epic narrative of history. The contours of this narrative, as we saw in Chapter 1, are recognizably Virgilian in the Son's subsequent imperial triumph through heaven to the side of his father, "at the right hand of bliss" (6.891); His successful battle represents the victory of a principle of ending—and hence of narrative and historical intelligibility—over the cyclical repetition of Satanic evil. Satan expects a "triumph" (10.546) of his own to celebrate his seduction of Adam and Eve on his return to Hell, but instead is transformed, just as he proclaims the happy ending of his expedition with the word "bliss" (503), into a (bl)hissing serpent. He ends "on his belly prone" (514) in the same position where he started his course in the poem: "Prone on the flood" (1.195). The legend that he and his fellow devils are forced each year "to undergo / This annual humbling" (10.575–76) reinforces the cyclical quality of repeated failure that characterizes his epic career.[30] The Son's victory is a figure of the Passion, His victory over the natural cycle of life and death itself. The opposition of the victors' teleological narrative, here authorized by the Christian apocalypse, the ending of endings, to the losers' condition of endless, circular repetition—this condition being part of what the victor must overcome—should by now be familiar to us as an organizing structure of epic poetry after Virgil.

By contrast, Adam and Eve, at least before their Fall, seem to inhabit a world at a remove from the epic struggles and grand transhistorical narrative taking place at the level of the poem's divine machinery. Eden and the unfallen earth itself belong within epic tradition to the romance topos of Calypso's island—the terrestrial paradise, locus of lovemaking, site of immortality, literally insulated from the rest of history—a topos studied by A. Bartlett Giamatti through its development in the island love-gardens of Ariosto's Alcina and Tasso's Armida.[31] Milton's relationship to this traditional topos and its later version in the Cyprian garden of Venus in Marino's *Adone* will be taken up in the last section of this chapter. The inward-looking and narcissistic quality of this already highly conventionalized realm of erotic enthrallment has caused some critics to detect in *Paradise Lost* a moving away from the public engagement of martial and political epic; and Milton famously bids farewell to the traditional epic of war in the *recusatio* at the beginning of Book 9 (27–47). Instead, he moves the story to a private realm that is at once the figure of the inner, spiritual heroism of Christian fortitude and of a domestic sphere that would newly become the subject of the novel, the principal literary heir to romance and its structures. Family life, particularly, as Tolstoy would observe, the kind of unhappy family life that Adam and Eve come to share by the end of Book 9, would be the area explored by the emerging genre that appealed to the experience of a bourgeois as well as an aristocratic reading public.[32]

There is much to be said for this critical line that also links the Protestant emphasis on companionate marriage to a division enforced by nascent capitalism between the spheres of work and of home and family.[33] It may suggest, however, too complete a split between private and public worlds, as if Eden and the marriage of Adam and Eve represented a kind of passive escape or refuge from politics and history, especially for Milton after the Restoration. This is indeed the character of the earthly paradise in earlier epics, where the hero—Odysseus, Ruggiero, Rinaldo—is sidetracked from his larger destiny; Aeneas's pseudomarriage with Dido, which imitates the Calypso episode among other Odyssean models, is another version of this epic pattern. But just as Milton reverses epic tradition by giving the private world of Eden prominence over a public arena of military-political exploits—a reversal so remarkable that it almost seems to create a new genre—he also disputes the conventional epic wisdom that separates them. *Paradise Lost* suggests, to the contrary, that individual choices of conscience, themselves the product of complicated psychological processes, can have far-reaching, indeed world-historical consequences. Private life is thus continuous with the public, political world; personal actions in one sphere reveal states of mind that have implications for and impact upon behavior in the other. And it is in this light that the poem can find analogies between its account of the Fall and the fall of a godly Commonwealth: character flaws that lead Adam and Eve to sin may indicate what Milton saw as deficiencies in the political character of his fellow Englishman as well.

We may approach this nexus of individual character psychology, of spiritual disposition and choice, and of their temporal, political application by considering two instances before and after the Fall where *Paradise Lost* both uses the language of theology and alludes to a contemporary doctrinal debate.

Adam initially finds it hard to believe that he and Eve could fall. He declares to Raphael his certainty of their ability to stand, even though Raphael has been sent expressly to warn them of Satan's wiles, and will tell them about the fall of the angels as an exemplary story:

> nor knew I not
> To be both will and deed created free;
> Yet that we never shall forget to love
> Our maker, and obey him whose command
> Single, is yet so just, my constant thoughts
> Assured me, and still assure: though what thou tell'st
> Hath passed in heaven, some doubt within me move . . .

(5.549–54)

Adam is rather too quick to tell the angel that he already knew what he has just been told; he has naively asked Raphael, only a few verses earlier, "What meant that caution joined, *If ye be found / Obedient?*" (513–14). Adam, that is, knew that he and Eve had been created free, but he had not grasped the responsibilities and potential perils of freedom. And now that these are impressed upon him, he seeks reassurance in his "constant thoughts," a self-examination that grants him what will turn out to be a false sense of security.

This reassurance—textually spelled out by the repetition "Assured . . . assure"—that Adam looks for and finds is a form of *assurance*, the spiritual comfort that orthodox Calvinists received when, upon examining their consciences, they came to the conclusion that they were among the predestined elect. For many this comfort was a feeling of overwhelming relief arrived at after long and terrifying consideration of the prospect of their possible damnation, and the failure to achieve assurance could produce a suicidal despair. The believer who did attain assurance was confident that he or she would persevere until death without falling away from God's grace into sinful perdition.[34]

But the Arminian dimension of Milton's theology rejected a doctrine of predestination that seemed to give human beings no share or role in their individual salvation—no freedom to persevere or to fall. Thus Raphael in this same passage tells Adam and Eve that "to persevere / He [God] left it in thy power" (5.525–26). In Book 1, Chapter 25, of his *De Doctrina Christiana*, Milton equivocally defines ASSURANCE OF SALVATION as

A CERTAIN DEGREE OF FAITH. IT MEANS THAT A MAN IS PERSUADED BY THE TESTIMONY OF THE SPIRIT, AND FIRMLY BELIEVES THAT IF HE BELIEVES AND PERSISTS IN FAITH AND CHARITY, HE WILL WITHOUT ANY DOUBT ATTAIN ETERNAL LIFE AND PERFECT GLORY, SINCE HE IS ALREADY JUSTIFIED, ADOPTED AND PARTIALLY GLORIFIED BY UNION AND COMMUNION WITH CHRIST AND THE FATHER.[35]

. . . .

THE PERSEVERANCE OF THE SAINTS IS A GIFT OF GOD THE PRESERVER. IT MEANS THAT THOSE WHO ARE FOREKNOWN, ELECT, REGENERATE AND SEALED THROUGH THE HOLY SPIRIT, PERSEVERE TO THE END IN THE FAITH AND GRACE OF GOD. NO POWER OR GUILE OF THE WORLD OR DEVIL MAKES THEM ENTIRELY FALL AWAY, SO LONG AS THEY DO NOT PROVE WANTING IN THEMSELVES, AND SO LONG AS THEY CLING TO FAITH AND CHARITY WITH ALL THEIR MIGHT.[36]

It is the "if" and "so long" clauses in these two passages that make the assurance that Milton states is a "great joy" for the believer rather less of a comfort than it might seem. For in spite of the assurance human individuals may feel, they must keep and live up to their faith—and it is still possible for them to fall away. For an orthodox Calvinist, this is not assurance at all. The same kind of provisionary "if" clause—"If ye be found obedient"—sticks out uncomfortably for Adam in Raphael's words.

Only in Book 11, after he and Eve have fallen, and after they have through the motion of "Prevenient grace" (11.2) turned to God in prayer, does Adam experience something like Milton's kind of assurance, as he says

> persuasion in me grew
> That I was heard with favour; peace returned
> Home to my breast, and to my memory
> His promise, that thy seed shall bruise our foe;
> Which then, not minded in dismay, yet now
> Assures me that the bitterness of death
> Is past, and we shall live.

> (11.152–58)

The inner peace that Adam receives is the knowledge of God's pardon for his transgression, of his and his progeny mankind's eventual victory over Satan ("our foe") and death; in the short term, he and Eve realize that they are not going to die just yet. This Miltonic assurance, as Milton explains in *De Doctrina Christiana*, is a form of inward persuasion based on God's promises or covenants with his faithful elect.

> God here promises to put reverence for him into their minds, so that they may not depart from him. In other words he promises to fulfill his own responsibility and give them enough grace to prevent their departure. He also makes a covenant, however, and the conditions of the covenant have to be fulfilled not by one party but by both.[37]

The judgment oracle uttered by the Son against the serpent in Book 10 (175–81), a prophecy of His Passion, is thus a kind of divine covenantal pledge from which Adam and Eve can derive comfort—and Michael's narration to Adam in Books 11–12 as well as the dreams sent to Eve fill in the details of this promise: Adam receives "peace of thought" (12.558), Eve the "consolation yet secure" (620) that "By me the promised seed shall all restore" (623). But the moment of assurance that follows prayer at the opening of Book 11 is immediately followed by the disruption of nature that presages the loss of Eden, "to warn / Us," Adam correctly surmises, "haply too secure of our discharge / From penalty, because from death released /Some days" (11.196–98). The physical contingency of death is a constant fearful reminder of the contingency of human salvation. Humans can never enjoy full assurance or security because they have their part to uphold in their covenant with God, who has given them "enough grace" to keep their faith—or, as the God of *Paradise Lost* says, created them "Sufficient to have stood, though free to fall." (3.99). But they are required to persevere in faith and righteousness *through time* and its vicissitudes, free to fall at any contingent occasion, even or especially in the face of a death that intervenes before the divine promises can be fulfilled.

When Milton depicts Adam twice asserting assurance—a false assurance before his Fall, a truer, more limited assurance in its wake—he evokes, perhaps quite directly, an earlier theological controversy that raged during the early years of the Commonwealth. In 1651 John Goodwin, the Puritan preacher with whom Milton shared both republican and Arminian convictions, published his lengthy manifesto *Redemption Redeemed* in which he argued that Christ had died for the salvation of all men, including the heathen, rather than for a predestined Elect, whose very existence Goodwin effectively denied.[38] He included in Chapters 9–15 of his work a "digression" that attacked the idea of assurance, the "Perseverance of the Saints," arguing that it was always possible for even the seemingly truest believer to fall away, and citing various scripturally attested cases of apostasy on the part of faithful saints. *Redemption Redeemed* caused a scandal among Puritan divines and occasioned at least ten published refutations of its doctrinal positions.[39] Two large treatises of 1654, *Sancti Sanciti, or The Common Doctrine of the Perseverance of the Saints . . . Vindicated*, by the Presbyterian George Kendall, and *The Doctrine of the Saints Perseverance Explained and Confirmed*, by the Independent John Owen, specifically addressed themselves to Goodwin's digression on assurance.

Kendall, in his attack, lumped with Goodwin's work a 1653 tract by the great nonconformist divine Richard Baxter, *The Right Method for a Settled Peace of Conscience and Spiritual Comfort*. Baxter was not, in fact, denying the doctrine of assurance, but humanely instructing worshipers not to be overly concerned if they did not find assurance in themselves, for assurance was not necessary for salvation, nor was its absence a sign of damnation. He sought rather to prove that "a Christian may live a joyful life without assurance." Baxter cited the case of Adam.

> No doubt but Adam in innocency, had peace of conscience, and comfort, and communion with God, and yet he had no assurance of salvation; I mean, either of continuing in paradise, or being translated to glory. For if he had, either he was sure to persevere in innocency, and so to be glorified, (but that was not true,) or else he must foreknow both that he should fall and be raised again, and saved by Christ. But this he knew not at all. 2. Experience tells us, that the greatest part of Christians on earth do enjoy that peace and comfort which they have, without certainty of their salvation.[40]

Kendall argues that Adam's example is beside the point, for Adam, created in a state of innocency, was in a qualitatively different position from his descendants who inherited original sin from his Fall. Assurance is rather the gift of grace, the result of Christ's redemption of a sinful humanity on the cross.

> ADAM had no such *arreares* to reckon for, and consequently he had not the same *disturbances in his Spirit*, that all his children must needs have. . . . *Adam* had no *corruption in him*, to draw him under the *fear of Damnation*; the best of

his children are conscious to themselves of an unhappy plenty of this damnable commodity. And therefore albeit they were assured of pardon for *all former* transgressions, they could have little peace, unlesse they had a superadded *assurance of like pardon* for their *future* sinnes, though never so *small*, and *grace* to prevent them from committing, at least continuing in *greater* . . . and therefore though *Adams condition* might admit *peace and comfort* without an *assurance of salvation*, yet *no mans else* can, all being so obnoxious to *damnation*.[41]

Kendall agrees with Baxter that Adam did not possess assurance—but only because assurance was superfluous in his prelapsarian condition. Up to a point Milton seems to agree with both divines and may even echo their debate: his Adam enjoys a genuine form of assurance only after his Fall and as a product of grace based on the promise of Christ's future sacrifice. But Milton's Adam nonetheless *claims* that he is assured of the impossibility of his fall, even if this assurance turns out to be a mistaken and short-lived comfort. *Paradise Lost* here collapses the difference—or at least finds a close analogy—between prelapsarian and postlapsarian religious experience in order to argue, as Goodwin does, that assurance, in the orthodox Calvinist sense, is a kind of delusion.[42]

If the structure of religious life is, according to Milton, the same before and after the Fall, what is it in Adam's experience and psychology that corresponds to the anxiety and insecurity that caused Puritan believers to look for assurance of their election? For, as Goodwin makes clear, it was *fear*, based on the knowledge of original sin and human depravity, that was thought to be assuaged by the doctrine of assurance. His entire digression against assurance may be understood as a refutation of the aphorism he cites at its beginning: " 'pessimus consiliarius timor,' fear is a very bad counselor."[43] The Christian's fear of God was not, as his opponent Owen would counter, servile and unworthy, because, Goodwin asserted, such fear was accompanied by hope; rather, it was assurance that, by removing fear, made the believer more liable unwarily to lapse from the paths of righteousness.[44]

> As that doctrine of perseverance whereof professors make such a treasure, is deeply accessary to the greatest part of those fears, those wringings and gripings of conscience, wherewith their peace is interrupted, and their comforts appalled and shaken, so is it exceedingly to be feared that it hath a potent and pernicious influence of causality into those frequent, daily, and most sad apostasies and declinings from ways of holiness unto looseness and profaneness, which are found amongst them. . . . When a man that stands is in any capacity of falling, is it not the only way to educe that power or capacity into act, and to cause him to fall indeed, to persuade him that he is no possibility of falling?[45]

The Calvinist claim to assurance, Goodwin maintains here, grows out of an inability to live with fear—and so without hope as well—as the believer is afflicted by conscience and by the possibility of his or her falling away. But it is precisely this doctrine that, by creating a false spiritual peace, can cause such an apostasy. To have one's spiritual peace interrupted, to be always on guard against sin is for Goodwin a good thing: whereas the certainty that one is already of the Elect lets one's guard down. But Milton's Adam is without sin, and his insecurity is thus of another kind: it is a lack of what Raphael in Book 8 labels "self esteem."

What Adam shares with the seventeenth-century Calvinist is a deep sense of his creatureliness. At the moment of his creation, he tells Raphael, he addressed the sun overhead to learn "who I was, or where, or from what cause" (8.270).

> Thou sun, said I, fair light,
> And thou enlightened earth, so fresh and gay,
> Ye hills and dales, ye rivers, woods, and plains,
> And ye that live and move, fair creatures, tell,
> Tell, if ye saw, how came I thus, how here?
> Not of my self; by some great maker then,
> In goodness and in power pre-eminent;
> Tell me, how may I know him, how adore,
> From whom I have that thus I move and live,
> And feel that I am happier than I know.
>
> (8.273–82)

Adam does not make the mistake of identifying the sun itself as his creator, as Satan will suggest in his temptation of Eve (9.720–22), but he speaks to it as a fellow creature; nor does he claim, as Satan does at the moment of his rebellion from God, to be "self-begot, self-raised / By our own quickening power" (5.860–61).[46] And looking upwards toward heaven, he is not momentarily transfixed by his own reflected image as is Eve at her creation (4.449f.) when the admonishing heavenly voice both addresses her as and reminds her that she is a "fair creature" (468). Adam, that is, understands correctly from the beginning his subordinate status in relationship to God. But, however preferable it may be to the experience of Satan and Eve, this understanding has its burdens.

Book 8 of *Paradise Lost* is from beginning to end an exploration of how Adam's consciousness of being God's creature produces in him a sense of inferiority. The book opens with Adam's asking Raphael why "this earth, a spot, a grain / An atom, with the firmament compared" (17–18) should be served by the infinite stars of heaven. His question not only reflects the new astronomy of Milton's century, but a larger doubt about Adam's place as man at the center of the newly created universe. The angel's response is not completely reassuring. On the one hand, Raphael does make Adam the prime reason for the presence of the heavenly bodies: "not to earth are those bright luminaries / Officious, but to thee earth's habitant" (98–99). Yet if they shine for him, their vastness is also designed to put him in proportion: "That man may know he dwells not in his own" (103). The universe is a constant reminder both of man's centrality and of his incalculable smallness next to his Creator, who resides, the angel goes on to tell Adam, at a "distance inexpressible / By numbers that have name" (113–14). Adam next relates to Raphael his own experience of his absolute distance and difference from the God in whose image he is made when he tells Raphael about his bargaining with the Deity for the creation of Eve. To God's declaration that He is "alone / From all eternity," Adam replies:

> Thou in thy self art perfect, and in thee
> Is no deficience found; not so is man,
> But in degree, the cause of his desire
> By conversation with his like to help,
> Or solace his defects.

$$\text{(8.415–19)}$$

It is by measuring himself "in degree" against God that Adam finds himself deficient and wanting: and what he wants is Eve.[47]

But if Eve is supposed to make up for and console Adam for his defects *as creature*, he confides in Raphael that her creation seems only to have taken more away from him, and not simply the rib from which she was formed: "from my side subducting, took perhaps / More than enough" (536–37). Adam's precarious sense of selfhood, when he measures himself now not beside the deity but beside his wife, is suggested a few lines earlier in his description of their first encounter, when Eve turned away from him.

> She heard me thus, and though divinely brought,
> Yet innocence and virgin modesty,
> Her virtue and conscience of her worth,
> That would be wooed, and not unsought be won,
> Not obvious, nor obtrusive, but retired,
> The more desirable, or to say all,
> Nature her self, though pure of sinful thought,
> Wrought in her so, that seeing me, she turned;
> I followed her, she what was honour knew,
> And with obsequious majesty approved
> My pleading reason.

$$\text{(8.500–510)}$$

The tortured syntax of the first seven verses, with the multiple subjects proposed for "wrought" and the gap between "she heard" and "she turned" acutely convey Adam's bewildered attempt to explain the painfully inexplicable: Eve's initial rejection of his advances. Her turning away is alternately ascribed to a modest shyness or to coquettishness—"sweet reluctant amorous delay" (4.311).[48] Or, most revealing of Adam's own psychology, Eve's reluctance is explained by her self-possession, her possession that is, of the very sense of self-worth that Adam seems to lack: "virtue and the conscience of her worth." This Virgilian phrase—"conscia virtus" (12.669)—that describes Turnus shortly before his death in the *Aeneid*, has appeared earlier in *Paradise Lost* to describe the "monarchal pride / Conscious of highest worth" (2.428–29) of Satan before the assembly in Pandemonium. There is something premonitory in Adam's projection upon Eve of a confident selfhood—suggested again in her "knowledge" of her honor and her "majesty"—that the poem has equated with the devil's attempt to emulate God's kingship over the universe, for Satan will subsequently tempt Eve in Book 9 with the titles of "Empress" (567, 626), "Queen" (684), and "Goddess" (537, 732), and Satan has first tempted her in her dream, telling Eve that she could not be "worthier" (5.76). But the point is that Adam has already made Eve his queen and goddess before Satan tells her that she is one. And the most remarkable aspect of the passage is the way in which Adam's version of his first meeting with Eve simply ignores her side of the story that she has recounted to him earlier in Book 4 (449f.). There, Eve both suggests her sexual fear of Adam and her initial preference to him of her "beauty" (490), which, through its retelling of Ovid's Narcissus story, Milton's poem equates with mere surface—in the terms of Book 8, mere external "show" (538, 575). Moreover, Adam leaves out the moment of force—Eve recalls how "thy gentle hand / Seized mine, I yielded" (488–89)—that must always leave a lingering doubt in his mind about whether Eve would ever have turned back to his pleadings on her own, after turning away from him in the first place. Rather her turning away—her seeming ability to do without him—seems to have inflicted upon him a psychic wound that confirms his sense of his own creaturely insufficiency.

And so Adam famously confesses to Raphael toward the end of Book 8 his helplessness "Against the charm of beauty's powerful glance" (533). For while he knows intellectually Eve's subordinate position to him in the hierarchy of creation—"well I understand in the prime end / Of nature her the inferior" (540–41)—his emotions tell him otherwise:

> yet when I approach
> Her loveliness, so absolute she seems
> And in her self complete, so well to know
> Her own, that what she wills to do or say,
> Seems wisest, virtuousest, discreetest, best;
> All higher knowledge in her presence falls
> Degraded, wisdom in discourse with her
> Looses discountenanced, and like folly shows;
> Authority and reason on her wait,

> As one intended first, not after made
> Occasionally; and to consummate all,
> Greatness of mind and nobleness their seat
> Build in her loveliest, and create an awe
> About her, as a guard angelic placed.
>
> (546–59)

This is, in no small part, the voice of infatuation. But Adam's "uxorious-ness," which makes him feel as if Eve should have come first in God's plans, combines his love for her with a desire to be in his *own* "self complete." Eve's outward beauty makes her seem the embodiment of that absolute selfhood he knows himself to lack when weighed with the God who has created him, and in the last verse Adam's version of Eve has become in metaphor like that God surrounded by his angels. "Was she thy God?" (10.145) the Son will accusingly ask Adam after the Fall when Adam complains that Eve was bestowed on him as a "perfect gift" (138). But this perfection was Adam's transference onto his wife of the trait ("Thou in thyself art perfect") he had earlier correctly ascribed to his Creator. As Adam gives up in Eve's presence the discursive reason that is the highest human faculty—and, in degree rather than kind, the source of his real superiority over her—he separates out and exalts in her the charismatic, aristocratic qualities—"Greatness of mind and nobleness"—that Raphael had earlier declared to depend on that reason (7.508–11). The awed Adam describes Eve as royalty because he knows *himself* to be one "after made / Occasionally," a creature abased, as Satan had once been with his fellow angels, before "Heaven's awful monarch" (4.960).

Hence Raphael's rebuke:

> weigh with her thy self;
> Then value; oft times nothing profits more
> Than self esteem, grounded on just and right
> Well managed; of that skill the more thou know'st,
> The more she will acknowledge thee her head,
> And to realities yield all her shows.
>
> (571–75)

The angel's marital counsel needs to be read as something more than the warning that he goes on to give Adam against letting his carnal senses get the better of him. It amounts to a defense of the dignity of man—and not simply measured beside that of woman, but in the larger scheme of the creation. If Adam will recognize his own worth, the worth that God has granted him even as He has given him the knowledge of his creatureliness—and indeed the two are inseparably bound together—he will not transform a proper fear of God into feelings of inferiority. He will have a sufficient, if incomplete, sense of self: what Raphael calls "self esteem" is a more robust type of self-regard than the term conveys in present-day usage. Adam will therefore not "attribute overmuch" (565) to Eve—to project onto her a full, undivided selfhood and to offer her his "subjection" (570), thereby treating as God another human or wordly authority. Moreover, Raphael tells him, Adam's own self-confidence will make Eve respect him the more and follow his lead.

In spite of Adam's "half-abashed" reply reassuring Raphael and himself that his inner feelings do not govern his outward action (595–611), the angel's advice goes for naught as the separation scene unfolds in Book 9. The dynamics of the relationship of Adam and Eve that are set forth—from Adam's point of view—in the preceding book work themselves out as Eve seeks distance between herself and Adam. Her external motive is the dream that Satan has whispered in her ear and that she described in Book 5 (28–93). But the scene also repeats her turning away from Adam at their first meeting, and it seems to confirm his sense of her as complete in herself and self-sufficient. The center of his debate with Eve—quite apart from the doctrinal issue about the testing of virtue by temptation that has received the bulk of critical attention—is Adam's anxious question about their mutual interdependence:[49]

> nor think superfluous others' aid.
> I from the influence of thy looks receive
> Access in every virtue, in thy sight
> More wise, more watchful, stronger, if need were
> Of outward strength; while shame, thou looking on,
> Shame to be overcome or over-reached
> Would utmost vigour raise, and raised unite.
> Why shouldst not thou like sense within thee feel
> When I am present, and thy trial choose
> With me, best witness of thy virtue tried.
>
> (9.308–17)

"I need you," Adam is saying, "Don't you need me as well?" In their conversation at cross-purposes Eve does not answer, which may be the most devastating possible response. In his next speech Adam permits his wife to go (372) off by herself in the garden where she will fall to Satan's snares. Eve's seeking of independence thus grows out of her relationship with Adam as much as from diabolic suggestion. The more he communicates his feeling of dependence on Eve, and his feelings that she may *not*, in the self-sufficiency he envisions in her, stand in need of him, the more he encourages her to strike off on her own, which in itself gives further rise to his feelings of creaturely inadequacy.

As I have argued, Adam's lack of self-esteem causes him to overestimate Eve, ascribing to her a perfection that verges on idolatry. And he took this perfection for a *spiritual* perfection as well, as he ruefully admits at the end of Book 9, when the couple accuse each other after the Fall.

> But confidence then bore thee on, secure
> Either to meet no danger, or to find
> Matter of glorious trial; and perhaps
> I also erred in overmuch admiring
> What seemed in thee so perfect, that I thought
> No evil durst attempt thee.
>
> (9.1175–80)

In retrospect Adam blames Eve for *her* false assurance, her confident belief in her immunity to sin. But he also half acknowledges his own error by intimating that her sense of security was reinforced, if not indeed created, by the self-sufficiency he himself projected upon her. For although, as he defensively asserts, he had been trying to warn Eve: "I warned thee, I admonished thee, foretold / The danger" (1171–72)—just as Raphael had been sent by God to warn them both of the perils of Satan and sin, lest they claim to have fallen "unadmonished, unforewarned" (5.245)—Adam had been sending his wife mixed signals, encouraging her independence and confidence that she was "securer than thus warned thou seem'st" (9.371).

The last passage links the assurance that Adam had earlier claimed for himself to his overestimation of Eve. There is a homology between the two: both share an all or nothing logic concerning the authority of the self. For, as Goodwin implied, it was those men and women who were fearfully unsure of themselves who paradoxically asserted their assurance: orthodox Calvinists, who thought themselves to be the heirs of an original sin that impaired the will and allowed it no freedom or power to stand against sin, persuaded themselves that their wills had been taken over and made perfect by the special election of grace. They thus avoided the contingent responsibilities of a will that, according to the Arminian positions of both Goodwin and Milton, is free to accept or reject the gift of grace extended to all human beings—who are thus rendered, like the first created Adam, "Sufficient to have stood." For the prelapsarian Adam, the Calvinist's anxiety of sinfulness finds its equivalent in an acute feeling of creaturely incompleteness and insecurity: his reassuring of himself of the certainty that he will keep the divine injunction against the eating of the forbidden fruit is a defense precisely against the doubts that Raphael has come to instill in him. At the same time, he displaces his desire for an escape from his creaturely condition and its limitations on Eve, whom he makes his God. Both yearnings to transcend his own contingent middle realm as creature, where he is dependent *and* free, are delusory, and they reveal a self that would be all or nothing (as the Calvinist would be persuaded of a guaranteed salvation or equally certain damnation) in Adam's twofold declaration at his Fall: his assertion to the deceived Eve that, like her, he aspires "to be gods, or angels, demigods" (9.936), his "undeceived," inward thought: "Certain my resolution is to die" (9.907).

But in the lines that immediately precede Adam's berating of both Eve's confidence and his overconfidence in her, *Paradise Lost* spells out the dilemma inherent in human freedom: the contingency which is its very condition and which Adam finds so difficult to live with. It is here that the poem's psychologizing theological argument shades into an argument about religious and finally civil politics. To Eve's charge that he should have commanded her, as the Pauline "head" of their marriage, "absolutely not to go" (9.1156), Adam replies that he had tried persuasion.

> Beyond this had been force,
> And force upon free will hath here no place.

> (1173–74).

Because God has created human beings as individually free to stand or fall, they have—"here," that is, in matters of religious choice—no right to coerce the freedom of one another.[50] This is the burden of the similes that Goodwin uses in *Redemption Redeemed* to contest the imprisonment of the will implied by the doctrine of assurance. He draws on the Pauline characterization of Christ as the husband of His Church in Eph. 5:23.

> For, to follow the ducture of the parable or similitude here used by the apostle, the husband is the conservator or keeper of his wife; yet, notwithstanding, the wife may possibly miscarry, and break the marriage covenant, yea though the husband acts his part upon the best and most commendable terms, for the preserving of her from that folly, that may be. The reason is, because the wife, being a reasonable creature, is to be dealt with, in order to her preservation or keeping in that kind, as, viz., by rational arguments or motives only, as by an exemplary, loving, and prudent carriage in the husband towards her, by seasonable instructions, gentle admonition upon occasion, &c., not by keeping her under lock and key as in a prison, where no man may come near her, nor by any compulsory or violent means, in one kind or other. . . . In like manner Christ is the Saviour of his spouse, the church, and not only of the church in general, but of every member therof: but he executes and performs the interest or office of a Saviour . . . by inward motions and excitements of his Spirit, unto well doing, and to a continuance therein, by vouchsafing the ministry of his word, the examples and converse of his saints, many providential opportunities, apt and proper to prevail with rational creature, to mind the things of God, and of its own peace, &c., but not by any necessitating administrations or applications of

himself whatsoever. So that though Christ performs the office of a Saviour towards his body, upon the most faithful, careful and honorable terms that can be imagined, yet there must needs be a possibility, at least, for any member thereof to miscarry.[51]

Christ saves by persuasion, not by force, conforming to—and at the same time providing—a model for marital relations. As husband, Milton's Adam had the duty to guide his wife, but he still could not use coercion on what was Eve's freedom of conscience or restrict her movement. So Eve, looking back in the same passage at the end of Book 9, herself suggests,

> Was I to have never parted from thy side?
> As good have grown there still a lifeless rib.
>
> (9.1153–55)

It was possible for Adam to err on the side of overprotectiveness and to confine Eve, out of harm's way, against her will; when persuasion failed, he had little choice but to let her go off on her own and risk the consequences.

This view of domestic politics had, as a second analogy in Goodwin's treatise suggests, its corollary in the public political world as well.

> For as in a politic or civil corporation, it is better that the governors should permit the members respectively to go or to be at liberty, that so they may follow their business and occasions in the world upon the better terms, though by occasion of this liberty they may behave themselves in sundry kinds very unworthily, than it would be to keep them close prisoners, though hereby the said inconveniences might certainly be prevented: in like manner, it is much better for the body of Christ, and for the respective members of it, that he should leave them at liberty, (especially upon such terms as he doth, and which have formerly been declared,) to obey and serve God, and follow the important affairs of their soul freely, and without any physical necessitation, though some do turn this liberty into wantonness, and so into destruction, than it would be to deprive them of this liberty, and to cause and constrain them to any course whatsoever out of necessity, though, it is true, the committing of much sin and iniquity would be prevented hereby in many.[52]

Where Christ the husband in Goodwin's first comparison would not keep his wife under lock and key, here Christ the magistrate would not imprison his citizen-subjects, even to protect them from sin. What is at stake theologically in this passage is well brought out in Kendall's brilliant rebuttal of Goodwin's "simile," which clearly indicates the difference between their respective Calvinist and Arminian positions.

> Mr. *Goodwin* highly deserves of his generation of *Saints*, for shewing them by his Doctrine how happy they may be in this [liberty of following their business

and occasions in the world] in comparison of what they should be, by being tied up too close in a sad bondage under Christ, according to the dangerous project of our assertions concerning their Perseverance. *Our Doctrine* doth not know what belongs to a *free State*. But upon second thoughts, Good Mr. *Goodwin*, is it not better for a man to be kept in *prison* in his *house*, then to be left to *banish himself* out of his *Country*? Is it not better to have his *hands manacled* and *tied behind his back*, then to be left to *embrue his knife* in his *blood*? Is it not better for him to be *confined to his chair*, then to be left to *throw* himself down the *stairs*? This is our case: Christ, according to our Doctrine, *overrules* us by *his Spirit*, that we may not be *overthrown* by our own *flesh*. I must needs say, had the Saints as great an *averseness* from any *deadliest sins*, as men *naturally have from killing themselves*, you might be in a possibility of justifying this your Simile.[53]

Here as elsewhere in his polemic against Goodwin, Kendall insists upon the effects of original sin, which leads human beings irresistibly toward a spiritual death, like the suicidal frenzy that would cause the madman to bring about his natural death. As the madman is restrained, so the saint with the gift of assurance is bound by the grace of Christ to prevent him or her from committing sin. Kendall's own simile quickly conflates political constraint—a kind of house arrest—with therapeutic coercion in order to argue that both are for the individual's own good, and to bear out the acknowledgment that his doctrine does "not know what belongs to a *free state*." For human beings in this view are not free: they must fall into the bondage of sin unless they are held up by a "bondage under Christ."

But, as Milton's poem suggests, such analogies were reversible. Goodwin's figures of coercive authority, both domestic and magistrative, are pointedly chosen: for the Christian liberty asserted by the Arminian opponents of predestined election and assurance argued, by extension, for freedom as well in Church and in civil political organization. The orthodox Calvinist position they opposed correspondingly argued for political constraint; there existed a link, perhaps more often implicit than explicitly voiced, between an assurance that the human will of the saint was controlled by divine grace and the support for a strong Church government that monitored the belief and behavior of its members. Henry Jacob, the early seventeenth-century divine who would be an intellectual founder of independent Congregationalism, saw the two as indivisible: the Church's discipline was "the only true complete means to get assurance of salvation to our souls, which otherwise we, for our parts, cannot find."[54] The idea is present in the insistence by both Independents and Presbyterians that individual churches should be constituted and governed by "visible saints," those who both felt themselves and were perceived by others to be assured of salvation. This emphasis on godly discipline—which sought to entwine ecclesiastical and civil power and which did not know a "free state"—was opposed to the broad toleration for which Goodwin, like Milton by the time of *Areopagitica* in 1644, was a leading proponent. The writing of *Redemption Redeemed* was conditioned by the defeat of a national Presbyterian Church in the Rump Parliament of 1649 and by an ensuing campaign for liberty of conscience in the first years of the Commonwealth; in his *Thirty Queries* of 1653, Goodwin refuted the idea that "the Civil Magistrate stands bound to interpose his powers in matters of religion and worship of God."[55] This was the cornerstone, too, of Milton's political thought, spelled out in the title of his 1659 tract, A *Treatise of Civil Power in Ecclesiastical causes: Shewing That it is not lawfull for any power on earth to compell in matters of Religion.*

It is in this context of religious politics that the response to *Redemption Redeemed* by the Presbyterian Kendall should be understood, as should the attack on the work by John Owen, the leading Independent minister and spiritual adviser to Cromwell. *The Saints Perseverance* opens with a dedicatory letter to Cromwell, now the Lord Protector, that reminds Cromwell of his own attainment of assurance.

> The series and chain of eminent providences whereby you have been carried on and protected in all the hazardous work of your generation, which your God hath called you unto, is evident to all. Of your preservation by the power of God, through faith, in a course of gospel obedience, upon the account of the immutability of the love and infallibility of the promises of God, which are yea and amen in Jesus Christ, your own soul only is possessed with the experience. Therein is that abiding joy, that secret refreshment, which the world cannot give. . . . Unto your Highness I have not any thing more to add, nor for you greater thing to pray, than that you may be established in the assurance and sense of that unchangeable love and free acceptance in Christ which I contend for, and that therein you may be preserved, to the glory of God, the advancement of the gospel, and the real advantage of these nations.[56]

Although Owen distinguishes the external signs of God's favor to Cromwell—the "providences" that have brought him to power—from the assurance that he may find from the inward workings of sanctifying grace, the two nonetheless appear connected: his assurance of his own godliness seems to be the warrant for the Lord Protector's authority.

This political warrant extended not only over the secular realm but also into matters of religion. In 1654, the year of his treatise against Goodwin, Owen led the commission of "Triers" that Cromwell had authorized to enforce a degree of uniformity upon individual parishes. Consistent with his principles, Goodwin attacked Owen and this state regulation of religion in his *Basanistae or The Triers or Tormentors Tried and Cast* (1657) and *Triumviri* (1658). In the former tract he compared the Triers to Spanish inquisitors: "they act so Inquisition like that not milk to milk, nor egge to egg, more like, was" (the typographer has somewhat vitiated Goodwin's rhetorical point).[57] After *Basanistae* was answered by Marchamount Nedham in *The Great Accuser Cast Down, or a Publick Trial of Mr. John Goodwin* (1657),[58] there appeared an anonymous defense of Goodwin, *A Letter of Addresse to the Protector . . . by a Person of Quality* (1657), which directly accused Cromwell of doing just what Owen had only implied he might do: of taking his belief in his personal election as the sanction for his government—and for his persecution, through the Triers, of all those who did not share his Calvinist assurance or, for that matter, did not believe in the doctrine of assurance itself.

> My Lord, you are taught to believe Christ died not for all, how should we then expect you should do us all good in the administration of your justice and judgment? . . . It appears . . . that the day of judgment is already come, that you are set upon your throne, and have begun to separate the sheep from the goates, and to distinguish betwixt the vile and the precious, the clean and the unclean, the elect and reprobate: you have set the Calvinists on your right hand, and invited them to rule with you and participate of your glory and greatness in your kingdom; you have set the Primitive Christians on your left, and said unto them, come not into any living, keep out of all imployment and trust under me, &c. . . . Sure I am my Lord, you perswade your self God Almighty loved you, personally before you had any real being and existence, and that you were with some few comparatively Elected to glory and blessedness *ab aeterno* . . . and therefore not unsuitable to your faith and opinion receive the reputed Saints into your bosome, preferr them at your pleasure, and herein comport with the divine decree; leaving the great rout of people (over which you are imposed) as the sad forlorn of Hell, unavoidably appointed to ruine, justly to beare whatever partiality in justice, cruelty can lay upon them here on earth.[59]

The Lord Protector's assurance of salvation, the premature closure on his own life that to the anonymous Arminian author is a denial of the Christian liberty to persevere or fall, causes him to tyrannize over the religious liberty of his subjects. This closure is carried over into Cromwell's politics, where he plays God and already metes out the punishments of the Last Judgment upon those he has prejudged as reprobate, setting up his fellow self-proclaimed Calvinist saints as arbiters over the religious practices and consciences of their fellow citizens, including (especially) the Arminians who have here, as "Primitive Christians," taken over the cause of True Reformation. But even a relatively orthodox Calvinist might call into question the tie between a sense of election and a claim to power in state and church government, an argument spelled out in the title of Edward Bagshaw's *Saintship no ground for Sovereignty* of 1660. While Bagshaw believed in both predestination and assurance, he argued for what the Restoration would in any event make a fait accompli, the saints' renunciation of a temporal power that could only lead to popery: "for men first to call themselves, *The Godly*, (a stile which *Paul*, after all his Revelations, did not so boldly assume) and then to make themselves our Governors, is without any streining the road thither."[60]

Both the polemical references to the doctrine of assurance in *Paradise Lost* and the poem's portrait of an Adam who suffers from a lack of proper self-esteem—and I have tried to suggest how these may be connected—are thus implicated in a much wider network of contemporary religious and political thought. Milton's Arminianism stands in opposition to a Calvinist orthodoxy, shared by both Presbyterians and most Independents, that, by asserting at a theological level the unworthiness of the human creature and the bondage of the will, sanctioned state intervention into church discipline during the Commonwealth. Moreover, by the time he wrote his epic, Milton confronted not merely the curbing of religious toleration and freedom, but the loss of republican freedom and the imposition of the restored monarchy, the "Egyptian bondage" toward which he had earlier seen England heading in *The Readie and Easie Way*. At the time of that treatise he had nonetheless detected the *same structure of thought* in his countrymen's rushing to enslave themselves once again. In his short 1660 pamphlet, *Brief Notes upon a Late Sermon*, Milton spelled out what he saw as the choice confronting the English people.

> Free Commonwealths have bin ever counted fittest and prosperest for civil, vertuous and industrious Nations, abounding with prudent men worthie to govern: monarchie fittest to curb degenerate, corrupt, idle, proud, luxurious people. If we desire to be of the former, nothing better for us, nothing nobler then a free Commonwealth: if we will needs condemn our selves to be of the latter, despairing of our own vertue, industrie and the number of our able men, we may then, conscious of our own unworthiness to be governed better, sadly betake us to our befitting thraldom;[61]

There is a continuity between Milton's theological critique of the Calvinist fear of a human will that, left free, must necessarily fall to sin—hence the need for an assurance that the will had been taken under the control of the higher power of grace—and his political critique of a people who despaired of their ability freely to govern themselves and invited a king to rule over them. Milton's Adam exemplifies the condition of being "conscious of our own unworthiness" that may stand at the opposite pole of Satan's "monarchal pride / Conscious of highest worth," but is equally conducive to both religious and political sin. Adam and the English people, whose collective psychology Adam can now be seen to share, fell because they did not have sufficient faith in their own liberty.

Such liberty must contain the potential for failure, whether it is the spiritual lapse of the Christian into sin and perdition, or mistaken political choices, including the choice for a king: such potential is the essence of human freedom, which must be contingent in order to be free. This contingency makes the way constantly difficult, rather than ready and easy, for men and women to stand in godliness or for republics to last. And this is the sobering essence of Adam and Eve's retrospective view of their Fall at the end of Book 9: there was no way that they could have ensured themselves—certainly not by force—against the occasion of temptation, which may be the delusion of escaping the contingency of occasion itself. For the surest way to fall was to look for some final guarantee or fixed condition—whether godhead or self-abjecting despair—that would enable them to drop their constant vigilance against sin, to give up, in short, the exercising of their freedom. Conversely, in his political tracts on the eve of the Restoration he tried to prevent, Milton argued that all political measures were to be justified by one standard: whether they preserved liberty. And here, apparently inconsistent with his principles, he was willing to justify the use of force by a minority to rule over the majority "They who seek nothing but thir own just libertie, have alwaies right to winn it and to keep it, when ever they have power, be the voices never so numerous that oppose it."[62]

The unfallen Adam and Eve enjoyed a freedom that is described by Adam of his state immediately after his creation:

> thus I move and live
> And feel that I am happier than I know.
>
> (8.281–82).

A pun on "happy" and "happiness" runs through *Paradise Lost*. We have seen it already in the references to the earth and stars as "happy isles" (2.411; 3.567), which turn them into versions of the Fortunate Islands. Milton emphasizes the "hap" in happiness: the element of fortune, chance, and contingency. As Fowler's notes observe, Adam echoes, with some irony and premonition, the hymn of praise that Raphael recounts the angels sang when God created the new human species:

> thrice happy if they know
> Their happiness, and persevere upright.[63]
>
> (7.631–32)

The problem for Adam and Eve, as has been often pointed out, is that they cannot *know* the full precariousness of their happy state until they have lost it: this is the real knowledge they receive from the forbidden fruit.

The burden of Raphael's visit is precisely to tell them that they are in a "happier" position than they think: though one which they have the freedom to lose. So God Himself instructs the messenger angel:

> such discourse bring on
> As may advise him of his happy state,
> Happiness in his power, left free to will,
> Left to his own free will, his will though free
> Yet mutable; whence warn him to beware
> He swerve not too secure.
>
> (5.233–37)

But in such contingent freedom lies their real human happiness, in the sense of "contentment." It is opposed to an excessive sense of security or assurance that may lead to their fall—especially once they make the mistake, like Eve, in the separation scene of Book 9, of identifying security with happiness. Her argument, in fact, echoes as it inverts those earlier words of God to Raphael.

> Let us not then suspect our happy state
> Left so imperfect by the maker wise,
> As not secure to single or combined;
> Frail is our happiness, if this be so
> And Eden were no Eden thus exposed.
>
> (9.337–41)

Here it is Eve, rather than Adam, who takes the all or nothing Calvinist position, assuming that a state that is contingent and imperfect—"not secure"—must contain no possibility of security at all, that happiness must be absolute, without any dangers or difficulties, in order to be happy, that she and Adam do not need to work for and at their happiness. Her logic implies a swing to the opposite extreme and to an overconfident assurance—"too secure"—that the happiness God has granted them will continue forever without any effort on their part.

A final gloss on Miltonic happiness is found in *Paradise Regained*, where the "happy station" (1.360) that Satan lost in heaven—like the "happy garden" of the poem's first line lost by Adam and Eve in the earlier epic—is contrasted to the "uneasy station" (4.584) that Milton's Jesus manages to keep, balancing on the pinnacle of the Temple. What Jesus, the man-god without sin, can do by himself is a model for all men and women upheld by grace, but also by their own striving. Happiness, for Milton, is always contingent and uneasy, conditioned by the terrifying possibility for failure—the drop before Jesus' feet—but maintained by the human will whose free exercise is in itself the source and essence of happiness.

The identifying of happiness not with security but with contingency further links Milton's fictions with a tradition of republican thinking. For as J.G.A. Pocock has shown, the theorists and promoters of republican institutions often acknowledged, with Machiavelli, that the dynamism of these institutions was also the cause of their potential instability.[64] In *The Readie and Easie Way*, Milton takes pains to balance the contingent liberty of the free Commonwealth he is designing with the promise that this Commonwealth would be "firmest, safest, and most above fortune," exempt from the corrupting attacks of Machiavelli's *fortuna*.[65] He draws on millenarian language to claim for republican institutions that

> with as much assurance as can be of human things, that they shall so continue (if God favour us, and our willfull sins provoke him not) even to the coming of our true and rightfull, and only to be expected King, only worthie as he is our only Saviour, the Messiah, the Christ.[66]

Milton the casuist appears ready to transfer to his republic the kind of assurance of persevering to the end that he denies to the individual believer: he has both secularized the doctrine of assurance and granted the Commonwealth (which he may well feel is godly or preserves the possibility of godliness) a divine sanction and guarantee of success. This historical closure does not seem so different from the Arminian caricature of Cromwell as would-be apocalyptic judge. Yet the parenthetical "if" clauses characteristically hedge the assertion of certainty and insist, precisely in Arminian terms, on the necessary cooperation of the human will with divine grace. Furthermore, the reference to Christ as the only "King" worthy to reign over the English people is aimed polemically against those who look to an earthly king for "the chief hope of thir common happiness or safetie"—and who mistrust a shaky republican freedom.[67] For in spite of Milton's protestations to the contrary, his countrymen turned to monarchy for a return to political stability and security. They confused, as does Milton's Eve, their happiness with safety, unwilling to endure any longer in the uncertainty of the Commonwealth and to wait for their true, eschatological King.

In spite, then, of the apocalyptic imminence that Milton's blueprint for a free Commonwealth evokes, the contingency that conditions human freedom, including republican freedom, creates a historical space that is *for practical purposes* open-ended—within the larger closed narrative of Christian history that is given shape by its promised end. In *Paradise Lost* this space corresponds to the world of Adam and Eve in Eden that seems to exist at a remove, both cosmic and generic, from the epic apocalyptic battles between Satan and the Son taking place at the level of the poem's divine machinery. "It is difficult," Patricia Parker writes, "to decide which is the crucial Miltonic focus, the middle period of suspension, wandering and trial, or the final movement towards resolution and end."[68] In its own internal freedom and open-endedness, the human arena of Milton's epic participates, as Parker has brilliantly shown in her reading of the poem, "in a tension ... identified with the uncertain middle term of 'romance.' "[69] We might build on Parker's analysis by suggesting the *political* ramifications of this in-between ground of romance: it allows the poem to enact—at the level of its narrative structure—an Arminian middle way that avoids the all or nothing extremes of Calvinist orthodoxy and preserves the liberty of its human protagonists.

At the same time, the human plot of *Paradise Lost*, no less than its divine superplot, can now be seen to be structured by the classic opposition between epic teleology and romance deviation and deferral that we have traced through the epic tradition. This opposition is construed with different political significance by the Virgilian victors' epic and by the losers' epic of Lucan and his imitators; and Milton's poem, with its double plot, divides between the two modes: it is Virgilian at the level of God and Satan, it follows Lucan at the level of the fallen Adam and Eve—which is also the level of the politically defeated Milton and his English countrymen. In the first case, the epic-romance dichotomy defines the all or nothing struggle of good and evil, and romance structures characterize the aimlessness of the eternally fallen Satan, the endless circularity of his repeated, failed revolts against God. In the second, those same structures are viewed in a positive light for permitting a suspended period of free choice for Adam and Eve before the premature ending that is the Fall, and—perhaps more crucially—for allowing their hope and free choice to surface again after the Fall, to resist the notion that the Fall and its consequences are final and irreversible.

The difference between these two plots is spelled out in the final verses of Book 9, where Adam and Eve have fallen out with each other.

> Thus they in mutual accusation spent
> The fruitless hours, but neither self-condemning,
> And of their vain contest appeared no end.
>
> (9.1187–89)

The strife dividing the human family repeats in little the structure of the potentially endless internecine War in Heaven. On that occasion God declared of the rebel angels:

> I suspend their doom;
> Whence in perpetuall fight they needs must last
> Endless, and no solution will be found.
>
> (6.692–94)

But this perpetual fighting, as we saw in Chapter 1, was the essence of Satan's strategy, to prolong his war against God for "eternal days" (6.424). The wrangling Adam and Eve thus share in the bad romance suspension and endless repetition of the devil; like Satan, neither of them are willing to repent: each prefers to blame the other. But just as the Son stepped in to break the impasse of the angelic war, He here intercedes, coming at the opening of Book 10 to judge Adam and Eve but also to offer them the promise of redemption. And that, of course, is the difference between His treatment of the fallen angels, whose defeat is also a kind of (Last) judgment, and His treatment of humanity. The covenantal promise begins the operation of grace that by the book's end has reconciled Adam and Eve to each other and then to God. The Son's sacrifice of Himself shapes history into a closed plot, just as His exaltation in heaven (5.600f.) initially differentiates historical, sequential time out of eternity. This redemptive plot provides the narrative telos that, for Parker, would distinguish the bad romance wandering of the fallen angels, "in wand'ring mazes lost" (2.561), from the purgatorial progress, "with wandering steps and slow" (12.648), of Adam and Eve and of their descendants throughout history.[70] The sublime close of the epic describes a world of almost infinite, contingent possibility:

> The world was all before them, where to choose
> Their place of rest, and providence their guide:
> They hand in hand with wandering steps and slow,
> Through Eden took their solitary way.
>
> (12.646–49)

Once history has disclosed its final shape in the angel Michael's prophecy—"providence their guide"—it becomes open-ended for practical human experience, a romance locus of choice, trial and error, and, above all, freedom.

Parker emphasizes that an analogous, if not indeed identical, structure governs the experience of Adam and Eve *before* the Fall. Raphael suggests that humanity may eventually rise spiritually to the level of the angels, and "at choice" (5.499) move between Eden and Heaven, and Adam interprets this as a contemplative ascent "by steps" (511) to God. These steps would be less wandering than the historical course that humanity takes toward its place of rest, but Milton's depictions of *both* prelapsarian and postlapsarian states are dynamic: they both depend on the "tract of time" (5.498) or "race of time" (12.554) necessary for the accomplishment of divine plans, a period that human actors must patiently wait out. The dangerous alternative is a leap to conclusions. Parker observes:

> The Fall, then, is from this perspective, an attempt to hasten the ascent, to circumvent the process of education by degrees, and to repeat the error of the angel who thought that "one step higher" would set him "highest" (4.50–51) and who enters Paradise in one "bound." (181)[71]

To seek to be all, like God, is to wish to have all one's story be told: to turn immediately to the last page and find how it all turns out instead of living with the suspense, the incompleteness of being a creature. In narrative terms, this is to opt for a fixed epic end, rather than a romance middle. Milton importantly makes this middle dynamic, if gradual and gradated, allowing to Adam and Eve the potential for spiritual education and growth even in prelapsarian Eden, so that his romance garden paradise will not be, as in earlier epics, a place merely of passive detachment from historical process or of avoidance of choice. Waiting obediently on God is a choice to preserve the freedom of choice itself.[72]

There are precedents in Lucan's tradition of the losers' epic for this choice of open romance process over final epic goals—which constitutes a reversal of the narrative values of the Virgilian victors' epic—and for the injunction against hasty action that would preempt and foreclose the possibilities of history: a warning given plain formulation by the Jesus of *Paradise Regained*, who, in answer to Satan's urging to speed up the coming of His Kingdom, calmly replies, "All things are best fulfilled in their due time / And time there is for all things" (3.182–83). In the retrospective view of the losers, their defeat came about all too quickly (while, for the victors, victory could not come quickly enough). In the *Pharsalia* Lucan suggested that the vanquished republicans had allowed themselves to be swept into the decisive battle at Pharsalia instead of keeping to Pompey's strategy of waiting Caesar out; they had played into the hands of the precipitate—"praeceps"—Caesar. The episodic, crosscutting of the *Pharsalia's* narrative offered a resistance to the teleological structures of the *Aeneid* and of the closed plot it told of a Roman history culminating in Caesarian imperial rule. Ercilla identified this narrative resistance both generically with the wandering of romance and ideologically with the continuing resistance of his Araucanian protagonists to final Spanish conquest. Closer in theological outlook to Milton, d'Aubigné redescribes the wandering of romance as the desert wandering of the Church waiting for apocalypse.

Milton's depiction of the Fall shares the same retrospect on defeat in which Adam and Eve, promised an eventual initiation into divinity, seem to have acted overhastily and thereby lost Eden. The depiction is further colored by its analogy to the defeat of the Commonwealth, which, according to the *Readie and Easie Way*, had only to stand and wait for its "expected" apocalyptic king. And already in that tract Milton had several times remarked upon the unholy rush in which the English people were seeking to go back to the bondage of monarchy: "returning precipitantly, if he [God] withold us not, back to the captivitie from whence he freed us,"[73]

> and may reclaim, though they seem now chusing them a captain back for *Egypt*, to bethink themselves a little and consider whether they are rushing . . . to stay these ruinous proceedings; justly and timely fearing to what a precipice of destruction the deluge of this epidemic madness would hurry us.[74]

The structures of romance suspension in *Paradise Lost* thus put a brake upon, and offer an alternative to, what, from a postlapsarian perspective, seems to have been a mad dash by Adam and Eve to their Fall: "And me with thee hath ruined" (9.906), Adam says of Eve as he prepares to fall with her, and Milton plays on the Latin etymology (*ruo*) of his verb to suggest how both are "on a sudden lost" (900). And such romance suspension might also characterize the alternative political choice—a choice to hold steady, even if this just means to muddle on, through the contingent and uncertain turns of republican liberty—that Milton had held out in place of his countrymen's precipitate haste to seek out security and certain enslavement under the restored king.

The closest model in *Paradise Lost* for this republican experience is the wilderness existence of the Israelites described by Michael to Adam in Book 12.

> the race elect
> Safe towards Canaan from the shore advance
> Through the wild desert, not the readiest way,
> Lest entering on the Canaanite alarmed
> War terrify them inexpert, and fear
> Return them back to Egypt, choosing rather
> Inglorious life with servitude; for life
> To noble and ignoble is more sweet
> Untrained in arms, where rashness leads not on.
> This also shall they gain by their delay
> In the wide wilderness, there they shall found
> Their government, and their great senate choose
> Through the twelve tribes, to rule by laws ordained:
> God from the mount of Sinai, whose grey top
> Shall tremble, he descending, will himself
> In thunder lightning, and loud trumpets' sound
> Ordain them laws; part such as appertain
> To civil justice, part religious rites
> Of sacrifice, informing them, by types
> And shadows, of that destined seed to bruise
> The serpent, by what means he shall achieve
> Mankind's deliverance.

(12.214–35)

The risk that the Israelites will return to Egyptian servitude clearly recalls Milton's charge against his fellow Englishmen in the *Readie and Easie Way*. The alternative, ready way of the sojourn in the wilderness turns out to be not the "readiest" way, an apocalyptically immediate or triumphalist epic entrance into the Holy Land, but rather a period of romance wandering that is also a time of political education. The Israelites have the freedom to choose their "great senate" like the one that Milton outlined for England in the *Readie and Easie Way*. And just as Adam and Eve have providence as the guide to their wandering steps, here God steps in Himself to ordain laws: what appears to be a divine doubling or ratification of the people's own choice to live by the senate's law. The romance state of delay in the wilderness is thus not static but informed by the dynamism of salvation history: it affords the time necessary to prepare the Israelites not only for their eventual entrance into Canaan but also for the later advent of Christ. Milton similarly had described his model commonwealth in the *Readie and Easie Way* as open to the Second Coming. But the delay does nonetheless defer expectations and rules out a quick victory and acquisition of the Promised Land as well as an equally quick defeat and return to Egypt. Both alternatives would be the product of a martial, and hence *epic* "rashness:" an end-directed, if premature drive similar to the impulse leading on the "rash hand" (9.780) of Eve at the moment she plucked and ate the forbidden fruit.

This haste to have things done with is both a flight from freedom and the sign of despair: so Adam after the Fall longs for death to come and complains, "Why do I overlive?" (10.773) and Eve suggests the recourse of suicide (10.1000f.). They are too quick to draw conclusions about their defeat—as if it were conclusive and final—and only slowly realize in Book 10 that God promises them "revenge" against their "grand foe / Satan" (1033–34). By insisting upon the open-endedness of history, Lucan's losers' epic not only nostalgically suggests that the events that led up to defeat could have turned out differently, but also asserts that the setback may only be temporary, that continuing resistance may turn the tables on the victorious enemy. *Paradise Lost* most fully belongs to the tradition of Lucan in the resistance to closure that makes its ending into a new beginning for Adam and Eve, in their carrying on the memory of Eden as a "paradise within thee happier far" (12.587).[75] This inner reconstitution of the contingent freedom, the happiness of Eden, requires a new acknowledgment of their condition as creatures, imperfect and now flawed by sin, but also sufficient by the aid of grace. It is the acceptance of this creaturely condition—which means maintaining a sense of worthiness even while forgoing the assurance of salvation—that was earlier summed up in Raphael's parting advice: "Be strong, live happy" (8.633). In the initial failure of Adam and Eve to keep their happy state, Milton found the psychological analogies to explain the downfall of republican freedom in England: his countrymen were affected by a kind of mass inferiority complex, a loss of nerve or belief in themselves that made them give over their liberty, religious and civic, into the hands of another. But by the end of *Paradise Lost* Adam and Eve have become models of how that liberty might be reachieved, by once again embracing the contingency of history and its surprising possibilities.[76] The Miltonic formula demands giving up the assurance of all certain endings—except for the promised, if indefinitely deferred eschatological end. But, in exchange, to abide in the middle of a still incomplete history is the condition of both personal and political faith.

Milton, Marino, and Seventeenth-Century Epic

For all that Adam and Eve receive an inner paradise, "happier far" than the Eden they have left, the tragic sense of loss that accompanies the Fall at the very least counterbalances the offical theological conclusion that it was a Fortunate Fall, all for the best. "Happier" yes, if the punning, secondary sense of "happy" is kept in mind: as death comes into the world under the curse of original sin, human existence becomes that much more contingent; men and women must work all the harder to achieve their salvation, though in that work lies their contentment. Milton, we have seen, revises in two ways the traditional epic opposition between the narrative suspension of romance and epic's own plot of historical destiny: there is the promise of some narrative, historical progress in his romance Eden where Adam and Eve would both increase and multiply the human race and rise spiritually to the ranks of the angels. More significantly, the history into which Adam and Eve are cast remains itself a romance world of contingency and wandering, rather than a clearly end-directed epic narrative. Their Fortunate Fall is a fall into the world of Fortune, however much Providence may act as guide.

At the level of genre, therefore, the choice of the human actors of *Paradise Lost* to fall and leave Eden is a choice not between romance and epic, but between two dynamic forms of romance. Effectively eliminated from the human experience of the poem is the conventional epic narrative of a history organized by collective human power. Such martial and imperial plots are criticized in Michael's account of the giants (11.638f.)—with its extensive imitation of the shield of Achilles in the *Iliad*—and of Nimrod and the first world-empire of Babel (12.24–62). These episodes are subsumed as passing moments, destroyed by the Flood and the confusion of tongues, within the archangel's larger narrative of salvation history. Michael's narrative is pointedly substituted for the prophetic catalogue or procession of national history such as Anchises' speech to Aeneas in Book 6 of the *Aeneid* or, a closer model, for the geographical and historical overview of imperial expansion that concludes the *Lusíadas*. Michael sets Adam on top of the highest hill of Eden from where he might have seen—as Jesus, tempted by Satan, would later behold (11.381–84)—the kingdoms of the world, including the Portuguese conquests of "Mombasa, and Quiloa, and Melind" (399) celebrated in Camões' epic.[77] Milton invokes these epic models for Michael's narrative in order to reject them, and he satirizes the epic of empire in the role of Satan as colonialist explorer of space and the New World.

While I have argued above, then, that the focus on a private, domestic realm in Eden does not necessarily constitute a passive retreat from the public world of politics, *Paradise Lost* nonetheless turns away *generically* toward romance from an epic organization of that political world. In doing so, however, Milton's poem conforms to a general pattern in the history of epic poetry in the seventeenth century. We can observe in several other poems of the age, notably in the *Adone* (1623) of Marino, the deformation of epic in the direction of the romance genre from which it had traditionally differentiated itself. And the sociopolitical factors that underlie this larger literary-historical development may, in turn, offer a base of comparison that will shed some light on the politics of Milton's poetry.

How well Milton knew Marino's *Adone* is open to question. He acknowledges the poem in his own *Mansus* (11), written to celebrate Giovanni Battista Manso, the friend of both Tasso and Marino; by praising Manso's hospitality to him when he was traveling in Italy, Milton was placing himself in the line of the other two famous poets. Direct allusions to the *Adone* in *Paradise Lost* are harder to detect. The immediate similarity between the two poems lies in their respective settings. Both take place largely inside pleasure gardens of love; in the *Adone* this is the garden of Venus on Cyprus.

Marino's Adonis sails to Cyprus, in the first canto of the poem, aboard the boat of Fortune, invoking the fictions of both Tasso and Boiardo explored in our last chapter, and this romance Fortune will remain, in different personifications, the presiding figure over the entire work. Adonis is hunting on the shores of Palestine when the allegorical figure of Fortune approaches him in her bark, singing.

> Chi cerca in terra divenir beato
> goder tesori, e possedere imperi
> stenda la destra in questo crine aurato.[78]

(1.50)

(Whoever seeks to be blessed on this earth, to enjoy riches and possess empires, let him stretch his right hand towards this golden lock.)

The song clearly imitates a similar song of Boiardo's Fata Morgana, the fortune fairy of the *Innamorato*, who similarly invited Orlando to seize her by her golden forelock, the forelock of occasion.[79] Adonis enters into the boat of Fortune and after an Odyssean storm is carried to Cyprus and eventually to the garden of Venus. The action and geography recall and pointedly reverse the plot of the *Gerusalemme liberata*, where the boat of Fortune is employed to ferry Rinaldo from Armida's island back to Palestine and the

Crusader army before Jerusalem. Here Fortune, no longer as in Tasso's poem the instrument of a divine providence or of the epic's teleological plot, takes Adonis not *away from* but *to* a realm of romance, an island of adventure and erotic idyll, where he remains for the entire course of Marino's poem.

Adonis might remain forever beside Venus, where for the following ten cantos—and Marino's cantos are very long—the story of his courtship and marriage to the goddess of Love is accompanied by an education, first in the five senses (cantos 6–8), then, in an ascent through the heavens (10–11), in the secrets of nature and in the human liberal arts. But Mars, the god of martial epic, invades the realm of Venus in canto 12, and the arrival of his rival forces Adonis to flee, described in verses (96) that recall the frightened Angelica at the beginning of the *Orlando furioso* as she is fleeing from the battlefield into a forest, the romance wood of error. (These verses, we have seen in Chapter 1, go back ultimately to Virgil's Cleopatra escaping from Actium.) Adonis similarly escapes into a wood, where he immediately encounters an enchanted stag sent his way by the fairy Falsirena (105f.). The beast, which jumps into the arms of Marino's passive hero and spares him the trouble of hunting it down, reproduces almost in toto the stag of Boiardo's Morgana with its golden antlers, although it molts its valuable headgear only twice instead of six times a day. Falsirena, the "fairy of gold" (117), is a second figure of Morgana-Fortune who, like Venus, falls in love with the beautiful Adonis and takes him to her own garden of pleasure. She spells out her allegorical identification when she offers herself to the unwilling youth.

> Intenerisci il tuo selvaggio ingegno,
> prendi il crin che Fortuna or t'offre in dono.
>
> (12.249)

(Soften your hardhearted disposition; take the forelock that Fortune now offers you as a gift.)

The two succeeding cantos, in which Adonis escapes from the erotic prison of Falsirena, first transformed into a parrot (!), then in his own body, will implicate the hero in a whole series of romance adventures: especially in canto 14, where the fairy sends after Adonis a troop of bandits imitated from the *Ethiopian Romance* of Heliodorus. Mixing together elements from both Greek romance and the earlier Italian chivalric romances, Boiardo's *Innamorato* preeminent among them, Marino illustrates the generic affinities between the two and confirms the observations of late-sixteenth-century literary theorists like Paolo Beni who grouped together these two historical forms of romance.[80]

As she instigates these adventures, the Fortune fairy Falsirena becomes identified—again like Boiardo's Morgana—with romance itself. And it is

Falsirena who will return in canto 18 to put in motion the intrigue that leads to the death of Adonis, a death that he himself perhaps brought upon himself when he stole the fatal arms of Meleager from her treasure house (13.248–52). Falsirena is the source of much of the plot—to the extent that there is a plot in Marino's static poem—and is a double of that Fortune who initiated the action of the poem: a Fortune that in the end is transformed into Nemesis. She is also the double of the Venus whose divine beauty captivates Adonis. When Falsirena attempts to seduce Adonis a second time, she disguises herself in the dress and features of Venus (12.144f.), literally becoming a counterfeit copy. And Marino could have known of a mythographic tradition according to which Nemesis-Fortune was depicted in the guise of Venus.[81]

The effect of all these doublings is that—particularly so far as the generic identity of the *Adone* is concerned—there is not much to choose from between Venus and Falsirena. What was in the earlier epic tradition (the case, for example, of Tasso's Rinaldo on the island of Armida) an Achillean choice between uneventful romance pleasure and epic duty and history collapses in the *Adone*. Adonis commutes back and forth between the garden of Venus and the garden of Falsirena, both idyllic *loci amoeni*. There is no arena for heroic action for Adonis, aside from his gaining the Cyprian throne by winning a beauty pageant in canto 16, a reversal of gender roles and an obvious parody of epic political conquest. And this contest for Beauty King or Mr. Cyprus is accompanied by a romance foundling plot through which Adonis, by the usual birthmark, is discovered after all to be the island's true heir (16.247f.). Wherever Adonis turns, then, he encounters some form of romance, and in all cases he is turned into the passive, childish recipient of the gifts of Fortune—the caresses of Venus, the stag of Falsirena, the crown of Cyprus—and these come his way because of still anterior gifts of Fortune: his beauty, his royal birth. Even when Falsirena turns nasty and sends him into a succession of misadventures, Adonis remains passive, taking the role of the heroine assaulted by Fortune in Greek romance, in a kind of Perils of Pauline cliff-hanger: and he in fact spends a good part of canto 14 in drag, disguised as a woman. Adonis himself grows tired of this passivity and of his static life (the boredom of the long poem itself, which fills its fifteenth canto with the diversion of a game of cards) and goes hunting in the forbidden park of Diana, returning to the action where he began in the epic. But there he meets his death from the boar on whom he has himself inflicted both physical and erotic wounds (18.97–98).

The parallels to the plot of *Paradise Lost* are instructive, if superficial. Geoffrey Hartman has referred to Milton's Eden as a "consumer's paradise," and this is the nature par excellence of the garden of Venus in the *Adone*, a paradise both of the senses and of human culture.[82] The latter, in fact, appears to offer the opportunity for self-cultivation and education that literally raises Adonis to the heavens—a secularized, humanistic equivalent of that spiritual, contemplative ascent that Milton's Adam is promised if he can remain obedient to the divine command. Adonis is, however, not much interested in exploring these cultural possibilities: he falls asleep during a theatrical performance (5.147) of the story of Diana and Actaeon, which has the purpose of warning him against the dangers of hunting in Diana's precinct, much as Raphael's narrative admonishes Adam and Eve against the dangers of their disobedience. Ignoring as well the pleas of Venus, who goes off to seek a method of making him immortal, Adonis leaves her garden, violates Diana's prohibition, and dies, at the hands both of the goddess and of a malignant Fortune. Adam and Eve eat the forbidden fruit, are banished from Eden, and bring death into a world whose contingency and subjection to fortune they have newly come to discover. The differences are of course crucial: for Milton the romance contingency of Eden and of the human history that follows it provides the opportunity—fortune as *occasio*—for human action, above all for active spiritual choice; but the romance Fortune governing the world of Marino's cynical, Ovidian poem is an omnipotent chance that reduces the human agent to her plaything and eventually deforms him—through the metamorphoses undergone by Adonis and other mythological figures recalled in canto 19—from his human state.

Nonetheless, when *Paradise Lost* is held up beside the *Adone*, the consolation of the Fortunate Fall feels even less cheering than it does on an ordinary reading of Milton's epic: Adam and Eve would, like Marino's Adonis, have done much better to have stayed at home in paradise, enjoying their immortal happiness or good luck. Eden, like the garden of Venus, provided a private, timeless escape from a historical world of human politics—of Nimrod-like kings. This traditional world of epic is revealed by the *Adone* to be governed by a capricious Fortune rather than by national or imperial destiny: so Marino's Venus remarks, as she foretells the eventual historical fall of her island of Cyprus to the Turks.

> Con strage alfin cui non fia pari alcuna
> lo spietato Ottomano a forza il prende.
> Vedi quanto alternar sotto la luna
> così lo stato uman varia vicende.
> Solo per te non girerà Fortuna,
> Fortuna ch'altrui dona e toglie e rende,
> ch'Amor con l'aureo stral per farla immota
> inchioderà la sua volubil rota.

(15.225)

(At last with slaughter that will have no equal, the pitiless Ottoman takes it by force. See how much things are in flux beneath the moon: just so human affairs vary their events. Only for you will Fortune not turn, Fortune that gives and takes and gives again to others, for Love with its golden arrow will nail down her changing wheel to render it immobile.)

Venus promises to make Adonis immune to the Fortune that rules over kings and nations. In this same passage Adonis places venery—hunting and loving—above the throne of Cyprus that he is to win in the next canto; he willingly forswears the burdens of royalty that transform the prince into a "public servant" (230). He prefers the gold of Venus's blonde hair to the riches of state (235).

> Se'l regno di quel cor che mi donasti
> conservato mi fia, tanto mi basti.
>   Altri con l'armi pur seguendo vada
> schiere nemiche e pace unqua non aggia.
> A me l'arco e lo stral più che la spada
> giova e mostri cacciar di piaggia in piaggia.
> Più che la reggia il bosco e più m'aggrada
> che l'ombrella real, l'ombra selvaggia.
> Se vuoi servi e vassalli, ecco qui tante
> suddite fere e tributarie piante.
>
> (15.227–28)

(It will suffice me if the realm of the heart you have given me is preserved.
   Let another go in arms in pursuit of enemy troops and nowhere find peace.
I prefer the bow and arrow to the sword and to hunt beasts from shore to shore.
The wood is dearer to me than the palace, and I enjoy the shade of the forest more than the royal canopy. If you want servants and vassals, here are so many subject animals and tributary trees.)

The rejection of epic martial prowess and political conquest could not be clearer, and the taking of refuge from the storm of history in the pastimes of love and hunting is a romance alternative to epic that goes back to the lovemaking of Aeneas and Dido in Book 4 of the *Aeneid*. Jean Chapelain, in his French preface to the *Adone*, praises the originality of Marino's "nouvelle Idée de Poëme de Paix."

The very fact, however, that this Italian poem should have been published in Paris, where Marino enjoyed the patronage of the French queen, Marie de' Medici, suggests the historical factors that led to the poet's generic innovation. The *Adone* includes encomiastic passages and, at its middle and end, two historical surveys of the French wars of religion (10.184–285; 20.486–514). The funeral games for Adonis concluding the poem in canto 20 feature an allegory of an ideal political alliance between France and Spain. The recognition that real political power belongs to the great European states outside of the Italian peninsula conditions the inward turning of Venus's garden, which may offer a kind of contemporary portrait of the small Italian princely court. Evading a history they have less and less ability to affect, its denizens retreat into a life of hedonism and of consumption of Italy's patrimony of art and culture—where Marino's countrymen still enjoy preeminence. And the *Adone* itself can be seen to be living off the past of poetic tradition—whose Greek, Latin, and especially modern Italian authors it catalogues in canto 9 (173–83)—that Marino recycles through imitation and allusion, just as the poem offers itself as a pastime of timeless art like the immortal garden it depicts. It should be pointed out that the philistine Adonis is less interested in cultural pursuits than in the usual aristocratic pleasures of sex and the hunt: here, too, Marino may present a realistic depiction of princely and noble life in an increasingly decadent Italy.

The leisure-class existence of the garden of Venus is decidedly aristocratic, as opposed to the more middle-class domestic space of Milton's Eden, where Adam and Eve both toil in the garden and where Eve has to prepare dinner. As a retreat from the political world of the seventeenth century—the world of the capital city and the centralized royal court—the garden in the *Adone* resembles not the bourgeois household but the great country house of the landed nobleman. The rusticated aristocrat suggested by the poetic fiction may thus reflect the condition not only of disempowered Italian rulers but also of local, provincial grandees throughout Europe who have similarly lost ground to emergent national monarchies.[83] The collapse of Marino's poem into romance evasion could thus speak for an aristocracy that feels itself growingly alienated from the "epic" schemes of state-building kings.

A glimpse of the English version of this aristocratic ethos can be found beneath the eighth-century-Lombard setting of the country house of Astragon in cantos 5–8 of Book 2 of *Gondibert* (1651), the unfinished "heroick poem" of William Davenant, the Royalist court poet and contemporary of Milton. The hero Gondibert, wounded in a duel in which he kills his rival Oswald (1.4)—the only combat in the poem and one quickly gotten out of the way—is taken to be healed in the dwelling of Astragon, "His House (where Art and Nature Tennants were)" (2.5.5). Astragon is both a Baconian scholar—investigating the secrets of nature (2.5.7–35) and the books of the past (36–64), last but not least among them books of poetry (65–68)—and a religious contemplative who has built on his estate three temples dedicated "To daies of *Praise*, of *Penitence*, and *Pray'r*" (2.6.4); their description takes up the better part of canto 6. This rural retreat from the arena of heroic action thus combines the scientific and cultural lore of Marino's garden of Venus and the possibilities for spiritual ascent of Milton's Eden. And, like these other romance realms, it contains a love interest: Gondibert becomes enamored of Birtha, Astragon's daughter, and for her sake appears ready to forgo the hand of the princess Rhodalind and the throne of Verona. So Gondibert expresses his admiration for Astragon's house and his new-found contempt for the world of war and politics outside it.

> A Minde long sick of Monarchs vain disease;
> Not to be fill'd, because with glory fed;
> So busy it condemn'd even War of ease,
> And for their useless rest despis'd the Dead.
>
> But since it here has Vertue quiet found,
> It thinks (though Storms were wish'd by it before)
> All sick at least at Sea, that scape undrown'd,
> Whom Glory serves as winde to leave the shore.
>
> All Vertue is to yours but fashion now,
> Religion, Art; Internals are all gon,
> Or outward turn'd, to satisfie with show,
> Not God, but his inferiour Eie, the Sun.
>
> And yet, though vertue be as fashion sought,
> And now Religion rules by Art's prais'd skill;
> Fashion is Vertue's Mimmick, falsely taught;
> And Art, but Nature's Ape, which plays her ill.
>
> To this blest House (great Nature's Court) all Courts
> Compar'd, are but dark Closets for retreat
> Of private Mindes, Batails but Childrens sports;
> And onely simple good, is solid great.[84]

$$(2.7.80–84)$$

The desire for rest from heroic travails that had characterized the romance *locus amoenus* in earlier epic is conjoined here to a nostalgia for a natural, simpler virtue that has been corrupted by the fashion of the court—though the highly wrought conceits of Davenant's verse suggest that this simplicity may now be irrecoverable. And whereas, from Dido's Carthage on, the romance retreat that detains the epic hero from his political destiny is discovered to conceal hidden moral dangers, this nobleman's estate is the true seat of an inner virtue, a virtue of "Internals"—or a "paradise within"—that has become the hero's true goal and from which the royal court, paling in comparison, now becomes seen as a "retreat." For all of Davenant's royalism— he wrote *Gondibert* in exile in Paris—his poem presents a literary version of the conflict between court and country where the country—an aristocracy that maintains its distance and autonomy from royal authority—seems decidedly favored.[85] The political configuration of *Gondibert* bears out this bias toward the high nobility rather than the monarch. Aribert, the king of Verona, is old and weak and without male heir: the poem describes the competition between two factions of his leading nobles to win Rhodalind and the crown.

Because there is a power vacuum where its central royal authority should be, the political world of Verona cannot offer much of an arena for heroic action or the pursuit of national greatness to counterbalance the contemplative and erotic attractions of Astragon's house. The rest of *Gondibert* is taken up in court intrigues and complications of its love plot: for political reasons Gondibert is betrothed to Rhodalind. While Davenant did not complete its last two books, it seems probable that the poem would have taken the five-act form of tragicomedy—the favorite genre of Davenant's dramatic works—with little or no martial action required for its resolution. More likely there would have been a foundling recognition scene revealing Gondibert to be the long-lost brother either of Birtha or Rhodalind, the stroke of Fortune that would make the choice between his two affianced brides for him.[86] Here too, then, the alternative in the world of public, political action to the romance retreat toward the cultivation of private virtue turns out to be *more* romance, rather than a conformity to epic generic models.

The true model for Davenant's "heroick poem," it has been suggested, was not epic at all but the aristocratic prose romance.[87] In England, this literary form already had a distinguished prototype in Sidney's *Arcadia*, and its popularity in France had been renewed by the *romans* of Madeleine de Scudéry. Scudéry's model and the greatest European version of the genre was the *Astrée* of Honoré d'Urfé, whose four parts were published, respectively, in 1607, 1610, 1619, and 1627; in 1620 an English translation of the First Part appeared. Few modern readers are willing to negotiate its five thousand pages, but the *Astrée* was perhaps the most significant work of French literature of the first half of the seventeenth century. Set among the shepherds and knights of a mythological fifth-century Gaul, it combines the precious gallantry, neoplatonic sentiments, and sexual titillation of pastoral love plots with an endlessly inventive, if repetitive, series of chivalric adventures of the kind that Cervantes was contemporaneously subjecting to parodic destruction in *Don Quixote*. The book's influence was enormous, not least because it summed up what the French classicism of the second part of the century wished to overthrow. This was not only the unclassical multiple plotting and digressions of chivalric romance—and d'Urfé's *Astrée* remains open-ended: his secretary, Balthazar Baro, added a Fifth Part in 1628 that finally resolves its many plots, including the usual contrivance of a last-minute discovery of the identity of a lost foundling child—but the *Astrée*, as

Norbert Elias has acutely argued, also expressed an "aristocratic romanticism," both in its subject matter and in its romance form. The book's retreat into the pastoral countryside, into Nature as opposed to the Art or artificiality of the court, represents the ethos of a nobility—particularly of the middle ranks of this nobility—that was estranged, and claiming its independence from, the centralizing projects of the French monarchy and the new court society it sponsored.[88] One of these projects was the regularizing of literary taste itself. Doctrinaire classical strictures increasingly emerged after the personal rule of Louis XIV began in 1661. They are reflected in Boileau's dialogue, *Les Héros de Roman* (written 1664–1665, published in an "unauthorized" edition in Holland in 1688, then in Boileau's revised version in 1713), a satirical attack upon the imitators of the *Astrée* and ultimately upon d'Urfé's romance itself.[89] Boileau's work should be understood as an expression of a cultural politics aimed not only at what he declared to be outmoded literary forms but also at a nostalgic ideology that those forms preserved for an aristocracy which the crown, particularly after the rebellions of the Fronde, was determined to tame.

That Boileau should have included in his satire on the *romans La Pucelle* (1656), the long-awaited epic poem on Joan of Arc by Jean Chapelain, may initially seem like a gratuitous sideswipe at a favorite target in the literary establishment.[90] But Chapelain, in his unpublished *De la Lecture des Vieux Romans* (1647), had acknowledged that he had modeled the character of his poem's male hero, Dunois, upon the Lancelot he had found in an old prose *Lancelot* that he thought to be of the twelfth or thirteenth century.[91] And Chapelain's defense of the mores of the knights and ladies in these ancient *romans* is filled with admiration for old-style valor and feudal loyalty, as opposed to the artifice of the modern peacetime courtier.

> Indeed, I should have great trouble in answering him who, wishing to defend it, should represent to me how noble is the gallantry that proves its passion by searching out dangers, by sacrifice of blood and by victories, and what superiority it has over that which proves itself only by coquetries and assiduous attentions or, at the most, by banquets, by music, and by jousting at rings.
>
> I should have great trouble in persuading him that a pretty dance step was more worthy than good swordstrokes, that pretty ringers or riding were more considerable than jousts with sharpened steel, than stubborn combat to the point of death, than the gifts of vanquished opponents and of prisoners ... jousts, combats, and quests were the custom of those centuries, as the promenade on the Cours-la-Reine, the comedy, and the ball are of this one; if I were not to agree with him that he was right to prefer that gallantry to ours, I could not, at least, help but agree that such gallantry could not be deemed ridiculous.[92]

Here was aristocratic romanticism: it already groups Chapelain with the side of the Moderns against the Ancients in the later *Querelle*, and it suggests how this quarrel, too, lined up proponents of an older, yet "modern" aristocratic culture of the great *hôtels* against the new, yet classicizing culture of the court. It is true that Chapelain, as he himself tried to write an epic according to classical rules, removed many of the romance adventures contained in his initial prose design of *La Pucelle*, including the burning of Joan of Arc's double and the miraculous salvation of the shipwrecked saint on the shores of a hermitage (modeled on the rescue of Ruggiero in the *Orlando furioso*).[93] But the poem's author, nonetheless, cannot let the poem be identified with a central royal power that had by now claimed to be indistinguishable from the destiny of France and that was unavoidably the subject matter of any national epic. Boileau may have detected this reticence when he lumped *La Pucelle* with the *romans*. In spite of its fulsome encomiastic praise of Louis XIV, *La Pucelle* depicts its royal character, Charles VII, as the feckless historical monarch that he was, in the words of a modern biographer of Chapelain, a king "aussi peu épique que possible."[94] The poem's preference for the Lancelot-like Dunois over this Arthur figure indicates sympathies for aristocratic heroism at cross-purposes with its epic plan, an imaginative division that contributed (though Chapelain's thoroughly mediocre poetic abilities contributed much more) to the poem's thunderous failure.

It is in another ambitious, but hardly more successful "Poëme Heroïque," the *Clovis* (1657) of Jean Desmarets de Saint-Sorlin, published one year after *La Pucelle*, that we can see a clear French parallel to the transformation of the epic project into romance at work in the *Adone* and *Gondibert*. Desmarets would be Boileau's initial opponent on the modern side in the *Querelle des Anciens et Modernes*, later succeeded by Perrault.[95] In addition to writing *Clovis*, he was the author of the prose romance *Ariane*, for which he is included as a target in *Les Héros de Roman*.[96] *Clovis* contains a tribute to d'Urfé, whose fifth-century ancestor appears as a minor character in the poem.

> Le brave Urfé commande un corps de ces guerriers,
> Dont le casque d'argent, orné de deux lauriers,
> Des armes & des vers porte un double trophée;
> Urfé, qui se vantoit de la race d'Orphée;
> Et dont tira son sang, celuy qui dans nos jours
> Des bergers de Forests, a chanté les amours.[97]

(13.5135–40)

(Brave d'Urfé commands a band of these warriors, whose silver helmet, adorned with two laurel wreaths, bears a double trophy for arms and verses. Urfé who boasts of descent from Orpheus and from whose blood will come he who in our days sang the love of the shepherds of Forez.)

"The composer of the *Astrée*," Desmarets's own marginal gloss helpfully comments. Indeed, the action of *Clovis* is hardly distinguishable—except for its frenetic pace—from the intricate plots of d'Urfé's romance, as the following modern summary of the contents of Book 7 suggests.

> Gondebaut at last promises the hand of Clotilde [to Clovis]; the envoys of Clovis leave Vienne, after Clotilde has confided her worries to Aurèle. Two weeks later, near Dijon, before Clovis and his assembled nobles, there appears an unknown knight who demands to joust with a warrior; Amalagar and Clodéric are vanquished by him. When Clovis, angered, wishes to break a lance in his own turn, the unknown knight takes him apart and reveals that she is Clotilde. She declares that she wishes to remain beside the king in this disguise, and that she wishes to become a pagan. Clovis, the false Clotilde (for in reality she is no other than Albione in disguise), and their soldiers go to Paris. Yoland, out of amorous spite, decides to avenge herself on Clovis; she rides to encounter him at Arcueil. Lisois, having fallen in love with her wants to joust with her, as does the woman warrior Argine; but Yoland announces that she will fight only with Clovis, and that she wants to kill him. Clovis, astonished, halfheartedly accepts her challenge, but decides secretly to save the life of the young girl (whom he does not recognize): in the course of the joust, he lifts Yoland off of her horse and carries her off in his arms.[98]

All of this in one book, in the space of 360 verses. The royal hero Clovis, still a pagan, not only seeks the Christian princess Clotilde—and his final conversion and marriage will create a dynasty of Christian kings of France—but is also pursued by two other amorously enthralled heroines, disguised even in their romance disguises. And other love intrigues, adventures, enchantments, and historical digressions emerge around this "central" plot to the point of displacing it for whole books (10, 12, 18) at a time.

In a letter answering one of his critics, the Abbé de Villeloin, published in 1673 when he was reissuing a revised version of his poem, Desmarets defended these modern romance inventions precisely because of their inventiveness and their abundance—in contrast to the relative imaginative poverty of the *Aeneid*, held up by the abbé as the normative ancient model. As a second line of defense however, Desmarets pointed to the romance elements of Virgil's poem as well.

> In [the abbé's] *Considerations on the Poem of Clovis*, after having seen everywhere an Invention so rich and plentiful, in comparison with that of Virgil, he found no other means to decry it except to say, as he does almost constantly, that these are Romance (*Romanesques*) extravagances, and Books of Chivalry, and denouements of Comic plots, and that all that could not be verisimilar or fitting in a heroic Poem. . . . Whereas Virgil piles up in his First Book so many Apparitions of Divinities, Jupiter, Aeolus, Neptune, Venus speaking in heaven

with Jupiter, who makes her so many Prophecies; the same Venus who speaks to Aeneas on the shore of Libya, Aeneas who goes about inside a cloud to the presence of Dido and of her Nobles, to whom he suddenly appears . . .[99]

. . . .

What kind of Invention is that of Laocoon, with his two Sons entangled by two horrible Serpents? And, again, what Invention is that of the Ships turned into Nymphs of the Sea, and the death of Misenus by the jealousy of Triton, and that of Palinurus by the malice of the God of Sleep. . . . All that and a quantity of similar things, as, again, that Dira who transforms herself into a Bird to frighten Turnus, beating his face with her wings, are true and continous extravagances.[100]

. . . .

In his Observations on the first and second Books, he condemns their Adventures, as so many Digressions that hinder the coming to a conclusion. He wishes that from these first Books one came to the conclusion of the Poem. Similarly he should condemn the First Book of the *Aeneid*, for the Storm turns Aeneas away from Italy where he was called by the Fates.[101]

Like Chapelain, Desmarets was a far better critic than poet, and he seizes upon those romance features of the *Aeneid*—its epic machinery and episodes of the marvelous, the digressive nature of the narrative in its Odyssean first half epitomized by the opening storm—as precedents that justify the inventions of his own poem. In what was a key argument for the superiority of modern culture over the works of the ancients, Desmarets points out that he has replaced the false gods of classical epic with the true Christian God and His adversary the devil, and substituted the miraculous for the marvelous.[102] And he acutely notes that digressions and episodic "extra-vagances" that wander away even from the classically teleological plot of Virgilian epic are necessary if poems are not to end where they begin. But Desmarets fails to note that the romance structures of the *Aeneid* are held up as the politically charged "other" of the epic narrative of Roman historical destiny. And, as his critic had objected, the extravagances of the *Clovis* have all but taken over the poem and removed any urgency that it reach its end. The model for the long-delayed marriage and conversion of Clovis and, in the poem's concluding lines, for the duel between Clovis and Alaric is the career of the hero Ruggiero in Ariosto's *Orlando furioso*, the prototypical Italian *romanzo*: *Clovis* is unmistakably a "Livre de Chevalerie," combining the romance models both of Ariosto and of Desmarets's acknowledged master, d'Urfé.

The effect of celebrating the founder of the French monarchy as a romance hero—one knight jousting and accepting individual challenges from other similar knights, even from lovers disguised as knights—is both to legitimize the nostalgic culture of a nobility that still invoked the ideals of chivalric honor and courtesy and to make the king one more participant of that culture: the first among equals who indeed asserted their equal footing with and independence from the king. Whereas Chapelain, like Davenant, placed a weak and vacillating monarch at the center of his poem, the decentralizing impulses of romance in *Clovis* similarly correspond to an aristocratic distrust of and resistance to the new absolutism of the French crown, a resistance that looked back to earlier feudal arrangements that placed the monarch at the top, but still laterally within his realm's political hierarchy rather than in a position of vertical domination above and outside the hierarchy altogether. The concentration of royal state power that had its formal corollary in the unity of epic fiction is here imaginatively broken up and collapsed in the errors of romance.

The seventeenth-century writers discussed here were variously connected. Marino's letters testify that he and D'Urfé were acquainted and may have reciprocally influenced each other.[103] Chapelain's first and perhaps finest work was his preface to the *Adone*. Davenant used Chapelain's preface as a model for his Preface to *Gondibert*, a work that, unlike the poem itself, still commands modern interest;[104] Davenant's masque, *The Temple of Love* (1635), was written, apparently at the behest of Charles I of England's French queen Henrietta Maria, along the lines of the *Astrée*.[105] Together, these writers represent a literary culture that in its broad outlines may be described as "modern" and anticlassical, as given to refined politeness of speech bordering on preciosity and to a generally brilliant and witty superficiality, and as the ideological expression of an older aristocracy. In spite of the professed wish of Davenant's *Gondibert* to recapture the "Internals," some essential inward life or noble identity lost in the formalized society of the court, this literature is no less fixated on the outward gesture of aristocratic grandeur: what may be summed up by the preference expressed in Davenant's own Preface for a culture of Fame over a culture of Conscience.

Because this literature was so much concerned with externals—externals, moreover, that could be easily enough reproduced by mediocre literary talents—it has for the most part not survived the social formation for which it spoke. Its predilection for romance is readily understandable. From the initial critical debates over the *Orlando furioso* in the preceding century, the romance had been recognized as a distinctly modern genre: only gradually were generic resemblances noted between the chivalric romances and the ancient prose novel. And the fairy-tale stories of knights-errant and amorous shepherds codified aristocratic ideals of individual honor and gallantry and placed those ideals in an ahistorical setting, an escapist pastoral removed from a real political world in which those ideals and the nobility who upheld them were losing out to new historical forces: competition from below from a new mercantile bourgeosie (whose reflection in epic was discussed in Chapter 6), pressure from above exerted by the centralizing, absolutist state.[106]

The literary taste for romance evasion, which represented a defection or alienation from the national projects of the crown on the part of an aristocracy that no longer felt itself to be a full partner with the monarch, emerged at the expense of epic. Sixteenth-century epic poetry might receive some of its energy from aristocratic discontent, depicting—under the guise of Ercilla's Araucanian chiefs or d'Aubigné's militant Huguenots—armed resistance to royal power. And the *Gerusalemme liberata*, though it sides with the central power of the commander Goffredo and ultimately restores his partnership with the Achillean warrior Rinaldo to achieve his epic purpose of conquering Jerusalem, nonetheless dramatizes the conflict between this sovereign and his leading noble. The career of Rinaldo is instructive for the fortunes of seventeenth-century epic, for which Tasso's poem was such a preeminent model. Rinaldo both rebels against Goffredo, barely persuaded to forgo violent confrontation with his ruler, and defects from the military life altogether in the romance pleasures of Armida's garden—before his eventual reintegration into the Crusade. Both options may be understood as forms of resistance to Goffredo's sovereign authority and epic project. But in the epic of the following century, it is the second option that will predominate—already signaled in Adonis's imitation of Rinaldo's trip to Armida's island in the first canto of the *Adone*—as aristocratic disaffection from the crown and national destiny finds expression in escapism. As a consequence, with its key warrior-class on permanent furlough, epic suffered a demise from which it would not recover. Seventeenth-century epic closed itself off from its traditional subjects of conquest and empire, and became a "heroic poem" of which the author of *Clovis* revealingly wrote: "The *roman* and the poem are in no way different except that one is in prose and the other in verse."[107]

How well do Milton and his poetry fit into this picture of aristocratic literary culture of the first half of the century? At first glance, hardly at all. It is true that he had once planned, as he excitedly forecast in *Epitaphium Damonis* (161–68), to write a heroic poem about King Arthur—in the later words of *Paradise Lost*, "what resounds / In fable or romance of Uther's son / Begirt with British and Armoric knights" (1.579–81). And for all the humanist learning of his poetry, Milton's eventual choice of biblical epic marked him as a "Modern," as Jesus' rejection of the classical learning of Athens attests in *Paradise Regained*. But this very choice and the forsaking, on maturer consideration, of his earlier Spenserian project to "dissect /With long and tedious havoc fabled knights / In battles feigned," voiced at the beginning of Book 9 of *Paradise Lost* (29–31), suggests Milton's distancing of himself from the aristocratic ethos of romance. Milton might, indeed, be seen as the prototype of that class of authors who, as Davenant disapprovingly puts it in his Preface, "write by the command of Conscience (thinking themselves able to instruct others, and consequently oblig'd to it)"; he belonged, that is, among the Puritan fomenters of disobedience to ecclesiastical authority—an authority that, like the "hereditary Power" of the crown and aristocracy, is conversely upheld, according to Davenant, by the poetry and culture of Fame.[108] In *Paradise Lost* the romance retreat of Eden is the site—and the figure—of psychological inwardness and of contingent choices of conscience; the literary exploration of such subjects points, as I have suggested above, toward the bourgeois novel rather than to the aristocratic romance, however these two genres may be related. And, as Annabel Patterson has shown, Milton's attack in *Eikonoklastes* on the prayer of Charles I recorded in *Eikon Basilike*, a prayer lifted from Sidney's *Arcadia*, turns into an assault on all the romances, with their suspiciously foreign, that is, Catholic, provenance.[109]

> For he certainly, whose mind could serve him to seek a Christian prayer out of a Pagan Legend, and assume it for his own, might gather up the rest God knows from whence; one perhaps out of the French Astraea, another out of the Spanish Diana; Amadis and Palmerin could hardly scape him.[110]

For the anti-Royalist Milton, the prose romance belongs to a profane cavalier culture that does not distinguish an estranged aristocracy from its king, but separates monarch and his loyal nobles together from the sober and pious citizens of the Commonwealth.

And yet, the federally planned Commonwealth that Milton envisions in *The Readie and Easie Way* retains an aristocratic flavor. For while this Commonwealth would remove from the parliamentary level of its one-chamber national senate "all distinctions of lords and commoners, that may any way divide or sever the publick interest," at the level of local government organized in provincial urban centers, "the nobilitie and chief gentry from a proportionable compas of territorie annexed to each citie, may build, houses or palaces, befitting thir qualitie, may bear part in the government, make thir own judicial laws."[111] For Milton, such regional arrangements make possible "the civil rights and advancements of every person according to his merit," and his projected Commonwealth would provide the means of education to promote the eventual social mobility of its citizens. But for the moment, "merit" seems to be tied to class position, and this vision of local grandees settling for themselves the political affairs of their vicinity without interference from the central government is quite close, indeed, to the nostalgic aristocratic autonomy imagined in the pastoral enclaves and great houses scattered through the countryside of Marino's and d'Urfé's fictions.

The similarity of Milton's Eden to these romance retreats—however different the activities that go on inside them may ultimately be—is produced by a distrust of central authority shared by republican and aristocrat alike; and both Milton, the Commonwealth man, and the noble opponents of royal "tyranny," like d'Aubigné, could look for inspiration to the patrician republic of Venice with its largely symbolic head of state, the doge. When juxtaposed beside other attempts to write epic in the seventeenth century, *Paradise Lost* exhibits an analogous flight into romance from an epic domain of kings and national histories, a domain that effectively ceases meaningfully to exist once the world outside of Eden is recognized to share the same romance contingency as the garden itself, and once the human history embarked upon by Adam and Eve becomes a quest to restore a "paradise within." To be sure, this rejection of epic nationhood is a response to a particular national situation, the end of the Commonwealth and the return of Charles II. But within the resistance of the defeated republican to the restored monarchy there appears to lie a second strain of resistance to statism, to centralizing projects—such as Cromwell's Triers—that intruded on individual and local liberty. This twofold resistance can be perceived more clearly in *Paradise Regained,* and in the next chapter I shall try to show how the criticism of kingship in Milton's sequel epic is framed in terms that implicate state power itself. The Miltonic emphasis on inward, spiritual choice, I will further argue, is partly conditioned by and shaped as a defense of the individual against the state, against its instruments of surveillance and control. A common logic of decentralization links the turn toward romance in Milton's poetry to the larger fate of epic in the course of the century.

EIGHT

DAVID'S CENSUS: MILTON'S POLITICS AND

PARADISE REGAINED

THE POLITICAL allusions in Milton's poetry after 1660 are not always easy to detect; nor, perhaps, were they meant to be. It has not, to my knowledge, been noted that the temptation of Parthia in the third book of *Paradise Regained* is based in its larger outline upon the episode in the *Pharsalia* (8.262f.) where Pompey, after the defeat of his forces at Pharsalia, proposes to seek the aid of the Parthian king in order to continue the war against Julius Caesar. His lieutenant Lentulus, we remember from our discussion of Lucan's poem in Chapter 4, dissuaded him from this course, protesting against an alliance with Rome's enemies and criticizing the Parthians for their Eastern effeminacy and unreliability as soldiers.[1] This epic model suggests that the temptations of Parthia and Rome in *Paradise Regained* are really the same temptation: Pompey wants Parthian arms in order to regain possession of Rome.[2] It also explains the presence of Pompey at the opening of Book 3 among Satan's examples of youthful conquerors (35–36), his name followed four lines later by that of "Great Julius" (39). It colors the final verse (385) of Satan's peroration on the benefits of a Parthian alliance: "and Rome or Caesar not need fear." The enemy may be not so much Rome as Caesar or Caesarism.

For, most importantly, the model of Lucan's Pompey places Milton's Jesus in the position of a defeated republican, the loser of the civil war who now considers what form of resistance to pursue against the new Caesarian monarchy; that is to say, roughly in the same position as John Milton himself during the Restoration. The lost tribes of Israel which Satan calls upon Jesus to restore with Parthian arms (3.371–85, 414–40) have been associated by critics of *Paradise Regained* with Milton's backsliding compatriots, the adherents of the Good Old Cause who made their settlement with Charles II.[3] This association gains strength when in the ensuing temptation of Rome, Satan suggests that Jesus replace Tiberius and free a "victor people" from their "servile yoke" (4.102): the Romans are to be restored to the liberty of their republic. Jesus' reply, that the Romans have fallen away from republican virtue—which he earlier praised in the figures of "Quintius, Fabricius, Curius, Regulus" (2.466)—and brought about imperial oppression, "by themselves enslaved" (4.144), matches his denunciation of the ten lost tribes who "wrought their own captivity" (3.415). The idolatrous Israelites are paired with the politically degenerate Romans, and their respective sins appear to be causally related. Milton's Jesus rejects any worldly political action to deliver these figures for the fallen citizens of the Commonwealth: they are left to God's "due time and providence." The Jesus who had once dreamed as an adolescent of "victorious deeds" and "heroic acts" to "rescue Israel from the Roman yoke" (1.215–17), preaches now instead the way of persuasion and the spiritual regeneration of individual souls.

Evident as this allusion may or may not be, it is Milton's most explicit alignment of his epic poetry with the anti-Virgilian, anti-imperial epic tradition of Lucan. The Jesus of *Paradise Regained* is identified with the republican cause, even if his mission is much larger than that cause. The episode of the temptation of the kingdoms contains a further series of buried political allusions, clustered around the pivotal reference to David's census at the end of Book 3. They point in this case not to the classical literary tradition in which Lucan is a republican touchstone, but to texts more contemporary with Milton: they suggest the extent to which the language and terms of *Paradise Regained* are in dialogue with the political writings, Royalist and anti-Royalist, of the first decade of the Restoration. Like the topical elements of *Paradise Lost*, they demonstrate Milton's continuing engagement in political controversy. It is pleasing to see Milton keeping his revolutionary faith in dark times, but new problems of interpretation arise. In *Paradise Regained* Satan criticizes Jesus for his "retiring"(3.164) into the desert, and the poem's opening lines declare that this desert will, as the scene of temptation, become an "Eden raised in the waste wilderness" (1.7): like the Eden of *Paradise Lost*, it is a private romance locus separated from an epic world of history and battle, yet nevertheless the locus of an all-determining spiritual warfare—for the inwardness and individuality of which it is also a figure. But how are we to understand a poetry that expressly preaches inner withdrawal from worldly politics while, through indirect means of allusion, it criticizes the poet's political world? The temptation of the kingdoms is particularly double-edged in this regard, for Jesus' rejection of kingship is both a renunciation of all temporal force and carnal power and, at the same time, a pointed attack on the Stuart monarchy.

Critics have found it easy enough to square Milton's call for individual piety and meek witness—the behavior summed up in Adam's speech at the end of *Paradise Lost* that was cited at the beginning of the last chapter— with his supposed disillusionment and retreat from the political stage.[4] But the conventional image of Milton, the defeated Commonwealth man, turning in upon himself and his spiritual resources must be supplemented, if not replaced, by an image of the same Milton carrying on as polemicist against the Restoration. The problem is to explain how these two, more contradictory images should coexist. Why should a still-active opponent of monarchy espouse an extreme individualism—what appears to be a political renunciation? Perhaps this contradiction is not so surprising. Other defeated revolutionaries have turned to protest without advancing an alternative program of political action. But it may be possible, once the political content and context of Milton's poetry are more exactly identified, to offer a tentative explanation of why he proposed no alternative except his individualist religious doctrine. For all its claims to a universality that would displace, transcend, or subsume the political, this doctrine may itself respond to a specific historical and political climate.

Numbering Israel

Like the allusion to Lucan's Pompey, Jesus' evocation of the sin of David's census provides a connecting link between the alternative temptations of Parthia and Rome.

> But whence to thee this zeal, where was it then
> For Israel, or for David, or his throne,
> When thou stood'st up his tempter to the pride
> Of numb'ring Israel, which cost the lives
> Of threescore and ten thousand Israelites
> By three days' pestilence? such was thy zeal
> To Israel then, the same that now to me.
>
> (3.407–13)

It is to recover David's throne (1.240; 3.153, 169, 357, 383; 4.108, 147, 379, 471) that Satan proposes the temptation of the kingdoms in the first place. This "royal seat" (3.373) connects the kingdoms imagistically with the earlier banquet temptation where Satan bids Jesus "only deign to sit and eat" (3.335), a scene that recollects, in turn, Spenser's Mammon and his treacherous golden fruit and silver stool (*Faerie Queene*, 2.7.63);[5] in the wisdom temptation of Athens, this paralyzing seat becomes "Moses' chair" (4.219). David's throne, which Satan offers as the goal of Jesus' mission, may become instead a worldly deviation into immobility and spiritual sloth, paradoxically a demonic form of retirement, like the isolated condition of the emperor Tiberius "from Rome retired / To Capreae" (3.91–92): Jesus' true posture is to "stand"—"to stand upright / Will ask thee skill" (4.551–52)—rather than to sit.[6]

Jesus' recollection of the disastrous census of 2 Samuel 24 and 1 Chronicles 21 calls both David and his kingship into question and reaffirms that Jesus' own kingdom is not of this world: it is "allegoric" as Satan sarcastically concludes (4.390). Placed between the offers of Parthia and Rome, the royal sin of "numb'ring Israel" reflects upon both. The Parthians are the temptation of numbers itself, or raw military might, the "thousands" (3.304) and "numbers numberless" (310) who pour out of Ctesiphon. The gathering of the Parthian host may serve the same purpose as David's census, which, like the archetypal biblical census of the Book of Numbers that records "all that are able to go forth to war in Israel" (Num. 1:3), is a military census: David learns of Israel's "thousand thousand and an hundred thousand men that drew sword" (1 Chron. 21:5). But the Parthian forces are "numberless"—only loosely ordered and organized. David's numbering is more properly aligned with the ensuing temptation of Rome, which is presented as the center of an administrative empire, its praetors and proconsuls crossing paths with embassies from its far-flung provinces (4.61–79).[7] It may thus recall a third biblical census, the census ordered by Augustus to tax all the world at the time of the Nativity, during the rule of the proconsul Cyrenius (Luke 2:1–2).[8] Royal power is identified with the state's ability to place its population under bureaucratic scrutiny and control; and this power conduces to the sin of pride, David's reliance upon the military strength and human resources of his kingdom rather than upon God.[9]

Davidic kingship thus becomes one, perhaps even the most important, of the kingdoms of the world that Jesus rejects. The best of all biblical kings becomes difficult to distinguish from the "proud tyrannick power" of the Parthian and Roman rulers. Milton's target is monarchy itself, and his poem recalls his earlier polemics against a self-styled Davidic king. The author of *Eikon Basilike* had presented a chapter of penitential meditations and vows that Charles I had purportedly made during his "solitude" and captivity at Holdenby: these include a somewhat garbled version of the prayer (2 Sam. 24.17) that David raised when God sent a plague upon Israel to punish him for the census.

> And if Thy anger be not yet to be turned away, but Thy hand of justice must be stretched out still, let it, I beseech Thee, be against me and my father's house: as for these sheep, what have they done?[10]

Milton seized upon this passage in *Eikonoklastes* and accused the dead king of hypocrisy: "the vain ostentation of imitating David's language, not his life."

> For if David indeed sinn'd in numbring the people, of which fault he in earnest made that confession, & acquitted the whole people from the guilt of that sin, then doth this King, using the same words, bear witness against himself to be the guilty person; and either in his soule and conscience heer acquitts the Parlament and the people, or els abuses the words of David, and dissembles grossly eev'n to the [very] face of God.[11]

Charles, Milton concludes, has not understood or chosen not to understand the implications of his Davidic imposture: for David was a sinner, and was justly punished. The king, in fact, has brought "a curse upon himself and his Fathers house (God so disposing it) by his usurp'd and ill imitated prayer."[12]

David's census is the type that Charles himself has invoked for his own irrefutable crimes. Its reappearance in *Paradise Regained* continues to affirm the guilt of the king, self-condemned by his scriptural analogy.

But Charles I was not the only Stuart to present himself as a second David; the Davidic analogy figures even more prominently in the propaganda of his son, whose restoration was frequently compared by his apologists to David's return to the throne after the revolt of Absalom: this typology would later be reworked by Dryden at another period of royal crisis.[13] Sermons of 1660, written and published to celebrate the birthday of Charles II or to be presented upon national days of thanksgiving for his return, spelled out the king's resemblance to David. Analogies, however, multiply in these texts. In *David's Devotions upon his Deliverances*, Joseph Swetnam sees typological significance in Charles's age.

> Here is no *childe*, to bee carried to and fro by the breath of self-seeking syco-
> phants, but of that age the Lord Christ was, when he undertook his spiritual
> kingship, and David his temporal, thirty years old.[14]

Swetnam suggests that the years of the interregnum and of Charles's exile have been a period of preparation and maturation; Dryden describes them in *Astraea Redux*, also of 1660, as the time of Charles's political education, when like the "banish'd *David*" (79) he examined the workings of foreign governments and viewed the "Monarchs' secret Arts of sway" (77).[15] The period also resembles the "hidden" life of the child Jesus, who "grew, and waxed strong in spirit, filled with wisdom" (Luke 2:40), between the time of his debate with the doctors in the temple and his baptism, the starting point of his ministry and the starting point of *Paradise Regained*. Milton's poem about the inauguration of the career of Jesus thus reverses and rejects Charles's inaugural typology: for Swetnam, Charles is like David who is like Christ, but Milton's Jesus declines to follow David's model and enter a kingship for which, as Satan reminds him, his years "are ripe, and overripe" (3.31). Satan's temptation of the kingdoms begins (3.236–50) as an offer to instruct Jesus "in regal arts / And regal mysteries" (3.247–48), a kind of catch-up course for a student who has spent his schooltime on other subjects.[16]

Swetnam develops other Christological parallels for Charles:

> Heresie and blasphemy like *Apolloes* oracles at Christ his birth being silenced,
> *oracula cessant*, as Juvenal said A canting *Augustus*, as Suidas hath it, enquiring
> about his successor, might if hee could return, write *hic est ara primogeniti dei*;
> this is hee whose right is from God; in a sound sense I may say, the son of God,
> the sonne of his care, and delight, witness those wonderful providences in his
> preservation, and restauration.[17]

Suidas recounts that when Augustus asked the oracle at Delphi who was to reign after him, the oracle ceased to prophesy altogether; the astonished emperor built an altar to the firstborn son of God, an intimation of the coming of Christ.[18] In Swetnam's version, Charles-as-Christ becomes Augustus's true "successor." There is an evident parallel—with a difference—in *Paradise Regained*, where a Jesus who has announced the cessation of oracles (1.456–64) rejects Satan's proposal that he replace Tiberius, Augustus's heir. Milton's objection to an Orosian linking of Christ and Caesar is that it leads, by a somewhat roundabout historical route, to the kind of claim that Swetnam makes for the divine right of kings.

Were Jesus to succumb to the temptation of Rome and the inheritance of Caesar, it would suggest that he had placed his Church under the Roman jurisdiction of the papacy.[19] Further, it would allow the Roman Church to claim—as it did—the temporal goods and power of the Roman Empire, what it claimed to receive in the infamous Donation of Constantine; in *Of Reformation in England* Milton saw Constantine's enrichment of the Church as the primary source of Christianity's corruption, a confusion of temporal and spiritual power that was the worst of the papacy's errors and one that had been communicated to reformed churches as well.[20] When the Jesus of *Paradise Regained* rejects the gift of the kingdoms of the world that Satan proffers him, he pointedly contests Satan's claim to ownership.

> The kingdoms of the world to thee were given,
> Permitted rather, and by thee usurped,
> Other *donation* none thou canst produce.
>
> (4.182–84; my italics)

The imperial papacy, moreover, by accepting the structures of pagan kingship within the Church, has, in turn, made itself the model and prop for monarchy: especially, perhaps, for the English monarchy whose king is head of both state and Church. So Milton implies in *The Readie and Easie Way to Establish a Free Commonwealth*.

> All Protestants hold that Christ in his church hath left no viceregent of his power, but himself without deputie, is the only head thereof governing it from heaven: how then can any Christian-man derive his kingship from Christ, but with wors usurpation then the Pope his headship over the church, since Christ not only hath not left the least shaddow of a command for any such viceregence from him in the State, as the Pope pretends for his in the Church, but hath expressly declar'd that such regal dominion is from the gentiles, not from him, and hath strictly charg'd us, not to imitate them therein.[21]

Monarchy and the papacy are unholy, mutually dependent twins, each upholding the other's claim to derive its authority from God. Milton hints that the king's return may open the way for Catholicism in England, for Charles was "traind up and governd by *Popish* and *Spanish* counsels, and on such depending hitherto for subsistence."[22] His poem's dissociation of Jesus from Rome and her emperor attempts to redress the historical error by which kingship has received a false Christian legitimation: it attacks the Christo-logical pretenses of the Stuart monarchy.

Striking as the coincidences are between the scriptural figures of *David's Devotions* and of *Paradise Regained*, I am not arguing that Milton knew Swetnam's sermon: these figures were commonplaces. It is important to note, however, that they were contested ground, that they could be invoked to support the Restoration monarchy as well as to condemn it. Milton's task is partly to reclaim these figures and "purify" them of their Royalist asso-ciations. This is even true of the larger subject of the temptation of the kingdoms itself. An anonymous tract, published in 1659 and reprinted the following year, A *Character of His Most Sacred Majesty King Charles II, Written by a Minister of the Word*, closes with a meditation on Christ's temptation that turns rather surprisingly into an apology for kingship.

The *Tempter* in the Gospel *presented* unto our Blessed Saviour the *sight* of the *Kingdoms* of the *world* and the *glory* of them: The Kingdoms and their glory! and we may *confess* that there is no such Beauty, Splendor, Bravery, Riches, Pleasures, Majestie to be found in the world as in the *Courtes* of Princes, who are Gods *Deputies* here on *earth*; there is *soft rayment*, there are sumptuous Feasts, rich Jewels, glorious Triumphs, royal State; there is honourable Atten-dance and what not? And all those (no doubt) Satan presented on their *fairest side*, to their best *advantage*: But he did not tell him how many *Cares* and anxieties attend *Greatness*: He did not *acquaint* him with the abundant troub-les and great disquiet, and marvellous perplexities; which usually attend *earthly Crowns*; all these Satan *hides* out of the *way*, nothing may be *seen* but what might both *please* and *allure*. But most certain it is, that the *Crowns* of *Gold* that adorn the *heads* of *Kings*, though they shine and glister all is not gold in *them*, because they are *in-layed* with *Bryars* and *Thorns*. High *Seats* are always *uneasie*: And there is no good *Prince* who desires to manage his *Scepter* well, if he could view it round on all *sides*, but shall find that there is a great deal more attending earthly *Diadems* beside *Pomp* and *Glory*. And for this *reason*, First, *Prayers must be made for Kings* that desire to rule well, because their troubles, cares, and fears are greater than other *mens*. *Secondly*, their *Temptations* are likewise *greater* than those of private *Persons*, and therefore they stand more in need of joynt, *publick*, and private *Prayers*. And, *Lastly*, they must in a special manner be prayed for by their *people* upon the account of *good* which may be received under them; *that they may lead a quiet and peaceable life in all godli-ness and honesty*.[23]

It is not quite clear just what the "Minister of the Word" takes to have been the source of temptation in Satan's offer of the kingdoms. Presumably Christ was tempted to accept the material comforts and personal prestige of kingship—for which the Minister nonetheless cannot conceal his admira-tion, even his sense that they are the due of "Gods *Deputies*"—without assuming its cares and responsibilities. Such duties, as the conceit of a crown "*in-layed* with *Bryars* and *Thorns*" suggests, transform the conscientious king into a Christ-like suffering servant for his people: here, too, kingship becomes confused with the office of Christ, from whom the king claims deputyship or "viceregence." The terms of this apology for monarchy are conventional, and Milton's Jesus goes to some pains to discount them.[24]

> What if with like aversion I reject
> Riches and realms; yet not for that a crown,
> Golden in show, is but a wreath of thorns,
> Brings dangers, troubles, cares, and sleepless nights
> To him who wears the regal diadem,
> When on his shoulders each man's burdens lies;
> For therein stands the office of a king,
> His honour, virtue, merit, and chief praise,
> That for the public all this weight he bears.
> Yet he who reigns within himself, and rules
> Passions, desires, and fears, is more a king;
> Which every wise and virtuous man attains.
>
> (2.459–67)

Jesus makes it clear that he does not shun kingship for lack of public spirit or an unwillingness to sustain the ruler's burdens. He prefers a spiritual leadership, "to guide nations in the way of truth / By saving doctrine" (473–74), over the king's reign "oft by force" over the bodies of his subjects. And he notes that it has been thought nobler "to give a kingdom" (481) and "to lay down" (482) rulership: this last bit of moral wisdom probably recalls Cromwell's several refusals of the crown. At the same time, Jesus redefines true kingship as an interior self-mastery that is available to all men of virtue and is independent of any political institution. This passage at the end of Book 2 of *Paradise Regained* actually precedes the kingdoms temptation proper: Jesus turns down worldly kingship before it is even offered to him, and the example of David's census at the corresponding end of Book 3 merely confirms the wisdom of his choice.

David's census was punished by God with a plague that cost seventy thousand Israelite lives. The idea that plagues were divine visitations for political sins had acquired a new currency in the 1660s. Writing in his *Natural and Political Observations Made upon the Bills of Mortality* in 1662, John Graunt notes that the return of Charles II had restored health to a blighted England.

> As to this year 1660, although we would not be thought *Superstitious*, yet is it not to be neglected that in the said year was the *King's Restauration* to his Empire over these three Nations, as if God Almighty had caused the healthful-

ness and fruit fulness thereof to repair the *Bloodshed,* and *Calamities* suffered in his absence. I say, this conceit doth abundantly counterpoise the Opinion of those who think great *Plagues* come in with *Kings* reigns, because it hapned so twice, *viz. Anno* 1603, and 1625, whereas as well the year 1648, wherein the present *King* commenced his right to reign, as also the year 1660, wherein he commenced the exercise of the same, were both eminently healthfull, which clears both *Monarchie,* and our present *King's Familie* from what seditious men have surmised against them.[25]

Graunt writes against the opinion of certain "seditious men" who had linked pestilence with monarchy, particularly with royal accessions. Who were these seditious men? One was John Milton, who at the close of *The Readie and Easie Way* admonished his compatriots not to give up their freedom for false hopes of greater commercial prosperity.

But if the people be so affected as to prostitute religion and libertie to the vain and groundless apprehension that nothing but kingship can restore trade, not remembering the frequent plagues and pestilences that then wasted this citie, such as through God's mercie we never have felt since . . .[26]

The Commonwealth rescued England from plague, which, Milton implies, will return again with the monarchy. And when Graunt's *Observations* was reprinted in 1665, his words had acquired a new relevance, for the Great Plague had visited London and the rest of England. It produced murmurings among the old republicans, as John Burnet testified in his *History of His Own Time.*

All the King's enemies and the enemies of monarchy said, here was a manifest character of God's heavy displeasure upon the nations, as indeed the ill life the King led, and viciousness of the whole court, gave but a melancholy prospect. Yet God's ways are not as our ways. What all had seen in the year 1660 ought to have silenced those who at this time pretended to comment on providence.[27]

Contemporaries found a scriptural analogy for the plague in the pestilence that followed David's census. In *A Memorandum to London* (1665), the aged satirist George Wither recollected how "King David's pride, made manifest in him / (By numbring of the people) brought on them / A *Pestilence.*"[28] Wither had been imprisoned for three years at the time of the Restoration, and his sympathies, although disguised, belong fairly clearly to the Good Old Cause. By contrast, Royalist writers shifted the blame for the plague to the killing of Charles I and the sins of the Commonwealth. This is the strategy of John Tabor's version of the plague of 2 Samuel 24 in his *Seasonable Thoughts in Sad Times* (1667).

In *David's* time, a Plague on *Israel*
For what *Saul* did to th' *Gibeonites* befel.[29]

Tabor drastically rewrites Scripture so that the plague falls as a divine punishment not upon Royal David and his census but upon the bloodstained career of his predecessor Saul—a transparent figure for Cromwell. Here, too, the text of the Bible becomes open to the manipulation of competing propagandists, disputing over precisely whose political sins had occasioned the Great Plague. By its evocation of David's census, *Paradise Regained* appears to echo and enter into these contemporary disputes; it sees Milton's earlier prophetic warnings confirmed and points an accusing finger at the restored king.

Individual and State

Paradise Lost had already coupled disease and kingship in two parallel passages (11.471–525; 12.79–104) in Michael's narration to Adam; both are the results of the Fall and of an inner servitude to the lower appetites: sickness is "inductive mainly to the sin of Eve" (11.519), while monarchy follows Adam's "original lapse" (12.83). The juxtaposed passages suggest that kingship is a kind of disease of the body politic.[30] But here, too, in the idea that kingship is a product of sin, is the basis of the Miltonic position that political reform can only be founded upon, and hence must give way to, individual spiritual regeneration. *Paradise Regained*, inscribed in a whole web of contemporary political discourse, demonstrates that the poet has not given up the fight against monarchy. But if Milton did not opt for simple quietism, neither did he find a formula for political action that goes beyond individual acts of piety. Christopher Hill may be correct when he argues that Milton's political thought "represents a dead end, with its blind assertion that good will triumph,"[31] though Hill also acknowledges Milton's crucial importance in the formation of a nonconformist conscience whose effects on British political history have not been negligible. The reasons for the impasse in Milton's thought need to be sought in the larger historical factors and patterns that Hill has done much to outline and clarify: these may perhaps be suggested by one more look at David's census.

The census, we remarked earlier, is the sin of the king as the head of a statist power. The regime's ability to know its resources, human and material, allows it to organize them to its own ends. It was precisely in Milton's own time that the first scientific population studies were being developed, and these were expressly allied to statist projects. John Graunt's *Natural and Political Observations* of 1662, mentioned above, was a pioneering work of modern demography. Graunt confesses to his initial reluctance to undertake an estimate of the population of London.

I had been frighted by that mis-understood Example of *David* from attempting any computation of the People of this populous place; but hereupon I both examined the lawfulness of making such enquiries, and, being satisfied thereof, went about the work.[32]

Having argued away the scruples that David's census had caused him to have, Graunt began his study. Nonetheless, the biblical example and the fear of divine displeasure and visitation continued to be cited in the following century by parliamentary opponents to a national census; the Census Act was not, in fact, passed until 1800.[33] Graunt presents his findings as an instrument of royal policy, and Charles II seems to have appreciated the offer, for the king himself recommended the election of Graunt, a London merchant and shopkeeper, to the aristocratic Royal Society. He added, according to Thomas Sprat, "this particular charge to His Society, that if they found any more such Tradesmen, they should be sure to admit them all, without more ado."[34] Graunt's concluding remarks spell out the utility of population studies for his sovereign.

It is no less necessary to know how many People there be of each Sex, State, Age, Religion, Trade, Rank, or Degree &c by the Knowledg whereof Trade, and Government may be made more certain, and Regular.[35]

This census would do much more than count: it would be a form of state scrutiny that would permit greater control over a population that, as Graunt describes it, is underemployed in productive pursuits.

How many Women, and Children do just nothing, onely learning to spend what others get? how many are meer Voluptuaries, and as it were meer Gamesters by Trade? how many live by puzzling poor people with unintelligible Notions in Divinity and Philosophie? how many by perswading credulous, delicate, and Litigious Persons, that their Bodies or Estates are out of Tune, and in danger? how many by fighting as Souldiers? how many by Ministeries of Vice, and Sin? how many by Trades of meer Pleasure, or Ornaments? and how many in a way of lazie attendance, &c upon others? And on the other side, how few are employed in raising, and working necessary food, and covering.[36]

The tradesman Graunt's horror at idleness and parasitism contains an implicit call upon the state to use his new *statistical* methods to intervene and monitor economic activity: to increase the country's level of production. The gathering of information about the citizenry would not only promote trade but would also regularize the administrative processes of government. Graunt earlier suggests that his figures would have corrected and facilitated the gathering of the poll tax, ordered by Charles II in 1660 and again in 1666: "the number of Heads is such, as hath certainly much deceived some of our *Senatours* in their appointments of *Pole-money, &c.*"[37] Here, Graunt's friend and colleague, Sir William Petty, concurred. In his *Treatise of Taxes and Contributions*, which was also published in 1662 and which at several junctures cites the *Natural and Political Observations*, Petty similarly commented on the shortcomings of the 1660 taxation.

> Ignorance of the Number, Trade, and Wealth of the people, is often the reason why the said people are needlessly troubled, *viz.* with the double charge and vexation of two or many Levies, when one might have served: Examples whereof have been seen in late Poll-moneys; in which (by not knowing the state of the people, *viz.* how many there were of each taxable sort, and the want of sensible markes whereby to rate men, and the confounding of Estates with Titles and Offices) great mistakes were committed.[38]

As Petty's remarks suggest, Charles's poll taxes were unpopular, and when Parliament threatened to add to the tax bill of 1666 a proviso that called for a commission to oversee how the tax revenue was spent, it must have seemed as if the struggles of the 1640s over royal taxation were about to repeat themselves.[39] Petty's and Graunt's proposals to improve the efficiency of the tax collection through better studies of the population probably only increased resentment at a government that would inquire too closely into its subjects' affairs. Petty answers an imaginary critic:

> The next objection against this so exact computation of the Rents and works of lands, &c is, that the Sovereign would know too exactly every man's Estate; to which I answer that if the Charge of the Nation be brought as low as it may be, (which depends much upon the people in Parliament to do) and if the people be willing and ready to pay, and if care be taken, that although they have not ready money, the credit of their Lands and Goods shall be as good; and lastly, that it would be a great discommodity to the Prince to take more than he needs, as was proved before; where is the evil of this so exact knowledge?[40]

Petty's argument rests upon an idea of economic rationality that governs king and subject alike. This rationality sanctions in its name a total, scientific organization of state finances; Petty dismisses any objection that the citizen might have to becoming a numerical figure in what he would later call "political arithmetick." It is precisely the impersonal and objective nature of the tax survey that should allay the loyal citizen's qualms about the state's invasion of his privacy—even though the issue of privacy may be really one of local privilege and traditional prerogative resisting the fiscal encroachments of a centralized and rationally uniform state power. Petty was in a position to know how individuals did in fact react to measures of government scrutiny, for he had been in charge of the enormous and astonishingly efficient Down Survey of army lands in Ireland from 1655 to 1656, and he also completed an unpublished census of the Irish population in 1659. These colonialist surveys, which were not carried out without controversy, were what he proposed to transfer and apply to the home country.[41]

In Ireland, Petty had been the servant of Cromwell and the Commonwealth. His and Graunt's ideas belonged to a tradition of Baconian thought developed by Puritan reformers, particularly by the circle of Samuel Hartlib; the young Petty was Hartlib's protégé. These savants sought to place science and technology in the service of economic progress and national greatness; they were loyal to the new republican regime, which they also saw as an instrument to further their projects.[42] Hence they favored a strong central government to regulate trade and to carry out an aggressive foreign policy of empire and expansion. These policies also found special support during the first years of the Commonwealth from members of a newly emergent sector of the London merchant community that had originally risen to wealth through trade to the Western colonies and which now sought its share of the East Indian market as well.[43] Together with the scientific reformers, these mercantile interests contributed in 1650 to the formation of the Council of Trade, which, though short-lived, produced the landmark Navigation Act of 1651; these two groups, whose membership sometimes overlapped, variously supported the other notable efforts of the Cromwellian government's pursuit of commercial expansion: the Western Design, the conquest and colonial resettlement of Ireland, and the war with the Dutch of 1652–54. When viewed in light of these developments of the 1650s, Graunt's and Petty's writings of the 1660s appear to be not so much Royalist as more generally statist: their plans to rationalize government and the national economy through statistics had grown out of the Puritan Commonwealth's own intellectual circles, and their implicit ideal of a powerful, interventionist state had been partly realized in Cromwell's policies. Nonetheless, these statist policies—and the allegiances of the scientist-projectors—were soon appropriated by Charles II. The renewed and revised version of the Navigation Act in 1660 was part of the Restoration settlement, and the king embarked on two further wars against the Dutch.[44]

Milton had seen this coming, this easy transition and slide from republican to Royalist statism, just as he saw his countrymen's hunger for trade as a threat to their freedom. As early as 1654, he had closed his *Second Defense of the English People* with a famous passage warning his fellow citizens not to fall from true liberty into a worship of the state and its workings.

> For if the ability to devise the cleverest means of putting vast sums of money into the treasury, the power readily to equip land and sea forces, to deal shrewdly with ambassadors from abroad, and to contract judicious alliances and treaties has seemed to any of you greater, wiser, and more useful to the state than to administer incorrupt justice to the people, to help those harassed and

oppressed, and to render to every man promptly his own deserts, too late will you discover how mistaken you have been. . . . If you begin to slip into the same vices, to imitate those men, to seek the same goals, to clutch at the same vanities, you actually are royalists yourselves, at the mercy either of the same men who up to now have been your enemies, or of others in turn.[45]

The language is that of biblical prophecy—compare Hosea's condemnation of foreign alliances (5:13; 8:8–10) and Isaiah's call for justice and reform (1:17); but the application is contemporary. Milton polemicizes against Commonwealth statesmen who are devoted to the state as an end in itself. As a friend of Hartlib's and one familiar with the ideas of his scientific circle, Milton singles out first of all those projectors, as Graunt and Petty were later to be, of schemes for the nation's fiscal management. The efforts of statist politicians to build England into an economic and military power, engaged in a dynamic foreign policy, would transform the republic into a mirror image of the deposed monarchy—and, Milton implies, would pave the way for the king's return. Milton equates with royalism a preoccupation with statecraft that places the aggrandizement of state power above individual considerations of justice: the centralizing tendency of that power is opposed to what is due to "every man" according to "his own deserts." When Milton later outlined his own utopian political plans in *The Readie and Easie Way*, he proposed a federation of local county governments, partly modeled on the Dutch United Provinces. Each county was to be "a kinde of subordinate Commonaltie or Common-wealth" with relative judicial autonomy: "they shall have none than to blame but themselves, if it be not well administered: and fewer laws to expect or fear from the supreme authoritie."[46]

This fear of central state authority, it needs always to be emphasized, is linked with—to the point of being the reflection of—Milton's religious politics: his opposition to Presbyterianism, to tithes and a stipendiary clergy, to censorship, and to a state religion, even one constituted by the Independents themselves. When the Jesus of *Paradise Regained* rejects the use of fear (1.223) and of force (2.479) to build his kingdom, it is especially the forcing of conscience that is at stake.[47] The more powerful the state and the more developed its instruments of scrutiny and control, the greater will be its ability to impose conformity. Rather ominously, Graunt's population survey seeks to learn the religion of every citizen as well as the citizen's sex, state, trade, rank, and degree.

If the allusion to David's census contains specific attacks upon the Stuart monarchy, it may also attack that monarchy as part of the larger configuration of the modern nation-state, the sponsor, whether in Royalist or republican guise, of a new statistical science and instrumental rationality. This double perspective—the convergence of related but not fully congruent ideas in Milton's political thought—might help to account for, if not resolve, the political contradiction of his great poetry: its persistent, genuinely subversive criticism of kingship, its lack of any political alternatives to kingship beyond individual spirituality. The Commonwealth alternative had produced its own forms of statism, which, Milton seems to have thought, contributed to its drift back to monarchy. Milton's refuge in a passive individualism may thus have been an antithetical response to the very idea of the state, especially to the modern Leviathan that drew power to its center and constantly expanded its spheres of government control. He was, perhaps, responding to a state that did not yet exist: for all the achievements and schemes of the English projectors, it was in France and Prussia, rather than in Britain, that seventeenth-century governments began to run along comprehensive, scientific principles of organization. And Milton may well, as Hill suggests, have been swimming against the historical tide. In the 1670s, resistance to royal absolutism would be effected by the emergence of political parties: individuals could join shifting coalitions in order to influence and guide state policy.

Yet if Milton could foresee little political role for the individual against the authoritarian state and urged a withdrawal to inward piety, this recourse may not have been a wholly negative gesture. It maintained an area of personal autonomy from a state that seemed increasingly to intrude upon local and private reserves. One such reserve may be figured in the domestic bower of Adam and Eve trespassed upon by a voyeuristic Satan who, like a government surveyor, takes the measure of Eden.

> But first with narrow search I must walk round
> This garden, and no corner leave unespied.
>
> (PL 4.548–49)

After this Eden of privacy (and property) has been invaded and desecrated by satanic forces, the dispossessed Adam and Eve fall back upon a "paradise within," its boundaries contracted into the individual conscience. In Milton's sequel poem, Satan will attempt to penetrate this latter paradise as well with his "nearer view / And narrower scrutiny" (4.514–15), as he tries to learn the true nature of God's Son. The Prince of this world seeks ever more detailed information on those he would make his subjects, and his field of knowledge would include the inner realm of identity itself. But Jesus keeps his adversary guessing until true knowledge comes too late to help him. The hero of *Samson Agonistes* similarly reveals his returning strength only at the moment when he brings his enemies down. But the fallen Samson had earlier yielded up his "capital secret" (SA 394) to Dalila and the Philistine authorities; he has had to endure the continuing probing of Harapha who comes "to survey" him (1089; 1227–30), in a scene that suggests a blind man's horror of being observed by those he cannot see. Milton's last two poems share a common concern with maintaining inwardness under the scrutiny of others, even when, in the case of Samson, one is made into a public spectacle. Milton's Jesus defends his individuality from the observation and reckoning of external power and shows the way that paradise can be regained.[48]

Milton's rejection of statism, whether monarchical or republican, offers a further political gloss on the shift in genre of his epic poetry towards romance, a shift that we traced in *Paradise Lost* in the preceding chapter and that is also felt in the wilderness wandering of Jesus in *Paradise Regained*. God's "exercise" and testing of His Son before sending him forth to "conquer" Sin and Death (1.155–60), typologically repeats the Exodus experience of the Israelites described by Michael in *Paradise Lost* (*PL* 12.214–35; see above, pp. 306–7): the prolonged period of contingency, trial, and choice that is a preparation for the conquest of the Promised Land and that acquires a higher value than—and so displaces—that imperial conquest itself. Jesus' criticism of the census, with its link to the epic catalogue that musters imperial resources into a parade or triumph—the first such catalogue in *Paradise Lost* (1.376–571) is significantly a catalogue of devils—suggests Milton's own resistance to the idea of concentrated human power, and this resistance has generic consequences. Milton opposes *both* of the aspects of empire linked and celebrated by Virgilian epic, the kingship of an Augustus-like emperor and the expansionist territorial state. He thus goes even further than the losers' epics of Lucan's tradition to which his poems bear and claim affinity, for those earlier epics still remain committed to one or the other kind of imperial power. *Paradise Lost* and *Paradise Regained* carry further, too, the movement toward and valorization of romance that Lucan's tradition had begun, to the point where Milton's poems effectively create their own new genre. In their fictions, the epic of empire is already part of a superseded literary past: the classics that the adolescent Jesus may or may not have read, a War in Heaven that Raphael relates to Adam and Eve and that is placed so far in the past that it precedes human history. Milton pronounces the demise of epic as a genre, and since he had no great successors, he appears from the perspective of a later literary history to have fulfilled the ambition of every epic poet: to have written the epic to end all epics. This final assimilation of epic with that romance which, from the *Aeneid* onward, epic had projected as its generic and narrative antithesis is informed by Milton's particular political vision—a vision no less political for its distrust of organized power.

PART FOUR

A MODERN EPILOGUE

NINE

OSSIAN, MEDIEVAL "EPIC," AND EISENSTEIN'S

ALEXANDER NEVSKY

ALEXANDER THE GREAT kept a copy of the *Iliad* beside him on his campaigns. Napoleon Bonaparte, the new Alexander, carried to the battlefield a copy of the *Poems of Ossian*. His edition included the "epic poems" *Fingal* and *Temora*, published, respectively, in 1761 and 1763 by James Macpherson, who claimed to have translated them into English from ancient Gaelic manuscripts he had collected in the Scottish Highlands. Napoleon is said to have remarked that "Alexander had chosen Homer for his poet ... Augustus had chosen Virgil, the author of the *Aeneid*.... As for me, I had nothing but Ossian: the others were taken."[1] The anecdote suggests a devotion not untempered by wry feelings of romantic belatedness. Napoleon's fondness for Ossian was nonetheless real, and he was still thumbing and discussing his copy of Macpherson's work during his last years on Saint Helena. His case is typical of a peculiar afterlife that epic itself enjoyed in the late eighteenth and nineteenth centuries. Unsuccessful attempts might be made by writers to continue the classical epic tradition of Virgil, but the significant national epics of the age were not written but instead were recovered and translated from a medieval, nonclassical past: a scholarly enterprise that may have taken the semispurious poems of Ossian as its model and inspiration, but that also brought to light the Norse eddas, the *Nibelungenlied, Beowulf*, the *Poema de Mio Cid*, the *Song of Igor*, and the *Chanson de Roland*. These are now canonical works in their respective national literatures, and are often read and studied alongside ancient and Renaissance epics. By way of an epilogue to this study of the politics of epic, the present chapter examines the cultural politics that helped to make medieval heroic poems into "classics." The chapter concludes with a discussion of Sergei Eisenstein's film classic, *Alexander Nevsky*, perhaps the last medieval epic in the line that the *Poems of Ossian* began.

How could anyone have been taken in by Macpherson's work? At the opening of *Fingal*, Swaran, the invading king of Lochlin, is described by a messenger to the Irish chieftain Cuthullin:

"I beheld their chief," says Moran, "tall as a glittering rock. His spear is a blasted pine. His shield the rising moon! He sat on the shore! like a cloud of mist on the silent hill!"[2]

(*Fingal* 1; 2:262–63)

This brief passage gives a good idea of Macpherson's heroic style: the parallelism that imitates biblical verse, the short, "primitive," declarative sentences that can quickly fall into the bathetic—"He sat on the shore!" Also, the overload of metaphors, often less apposite than deliberately vague and evanescent: a glittering rock, a cloud of mist. Swaran's spear and shield, however, are the giveaway. The shield of Achilles is compared to the moon in the *Iliad* (19.373), and his mighty spear is made of an ash tree hewn on Mount Pelion (390–91); Milton's Satan has a shield compared to the moon (*Paradise Lost* 1.287) and a spear compared to a Norway pine (2.292–93).[3] The unlettered Celtic bard Ossian appears somehow to have had possession of a long-term classical tradition.

Macpherson could, of course, defend Miltonic echoes in his translation: there were similar echoes in Pope's translation of the *Iliad*.[4] And if there were resemblances between the primitive Ossian and Homer, these were only to be expected. By the mid-eighteenth century, Vico, Voltaire, and others had recast Homer as a primitive himself at the infancy of Greek civilization; the ancient testimony of Josephus that Homer had not written his poems was revived, provoking a gradual recognition of their oral composition and casting doubts on their unity and on the authenticity of the author Homer himself. Macpherson, who loosely based some episodes of his epics upon real heroic songs preserved in Highland folk tradition, might have looked at himself as a new Peisistratus who, according to Richard Bentley in 1713, collected the "loose songs" of Homer "together in the form of an epic poem" some five hundred years after the bard's death.[5] And Macpherson would later publish his own translation of the *Iliad* (1773) in the same style as his Ossianic poetry. The Abbé Cesarotti, the great Paduan man of letters and antagonist of the Homerist Friedrich Wolf, similarly translated into Italian both Macpherson's own *Poems of Ossian* and the *Iliad* as parallel projects: it was probably Cesarotti's translation that Napoleon had with him at the end on Saint Helena.[6]

It was, moreover, the "cloudy" style of the Ossianic poems—the "cloud of mist on the silent hill"—that gave them their great vogue. Comparing Homer and Ossian, Herder wrote of the objectivity of the former, and his brilliantly lighted descriptions of heroes and gods alike: this is the traditional German romantic view of Homer as all foreground that survives in the opening pages of Auerbach's *Mimesis*. Ossian, by contrast, was all subjectivity, a "lyrical-epic" poet.

> His figures are all cloud-figures (*Nebelgestalten*) and were meant to be; they are created from the light breath of sensibility, and they glide past like zephyrs. So they not only appear as ghosts dwelling in clouds through which the stars shimmer; but also Ossian suggests more in these figures of his loved ones than if he had represented and depicted them. One hears their step or their voice;

one sees the glimmer of their limbs, of their faces like a moonbeam sliding past. Their hair flows softly in the wind; so they glide hither and away. He paints similar figures of his heroes, not as they are, but as they draw nigh, as they appear and vanish. It is a ghostworld in Ossian, while in Homer a fleshly bodily world stirs with life.[7]

Macpherson, that is, had invented Ossian as a preromantic. The ancient heroic characters described in the poems become hard to distinguish from the ghosts—often those characters' very own ghosts—whom the bard invokes at the beginning of his songs as the traditional epic poet might call on his muse. The opening of the *Songs of Selma* is characteristic, a passage that Goethe's young Werther translates and that moves Charlotte to tears when she reads it. "Farewell thou silent beam," Ossian declares to the evening star in a typical scene of romantic inspiration, and then seeks his own inner illumination.[8]

> Let the light of Ossian's soul arise! And it does arise in its strength! I behold my departed friends. Their gathering is on Lora, as in the days of other years. Fingal comes like a watry column of mist! his heroes are around: and see the bards of song . . .
>
> (1:425)

Like the living Swaran, the dead Fingal appears as misty cloud.

If this kind of Ossianic invocation seems faintly silly coming from the overwrought Werther, Goethe could nonetheless take it seriously and transform it into the great poetry of the Dedication to the first part of *Faust*.

> Ihr naht euch wieder, schwankende Gestalten,
> Die früh sich einst dem trüben Blick gezeigt.
> Versuch' ich wohl euch diesmal fest zu halten?
> Fühl' ich mein Herz noch jenem Wahn geneight?
> Ihr dräht euch zu! nun gut, so mögt ihr walten,
> Wie ihr aus Dunst und Nebel um mich steight;
> Mein Busen fühlt sich jugendlich erschüttert
> Vom Zauberhauch, der euren Zug umwittert.
>
> (1–8)

> . . . .
> Was ich besitze seh'ich wie im Weiten,
> Und was verschwand wird mir zu Wirklichkeiten.[9]
>
> (31–32)

(You draw nigh again, you wavering Forms, that once long ago appeared to my beclouded sight. Do I seek this time to hold you fast indeed? Do I feel my heart still under the power of that delusion? You press closer! Very well, so may you command me as you rise around me from the mist and cloud; my breast feels itself youthfully shudder, from the magical inspiration that breathes from your airy course.

. . . .

What I possess I see as if in the distance, and what has vanished becomes reality.)

The poet's inspiration becomes a recapturing of a ghostly past, of an earlier time of youth. Macpherson's Ossian sings from the vantage point of old age on heroic events in which he himself had participated and sometimes appears as a character: he is the son of the great hero Fingal whom he celebrates. The subjective cast of his poetry is bathed in nostalgia and melancholy, a mourning for times gone by, for a greater paternal generation and for his dead comrades-in-arms. Herder took this as an indication that the Ossianic poems came from the end of the Gaelic heroic age.

> As there are several seasons in Nature, so are there also in human history. Peoples too have their Spring, Summer, and Autumn, and Winter. Ossian's poetry denotes the Autumn of his people. The leaves turn colors and crumple; they fade and fall. The breeze that loosens them has none of the vigour of spring in it; but as it plays with the falling leaves, it is sadly pleasing.[10]

With its elaborate puns in the original German—*Blätter* as leaves, pages, and sheet music and *Spiel* as the wind playing and as music playing—this description of the breeze of inspiration is decidedly elegiac. William Hazlitt noted a similar opposition between Homer and Ossian.

> As Homer is the first vigour and lustihed, Ossian is the decay and old age of poetry. He lives only in the recollection and regret of the past. There is one impression which he conveys more entirely than all other poets, namely the sense of privation, the loss of all things, of friends, of good name, of country— he is even without God in the world. He converses only with the spirits of the departed; with the motionless and silent clouds.[11]

Primitive though he may be, Ossian already experiences the belatedness of his romantic readers.

This pervasive sense of loss, almost of a survivor's guilt, in Ossian could also be read as an experience of defeat: Friedrich Schlegel wrote that "in the Ossianic poems there prevails that tone of lamentation which might be supposed to be most in harmony with a vanquished, depressed, and almost expiring people."[12] Macpherson's work was linked to real political defeat, to the failed Jacobite risings of 1715 and 1745–46 in his native Scottish Highlands. As a child he had witnessed the latter rebellion and the repressive measures of the British government that followed. Among these was the banning of the use of Gaelic in the schools, which henceforth exclusively taught the English language of the conquerors. The composition of the Ossianic poems was thus motivated as much by the desire to vindicate a fallen national tradition as by Macpherson's personal ambition to ascend to social eminence by his literary talents. The cultural and political interests at work in the creation and reception of Ossian were understood by early discerning readers. Schlegel, who by 1812 realized that Macpherson had been very free in his version of the poems, nonetheless held that genuine Gaelic originals lay at their basis; he also recognized that nationalist issues were at stake.

> The patriotism of the Scotch being, after that catastrophe [the rebellion of 1746], forcibly repressed, concentrated itself, as is frequently the case, in a more fervent love and veneration of old national traditions, and the memorials of their ancient fame. This disposition prompted the sedulous preservation of the songs of the Gaelic bards, and possibly also contributed to the enthusiastic love and veneration with which they were received in their mother country. All Europe, too, soon imbibed the spirit of enthusiasm, and joyfully hailed the new apparition of the North which harmonised so wonderfully with the general feeling and poetical aspirations of the time.[13]

Schlegel suggested, too, that the hostility of English critics, such as Doctor Johnson, to the Ossianic poems, and their eagerness to prove their inauthenticity, were colored by "some tinge of prejudice" and "party spirit."

In *Fingal*, the bitterness of loss and the shame of defeat emerge as the dominant note of an epic that has apparently ended in total victory. The Highlander hero Fingal sails to Ireland to the rescue of Cuthullin, routing Swaran's forces and taking the invading king captive in battle. But Fingal's youngest son, Ryno, has been killed in the fighting, and the mourning father perceives the transience of all things.

> Rest, youngest of my sons! rest O Ryno! on Lena. We too shall be no more. Warriors one day must fall!
>
> Such was thy grief, thou King of swords, when Ryno lay on earth. What must the grief of Ossian be, for thou thyself art gone! I hear not thy distant voice on Cona. My eyes perceive thee not. Often forlorn and dark I sit at thy tomb, and feel it with my hands. When I think I hear thy voice, it is but the passing blast. Fingal has long since fallen asleep; the ruler of the war!
>
> Then Gaul and Ossian sat with Swaran, on the soft green banks of Lubar. I touched the harp to please the king. But gloomy was his brow. He rolled his red eyes towards Lena. The hero mourned his host.
>
> (*Fingal* 5:349–50)

Fingal's grief over Ryno occasions Ossian's characteristic lament for Fingal himself, and when he returns to his narration he describes the mournful Swaran, who in the following Book 6 is still looking toward Lena with reddened eyes: "He remembered that he fell" (356). Fingal comforts his defeated enemy by making peace with Swaran and sending him back to Lochlin and—more importantly—by suggesting the power of poetry to perpetuate their fame.

> "Swaran," said the king of hills, "to-day our fame is greatest. We shall pass away like a dream. No sound will remain in our fields of war. Our tombs will be lost in the heath. The hunter shall not know the place of our rest. Our names may be heard in song. . . ." The face of Swaran brightened, like the full moon of heaven . . .
>
> *(Fingal* 6: 362)

The ambiguity of "may," which could suggest the certain capacity or the barest possibility of the survival of the warriors' name, nicely captures the gloom and the perception of a shared mortality that engulf both victor and vanquished alike and that underlie Fingal's magnanimous reconciliation with Swaran. Behind this scene undoubtedly lies the great reconciliation scene between Achilles and Priam, each weeping for his own loss, in the last book of the *Iliad*.

But Macpherson does not end here, for Fingal must also give comfort to his ally Cuthullin, the Irish king, who is mortified by his own rout at Swaran's hands and who now

> lies in the dreary cave of Tura. His hand is on the sword of his strength. His thoughts on the battles he lost. Mournful is the king of spears; till now unconquered in war. He sends his sword to rest on the side of Fingal.
>
> (362–63)

Fingal nobly refuses Cuthullin's despairing gesture of submission and renunciation. He applies his sententious response to both Cuthullin and Swaran alike.

> Many have been overcome in battle; whose renown arose from their fall. O Swaran! king of resounding woods, give all grief away. The vanquished, if brave, are renowned.
>
> (363)

Fingal goes to find Cuthullin in his cave and consoles his Irish confederate for the shame of his defeat, promising him that "hereafter thou shalt be victorious" (367). The epic concludes with this hope for the future and gesture of solidarity between the Gaelic-speaking peoples. The glory that Fingal proclaims may lie in defeat is the goal sought by Macpherson's Ossian poems themselves, poems that give to his vanquished but valiant Scots their own voice, and a commemoration that is by turns mournful and celebratory.

When Macpherson published his first collection of Ossianic poetry, the *Fragments of Ancient Poetry*, in 1760, he placed as an epigraph upon the title page the following verses from the *Pharsalia*:

> Vos quoque qui fortes animas, belloque peremptas
> Laudibus in longum vates dimittitis aevum
> Plurima securi fudistis carmina Bardi.

(1.447–49)

(You vatic bards, too, who, by your praise transmit into long ages to come the feats of great heroes slain in battle, poured forth your many songs safe from harm.)

Here was classical testimony for the poetry of the Celtic bards that Macpherson sought to recover. But Fiona Stafford suggests that Macpherson, a survivor of the losing side of the 1746 civil war in the Highlands, felt an affinity between his work and Lucan's epic of lost freedom: "The overwhelming sense of a world in the process of disintegration, which is conveyed in the *Pharsalia*, also emerged in the *Fragments*."[14] The context in the *Pharsalia* suggests a further meaning. The reason the bards can sing in safety is that Roman might has turned upon itself, and the occupying legions of Caesar have left Gaul: this is a period of Celtic liberty. Macpherson's evocation of the *Pharsalia* thus appears both to look back at an age of Scottish independence, the age of heroic song, and to lament its passing. In fact, two of the shorter Ossianic poems, *Comala* and *The War of Caros*, depict the ancient Celts fighting against third-century Roman invaders, the emperors Caracalla and Carausius. Schlegel comments that "Macpherson, anxious from mistaken patriotism to give greater antiquity to these poems, and carry them back even to the period of the Romans, has allowed himself in many instances to falsify the text."[15] But it is not hard to see in the Caledonian resistance to the Roman army of occupation, which in *The War of Caros* is rebuilding Agricola's wall, a backdating into antiquity of the native struggles against British forces that after 1715 had built a system of garrisons and roads throughout the Highlands. This backdating of heroic legend to classical antiquity may, moreover, have influenced the *Nibelungenlied* scholar F. J. Mone, who suggested in 1830 that Siegfried was to be identified with the German chieftain Arminius who defeated the army of Augustus under Varus in A.D. 9; later-nineteenth-century scholars argued that the dragon Siegfried kills represented the Roman legions.[16]

The struggle of Ossian's Celts against imperial Rome may be viewed as a figure not only of the defense of Scottish liberty against the tyranny of the British state, but also of Macpherson's very project: the creation of a new epic that could rival or supplant the classical epic tradition, especially insofar as that tradition was identified with the Roman Virgil and his epic of empire. The *Fragments* is symptomatically aligned with the *Pharsalia*—with Lucan's alternate, anti-Virgilian current of resistance within that tradition. When Macpherson published *Fingal* in 1762, he replaced the epigraph from Lucan on the title page with one from Virgil: "Fortia facta patrum" (*Aeneid* 1.641). The "greater deeds of one's ancestors" refers in its original context not to the forefathers of Trojan Aeneas but to those of *Tyrian Dido*; their exploits are engraved in the Carthaginian queen's dinnerware. *Fingal* is meant to celebrate not the Virgilian imperial victor, but the "other" tradition of Rome's historically defeated enemies.[17]

Howard Weinbrot has documented how the *Aeneid* suffered a decline in prestige as Virgil was accused of being an imperial propagandist and a servile adulator of Augustus.[18] In the French version of his essay on epic, Voltaire paraphrases Ariosto's sardonic view of Virgil in the *Orlando furioso* (35.26):

> He and Horace were loaded with gifts by Augustus. This fortunate tyrant knew well that one day his reputation would depend on them: thus has it come about that the idea that these two great writers have given us of Augustus has effaced the horror of his proscriptions; they have made us love his memory; they have, if I dare to say it, imposed upon the whole world.[19]

Virgil, the courtier poet, is identified with absolutism and the *ancien regime*, and, as a Roman, with the Catholic South. For an alternative in epic poetry to the political universalism of the Roman Empire in the *Aeneid*—a universalism that Tasso, following timeworn tradition, easily transferred in the *Gerusalemme liberata* to the Church of Rome, a universalism that persisted in the Latin-speaking republic of letters—preromantic and romantic thinkers could look to heroic verse either written before Virgil or in native traditions outside the culture of Latinity. Hence, in part, came the rise in the reputation of Homer, a Homer whose "primitive" times place him in a virtually prepolitical world of petty kings and chieftains, whose princess daughters do the laundry, not in a world of great states and imperial destiny. Hence, too, came the rise of interest, at first antiquarian but soon much broader, in medieval sagas and heroic poems, an interest that Macpherson's Ossian poems both stem from and did so much to create. Though Schlegel decided that the Ossianic works could not go back to a Roman period, as Macpherson tried to suggest, he placed them instead in the ninth and tenth centuries, the period also, he contended, of the Icelandic eddas, of the Roland poems, of *The Cid*, and of the *Nibelungenlied*.

> All these works appeared in the very heart of that long period of time usually designated the "night of the middle ages," a term, perhaps, well fitted to express the isolated existence of nations and individuals, and the interruption of that universal, active intercourse prevailing in the later period of Roman dominion.[20]

It is at the moment when Rome's power failed, and with it a shared civilization, that national traditions could emerge in their isolated splendor: "How radiant was that night!" of the Dark Ages, Schlegel declares.[21]

Schlegel's remarks are a transparent allegory of a romantic nationalist culture arising as a welcome alternative to a cosmopolitanism represented by Catholicism or by its warring twin: a (French) enlightenment culture of neoclassicism, universal reason, and progress. Schlegel also asserts a general gravitation of the center of European literary culture northward into Protestant regions and away from the Latin Mediterranean: his essay is entitled "On the Poetry of the North," and it eventually couples Ossian with Shakespeare, "the favourite poet not only of the English, but of all nations of Teutonic origin: excepting only when a foreign and ungerman influence intervenes, and people have already become false to their original character and better feeling."[22] Such xenophobic sentiments, uttered even as he and his translator brother, August Wilhelm Schlegel, "Germanize" the foreigner Shakespeare, are the by-product of the quest for the pure origins of a national culture that Schlegel describes at the essay's beginning.

> Poetry, indeed, in its earliest, original form, is not strictly confined within the actual limits of that art, but, as a record of the noble word and actions of ancient heroes, appears rather to belong to history, the primitive history, of nature and mankind. Contrasted with that poetry that flows from the false channels of conventional art and social habits, the last mentioned may be likened to the clear, pure water gushing from a mountain spring, but compared with the exterior charm, the richness, and glittering flower-like hues of that poetry which springs from the impulses of youthful life and love, it seems rather to resemble the rude majesty of a primitive rock, whose aspect fills the lonely wanderer with astonishment, placing him, as it were, amid the giant features of the olden time.[23]

. . . .

> It is in a similar frame of mind that we should approach and contemplate the vestiges of heroic tradition; and I might, perhaps advantageously, attempt here to impart to my readers certain of my meditations on this subject, at least in as far as relates to the poetry of our fatherland, but I shall confine myself rather to the task of rescuing from oblivion the solid, pure metal, of our earliest poetry, and bringing it once more into life and notice. . . . During the last ten or twelve years especially, a stronger national feeling has stirred within us, and the love thus kindled for the early poets of our fatherland has become warmer and more universal. . . . Even in poetry, to which the genius of our nation and the taste of our investigators has ever been peculiarly directed, much remains to be sought out in a still more remote antiquity, and drawn from a far deeper source, before the spirit of German poetry, as it once reigned among our ancestors, can be awakened and rekindled amongst ourselves.[24]

As the mixture of metaphors suggests, the scholarly recovery of the medieval poetry is conceived as an excavation into the depths of time in search both of a source of inspiration ("einer reinen und starken Felsenquelle") and of a pure national vein ("das gediegene Metall der alten Poesie") that approximate nature itself: that undiluted national treasure that Wagner, making a punning combination of the wellspring and mining figures, would later call "Rhein[rein]gold."

The same metaphor was exploited in 1797 by the great Russian scholar N. N. Karamzin, when he announced to the larger European world in the pages of *Le Spectateur du Nord* the discovery of the *Song of Igor*; here, too, Macpherson's Ossian poems provided a model for appreciating the new nationalist epic.

> But what will perhaps surprise you further, Sir, is that two years ago there was unearthed [*déterré*] in our archives the fragment of poem, titled *The Song of the Warriors of Igor*, which can be placed alongside the most beautiful bits of Ossian, and which was made in the twelfth century by an unknown author. An energetic style, feelings of sublime heroism, striking images, dug up [*puisées*] from the horrors of nature, constitute the merit of this fragment, where the poet, tracing the picture of bloody combat, calls out to himself: "Ah! I feel that my paintbrush is weak and feeble; I do not have the talent of the great *Bayan*, that nightingale of times past." There were thus in Russia before him, great poets, whose works are swallowed up by the centuries. Our annals do not name this *Bayan* at all; we do not know when he lived, nor what he sang. But this homage, paid to his genius by such a poet, makes us acutely regret the loss of his works.[25]

In this letter to *Le Spectateur du Nord*, Karamzin is defending a Russian literature that, he proclaims, possesses epic poems that equal the beauty of Homer, Virgil and Tasso.[26] The roots of this national literature, as the hoary *Song of Igor* itself attests to the still earlier poet Bayan, go back into ages so dark that they cannot be plumbed: into depths of time that are in some way equivalent to an eternal and mysterious nature, that wellspring from which the *Igor* poet draws up his imagery. The equivalence points to the analogy between the poet and the scholar who recovers the lost poem from a devouring history: the analogy that became a confusion of identity in Macpherson's treatment of the Highland songs. A similar confusion reappeared in Elias Lönnrot's compilation of old Finnish runes into the *Kalevala* (1835). His critic Carl Axel Gottlund, himself a collector of Finnish songs and folk poetry, had suggested the project in an article in 1817.

> We are so bold as to propose that if we collected these ancient folk poems and created some kind of ordered whole of them, be it then an epic, a drama, or whatever, another Homer, Ossian, or *Niebelungenlied* might be created of

them, and through this our Finnishness could yet be celebrated nobly with honor—by the brilliance of its own worth, in its own self-knowledge and beautified by the knowledge of its own creation—to awaken the wonder of our contemporaries and of those to come.[27]

Gottlund was later bitter that Lönnrot had not given him credit for the idea of making a new Finnish epic. But the nationalist ambitions and implications of the future *Kalevala* are already spelled out here, as is Lönnrot's ambiguous Macpherson-like role as arranger-collector and creator of the poem. Later in the century the comparison to Macpherson would be disparaging, as the authenticity of the *Kalevala* would be called in doubt, characteristically enough by Swedish-speaking Finns.[28] Polemical as it was, this comparison was unfair insofar as it concerned Lönnrot's scholarship—which was far more serious and painstaking than that of Macpherson. And the *Kalevala* provides a unique instance in which a "revived" medieval epic did indeed become the basis for a new national consciousness and self-conception of a people. February 28, the day on which Lönnrot signed the preface to his work, would become a national holiday in Finland.[29]

In the European-wide quest for national origins and identity of the early nineteenth century, heroic poetry held a special allure. It could embody a pure state of national feeling because its martial subject not only invokes the patriotic unity of a people at war but also provides the mythic memories that can mobilize them. In his *Lectures on the History of Literature*, written in the same period as "On the Poetry of the North," Schlegel expresses his particular admiration—even his envy as a German—for the *Poema de Mio Cid* and the romance ballads based on it.

> The literature of Spain possesses a high advantage over that of other nations in its historical heroic romance of the Cid. This is exactly that species of poetry which exerts the nearest and the most powerful influence over the national feelings and character of a people. A single work, such as the Cid, is of more real value to a nation than a whole library of books, however abounding in wit or intellect, which are destitute of the spirit of nationality.[30]

The story of the Cid became a rallying point in the history of the long struggle between Christian Spain and its Moorish and Jewish communities, a history that its fiction distills.[31] Schlegel, who was to his credit a champion of civil rights for German Jews, notes approvingly the comic trick by which the Cid extorts funds for his campaigns from the Jewish moneylenders of Burgos (1.6–11).[32] The creation of Spanish national identity by a process of conflict with and separation from surrounding alien cultures is not only narrated by the *Poema de Mio Cid* but paralleled in the making of the poem itself, a work that breathes a "pure, true-hearted, noble old Castilian spirit" and whose shape, Schlegel notes, was achieved before the Crusades brought into European heroic poetry a taste for Oriental fantasy.[33] He similarly praises the final redactor of the *Nibelungenlied* for keeping it "perfectly free of all allusions to the Crusades," thus preserving the German poem from contamination by foreign influences in a period when "the nations of the west came in closer contact with each other than they had ever before experienced and the fictions of all ages and all countries became inextricably mixed and confounded":[34] a new cosmopolitanism that provided its own version of the cultural unity formerly enjoyed beneath the Roman Empire.

The Dark Ages, because they intervene between the periods of international commerce in European civilization, are thus the bedrock in which an original national spirit and culture can be located and mined. But this spirit and culture are already lost in the very darkness of the times. Schlegel begins the *Lectures* by asserting that "there is nothing so necessary to the whole improvement, or rather to the whole intellectual existence of a nation, as the possession of a plentiful store of those national recollections and associations, which are lost in a great measure during the dark ages of infant society, but which it forms the great object of the poetical art to perpetuate and adorn."[35] National pride depends on the possession of a national poetry, which Schlegel appears to elide here, as in the above passage from "On the Poetry of the North," with the posession of a history, a people's consciousness of their own making of their collective destiny.[36] Epic, he declares in a later lecture, is the privileged literary form for the creation of such a consciousness.

> The first and original end of all poetry, if we consider it as it is to have influence on men and on life, and, in one word, as it is to be national,—is, to preserve and embellish the peculiar traditions and recollections of the people; and to preserve alive, in the memories of men, the magnanimity and greatness of ages that are gone by. The peculiar sphere of this poetry is epic narrative where there is the utmost scope for the introduction of the marvellous, and where the poet cannot move a step without the assistance of mythology.[37]

Schlegel's logic wavers uneasily here between, on the one hand, a Viconian vision of myth and heroic poetry as the preserver, through euhemerist distortion, of the real historical experience and collective memory of a people (the process that turns a Roman army into Siegfried's dragon) and, on the other hand, a view of this poetry as an embellishment ("verschönern"), a necessary myth that creates or replaces national memory and that uses the resources of the marvelous to compel an irrational assent to its fiction. Thus, for the purpose of "forging" a national identity, the scholarly recovery of this poetry, which may be a genuine-enough product of medieval song, confronts the same problem of authenticity that surrounded Macpherson's largely invented Ossianic works. Only now it may be the poetry itself that invented a national past, an invention the romantic scholar both colludes with and repeats as he holds up the newly excavated medieval epic as the repository of national spirit and collective memory. The scholar digs up the old heroic poetry *as*—and thereby *creates*—a new national epic for the nineteenth-century European state. In doing so he helps to create the very essence of national consciousness.

Schlegel's purposes were practical and political. The *Lectures*, delivered in Vienna in 1812, reflect and form part of a by then decade-old nationalist agitation for a *Befreiungskrieg*, a war of liberation of German-speaking peoples from the domination of Napoleon's armies; Prussia and then Austria would finally rise against the emperor in 1813. If Napoleon could be inspired by Ossian, Schlegel and others looked to the *Nibelungenlied*. Napoleon's atttraction to the Ossianic poems can be variously explained: as a prevalent preromantic or romantic enthusiasm shared by readers of his period, as the response of a soldier to a warrior's poetry, as the identification of a Corsican outsider in France with Ossian's Highlanders (all the more so given their common opposition to the perfidious Albion). Macpherson's celebration of the deeds of a historically vanquished people—even as the depiction of their past victories suggests that they may arise victorious again—might also fit the originally revolutionary impetus of Napoleon's military adventures. This same celebration of a glorious past is the role to which Schlegel for his part summons a truly national poetry.

> A people are exalted in their feelings, and ennobled in their own estimation, by the consciousness that they have been illustrious in ages that are gone by,— that these recollections have come down to them from a remote and heroic ancestry.[38]

This poetry proclaims the once *and future* greatness of a nation, a greatness that is heroic and martial. It makes possible a revival, or *Erneuerung*, both of language and of the nation, as F. H. von der Hagen, the 1807 translator of the *Nibelungenlied*, promised of the work he held up as the German national epic.[39] In an 1831 essay on the *Nibelungenlied*, Thomas Carlyle commented on the patriotic feelings the poem evoked in the German academic community: "Learned professors lecture on the *Nibelungen* in public schools, with a praiseworthy view to initiate German youth in love of their fatherland; from many zealous and nowise ignorant critics we hear talk of 'a great Northern Epos,' of a 'German Iliad.'"[40] One of these professors was August Wilhelm Schlegel, who in his Berlin lectures of 1802 suggested a close likeness of the *Nibelungenlied* to the *Iliad*.[41] With evident satisfaction, Friedrich Schlegel gives preeminence to the *Nibelungenlied* among medieval epics (the Germans turn out to be even more fortunate in their heroic poem than the Spaniards in the *Cid*): "But among the heroic poems of those of other nations which have remained satisfied with a more simple mode of poetry, this German poem claims a very high place—perhaps among all the heroic chivalrous poems of modern Europe it is entitled to the first." [42] In 1815, August Zeune produced a pocket-size school edition of the *Nibelungenlied*, and ended his introduction with the hope that "this edition, in these so suddenly changing historical circumstances, may still fulfill the wish of one hundred students in my audience of the Spring of 1813 and be their intimate and faithful field and tent companion."[43] The German epic was to be carried along on the campaign against the Ossian-bearing Napoleon: as its epigraph by Franz Horn proclaimed, "Let us regard this German poem as an eternal column, around which the valiant German people readily assemble together, to renew their holiest vows."

This conflict between France and Germany, played out through rival medieval epic poems, would be repeated half a century later. In the interim, the Oxford text of *La Chanson de Roland* had been discovered and published by Francisque Michel in 1837. As Joseph Duggan has shown, the poem was immmediately hailed as France's oldest and most authentic national epic.[44] In 1862, Gaston Paris, the dean of French literary medieval scholars, published an essay, "La Chanson de Roland et les Nibelungen." Its appearance in the *Revue Germanique* was a provocation. The *Chanson* had recently been translated into German by Wilhelm Hertz. Paris praised the translation but noted that Hertz followed his countrymen's opinions on the merits of the *Chanson* and on its relative inferiority to the *Nibelungenlied*: in his essay, Paris intended to convince "impartial minds on the other side of the Rhine" of the claims of the French epic.[45] To do so, Paris assigned to the *Chanson de Roland* the title of national poem, which the Germans had—with much less cause, he argued—bestowed upon the *Nibelungenlied*. This was to demote the German poem from the ranks of epic itself, even as Paris conceded that it might be of higher aesthetic interest than its French counterpart. At the beginning of his argument he declares that

> The character of epic is, first of all, to be truly national, to have issued from the entrails of the people that has produced it, to summarize in poetic form the great ideas of its epoch, and principally those that touch on religion and the fatherland.[46]

By these criteria, Paris asserts, one would hesitate to call the *Aeneid* and the *Gerusalemme liberata* epics, fine poems that they are; the *Nibelungenlied* will be in good company. He goes on to note that *La Chanson de Roland* expressed the ideals not of all of French medieval society, but of its martial nobility: "it was above all for the aristocratic and warrior class of the nation that it was truly epic."[47] But this limitation—the poem's single-minded concentration on the ethos of a military class—is also its strength: what gives to the *Chanson* its national, epic character.

Tradition had consecrated in the memory of all the deeds that it celebrates, and the ideas that inspired it fill all hearts. The crusades are but the realization of these ideas, which constituted the common atmosphere that everyone breathed. Like the *Iliad*, *La Chanson de Roland* celebrates the great struggle of Europe against Asia, like the *Iliad*, it exploits and exalts national feeling, like the *Iliad*, it is entirely pervaded by the religious ideas of its time. Powerful families find mention in it and seek their genealogies there, as the princes and peoples of Greece in the verse of Homer. . . . This character is completely absent from the *Nibelungenlied* and it is this, in my opinion, that constitutes its inferiority to our poem.[48]

National identity is created by war against the Eastern other—for Paris the Crusades are not, as for Friedrich Schlegel, an international event but an outgrowth of a peculiarly French historical impulse[49]—and it is likewise created by the poem that celebrates it. Thus a *literary*-historical event may become so decisive that it achieves the status of patriotic origin for later generations of noble warriors. Noting that the *Nibelungenlied* does not recount, as he claims *La Chanson de Roland* does, an event held in the recent memory of a people, but instead mixes protagonists from different historical periods, Paris denies such genealogical power to the German poem. This freedom from history and from a strictly martial subject, however, allows the *Nibelungenlied* to explore a greater range of human experience and character.

> In a word, the *Nibelungenlied* is a human poem, *La Chanson de de Roland* is a national poem. One feels that that which the German epic loses in force, in inspiration, in historical importance, it regains in truth, in interest and in aesthetic worth. If in literary history, envisioned from the point of view of different national manifestations of the thought, genius, and diverse ideas of peoples, *La Chanson de Roland* should occupy a more important place, one must assign to the *Nibelungenlied* a higher rank in the history of literature envisioned with relationship to art. But the balance of the scale which leans toward the German poem, if one makes an abstraction of the genre to which it claims to belong, tilts sensibly toward our old *chanson de geste* once it is a question of comparing them as two epics; for, in spite of its imperfections and lacunas, *La Chanson de Roland* completely deserves this fine name, which it is not permitted to accord to the *Nibelungenlied* except with much greater reservation.[50]

Paris thus uses philology, the Germans' own weapon of choice, to separate out the history and mythology that Friedrich Schlegel had seen operating together in the national, heroic poem. The *Chanson*, deriving from authentic events, stakes its claim on a history on which it can continue to exert an important "force"; the *Nibelungenlied* is by contrast a mythic, even Ossianic fabrication, the object properly of aesthetic contemplation.[51] The apparent evenhandedness of Paris's scholarly criticism, of impartial weighing in a scale that now inclines first for the German, now for the French poem, is in reality ironic in its effect: Paris deprives the *Nibelungenlied* of the nationalist aura in which its romantic admirers had set greatest store. Paris ends his essay by acknowledging that neither *La Chanson de Roland* nor the *Nibelungenlied* measures up to the *Iliad*; the first is not so national and epic, the second is not so artistic and profound as Homer's poem. But the tribute paid to the *Iliad* does not invalidate its earlier coupling with *La Chanson de Roland*: these are the only true epics.[52]

On December 8, 1870, the city of Paris was under siege from German armies during the Franco-Prussian War, and it would ultimately capitulate the following January 28, 1871. At this dark hour, Gaston Paris chose for his opening lecture at the Collège de France a talk titled "*La Chanson de Roland* et la nationalité française"; while he warned at the outset against injecting patriotism into a scholarship whose sole goal was the truth, his lecture was obviously designed to boost morale. For, Paris argued, it was literature that gave a people its sense of identity—which was nothing else than the love of their nation itself—and the *Chanson*, as the first great document of French literature, already defined that identity in Roland's sense of national honor and his love for his country, "*la douce France*."[53] The poem also expressed the two great ideas that continue to animate French national experience: "the tendency to unity and the tendency to expansion."[54] Duggan suggests that the latter imperialistic urge, the impulse of the Crusades that Paris locates in the *Chanson*, would have struck a resonant chord with Frenchmen who could take pride in their colonial activities in Algeria:[55] here, as in Paris's earlier essay, it is war against the non-European Muslim that creates Frenchness. But Paris is, in fact, uneasy about French colonialism and its "mission civilisatrice."

> Today, even as we conserve this noble need of expansion which created and will create the greatness of our nation in the world, we understand, instructed by experience and philosophy, that liberty is the first of all rights, and that oppression, without being less criminal, becomes even more hateful when it gives itself the mask of fraternity and is considered to establish the happiness of those it crushes.[56]

These misgivings of the conquering Western power may have been intensified by the desperate situation in which France now found itself, about to be conquered in turn by German arms. They may even suggest that the German invasion is a retribution for France's oppression of its colonial subjects. Paris's lecture seeks to reassure its audience that a sense of French unity and nationhood can survive the present defeat, and the story of Roland's death admirably suits his purposes: a story of heroism in disaster and defeat that is followed by Charlemagne's ultimate victory against the Moors. He ends his lecture by calling upon his listeners:

> Let us make ourselves recognized as the sons of those who died at Roncesvalles and of those who avenged them . . . let us feel like them responsible in solidarity for the honor of France, and let us wish above all other things, like Roland, that none may ever say of us that, on our account, France has lost its valor![57]

La Chanson de Roland, like the *Nibelungenlied*, could therefore be enlisted for the battlefield, perhaps precisely because both poems recount terrible defeats. It was a vanquished Germany that turned for a source of national inspiration to the death of Siegfried, and even more to the deaths of Gunther and Hagen in the awful revenge of Kriemhild. Similarly, a defeated France was exhorted to emulate the gallantry of Roland. In fact, the great medieval poems that had been recovered by the nineteenth century typically contain elements of defeat and tragedy: in the *Song of Igor*, Igor is vanquished and taken prisoner by the Polovetsians, and the poem celebrates his rather ignoble, if successful, flight from their camp; Beowulf slays Grendel, Grendel's mother, and the treasure dragon, but in the last fight he is mortally wounded; the Icelandic *Njalssaga* ends with the burning of Njal and his family; even the relatively triumphalist *Poema de Mio Cid* begins with the banishment and disgrace of the Cid. Macpherson's Ossian poems had already sounded the notes of defeat and loss even as they celebrated the victorious exploits of Fingal, and they set the tone for the reception of these more authentic medieval epics. Friedrich Schlegel could be echoing Herder on Ossian when he drew a general conclusion:

> Even among the most cheerful nations, the traditions and recollections of the heroic times are invested with a half mournful and melancholy feeling, a spirit of sorrow, sometimes elegiac, more frequently tragical—which speaks at once to our bosoms from the inmost soul of the poetry in which they are embodied: whether it be that the idea of a long vanished age of freedom, greatness and heroism, stamps of necessity such an impression on those who are accustomed to live among the narrow and limited institutions of after times; or whether it be not rather that poets have chosen to express, only in compositions of certain periods, those feelings of distant reverence and self abasement with which it is natural to us at all times to reflect on the happiness and simplicity of ages that have long passed away.[58]

This nostalgia and sense of loss that seemed for romantic readers to emanate from the medieval heroic poems themselves, rather than from the readers' own Schillerian sentimentality, could be variously construed. At one level they could stand for the loss of the native, vernacular literary traditions themselves, suppressed by the domination of a more cosmopolitan culture of Latinity and polite letters and now only recovered from the darkness of time by loving scholarly study. But, as Paris's remarks on the *La Chanson de Roland* further suggest, the nostalgia is also a nostalgia for aristocracy expressed from the "narrow and more limited institutions" of nineteenth-century bourgeois culture, an example of the uneasy accommodation that the bourgeoisie sought with the class it was superseding and with the outmoded cultural forms of that class. Epic and the heroic style were, as our earlier chapters have argued, tied to the fortunes of a martial aristocracy, and as these fortunes waned in the seventeenth century, the classically modeled epic poem gave way to the "modern" romance and the novel. The nationalist revival of medieval epics in the nineteenth century necessarily acknowledged their feudal ethos, even as these poems were enlisted as patriotic inspiration for nations embracing all classes. In times of war especially, the literature that could be invoked to gather popular support had to derive from or at least mimic available aristocratic forms. The content of the medieval heroic poems, however, of which the dying Roland could be the emblem, already suggested that they belonged to a historically doomed class: the bards seem to lament the passing of the very heroic ages they describe. It was this elegiac dimension that set these poems at a safe historical remove, and allowed a post-Revolutionary Europe to summon up the fighting spirit of the old nobility (and aristocrats still predominated the military establishments of nineteenth-century Germany and France) without inviting back the wholesale hegemony of the nobility itself. It permitted scholars like Friedrich Schlegel and Paris to indulge in fantasies of combat without compromising fatally their love of reason, cosmopolitanism, and liberal progress.[59]

A further construction can be placed on this appropriation by romantic nationalism of medieval epics that seemed to speak of loss and defeat. In order to build a narrative of national resurgence and redemption, the nation in question is first depicted as vanquished: it receives its identity in its moment of prostration—from which, historically, its only way can be up. Present national greatness is thus a redressing of or taking of revenge on the past. *La Chanson de Roland* enacts the double process within its action: the defeat of Roland that produces the revenge and triumph of Charlemagne. Thus, on the one hand, the medieval epics were taken, as Macpherson's epigraphs indicate he hoped the Ossian poems would be, to constitute an alternative to Virgilian classical epic, even to be aligned with Lucan's tradition of epics of lost causes. But, on the other hand, they were put to an ideological use that recalls nothing so much as the *Aeneid*, the epic narrative of Trojan victims turning into Roman victors. As in Virgil's poem, the suffering of the defeated people not only attracts sympathy but also makes a moral claim that justifies the logic by which that people rise back to power at the expense of others: as often as not a vengeance taken not upon the original oppressors but upon new peoples and nations altogether. To rein-voke the Freudian pattern discussed in relationship to the *Aeneid* in Chapter 2, this process can be conceived as therapeutic—a restoration of health to a nation suffering from its earlier trauma—but it still takes the form of a compulsion: what Karen Horney calls a "drive towards a vindictive triumph."[60] The clinging to victimization is familiar to us in nationalist and irredentist movements of our own century. To take an instance close to home, and that occurred during the writing of this book, the destruction visited on the Iraqi military and civilian population in 1991 was widely talked about in the United States as a psychic "healing" for the defeat in Vietnam. Virgil is still with us, though we may have lost his clear sense of the vindictiveness of this logic.

Film Epic: *Alexander Nevsky*

Directed by Sergei Eisenstein and written by Eisenstein and Pyotr Pavlenko, the film *Alexander Nevsky* (1938) draws on the nineteenth-century revival of medieval epic and on the classical epic tradition as well. The label of "epic" describes many kinds of movies, but Eisenstein's account of the thirteenth-century victory of Russian arms over the invading Teutonic knights is one of the few films that comes self-consciously to terms with the literary genre itself. The film was made at a time when Soviet Russia was bracing for war with Nazi Germany—before the Hitler-Stalin pact of the following year—and its broader patriotic and propagandistic messages are fairly clear. The messages are conveyed, however, by the manipulation of epic conventions that, the film suggests, have now played out their historical destiny. For if we return to the ideological dichotomies of the shield of Aeneas—West victorious over East, Male over Female, Reason over Nature, the unified One over the disorganized Many, Permanence over Flux—*Alexander Nevsky* can be seen to reverse the entire Virgilian imperialist pattern.

It is now the sinister German bishop guiding the Teutonic knights who gives voice to the traditional imperial ideology as he sanctions the atrocities the knights carry out against the civilian population of Pskov (an accurate prophecy of the Nazi genocide to come). The bishop declares:

> There is but one God in Heaven, and one deputy of God on earth. One sun lights up the universe, and lends its light to other luminaries. There can be but one Roman emperor on earth. All who refuse to bow to Rome must be destroyed.[61]

The bishop's logic has been deliberately confused, since it is not clear whether the unique sun refers to the pope or the emperor—and herein lay the great political debate of the Middle Ages in the West, and the origin of

Dante's doctrine of the *two* suns. For the film's contemporary Russian audience, the bishop's confusion suggests the continuity between the expansionist Nazi Reich, with its pretensions of renewing the Holy Roman Empire, and the hated Catholic Church, with its global, universalist ambitions. That audience would know, in spite of the film's virtually total suppression of the fact, that Alexander Nevsky was a major warrior-saint of the Russian Orthodox Church who had once turned down the invitation of Catholic emissaries to convert to the religion of Rome.[62] The bishop identifies the Germans as a Roman imperial power, and their garbled Latin hymn set to Prokofiev's music—"Peregrinus expectavi"—identifies them, like Tasso's heroes, as Western crusaders against the Eastern infidel. Like the typical Western conquerors in Virgilian epic, the Teutonic knights seem to enjoy a greater unity than the Russians, who are wrangling among themselves. The Germans seem to enjoy a technological superiority as well in the quality of their spears, swords, and armor.[63] They are consistently seen in ordered groupings from the first view of four knights standing at attention in a row, a motif carried over in the two celebrations of the Mass before the bishop's pavilion, to their battle formations: their attacking wedge and, most terrifying of all, their defensive wall that seems impossible to attack. By contrast the Russians are shown in crowd scenes that emphasize confusion, and even on the battlefield their dense ranks seem only loosely organized—in spite of Alexander's master plan for the battle. The contrast is sharpened by the spotless white robes and clean-shaven faces of the Germans and the dark armor of the bearded Russians—though the black monk who accompanies the Teutonic knights at his organ betrays their true colors.[64] The German army is all-male while, as the defenders of their homeland, the Russians are fighting alongside, and for, their women and children. The "bravest" of the Russian soldiers will be declared by Vaska Buslai to be Vasilisa, the woman warrior—reminiscent of Virgil's Camilla, Ariosto's Bradamante, and Tasso's Clorinda—who fights to avenge the death of her father in Pskov. In the subplot, Vaska and his comrade Gavrilo contend as friendly rivals for the Novgorod maiden Olga, paralleling Alexander's own wooing of the city. The very strategy of the battle on the ice, where Alexander has his army construct a V-shaped trap to receive the onslaught of the German wedge, "feminizes" the Russian soldiers.[65]

And yet this strategy of engulfment works, and the "Eastern" hordes defeat their would-be Western conquerors. There is a sense that the Teutonic knights are defeated by the Russian land itself—the revenge of nature over a fascistic instrumental or technocratic reason. The land seems literally to pour forth autochthonous troops from its soil when, in a stunning visual effect, the army of peasants that Alexander decides to recruit rise from their huts built into the earth; and later, in the even greater *coup de cinéma*, when the ice on Lake Peipus breaks at the end of the battle and its waters swallow up the routed Germans. Leon Balter comments that if the film seems in retrospect prophetic of the defeat of Hitler's army in the Russian winter, it also repeated a scenario the Russians had been through before.

> This was also the collective behavior of the Russians when Napoleon launched his invasion of an unprepared Russia in 1812. Then, also, the Russians fell back before a painful and penetrating assault into their heartland, only subsequently to engulf and viciously destroy the enemy. If one is willing to speculate in the very hazardous area of national psychological character, one could make the argument that Eisenstein in *Alexander Nevsky* touched upon a very profound psychological wellspring of the Russian national character.[66]

Equally, one could argue that Eisenstein dramatized the worst psychic nightmares of the fascist enemy, who, as Klaus Theweleit has shown, characterized the Red Menace as an uncontrolled flood, closely identified with the " 'flowing' non-subjugated woman."[67] And this metaphor of the Red Tide comes to life when Lake Peipus opens up to drown the Teutonic knights in the film. Yet however historically determined the watery end of the Germans may be, it is also determined by an epic tradition in which we have seen Western imperial conquest characterized as a victory of atemporal reason over nature, over an Eastern principle of natural flux—the kind of thinking that conflates the Eastern woman Cleopatra on the shield of Aeneas with the Nile that gathers her and Antony into its depths, with the river Araxes that chafes angrily and throws off the bridge of its conqueror. Eisenstein has turned this pattern around so that Eastern flux now prevails, and he has reversed as well the ideology that equates empire building with history making, when historical meaning is defined monumentally *in opposition* to temporal process. As a believer and agent in the historical dialectic, the Marxist artist has time on his side. And if the Germans are destroyed by the icy waters of Lake Peipus, the Russians seem to be in their element in the opening scenes of the film, where Alexander is first viewed standing in Lake Pleshcheyevo by Pereslavl as he supervises the fishing: he later seems almost to walk on water as he rushes out to gather in the nets.

The opening scenes of *Alexander Nevsky* also qualify and complicate the West-East pattern of the film. For if the Russian Easterners will successfully resist the German Westerners, here they confront a people farther to the east than Russia itself: the Mongols. The Golden Horde was the true master of Russia during the thirteenth century, and the film begins by surveying the skeletons of men and horses on a battlefield where the Mongols have inflicted a terrible defeat upon Russian arms. A convoy of Mongol warriors passes by Alexander's dwelling at Pereslavl, dragging a human tribute of enslaved Russians behind it. The Russians, that is, begin the film as *losers,* and the old fisherman (called Nikita in the scenario) calls for vengeance upon the Mongols—a vengeance that is transferred instead upon the Teutonic knights, whose defeat thus redresses past victimization.[68]

Moreover, the film's beginning casts the Russians as *Westerners* in relationship to the Mongols, who are the real Oriental menace—the teeming horde that has flooded in from the East. In this sequence, it is the Russians who are wearing white or light-colored clothing, while the Mongols are dressed in darker, fur-lined materials; the Russians, especially as they are represented by the young blonde-haired Mikhalka and Savka, are clean-shaven, while the Mongols are bearded. The Russian fishermen are spaced apart in the lake in an ordered formation, while the Mongols, shouting and rushing forward, are a ragtag band, and they immediately start a skirmish that only Alexander's authoritative voice can stop. In fact, the Mongol potentate, riding inside the palanquin that the soldiers are accompanying, tells Alexander that the Golden Horde needs military commanders and invites the prince to serve the khan, an offer Alexander patriotically refuses. The potentate, fat and wrapped in silks, suggests a decadent effeminacy underlying the ferocity of the Mongol oppressor—especially when he steps on the back of one of his men in order to climb into the palanquin.[69] The Mongols have taken over the role and negative connotations that epic ideology assigns to the Easterners: they are undisciplined, they lack leadership, they are womanish, and they are racially distinct from the Russians (and Germans) as well.

This opening of the film may be viewed as its ideological safety valve. If Eisenstein wishes to reverse Virgilian epic conventions and show the triumph of an unregimented and "free" East over a hyperorganized and imperial West—of a patriotic, popular Russia over a universalist, fascist Germany—he does not want to depict Russia as overly Eastern either: to the point of its becoming non-European or nonrational, a nature gone out of control. The ideological terms East and West are thus relative, and by positing from its beginning the presence of the Easterner Mongols to whom the Russians play the role of Westerners—in the same visual terms that the Teutonic knights will play this role to the Russians in turn—the film can portray Russia as a balanced mean between two politically undesirable extremes. Eisenstein thus contests Virgilian ideological categories only to keep them alive as well.

The balance between the ordered (fascist) West and the chaotic (leaderless) East is maintained within Eisenstein's Russia by the alliance that Prince Alexander strikes with the rural peasantry and the workers in Novgorod: in twentieth-century terms an alliance between the Communist party, with its charismatic leader Stalin, and the people. In the film's own terms this is a patriotic alliance between the warrior aristocracy and the common people. Together they oppose the merchant bourgeoisie of Novgorod, who at once resist Alexander's rulership—a situation attested to in the chronicles that Eisenstein followed—and are narrowly concerned with protecting their own financial interests. The film thus suggests how the current revolutionary situation has restored—in a form that no longer involves class exploitation—the "feudal, patriarchal, idyllic relations" that prevailed, according to Marx and Engels in *The Communist Manifesto*, before an ascendant bourgeosie put an end to them.[70] Marx and Engels had also noted the cosmopolitan nature of bourgeois society and of the culture it produced.

> National one-sidedness and narrowmindedness became more and more impossible, and from the numerous national and local literatures there arises a world literature.[71]

Patriotic art, such as the film itself, becomes possible in either a prebourgeois or a postbourgeois society. *Alexander Nevsky* offers a revolutionary gloss on the turn toward medieval epics on the part of a nineteenth-century European bourgeoisie seeking its national origins and identity in the martial exploits of an aristocratic class that it was simultaneously displacing. If the mournful quality that romantic scholarship felt in these heroic poems kept them at a safe distance from bourgeois culture, Eisenstein's film version of medieval epic suggests how this potentially reactionary nationalist nostalgia for the feudal order could become transformed into a revolutionary ideological weapon against the same bourgeois culture. In the process, of course, the international quality of the communist revolution becomes itself nationally one-sided and narrow-minded.[72]

The feudal, patriarchal, idyllic relations of which Marx and Engels wrote are exemplified in the film's opening shot of Alexander among the fishermen at Lake Pleshcheyevo. Fishing is an aristocratic leisure-class activity as well as work for common people: in this first pastoral sequence—a piscatorial eclogue, one might say—the film leaves deliberately ambiguous Alexander's role in the fishing, which he appears both to supervise and to take part in, and suggests what William Empson, writing on the pastoral, called "a beautiful relation between rich and poor."[73] This relation, linking prince and people, continues throughout the film: in his calling for and recruiting of a peasant army (that overawes the recalcitrant Novgorod merchants), in the inspiration for the plan of battle that he draws from the folktale of the armorer Ignat, and in the film's final scenes of celebration in Pskov, where, as Balter has pointed out, Alexander becomes a kind of benign father—if one who threatens punishment—to his people, the film's clearest contribution to a "cult of personality" around Stalin.[74] A comic double to this relation is provided by the film's most vivid figure, Vaska Buslai, an aristocratic Novogorod warrior and voivod who acts as one of Alexander's officers, but who is presented as a folksy bumpkin: he is initially compared to a bear, and in the battle on the ice he swigs down a bucket of ale before throwing the bucket as a weapon against the helmet of a German knight. Just previously, Vaska has swung a giant wooden pole against the enemy—also with effects of folk humor—and the scene belongs to a whole symbolism of weaponry in the film that turns the fight against the Germans into popular resistance. Vaska's pole is a comically outsize version of the staves and clubs that the mobilized peasantry are seen carrying into battle; their other weapons are agricultural implements: pruning hooks and axes. The former prove useful in pulling the enemy knights down off their horses. But it is the ax, with its ambiguous double identity as weapon and tool (and it was also a traditional heraldic emblem of medieval Russia), that becomes the hallmark of the Russian combatant and effects the film's rapprochement of aristocratic warrior and peasant fighter.[75]

The theme is anticipated, and in a typically comic way, by Vaska, who, in his first scene in the movie, fingers a battle-ax in the marketplace of Novgorod while his beloved Olga fingers textiles. In the battle on the ice, all the major Russian characters—Alexander, Vaska, Gavrilo, Ignat—begin the fighting with sword in hand only to end up with an ax. Vaska has his sword knocked out of his hand and resorts—as we have seen—to pole and bucket before he is later seen attacking the Germans from the rear, disguised in their armor, wielding an ax. Gavrilo switches to an ax when a German kills the young Savka—significantly this is one time when a German is also portrayed using a battle-ax—and then, like Aeneas after the death of Pallas, performs an *aristeia* that breaks through the lines of the Teutonic knights' defensive formation. Alexander, according to the scenario, breaks his sword in his duel with the Grand Master of the knights—perhaps another comment on the inferior make of Russian armaments—and takes from the hands of a peasant onlooker an ax with which he defeats the enemy commander. (In the prints I have seen, Alexander is shown in one frame fighting the duel with a sword, in the next with an ax.)[76] Ignat hews down the German bishop's tent like a woodchopper with his ax, and the routed Germans in the last scenes of the battle are being hunted down by peasants armed with clubs and axes. In the fighting, the film's imagery suggests, aristocrats and folk have merged: the warrior's profession is seen as a form of work, while the peasant worker is raised into a hero.

This transformation of epic heroism into the exploits of a workers' army, the heroism not of an individual but of the masses, takes place under the aegis of Alexander, the strong leader who emerges to unify the nation at a time of crisis. It is Alexander who rises above regional rivalries and class differences and sustains a vision of a united Russia: "For Rus," he shouts as he leads his troops into battle, and "Rus" was the original title of Eisenstein's filmscript. A great antifascist work of art, *Alexander Nevsky* is also an apologia for Stalin's tyranny: an epic film that seems no less a piece of imperial propaganda—a brief for totalitarian one-man rule—than is the *Aeneid* in its glorification of Augustus. Eisenstein intended, however, to complicate his portrait of Alexander, the idealized Stalin, by ending his film not with the prince's triumphal march through Pskov in the present version—much like the satisfying triumph of Augustus on the Palatine that concludes the description of the shield of Aeneas—but with an episode based on the later career of the historical Alexander, who was continually forced to appease the Mongol masters of Russia.[77]

The original ending of the film was designed to link up with its beginning: where the Mongol envoy visited him, now Alexander travels to the court of the khan. Such summonings of Russian princelings to the Golden Horde were in fact common and commonly fatal: Alexander's father had died as a captive guest of the Mongols. Alexander repeatedly humbles himself before the Mongol ruler, but stops short of giving up his claim to rule the Russian people. The khan's wife meanwhile contrives to poison Alexander, who succumbs on his return home, but not before prophesying a great battle on the spot where he dies. The final scene of the film would have shown a great Russian army, led by Alexander's grandson, the prince of the newly powerful Moscow, routing the Mongols at Kulikovo: "The heavy Russian wedge silently carves through the Tartar horde."[78] In his memoirs, Eisenstein explained the idea of the original ending: Alexander would be shown "winning time by his humility for building up strength so that this enslaver of our land might also with time be overthrown, though not by his own hand, but by the sword of his descendant and follower, Dmitri Donskoi."[79]

Eisenstein movingly goes on to suggest that this "heroic deed of self-abasement" and temporizing reflected his own relationship to Stalin and the Communist party officials. The originally planned ending to *Alexander Nevsky* would have imaginatively reversed this relationship. The Alexander-Stalin who sacrifices his pride and his own life for the future good of Russia is an epic character on his way to being a tragic one: the Ivan the Terrible of Eisenstein's later film project. Eisenstein notes with some satisfaction that he was able to depict "the Russian state's first crowned autocrat" abasing himself before his boyars, even if he was not allowed to bring the "saintly prince . . . to his knees."[80] For the party censor appears to have felt that there was something subversive in this masochistic ending, where Alexander becomes heroic in the exercise not of strength but of restraint and humility; he may even have detected in it the suggestion that the best Stalin was a dead Stalin. Eisenstein recalled:

> A hand other than mine drew a red pencil mark after the scene about the defeat of the Germans.
> "The scenario finishes here," the words were passed on to me. "Such a fine prince could not die!"[81]

But perhaps it could not have been otherwise, and the censor-hack—was it Stalin himself?—was a good critic after all. *Alexander Nevsky* may represent itself as belonging to an epic genre that has run its historical course—to the point where the genre reverses its original political and class suppositions and becomes a revolutionary epic celebrating victory against imperial aggression and the triumph of the historically oppressed masses. But the film remains an epic of empire, for the emperor, the strongman Alexander, has not disappeared. If anything, the prince—and the Stalinist regime he allegorizes—seems a necessary condition for a film "epic" itself. When Eisenstein does try to do away with the Alexander in his proposed epilogue and alternate ending, his film reverts to generic type in a different way, for its final scene pictures the Russians not only as throwing off the Mongol yoke, but also as acting like Western imperialists in turn, their attacking wedge a successful version of the German wedge that was defeated at Lake Peipus, their victory the beginning of that conquest of central Asia and its peoples that Eisenstein would continue to depict in the campaign against Kazan in *Ivan the Terrible* and that would be the foundation of a greater Russian or Soviet state. The *Aeneid*, we have seen, coupled emperor *and* empire—centralized monarchy within the state *and* imperial conquest over other subject peoples—as if the two were mutually dependent. Lucan's critique of this formula in the *Pharsalia* would have removed the emperor and restored republican liberty, but kept the empire intact; and the same can be said for Eisenstein's original ending, which would have sacrificed Alexander so that—in the typical romantic construction of medieval epic where loss and humiliation lead to national redemption—Russia could fulfill her Manifest Destiny in the conquest of the East. The two endings of *Alexander Nevsky* may thus contest Virgil's epic ideology, but only by alternately choosing emperor *or* empire: as if the genre's fascination with the concentration of power demanded an identification either with the charismatic leader or with imperial expansion. Perhaps only Milton among epic poets could reject both kingship and territorial empire, displacing this concentrated power from human politics onto his God, and onto the will of the individual believer; but in doing so, he seemed to denature the genre itself. Eisenstein revived an epic tradition that he simultaneously subjected to an internal critique and revision: he continued the nineteenth-century quest for an alternative epic in the medieval past of the nation. And yet his film is emblematic of the ways in which this "new" epic could still look very like the old. To enter the genre at all was again to evoke ideological categories and patterns of thought that had proved suprisingly tenacious across two millennia: like the "fine prince," epic could not die.

NOTES

INTRODUCTION

1. Citations of the *Iliad* are taken from *The Iliad of Homer*, trans. Richmond Lattimore (Chicago and London, 1951).

2. See M. I. Finley, *The World of Odysseus* (New York, 1954; 2d rev. ed. London and New York, 1978).

3. Plutarch, *Life of Alexander* 15.7–8; *Plutarch's Lives*, trans. A. H. Clough (New York, 1902), 4:16–17.

4. See Cicero, *Pro Archias* 10.24, for the anecdote of Alexander standing at the tomb of Achilles and envying the hero who had Homer to sing his praises.

5. Herodotus, *Persian Wars* 7.43.

6. See the episode in Plutarch's *Life of Alexander* (37.5) where Alexander passes by the fallen statue of Xerxes; *Plutarch's Lives* 4:45.

7. Euripides, *Andromache* 695–98. I cite the translation of John Frederick Nims in *The Complete Greek Tragedies*, ed. David Grene and Richmond Lattimore (Chicago, 1959) 3:695–96. For the episode, see the *Life of Alexander* 50–52.2, especially 51.8; *Plutarch's Lives* 4:59–62.

8. Plutarch, *Life of Caesar* 11.5–6; *Plutarch's Lives* 4:99.

9. Valerius Maximus, *Factorum et Dictorum Memorabilium Libri* 8.14.2.

10. Juan Luis Vives, *De Causis Corruptarum Artium*, chap. 6; *Joannis Ludovici Vivis Valentini Opera Omnia* (1745; London, 1964), 6:105. I have not been able to trace a classical source for Vives's passage. For another humanist version of this formulation, see Jean Bodin, *Method for the Easy Comprehension of History*, trans. Beatrice Reynolds (New York, 1969), 13. Bodin asserts that the Turkish conqueror Selim modeled his career on that of Julius Caesar. See also Francisco Guicciardini, *Storia d'Italia* 13.9 (Bari, 1929), 4:44, who reports that Selim frequently read over the deeds of Alexander and Julius Caesar.

11. For critical discussions of this scene, see Otto Zwierlein, "Lucans Caesar in Troja," *Hermes* 114 (1986): 460–78; Frederick M. Ahl, *Lucan* (Ithaca and London, 1976), 214–22; W. Ralph Johnson, *Momentary Monsters* (Ithaca and London, 1987), 118–23.

12. All citations of the *Pharsalia* are taken from *Lucan*, trans. J. D. Duff, Loeb Classical Library (Cambridge, Mass., and London, 1962).

13. Roman epic had already contained political poems, notably the *Annales* of Ennius, before the *Aeneid*; still, the greatness of Virgil's poem lent a definitive power to its intervention into the tradition of the genre.

14. See Thomas M. Greene, *The Descent from Heaven: A Study in Epic Continuity* (New Haven and London, 1963).

15. For this useful distinction, see the first chapter of C. M. Bowra, *From Virgil to Milton* (London, 1945), 1–32. Like Bowra, I am interested primarily in this literary tradition of epic, and as the subtitle of my book suggests, it is intended as a rewriting of his still fundamental study.

16. See the pages on medieval epic and romance in Erich Auerbach, *Mimesis*,

trans. Willard Trask (Garden City, N.Y., 1957), 83–124. Of particular interest for this study are Auerbach's remarks, 107, on the "historico-politico function" of epic: "And indeed, the heroic epic *is* history, at least insofar as it recalls actual historical conditions—however much it may distort and simplify them—and insofar as its characters always perform a historico-political function."

17. On the dialectical relationship between quest and adventure in romance, see Riccardo Bruscagli, "*Ventura e inchiesta* fra Boiardo e Ariosto," in *Stagioni di civiltà estense* (Pisa, 1983), 87–126.

18. Joseph Schumpeter, "The Sociology of Imperialisms," in *Two Essays by Joseph Schumpeter*, trans. Heinz Norden (Cleveland and New York, 1955), 3–98.

19. Ibid., 61.

20. The eclectic critical practice referred to as the New Historicism has found, among students of Early Modern literature, its most influential voices in Stephen Greenblatt and Louis Adrian Montrose. For brief methodological statements, see Greenblatt, "The Forms of Power and the Power of Forms in the Renaissance," *Genre* 15 (1982): 1–4, and Montrose, "The Elizabethan Subject and the Spenserian Text," in *Literary Theory/Renaissance Texts*, ed. Patricia Parker and David Quint (Baltimore and London, 1986), 303–40, especially 303–7. Greenblatt's own practice moves adroitly between analogy and allusion, particularly in the essays on *King Lear* and *The Tempest* in *Shakespearean Negotiations* (Berkeley and Los Angeles, 1988), where his point of departure is a reinvestigation of Shakespeare's sources, clear cases of allusion; these may be compared to his earlier essay on *1 Henry IV* collected in the same volume.

The dependence on analogy in New Historical practice is reminiscent of the earlier structuralist criticism by Lucien Goldmann: see the discussion by Fredric Jameson in *The Political Unconscious* (Ithaca, 1981), 43–45. For a searching critique of the anti-humanist qualities of poststructuralist critical practice and theory, including Jameson's, and for the objection that the search for the analogy or *conjoncture* has been apt to make for bad history, see David Bromwich, *A Choice of Inheritance* (Cambridge, Mass., and London, 1989), 264–91.

21. Coming to this new critical practice from the field and perspective of a historian, Lynn Hunt, the editor of the influential volume of essays, *The New Cultural History* (Berkeley, Los Angeles, and London, 1989), is explicit: "history has been treated here as a branch of aesthetics rather than as the handmaiden of social theory" (21).

22. Jameson, *The Political Unconscious*, 79.

23. For Jameson on master narratives and the ideology of form, see *The Political Unconscious*, 34, 98–100.

24. Citations of *La Araucana* are taken from the text prepared by Ofelia Garza de del Castillo (Mexico City, 1972).

25. Caupolicán is echoed nine stanzas later by another chieftain, Tucapel, who says that he will alone defeat the Spaniards, "ahora sean divinos, ahora humanos" (8.27). The conquistadors apparently misunderstood the Amerindian expression, "to come from the sky"—which means something like "to come out of nowhere"—and thought that the Indians believed them to be gods; they then tried to use this claim to divinity to awe the natives. See Rolena Adorno, "The Negotiation of Fear in Cabeza de Vaca's *Naufragios*," *Representations* 33 (1991): 162–99, 183–84.

CHAPTER ONE
EPIC AND EMPIRE: VERSIONS OF ACTIUM

1. The scene of Actium has been discussed by other critics and readers of the *Aeneid*, and my analysis is variously indebted to them. My argument differs in its attempt at comprehensiveness and in its effort to demonstrate how metaphorical analogies relate the metonymically contiguous descriptions of the shield and unite the passage into a single whole. See the analysis in Ronald Syme, *The Roman Revolution* (Oxford, 1939), 296–98; Gerhard Binder, *Aeneas und Augustus* (Meisenhiem am Glan, 1971), 213–70; Philip Hardie, *Virgil's Aeneid, Cosmos and Imperium* (Oxford, 1986), 97–110; Eugene Vance, "Warfare and the Structure of Thought in Virgil's *Aeneid*," *Quaderni urbinati di cultura classica* 15 (1973): 111–62, especially 124–30, where Vance presents his own table of binary ideological oppositions; Page Dubois, *History, Rhetorical Description and the Epic* (Cambridge and Totowa, N.J., 1982), 43–47; and Sergio Zatti, *L'uniforme cristiano e il multiforme pagano* (Milan, 1983), 51–56, for a discussion of Tasso's imitation of the scene.

2. On Satan as Oriental despot, see Stevie Davies, *Images of Kingship in Paradise Lost* (Columbia, 1983), 57–88.

3. For an analysis of the enrichment of the patriciate through Rome's Eastern conquests, see E. Badian, *Roman Imperialism in the Late Republic* (1968; Ithaca, 1971). The rise of luxury in the second century B.C. is discussed by William V. Harris in *War and Imperialism in Republican Rome 327–70 B.C.* (Oxford, 1979), 86–93.

4. On Numanus, see N. M. Horsfall, "Numanus Remulus: Ethnography and Propaganda in *Aeneid* 9.958ff.," *Latomus* 30 (1971): 1108–16.

5. The real epic *locus classicus* for this anti-Eastern propaganda is Lentulus's condemnation of the Parthians in the *Pharsalia* 8.331–439. This passage is the model, in turn, for Jesus' rejection of Parthian arms in Book 3 of *Paradise Regained*. See below, Chapters 4 and 8.

6. So this Iliadic passage was read by Polybius (15.12), who cites it when he describes the confusion of the polyglot Carthaginian forces at the battle of Zama.

7. Tasso's passage imitates Caesar's assessment of Pompey's multinational troops in *Pharsalia* 7.272–74. As we shall see, Lucan's Pharsalia is an epic battle modeled on Virgil's Actium.

8. See Syme, *The Roman Revolution*, 465–66.

9. On these cosmocratic analogies, and for a larger discussion of the motif of gigantomachy in the *Aeneid*, see the excellent chapters in Hardie, *Virgil's Aeneid*, 85–156.

10. Virgil exploits a preceding classical tradition of gender definition and distinction. The chart of oppositions that I have drawn up for the description of Actium can be compared to the table of opposites that Aristotle attributes to the Pythagoreans in *Metaphysics* 986a, a table that includes a polarity between the sexes.

limit	unlimited
odd	even
one	plurality
right	left
male	female

resting	moving
straight	curved
light	darkness
good	bad
square	oblong

See *The Complete Works of Aristotle*, ed. Jonathan Barnes (Princeton, 1984), 2:1559. This Pythagorean Table of Opposites was to be a cornerstone in a subsequent tradition of misogyny. See Prudence Allen, *The Concept of Woman* (Montreal, 1985), 19–24, and, for her survey of ideas of gender in Aristotle and later classical writers to the time of Virgil, 83–167. I am indebted to Patricia Parker, *Literary Fat Ladies* (London, 1987), 181–85.

11. See W. W. Tarn and M. P. Charlesworth, *Octavian, Antony, and Cleopatra* (Cambridge, 1965), 101–5.

12. "Ventisque uocatis" appears at 3.253 and 5.211 without any Junonian implications; in Cleopatra's case, the winds do come, but only to sweep her toward her death. As we shall see below, Lucan interprets Cleopatra's passivity as an abandonment of control: his simile (*Pharsalia* 7.125–27) compares Pompey at Pharsalia to a pilot who forsakes the rudder and literally gives the ship to the winds. For Juno as air, see Michael Murrin, *The Allegorical Epic* (Chicago and London, 1980), 3–25.

13. This passage has been eloquently discussed by John Arthur Hanson in pp. 686–88 of his essay, "Vergil," in *Ancient Writers: Greece and Rome*, ed. T. James Luce (New York, 1982), 2:669–701.

14. *Orlando furioso* 41.42–45; *Gerusalemme liberata* 19.41, 20.73–74; *La Araucana* 34.5–15, 22–23; *Paradise Lost* 4.32–113. In the *Austriada* (1582) of Juan Rufo, Ali Baja, the commander of the Ottoman fleet at Lepanto, learns from his astrologer that the stars look unfavorably on his enterprise in the coming battle, that the *fates* (*hados*) are preparing *misfortunes* (*desventuras*) for the Muslim forces. Ali replies to this wager of chance with his own stoic fatalism and constancy.

> El cielo y el infierno echen el resto
> Que yo seré mas firme que diamante;
> De la vida triunfar puede la muerte,
> Que no de la virtud del varon fuerte.

> (22.85)

Ali is killed in the subsequent battle, fighting to the end, cursing Mohammed (24.26). The text of the *Austriada* is printed in *Poemas Epicos*, vol. 2, ed. Don Cayetano Rosell (Madrid, 1854), 1–130.

15. See Frederick Kiefer, "The Conflation of Fortuna and Occasio in Renaissance Thought and Iconography," *Journal of Renaissance and Medieval Studies* 9 (1979): 1–27. Fortune's boat is already a classical motif: Kiefer, 4, notes that both Ovid and Seneca "liken Fortune to a breeze filling the sails of a ship."

16. Polybius, *Histories* 1.3. *Polybius*, trans. W. R. Paton (New York and London, 1922), 1:7–9. On Polybius and universal history, see F. W. Walbank, *Polybius* (Berkeley, Los Angeles, and London, 1972), 67–68, and the review of Walbank by Arnaldo Momigliano, "The Historian's Skin," collected in *Essays in Ancient and Modern Historiography* (Oxford, 1977), 67–77.

17. Such flooding, which also recalls Achilles' battle with the overflowing Scamander in *Iliad* 21, becomes an epic topos in *Pharsalia* 4.48–120, where Caesar's camp and army are almost "shipwrecked" (87) and carried away by the flooding spring rivers of Spain. Here, significantly, the rain clouds come from the *East*, from Arabia and India (61–70). Francesco Bracciolini imitates this passage in the opening episode of his *La Croce Racquistata* (1613)—a less than great heroic poem—where the fallen angel and water demon, Hidrausse, causes the Euphrates, swollen with the streams of Mount Taurus, to flood the camp of the emperor Heraclius (1.9–25). Heraclius's first speech imitates the opening words of Aeneas caught in the sea storm of *Aeneid* 1: Heraclius wishes that he had found death in a battle worthy of memory (26–27). In answer to the prayers of the saintly Niceto, an angel of God descends and causes the flooding river to subside; Heraclius now imitates (938–39) the "O socii" speech that Aeneas makes after his fleet has safely reached the Libyan shore. Bracciolini's conflation of Lucan and Virgil demonstrates how the dread of submersion—in "Eastern" waters—may be the single greatest fear experienced by the Western epic hero.

18. For a particular version of the relationship of the epic verse scheme to a unified vision of history, see John Freccero, "The Significance of *Terza Rima*," in *Dante: The Poetics of Conversion* (Cambridge, Mass., and London, 1986), 258–71.

19. The analogy between imperial permanence and eschatology has received rich discussions in two works of Frank Kermode, *The Sense of an Ending* (London, Oxford, and New York, 1966), 3–31, and *The Classic* (Cambridge, Mass., and London, 1983), 15–45.

20. Polybius, *Histories* 3.1; *Polybius* 2:3.

21. The ideological closure to which this epic insistence upon a single narrative corresponds has elicited some suggestive remarks by M. M. Bakhtin, who sees in epic a sealed-off, sacrosanct vision of a national past. See the essay "Epic and Novel" in *The Dialogic Imagination*, ed. Michael Holquist (Austin and London, 1981), 16–17. In *De la Grammatologie* (Paris, 1967), Jacques Derrida has spoken, 130, of linearity as the "modèle *épique*" of Western thought and logic, a model that suppresses a "pluri-dimensionalité" of meaning.

22. Northrop Frye, *The Secular Scripture* (Cambridge, Mass., 1976), 15, 30. For the idea of adventure, an animating principle of romance, as an "island" of experience, see Georg Simmel, "The Adventurer," in *Georg Simmel 1858–1918: A Collection of Essays*, ed. Kurt H. Wolff (Columbus, 1959), 244. On the relationship of the digressive romance episode to epic teleology I am most indebted to Patricia Parker, *Inescapable Romance* (Princeton, 1979), and to James Nohrnberg, *The Analogy of the Faerie Queene* (Princeton, 1976), especially 1–22. See also my essay, "The Figure of Atlante: Ariosto and Bioardo's Poem," *MLN* 94 (1979): 77–91. In the present study I wish to show how the epic-romance dichotomy can yield political ideological meanings.

23. I follow the analysis of this episode by Nohrnberg, *The Analogy of the Faerie Queene*, 9–10.

24. On this central motif of the Italian romances, see A. Bartlett Giamatti, "Headlong Horses, Headless Horsemen: An Essay on the Chivalric Epics of Pulci, Boiardo, and Ariosto," in Giamatti, *Exile and Change in Renaissance Literature* (New Haven and London, 1984), 33–75.

25. Alcina's flight seems to be repeated and echoed by Agramante's flight—

"Fugge Agramante" (40.9)—from the climactic sea battle before Biserta. Thus this battle also becomes a kind of Actium; and like the defeated Cleopatra and Antony, Agramante contemplates suicide at 40.36.

26. The ineradicability of Alcina's presence—often as a double of the "reason" that would control or displace her—is discussed by Albert Russell Ascoli in *Ariosto's Bitter Harmony* (Princeton, 1987), 121–46. Ascoli writes, 221, of the "blindness, madness, and error which Platonism and Ariosto believe to be essential characteristics of life in the body."

27. For the prose allegory, see *Le prose diverse di Torquato Tasso*, ed. Cesare Guasti (Florence, 1875), 1:301–8. The *Liberata* spells out the allegory at 17.62–63, where Rinaldo is instructed to use his wrathful faculty to subdue "le cupidigie, empi nemici interni" (63), and to submit to a commander in chief who is either Goffredo, or reason, or both at once. See Murrin, *The Allegorical Epic*, 87–107.

28. For Tasso's treatment of Actium, see Zatti, *L'uniforme cristiano*, 51–56.

29. There is a further Miltonic version of this scene, where Tasso's Virgilian line is echoed, in turn, in Eve's urging suicide to Adam after the Fall in Book 10 of *Paradise Lost*: "so much of death her thoughts / Had entertained, as dyed her cheeks with pale." (10.1008–9). Eve, like the suicidal Armida and Virgil's Cleopatra and Dido before her, has taken on the pallor of death. But Adam dissuades her from this rash, if potentially "sublime" (1014) heroic act, arguing that they should not cut themselves and their descendants off from hope in God's mercy.

30. See Robert Durling, "The Epic Ideal," in *The Old World: Discovery and Rebirth*, ed. David Daiches and Anthony Thorlby (London, 1974), 105–46, 120–23. The revival of Aristotelian ideas of unity in sixteenth-century literary theory are, as Durling points out, deeply connected to the (re)unifying imperialist projects of the Counter-Reformation and of emergent nation-states.

31. The classic essay on the War in Heaven remains Arnold Stein, "Milton's War in Heaven—An Extended Metaphor," *ELH* 18 (1951): 201–20; also a chapter in Stein, *Answerable Style* (Minneapolis, 1953), 17–37, in which Stein points out that the war is funny. More recent commentators stress, as I do, more serious aspects of the episode. See Michael Lieb, *Poetics of the Holy* (Chapel Hill, 1981), 246–312; Stella Purce Revard, *The War in Heaven* (Ithaca and London, 1980); and James M. Freeman, *Milton and the Martial Muse* (Princeton, 1980).

32. For Charles and solar imagery, see Joan S. Bennett, *Reviving Liberty: Radical Christian Humanism in Milton's Great Poems*, (Cambridge, Mass., and London, 1989), 36–39, and Davies, *Images of Kingship*, 14–19. Davies, 121, mentions the cult of *sol invictus* in a larger discussion of Roman imperial imagery in *Paradise Lost*, 89–126.

33. Alastair Fowler notes that the Triumph of the Son falls at the very middle of the 10,550 verses of the first edition of *Paradise Lost* (1667); see Fowler, *Triumphal Forms* (Cambridge, 1970), 116–17.

34. See Harold Bloom, *A Map of Misreading* (New York, 1975), 125–40; Parker, *Inescapable Romance*, 130–35; David Quint, *Origin and Originality in Renaissance Literature* (New Haven and London, 1983), 207–18.

35. For a discussion of Milton's Chaos that stresses the split between poetic representation and explicit doctrinal formulation, see Regina Schwartz, "Milton's Hostile

Chaos: ... And the Sea Was no More," *ELH* 52 (1985): 337–74. See also A. B. Chambers, "Chaos in *Paradise Lost," Journal of the History of Ideas* 24 (1963): 55–84.

36. On Chaos and Babel, see Quint, *Origin and Originality*, 210–11. One might note how the Babelic quality of the War in Heaven repeats the linguistic multiplicity attributed by epic to defeated Easterners, the many nations, "variae linguis," who march in Augustus's triumph. Babel is itself the Bible's figure for the world-empire that gathers different nationalities under its rule.

37. See the illuminating chapter, "War," in Lieb, *Poetics of the Holy*, especially 277–82 on the humiliation of God's soldiers.

38. Uvedale's poem, which begins "Welcome, Dread Sir, to this now happy Ile," is included in *Britannia Rediviva* (Oxford, 1660). There are no page numbers in this anthology of poems, Latin and English, written by Oxford wits to greet the returning king.

39. The Achillean Iliadic model has long been noted by critics of the War in Heaven. Addison's commentary on Book 6 in the *Spectator* 333 (1712) also discusses models for the war in Hesiod's treatment of the battle of the Titans and Gods in the *Theogony*, Claudian's *Gigantomachy*, and the *theomachia* of *Iliad* 20; see Joseph Addison, *Criticism on Milton's Paradise Lost*, ed. Edward Arber (1869; New York, 1966), 92–96. For a more recent discussion, see Barbara Kiefer Lewalski, *Paradise Lost and the Rhetoric of Literary Forms* (Princeton, 1985), 59–62.

40. For a late antique version of Achilles' death that depends on the *Iliad* and appropriately uses the model of the death of Patroclus in Book 16, see Book 3, 21–185, of Quintus Smyrnaeus, *The Fall of Troy*, trans. Arthur S. Way (London and Cambridge, Mass., 1913). Wounded by the arrow of Apollo, Achilles protests against an enemy who has not fought him face-to-face.

41. See for example the funeral oration for the Venetian dead at Lepanto by Paolo Paruta (1572), included in *Orazioni scelte del secolo XVI*, ed. Giuseppe Lisio (1897; Florence, 1957), 306–7. Ferrante Carrafa composed the following sonnet in his collection of celebratory poems on Lepanto, *Dell'Austria* (Naples, 1572), Third Part, 19.

> Ottenne Augusto glorioso vanto
> D'aver nel seno Ambratio il gran Romano
> Vinto, dove vinceste l'Ottomano
> Voi signor degno d'altro grido, e canto.
> Che Cleopatra vinse quel, ch'a canto
> Huomini inermi havea, perche la mano
> Di Marco Antonio, anzi guerrier sovrano
> Soggettto era a colei col mortal manto.
> D'ebeno navi havea la gente imbelle,
> Ma Nembroth, Goliji, Tifei, giganti
> Vinceste voi, galee di quercie antiche.
> Ond'a l'ottava spera i sommi amanti
> Vostre glorie fatto han, vostre fatiche
> Di pingere, e scolpir di chiare stelle.

42. Juan Latino, *Ad Catholicum pariter et invictissimum Philippum ... Austrias Carmen* (Granada, 1573), 20; the text of the *Historia del Monserrate* is included in

Poemas Epicos, vol. 1, ed. Don Cayetano Rosell (Madrid, 1851), 503-70. I am indebted to Jack Winkler for the first reference, to Michael Murrin for the second.

43. For the text of the *Araucana*, I follow Alonso de Ercilla, *La Araucana*, introduced by Ofelia Garza de del Castillo (Mexico City, 1972).

CHAPTER TWO
REPETITION AND IDEOLOGY IN THE *AENEID*

1. Patricia Parker writes in *Inescapable Romance*, 42-43, "Commentators from Servius to the present have noted the way in which Virgil's poem incorporates not just the epic *agon* of the *Iliad* but also the 'errores' of the *Odyssey*, the poem customarily assimilated by Renaissance critics to romance." The idea that the *Odyssey* is to be assimilated with romance goes back to the first theorists of romance (of the chivalric *romanzo*), Giovambattista Pigna in his treatise *I romanzi* (Venice, 1554), 23-24, and Giovambatista Giraldi Cinzi, *Discorsi* (Venice, 1564), 65. See Bernard Weinberg, *A History of Literary Criticism in the Italian Renaissance* (Chicago and London, 1961), 445, 970. Parker suggests in a note (248, n. 36) that this epic/romance dichotomy fits Viktor Poschl's study of Iliadic versus Odyssean elements of the *Aeneid* in *The Art of Vergil*, trans. Gerda Seligson (Ann Arbor, 1962), 24-33. See also the remarks of James Nohrnberg in *The Analogy of the Faerie Queene* (Princeton, 1976), 9-11.

2. Peter Brooks, *Reading for the Plot* (New York, 1985), 99-100.

3. A discussion of the implications of these virtues, together with a survey of the critical literature on the issue, can be found in Gabriele Thome, *Gestalt und Funktion des Mezentius bei Vergil—mit einem Ausblick auf die Schlusszene der Aeneis* (Frankfurt, Berne, and Las Vegas, 1979), 297-347. Alessandro Barchiesi sees the same conflict between *clementia* and *pietas*—which he describes in terms of *misericordia* and *ultio*—informing the ending of the *Aeneid* in a reading that has been very helpful to my own interpretation of the epic; see Barchiesi, *La traccia del modello* (Pisa, 1984), 91-122, especially 119-22.

4. Fredric Jameson has made it his critical project to uncover such ideological workings in the strategies of repression of the social body; see his exciting pages on Northrop Frye and Levi-Strauss in the opening chapter of *The Political Unconscious* (Ithaca, 1981), 68-79. But Jameson's implicit faith that criticism can undo the ideological force of literary (and social) fictions and restore health to a human community should be compared with Franco Moretti's sardonic view that "health" or the reality principle resides in those fictions themselves: "[Literature] makes us realize that 'consent'—feeling that we 'want' to do what we 'have' to do—can be one of the highest aspirations of the individual psyche. It tells us, in other words, that in the absence of great battles (and therefore—the point cannot be suppressed—in the absence of what could be great tragedies), it is inevitable that from time to time one will try to convince oneself that this is really the best of all possible worlds." Moretti, *Signs Taken for Wonders* (London and New York, 1988), 40. The *Aeneid* has its battles and tragedies: its psychic analogy may not, perhaps, suggest that Augustan Rome is the best of all possible worlds, but that it is, nonetheless, the only world possible and the one we must make the best of.

5. See Frank Kermode, *The Classic* (Cambridge, Mass., and London, 1983), and

W. R. Johnson, *Darkness Visible* (Berkeley, Los Angeles, and London, 1976). Both attack the politically disreputable aspects of Eliot's particular canonization of Virgil. But while Kermode seems tacitly to accept Eliot's view of the *Aeneid*, Johnson, 1–22, offers a brilliant rebuttal; the burden of *Darkness Visible* is to demonstrate a nihilistic pessimism running through Virgil's epic that swallows up altogether the political and propagandistic dimensions of the poem. I contend that these are central to the *Aeneid*, and that the power and complexity of the poem lie precisely in its exploration of the terms of imperial ideology that inform its fictions.

6. For the *Aeneid's* identification of Aeneas—and Augustus—with Romulus, see Gerhard Binder, *Aeneas und Augustus* (Meisenheim am Glan, 1971), 31–38, 118–22, 137–41. Binder surveys the figure of Romulus in Augustan propaganda before and after Virgil's epic at pp. 157–69.

7. For readings of Book 3, see the studies of Robert B. Lloyd, "*Aeneid* III: A New Approach," *AJPh* 78 (1957):133–51, and "*Aeneid* III and the Aeneas Legend," *AJPh* 78 (1957):383–400; Michael C. J. Putnam, "The Third Book of the *Aeneid*: From Homer to Rome," *Ramus* 9 (1980):1–21, reprinted in Putnam, *Essays on Latin Lyric, Elegy, and Epic* (Princeton, 1982), 267–87. Sections devoted to Book 3 are found in Brooks Otis, *Vergil: A Study in Civilized Poetry* (Oxford, 1963), 251–64; Friedrich Klingner, *Virgil* (Zurich and Stuttgart, 1967), 420–36; and Mario di Cesare, *The Altar and the City* (New York and London, 1974), 61–76. A fine reading of the Buthrotum episode that describes Andromache and Helenus as the "living dead" is contained in Lowry Nelson, Jr., "Baudelaire and Virgil: A Reading of 'Le Cygne,'" *Comparative Literature* 13 (1961):332–45.

8. In Thrace, Aeneas proffers the portent of Polydorus for Anchises' interpretation (58). While Aeneas asks Apollo for his oracle on Delos (84–89), Anchises explicates—incorrectly, as it turns out—its meaning. Confronted by plague on Crete, Anchises urges a return to Delos (144–46), but his plan is scrubbed when the Penates appear to Aeneas (147–71) and send him on his true course to Italy; it is Anchises, nonetheless, who gives the orders to leave Crete (182–89). Similarly, on the Strophades Anchises prays to the gods to avert Celaeno's prophecy and orders the Trojans to put to sea (264–67). Aeneas sets up his Trophy at Actium (286–88), and he is the main protagonist of the encounter with Andromache and Helenus at Buthrotum. But Anchises, too, is honored by gifts (469) and by the praise of the seer (475–81), and he commands the ships to set sail (472–73). Anchises performs the libations at the sighting of Italy (525–29), and he interprets the omen of the horses (539–43). He gives warning when Charybdis is near (558–60), and extends his hand to the suppliant Achaemenides (610–11).

For a similar summary and a discussion of the roles played by the hero and his father in Book 3, see the valuable commentary of R. D. Williams in his edition of *Aeneidos Liber Tertius* (Oxford, 1962), 3–7. The discrepancy between the Anchises of Book 2 and the one of Book 3 is noted by W. H. Semple, "A Short Study of *Aeneid, Book III*," *Bulletin of the Rylands Library* 38 (1959):225–40. Semple, 229, explains the discrepancy away by arguing that Book 3 may originally have been the first book of an earlier version of Virgil's poem.

9. This Odyssean echo is noted by G. N. Knauer in *Die Aeneis und Homer*, "Hypomnemata" 7 (Göttingen, 1964), 383. Klingner, *Virgil*, 426–27, suggests parallels with the Odyssean underworld.

10. David F. Bright, "Aeneas' Other Nekyia," *Vergilius* 27 (1981):40–47.

11. See Bright, "Aeneas' Other Nekyia," 43, and, for an analysis of the whole scene, Richard E. Grimm, "Aeneas and Andromache in *Aeneid* III," *AJPh* 88 (1967):151–62.

12. One might add that the episode on Crete also adumbrates this theme, for the plague that ravages the island may be identical to the one that drove away Idomeneus (121–23) after he sacrificed his own son. M. Owen Lee discusses Virgil's themes of filial relationship in *Fathers and Sons in Virgil's Aeneid: Tum Genitor Natum* (Albany, 1979). See especially 1–7, 46–50, 96–104. For some remarks on the role of fatherhood in the *Aeneid* and in epic in general, see A. Bartlett Giamatti, *Play of Double Senses: Spenser's Faerie Queene* (Englewood Cliffs, N.J., 1975), 17–24.

13. At the climax of Book 4, when Dido falls on Aeneas's sword, the wailing of her women is compared to a lamentation for the city of Carthage itself, falling before its enemy and in flames (669–71). This simile, proleptic of the history of the city that Rome will eventually destroy in 146 B.C., is modeled on the Homeric simile describing the lament that goes up in Troy at Hector's death in *Iliad* 22.410–11: "It was most like what would have happened, if all lowering / Ilion had been burning top to bottom in fire."

14. See Robert B. Lloyd, "The Character of Anchises in the *Aeneid*," *TAPA* 88 (1957):44–55.

15. While it overstates its case, D. L. Drew's *The Allegory of the Aeneid* (Oxford, 1927) remains a useful starting point for an examination of the historical allusions in the *Aeneid*. See also the fine pages of W. A. Camps, *An Introduction to Virgil's Aeneid* (Oxford, 1969), 95–104, 137–43.

16. Ronald Syme, *The Roman Revolution* (Oxford, 1939), 317.

17. Ibid., 317–18.

18. The genealogies contained in the *Aeneid* are inconsistent, probably deliberately so. In Book 6, the line of Romulus is descended through Silvius (762), Aeneas's Italian son by Lavinia; but in Book 8 (629) and perhaps also in Book 1 (267ff.), this line seems to derive from Ascanius. Dionysius of Halicarnassus (*Roman Antiquities* 1.70.3–4) recounts that Silvius, the ancestor of Romulus, ascended the throne of Alba Longa after the death of his older brother Ascanius and in opposition to Ascanius's eldest son Iulus, from whom the Julian house descended. Dionysius's version looks suspiciously like official propaganda: by its terms, Augustus's new foundation of Rome also restores the Julii to a rightful place of sovereignty from which all previous Roman history had dispossessed them. See also Livy's account (1.3), which suggests the possibility that there were two different sons of Aeneas named Ascanius: the elder one the son of Creusa, from whom the Julian line claims descent; the younger the son of Lavinia and the father of Silvius. For the background, see R. M. Ogilvie, *A Commentary on Livy, Books 1–5* (Oxford, 1965), 42–43.

19. There was, however, an extensive and long-standing tradition that Trojan refugees had come to Italy. See Arnaldo Momigliano, "How to Reconcile Greeks and Trojans," *Mededelingen der Koninklijke Nederlandse Akademie van Wetenschappen, Afd. Letterkunde* N. R. 45 (1982):231–54. See also *Enea nel Lazio: Archeologia e mito* (Rome, 1981) and F. Castagnoli, "La leggenda di Enea nel Lazio," *Studi Romani* 30 (1982):1–15.

20. William S. Anderson, "Vergil's Second *Iliad*," *TAPA* 88 (1957):17–30.

21. Ibid., 24–25.

22. The double Iliadic model for the stone-throwing Turnus, the textual starting point for the reading that follows, was noted by Margery W. Mackenzie in "Who Is Vergil's Aeneas? (A plea to let him be himself)," *Vergilius* 10 (1964):1–6. This short essay does not relate the scene to its earlier anticipations in the *Aeneid*, and its findings are inconclusive. Mackenzie's work is briefly touched on by W. R. Nethercut in "The Imagery of the *Aeneid*," *Classical Journal* 67 (1971–1972):123–43, 137. See also the more recent treatment of Virgil's Homeric imitation in Lawrence Lipking, *The Life of the Poet* (Chicago and London, 1981), 86–88.

23. Mackenzie, "Who Is Vergil's Aeneas?" 5, notes that the Iliadic Aeneas, like Turnus at the end of the *Aeneid*, is wounded in the thigh.

24. This verse has been considered an interpolation by editors because it so closely resembles 2.197. It is, however, attested to in all manuscripts of the poem. The fact that it fits into a larger pattern of verses coupling Achilles and Diomedes suggests that it is indeed genuine and belongs where it is. See the commentary of R. D. Williams to *The Aeneid of Virgil*, Books 7–12 (London, 1973), 409.

25. *The Standard Edition of the Complete Psychological Works of Sigmund Freud*, ed. James Strachey et al., 24 vols. (London, 1953–1974), 18:17.

26. But see, for another view, the important essay of Michael C. J. Putnam, "Possessiveness, Sexuality and Heroism in the *Aeneid*," *Vergilius* 31 (1985):1–21. Putnam persuasively uncovers the poem's suggestion of a love relationship between Aeneas and Pallas, one that would correspond to the physical love that a post-Homeric tradition ascribed to the relationship between Achilles and Patroclus. Putnam reads the end of the poem and the killing of Turnus as an explosion of repressed sexual passion that calls into question the possibility of a Roman civilizing mission.

27. See, for instance, Johnson's analysis of this scene in *Darkness Visible*, 123–34. Some consideration of the Odyssean model might have qualified the unremitting pessimism that he sees in Virgil's scene.

28. The Odyssean parallel is noted by Knauer, *Die Aeneis und Homer*, 430.

29. *The Odyssey of Homer*, trans. Richmond Lattimore (New York, 1965), 357.

30. On *pietas*, see Syme, *The Roman Revolution*, 156; see also Syme, *Tacitus* (Oxford, 1958), 1:414–15, on both *pietas* and *clementia*.

31. Citations from the *Metamorphoses* are taken from the Loeb Classical Library edition, with a translation by Frank Justus Miller (Cambridge, Mass., and London, 1971), 2 vols.

32. Against an ironic reading of the panegyrical passages of the *Metamorphoses*, see the arguments of Gordon Williams in *Change and Decline: Roman Literature in the Early Empire* (Berkeley, Los Angeles, and London, 1978), 87–96.

33. See Propertius 2.31.1–4 for a description of the temple. Paul Zanker has studied the Augustan building projects and the propagandistic symbolism of the art of the new regime in *The Power of Images in the Age of Augustus*, trans. Alan Shapiro (Ann Arbor, 1988). He discusses the temple of Apollo on the Palatine, 65–70 and 84–89, and he sugggests, 85–86, that the statues of the Danaids "prompted thoughts of guilt and expiation."

34. This political dimension of the baldric of Pallas adds another layer of meaning to the reading of the baldric advanced by Gian Biagio Conte in *The Rhetoric of Imitation* (Ithaca and London, 1986), 185–95.

35. Barchiesi, *La traccia del modello*, 111–19. The connection between the two

passages is also drawn by Michael C. J. Putnam in *"Pius* Aeneas and the Metamorphosis of Lausus," *Arethusa* 14 (1981):152–53, reprinted in Putnam, *Essays on Latin Lyric, Elegy, and Epic* (Princeton, 1982), 324–25.

36. When Turnus invokes Anchises, the scene also looks back to the pleas of the suppliant Mago in Book 10.521f. Mago calls upon the "patrios manis" (524) of Anchises, only to be told by Aeneas that the "patris Anchisae manes" (534) enjoins him to take the enemy warrior's life: "hoc patris Anchisae manes, hoc sentit Iulus." (The inclusion of Iulus may help to remind us of the connection between Anchises and Julius Caesar.) This line is recalled when Aeneas kills Turnus and claims to be authorized by Pallas himself: "Pallas te hoc vulnere, Pallas" (12.948). But see the argument of W. A. Camps, *An Introduction,* 141–42, that links both Anchises *and* Pallas as figures of the dead Caesar whom Aeneas-Augustus must revenge. For Pallas and Julius Caesar, see also C. M. Bowra, *From Virgil to Milton* (London and Basingstoke, 1945), 68–69.

37. Rene Girard has provided a model for thinking about doubling, violence, and civil war. My thinking is variously indebted to Girard, *La Violence et le sacré* (Paris, 1972).

38. These doubling echoes have been noted by Michael C. J. Putnam in *The Poetry of the Aeneid* (1965; Ithaca and London, 1988), 200–201; 228, n. 20.

39. I am citing the translation of Michael Grant of *The Annals of Imperial Rome* (Hammondsworth, 1971), 37–38.

40. See the analysis in Syme, *Tacitus,* 1:431–32.

41. William Butler Yeats delivered the most crushing verdict on Virgil's hero by retelling the reaction of a "plain sailor man" who took a notion to study Latin and the *Aeneid*: "Ach a hero, him a hero? Bigob, I t'ought he waz a priest." The story is recounted by Ezra Pound in *A B C of Reading* (New Haven, 1934), 31. For a probing discussion of the character of Aeneas to which I am much indebted in what follows, see Thomas Greene, *The Descent from Heaven: A Study in Epic Continuity* (New Haven and London, 1963), 85–93. See also Richard Heinze, *Virgils Epische Technik* (Leipzig and Berlin, 1908), 269–77, for a discussion of the character development of Aeneas, particularly from the first to the second half of the poem.

42. Syme, *The Roman Revolution,* 442.

43. The fate that Venus proposes for Ascanius echoes the one that Hippolytus-Virbius is said to enjoy at 7.776–77. For the epic tradition of the romance garden, see A. Bartlett Giamatti, *The Earthly Paradise and the Renaissance Epic* (Princeton, 1966).

44. For a thorough examination of the discrepancies in the two versions of the death of Palinurus, and for the argument for Virgil's change of plan, see Gordon Williams, *Technique and Ideas in the Aeneid* (New Haven and London, 1983), 281–82. Putnam offers a valuable reading of the Palinurus episode, placing it in relationship to the boat race during the funeral games for Anchises earlier in Book 5; see *The Poetry of the Aeneid,* 64–104.

45. Knauer, *Die Aeneis und Homer,* 373, sees the death of the falling Orontes as a parallel to the death of the unnamed steersman of Odysseus. For the connection between Orontes and Palinurus, see James J. O'Hara, *Death and the Optimistic Prophecy in Vergil's Aeneid* (Princeton, 1990), 7–24, 107–11.

46. Greene, *The Descent from Heaven,* 20–22.

47. Putnam, *The Poetry of the Aeneid,* 97.

48. See Seneca, *De Beneficiis* 5.17.5 and also *Epistulae* 12.9.

49. For a similar distinction, see the discussion of Frederick M. Ahl in *Lucan: An Introduction* (Ithaca and London, 1976), 300.

50. On Caesar and *Fortuna*, particularly for the relationship of Venus Victrix with Fortune, see Ahl, *Lucan*, 287–93.

51. See Greene, *The Descent from Heaven*, 92, on Aeneas in this scene: "he also reveals—the impassivity of the public executioner."

52. See Book 3 of the *Discorsi del poema eroico* in Tasso, *Prose*, ed. Ettore Mazzali (Milan and Naples, 1959), 611. For a recent critical justification of the killing of Turnus, see H.-P. Stahl, "The Death of Turnus: Augustan Vergil and the Political Rival," in *Between Republic and Empire*, ed. Kurt A. Raaflaub and Mark Toher (Berkeley, Los Angeles, and Oxford, 1990), 174–211. Stahl credits Virgil with little ambiguity of thought or feeling in the episode.

CHAPTER THREE
THE EPIC CURSE AND CAMOES' ADAMASTOR

1. So Villagrá's Zaldívar proclaims at the end of canto 33: "A qui fue Troia"; Gaspar Perez de Villagrá, *Historia de la Nueva Mexico*, (Alcalà, 1610), 276v. The poem has been translated by Gilbert Espinosoa and annotated by F. W. Hodge as *History of New Mexico* (Los Angeles, 1933).

2. Villagrá, *Historia de la Nueva Mexico*, 285r; my translation.

3. See, for example, Paul Horgan, *Great River: The Rio Grande in North American History*, 2 vols. (New York, 1954), 1:209.

4. The indebtedness of Villagrá's episode to the *Araucana* has been noted by Daniel Wogan in "Ercilla y la poesía mexicana," *Revista iberoamericana* 3, no. 6 (1941):371–79, especially 374–75.

5. Gerónimo de Bibar, *Crónica y relación copiosa y verdadera de los regnos de Chile hecha por Gerónimo de Bibar natural de Burgos MDLVIII*, ed. Irving Leonard, 2 vols. (Santiago, 1966), 2:203.

6. Alonso de Góngora Marmolejo, *Historia de Chile*, chap. 26, in *Colleción de historiadores de Chile y documentos relativos a la historia nacional*, vol. 2 (Santiago, 1862), 76. Marmolejo may have written to counter Ercilla's poem, and he shows little of Ercilla's sympathy for their Araucanian foes. See his remarks on Ercilla in his dedicatory letter (xii). But his description of the aftermath of Millarapue presumably cannot be a response or rival version to Ercilla's account, which he would not have known: it appeared in the second part of the *Araucana* in 1578, two years after Marmolejo's death. Since Ercilla, Bibar, and Marmolejo all claim to present eyewitness reports, there is little way to determine the actual historical facts over which they disagree.

7. Villagrá, *Historia*, 280r. See also Bibar, *Crónica* 2:203, who compares the Araucanians who hang themselves to "aquellos antiguos numantinos." For the sixteenth-century sources that lie behind Cervantes' *Cerco de Numancia* (and also Francisco de Rojas-Zorilla's two Numantia plays), see Cervantes, *Comedias y entremeses*, ed. Rodolfo Schevill and Adolfo Bonilla, 6 vols. (Madrid, 1922), 6:38–60. For an anti-imperialist reading of the Cervantes play that links it to the *Araucana*, see Willard F. King, "Cervantes' *Numancia* and Imperial Spain," *Modern Language Notes* 94 (1979):200–221.

8. See the chillingly cynical comments of Appian in the *Roman Histories* 6.15.98.

9. Along with the *Historia*, Villagrá two years later published a pamphlet, exonerating Oñate: *El Capitan Gaspar de Villagrá para justificcación de la muertes, justicias, y castigos que el Adelantado don Iuan de Oñate dizen que hizo en la Nueva Mexico* (Madrid, 1612). I am indebted for this reference to Michael Murrin, who is preparing a full discussion of Villagrá and Acoma. The documents surrounding Oñate's career and trial have been collected and translated by George P. Hammond and Agapito Rey in *Don Juan de Oñate: Colonizer of New Mexico, 1595–1628*, 2 vols. (Albuquerque, 1953). Villagrá was himself tried and ultimately found guilty, but for unrelated charges: he had executed two deserters without trial and written a letter to the Mexican viceroy falsely extolling the richness and fertility of New Mexico. See *Don Juan de Oñate*, 2:1116.

10. Max Horkheimer and Theodor W. Adorno, *Dialectic of Enlightenment*, trans. John Cumming (New York, 1972), 43–69. See also Norman Austin, *Archery at the Dark of the Moon* (Berkeley, 1975), 143–49.

11. See John H. Finley, *Homer's Odyssey* (Cambridge, Mass., 1978), 61–63; and, for a negative argument, M. I. Finley, *The World of Odysseus* (New York, 1980), 156.

12. Tieresias tells Odysseus (*Odyssey* 11.126–31) that he must sail to a place where shipping itself is unknown—where his oar will be mistaken for a winnowing fan. Just where this might be in the Mediterranean world is unclear, and suggests that this will be a very long, if not endless, quest.

13. One can compare the famous passage in Chapter 3 of Rousseau's *Essay on the Origin of Languages*: "Upon meeting others a savage man will initially be frightened. Because of his fear he sees others as bigger and stronger than himself. He calls them *giants*"; *On the Origin of Language: Two Essays by Jean-Jacques Rousseau and Johann Gottfried Herder*, trans. John H. Moran and Alexander Gode (New York, 1966), 13. Rousseau is anticipated—perhaps inspired—by a narrative of a Renaissance European explorer in the New World. In his celebrated account of his wanderings, Cabeza de Vaca remarks of the Indians that he and his companions first encountered after being shipwrecked off the coast of Texas in 1528: "Whatever their stature, they looked like giants to us in our fright." See Chapter 18 of de Vaca, *Adventures in the Unknown Interior of America*, trans. and ed. Cyclone Covey (New York, 1961), 56.

14. This backward pattern, to which Virgil tips off the reader at 3.690–91—"talia monstrabat *relegans errata retrorsus* / *litora* Achaemenides comes infelicis Vlixi" (my emphases)—has been discussed in Chapter 2 of this book. The visit to the Cyclopes' coast and to Carthage belong to the *end* of Aeneas's Odyssean wanderings, while the episode of Polyphemus in *Odyssey* 9 takes place toward the beginning of the wanderings of Odysseus; similarly, the eating of the cattle on the island of the Harpies, which occurs earlier in the journey of Aeneas (3.209–67), corresponds to the eating of the cattle of Helios in *Odyssey* 12, the final episode of Odysseus's narrated wanderings. But this pattern of reversal is also countered by the storm of *Aeneid* 1, which, in the chronological order of Aeneas's voyage, follows the episode of the Cyclopes at the end of Book 3 and partly corresponds to the storm at the end of *Odyssey* 12 that drives Odysseus to Calypso's island (here the *Aeneid* seems to follow the order of its Homeric model). Similarly, Virgil places a prophetic curse in the mouth of the Harpy Celaeno that recalls the curse of Polyphemus and suggests a correspondence be-

tween the Harpy episode and the Homeric episode of the Cyclopes—again conforming to the narrative order of the *Odyssey*.

Celaeno's curse—that the Trojans will be so consumed with hunger that they will eat their tables (3.255–57)—turns out to have a happy resolution in Book 7 when Ascanius jokes that the Trojans' bread cakes are edible tables (7.116f.). The monster's curse is thus comically appropriated by her enemies—and Aeneas, in fact, attributes her prophecy to Anchises (123), completely removing Celaeno from memory. Celaeno is related to Dido through her curse and her gender (both are female versions of Polyphemus), and the impotence of her prophecy may reflect in miniature upon Dido's own curse, which, however effective it may be in summoning up Hannibal and the Punic Wars, and perhaps Cleopatra after them, cannot stop the eventual victory of Roman power.

15. Dido here recalls not only Penelope but also Nausicaa, at *Odyssey* 6.283–84. Nausicaa, like the other women Odysseus encounters in his wanderings (Arete, Circe, Calypso), is a kind of prefiguration—or a representative of certain aspects—of Penelope, the goal of his voyage.

16. The view of the Carthaginian coast in Book 1 is, in fact, a *conflation* of the description of Ithaca in *Odyssey* 13 with the description of the harbor of the Laistrygonians in *Odyssey* 10.87–94. Thus from the very beginning Carthage is seen in its double aspect: as a potential homeland and site of a high civilization rivaling Rome *and* as a place of monstrous cannibalism. Moreover, the allusion to the Laistrygonians frames the entire Carthage episode. For while Aeneas's cutting of the anchor cables of his ships to escape in haste from Carthage echoes within the *Aeneid* his flight from the coast of the Cyclopes, it also imitates *Odyssey* 10.126–27, where Odysseus similarly cuts the ship ropes in order to save his crew from the Laistrygonians. The Cyclopes and the Laistrygonians are coupled in the *Odyssey* (10.199–200) by their monstrous size and cannibalism.

17. See the preceding note for the Odyssean parallel.

18. In the case recorded in Chapter 2 of *The Psychopathology of Everyday Life*, Freud describes a young Jewish man "of academic background" obsessed with the (misquoted) words of Dido's curse. See *The Standard Edition of the Complete Psychological Works of Sigmund Freud*, ed. James Strachey et al., 24 vols. (London, 1953–1974), 6:8–14. It seems likely that Freud was referring to himself, for in *The Interpretation of Dreams*, Chapter 5b, he describes his own identification with Hannibal and the Carthaginians and his inability to reach Christian Rome; *Standard Edition*, 4:195–98. In *Fin-de-Siècle Vienna* (New York, 1980), 181–207, Carl E. Schorske discusses this latter passage in a stimulating reading that shows how Freud's feelings of political resentment and resistance could be internalized by his psychoanalytic theory.

19. There are two versions of the myth of the Phoenix. The one in which the bird immolates itself and is reborn from its ashes can only be unambiguously attested after the time of Virgil: in poems of Statius (*Sylvae* 2.4.37) and Martial (5.7). An earlier attested version describes the young Phoenix generated out of the decomposing body of its parent and then burning the parent's body in an act of piety: see the version attributed to Manilius in Pliny's *Natural History* 10.4 and, for a parallel account, Pomponius Mela, *De Chorographia* 3.84. But see the persuasive arguments of R. Van den Broek for the equal antiquity of the myth of generation from self-immolation in *The Myth of the Phoenix* (Leiden, 1972), 409–11.

20. Servius on *Aeneid* 4.581, in *Servianorum in Vergilii carmina commentariorum,* ed. A. F. Stocker and A. H. Travis (Oxford, 1965), 420.

21. See the excellent discussion in Frederick M. Ahl, *Lucan: An Introduction* (Ithaca and London, 1976), 88–107.

22. Tasso's imitations of Silius are particularly numerous in canto 9, where Solimano's attack on the Crusader army is modeled on the battle of Cannae in Books 9–10 of the *Punica.* Solimano's promise of booty to his Arab troops repeats Hannibal's exhortation on the eve of Cannae (9.195f.); the episode of Latino and his sons (9.27–39) imitates Silius's Crista (10.92–169), and the simile of the lioness at octave 29 repeats 10.124–27. Further, the death of Lesbino, the object of Solimano's pederastic affection (9.81–88), is modeled upon the death of Cinyps, the favorite of Hannibal, in *Punica* 12.226–52.

23. I risk oversimplification here, for, as usual, Virgil has it at least two ways. Dido seems to regain her composure and dignity following her curse and at the moment of her suicide, 4.651f.; her words at verse 653—"uixi et quem dederat cursum Fortuna peregi"—earned the admiration of Seneca (*De Beneficiis* 5.17.5). Thus her death combines stoic autonomy and fatalism with an erotic loss of self-mastery. See the commentary of R. G. Austin to P. *Vergilii Maronis Aeneidos liber quartus* (Oxford, 1955), 188–90.

24. See W. W. Tarn and M. P. Charlesworth, *Octavian, Antony, and Cleopatra* (Cambridge, 1965), 137–39.

25. The classical models of the Adamastor episode have been excellently traced by Américo da Costa Ramalho in his *Estudios Camonianos* (Coimbra, 1975), 33–53.

26. Ibid., 35.

27. Frank Pierce notes parenthetically that the waterspout is "a kind of natural Adamastor" in his essay, "Camoes' Adamastor," in *Hispanic Studies in Honour of Joesph Manson* (Oxford, 1972), 207–15. There are helpful remarks on the Adamastor episode in C. M. Bowra, *From Virgil to Milton* (London and Basingstoke, 1945), 123–25.

28. Cf. Decade 1, Book 3, Chapters 3–4, of the *Asia de Joam de Barros,* ed. António Baiao (Coimbra, 1932), 127–29; Part 1, Chapter 35, of Damião de Góis, *Cronica do Felicissimo Rei D. Manuel,* ed. David Lopes Gagean (Coimbra, 1949) 1:74–75. For the log of da Gama's voyage, see *Portuguese Voyages 1498–1663,* ed. Charles David Ley (London and New York, 1947), 5–6.

29. De Góis, *Cronica,* 1:75.

30. Ramalho, *Estudios,* 44–45, sees a connection between the allusion to Antaeus and the giant Adamastor.

31. For a description of the "dialectical" literary imitation at work here in Camões' rewriting of Homer, see the heuristic model proposed by Thomas M. Greene in *The Light in Troy* (New Haven and London, 1982), 45–47.

32. This was a not untypical expression of Portuguese attitudes toward the natives of black Africa, although these attitudes could vary considerably with respect to different African peoples and in different regions. See C. R. Boxer, *Race Relations in the Portuguese Colonial Empire, 1415–1825* (Oxford, 1963).

33. See for example Giovanni Boccaccio in Book 3 of the *Genealogie deorum gentilium libri,* ed. Vincenzo Romano, 2 vols. (Bari, 1951), 1:122–23; and Natalis Comes in Book 8, Chapter 2, of *Natalis Comitis mythologiae* (Padua, 1616), 428–30.

34. On the critical debates over narrative discontinuity in the *Orlando Furioso*, see Daniel Javitch, *Proclaiming a Classic* (Princeton, 1991), 86–105.

35. This conclusion is briefly considered by Cleonice Berardinelli in her *Estudios camonianos* (Rio de Janeiro, 1973), 40.

36. The comparison of daring seafarers to rebellious giants has a classical model in the *Silvae* of Statius (3.2).

> Quis rude et abscissum miseris animantibus aequor
> fecit iter solidaeque pios telluris alumnos
> expulit in fluctus pelagoque immisit hianti
> audax ingenii? nec enim temeraria virtus
> illa magis, summae gelidum quae Pelion Ossae
> iunxit anhelantemque iugis bis pressit Olympum.
>
> (61–66)

(Who made the rough and sundered sea a path for miserable mortals, and, daring of character, cast the devoted children of the firm earth out onto the waves and threw them into the yawning ocean? For not more presumptuous was the valor that joined frozen Pelion to the top of Ossa and pressed upon panting Olympus with the double mountains.)

See *Statius*, trans. J. H. Mozely, 2 vols., Loeb Classical Library (London and Cambridge, Mass., 1961), 1:160. For Rabelais's treatment of this topos, see the *Tiers Livre*, Chapter 51.

37. Herman Melville, *Billy Budd*, chap. 7, in *Shorter Novels of Herman Melville*, ed. Raymond Weaver (New York, 1928), 255.

38. On Celaeno, see note 14 above.

39. Both text and translation are cited from *Fracastoro's Syphilis*, ed. and trans. Geoffrey Eatough (Liverpool, 1984).

40. *The Works of Joel Barlow*, facsimile reproduction, ed. William K. Bottorff and Arthur L. Ford (Gainesville, 1970), 2:672. All passages from the *Columbiad* are cited from this edition.

41. On the importance of Mickle's translation for Barlow, see William C. Dowling, *Poetry and Ideology in Revolutionary Connecticut* (Athens, Ga., and London, 1990), 139–40. Dowling offers a compelling protrait of Barlow, in relationship both to British Augustanism and to his other "Connecticut Wits": John Trumbull, David Humphreys, and Timothy Dwight. See also, for a critical description of the Atlas episode in the *Columbiad*, Emory Elliott, *Revolutionary Writers* (New York and Oxford, 1982), 118–22.

CHAPTER FOUR
EPICS OF THE DEFEATED: THE OTHER TRADITION OF
LUCAN, ERCILLA, AND D'AUBIGNE

1. All citations from Statius's poetry are taken from *Statius*, trans. J. H. Mozley, 2 vols., Loeb Classical Library (London and Cambridge, Mass., 1961).

2. Harold Bloom outlined his psychoanalytical model of poetic influence in *The Anxiety of Influence* (London, Oxford, and New York, 1973) and *A Map of Misread-*

ing (New York, 1975). Perhaps of special interest for the case of Lucan are Bloom's brief remarks on hyperbole and its psychic cost in *Poetry and Repression* (London and New Haven, 1976), 23–27.

3. *The Works of Joel Barlow*, facsimile reproduction, ed. William K. Bottorff and Arthur L. Ford (Gainesville, 1970), 2:380–81.

4. Ibid., 2:380.

5. See Book Three of the *Discorsi del poema eroico* in Tasso, *Prose*, ed. Ettore Mazzali (Milan and Naples, 1959), 567. In this passage Tasso also cites the judgment of Quintilian (*Inst. or.* 10.1.90) that Lucan was a better model for orators than for poets.

6. See Eva Matthews Sanford, "Lucan and His Roman Critics," *Classical Philology* 26 (1931):233–57. See also the fine discussion of the debates over Lucan's status as a historical poet, particularly in the politically charged literary world of seventeenth-century England, in Gerald M. MacLean, *Time's Witness* (Madison, 1990), 26–44.

7. *Voltaire's Essay on Epic Poetry*, ed. Florence Donnell White (Albany, 1915), 101. Voltaire's remark is, in turn, apparently echoed by Barlow, 2:384: "We ought to consider that, in the epic field, the interest to be excited by the action cannot be sustained by following the gazette, as Lucan has done."

8. See A. W. Lintott, "Lucan and the History of the Civil War," *Classical Quarterly* 21 (1971):488–505; Pierre Grimal, "Le poète et l'histoire," in *Lucain*, Fondation Hardt Entretiens 15 (Geneva, 1970), 53–117; Elaine Fantham, "Caesar and the Mutiny: Lucan's Reshaping of the Historical Tradition in the *De Bello Civili* 5.237–383," *Classical Philology* 80 (1985):119–31; and Gordon Williams, *Change and Decline: Roman Literature in the Early Empire* (Berkeley, Los Angeles, and London, 1978), 249. The issue is overstated by W. R. Johnson in *Momentary Monsters* (Ithaca and London, 1987), 103: "The poem is not history or even about history."

9. See the pages of J. C. Bramble on the Augustan precursors of Lucan, whose works have not survived except in a few fragments, in *The Cambridge History of Classical Literature 2: Latin Literature*, ed. E. J. Kenney (Cambridge, 1982), 485–91. Some of these poets took up the subject of the civil wars.

10. See Frederick M. Ahl, *Lucan* (Ithaca and London, 1976), 67–75.

11. See Ahl, *Lucan*, 293–305; Wolf-Hartmut Friedrich, "Cato, Caesar und Fortuna bei Lucan," *Hermes* 73 (1938):391–421. An abridged version is reprinted in Werner Rutz, *Lucan* (Darmstadt, 1970), 70–102.

12. Bernard F. Dick has addressed the issue of prophecy in two studies of the *Pharsalia*: "The Role of the Oracle in Lucan's *De Bello Civile*," *Hermes* 93 (1965): 460–66, and "The Technique of Prophecy in Lucan," *TAPA* 94 (1963):37–49. In the latter he concludes, 49, that Lucan forgoes and criticizes prophecy because "knowledge of the future annihilates hope." See also Ahl's analyses of Appius's consultation with the Delphic oracle in Book 5 and of the great scene of Erictho's conjuration and prophecy in Book 6; Ahl, *Lucan*, 121–49.

13. The courage, as well as the faith, that allows Lucan to portray history as open-ended and contingent—without final settlements either of republican liberty or imperial tyranny—need not be confused with despair, as Johnson suggests in *Momentary Monsters*, 30, where he writes of the struggle between these principles as a " 'fearful zizag' and 'stalemate': 'the brutal, useless contest repeats itself endlessly."

14. The question of Lucan's relationship to Virgil is inevitable in criticism of the

Pharsalia. For some important discussions, see Ahl, 64–67 and passim; Andreas Thierfelder, "Der Dichter Lucan," *Archiv für Kulturgeschichte* 25 (1934):1–20, reprinted in Rutz, *Lucan*, 50–69; Emanuele Narducci, *La provvidènza crudele* (Pisa, 1979), 25–62; Lynette Thompson and R. T. Bruère, "Lucan's Use of Vergilian Reminiscence," *Classical Philology* 63 (1968):1–21.

15. For discussions of this episode, see Fantham, "Caesar and the Mutiny"; Ahl, *Lucan*, 205–9; Johnson, *Momentary Monsters*, 105–12; M.P.O. Morford, *The Poet Lucan* (New York, 1967), 37–42; Narducci, *La provvidènza*, 107–9; Thompson and Bruère, "Lucan's Use of Vergilian Reminiscence," 10–16. See also Pamela Barratt, *M. Annaei Lucani Belli Civilis Liber V: A Commentary* (Amsterdam, 1979), 164–224.

16. Thompson and Bruère, "Lucan's Use of Vergilian Reminiscence," 14.

17. Cicero writes of Fortune in *De Officiis* 2.6: "Who fails to comprehend the enormous, two-fold power of Fortune for weal and for woe? When we enjoy her favouring breeze, we are wafted over to the wished-for haven; when she blows against us, we are dashed to destruction. Fortune herself, then, does send those other less usual calamities, arising, first, from inanimate Nature—hurricanes, storms, shipwrecks, catastrophes, conflagrations ..."; *De Officiis*, trans. Walter Miller, Loeb Classical Library (Cambridge, Mass., and London, 1975), 187. The passage is cited in Frederick Kiefer, "The Conflation of Fortuna and Occasio in Renaissance Thought and Iconography," *JMRS* 9 (1979):1–27, 4.

18. Johnson, *Momentary Monsters*, 107f., emphasizes Caesar's will to power in the scene of the boat ride as part of his larger reading of Lucan's poem as a depiction— and disclosure—of the irrationality of the political world. This absurdist reading of the poem gets at a strain that is undeniably present in the *Pharsalia*, and Johnson's study is full of valuable insights. His position, nonetheless, leaches the poem of all political meaning, as Johnson also does to the *Aeneid* in *Darkness Visible*. In fact his readings of Virgil and Lucan become all too similar. I shall argue that Lucan's angry wit is directed at a particular political arrangement and history, and is not simply a statement of blanket despair: a rather too facile way of confronting unhappy political situations. Caesar's superhuman energy, suggested from the beginning of the poem in the famous simile that compares him to a bolt of lightning (1.151f.), is also emphasized by Ahl, *Lucan*, 197f.

19. See John Henderson, "Lucan/The Word at War," *Ramus* 16 (1987):122–64, 124: "When Victim is Victor, when the differences constructed and confirmed by war have shrunk toward zero, when there is only one side ... You have, you find, no way to tell the story. This is not what narrative *can* narrate. Such is the 'Caesar-Epos' of Lucan." Henderson's provocative essay attempts to imitate the fragmentation and fractured logic of the *Pharsalia* itself; it is a deliberate critical outrage, aimed to demonstrate the incommensurability of traditional critical categories to Lucan's outrageous poem.

20. On the storm and its tradition, see Morford, *The Poet Lucan*, 20–44.

21. Williams, *Change and Decline*, 248. Williams goes on to suggest, 249–53, that the "cult of the episode" in later Latin poetry was a function of the practice of recitation; short, self-contained passages could be performed without tiring poet and audience.

22. *The Complete Works of Aristotle*, ed. Jonathan Barnes (Princeton, 1984), 2:2322.

23. For metaphors of the speech as body in the rhetorical tradition, see Elaine

Fantham, *Comparative Studies in Republican Latin Imagery* (Toronto and Buffalo, 1972), 164–75.

24. Fantham, *Comparative Studies*, 165. All citations from the Platonic corpus are taken from *The Collected Dialogues of Plato*, ed. Edith Hamilton and Huntington Cairns (Princeton, 1963).

25. Fantham, *Comparative Studies*, 165.

26. For another analysis of this passage and of the self-referential, emotionally charged nature of Lucan's descriptive language, see Gian Biagio Conte, "La guerra civile nella rievocazione del popolo: Lucano, 2.67–233," *Maia* 20 (1968):225–53, especially 234–36.

27. Johnson, *Momentary Monsters*, 45–46, 56–57, would read this wit as "gallows humor" or "black comedy" suffusing the whole *Pharsalia* and turning it into a "deadly serious" burlesque. In episodes such as the confrontation with Erictho in Book 6 and with the snakes of Libya in Book 9, it seems hard to disagree with him. But here, too, Johnson's absurdist reading would swallow up the political ideas and hopes of the epic: Johnson, in fact, sees the poem addressed to the "hope that he [Lucan] sensed was about to fail him" (25). We may ask whether this sense of failure and despair belong more to the poet or the critic; Johnson's contention that Lucan is laughing at Cato may not convince many readers of the poem.

28. For a discussion of this scene and of the larger Stoic framework of thought in the *Pharsalia*, see Berthe Marti, "The Meaning of the *Pharsalia*," *TAPA* 66 (1945): 352–76. For a critique of Marti's position, see Otto Steen Due, "An Essay on Lucan," *Classica et Mediaevalia* 23 (1962):68–132, 108–9.

29. My translation is based on the Latin text in *Ad Lucilium Epistulae Morales*, ed. and trans. Richard M. Gummere, 3 vols., Loeb Classical Library (London and New York, 1920).

30. Suetonius, *Caesar*, 82; Plutarch, *Caesar*, 66; Appian, *Civil Wars*, 2.16.117.

31. We can add to these passages an analogous one, 2.166–73, immediately preceding the dismemberment of Marius Gratidianus, where the anonymous speaker of Book 2 recalls how the relatives of the leading Romans killed during Sulla's proscriptions attempted to recognize and bury their kinsmen, whose heads, exposed on pikes, had lost their features (166–68); the speaker himself had searched through myriad headless trunks to find one that would match up with the now featureless remains of his brother's severed head—"deformia . . . ora" (169–70).

32. Due, "An Essay on Lucan," 99–100, also notes the parallel between the matron's speech and the prophecy of Nigidius Figulus in his discussion of the *Pharsalia*'s proem in (sarcastic) praise of Nero.

33. In "Lucan's Narrative Techniques," *La parola del passato* 30 (1975):74–90, Berthe Marti has described the way that Lucan will on occasion switch to a narrator persona who seems to have a limited knowledge of the outcome of the historical events the poem recounts: "Through it the poet imaginatively participates in a past seen as still unfolding and not irrevocably lapsed, where some options are felt to be still available" (88). And earlier in the essay, she comments on the same device: "It seems to me to place the reader in a state of uncertainty and apprehension and keep him in suspense" (77). I would suggest that this vicarious experience of a history still open to change is meant to be carried over into the present of Lucan's contemporary readers.

34. Just what is it that Lucan is still fighting for? Does he really believe in the restoration of the republic? Under the principate, Chaim Wirszubski argues, the cause of *libertas* meant chiefly the struggle to persuade or compel the emperor to hold to the rule of law and to respect the advisory and legislative role of the senate; by the time of Tacitus, the concept of freedom had shrunk to "merely the courage to preserve one's self-respect in the face of despotism and amidst adulation" (166); Wirszubski, *Libertas as a Political Idea at Rome during the Late Republic and Early Principate* (Cambridge, 1950), especially 124–71. The failed Pisonian conspiracy against Nero in which Lucan participated aimed, Tacitus implies (15.52), merely to replace one emperor with another more attuned to the ideals of the senatorial class. But the motives of the conspirators appear, by Tacitus's own account, to have been mixed and varied. Ahl, *Lucan*, 343–46, cautions against accepting Tacitus's hostile view of Lucan (15.49) as vain and self-serving and argues for the poet's leading place in the senatorial opposition. Ahl, 57, nonetheless, reads the poem in terms that are very close to Wirszubski's description of the fate of the concept of liberty: "When Lucan assures us that the battle of Pharsalia is the great catastrophe of the republic, he is telling us that this is the moment when constitutional government, or what was left of it, fell. From Pharsalia onwards, *libertas*, the republic, no longer exists at Rome, though it continues as an ideal, enshrined in men like Cato. . . . Pompey is the representative of the last moments of the republic itself, Cato the man who keeps the disembodied ideal alive, and Caesar the evil genius who brings an end to the republic as a political reality, but who, one suspects, will not be so successful in destroying the ideal." At times the *Pharsalia* seems to envision a rolling back of history to the republic and its *libertas*, but this may be a largely internal process, a keeping alive of historical memory and of a Stoic philosophical freedom (the two become confused) while adjusting to the new political reality of the empire. And this may help to explain the opposing moods of Book 7: the admission that imperial rule may be here to stay, the imperative to keep faith with the republican past. Still, it was *not* a purely internal process, as Lucan's own failed act of political engagement attests. See Richard C. Lounsbury, "History and Motive in Book 7 of Lucan's *Pharsalia*," *Hermes* 104 (1976):210–39, for the argument that Book 7 was revised and turned into a manifesto for the Pisonian conspiracy.

35. Henderson, "Lucan/The Word at War," 133–34: "This narrator loathes the progress of his story of Caesarian triumph, loves *mora*, delay, obstruction, diversion. . . . Lucan hates, spurns, defers, resists his projected narrative. The *end* of his text is to establish incompleteness as pre-destined objective. His (anti-)epic triumph is to make writing itself the drama of political resistance in the name of history. Thus, Lucan 'refuses to narrate.' "

36. See Ahl, *Lucan*, 305–32; Berthe Marti, "La Structure de la *Pharsale*," in *Lucain*, 3–38; Richard T. Bruère, "The Scope of Lucan's Historical Epic," *CP* 45 (1950):217–35; Due, "An Essay on Lucan," 120–32.

37. The unlikely thesis that the poem is complete in its present form has been advanced by M. Haffter, "Dem Shwanken Zünglein lauschend Wachte Cäsar dort," *Museum Helveticum* 14 (1957):118–26. Henderson, *Lucan*, 132, meditates on the fittingness of the final lines of the version that has come down to us. Within the epic tradition, Ariosto models the "ending" of his own unfinished fragment, the *Cinque Canti*, on the last scene of *Pharsalia* 10: his Charlemagne, like Lucan's Caesar,

stands on the verge of imminent defeat and is crowded off a bridge into the water below by the press of his own retreating soldiers.

38. Johnson, *Momentary Monsters*, 88. My argument overlaps with Johnson's acute discussion of the issue, 86–97.

39. On this episode, see Ahl, *Lucan*, 22–225; Morford, *The Poet Lucan*, 13–19. For other scenes, the mutiny in Book 5 and Caesar's tour of Troy in Book 9, that connect Caesar to Alexander, see Fantham, "Caesar and the Mutiny"; Otto Zwierlein, "Lucans Caesar in Troja," *Hermes* 114 (1986):460–78.

40. Seneca, *Naturales Quaestiones*, 6.8.3.

41. See Eva Matthews Sanford, "The Eastern Question in Lucan's *Bellum Civile*," in *Classical and Medieval Studies in Honor of E. K. Rand*, ed. Leslie Webber Jones (New York, 1938), 255–64, and also M. P. Charlesworth, "The Fear of the Orient in the Roman Empire," *Cambridge Historical Journal* 2 (1926):1–16.

42. Ahl, *Lucan*, 170–73.

43. See Richard J. A. Talbert, *The Senate of Imperial Rome* (Princeton, 1984), 392–430; F. Millar, "The Emperor, the Senate and the Provinces," *Journal of Roman Studies* 56 (1966):156–66.

44. Hardie, *Virgil's Aeneid*, 381. See also Michael Lapidge, "Lucan's Imagery of Cosmic Dissolution," *Hermes* 107 (1979):344–70.

45. On Lepanto and Actium, see Appendix 2 to Chapter 1 above.

46. On Lucan's influence on Ercilla, see Dieter Janik, "Ercilla, lector de Lucano," in *Homenaje a Ercilla* (Concepción, 1969), 83–109; Gareth Davies, "'El incontrast-able y duro hado': *La Araucana* en el espejo de Lucano," in *Estudios sobre literatura y arte dedicados al Profesor Emilio Orozoco Díaz* (Granada, 1979), 1:405–17; Barbara Held, *Studien zur Araucana des Don Alonso de Ercilla* (Frankfort, 1983), 114–43; Frank Pierce, *Alonso de Ercilla y Zuniga* (Amsterdam, 1984), 71. An argument against the importance of Lucan's model, wrongheaded in my opinion, is advanced by Maxime Chevalier in *L'Arioste en Espagne* (Bordeaux, 1966), 144–46.

47. See the prologue to the *Arauco domado*, ed. J. T. Medina (Santiago, 1917), 26: "Accordé dalle título de *Arauco domado*, porque, aunque sea verdad que agora, por culpas nuestras, no lo esté . . ."

48. See the discussion of nautical metaphors in Ernst Robert Curtius, *European Literature in the Latin Middle Ages* (New York, 1953), 128–30. The most important instance of the metaphor for Ercilla was undoubtedly the opening of the final, forty-sixth canto of the *Orlando furioso*; see the argument below.

49. Chevalier, *L'Arioste*, 153; Pierce, *Ercilla*, 72–73. Many commentators have pointed out that the suspension of the duel between Tucapel and Rengo is a model for the breaking off of the "manuscript" of *Don Quixote* at the beginning of the duel between Don Quixote and the Biscayan in Chapter 8 of the First Part of Cervantes' novel.

50. The poem's central scene of mutilation is the amputation of Galbarino's hands (22.45f.), discussed in the previous chapter. In addition to the slaughter at Penco, the poem emphasizes the laceration of bodies in the battle at Mataquito (14.34–35; 15.46). See Jaime Concha, "El Otro Nuevo Mondo," in *Homenaje a Er-cilla*, 31–82, 59; Ramona Lagos, "El Incumplimiento de la programación epica en *La Araucana*," *Cuadernos Americanos* 40 (1981):157–91, 173–74.

51. This pattern is noted by Chevalier, *L'Arioste*, 153.

52. On Indian honor, see José Durand, "El chapetón Ercilla y la honra araucana," *Filología* 10 (1964):113–34, 126–31. See also the discusssion by Beatriz Pastor in the chapter on the *Araucana* in her *Discursos narrativos de la conquista: Mitificación y emergencia* (Hanover, 1988), 368–71.

53. This passage, I think, should question the reading of Jaime Concha in "Observaciones acerca de *La Araucana*," *Estudios Filológicos* 1 (1964):63–79, which sees Caupolicán's death—accompanied by baptism—as the culminating victory of a Providential plot over the workings of Fortune. Concha's Christological view of Caupolicán's execution as a kind of crucifixion, advanced both here, 71, and in "El otro Nuevo Mundo," 63–66, lacks persuasive textual support. For the historical reality of Ercilla's Caupolicán, see José Durand, "Caupolicán, clave historial y épica de *La Araucana*," *Revue de Littérature Comparée* 52 (1978):367–89.

54. This stanza, it should be pointed out, is found only in the 1597 expanded edition of the poem that appeared three years after Ercilla's death. The new material, which deals with the journey to the South—the last twenty stanzas of canto 34, canto 35, and canto 36 except for its last four stanzas—is surely from the poet's hand, and its inclusion presumably reflects his intentions; though, of course, it may not. But the 1589 Third Part, which ends its Chilean narrative with the calling of a new Indian council in canto 34 before turning away to the war in Portugal in canto 35, suggests a similar return to the beginning of the poem and a similar sense of a cycle starting over again.

55. On theories of the just war, see Held, *Studien zur Araucana*, 65–98.

56. Readings of this episode are offered by Pastor, *Discursos*, 418–22, and by Concha, "El otro Nuevo Mundo," 73–81. Pastor views the voyage south as a version of what her study defines as a shipwreck or calamity (*fracaso*) narrative that questions the Spaniards' conquest ideology; at the same time she sees in the idyllic and as yet uncorrupted Indian communities that the Spaniards finally encounter in the South a utopian vision of a pre-Columbian America. Concha emphasizes the whiteness of the skins of the southern Indians and reads the episode as a reflection of contradictions in Spanish racial thinking about the Native Americans.

57. I borrow these observations on the ways in which the military technology and tactics of the conquistadors shape Ercilla's representations of epic battle from Michael Murrin, who is preparing a larger discussion of the subject.

58. J. H. Parry, *The Spanish Theory of Empire* (Cambridge, 1940), provides an excellent, concise overview of the ideological debate over the encomienda and the legal and human status of the Indians; see also the chapter, "Rights and Duties," in Parry's *The Spanish Seaborne Empire* (New York, 1966), 137–51. Parry's work has been superseded by the more philologically rigorous studies of Anthony Pagden, *The Fall of Natural Man* (Cambridge and New York, 1982), and "Dispossessing the Barbarian: The Language of Spanish Thomism and the Debate over the Property Rights of the American Indians," in Pagden, ed., *The Languages of Political Theory in Early-Modern Europe* (Cambridge and New York, 1987), 79–98. In his attention to the Scholastic framework and terms of the debate, Pagden may sometimes play down the social and political pressures that operated upon it, and he does not give weight to the moral urgency of Las Casas, who participated in the controversy as a firsthand witness to the mistreatment and decimation of the Indians. For a corrective view, critical of Vitoria, see Gustavo Gutiérrez, "Si fuesimos indios . . . ," *Socialismo y*

Partipación 40 (1987):17–27. See also the stimulating discussion of Las Casas and Sepúlveda in Tzvetan Todorov, *The Conquest of America*, trans. Richard Howard (New York, 1984), 146–82. For the continuation in Ercilla's Chile of the debate over the status of the Indians and of the justification of the Spanish war policy, see Eugene H. Korth, *Spanish Policy in Colonial Chile* (Stanford, 1968), especially 1–58.

59. Bartolomé de Las Casas, *History of the Indies*, trans. Andrée Collard (New York, Evanston, and London, 1971), 106–15.

60. Juan Ginés de Sepúlveda, *Demócrates segundo o de la justas causas de la guerra contra los indios*, ed. Angel Losada (Madrid, 1951), 35–36.

61. But perhaps, whether they resisted or, as Sepúlveda suggests, merely capitulated, the Indians could not win in Spanish eyes. See Inga Clendinnen, who argues against Todorov's interpretation of Cortés as a master decipherer of the alien Mexica culture in her " 'Fierce and Unnatural Cruelty': Cortés, Signs, and the Conquest of Mexico," in *The Transmission of Culture in Early Modern Europe*, ed. Anthony T. Grafton and Ann Blair (Philadelphia, 1990), 84–130. The obstinate—and from a European viewpoint unreasonable, even inhuman—defense that the Mexica put up during the siege of Tenochtitlán, Clendinnen argues, clouded the Spanish attitude toward them after the end of hostilities. I have similarly argued in the preceding chapter that Villagrá's *Historia de la Nueva Mexico* depicts the unremitting resistance of the Acoman pueblo dwellers as a justification for the draconian measures taken against them.

62. Las Casas, *In Defense of the Indians*, ed. and trans. Stafford Poole (De Kalb, 1974), 25–49.

63. Ibid., 43. See in this context the parallels drawn between the *Araucana* and the *Numancia* of Cervantes by Willard King in "Cervantes' *Numancia* and Imperial Spain," *Modern Language Notes* 94 (1979): 200–221.

64. Ibid., 47.

65. Ibid., 297.

66. Todorov, *Conquest*, 163–64. Todorov's picture of Las Casas's characterization of the Indians as docile and meek—already Christian in spirit—is, however, one-sided and misleading. Las Casas could also depict the Indians as valiant freedom fighters, as in the case of the rebellion of Enriquillo, whom he compares to the Maccabees. See Las Casas, *History of the Indies*, 246–56.

67. Ercilla in this instance follows a line of argument that Sepúlveda would himself take subsequent to the *Demócrates secundus*; for this switch in Sepúlveda's position and for a sixteenth-century historiographic tradition that idealized the Amerindians as noble warriors, see Rolena Adorno, "The Warrior and the War Community: Construction of the Civil Order in Mexican Conquest History," *Dispositio* 14 (1989):225–46.

68. The most thorough attempt to locate the *Araucana* vis-à-vis contemporary debates over the status of the Indians and the moral legality of the *conquista* is offered by Held, *Studien*, 26–58. Ercilla sailed on the same ship and undoubtedly came in contact in Chile with Fray Gil González de San Nicolás, a Dominican who accompanied Mendoza's expedition and who declared the war against the Araucanians to be illegal in a debate with his Franciscan opponent Gallego; the troublemaking and undiplomatic González was sent back to Peru in 1563. See Korth, *Spanish Policy*, 40–58; Held, *Studien*, 41–44.

69. On Ercilla's position as outsider and royal servant, see Durand, "El chapetón Ercilla," to which my argument is particularly indebted. See also Concha, "El otro Nuevo Mundo," 68–73. For the biography of the poet, see the fundamental work of José Toribio Medina, Vida de Ercilla (Mexico City and Buenos Aires, 1948). On the development of a colonial identity in Spanish America, see Anthony Pagden, "Identity Formation in Spanish America," in Colonial Identity in the Atlantic World, 1500–1800, ed. Nicholas Canny and Anthony Pagden (Princeton, 1987), 51–93.

70. See the prologue to de Oña's Arauco Domado, 25, and also stanza 19 of the "Exordio" to de Oña's epic, 35.

71. Durand argues in "El chapetón Ercilla," 132–33, that in this passage Ercilla has scrupulously spelled out the justifications for the present Spanish campaign against the Araucanians: the Indians are accused of having lapsed from their earlier conversion to Christianity. Durand points out that war could be defended if it was waged to protect the newly baptized; the latter, however, are not explicitly mentioned by Ercilla's text. Although the Araucana makes occasional gestures toward religion, the invocation of Christianity is insufficient in itself to resolve the poem's divided allegiances and ideological fissures.

72. De Oña, Arauco Domado, 97.

73. Ibid., 106–7.

74. On codicia as a symptom of Spanish tyranny and a cause of the war in Chile, see Held, Studien, 132–33, and Pastor, Discursos, 405–10. Pastor argues that the Spaniards are consistently viewed in an unflattering light by the poem, but her examples all come from the First Part, where the Spaniards in question are the doomed Valdivia and his shattered command before Francisco de Villagrán reorganizes them; this part of the poem precedes the poet's own arrival in Chile along with Mendoza. Ercilla is more respectful toward the Spaniards alongside of whom he himself fought.

75. Durand, "El chapetón Ercilla," 126–31.

76. The classic studies of this trans-European phenomenon take up the English and French cases: see Lawrence Stone, The Crisis of the Aristocracy 1558–1641 (Oxford, 1965), and Norbert Elias, The Court Society (Oxford, 1983); see also Mervyn James, Society, Politics and Culture: Studies in Early Modern England (Cambridge, 1986), especially 148–75, 308–465; George Huppert, Les Bourgeois Gentilshommes (Chicago and London, 1977); Davis Bitton, The French Nobility in Crisis, 1560–1640 (Stanford, 1969). For Spain, see the studies of José Antonio Maravall, Poder, honor y elites en el siglo XVII (Madrid, 1979) and Culture of the Baroque (Minneapolis, 1986).

77. On the duel, see Francesco Erspamer, La biblioteca di Don Ferrante: Duello e onore nella cultura del cinquecento (Rome, 1982); V. G. Kiernan, The Duel in European History: Honour and the Reign of Aristocracy (Oxford, 1988); François Billacois, Le duel dan la société française des XVIe–XVIIe siècles (Paris, 1986).

78. Concha, "El otro Nuevo Mundo," 58; Durand, "El chapetón Ercilla," 132; Pierce, Ercilla, 66; Held, Studien, 95–96.

79. On fortune and fate in the Araucana, see Julio Caillet-Bois, "Hado y fortuna en La Araucana," Filología 8 (1962):403–20; Concha, "Observaciones"; Luis Muñoz, "Ercilla, protagonista de La Araucana," in Homenaje a Ercilla, 16–22. Held, Studien, 174–80, follows Muñoz in locating an opposition between Providence and Fortune in the poem, but where the latter asserts that the poet's faith in Providence ulti-

mately resolves the opposition, Held, in my view correctly, argues that the *Araucana* fails to give poetic form to a Providential plan—for which the poet narrator may express an unfulfilled wish—and instead turns the destinies of its heroes over to Fortune.

80. On the role of the poet in his epic, see Pastor, *Discursos*, 427–39; Munoz, "Ercilla, protagonista"; Pierce, *Ercilla*, 62–69; Juan Bautista Avalle-Arce, "El poeta en su poema (El caso Ercilla)," *Revista de Occidente* 94 (1971):152–70. Both Pierce and Avalle-Arce compare Ercilla's narrator to the narrator of the *Orlando furioso*, and Avalle-Arce is heavily indebted to the fundamental study by Robert Durling on the Renaissance epic narrator, *The Figure of the Poet in Renaissance Epic* (Cambridge, Mass., 1965).

81. The history of the critical debates over the *romanzo*, which culminated in the debate over the merits of Ariosto versus those of Tasso, has been most thoroughly traced in Bernard Weinberg, *A History of Literary Criticism in the Italian Renaissance*, 2 vols. (Chicago, 1961), especially 1:433–77, 2:954–1073.

82. *Giraldi Cintio on Romances*, trans. Henry L. Snuggs (Lexington, 1968), 23.

83. Ibid., 53.

84. See Lia Schwartz Lerner, "Tradición literaria y heroínas indias en *La Araucana*," *Revista Iberoamericana* 38 (1972):615–25; Chevalier, "L'Arioste," 151–53.

85. Lagos, "El incumplimiento." Lagos provides a brilliant revision of Concha's argument, "El otro Nuevo Mundo," 38–52, that defends the historical "unity" of the *Araucana*.

86. See María Rosa Lida, "Dido y su defensa en la literatura española," *Revista de Filología Hispánica* 4 (1942):209–52, 313–82; her discussion of Ercilla's episode is found at the end of the essay, 373–80.

87. Lagos, "El incumplimiento," 181.

88. See note 72 above.

89. Pagden, "Dispossessing the Barbarian," 96, notes that at the end of his *De indis* (1539) the theologian Francisco de Vitoria contrasts the Portuguese empire of licit commerce to the Spanish empire of "illicit occupation."

90. All citations of *Les Tragiques* and of d'Aubigné's French works are taken from the Pléiade edition of the *Oeuvres* of d'Aubigné, ed. Henri Weber (Paris, 1969).

91. For discussions of the style of *Les Tragiques*, see Greene, *The Descent from Heaven*, 255–93, especially 258–69; Imbrie Buffum, *Agrippa d'Aubigné's Les Tragiques* (New Haven, 1951). Henry A. Sauerwein, Jr., distinguishes the styles of the individual books of the poem in *Agrippa d'Aubigné's Les Tragiques* (Baltimore, 1953), 97–121. French criticism has treated the question of style in terms of the biblicism of d'Aubigné's verse: see Henri Weber, *La création poétique au XVIe siecle en France* (Paris, 1955); Marguerite Soulié, *L'inspiration biblique dans la poésie religieuse d'Aubigné* (Paris, 1977), 437–502; Jacques Bailbé, *Agrippa d'Aubigné, Poète des Tragiques* (Caen, 1968), 428–61.

92. For the pervasive presence of the Book of Revelation in *Les Tragiques*, see Elliott Forsyth, "Le message prophétique d'Agrippa d'Aubigné," *BHR* 41 (1979):23–39. Forsyth is responding polemically to the thesis of Soulié in *L'inspiration biblique* that apocalyptic rhetoric only enters the poem in the last two books, superseding what had in the first five been the poetic persona's adaptation of the voice of Old Testament prophecy. Soulié was herself criticizing the arguments of Robert Regosin,

The Poetry of Inspiration: Agrippa d'Aubigné's Les Tragiques (Chapel Hill, 1970), 55–78, that Revelation provided a global model for d'Aubigné's poem. For a further intervention into this critical debate, see André Tournon, "Le cinquième sceau: Les tableaux des *Fers* et la perspective apocalyptique dans *Les Tragiques* d'Agrippa d'Aubigné," *Mélanges sur la littérature de la renaissance à la mémoire de V.-L. Saulnier* (Geneva, 1984), 273–83.

93. See Northrop Frye, *Anatomy of Criticism* (Princeton, 1957), 194, 199, 205; James Nohrnberg, *The Analogy of the Faerie Queene* (Princeton, 1976), 214.

94. This inverse relationship between human events and their real meaning in the scheme of salvation has been related to the topos of the world upside down by Jean Céard in "Le thème du 'monde à l'envers' dans l'oeuvre d'Agrippa d'Aubigné," in *L'image du monde renversé et ses représentations littéraires et para-littéraires de la fin du XVIe siècle au milieu du XVIIe*, ed. Jean Lafond and Augustin Redondo (Paris, 1979), 117–27.

95. For the figure of the Calvinist New Israel in the case of the Netherlands, see Simon Schama, *The Embarrassment of Riches: An Interpretation of Dutch Culture in the Golden Age* (Berkeley, Los Angeles, and London, 1988), 93–125.

96. On d'Aubigné and Henri, see Soulié, *L'inspiration biblique*, 204–20; Bailbé, "L'image d'Henri IV dans l'oeuvre d'Agrippa d'Aubigné," in *L'Image du souverain dans les lettres françaises des guerres de religion à la révocation de l'Edit de Nantes* (Paris, 1985), 27–40. See also the biographical studies of the poet, Armand Garnier, *Agrippa d'Aubigné et le parti protestant* (Paris, 1928), 3 vols.; Jeanne Galzy, *Agrippa d'Aubigné* (Paris, 1965).

97. The first edition of *Les Tragiques* appeared anonymously, its author indicated by the initials "L. B. D. D.," which stood for "Le Bouc du Désert," the scapegoat driven out into the wilderness. This nickname indicated d'Aubigné's intransigence, his refusal to make compromises with the French crown, and it, of course, shared the typology of the apocalyptic church wandering in the wilderness. For a sophisticated discussion of the poet's "je" in the context of his religious politics, see Ullrich Langer, *Rhétorique et intersubjectivité: Les Tragiques d'Agrippa d'Aubigné* (Paris, Seattle, and Tübingen, 1983), especially 35–51, 105–8.

98. Garnier's biography of d'Aubigné remains the fundamental scholarly work on the stages of composition of his epic. A judicious reconsideration of the problem is contained in Giancarlo Fasano, *"Les Tragiques": Un epopea della morte* (Bari, 1971), 2:9–78.

99. For a discussion of this famous passage, see Frank Lestringant, *Agrippa d'Aubigné: Les Tragiques* (Paris, 1986), 112–19.

100. For the text of the poem, see *Pages inédites de Théodore-Agrippa d'Aubigné*, ed. Pierre-Paul Plan (Geneva, 1945), 168. Part of the poem is cited by Bailbé in "Lucain et Aubigné," *BHR* 22 (1960):320–37, 321. Much of my discussion goes over material that Bailbé has treated in this essay. On the relationship of the two poets, see also Lestringant, *Agrippa d'Aubigné*, 29–32.

101. See Weber, *La création poétique*, 722–25.

102. For the heroic stature that Coligny acquired in Huguenot accounts of Saint Bartholomew, see Robert M. Kingdon, *Myths about the St. Bartholomew's Day Massacres 1572–1576* (Cambridge, Mass., and London, 1988), 28–50.

103. The passage in *Princes* conflates the laughter of Pompey with the smile of

Cicero's Scipio in the *Somnium Scipionis* segment of Book 6 of the *De Republica* (16–20); see the preceding verses 1428–30. On stoical elements in d'Aubigné's thought, see Bailbé, "Agrippa d'Aubigné et le stoicisme," *Bulletin de l'Association Guilluame-Budé* (1965):97–111.

D'Aubigné's identification of Huguenot constancy with the stoic firmness of the exemplary figure of Cato helps to gloss the other great work of French literature of the last decades of the sixteenth century, Montaigne's *Essais*. Montaigne's gradual disenchantment with Cato as a figure of virtue, felt particularly in "De la cruauté" (2.11), is due, I would suggest, precisely to this kind of characterization of Protestant intransigence as a form of stoic *constantia*. See Timothy Hampton, *Writing from History* (Ithaca and London, 1990), 159–71. The *politique* Montaigne, who proclaims from his first essay his own "mollesse," i.e., the "mollitia" to which Senecan stoicism constantly opposes itself, has confessional and political reasons to reject this stoic-Huguenot conjunction. "D'Aubigné" could sum up that which the *Essais* are against.

104. See Michel Jeanneret, "Les tableaux spirituels d'Agrippa d'Aubigné," *BHR* 35 (1973):233–45; Tournon, "Le cinquième sceau"; Lestringant, *Agrippa d'Aubigné*, 77–97.

105. Lestringant, *Agrippa d'Aubigné*, 38–47, makes a valuable distinction between *Feux* and *Fers*. The Protestant victims of the former book are juridically condemned and thus enjoy the doctrinally clear-cut status of martyrs, while those of the latter are killed in indiscriminate massacres and are therefore put to a much greater test, as d'Aubigné's Satan is well aware (*Fers* 111–74).

106. Lestringant, *Agrippa d'Aubigné*, 91–92, makes a similar argument about the use that d'Aubigné makes of the rivers in *Fers*, substituting geographical space for historical chronology as the book's organizing principle.

107. For some critical discussions of the role of the elements in *Les Tragiques*, see Soulié, *L'inspiration biblique*, 424–25, who relates the apocalypse of the elements to the apocryphal Fourth Esdras; Weber, *La création poétique*, 633–34; Bailbé, *Agrippa d'Aubigné*, 224–37.

108. *Oeuvres poétiques de Jean Dorat*, ed. Ch. Marty-Laveaux (Paris, 1875), 31.

109. For an analysis of this passage and its reference to du Haillan, see Fasano, *Les Tragiques*, 2:192f., which is part of a larger excellent discussion, 2:171–210, of d'Aubigné's relationship to republican, monarchomach traditions of thought.

110. The Venetian doge is pointedly invoked by d'Aubigné at the end of Chapter 5 of *Du Debvoir Mutuel des Roys et des Subjects* to affirm against the flattering courtiers of Henri III the legal checks against absolutism and the obligations of royal faith. See *Oeuvres*, 483–84.

111. Ibid., 477. For a succinct discussion of *De Debvoir* and of d'Aubigné's other political tract, the *Traité sur les guerres civiles*, see Keith Cameron, *Agrippa d'Aubigné* (Boston, 1977), 128–37.

112. D'Aubigné, *Oeuvres*, 467. Abridged translations of Hotman's *Francogallia* and the *Vindiciae contra tyrannos* are contained in *Constitutionalism and Resistance in the Sixteenth Century: Three Treatises by Hotman, Beza, and de Mornay*, trans. and ed. Julian H. Franklin (New York, 1969). On the *Francogallia*, see Kingdon, *Myths*, 136–49.

113. For the tradition of literary attacks on the court, see Pauline Smith, *The Anti-Courtier Trend in Sixteenth Century French Literature* (Geneva, 1966).

114. On the military ethos of the sixteenth-century French aristocracy and their culture of honor, see Kristen B. Neuschel, *Word of Honor: Interpreting Noble Culture in Sixteenth Century France* (Ithaca and London, 1989). Mervyn James, *Society, Politics, and Culture*, 308–415, has studied how, as a policy of state building, the English crown arrogated to itself the determination of honor, which now became the gift of the king rather than a product of the nobleman's self-authenticating military prowess or high birth; one result, as the granting—what was in fact a selling—of noble titles and offices became an important source of royal revenue under James I, was the "inflation of honors" discussed by Stone, *Crisis of the Aristocracy*, 37–61. The analogous situation in France produced the conflict between *noblesse de robe* and *noblesse d'épée*; see Huppert, *Bourgeois Gentilhommes*, 24–33; Bitton, *French Nobility*, 109–15.

115. Fasano, *Les Tragiques*, 2:46.

116. Richard C. McCoy, *The Rites of Knighthood* (Berkeley, Los Angeles, and London, 1989), 103–26.

117. Elias, *The Court Society*, 99, 150, 169.

118. François Cromé, *Dialogue d'entre le maheustre et le manant*, ed. Peter M. Ascoli (Geneva, 1977), 189–90

119. The *Dialogue* was thought to be a Royalist work until a copy of its original version came to light in 1851. For a discussion of the work and its place in *ligueur* political thought, see Frederic J. Baumgartner, *Radical Reactionaries: The Political Thought of the French Catholic League* (Geneva, 1976), 210–20. See also J. H. Elliott, *Europe Divided 1559–1598* (London and Glasgow, 1968), 351–57.

120. William Hazlitt, *Characters of Shakespear's Plays* (London, 1869), 50–51.

121. See David Bromwich, *Hazlitt: The Mind of a Critic* (New York and Oxford, 1983), 314–20, for a discussion of this passage in its context of romantic aesthetics and politics.

122. William Empson, *Some Versions of Pastoral* (1935; New York, 1960), 78–84.

CHAPTER FIVE
POLITICAL ALLEGORY IN THE *GERUSALEMME LIBERATA*

1. Francesco de Sanctis, *History of Italian Literature*, trans. Joan Redfern (New York, 1931), 2:628.

2. Ibid., 2:657: "The Italian spirit makes its last poetic appearance among the languors and laments of the idyll and the elegy, becoming sensitive and delicate and musical. Tasso's genius is in his sentiment."

3. Eugenio Donadoni, *Torquato Tasso* (Florence, 1921), 196–98; Giovanni Getto, *Interpretazione del Tasso* (Naples, 1951), 393–97, 415–17. A useful summary of the critical tradition on the *Liberata* is contained in Guido Baldassari, *Tasso: Il progetto letterario della "Gerusalemme"* (Turin, 1979), 44–53.

4. Two important studies of Tasso that examine the relationship between the poet's tormented psychology and the political repression of the Counter-Reformation are Sergio Zatti, *L'uniforme cristiano e il multiforme pagano* (Milan, 1983), and Margaret W. Ferguson, *Trials of Desire* (New Haven and London, 1983).

5. Fiordibello was secretary to the prominent humanist and churchman Sadoletus. The text of his oration can be found in *Jacobi Sadoleti Opera quae extant omnia* (Verona, 1758), 2:435.

6. Angelo Solerti, *Vita di Torquato Tasso* (Turin and Rome, 1895), 1:30–31. Solerti, 45, also cites a 1566 letter of Muzio to the poet Francesco Bologneti in whch the former describes his long-entertained idea to write an epic about the First Crusade. See also Albert N. Mancini, *I Capitoli letterari di Francesco Bolognetti* (Naples, 1989), 175–76. For Muzio's career as an anti-Protestant propagandist, see Friedrich Lauchert, *Die italienischen literarischen Gegner Luthers* (Freiburg im Breisgau, 1912), 653–65.

7. On Matthaeus Iudex and his oration, see Johannes Janssen, *History of the German People at the Close of the Middle Ages*, trans. A. M. Christie (London, 1905), 8:92–95.

8. *L'Heretico infuriato* (Rome, 1562), proemio.

9. Andrew Fichter has remarked on Argillano as an enthusiast in the Protestant mold in his *Poets Historical* (New Haven and London, 1982), 147.

10. *L'Heretico infuriato*, chap. 20. For another example of the Babel-Babylon typology applied to German Protestantism, see Robertus Bellarminus, *Opera omnia*, ed. J. Fevre (Paris, 1873), 9:533.

11. On Parisani, see Giuseppe Fabiani, *Ascoli nel cinquecento* (Ascoli Piceno, 1957), 1:299–300. Fabiani, 358, notes the possible connection between Tasso's Argillano and the civil strife endemic to sixteenth-century Ascoli, but he does not identify Argillano with Parisani. See also the study of sixteenth-century banditry in the Papal States by Irene Polverini Fosi, *La società violenta* (Rome, 1985), 54–56. In addition to Parisani, Polverini Fosi, 56, mentions the 1571 plan of the captain Odoardo Odoardi to make a company of five hundred or six hundred "uomini pericolosi" from among the Ascolan bandits and exiles and to send them, in the wake of Lepanto, to fight for Venice against the Turks: here, too, there is a parallel to the crusading Argillano.

12. Tasso's discussion of the head-body metaphor in his prose allegory of the *Liberata* has been extensively analyzed by Michael Murrin in *The Allegorical Epic* (Chicago and London, 1980), 102–7. Murrin follows the poet and reads this figure of the body politic in primarily moral terms. The reading that I am advancing here has been anticipated in Robert Durling's discussion of the *Liberata* in his essay, "The Epic Ideal," in *The Old World: Discovery and Rebirth*, ed. David Daiches and Anthony Thorlby (London, 1974), 118–25.

13. Gaspar Contarenus, *Opera* (Paris, 1971), 580.

14. John Calvin, *Responsio ad Sadoleti Epistolam* (1539), in *Joannis Calvini Opera Selecta*, ed. Peter Barth (Munich, 1926), 1:485–86.

15. Riccardo Bruscagli has argued that both of the major protagonists of canto 8, Argillano and more especially Sveno, are mirror figures of Rinaldo. See his chapter, "Il campo cristiano nella *Liberata*," in *Stagioni nella civiltà estense* (Pisa, 1983), 214–22. It might be added that Argillano and Sveno are themselves linked by the fact that both are killed in battle by Solimano. On Sveno, see Timothy Hampton, *Writing from History* (Ithaca and London, 1990), 110–33; Filippo Grazzini, "Sveno's Sword and the Story of Argillano," in *Western Jerusalem*, ed. Luisa del Giudice (New York, 1984), 71–92.

16. On the theme of exile in the *Liberata*, see Sergio Zatti, *L'uniforme cristiano*, 15. Argillano's exile from Ascoli can be added to Zatti's examples. See also Zatti's remarks on Argillano, 30–31.

17. The episode of "Ernando" in an early manuscript version of canto 5 is reprinted by Lanfranco Caretti at the back of his edition of the *Gerusalemme liberata* (Milan, 1979), 538–40. Caretti, 655, dates the manuscript to 1565–1566.

18. The simile of the escaping warhorse that portrays Argillano's re-entry into battle (9.75) may be compared to another simile of the warhorse eager for battle (16.28) that later will describe Rinaldo's eagerness to leave Armida's island and return to the war.

19. "Scrittura onde appaiono i ragionevoli sospetti che Sua Altezza ha di continuo potuto haver che i Pontefici de suoi tempi fossero per muoversi contra di lei." Modena, Archivio di Stato, Archivio Segreto Estense, Casa e stato, b. 512.

20. Venceslao Santi gives an excellent account of the precedence controversy and of the propaganda war it generated in "La precedenza tra gli Estensi ed i Medici e *l'Historia de' Principi d'Este* di G. Battista Pigna," *Atti e memorie della R. Deputazione di Storia Patria Ferrarese* 9 (1987):37–122.

21. "Scrittura . . ." The passage is labeled in the margin: "12 Ag. 1570 lega."

22. See Bernardo Canigiani's letter to Cosimo of December 12, 1567: "Quasi che ei sia poca atta a la generatione, della quale opinione io so che è anche intrinsecamente il Cardinale da Este, et qualche donna che io conosco: pur sarà quel che dio vorra." Florence, Archivio di Stato, Archivio Mediceo del Principato, f. 2890. See also the somewhat later report of the Venetian ambassador, Emilio Maria Manolesso, to the senate in 1575: "La commune opinione è che sia inabilie a generare," in *Relazioni degli ambasciatori veneti al Senato*, ed. Arnaldo Segarizzi (Bari, 1912), 1:42. Alfonso's doctor in 1589 secretly informed the Medici of a congenital defect that rendered the duke sterile, but of which Alfonso himself seems to have been unaware. See Alfonso Lazzari, "Il duca Alfonso II nelle note segrete del suo medico particolare," in Lazzari, *Attraverso la storia di Ferrara: profili e scorci* (Rovigo, 1953), 349–51.

23. Santi, "La precedenza," 81, n. 1, corrected the assertion of Solerti, *Vita di Torquato Tasso*, 1:179, that Alfonso's visit to Rome was aimed at regulating the line of succession in the duchy of Ferrara, but Solerti's contention, which goes back to Muratori, has been repeated by more recent writers, including Fabio Pittorru on pp. 96–99 of his *Torquato Tasso: L'uomo, il poeta, il cortegiano* (Milan, 1982); Pittorru's lively and popular biography otherwise makes many acute and helpful observations about the poet. Alfonso may have been too vain to think that he could not produce an heir: in any event his principal diplomatic concern in 1572–1573 was the precedence controversy. In the diplomatic correspondence from Rome to Ferrara from 1567 to 1575—the period of the composition of the *Liberata*—the one reference I have found to the bull of Pius V is in a group of notes and memoranda sent by the ambassador, Giulio Masetti, on July 18, 1573: "Il S. Cardinal Bobba ha havuto la cura d'ordine di Nostro Signore di riformare e moderar la bolla di Pio V contra li bastardi." Modena, Archivio di Stato, Archivio Segreto Estense, Ambasciatori, Roma, b. 87, 387-II-41. Canigiani, in a letter of July 31, 1570, reports rumors that Alfonso's brother, the cardinal Luigi d'Este, was considering giving up his cardinalship in order to marry and produce an heir. Archivio Mediceo del Principato, f. 2892. For Alfonso's later maneuverings in the 1580s, see Luciano Chiappini, *Gli estensi* (Varesi, 1967), 309–13.

24. Manolesso in *Relazioni*, 1:45.

25. Canigiani, Letter of July 12, 1568. Archivio Mediceo del Principato, f. 2891.

26. Canigiani, Letter of January 16, 1570. Archivio Mediceo del Principato, f. 2892.

27. In the minutes of the letter sent from Ferrara to Francesco Martello in Rome on July 22, 1569, are included instructions on how to excuse the Este of responsibility for the events of 1527; this passage is labeled in the margin of the document as section 7. See the "Minuta della lettera di xxij di Luglio al Martello." Modena, Archivio di Stato, Archivio Segreto Estense, Casa e stato, b. 512.

28. Janssen, *History of the German People*, 8:85. Feelings against Rome in the imperial court ran high again in 1570, and Pius's deciding the precedence controversy in favor of Cosimo contributed to the emperor's ire; see p. 91.

29. "Minuta," as cited in note 27.

30. "Servitij fatti dalla serenissima casa di Este alla Santa Sede Apostolica principiando l'anno 773 per tutto l'anno 1474." Modena, Archivio di Stao, Archivio Segreto Estense, Casa e stato, b. 512.

31. This passage of the "Minuta" is labeled section 5.

32. "Servitij," as cited in note 30.

33. Cited by Santi, "La precedenza," 104.

34. The oration has been reprinted, along with Guarini's preparatory drafts and a detailed description of the historical context, by Ermelinda Armigero Gazzera in *Storia d'un ambasciata e d'un orazione di Battista Guarini (1572)* (Modena, 1919).

35. One can compare the orations by the famous orator Marc Antoine Muret pledging the obedience of the French monarchy to the newly elected Pius IV, Pius V, and Gregory XIII: see *M. Antonii Mureti Opera Omnia*, ed. David Ruhnkenius (Leyden, 1789), 1:45, 107–17, and 173–79. The same Muret had been in the employ of the Este as well and wrote obedience orations on their behalf to Pius IV, 1: 95–99, and Pius V, 1:100–107. I am indebted to Eric MacPhail for drawing my attention to these texts.

36. Gazzera, *Storia d'un ambasciata*, 39.

37. Ibid.

38. Ibid., 28–29. The Medici ambassador in Rome, Alessandro de' Medici reported back to Cosimo that the pope was displeased and that he would allow the oration to be published only if the offending title of "Serenissimo" were removed: "Che se gli concedera quando levano dell'oratione il titolo di Serenissimo, altrimenti no." Alessandro de' Medici, Letter of January 23, 1573. Florence, Archivio di Stato, Archivio Mediceo del Principato, f. 3292.

39. Alessandro de' Medici, Letter of January 17, 1573. Archivio Mediceo del Principato, f. 3292.

40. Alessandro de' Medici, Letter of January 23, 1573.

41. See Santi, "La precedenza," 112–16, on Tasso's possible debt to Pigna's predecessor, Girolamo Faletti, author of a *Genealogia Marchionum Estensium et ducum Ferrariae*.

42. Here one might consider Pittorru's suggestive attempts, in *Torquato Tasso*, 173–92, to reconstruct the causes of Tasso's imprisonment in 1579. He conjectures that Tasso may have accused his patrons of heresy during his frequent visits to the Ferrarese Inquisition in the later 1570s. The Este locked him up.

43. This pattern of simultaneous filial revolt and identification with the father is well studied by Ferguson, in *Trials of Desire*, 54–136, and by Zatti, in *L'uniforme*

cristiano, especially 107–14. Zatti describes Tasso's resentment and paranoid response to his powerless position at the Este court, and speaks, 113, of Tasso's resistance to the "legge tirannica del principe-padre." Given this strategy of appealing to a higher authority or father over the law of the more immediate father, it is worth noting that Tasso punishes Goffredo himself: he is wounded in canto 11 for fighting on foot before Jerusalem in opposition to the plan of God, the "Padre eterno" (1.7). The importance of this central episode is studied by Fredi Chiappelli in *Il conoscitore di caos* (Rome, 1981).

44. Giuseppi Castiglione, *Expeditio ferrariensis et Ferraria recepta* (Rome, 1597), 9–14.

45. Giovanni Battista Ramusio, *Navigazioni e viaggi*, ed. Marica Milanesi, 6 vols. (Turin, 1978–1988), 2:380. For the earlier editions of the documents of the Ethiopian embassy to Clement VII, see Renato Lefevre, *L'Etiopia nella stampa del primo cinquecento* (Como, 1966), 52–67.

46. Ramusio, *Navigazioni e viaggi*, 2:365–66.

47. For an English translation of Alvarez's book, see *The Prester John of the Indies*, trans. Lord Stanley of Alderley, ed. C. F. Beckingham and G.W.B. Huntingford, 2 vols., Hakluyt Society Series 2 (Cambridge, 1961), 114–15. For an excellent popular history of the Portuguese contacts with Ethiopia in the sixteenth and seventeenth centuries, see Elaine Sanceau, *The Land of Prester John* (New York, 1944).

48. Ramusio, *Navigazioni e viaggi*, 2:379.

49. Ibid., 2:240.

50. Damião de Góis, *De Fide, Religione, moribusque Aethiopum* (Louvain, 1540); Sanceau, *The Land of Prester John*, 165–69.

51. Sanceau, *The Land of Prester John*, 105–62. The Portuguese histories of this heroic intervention in Ethiopia are collected and translated in *The Portuguese Expedition to Abyssinia in 1541–1543*, trans. and ed. R. S. Whiteway, Hakluyt Society Series 2, 10 (London, 1902). For the Ethiopian account, in which the presence of the Portuguese allies receives only passing mention (132–33), see the *Chronique de Galâwdêwos*, French trans. William E. Conzelman (Paris, 1895).

52. According to the *Chronique de Galâwdêwos*, 158–59, the king undertook learned debates with the Jesuit missionaries whose aim was "to criticize the true faith that had been brought from Alexandria to Ethiopia and to proclaim loudly the false belief that issued from Rome. When he [the Jesuit bishop Oviédo] said with pride, 'Our father Peter,' he forgot that, from the very stones that he tread with his feet, the glorious God on high can raise up children for Peter. At this time, King Galâwdêwos had two great cares. On the one hand were his controversies with the learned Franks on the subject of their little faith; he conquered them, confounded them, and blasted their false errors. He composed on this occasion a great number of dissertations where he found support in the holy texts chosen from the writings of the apostles, prophets, and heads and doctors of the Church." See Sanceau, *The Land of Prester John*, 175–78.

53. Sanceau, *The Land of Prester John*, 200–228.

54. *Appendice alle Opere in prosa di Torquato Tasso*, ed. Angelo Solerti (Florence, 1892), 164–65.

55. Quintus Smyrnaeus, *The Fall of Troy*, trans. Arthur S. Way, Loeb Classical Library (London and Cambridge, Mass., 1955), 55. The episode had already been

imitated by Giangiorgio Trissino in his epic, *L'Italia liberata dai Goti*, 18.856–86; Tasso criticized Trissino's poem, but imitated it nonetheless.

56. *Collected Ancient Greek Novels*, ed. B. P. Reardon (Berkeley, Los Angeles, and London, 1989), 432.

57. "Stabat ut Andromede monstris exposta marinis." *Fr. Baptistae Mantuani Georgius*, ed. Vinc Graumann, *Jahresbericht des K. K. Gymnasiums zu Pilsen für das Schuljahre 1857–1858* (Pilsen, 1858), 18.

58. Ramusio, *Navigazioni e viaggi*, 2:362. The figure of Saint George was indeed highly diffused in Ethiopian church art. See the three-part study of S. Chojnacki, "The Iconography of Saint George in Ethiopia," *Journal of Ethiopian Studies* 11.1 (1973):57–73; 11.2 (1973):51–92; 12.1 (1974):71–132.

59. Ramusio, *Navigazioni e viaggi*, 2:146. See also a later passage, 241, in Alvarez's account and a passage, 378, in one of Atani Tingil's letters to Pope Clement.

60. Ramusio, *Navigazioni e viaggi*, 2:118.

61. Ibid., 244.

62. Ibid., 261.

63. Ibid., 262.

64. *The Canons and Decrees of the Council of Trent*, trans. H. J. Schroeder (Rockford, Ill., 1971), 54.

65. *Notizia e saggi di opere e documenti inediti riguardanti la storia di Etiopia durante i secoli XVI, XVII e XVIII*, ed. Camillo Beccari (Rome, 1903), 244.

66. Ibid., 245.

67. Pêro Paez, *História da Etiópia*, intr. Elaine Sanceau, ed. Lopes Teixeira (Pôrto, 1945), 2:76.

68. Ibid., 59f.

69. Clorinda is closely linked to these other women characters in the poem. In Jerusalem, she and Erminia share the same bed, and Erminia famously dons the armor of Clorinda in canto 6 (87f.) to go out in search of Tancredi, the Tancredi whom Erminia loves, but who, in Tasso's triangle, is in love with Clorinda—who is unaware of his existence. The simile describing the mourning in Jerusalem at Clorinda's death (12.100) recalls the mourning in Virgil's Carthage at Dido's death (4.669–71), and links Clorinda to the Dido figure of the *Liberata*, Armida: when Armida goes into battle with her bow and arrow (17.33; 20.62f.), she appears to be a new Clorinda. The parallels among the three women characters go on and on.

70. Argante and Solimano are both given demonic traits. Tancredi's duel with Clorinda is paired with his later duel in canto 19 with Argante, Clorinda's partner on her night exploit in canto 12. Where the vanquished Clorinda asks for baptism, the fallen Argante wounds Tancredi in the heel (19:25), like the cursed serpent of Gen. 3:15. On this duel and its reworking of the end of the *Aeneid*, see Lauren Seem, "The Limits of Chivalry," *Comparative Literature* 42 (1990):116–25. Tancredi is compared to Hercules wrestling with Antaeus (19.17), and the figure of the earthborn giant links Argante to Solimano, whose identification as the "new Antaeus" (20.108) is discussed above in Chapter 3. Antaeus is one of the giants met by Dante in Hell (*Inferno* 31.113f.), in the passage that lies behind Tasso's description of Solimano, Argante, and Clorinda, too, as giants on the battlements of Jerusalem (11.27). Voltaire's sardonic comment is apposite here; he contrasts Tasso's treatment of the pagan adversaries to the Crusade with Homer's sympathetic treatment of Hector and

Priam on the losing side of the *Iliad*: "I will not decide if *Homer* hath done right or wrong, in gaining upon our Affections towards *Hector*, and in moving our Pity for *Priam*, but sure it is, that if *Tasso* had not represented *Aladin* and *Argante* rough and unamiable, if he had not skilfully created an Aversion to them, in the Mind of the Reader, he had defeated his own Intention; for in that Case, instead of being concern'd for the Cause of the *Christian* Princes, we should look upon them as Plunderers, united to waste a foreign Country, and to massacre in cold Blood, an old venerable *Eastern* Monarch, together with his innocent Subjects." Voltaire, *An Essay on Epick Poetry*, 115.

71. Tasso does not go quite so far as to put his hero into a dress. But a controlling subtext for Rinaldo's sojourn on Armida's island is Statius's *Achilleid*, where the young Achilles is disguised as a girl and concealed among the maidens of Scyros by Thetis, who is determined to keep him out of the Trojan War (1.317f.).

72. In the battle at Jerusalem, Clorinda, with the two other pagan champions, Solimano and Argante, is viewed and assimilated with the towers of the city,

> e quinci in forma d'orrido gigante
> da la cintola in su sorge il Soldano,
> quindi tra' merli il minaccioso Argante
> torreggia, e discoperto è di lontano.
> e in su la torre altissima Angolare
> sovra tutti Clorinda eccelsa appare.
>
> (11.27.7–8)

(And here, in the guise of a horrible giant, the Sultan rises from the waste up; there between the battlements the threatening Argante towers, and is seen from afar; and on the highest Corner tower, Clorinda appears lofty above all.)

in verses whose Dantesque echoes recall both the circle of the heretics in *Inferno* 10 (33) and the giant builders of Babel in *Inferno* 31 (43–45). Islam has already been compared by the poem to Babel (7.62, 69; 8.5), and in pagan hands, Jerusalem itself is the city of confusion. But in Clorinda's case the typology is doubled in much the way the Dantesque allusions suggest; as Ethiopian heretic as well as Muslim, she may be assimilated with the schismatic Argillano, who would have abandoned the Crusader enterprise of Jerusalem to carve out a separate Babylonian kingdom of his own. I am grateful to Albert Ascoli for pointing out to me the Babelic overtones of this passage. For Argante's earlier association with Babel, see 2.91.5–8. For another discussion of Clorinda and the siege towers of Goffredo as well as the towers of Jerusalem, see Georges Güntert, "L'eccelsa torre in fiamme: Il combattimento di Tancredi e Clorinda," in *Das Epos in Romania: Festschrift für Dieter Kremers zum 65. Geburtstag*, ed. Susanne Knaller and Edith Mara (Tübingen, 1986), 59–77.

73. *Canons and Decrees of the Council of Trent*, 90. I am grateful to Walter Stephens and Naomi Yavneh for this point. On the dewfall in canto 18, see Quint, *Origin and Originality in Renaissance Literature*, 112–16.

74. The hermit's ignorance here is thus a counterpart to Goffredo's limitations and error as a commander (see note 43); a divine vision similar to Clorinda's apparition to Tancredi, this time vouchsafed to the dreaming Goffredo, is needed at the beginning of canto 14 to fill in the gap in human knowledge. The hermit's misunder-

standing of the significance of Clorinda's death also parallels that of her fellow pagan champion Argante, who declares at the end of canto 12 that she succumbed to a "fated"—"fatal" (103)—death, and that for all of his efforts "it seemed otherwise to the counsel of men and of the gods"—"parve al consiglio / de gli uomini altramente e de gli dei." The line echoes the Virgilian formula, "dis aliter uisum," and the passage in the *Aeneid* (2.426–27) describing the seemingly unjust death of Riphaeus, the justest of the Trojans. Dante had placed Riphaeus among the blessed in heaven (*Paradiso* 20.67–69) in order to "correct" Virgil, to demonstrate the unfailing nature of divine justice and the inscrutable mystery of predestination. This opposition between Virgilian, pagan fate and Christian Providence at the end of the canto corresponds to Clorinda's own citation of the words of Virgil's Nisus (*Aeneid* 9.184–85) at its beginning: "Either God inspires me or man makes a God for himself of his own will"—"o Dio l'inspira / o l'uom del suo voler suo Dio si face." Clorinda's night exploit and death will turn out to have been divinely inspired all along.

75. For critical discussions of this episode see Murrin, *The Allegorical Epic*, 107–21; Ferguson, *Trials of Desire*, 126–35. Freud's evocation, in the third section of *Beyond the Pleasure Principle*, of Tancredi's wounding (again) the simulacrum Clorinda as an example of the repetition compulsion is perhaps not based on a reading of the *Liberata*; it is borrowed secondhand from Goethe's *The Apprenticeship of Wilhelm Meister*, 1.7.

76. See 12.57, where Tancredi wrestles with Clorinda and holds her in "nodi di fer nemico e non d'amante"; and the death blow at 12.64, where Tancredi pushes his sword point into Clorinda's fair breast ("bel sen") and drinks her blood: an act of penetration that is more explicitly phallic than its model in Virgil's description of the death of Camilla (11.803–4), killed by a thrown spear.

77. Rinaldo, in fact, exceeds those orders and single-handedly wins the battle: much as he storms and takes the walls of Jerusalem on his own initiative in canto 18 (72f.). The extent to which Rinaldo as a military actor is ever really controlled by Goffredo is not resolved by the poem.

78. Tasso's revisions of the *Liberata* into the *Gerusalemme conquistata* aimed to make the poem conform both to orthodoxy *and* to the single epic model of the *Iliad*, as if the two amounted to the same thing. He also expanded Clorinda's story by giving her a premonitory dream of her baptism (15.41–47). See Quint, *Origin and Originality*, 117–32.

CHAPTER SIX
TASSO, MILTON, AND THE BOAT OF ROMANCE

1. Torquato Tasso, *Rinaldo*, vol. 2 of *Opere*, ed. Bruno Maier (Milan: Rizzoli, 1963).

2. Georg Simmel, "The Adventurer," *Georg Simmel 1858–1918: A Collection of Essays*, trans. David Kettler, ed. Kurt H. Wolff (Columbus, 1959), 244.

3. On the magic boat as a digression from epic to romance, see James Nohrnberg, *The Analogy of the Faerie Queene* (Princeton, 1976), 9–11.

4. See Frederick Kiefer, "The Conflation of Fortuna and Occasio in Renaissance Thought and Iconography," *Journal of Medieval and Renaissance Studies* 9 (1979):1–27. See also Nohrnberg, *Analogy*, 309–11.

5. I have discussed the generic and ideological implications of Boiardo's episode in "The Figure of Atlante: Ariosto and Boiardo's Poem," *MLN* 94 (1979):77–91. See also Charles S. Ross, "Angelica and the Fata Morgana: Boiardo's Allegory of Love," *MLN* 96 (1981):12–22.

6. A *Spaniard in the Portuguese Indies: The Narrative of Martín Fernández de Figueroa*, ed. James B. Mackenna (Cambridge, Mass., 1967), 134–37. Menéndez y Pelayo brings up an anecdote about an early-seventeenth-century Portuguese soldier in India who believed in the literal truth of the books of chivalry and sought to emulate the deeds of their heroes in his combat against the natives, in *Orígenes de la novela I, Edición nacional de las obras completas de Menéndez y Pelayo* 13 (Madrid, 1943), 370–71n. This story of a Don Quixote *avant la lettre* is also cited by Irving Leonard in his study of the book trade to the Spanish New World, *Books of the Brave* (Cambridge, Mass., 1949), 26.

7. In Ariosto's fiction, the knight Astolfo is carried back from Alcina's enchanted island through the Indian Ocean on a boat accompanied by the allegorical figures of Fortitude and Temperance. For a discussion of the "imperial" interpretation of the New World discoveries that the *Orlando furioso* shares, see Frances A. Yates, *Astraea: The Imperial Theme in the Sixteenth Century* (London, 1985), 1–28; on Ariosto's passage, 22–26.

8. See Tasso's own remarks in the first of the *Discorsi dell'Arte Poetica*: "Poco dilettevole è veramente quel poema che non ha seco quelle meraviglie che tanto muovono non solo l'animo de gl'ignoranti, ma de' giudiziosi ancora." Torquato Tasso, *Prose*, ed. Ettore Mazzali (Milan, 1959), 353.

Rinaldo plays the role of an Achilles who wrathfully departs from the Crusader army not to sulk in his tent but to wander into the realm of romance fortune. While Tasso's specific allusions are to the *Orlando innamorato*, these are mediated by the poem that Tasso deeply criticizes in the *Discorsi*: Giangiorgio Trissino's *L'Italia liberata dai Goti* (1547). Trissino's Achillean hero Corsamonte leaves Belisario's army in canto 2.527ff., angered because the general has not granted him his beloved Elpidia in marriage. He eventually travels to Monte Circeo, the dwelling of the blind fairy Plutina (761ff.). Plutina, as her name implies, is a treasure demon and a Fortune figure, reminiscent of Boiardo's Morgana. In canto 13.271ff., the magician Filodemo divines Corsamonte's whereabouts and dispatches two knights, Trajano and Ciro, in search of the absent champion. Here clearly is the literary precedent for Tasso's Magus of Ascalon and for the mission of Carlo and Ubaldo. In this scheme Armida plays the role of Plutina. But Armida also recalls another of Trissino's demonic fairies, Acratia, who, together with her accomplice Ligridonia, imprisons Corsamonte earlier in cantos 4–5 of the *Italia liberata*; Acratia is a figure of lust and concupiscence, modeled on Ariosto's Alcina. Tasso models Armida on both Alcina and Morgana; his inspiration for this conflation of Ariosto's and Boiardo's heroines was Trissino's poem. It is, however, on Armida's symbolic nature as a Fortune figure that the model of the *Italia liberata* primarily insists, a negative and potentially demonic Fortune contrasted with the providential Fortune who serves divine ends. In Tasso's later revision of his epic into the *Gerusalemme conquistata*, Fortune becomes wholly and exclusively negative; the episode of the providential Fortune and her boat is cut, and Fortune appears as a literal demon (18.70) of the sea and storms. This change is remarked upon by Guido Baldassarri in "*Inferno*" e "*cielo*": *Tipologia e funzione del "mervaglioso" nella Liberata* (Rome, 1977), 34–35.

9. See James H. Sims, "Camoens' 'Lusiads' and Milton's 'Paradise Lost': Satan's Voyage to Eden," *Papers on Milton*, ed. Philip Mahone Griffith and Lester F. Zimmerman (Tulsa, Okla., 1969), 36–46. Sims brilliantly relates, 41, the second simile to Satan's farewell to Hope some fifty lines earlier, at 4.108–10. I intend here to fill out some of the details that confirm Sims's argument for the presence of the *Lusíadas* behind Satan's journey. See also two other pioneering studies by Sims: "Christened Classicism in *Paradise Lost* and the *Lusiads*," *Comparative Literature* 24 (1972):338–56, and "The Epic Narrator's Mortal Voice in Camões and Milton," *Revue de Littérature Comparée* 51 (1977):374–84.

10. I have discussed in more detail the link between Milton's Chaos and Camões' description of Neptune's ocean palace in *Origin and Originality in Renaissance Literature: Versions of the Source* (New Haven, 1983), 208–9.

11. Sims, "Christened Classicism," 348, argues that the conversation between Satan and Chaos recollects the descent of Camões' Bacchus to the palace of Neptune. The resemblance between Chaos and the primordial realm of Neptune bears out his point. Milton has thus conflated three separate episodes of Camões' poem into one: da Gama and the King of Melinde (Book 2), Bacchus and Neptune (Book 6), and da Gama and the Zamorin of Calicut (Book 7). One effect of this virtuoso display of allusion is to make da Gama inseparable from the demonic pagan god who tries to thwart his mission.

12. William Blisset, "Caesar and Satan," *Journal of the History of Ideas* 18 (1957):221–32, 229–31. The storm in *Lusíadas* 6 is itself partly modeled on Lucan's storm in *Pharsalia* 5, including the passage (6.84) I have cited above in Fanshawe's translation: compare *Pharsalia* 5.632–36.

13. See Alastair Fowler's note to *Paradise Lost* 2.935 in *The Poems of John Milton*, ed. John Carey and Alistair Fowler (New York, 1972), 551.

14. It hardly needs stressing that the Spanish nobility did nonetheless invest in mercantile ventures, particularly those to the New World. See Ruth Pike, *Aristocrats and Traders: Sevillian Society in the Sixteenth Century* (Ithaca, 1972), and Richard Konetzke, "Entrepreneurial Activities of Spanish and Portuguese Noblemen in Medieval Times," *Explorations in Entrepreneurial History* 6 (1953–1954), 115–20. The aristocratic prejudice against commercial activity could be reinforced by religio-juridical treatises that instructed the Renaissance merchant how to regulate his business on this side of usury. In a 1542 guide for merchants, Juan Sarabia de la Calle cites Cicero's condemnation of trade in *De Officiis* (1.42) and reminds his reader "Y por ser la mercadería officio tan vil se cuenta por una de las siete artes mecánicas, e si algún caballero públicamente le usase por sí mismo pierde la honra de la caballería por la ley de Partida." *Instrucción de mercaderes del Doctor Sarabia de la Calle* (Madrid, 1949), 24. A similar disapproval of merchants can be found in Tomás de Mercado, *Suma de tratos y contratos*, ed. Nicolás Sánchez-Albornoz (1569; Madrid, 1977), 72. For a comment on marriages between noble and merchant families, see Mercado, 63. Such scholastic treatises, however, had little to do with the merchant's real experience and should be carefully distinguished from the practical handbooks that taught arithmetic, accounting, and other business procedures. For discussions, see Henri Lapeyre, *Une famille de marchands: Les Ruiz* (Paris, 1955), 126–40, and Natalie Zemon Davis, "Sixteenth-Century French Arithmetics on the Business

Life," *Journal of the History of Ideas* 21 (1960):18–48. Davis sees in these handbooks an incipient attempt to give value and social dignity to the merchant's profession.

15. R. Hookyaas, "Humanism and the Voyages of Discovery in 16th Century Portuguese Science and Letters," *Mededelingen der Koninklijke Nederlandse Akademie van Wetenschappen, Afd. Letterkunde* 42 (1979):99–159, 125–29; Vitorino Magalhaes-Godinho, *L'économie de l'empire portugais aux XVe et XVle siècles* (Paris, 1969), 833–35. On the low social position of merchants in Portugal, who were, in effect, squeezed out by royal monopolies, see C. R. Boxer, *The Portuguese Seaborne Empire, 1415–1825* (New York, 1969), 318–39.

16. See Boxer, *The Portuguese Seaborne Empire*, as well as Bailey W. Diffie and George D. Winius, *Foundations of the Portuguese Empire, 1415–1580* (Minneapolis, 1977). Carlo Cipolla, *Guns and Sails in the Early Phase of European Expansion, 1400–1700* (London, 1965), 132–38, suggests that the idea of a crusade allowed the Renaissance conquistadors to reconcile "the antithesis between business and religion that had plagued the conscience of medieval Europe."

17. T. K. Rabb, *Enterprise and Empire: Merchant and Gentry Investment in the Expansion of England, 1575–1630* (Cambridge, Mass., 1967), 33–55. See also T. K. Rabb, "The Expansion of Europe and the Spirit of Capitalism," *Historical Journal* 17 (1974):675–89.

18. From Abraham Fleming's introduction in verse (a four-stanza "rythme decasyllabicall, upon this last luckie voyage of worthie Capteine Frobisher") to Dionyse Settle, *A true reporte of the last voyage into the west and northwest regions* (London, 1577), fol. Ai verso. This stanza is cited in John Parker, *Books to Build an Empire* (Amsterdam, 1965), 70.

19. Edmund S. Morgan, "The Labor Problem in Jamestown, 1607–1618," *American Historical Review* 76 (1971):595–611.

20. This passage is discussed in M. I. Finley, *The World of Odysseus*, 2nd ed. (New York, 1979), 69–71.

21. Aelian, *Variae Historiae*, 4.20. Aelianus, *A registrie of Hystories, containing Martial exploits of worthy warriours, Politique practice of Civil Magistrates . . .* , trans. Abraham Fleming (London, 1576), 58. James Joyce followed Victor Bérard's theory that the *Odyssey* reflects the experience of ancient Phoenician sailors and made his modern-day Ulysses into a Semitic commercial traveler; see Michael Seidel, *Epic Geography: James Joyce's Ulysses* (Princeton, 1976).

22. The first theorist of the romanzo, Giovanni Pigna, noted its resemblance to the *Odyssey*. See chapter 2, note 1.

23. There is an earlier French treatment of the Jason story as a chivalric romance to which Boiardo may be indebted: Raoul Lefèvre, *L'Histoire de Jason*, ed. Gert Pinkernell (ca. 1460; Frankfurt, 1971).

24. *Lettres d'un marchand venitien Andrea Berengo (1553–1556)*, ed. Ugo Tucci (Paris, 1957), 176, 132, 143, 152.

25. Christiane Bec, *Les marchands écrivains: Affaires et humanisme à Florence, 1375–1434* (Paris, 1967) 301–30.

26. See Ross (n. 5, above) for a discussion of Boiardo's allegory of riches, especially 13, n. 4; 20–21.

27. Erich Köhler, *L'aventure chevaleresque: Idéal et réalité dans le roman courtois*, French trans. Elaine Kaufholz (1956; Paris, 1974), has argued that the origins of chivalric romance in the twelfth century reflect the aspirations of a lower nobility

that sought to define its own ethos in opposition to the new central power of the crown, whose own ideology was expressed in the epic *chanson de geste*. The vestiges of this split between a strictly martial, nationalistic ethos and an ethos of aristocratic courtliness can still be found in the poems of Ariosto and Tasso, in the conflict between duty to a collective army and the individual pleasures, normally amorous, of knight-errantry. This split will still be a feature of seventeenth-century epic discussed in Chapter 7. But in Renaissance epic this same conflict may also have begun to express a division between the nobility and the ethos of the merchant classes, the latter clothed in the forms of romance. The relationship between adventure and commerce has been explored with Marxist insight and tendentiousness by Michael Nerlich, *Ideology of Adventure: Studies in Modern Consciousness, 1100–1750*, trans. Ruth Crowley, 2 vols. (Minneapolis, 1987).

28. Samuel Eliot Morison, *Admiral of the Ocean Sea: A Life of Christopher Columbus* (Boston, 1942), 364–67.

29. Ubaldo's Odyssean character is further reinforced by extended allusions in canto 16 (29, 32, 48) to the *Achilleid* (1.785–960) of Statius. In liberating Rinaldo from Armida, Ubaldo plays the role of Statius's Ulysses who, together with Diomedes, draws the young Achilles out of his hiding place among the maidens of Scyros and away from his beloved Deidamia.

30. Mercado, *Suma de tratos*, 71–72. One can compare to these merchants and to Tasso's Ubaldo Francus, the hero of Ronsard's unfinished epic *La Franciade* (*Oeuvres complètes*, ed. Gustave Cohen [1572; Paris, 1950], 1:663). Francus has been prepared for his present epic mission by having been sent on a Grand Tour, a kind of Odyssean preparation:

> En maint païs je l'ay fait voyager;
> Il a cognu maint peuple et maint danger,
> Cognu les moeurs des hommes pour se faire
> Guerrier pratiqu'en toute grande affaire.
>
> (1.498–501)

Here, too, the language suggests a confusion between Odyssean adventures in search of experience and business ventures. Francus the warrior seems also to be a man of affairs.

31. There is scholarly disagreement about how to translate "andava l'avolo a la cerca." See the commentary of Charles Singleton in his translation of the *Paradiso* (Princeton, 1982), 273.

32. The end of the *Liberata* thus coincides with its beginning, where God looks down on the Crusader army and compares the perfect zeal of Goffredo, who "ogni mortale / gloria, imperio, tesor, mette in non cale" (1.8), with all the other Crusaders, each of whom possesses some impure motive or moral deficiency. In the third book of his *Discorsi del poema eroico*, published in 1594, Tasso follows Plato (*Republic* 3.390e) in condemning Achilles for having sold the body of Hector back to Priam in the last book of the *Iliad*. Goffredo's refusal of Altamoro's offer of ransom may thus also reflect a traditional criticism of Achilles' avarice. See Tasso, *Prose*, 608–9.

33. See Ferdinand Braudel, *The Mediterranean and the Mediterranean World in the Age of Philip II*, trans. Sian Reynolds (New York, 1973), 873–80.

34. The mercantile and colonialist dimensions of Satan's mission to earth, which

I am outlining here, have also been discussed by J. Martin Evans in the commentary to his edition of *Paradise Lost: Books 9–10* (Cambridge, 1973), 46–47.

35. See Holden Furber, *Rival Empires of Trade in the Orient, 1600–1800* (Minneapolis, 1976).

36. *Early English Tracts on Commerce*, ed. J. R. McCullough (Cambridge, 1952), 83.

37. *Early English Tracts*, 108.

38. Today the aptly named *Fortune* magazine speaks of "the romance of big business."

39. *The Adventures of Don Quixote*, trans. J. M. Cohen (Hammondsworth, 1977), 658.

40. In the captive's tale in Part 1, Cervantes appears to locate ventures to the Indies squarely in the sphere of commerce. The captive and his two brothers are offered careers in the "Iglesia, mar, o casa real" (39). The sea represents "el arte de la mercancía," and the brother who chooses this profession and becomes rich in Peru (42) is pointedly contrasted with the captive, whose participation at Lepanto and the Goletta have placed him in the epic world of the sixteenth century; he is said to be of "más altos pensamientos" than his wealthy brothers. The captive returns penniless to Spain, confirming his father's words that although war "no dé muchas riquezas, suele dar mucho valor y mucha fama." Cervantes seems to suggest a kind of sibling rivalry between epic and the romance of the Indies, and he appears to subscribe to the epic ideology this chapter has described. See also the opening of Cervantes' *El celoso Extremeño*, where the title character successfully voyages to the Indies to recoup his fortune.

CHAPTER SEVEN
PARADISE LOST AND THE FALL OF THE ENGLISH COMMONWEALTH

1. For a description and critique of this view of *Paradise Lost* as a turning away from political engagement, see Mary Ann Radzinowizc, "The Politics of *Paradise Lost*," in *Politics of Discourse: The Literature and History of the Seventeenth Century England* (Berkeley, Los Angeles, and London, 1987), 204–29. Radzinowicz also criticizes approaches, such as my own, that look for encrypted political meanings in Milton's late poetry. I think, however, that her own essay cannot dispense with this kind of approach.

2. Northrop Frye, *The Return of Eden* (Toronto, 1965), 112–17; Christopher Hill, *Milton and the English Revolution* (New York, 1977), 421. In *John Milton and the English Revolution* (Totowa, N.J., 1981), Andrew Milner suggests that Milton's endorsement of a quietist withdrawal from politics should be understood as a temporary strategy rather than as a long-term solution. It is important to remember the extent of the persecution meted out upon dissenters by the Restoration regime: see Gerald R. Cragg, *Puritanism in the Period of the Great Persecution 1660–1688* (Cambridge, 1957).

3. "Nor were the expressions both of armie and people, whether in thir publick declarations, or several writings, other than such as testifi'd a spirit in this nation, no less noble and well-fitted to the liberty of a commonwealth, than in the ancient

Greeks or *Romans*. Nor was the heroic cause unsuccessfully defended to all Christendom, against the tongue of a famous and thought invincible adversarie . . . in a written monument likely to outlive detraction, as it hath hitherto convinc'd or silenc'd not a few of our detractors, especially in parts abroad." *The Readie and Easie Way to Establish a Free Commonwealth*, 2d ed., *Complete Prose Works of John Milton* [designated hereafter as *CPW*], ed. Don M. Wolfe, 8 vols. (New Haven, 1953–1982), 7:420–21.

4. Stevie Davies has succinctly sketched this history of Milton criticism in *Images of Kingship in Paradise Lost* (Columbia, Mo., 1983), 3–5. Davies' book is one of several recent studies that have reexamined Milton's poetry for anti-Royalist allusions; see also Joan Bennett, *Reviving Liberty* (Cambridge, Mass., and London, 1989), 33–58, and Hill, *Milton*, 341–448. It should be noted that the attacks on the Stuart monarchy, which seem to be the dominant political strain in Milton's late poetry, do not exclude retrospective criticism of aspects of the Commonwealth and Cromwellian Protectorate as well. Satan and the devils can play the roles of parliamentary debaters—as well as members of a papal conclave—in Book 2.

5. For the indeterminability of meaning in seventeenth-century political poetry, see John M. Wallace, " 'Examples are the Best Precepts': Readers and Meanings in Seventeenth-Century Poetry," *Critical Inquiry* 1 (1974):273–90. For the parallel case of Lucan, see Frederick Ahl, *Lucan* (Ithaca and London, 1976), 25–35.

6. See Josephine Waters Bennett, "Britain Among the Fortunate Isles," *Studies in Philology* 53 (1956):114–40. Bennett, 127, draws attention to *Paradise Lost* 1.519–21 for a more explicit identification of the Hesperian fields with the "utmost Isles" of the Celtic sea; that is, England.

7. Michael Drayton, *Poly-olbion*, ed. J. William Hebel (1933; Oxford, 1961), 16.

8. The two island motifs—the Fortunate Isles and Delos—come together in the following passage from a Latin ode written by Daniel Danvers of Trinity College, Oxford, to celebrate Cromwell and the end of the Anglo-Dutch War in 1654:

> Quis non inter Fortunata Insulas
> Posthac numerabit Angliam
> Cui denuo sunt Unitae Provinciae.
>   Sileat ergo Strada de bello Belgico:
> Constituit jam quieta Delos nostra,
> Quae diù jactata erat
>   fluctibus aequoreis
> Donec *Magnus Apollo* noster ortus est
>   ad culmen caeli Britannici,
>   faelix faustumq; Serenitatis signum.

Danvers' poem is found in the collection *Musarum Oxoniensium Halaiphoria sive Ob Faedera, Auspiciis Serenissimi Oliveri Reipub.Ang.Scot.&Hiber. Domini Protectoris* (Oxford, 1654), 28–29.

9. *Britannia Rediviva* (Oxford, 1660), n.p.

10. James Nohrnberg has explored the further invocations and symbolic uses of the symbolic figure of Delos in *Paradise Lost* in an unpublished paper, "Jerusalem Transposed: On the Axes of Western Epic," which he has kindly allowed me to read

in manuscript and which has helped to shape my own awareness of the importance of the figure in the poem.

11. See Frye, *The Return of Eden*, 83–84, on the figure of Xerxes and Milton's ideas of liberty.

12. For the most recent argument, see Stella Purce Revard, *The War in Heaven* (Ithaca and London, 1980), 87–107. Revard cites several of the sermons preached through the first half of the seventeenth century to commemorate the Gunpowder Plot.

13. David Norbrook has recently argued in *Poetry and Politics in the English Renaissance* (London, Boston, Melbourne, and Henley, 1984) for the importance of the Fletchers—Phineas and Giles—in forming and continuing a dissenting tradition of political poetry, militantly Calvinist and Low Church, to which the young Milton could claim affiliation. See 197–202, 234, 274–75. Norbrook notes, 240, that Milton's teacher, Alexander Gil, Sr., was a champion of the Spenserian poets.

14. The arguments over the dating of *In Quintum Novembris* and over its relationship to Fletcher's poems have been assembled and discussed by Douglas Bush in his commentary on Milton's Latin and Greek poetry in *A Variorum Commentary on the Poems of John Milton*, general ed. Merritt Y. Hughes (New York, 1970–), 1:167–71. Bush writes, 170–71: "While, then, it remains possible that Milton had seen a manuscript copy of Fletcher's poem, there is no plausible evidence that he had. If, as we may suppose, he read it later in print, one or two items may have lodged in his mind and given hints for *Paradise Lost*, but that is only a possibility." These hints, I will maintain, are more certain and substantial than Bush suggests. *In Quintum Novembris* is 226 lines long; *Locustae* has 836 lines; *The Apollyonists* is in five books and 199 modified Spenserian stanzas.

15. One striking exception is J. B. Broadbent, who, in *Some Graver Subject* (1960; New York, 1967), notes Milton's borrowings from *The Apollyonists* in the fiction of *Paradise Lost*: see 96, 126, 131, 183.

16. Broadbent, *Some Graver Subject*, 126. In his first edition of what has become one of the most wisely used school texts of *Paradise Lost* (New York, 1935), Merritt Hughes noted the parallel to *The Apollyonists* in his commentary on 2.650; the annotation disappeared in later editions, and out of sight is out of mind: it is now a forgotten fact. The original Hughes edition was the basis for a note by John M. Patrick, "Milton, Phineas Fletcher, Spenser and Ovid—Sin at Hell's Gates," *Notes and Queries*, n.s. 6, vol. 201 (1956), 384–86.

17. All citations from *The Apollyonists* are taken from the text printed by William B. Hunter, Jr., in his edition of *The English Spenserians* (Salt Lake City, 1977), 317–85.

18. See Alastair Fowler's comments on 2.650–66 in his indispensable annotations to *Paradise Lost* in *The Poems of John Milton*, ed. John Carey and Alastair Fowler (New York, 1972), 538.

19. "The originals of nature in their crude / Conception" should be compared to the earlier description of Chaos itself: "The womb of nature and perhaps her grave / Of neither sea, nor shore, nor air, nor fire, / But all these in their pregnant causes mixed / Confusedly" (2.911–14).

20. See Revard, *The War in Heaven*, 105–6.

21. Compare also Fletcher's version of this adage in his description of the devils in *The Purple Island* (7.10): "In heav'n they scorned to serve, so now in Hell they reigne."

22. Compare Moloch (*PL* 2.94–105) to *Apol.* 1.37; Belial (2.210–19) and Mammon (2.237–57) to *Apol.* 1.31–32; Beelzebub (2.330–40) to *Apol.* 1.38.

23. I owe the observation that the Son's mission is a version of the Nisus and Euryalus episode to conversations with James Nohrnberg.

24. It is obvious that my argument assumes that *Samson Agonistes* is a late work, possibly Milton's last poetic work, however earlier he may have conceived or begun its composition. I find persuasive the arguments advanced by Mary Ann Radzinowicz in *Toward "Samson Agonistes"* (Princeton, 1978). See especially her appendix, 387–407, on the dating of the play's composition.

25. For the events of the "Fatal Vespers" and the first pamphlet literature that chronicled them, see Arthur Freeman, "*The fatal vesper* and *The doleful evensong*: Claim-jumping in 1623," *Library* 5th Series 22 (1967):128–35.

26. Samuel Clarke, *England's Remembrancer* (London, 1657), 98.

27. Alexander Gil [Jr.], *Parerga sive Poetici conatus* (London, 1632), 12.

28. On the two Gils, see Donald Lemen Clark, "Milton's Schoolmasters: Alexander Gil and his Son Alexander," *Huntington Library Quarterly* 9 (1945):121–47. See also Bush in *A Variorum Commentary*, 1:171, and Bush's notes on *In Quintum Novembris* that suggest parallels to *In ruinam Camerae Papisticae*.

29. See Dennis H. Burden, *The Logical Epic: A Study of the Argument of Paradise Lost* (Cambridge, Mass., 1967), 57–60, for the suggestion that Milton's epic contains within it an alternative, pagan epic of the devils.

30. On Satan and repetition, see Regina Schwartz, *Remembering and Repeating: Biblical Creation in Paradise Lost* (Cambridge, 1988), 91–103.

31. A. Bartlett Giamatti, *The Earthly Paradise and the Renaissance Epic* (Princeton, 1966). For Giamatti's treatment of Milton's Eden, see 295–351. See also Joseph E. Duncan, *Milton's Earthly Paradise: A Historical Study of Eden* (Minneapolis, 1972); Barbara Kiefer Lewalski, *Paradise Lost and the Rhetoric of Literary Forms* (Princeton, 1985), 173–95.

32. Fredric Jameson baldly views Milton's Earth as the new bourgeois order suspended from an aristocratic Heaven that it will historically supplant. See the end of his "Religion and Ideology," in *Literature and Power in the Seventeenth Century*, ed. Francis Barker et al. (Colchester, 1981), 315–36. Broadbent, *Some Graver Subject*, 47–65, discusses *Paradise Lost* in the context of a decline in the taste for the heroic in the seventeenth century; he notes the century's interest in *Genesis*: "Behind this again there may be social factors: the aristocratic and lowest classes take their origins for granted; the bourgeois trace their pedigrees" (58). See also Greene, *The Descent from Heaven*, 364–65, 406–7; G. K. Hunter, *Paradise Lost* (London, 1980), 20–25, 181–88. Christopher Kendrick in *Milton: A Study in Ideology and Form* (New York and London, 1986) discusses Milton's reshaping of the epic genre, for which Virgil stands as a shorthand, in order to make *Paradise Lost* the poem of a new bourgeois ideology. Given its Marxian orientation, his argument is curiously abstract, however, and gives little historical instantiation of the ideology in question.

33. See the concluding argument, 120–24, of Mary Nyquist's study, "The Genesis of Gendered Subjectivity in the Divorce Tracts and in *Paradise Lost*," in *Remember-*

ing Milton: Essays on the Texts and Traditions, ed. Mary Nyquist and Margaret W. Ferguson (New York and London, 1988), 99–127. See also Kendrick, *Milton: A Study*, 188–96, on Milton's Eden.

34. For a case study of Nehemiah Wallington, a Puritan lathe-turner who spent his life seeking assurance of his election, see the fascinating work of Paul S. Seaver, *Wallington's World: A Puritan Artisan in Seventeenth-Century London* (Stanford, 1985).

35. *Complete Prose Works of John Milton* [hereafter referred to as *CPW*], ed. Don M. Wolfe, 8 vols. (New Haven, 1953–1982), 6:503. Milton's Latin original reads: "CERTITUDO itaque SALUTIS est FIDEI QUIDAM GRADUS, QUO QUIS TESTANTE SPIRITU PERSUASUS EST FIRMITERQUE CREDIT, SE CREDENTEM ATQUE IN FIDE ET CHARITATE PERMANENTEM, IUSTIFICATUM, ADOPTATUM, EX ILLA DENIQUE UNIONE ET COMMUNIONE CUM CHRISTO ET PATRE GLORIFICARI COEPTUM, SEMPITERNAM VITAM CONSUMMATAMQUE GLORIAM CERTISSIME ADEPTURUM." *The Works of John Milton* [hereafter referred to as *Works*], ed. Frank Allan Patterson et al., 20 vols. (New York, 1931–1938), 16:70.

36. *CPW*, 6:505. "PERSEVERANTIA SANCTORUM est DONUM DEI CONSERVANTIS, QUO PRAECOGNITI, ELECTI REGENITI ET PER SPIRITUM SANCTUM OBSIGNATI, IN FIDE ET GRATIA DEI AD FINEM USQUE PERSEVERANT, NEQUE ULLA VI AUT FRAUDE DIABOLI AUT MUNDI PENITUS EXCIDUNT, MODO UT IPSI SIBIMET NE DESINT, FIDEMQUE ET CHARITATEM PRO SUA VIRILI PARTE RETINEANT." *Works*, 16:74–76.

37. *CPW*, 6:506. "Promittit quidem his Deus, inditurum se reverentiam suam animo ipsorum, ut non recedant a se; quod enim suae sunt partes Deus promittit; sufficientiam nempe gratiae, ne recedant: attamen foedus pangit; in foedere autem non ab una parte sola, sed utrinque aliquid praestandum est." *Works*, 16:78.

38. Milton and John Goodwin presumably knew one another, though there is no direct evidence that they did. Their names were linked after the Restoration, when on June 16, 1660, the House of Commons ordered the public burning of Milton's *First Defense* and *Eikonoklastes* and of Goodwin's *The Obstructors of Justice* (which cites Milton's *The Tenure of Kings and Magistrates*) as well as the arrest of the authors of these anti-Royalist tracts. See Thomas Jackson, *The Life of John Goodwin, A. M.* (London, 1822), 377–79. See also Don M. Wolfe, *Milton in the Puritan Revolution* (New York, 1941), 91.

39. Jackson, *Life of John Goodwin*, 229–306.

40. Richard Baxter, "The Right Method for a Settled Peace of Conscience and Spiritual Comfort," Direction 16, *The Practical Works of the Rev. Richard Baxter*, 23 vols. (London, 1830), 16:104–5.

41. George Kendall, *Sancti Sanciti* (London, 1654), *To the Reader*, n.p.

42. The continuity between prelapsarian and postlapsarian spiritual situations in *Paradise Lost* is suggested by Hunter, *Paradise Lost*, 180–81, who shrewdly observes that Milton's Eden is "more a moral gymnasium than a place of relaxation." In this same passage, 181, Hunter alludes to the problem of " 'Security' or overconfidence" that I am taking up here. My thinking on the continuity of religious existence before and after the Fall is indebted to the work of Victoria Kahn; see her essay, "Allegory, the Sublime and the Rhetoric of Things Indifferent in *Paradise Lost*," in *Creative Imitation: New Essays on Renaissance Literature in Honor of Thomas M. Greene* (Binghamton, 1992), 127–52.

43. John Goodwin, *Redemption Redeemed* (London, 1840), 226–27.

44. Goodwin, *Redemption Redeemed*, 419–21. "For when men are secured, and this by the infallible security of faith, that the good things promised are already theirs, by the right and title of faith, and that they shall certainly persevere in faith unto the end, what need or occasion is there to persuade or move these men to do that which becomes them, in order to their perseverance, by any argument drawn from the promise of such things?" (420). See John Owen, *The Doctrine of the Saint's Perseverance Explained and Confirmed*, chap. 12, in *The Works of John Owen D. D.*, ed. William H. Goold (New York, 1863), 11:470–81.

45. Goodwin, *Redemption Redeemed*, 229–30.

46. On Adam and the sun, see the seminal essay of Geoffrey Hartman, "Adam on the Grass with Balsamum," collected in Hartman, *Beyond Formalism* (New Haven and London, 1970), 124–50. See also Joan S. Bennett, *Reviving Liberty: Radical Christian Humanism in Milton's Great Poems* (Cambridge, Mass., and London, 1989), 38–39; Broadbent, *Some Graver Subject*, 165–68.

47. In " 'The Invention' of Milton's 'Great Argument': A Study of the Logic of 'God's Ways to Men,' " *Huntington Library Quarterly* 9 (1945):149–73, Leon Howard maintained, 160–61, that Adam's sense of his "deficience" (8.416) when measured beside his Creator leads both to the creation of Eve and eventually to Adam's Fall. Howard's argument is taken up and developed by Patricia Parker in "Coming Second: Woman's Place," collected in her *Literary Fat Ladies: Rhetoric, Gender, Property* (London and New York, 1987), 195–201. My own reading variously overlaps with Parker's essay.

48. For an acute analysis that relates Eve's "coyness" to a long tradition of love poetry ultimately going back to Petrarch, see the chapter on Milton in William Kerrigan and Gordon Braden, *The Idea of the Renaissance* (Baltimore and London, 1989), 191–218.

49. Thomas H. Blackburn drew attention to the relationship of the separation scene at the beginning of Book 9 and the arguments of *Areopagitica* in " 'Uncloistered Virtue': Adam and Eve in Milton's Paradise," *Milton Studies* 3 (1971):119–37. See also Diane K. McColley, "Free Will and Obedience in the Separation Scene of *Paradise Lost*," *Studies in English Literature* 12 (1972):103–20; Stella Purce Revard, "Eve and the Doctrine of Responsibility in *Paradise Lost*," *PMLA* 88 (1973):69–78.

50. In *Reviving Liberty*, 94–118, Bennett similarly insists on the preservation of Eve's liberty in the Separation Scene. She reads Eve as an antinomian voluntarist, Adam as an antinomian humanist aware of the limits of human freedom imposed by God's test of obedience; I would suggest that Eve's overconfidence is to be related to an orthodox Calvinist sense of assurance rather than to a sectarian antinomian abrogation of the law.

51. Goodwin, *Redemption Redeemed*, 344.

52. Ibid., 434.

53. Kendall, *Sancti Sanciti*, 60.

54. Jacob is cited in Steven Brachlow, *The Communion of the Saints: Radical Puritan and Separatist Ecclesiology 1570–1625* (Oxford, 1988), 60.

55. Jackson, *Life of John Goodwin*, 310.

56. *The Works of John Owen*, 11:5–6. Cromwell himself used the language of assurance to describe in a letter his feelings before the battle of Naseby: "I could not (riding alone about my business) but smile out to God in praises, in assurance of

victory, because God would, by things that are not, bring to naught things that are. Of which I had great assurance; and God did it." *The Writings and Speeches of Oliver Cromwell,* ed. Wilbur Cortez Abbott and Catherine D. Crane (Cambridge, Mass., 1937), 1:365.

57. John Goodwin, *Basanistae* (London, 1657), 20.

58. On Nedham's tract, see Joseph Frank, *Cromwell's Press Agent: A Critical Biography of Marchamont Nedham* (Lanham, Md., 1980), 110–14.

59. A *letter of Addresse to the Protector Occasioned by Mr Needham's reply to Mr Goodwin's Book against the Triers* (London, 1657), 7.

60. Edward Bagshaw, *Saintship no ground for Soveraignty* (Oxford, 1660), 56.

61. *CPW,* 7:482–83. Compare as well this passage from the second edition of *The Readie and Easie Way:* "And why should we thus disparage and prejudicate our own nation, as to fear a scarcitie of able and worthie men united in counsel to govern us, if we will but use diligence and impartiality to finde them out and chuse them, rather yoking ourselves to a single person." *CPW,* 7:449.

62. Milton,*The Readie and Easie Way,* (2d ed.,) *CPW,* 7:455.

63. *The Poems of John Milton,* 830.

64. J.G.A. Pocock, *The Machiavellian Moment* (Princeton, 1975).

65. *CPW,* 7:436. Andrew Barnaby, in "Machiavellian Hypotheses: Republican Settlement and the Question of Empire in Milton's *Readie and Easie Way,*" *Clio* 19:3 (1990):251–70, has shown how Milton follows Machiavelli's distinctions in the *Discorsi* and designs for England a commonwealth modeled on Venice—a conservative, aristocratic republic for preservation—as opposed to the more popular, dynamic, and unstable Roman republic for empire that Machiavelli himself preferred.

66. *CPW,* 7:444–45.

67. *CPW,* 7:427.

68. Parker, *Inescapable Romance,* 142.

69. Ibid., 128.

70. Ibid., 140–41.

71. Ibid., 132.

72. See on this issue Leslie Brisman, *Milton's Poetry of Choice and Its Romantic Heirs* (Ithaca and London, 1973).

73. *CPW,* 7:450.

74. *CPW,* 7:463.

75. Milton's relationship to Lucan is also assessed by Charles Martindale in *John Milton and the Transformation of Ancient Epic* (London and Sydney, 1986), 197–224.

76. On this "surprising" creativity of God in history, see Bennett, *Reviving Liberty,* 59–93.

77. See James M. Sims, "Christened Classicism in *Paradise Lost* and the *Lusiads,*" *Comparative Literature* 24 (1972): 338–56.

78. All citations of the *Adone* are taken from the edition of Giovanni Pozzo (Milan, 1976), 2 vols.

79.

> Qualunche cerca al mondo aver tesoro
> Over diletto, o segue onore e stato
> Ponga la mano a questa chioma d'oro
> Ch'io porto in fronte, e quel farò beato.

> (*Orlando innamorato* 2.8.58)

80. Paolo Beni, *In Aristotelis Poeticam commentarii* (Padua, 1613), 80–81. For the status of the *Ethiopica* in the literary theory of the late Renaissance, see Alban Forcione, *Cervantes, Aristotle and the Persiles* (Princeton, 1970), 49–87. See also James V. Mirollo, *The Poet of the Marvelous: Giambattista Marino* (New York and London, 1963), 73–77.

81. See Lillio Giraldi, *De deis gentium* (Basel, 1548), 640, 648 (Syntagma 16). For the tradition of Fortune-Nemesis, see Erwin Panofsky, " 'Virgo et Victrix': A Note on Durer's Nemesis," in *Prints*, ed. Carl Zigrosser (New York, 1962), 13–38, 19, n. 28.

82. Hartman, "Adam on the Grass," 129.

83. See the brief, but suggestive remarks of Greene, *The Descent from Heaven*, 364.

84. Citations are taken from *Sir William Davenant's Gondibert*, ed. David F. Gladish (Oxford, 1971).

85. The hero Gondibert is from the first contrasted with his rival, the brilliant courtier Oswald (1.1.28–34). See also 3.2.100–108, the description of the school of virtue that Gondibert offers his young pages, and 3.6.9–11, where Ulfin contrasts military valor to court intrigue. The case for the court is offered by the plotting Gartha in 3.7.92–100.

86. See Gladish's introduction, xxii–xxiii, to *Sir William Davenant's Gondibert*.

87. See Cornell March Dowlin, *Sir William Davenant's "Gondibert," Its Preface, and Hobbes's Answer: A Study in English Neo-Classicism* (Philadelphia, 1934), 19–44, 73–83.

88. Elias, *The Court Society*, trans. Edmund Jephcott (New York, 1983), 246–67.

89. The *Discours* that prefaces *Les Héros de Roman* was written much later, in 1710. Here Boileau acknowledges the literary skill of *L'Astrée* and the fact that it was widely admired, even among people of the "most exquisite taste"; but he goes on to castigate d'Urfé's work: "its morality was very vicious, for it preached nothing but love and effeminacy, and sometimes went so far as to offend chastity." Boileau, *Oeuvres*, ed. Georges Mongrédien (Paris, 1961), 283.

90. See A. Fabre, *Les Ennemis de Chapelain* (Paris, 1897), 2:318–72; Geoges Collas, *Jean Chapelain* (Paris, 1911), 44–463.

91. Jean Chapelain, *De la Lecture des Vieux Romans*, ed. Alphonse Feillet (Paris, 1870), 3.

92. Ibid., 31–32.

93. Collas, *Jean Chapelain*, 234. The second twelve books of the poem, unpublished in Chapelain's lifetime, are more episodic and marvelous in invention: they move in the direction of romance.

94. Ibid., 241.

95. See Arthur Reibetanz, *Jean Desmarets de Saint-Sorlin: Scin Leben und seine Werke* (Leipzig, 1910), 87–91.

96. Boileau, *Oeuvres*, 284.

97. *Clovis ou La France Chrestienne*, ed. Félix R. Freudmann (Louvain and Paris, 1972), 360.

98. Ibid., 221.

99. Ibid., 755.

100. Ibid., 756.

101. Ibid., 761.

102. Ibid., 750.

103. Giambattista Marino, *Lettere*, ed. Marziano Guglielminetti (Turin, 1966), 204, 241. Maxime Gaume, *Les inspirations et les sources de l'oeuvre d'Honoré d'Urfé* (Saint-Etienne, 1977), 645–47.

104. Dowlin, *Sir William Davenant's "Gondibert,"* 21f.

105. See Alfred Harbage, *Sir William Davenant* (Philadelphia and Oxford, 1935), 55–58.

106. On the evasive, ahistorical nature of chivalric romance, see Timothy Hampton, *Writing from History* (Ithaca and London, 1990), 244–46.

107. Reibetanz, *Jean Desmarets de Saint-Sorlin*, 72. The passage from a letter to Desmarets's brother is worth citing at length: "The *roman* and the poem are in no way different except that one is in prose and the other in verse. Thus Tasso is a *roman*. Do you believe that all there is about Armida and Rinaldo in Tasso should be rejected because it is all *romanesque*? It's the longest and most beautiful part of the poem, and you could still find more to find fault in it, since Rinaldo is not the principal hero, but Goffredo; and that is much more episodic than the story of Aurèle which is the basis of my whole poem, since it is the basis of the loves of Clovis and Clotilde; for it is by the advice of Saint Daniel the Stylite that Aurèle went to find Clotilde, about whom he gave an account to Clovis, who fell in love with her. Episodes in poems are quite extended adventures without which the poem could survive, like that of Nisus and Euryalus in Virgil, that of Olindo and Sofronia in Tasso, that of the burning of the palace of Lisois in my poem, which are agreeable digressions and one is not pained to make a detour from one's path to see such agreeable things."

108. *Sir William Davenant's Gondibert*, 26.

109. Annabel Patterson, *Censorship and Interpretation* (Madison, 1984), 176–202. See also Barbara Lewalski, "Milton: Revaluations of Romance," in *Four Essays on Romance*, ed. Herschel Baker (Cambridge, Mass., 1971), 57–70. Lewalski cites, 58, the famous autobiographical passage from the *Apology for Smectymnus* where Milton recalls reading chivalric romances in his youth.

110. *Eikonoklastes* 1. CPW, 3:366–67.

111. CPW, 7:461, 458–59.

CHAPTER EIGHT
DAVID'S CENSUS: MILTON'S POLITICS AND
PARADISE REGAINED

1. Pompey's captains accuse the Parthian kings of mother-son incest, the crime of Oedipus: "Damnat apud gentes sceleris non sponte peracti / Oedipodionas infelix fabula Thebas: / Parthorum dominus quotiens sic sanguine mixto / Nascitur Arsacides!" (8.406–9). This passage may reinforce the Oedipal themes that surround Jesus in *Paradise Regained* and culminate in the simile at 4.572–75; these have been discussed by James Nohrnberg in "*Paradise Regained* by One Greater Man: Milton's Wisdom Epic as a 'Fable of Identity,' " in *Centre and Labyrinth: Essays in Honour of Northrop Frye*, ed. E. Cook et al. (Toronto, 1983), 83–114, and William Kerrigan, *The Sacred Complex* (Cambridge, Mass., 1983), 73–126.

2. See Northrop Frye, *The Return of Eden* (Toronto, 1965), 130–33; Barbara

Kiefer Lewalski, *Milton's Brief Epic* (Providence and London, 1966), 265–80; Arnold Stein, *Heroic Knowledge* (Minneapolis, 1957), 78–93. These scholars generally view Milton's Parthia as a figure for militant Genevan Protestantism: this view was earlier developed by Howard Schultz in "Christ and Antichrist in *Paradise Regained*," *PMLA* 67 (1952):790–808).

3. Frye, *The Return of Eden*, 132; Lewalski, *Milton's Brief Epic*, 270. The parallel between the lost tribes of Israel and the self-enslaved Romans has been noted by Stein, *Heroic Knowledge*, 89, and, more recently, by Andrew Milner in *John Milton and the English Revolution* (Totowa, N.J., 1981), 174–75.

4. This critical tradition is represented at its best by E.M.W. Tillyard, who offers a complicated and sympathetic assessment of Milton's spoiled political hopes and the inward turn of his poetry; see Tillyard, *Milton* (1930; rev. ed., New York, 1967), 249–51. Stein, *Heroic Knowledge*, 63–93, finds the political issues of the poetry more persistently problematic and unresolved.

5. Cf. Frye, *The Return of Eden*, 126, for the recollection of Spenser's Mammon.

6. On the theme of retirement, see Nohrnberg, "*Paradise Regained* by One Greater Man," 104.

7. *Paradise Regained* carefully contrasts the Parthian troops that the "city gates outpoured" (3.311) from Ctesiphon with the "conflux issuing forth, or entering in" (4.62) the gates of Rome. The two-way traffic of Roman administration is seen as an imperial advance over unidirectional Parthian conquest.

8. The census of Augustus figures prominently in two Neo-Latin nativity poems that Milton surely knew, Mantuan's *Primae Parthenices*, 3.1–26, and Sannazaro's *De partu virginis*, 2.116–234. For the importance of the *De partu virginis* as a model for the epic form of *Paradise Regained*, see Stewart A. Baker, "Sannazaro and Milton's Brief Epic," *Comparative Literature* 20 (1968):116–32. In *The Descent from Heaven* (New Haven and London, 1963), 161–62, Thomas M. Greene points out that the census of Augustus in Sannazaro's epic is treated as a figure for the universal, global claims of the Roman Church. The idea governs Catholic interpretations of Luke 2:1–2, which, following Orosius, not only viewed the Pax Augusta as the preparation for the birth of the Prince of Peace, but also regarded the census as the means for Jesus—and, by inference, all future Christians—to be enrolled as Roman citizens. See, for example, the great early-seventeenth-century compendium commentary of Cornelius a Lapide, the *Commentaria in Scripturam Sacram*, ed. A. Crampton (Paris, 1876), 16.53–56. By contrast and in reaction to this line of interpretation, Calvin argued that the census was merely a further extension of Roman tyranny that signified the total temporal servitude of the Jews: see John Calvin, *Commentary on a Harmony of the Evangelists, Matthew, Mark, and Luke*, trans. William Pringle (Edinburgh, 1846), 1.110. The Geneva Bible of 1560 comments that by the Roman census "the people were more charged and oppressed."

Milton's allusion to David's census may thus contain a critique of Augustus's census as it is celebrated in the poems of Milton's Catholic predecessors. In the *De partu Virginis*, moreover, the census is the occasion for a great epic catalogue of world geography, and in Book 11 of *Paradise Lost*, Adam's view from the high mountain of Eden, which is compared to and conflated with the vision of the kingdoms of the world that the tempter Satan offers to Jesus (11.381–384)—does the "His eye" of verse 385 refer to the eye of Adam or of Jesus?—occasions a similar long catalogue (385–411), the whole episode modeled on the vision of Camões' Vasco da Gama of the world and of Portugal's imperial possessions in it from the mountaintop of Venus's island in Book 10 of the *Lusíadas*. The descriptions of Parthian and Roman power in *Paradise Regained* present relatively short catalogue passages (3.270–91 and 4.69–79). David's census is a kind of figure and critique of the epic topos of the catalogue itself and of the imperial, state-building impulse behind it.

9. David's sin can be compared to Satan's military muster of the fallen angels in Book 1 of *Paradise Lost*: "Their number last he sums. And now his heart / Distends with pride, and hardening in his strength / Glories" (1.571–73). Behind this passage, as the last chapter demonstrated, is the Satan of Fletcher's *Apollyonists*: "his fiery eye / Much swol'ne with pride, but more with rage and hate, / As Censour, muster'd all his company" (1.18).

10. *Eikon Basilike: The Portraiture of His Majesty King Charles Ist* (London, 1879), 181.

11. *Eikonoklastes*, 25; *CPW*, 3.555; *Works*, 5.266.

12. *Eikonoklastes*, 25; *CPW*, 3.555; *Works*, 5.265.

13. For a discussion of the Davidic propaganda of Charles II, see Richard F. Jones, "The Originality of *Absalom and Achitophel*," *MLN* 46 (1931):211–18.

14. Joseph Swetnam, *David's Devotions upon his Deliverances* (London, 1660), 9.

15. John Dryden, *Astraea Redux, The Works of John Dryden*, ed. Edward Niles Hooker and H. T. Swedenberg, Jr. (Berkeley and Los Angeles, 1956–1979), 1.24.

16. Satan's offer to bring Jesus to the foreign monarchs' "radiant courts / Best school of best experience" (3.237–38) thus links the temptation of the kingdoms to the ensuing temptation of Athens and her "schools of ancient sages" (4.251). Jesus is tempted to continue his studies "Till time mature thee to a kingdom's weight" (4.282). In *Commentary on a Harmony of the Evangelists*, 1.165–72, Calvin discusses the hidden life of Christ and concludes that the child Jesus already possessed a fullness of knowledge and could not be said to learn as he grew older. For the parallel to Milton's own long sojourn as a scholar in his father's house, see Nohrnberg, "*Paradise Regained* by One Greater Man," 86–87.

17. Swetnam, *David's Devotions*, 8.

18. Suidas, *Historica caeteraque omnia . . . opera* (Basel, 1581), 151. See also Samuel Clarke, *The Life and Death of Julius Caesar, the first Founder of the Roman Empire, as also the Life and Death of Augustus Caesar* (London, 1665), 93.

19. Lewalski, *Milton's Brief Epic*, 273–80; Schultz, "Christ and Antichrist," 803.

20. Milton, *Of Reformation in England*, 1 *CPW*, 1.552–60; *Works*, 3.22–28.

21. *The Readie and Easie Way*, *CPW*, 7.429; *Works*, 6.142.

22. Ibid., *CPW*, 7.457; *Works* 6.142.

23. Anonymous, A *Character of His Most Sacred Majesty King Charles II* (London, 1660), 33–34.

24. One can compare the prefatory letter of James I to Prince Henry at the beginning of *Basilikon Doron*: "Being rightly informed hereby of the waight of your burthen, ye may in time beginne to consider, that being borne to be a king, ye are rather borne to *onus*, then *honos*: not excelling all your people so farre in ranke and honour,

as in daily care and hazardous paines-taking, for the dutifull administration of that great office that God hath laide upon your shoulders." *The Political Works of James I*, ed. Charles Howard McIlwain (Cambridge and London, 1918), 1.3.

25. John Graunt, *Natural and Political Observations Made upon the Bills of Mortality*, ed. Walter F. Willcox (Baltimore, 1939), 51.

26. *The Readie and Easie Way*, CPW, 7.461; *Works*, 6.147.

27. John Burnet, *History of His Own Time* (Oxford, 1833), 1.397. For the political charges and countercharges surrounding the Plague and Great Fire, see Michael McKeon, *Politics and Poetry in Restoration England* (Cambridge, Mass., and London, 1975), 138–46.

28. George Wither, *A Memorandum to London* (London, 1665), 13. For Wither's poetry of the civil war and Restoration, see Charles S. Hensley, *The Later Career of George Wither* (The Hague and Paris, 1969).

29. John Tabor, *Seasonable Thoughts in Sad Times* (London, 1667), 45.

30. Kingship and plague are also equated in a passage commenting on the *Iliad* in Chapter 5 of the first *Defense of the English People*, CPW, 4.441; *Works*, 7.312–13: "Achilles Agamemnonem, postquam eum ipsum esse pestem populi pestilentia tum laborantis comperisset" (Achilles, having found that Agamemnon was himself a pestilence unto his people who were then suffering under a pestilence.)

31. Christopher Hill, *The Experience of Defeat* (London, 1984), 318, 327.

32. Graunt, *Natural and Political Observations*, 67.

33. See Hyman Alderman, *Counting People: The Census in History* (New York, 1969), 41–42.

34. Thomas Sprat, *History of the Royal Society*, ed. Jackson I. Cope and Harold Whitmolre Jones (St. Louis, 1956), 67.

35. Graunt, *Natural and Political Observations*, 78–79.

36. Ibid., 4.

37. Ibid.

38. *The Economic Writings of Sir William Petty*, ed. Charles Henry Hull (1899; New York, 1963), 1.34.

39. See Ronald Hutton, *The Restoration* (Oxford, 1985), 255–57. A contemporary view of the poll-tax dispute is found in the December 8 and 11–12, 1666, entries in Pepys' diary. See *The Diary and Correspondence of Samuel Pepys, F.R.S.*, ed. Richard, Lord Braybrooks (London, 1929), 2.458, 460–61.

40. Petty, *Economic Writings*, 1.53.

41. For Petty's own account of the Irish survey, see *The History of the Survey of Ireland Commonly Called the Down Survey by Doctor William Petty* (1851; New York, 1967). See also Charles Webster, *The Great Instauration: Science, Medicine and Reform 1626–1660* (New York, 1976), 436–44.

42. See Webster's comprehensive study, *The Great Instauration*, especially 355–60, 369–84; for Graunt's parliamentary allegiance and friendship with Hartlib, see 445.

43. R. Brenner, "The Civil War Politics of London's Merchant Community," *Past and Present* 58 (1973):53–107. See also Webster, *The Great Instauration*, 462–65, and J. P. Cooper, "Social and Economic Policies under the Commonwealth," in *The Interregnum: The Quest for Settlement 1646–1660*, ed. G. E. Aylmer (London, 1972), 121–42.

44. See Gordon Jackson, "Trade and Shipping," in *The Restored Monarchy 1660–1688*, ed. J. R. Jones (Totowa, N.J., 1979), 136–54; David Ogg, *England in the Reign of Charles II* (Oxford, 1955), 1.234–51.

45. *Second Defense, CPW*, 4.681; *Works*, 8.242–45: "Nam pecuniae vim maximam in aerarium inferendi rationes posse calidissimas excogitare, pedestres atque navales copias impigrè posse instruere, posse cum legatis exterorum cautè agere, societas & foedera peritè contrahere, si qui majus utulius ac sapientius in republica existimavistis esse, quàm incorrupta populo judicia praestare, afflictis per injuriam atque oppressis opem ferre, suum cuíque jus expeditum reddere, quanto sitis in errore versati, tum serò nimis perspicietis. . . . Si vos in eadem vitia prolabi, si illos imitari, eadem sequi, easdem inanitates aucupari ceperitis, vos profecto regii estis, vel eisdem adhuc hostibus, vec aliis vicissim opportuni."

46. *The Readie and Easie Way, CPW*, 7.458–59; *Works*, 6.144.

47. These are the concerns of *A Treatise on Civil Power in Ecclesiastical Causes* (1659), *CPW*, 7.239–72; *Works*, 6.1–41.

48. Having placed Milton toward the beginning of a modern conflict between individual and state, I have inevitably evoked the figure of his contemporary, Thomas Hobbes. It was Hobbes, the apologist for royal sovereignty and religious uniformity, who defined individuality as a proprietary selfhood that could only come into being through a prior contractual relationship with the state. And of Hobbes's Baconian turn of mind, John Aubrey wrote: "He turned and winded and compounded in philosophy, politiques, etc., as if he had been at Analyticall [i.e., mathematical] worke." See *Aubrey's Brief Lives*, ed. Oliver Lawson Dick (London, 1950), 153. Aubrey also mentions Hobbes in a well-known passage of his brief life of Milton.

> His widowe assures me that Mr. T. Hobbes was not one of his acquaintance, that her husband did not like him at all, but he would acknowledge him to be a man of great parts, and a learned man. Their Interests and Tenets did run counter to each other. (203)

Aubrey is succinct. "Hobbes" could be the name for that which all the various political strategies of *Paradise Regained* converge to resist.

CHAPTER NINE
OSSIAN, MEDIEVAL "EPIC," AND EISENSTEIN'S
ALEXANDER NEVSKY

1. Paul van Tieghem, *Ossian en France* (Paris, 1917), 2:8. For the vogue of Ossian in France created by Napoleon, see 2:3–37 and the subsequent chapters of van Tieghem's classic study.

2. *The Poems of Ossian translated by James Macpherson, Esq.*, 2 vols. (London, 1807). References are given to page numbers in this edition.

3. On the Miltonic echo, see Fiona J. Stafford, *The Sublime Savage: A Study of James Macpherson and the Poems of Ossian* (Edinburgh, 1988), 137.

4. Johann Gottfried Herder acknowledged in his essay, "Homer und Ossian," in *Die Horen* (1795), that Macpherson's translation had been an act of creation: "Accordingly he cut out lowly traits of character; and he added analogies from the Hebrews, the Greeks, and the Moderns to his own, and gave to all, to his Fingal, to his

Ossian, to his Bragela the noblest and most sensitive form; so much the better." *Herders Sämmtliche Werke*, ed. Bernhard Suphan (Berlin, 1881), 18:452. For the case of Pope, see Steven Shankman, *Pope's "Iliad": Homer in the Age of Passion* (Princeton, 1983), 92, 152–57.

5. Shankman, *Pope's "Iliad,"* 82. On the new understanding of Homer whose origins reach back into the seventeenth century and perhaps the sixteenth as well in Julius Caesar Scaliger's comparison of Homer to Virgil, see Kirsti Simonsuuri, *Homer's Original Genius* (Cambridge, 1979), and Michael Murrin, *The Allegorical Epic* (Chicago and London, 1980), 173–96.

6. This was the opinion of Chateaubriand. See van Tieghem, *Ossian en France*, 10.

7. Herder, *Sämmtliche Werke*, 18:455.

8. See Geoffrey Hartman, "Reflections on the Evening Star: Akenside to Coleridge," in *New Perspectives on Coleridge: Selected Papers from the English Institute* (New York and London, 1972), 85–131.

9. *Goethe's Faust*, trans. Walter Kaufmann (Garden City, N.Y., 1963), 64–66.

10. Herder, *Sämmtliche Werke*, 18:458.

11. William Hazlitt, *Lectures on the English Poets*, in *Complete Works of William Hazlitt*, ed. D. P. Howe (1930; New York, 1967), 5:18.

12. Friedrich Schlegel, *Lectures on the History of Literature, Ancient and Modern*, 2 vols. (Philadelphia, 1816), 1:319; Schlegel, *Kritische Ausgabe*, ed. Ernst Behler (Munich, Paderborn, and Vienna, 1958–), 6:194.

13. Schlegel, "On the Poetry of the North" ["Über nordische Dichtkunst"], in *The Aesthetic and Miscellaneous Works of Frederick von Schlegel*, trans. E. J. Millington (London, 1859), 249; *Kritische Ausgabe*, 3:227.

14. Stafford, *The Sublime Savage*, 101.

15. Schlegel, *The Aesthetic and Miscellaneous Works*, 251; *Kritische Ausgabe*, 3:229.

16. Franz Joseph Mone, *Quellen und Forschungen zur Geschichte der teutscher Literatur und Sprache* (Aachen and Leipzig, 1830). See Mary Thorp, *The Study of the Nibelungenlied* (Oxford, 1940), 76–77.

17. The title page of the 1762 *Fingal* is reproduced opposite p. 61 of Stafford, *The Sublime Savage*.

18. Howard D. Weinbrot, *Augustus Caesar in "Augustan" England* (Princeton, 1978), especially 120–49. See also the excellent study by T. W. Harrison, "English Virgil: The *Aeneid* in the XVIII Century," *Philologia Pragensia* 10 (1967):1–11, 80–91. Harrison points out that as Virgil's politics were discredited, the *Aeneid* came to be valued for its pathetic passages: those, we might say, that identify with the sufferings of Aeneas and especially of his enemies, all victims of the hero's Roman destiny. The roots of the so-called "Harvard School" view of the *Aeneid* go back quite far indeed.

Alongside this specifically anti-imperial attack on Virgil—where the Roman poet was unfavorably compared to Homer—another strain of eighteenth-century criticism attacked both poets, and thus the epic genre itself, for its glorification of war: Claude Rawson has examined how this strain emerges full-blown in the burlesque critiques of epic of Shelley and Byron in "Byron Augustan: Mutations of the Mock-Heroic in *Don Juan* and Shelley's *Peter Bell the Third*," in *Byron: Augustan and*

Romantic, ed. Andrew Rutherford (London, 1990), 82–116. For Rawson's further comments on Pope's ambivalence—his admiration for ancient epic as a literary monument versus his sentiments against war, the central subject of that epic—see "Pope's *Waste Land*: Reflections on Mock-Heroic," in Rawson, *Order from Confusion Sprung* (London, 1985), 201–21. The romantic attachment to Ossian, the Highland Homer, thus revived epic as a martial genre—an inspiration to soldiers like Napoleon—even as romantic heirs of the Enlightenment continued to disparage epic precisely for its celebration of mayhem and slaughter.

19. *Oeuvres Complètes de Voltaire* (Paris, 1877), 8:321.

20. Schlegel, *The Aesthetic and Miscellaneous Works*, 256; *Kritische Ausgabe*, 234.

21. Ibid.: "aber eine *sternenhelle* Nacht war es!"

22. Schlegel, *The Aesthetic and Miscellaneous Works*, 267; *Kritische Ausgabe*, 244.

23. Schlegel, *The Aesthetic and Miscellaneous Works*, 245; *Kritische Ausgabe*, 224.

24. Schlegel, *The Aesthetic and Miscellaneous Works*, 246–47; *Kritische Ausgabe*, 224–25.

25. N. N. Karamzin, "Lettre au Spectateur sur la littérature russe," *Spectateur du Nord* 4 (1797):55–56.

26. Ibid. 57.

27. Cited in Juha Y. Pentikäinen, *Kalevala Mythology*, trans. and ed. Ritva Poom (Bloomington and Indianapolis, 1989), 16. See also John I. Kolehmainen, *Epic of the North* (New York Mills, Minn.,1973), 43–46.

28. Kolehmainen, *Epic of the North*, 87.

29. See Pentikäinen, *Kalevala Mythology* 68–72, 221–27.

30. Schlegel, *Lectures on the History of Literature*, 1:343; *Kritische Ausgabe* 6:207.

31. For a discussion of the criticism of the *Cid* of Ramón Menéndez Pidal, which carried the romantic nationalist reading of medieval epic into the twentieth century, see Richard Fletcher, *The Quest for the Cid* (London, 1989), 200–205. Menéndez Pidal was responding to the work of the Dutch Orientalist Reinhardt Dozy, who separated the poetic hero from the historical one.

32. Schlegel, *Lectures on the History of Literature*, 1:345; *Kritische Ausgabe*, 6:207.

33. Schlegel, *Lectures*, 1:344; *Kritische Ausgabe*, 6:207.

32. Schlegel, *Lectures*, 1:332, 326; *Kritische Ausgabe*, 6:200, 197.

35. Schlegel, *Lectures*, 1:15; *Kritische Ausgabe*, 6:15.

36. Schlegel, *Lectures*, 1:16; *Kritische Ausgabe*, 6:16.

37. Schlegel, *Lectures*, 1:98–99; *Kritische Ausgabe*, 6:59.

38. Schlegel, *Lectures*, 1:15; *Kritische Ausgabe*, 6:16.

39. Otfrid Ehrismann, *Das Nibelungenlied in Deutschland* (Munich, 1975), 69–71. See Ehrismann's larger discussion, 47–111, of the interest in the *Nibelungenlied* generated by the anti-Napoleonic wars, and Thorpe, *The Study of the Nibelungenleid*, 7–12. See also the chapter by Klaus von See, "Das Nibelungenlied—ein Nationalepos?" in *Die Nibelungen*, ed. Joachim Heinzle and Anneliese Waldshmidt (Frankfurt, 1991), 43–110.

40. Thomas Carlyle, *Critical and Miscellaneous Essays* (Boston, 1860), 2:298.

41. *Deutsche Vergangenheit und deutscher Staat*, ed. Paul Kluckhohn (Leipzig, 1935), 82. Compare Robert Southey in 1808 on the poet of the *Cid*: "for as a historian of manners, this poet, whose name unfortunately has perished, is the Homer of Spain." Southey, *Chronicle of the Cid* (London, 1808), xi.

42. Friedrich Schlegel, *Lectures on the History of Literature* 1:270; *Kritische Ausgabe* 6:169.

43. *Das Nibelungenlied*, ed. August Zeune (Berlin, 1815), xxi.

44. Joseph Duggan, "Franco-German Conflict and the History of French Scholarship on the *Song of Roland*," in *Hermeneutics and Medieval Culture*, ed. Patrick J. Gallacher and Helen Damico (Albany, 1989), 97–106, 98.

45. The essay is reprinted in Gaston Paris, *Poèmes et légendes du moyen âge* (Paris, 1900), 1–23.

46. Ibid., 6.

47. Ibid., 8.

48. Ibid., 14–15.

49. Paris, "*La Chanson de Roland* et la nationalité française," in *La Poésie du moyen âge*, 5th ed. (Paris, 1903), 104: "Cette disposition des esprits a produit dans l'histoire les Croisades, oeuvre française par excellence."

50. Paris, *Poèmes et légendes*, 18–19.

51. It was Paris's student, Joseph Bédier, who would deny to *La Chanson de Roland*, as well as to the *Nibelungenlied*, a firm historical basis, arguing that the poem did not go back through an oral tradition to the disaster that overtook Charlemagne's rear guard in 778, but was rather the product of the eleventh century itself. For a stimulating discussion of Bédier and his criticism of the romantic search for origins, see Hans Aarsleff, "Scholarship and Ideology: Joseph Bédier's Critique of Romantic Medievalism," in *Historical Studies and Literary Criticism*, ed. Jerome J. McGann (Madison, 1985), 93–113

52. The audience in the national military academy at Saint-Cyr was told in 1900 that "*La Chanson de Roland* est notre *Iliade*." See John Benton, "Nostre Français n'unt talent de fuïr: The *Song of Roland* and the Enculturation of a Warrior Class," *Oliphant* 6 (1979):237–58, 237. Cited in Duggan, "Franco-German Conflict," 106.

53. Paris, "*La Chanson de Roland* et la nationalité française," 97–99, 108–10.

54. Ibid., 103.

55. Duggan, *Franco-German Conflict*, 100.

56. Paris, "*La Chanson de Roland* et la nationalité française," 107.

57. Ibid., 118.

58. Schlegel, *Lectures on the History of Literature*, 1:34; *Kritische Ausgabe*, 6:27.

59. Paris, in "*La Chanson de Roland* et les *Nibelungen*," 7, speaks of the class divisions of the Middle Ages as the period's "grand malheur . . . en politique comme en littérature." In "*La Chanson de Roland* et la nationalité française," 116, he writes as a good liberal and anticleric: "Il faut qu'une éducation mieux comprise redonne aux âmes cette unité que le moyen âge leur assurait dans l'Église, et qui ne peut aujourd'hui se reconstituer que dans la science." Most remarkably, in this latter work, 99, Paris writes of a larger European civilization transcending national boundaries that he hopes to see restored at the end of the hostilities: "la civilisation européenne, patrie agrandie où nous ne désespérons pas, même dans les cruels moments que nous traversons, de voir se donner la main toutes les nations qui y participent."

60. *The Collected Works of Karen Horney* (New York, 1964), 2:26–27.

61. *Eisenstein: Three Films*, ed. Jay Leyda, trans. Diana Matias (New York, 1974), 103.

62. Jeremiah Curtin, *The Mongols in Russia* (Boston, 1908), 274–75; for Nevsky's larger career, see 261–90. The only reference to the Orthodox Church in the film occurs in its final section when the clergy are briefly seen emerging from the cathedral in Pskov to welcome the triumphant Russian troops.

63. These points are clearer in the scenario or screenplay of the movie, which contains the scenes in the "missing reel" of the film of which to this date only stills survive. See *Eisenstein: Three Films*. Alexander enters Novgorod during a pitched battle between the merchants and the commoners (106–8). The quality of Russian armaments—both medieval and contemporary—is specifically addressed in episodes (128–29) during the battle on the ice in the screenplay that were not transferred to or did not survive the editing of the film. The trace of this polemic is still evident in the death of the armorer Ignat, who complains as he expires that the chain mail he had made for himself was too short.

64. See Yon Barna, *Eisenstein* (Bloomington, 1973), 218: "The Teutonic knights always appear in strictly geometrical formation, contrasting with the irregularity and disarray of the Russian troops who advance in successive waves." Like Barna, Aldo Grasso, in *Sergej Ejsenstejn* (Florence, 1975), 97, notes the reversal of traditional identifications of white with purity and goodness, dark with evil, and draws a comparison to *Moby Dick*.

65. For a strong psychoanalytic and political reading of the sexual dyamics of the film, see Leon Balter, "Alexander Nevsky," *Film Culture* 70–71 (1983):43–87, who argues that these are prevalently sadomasochistic and homosexual. For Alexander as a "wooer" of Novgorod, see 69–70. Balter points out, among many other striking observations, the phallic overtones of the German wedge attack and the passive, "feminized" defense posture of the Russians before it; and he brilliantly shows how these sexual roles are reversed in Ignat's fable of the vixen pursuing the male hare who eventually takes her maidenhead (72–74). While Balter's main argument is generally plausible and persuasive, he can exaggerate: the rivalry of Vaska and Gavrilo for Olga may involve a Girardian, homoerotic dimension (67–68), but the pointed contrast of the two suitors suggests that while Gavrilo is indeed ready for a tranquil domestic life, Vaska, the war lover, is not (Balter uncharacteristically leaves out, given his penchant for flagellation imagery, Gavrilo's warning that Vaska will treat Olga with the birch, while he will show her reverence [*Eisenstein: Three Films*, 97]). In Vasilisa, Vaska has met his match—already suggested during the melee in Novgorod in the "missing reel" (*Eisenstein: Three Films*, 107) and in the similarity of their names. Vasilisa may well represent the subconscious threat—or pleasurable fantasy—of the "phallic woman" (82–84), but in the real, conscious world of the film, she is not, in spite of Vaska's praise, much of a warrior; nor should she be the source of any physical anxiety for Vaska, who is last seen dominating her in a kind of love tussle.

66. Balter, "Alexander Nevsky," 45.

67. Klaus Theweleit, *Male Fantasies*, trans. Stephen Conway (Minneapolis, 1987), 434; see especially 229–88, 382–435.

68. *Eisenstein: Three Films*, 95. In lines that do not appear in the finished film, Nikita says, "To you it's clearer which of them we should begin with, Prince, but to us they're all one scourge."

69. The idea of Oriental effeminacy was spelled out in the original ending of the film in the scenario, where it is the Mongol khan's wife who arranges to poison Alexander. See *Eisenstein: Three Films*, 183.

70. Karl Marx and Friedrich Engels, *The Communist Manifesto*, in *Essential Works of Socialism*, ed. Irving Howe (New York, 1970), 33.

71. Ibid., 34.

72. The ambiguities of the relationship of nationalism and communism were explored with some subtlety in Stalin's own early work of 1913, *Marxism and the National Question*. See Stalin, *Marxism and the National and Colonial Question* (New York, 1935), 3–61. As a Georgian, Stalin could speak with some personal insight on the issue. He, of course, wants it both ways. While he eloquently argues for the principal of ethnic self-determination and equality, he nonetheless concludes: "The only cure for this is organisation on internationalist lines.

"The aim must be to unite the workers of all nationalities in Russia into *united* and *integral* collective bodies in various localities and to unite these collective bodies into a *single* party.

"It goes without saying that a party structure of this kind does not preclude, but on the contrary presumes, wide autonomy for the *regions* within the single party whole" (59).

This was a recipe for the Soviet empire, an empire that would nonetheless be dominated by—and identified with—Russia. The volume also contains Stalin's further pronouncements on the issue.

73. William Empson, *Some Versions of Pastoral* (New York, 1960), 11.

74 Balter, "Alexander Nevsky," 78f.

75. The ax was to have figured even more prominently as a homely inspiration for Alexander's battle plan. According to Barna, *Eisenstein*, 209, "Pavlenko's first solution was a wood-chopping scene in which an axe becomes immovably stuck in a knot of wood, inspiring Nevsky to thoughts of a 'wedge' trap for the enemy." Eventually this idea was scrapped in favor of Ignat's fable of the vixen and the hare.

76. *Eisenstein: Three Films*, 132.

77. The original ending of the scenario is translated and printed as an appendix to *Eisenstein: Three Films*, 182–86.

78. Ibid., 186.

79. Eisenstein, *Immoral Memories*, trans. Herbert Marshall (Boston, 1983), 226.

80. Ibid.

81. Ibid.

INDEX